To Nigel,
In friendship 2 appreciation.

Marko, 11/11/2015

# THE LAW AND POLITICS OF THE KOSOVO
## ADVISORY OPINION

.

# The Law and Politics of the Kosovo Advisory Opinion

Edited by
MARKO MILANOVIĆ
and
MICHAEL WOOD

OXFORD
UNIVERSITY PRESS

UNIVERSITY PRESS

Great Clarendon Street, Oxford, OX2 6DP,
United Kingdom

Oxford University Press is a department of the University of Oxford.
It furthers the University's objective of excellence in research, scholarship,
and education by publishing worldwide. Oxford is a registered trade mark of
Oxford University Press in the UK and in certain other countries

Published in the United States of America by Oxford University Press
198 Madison Avenue, New York, NY 10016, United States of America

British Library Cataloguing in Publication Data
Data available

Library of Congress Control Number: 2014958037

ISBN 978–0–19–871751–5

Printed and bound by
CPI Group (UK) Ltd, Croydon, CR0 4YY

© Azem Ramadani / Gettyimages.co.uk

# Acknowledgements

The preparation of this volume took no small amount of time. We are grateful to our contributors and to Oxford University Press, especially Merel Alstein and Emma Endean, for their patience. We are particularly grateful to Vibheetha Santhaseelan, Gnanambigai Jayakumar, and their team for all the energy and hard work they invested in preparing this volume for press. We would also like to thank Haleema Wahid for compiling the bibliography.

# Contents

## II. THE OPINION

## III. REACTIONS AND IMPLICATIONS

## IV. THE ROAD AHEAD

# List of Abbreviations

| | |
|---|---|
| AO | Advisory Opinion |
| EULEX | European Union Rule of Law Mission in Kosovo |
| Decl. | Declaration |
| Diss. op. | Dissenting opinion |
| DoI | Declaration of Independence |
| FRY | Federal Republic of Yugoslavia |
| ICJ | International Court of Justice |
| ICTY | International Criminal Tribunal for the former Yugoslavia |
| KFOR | NATO Kosovo Force |
| Kosovo WC1 | Kosovo Written Contributions, First Round |
| Kosovo WC2 | Kosovo Written Contributions, Second Round |
| PISG | Provisional Institutions of Self-Government |
| OSCE | Organization for Security and Cooperation in Europe |
| Sep. op | Separate opinion |
| SFRY | Socialist Federal Republic of Yugoslavia |
| SRSG | Secretary-General's Special Representative (here, for Kosovo) |
| UNGA | United Nations General Assembly |
| UNMIK | United Nations Interim Administration Mission in Kosovo |
| UNSC | United Nations Security Council |
| UNSG | United Nations Secretary-General |
| WC | Written Contributions |
| WCM | Written Comments |
| WS | Written Statements |

# List of Contributors

**Richard Caplan** is Professor of International Relations at Oxford University and an Official Fellow of Linacre College Oxford. His books include *Europe and the Recognition of New States in Yugoslavia* (Cambridge University Press, 2005), *International Governance of War-Torn Territories: Rule and Reconstruction* (Oxford University Press, 2005) and, as editor, *Exit Strategies and State Building* (Oxford University Press, 2012).

**James Crawford** AC SC FBA is a Judge of the International Court of Justice (since 2015). He was Whewell Professor of International Law, University of Cambridge, and Research Professor of International Law, La Trobe University. He is a former member of the International Law Commission and was the Special Rapporteur on State Responsibility from 1997 to 2001. He was made a Companion of the Order of Australia in 2013.

**Vladimir Djerić** is attorney at law in Belgrade, Serbia. He has served as counsel before international courts and tribunals (ICJ, ECHR, ICTY) and as counsel and expert in international arbitrations. He was adviser to the Minister of Foreign Affairs of FR Yugoslavia/ Serbia and Montenegro from 2000 to 2004. During his service in the Ministry of Foreign Affairs, he was Co-Agent for FR Yugoslavia/Serbia and Montenegro in cases before the ICJ. He was formerly a substitute member and rapporteur of the Venice Commission of the Council of Europe. He acted on behalf of Serbia in the advisory proceedings.

**James Gow** is Professor of International Peace and Security, King's College London and Non-Resident Scholar, LISD, Princeton University. His numerous publications include *War and War Crimes, Prosecuting War Crimes: Lessons and Legacies of the International Criminal Tribunal for the former Yugoslavia* and *Security, Democracy and War Crimes* (as co-author) all in 2013. He received a Leverhulme Major Research Fellowship in 2013 for a study of the trial of General Ratko Mladić and the legacy of the UN International Criminal Tribunal for the former Yugoslavia.

**Mathias Forteau** is Professor at the Université Paris Ouest, member of the International Law Commission, and advocate and counsel for states in numerous cases before international courts and tribunals. He is the co-author of *Droit international public* with P. Daillier and A. Pellet, and author of many articles on various topics of international law.

**James Ker-Lindsay** is Senior Research Fellow in the Politics of South East Europe at the European Institute, London School of Economics. His books include *Kosovo: The Path to Contested Statehood in the Balkans* and *The Foreign Policy of Counter Secession: Preventing the Recognition of Contested States*.

**Bernhard Knoll-Tudor** is Director of Executive Education and Outreach at the Central European University's School of Public Policy. He previously worked in policy design and public relations for the Organization for Security and Co-operation in Europe, both at the level of field missions (Bosnia and Kosovo) and at the OSCE Office for Democratic Institutions and Human Rights (ODIHR) in Warsaw. His PhD thesis (European University Institute, Florence) on the subject of United Nation's governance of non-state territorial entities was published by Cambridge University Press in 2008.

**Harold Hongju Koh** is Sterling Professor of International Law at Yale Law School, where he has been a professor since 1985 and served as Dean from 2004–2009. As Assistant Secretary of State for Democracy, Human Rights and Labor from 1998–2001, he was the chief human rights official of the United States during the Kosovo crisis. As Legal Adviser to the US Department of State from 2009–2013, he argued before the International Court of Justice in 2009 as Head of Delegation and Advocate in the *Kosovo* case.

**Marko Milanović** is Associate Professor at the University of Nottingham School of Law. He is Vice-President and member of the Executive Board of the European Society of International Law, an Associate of the Belgrade Centre for Human Rights, and co-editor of EJIL: Talk!, the blog of the *European Journal of International Law*, as well as a member of the *EJIL*'s Editorial Board. He was an adviser to the legal team of Serbia in the *Kosovo* advisory proceedings.

**Daniel Müller** is a consultant in international law. He holds a PhD in Public Law from the Université Paris Ouest, Nanterre La Défense and the Humboldt-Universitätzu Berlin (cotutelle). He represented several states before the International Court of Justice, the International Tribunal for the Law of the Sea and other international courts and tribunals. He acted on behalf of Kosovo in the advisory proceedings.

**Sean Murphy** is the Patricia Roberts Harris Research Professor of Law at George Washington University, where he teaches international law and US foreign relations law. A Member since 2012 of the UN International Law Commission, he has appeared before numerous international courts and tribunals, including on behalf of Kosovo in the advisory proceedings.

**André Nollkaemper** is Professor of Public International Law at the Faculty of Law of the University of Amsterdam. He is also a Member of the Permanent Court of Arbitration, External Legal Adviser to the Minister of Foreign Affairs of the Netherlands, President of the European Society of International Law, and a member of the Royal Academy of Sciences of the Netherlands.

**Tatjana Papić** is Associate Professor in International Law at the Union University Belgrade School of Law. She was a Visiting Professor at the Washington and Lee University School of Law (Fall 2013), and previously Head of the Legal Department of the Belgrade Centre for Human Rights. She has published on various topics of public international law.

**Alain Pellet** is Professor at the University Paris Ouest Nanterre La Défense. He is a former member (1990–2011) and a former Chair (1997–1998) of the International Law Commission of the United Nations, member of the Institut de Droit International, and the President of the French Society for International Law since 2012. Pellet has been counsel in more than 50 cases before the International Court of Justice and the International Tribunal for the Law of the Sea, as well as in several international and transnational arbitrations. He acted as Counsel for France in the Kosovo advisory proceedings.

**Anne Peters** is Director at the Max Planck Institute for Comparative Public Law and International Law, Heidelberg, and a professor at the Universities of Heidelberg and Basel. She is member (substitute) of the European Commission for Democracy through Law (Venice Commission) in respect of Germany (since 2011) and served as the President of the European Society of International Law (2010–2012).

**Qudsi Rasheed** is qualified as barrister in England and Wales. He was part of the legal team representing Kosovo in the advisory proceedings. Having practised in the areas of public law and public international law, as well as working for the human rights NGO, Justice, he has been a member of the UK Diplomatic Service since 2010, initially as a Foreign Office legal adviser, and presently as a First Secretary in the UK Representation to the EU in Brussels.

**Marc Weller** is Professor of International Law and International Constitutional Studies at the University of Cambridge and the Director of the Lauterpacht Centre for International Law. He is the author, editor or co-editor of some 25 books, including *Contested Statehood: Kosovo's Struggle for Independence* (Oxford University Press, 2009) and, most recently, the Oxford University Press *Handbook on the Use of Force in International Law*.

**Stefan Wolff** is Professor of International Security at the University of Birmingham and an Associate Fellow at the Royal United Services Institute in London. Among his 17 books to date are *Disputed Territories: The Transnational Dynamics of Ethnic Conflict Settlement, Ethnic Conflict: A Global Perspective, Ethnic Conflict: Causes, Consequences, and Responses*, and, as co-editor, *The Routledge Handbook of Ethnic Conflict, Conflict Management in Divided Societies: Theories and Practice*, and *The European Union as a Global Conflict Manager*.

**Michael Wood** is a member of the International Law Commission, and a Senior Fellow of the Lauterpacht Centre for International Law, University of Cambridge. He is a barrister at 20 Essex Street, London, where he practises in the field of public international law, including before international courts and tribunals. He was Legal Adviser to the UK's Foreign and Commonwealth Office between 1999 and 2006, having joined as an Assistant Legal Adviser in 1970. He acted on behalf of Kosovo in the advisory proceedings.

Disclaimer: with regard to all of the contributors who participated in the *Kosovo* advisory proceedings on behalf of one of the participants, the views and opinions expressed in their contributions are strictly personal and not made in any official capacity. Similarly, in editing this book, neither editor was in any sense acting on behalf of his former client, nor should he be taken as necessarily endorsing the views expressed by the various contributors.

# 1

# Introduction

*Marko Milanović and*
*Michael Wood*

This volume is an edited collection of essays on various aspects of the 2010 *Kosovo* advisory opinion of the International Court of Justice. We drew inspiration for the book in part from the very successful collection, edited by Laurence Boisson de Chazournes and Philippe Sands, *International Law, the International Court of Justice and Nuclear Weapons*, dealing with the ICJ's *Nuclear Weapons* opinion and published by CUP in 1999, which is in many ways the definitive work on those decisions and is still widely read. We hope that this book will similarly make a significant and long-lasting contribution to scholarship.

This book, however, is different in purpose and scope from its *Nuclear Weapons* predecessor, and for two reasons. First, because the *Kosovo* opinion has (by design) much less substantive content. Second, because the *Kosovo* opinion has already attracted a significant amount of academic commentary—there is a reasonably comprehensive bibliography of works specifically dealing with the advisory opinion at the end of this book, which we hope will be a useful resource. As is normally the case, the existing commentary varies in quality, and much of it is less considered than perhaps it could have been. That said, we see little benefit in simply adding to the existing pile of commentary or incrementally developing the quality of scholarship further. In short, a traditional book focusing purely on a doctrinal analysis of the opinion would probably not be one that our authors would be interested in writing, or that others would be interested in reading.

We have thus opted for a different approach, one that we believe can produce novel and original results. The main theme of the book is the interplay between law and politics regarding Kosovo's independence generally and the opinion specifically. How and why did the Court become the battleground in which Kosovo's independence was to be fought out (or not)? How and why did *political* arguments in favour of Kosovo's independence (e.g. that Kosovo was a unique, *sui generis* case which set no precedent for other secessionist territories) change in the formal, *legal* setting of advisory proceedings before the Court? How and why did states supporting either Kosovo or Serbia choose to frame their arguments? How did the Court perceive them? What did the Court want to achieve, and did it succeed in doing so?

And how was the opinion received, and what broader implications has it had so far? These are the questions that we hope to shed some light on. Above all, we want to tell the *story* of the case, place it within its broader political context, and so advance our understanding of how such cases are initiated, litigated, and decided.

We assembled a stellar cast of contributors to help us address these questions. Naturally, most of them are international lawyers, since the book is mainly geared towards a legal audience. Indeed, many of the contributors (including the two editors) were directly involved in the case as counsel or advisors to different participants in the proceedings. Great care was taken that the chapters written by such insiders are not repetitive advocacy pieces. Of course, each contributor wrote his or her chapter in their individual capacity. This insider perspective is complemented by those authors who were observing the proceedings from the outside. In particular, we not only have lawyers among our contributors, but a number of eminent scholars of politics and international relations whose pieces further enrich the book and give it an interdisciplinary angle.

The book is divided into four parts. Part I places the *Kosovo* advisory opinion in its context. James Ker-Lindsay examines Serbia's motives for going to the ICJ. Marko Milanović looks at how the case was argued, and how arguments for or against Kosovo's independence made in the political arena had to be adjusted when the case came before the Court. Qudsi Rasheed and Michael Wood explain some practicalities of arguing a case with so many different participants. Bernhard Knoll-Tudor places the advisory proceedings in the context of the political process for the determination of Kosovo's final status.

Part II looks at the opinion itself, at what it said and left unsaid. Vladimir Djerić looks at issues of the Court's jurisdiction and its discretion to decline a request for an advisory opinion—the latter option indeed having attracted a sizable minority of the Court. Daniel Müller analyses the 'question question', namely how the formulation of the question drafted by Serbia and put to the Court by the General Assembly, as well as the Court's handling of that formulation, shaped the entirety of the case. Sean Murphy examines the Court's approach to interpreting Security Council resolution 1244 (1999), which was the main issue on merits. Mathias Forteau looks at the ambiguous position of the UN Secretary-General as an actor both inside and outside the advisory proceedings. Marc Weller then tries to makes sense of the sounds of silence in the Court's opinion and the various issues that the Court left unaddressed.

Part III discusses the reactions to the opinion and its wider implications. André Nollkaemper looks at whether the Court itself managed to satisfy its various constituencies in deciding the case as it did. Tatjana Papić analyses the opinion's political aftermath, specifically with regard to the relations between Serbia and Kosovo. Alain Pellet looks at questions that the Court left open, such as self-determination and recognition, while James Crawford discusses whether Kosovo satisfied the legal criteria for statehood. Anne Peters then examines whether either the opinion or Kosovo's secession have created an unfortunate precedent.

Finally, Part IV looks at the road ahead for Kosovo and Serbia. Richard Caplan and Stefan Wolff discuss the opinion's implications for the resolution of the

Kosovo/Serbia dispute, while James Gow advances the idea of an EU 'free territory' as a possible solution that would allow for the integration of both Serbia and Kosovo within the EU. Harold Hongju Koh then concludes the book with his reflections on the law and politics of the Kosovo opinion.

***

Why read this book? For some its intellectual content should be reason enough (time permitting), and it will obviously be of relevance to those with a direct interest in the status of Kosovo and the resolution of its dispute with Serbia. But Kosovo and the Court's opinion—and hence this book—may have bearing on other cases of secession and contested statehood, especially if such cases somehow fall within the remit of an (international) court. There are valuable lessons that the Kosovo example can teach us.

Consider, first, the Court's own efforts to produce a minimalist opinion, facilitated by the rather dubious formulation of the question put to it by the General Assembly. The Court was very conscious indeed of the imperative of future damage control, which led it to confine its examination of general international law issues to a couple of paragraphs. Note then how the formulation of the question, which proved to be so detrimental to Serbia's position before the Court, may have in the end produced the best of all political outcomes. The broader nationalist narratives of Serbia and Kosovo have remained unaffected by the opinion, and entrenched as they are would have remained as unaffected no matter what the Court had said—each side remains convinced of the justness of its cause. But the silences of the Court's opinion allowed the political elites of Serbia and Kosovo to move along the path of normalizing their relations towards integration into the EU, and, especially in Serbia, the proceedings bought enough time for nationalist passions to cool and a more *Realpolitik*-minded attitude to emerge.[1] In other words, even had Serbia 'won' the case on a similarly or somewhat better-worded question, for example if the Court said that Kosovo had *no right* to secede from Serbia, Serbia still would not have recovered Kosovo as a matter of fact. But having 'lost' the case in the precise way that it did, Serbia may have found a way of putting the whole Kosovo question behind it while continuing to maintain that it will not recognize Kosovo as an independent state.

But other consequences of the Kosovo episode are less salutary, as best evidenced by the unfolding tragedy in Ukraine. On one hand, the positions of Western powers with regard to Kosovo and (to a lesser extent) Iraq may have weakened their ability to criticize Russia's annexation of Crimea, for all that they claimed that Kosovo was somehow a special, *sui generis* case. This is not to say that as a matter of law there are no differences between Kosovo and Crimea—far from it. The most critical such difference is that Crimea's secession and subsequent annexation was the direct result of Russia's unlawful military intervention against Ukraine, whereas Kosovo's secession was not tainted to the same extent by NATO's 1999 intervention (which many would regard as illegal, and some as nonetheless legitimate) due to the subsequent adoption of resolution 1244 (1999), which authorized the

---

[1] We owe this point to Tatjana Papić.

presence of international forces in Kosovo while disabling Serbia from taking military action to suppress Kosovo's secession.

But even if Kosovo and Crimea are legally distinguishable, they are still close enough. At a normative or even purely rhetorical level the secession of Crimea was at least partly facilitated by the Kosovo 'precedent'.[2] This equally goes for the Court's opinion, despite all the care that the Court took to avoid precisely such adverse effects. Consider only President Putin's speech justifying the annexation of Crimea by explicit reference to Kosovo and the ICJ's advisory opinion:

Moreover, the Crimean authorities referred to the well-known Kosovo precedent—a precedent our western colleagues created with their own hands in a very similar situation, when they agreed that the unilateral separation of Kosovo from Serbia, exactly what Crimea is doing now, was legitimate and did not require any permission from the country's central authorities. Pursuant to Article 2, Chapter 1 of the United Nations Charter, the UN International Court agreed with this approach and made the following comment in its ruling of July 22, 2010, and I quote: 'No general prohibition may be inferred from the practice of the Security Council with regard to declarations of independence,' and 'General international law contains no prohibition on declarations of independence.' Crystal clear, as they say.

I do not like to resort to quotes, but in this case, I cannot help it. Here is a quote from another official document: the Written Statement of the United States America of April 17, 2009, submitted to the same UN International Court in connection with the hearings on Kosovo. Again, I quote: 'Declarations of independence may, and often do, violate domestic legislation. However, this does not make them violations of international law.' End of quote. They wrote this, disseminated it all over the world, had everyone agree and now they are outraged. Over what? The actions of Crimean people completely fit in with these instructions, as it were. For some reason, things that Kosovo Albanians (and we have full respect for them) were permitted to do, Russians, Ukrainians and Crimean Tatars in Crimea are not allowed. Again, one wonders why. [3]

The appeal of this critique is undeniable, even if it is ultimately contradictory and self-defeating. How can President Putin say all this while continuing to refuse to recognize Kosovo's independence, or for that matter after forcibly suppressing Chechnya's attempts to secede from Russia? His misinterpretations of the Court's advisory opinion are obvious, or at least obvious *to international lawyers*—the Court never said that Kosovo's separation from Serbia was legitimate, or that Kosovo is a state under international law. All it said was that the declaration of independence itself, as a piece of paper, did not violate international law, while adding that a declaration could do so if it was the result of an unlawful use of force by a third state (see, e.g., Crimea). The Court said absolutely nothing about self-determination, and rightly so.

And while President Putin was happy to quote from the US written statement in the Kosovo proceedings (with which everyone most certainly did *not* agree),

---

[2] On which, see Anne Peters' contribution to this volume.
[3] 'Address by President of the Russian Federation', Moscow, 18 March 2014, at <http://eng.kremlin.ru/news/6889>.

he failed to quote from Russia's own, which was at least as 'crystal clear' as the American one. Russia was in fact the only state in the pro-Serbia camp in the advisory proceedings, and, indeed, the only state among the permanent five members of the UN Security Council to argue that there *is* a right to remedial secession for peoples denied their right to internal self-determination, but one subject to exceptionally strict conditions. According to Russia's written statement:

[T]he Russian Federation is of the view that the primary purpose of the 'safeguard clause' [of the Friendly Relations Declaration] is to serve as a guarantee of territorial integrity of States. It is also true that the clause may be construed as authorizing secession under certain conditions. However, those conditions should be limited to truly extreme circumstances, such as an outright armed attack by the parent State, threatening the very existence of the people in question. Otherwise, all efforts should be taken in order to settle the tension between the parent State and the ethnic community concerned within the framework of the existing State.[4]

The statement later adds that:

[O]utside the colonial context, international law allows for secession of a part of a State against the latter's will only as a matter of self-determination of peoples, and only in extreme circumstances, when the people concerned is continuously subjected to most severe forms of oppression that endangers the very existence of the people.[5]

Russia thus claimed that on the facts Kosovo did not satisfy these stringent criteria even in 1999, let alone in 2008 when it declared independence. In the oral proceedings before the Court, Russia argued that the population of Kosovo did not constitute a people entitled to self-determination;[6] that even if they were entitled to self-determination they could exercise that right within Serbia;[7] and that the principle of territorial integrity stems from peremptory norms of international law which are not binding only upon states.[8]

If Kosovo, with all the systematic repression inflicted upon its population by Serbian authorities, could not in Russian eyes satisfy these criteria, then one fails to see how Crimea could begin to do so. Even when taking Russia's legal position at face value and accepting at their fullest Russia's descriptions of extremists influencing the Kiev Government, and even assuming that the population of Crimea constitutes a 'people', that people was on no reasonable appraisal of the facts 'continuously subjected to most severe forms of oppression that endangers [their] very existence.'

Governmental hypocrisy is of course nothing new, and with Crimea as with Kosovo there was plenty of it to go around. Our point here is different. President Putin's speech is the best example of how the Court's opinion (or any judicial opinion) can be twisted to serve a party's own ends, despite what the Court said or wanted to say. But, more importantly, this type of abuse was made possible by how

---

[4] Written Statement of the Russian Federation, 16 April 2009, available at <http://www.icj-cij.org/docket/files/141/15628.pdf>, p. 31, para. 88.
[5] Ibid., pp. 39–40.    [6] CR 2009/30, p. 42, para. 9.    [7] Ibid., p. 44, paras. 23–24.
[8] Ibid., p. 46, para. 34.

the Court itself chose to decide the case. Had the Court, for example, chosen to dispense with the case on grounds of discretion and propriety,[9] its opinion could not have figured in the Russian justifications of the secession and annexation of Crimea as it did.

In other words, the minimalist Court was perhaps not minimalist enough. Of course, whether minimalism was the best strategy in the first place and whether the Court as a general matter opted for the wisest of routes is a matter of reasonable disagreement, one of many examined in *The Law and Politics of the Kosovo Advisory Opinion*.

---

[9] For more, see the contributions by Marko Milanović and Vladimir Djerić in this volume.

# PART I

# THE ADVISORY PROCEEDINGS IN CONTEXT

# 2

# Explaining Serbia's Decision to Go to the ICJ

*James Ker-Lindsay*

## 1. Introduction

Following Kosovo's unilateral declaration of independence in February 2008, the Serbian Government initiated a range of steps to discourage international recognition of the new state. Perhaps the most controversial of these was the decision to seek an advisory opinion from the International Court of Justice (ICJ). As will be seen, the move served both internal and external goals. Internally, it provided further evidence that firm measures were being taken to challenge Kosovo's secession. Internationally, it was understood that even if the process did not result in an eventual legal victory that would force countries that had recognized Kosovo to reverse their decision, it would nevertheless serve to slow the pace of recognition as many countries would wait for the Court's decision. However, the decision to refer the matter to the Court also posed risks for Serbia. Most notably, it had the potential to disrupt relations with both the United States and key members of the European Union. As a result, Belgrade adopted a rather cautious approach when deciding how to frame the question to be put before the Court. Despite this effort not to antagonize key states, there was initially strong opposition to the move by a number of EU members. But this proved to be short-lived after it became apparent that efforts to pressure Serbia to drop the case were sending out the wrong message to the wider international community. As a result, on 9 October 2008, the United Nations General Assembly passed a resolution referring the question of the legality of Kosovo's declaration of independence to the ICJ.

## 2. The Declaration of Independence and Serbia's Response

By the middle of 2007, it was clear that Kosovo was preparing to declare independence. Although the Security Council had failed to reach an agreement on the Ahtisaari proposals, and a new process had been convened under the auspices of the Troika, few observers were left with any real doubt that the authorities in Pristina were determined to secede, with or without UN approval.[1] This perception was further reinforced by the strong statements of support coming from key Western countries, such as the United States, in particular,[2] as well as Britain, France, and, to a lesser extent at this stage, Germany. As a result, the Serbian Government was left with little choice but to begin to plan its strategy for the moment when the declaration of independence occurred.

Although Belgrade was adamant from the outset that it would not resort to the threat or use of armed force to pursue its sovereignty over Kosovo,[3] it nevertheless reserved the right to take all necessary legal, political, and economic steps required to defend its claim to the province. All ministries were therefore asked to prepare proposals outlining the steps they could take to manage the situation.[4] Within the Foreign Ministry a diplomatic campaign was designed to prevent the recognition of Kosovo by other states and prevent it from joining various international organizations; an effort that would be overseen by the foreign minister, Vuk Jeremic.[5] As part of this wider external effort to prevent Kosovo from being recognized and legitimized, in December 2007 President Boris Tadić raised the possibility that Serbia would even consider referring the question of Kosovo's unilateral secession to the International Court of Justice (ICJ).[6]

Serbia was therefore well prepared for the unilateral declaration of independence when it finally came, on 18 February 2008. Days beforehand, the Serbian Parliament passed a resolution annulling the decision.[7] This was followed by a decision to pursue treason charges against the president, prime minister, and speaker of the parliament in Kosovo.[8] Meanwhile, the campaign to prevent the international recognition of the new 'Republic of Kosovo' began in earnest.[9] From the outset, it was obvious that in many cases such efforts were pointless. There was never any doubt that the United States and many EU members would quickly recognize the new state, and that they would strongly encourage others to do so. As a result, within the first six weeks after the declaration of independence, 35

---

[1] For more on the status talks, see the chapter by Bernhard Knoll-Tudor in this volume. See also Marc Weller, 'The Vienna Negotiations on the Final Status of Kosovo', *International Affairs*, Volume 84, Number 4, 2008; and James Ker-Lindsay, *Kosovo: The Path to Contested Statehood in the Balkans* (London: I.B.Tauris, 2009).

[2] 'Bush says Kosovo to be independent, delights Albania', *Reuters*, 10 June 2007.

[3] 'Serbs to take West to International Court on Kosovo', *Reuters*, 10 December 2007; 'Kosovo declares Its independence from Serbia', *New York Times*, 18 February 2008.

[4] 'Serbs, Albanians totally opposed on Kosovo', *Reuters*, 26 November 2007.

[5] In the two years after Kosovo declared independence, it is estimated that Jeremic travelled to over 90 countries. 'Recasting Serbia's image, starting with a fresh face', *New York Times*, 15 January 2010.

[6] 'Serbs to take West to International Court on Kosovo', *Reuters*, 10 December 2007.

[7] 'Serbian government decides to "annul" Kosovo independence', *AFP*, 14 February 2008. 'Decision on the annulment of the illegitimate acts of the provisional institutions of self-government in Kosovo and Metohija on their declaration of unilateral independence', Serbian Ministry of Foreign Affairs, 14 February 2008. (Republished by *B92* <http://www.b92.net/eng/insight/strategies.php?yyyy=2008&mm=02&nav_id=47715>. Last accessed, 10 November 2014.)

[8] 'Serbia charges Kosovo leaders with treason', *Reuters*, 18 February 2008.

[9] For an analysis of Serbia's diplomatic efforts to prevent the recognition of Kosovo, see James Ker-Lindsay, *The Foreign Policy of Counter Secession: Preventing the Recognition of Contested States* (Oxford: Oxford University Press, 2012).

countries had explicitly accepted the new state of affairs.[10] However, Serbia was also able to claim some important victories. Most importantly, Russia issued a strongly worded statement condemning the declaration of independence, which it claimed violated, 'the sovereignty of the Republic of Serbia, the Charter of the United Nations, UNSCR 1244, the principles of the Helsinki Final Act, Kosovo's Constitutional Framework and the high-level Contact Group accords'.[11] The Chinese Government also noted its grave concern about the move.[12] The positions of Moscow and Beijing were crucial inasmuch as they signalled that Kosovo would be unable to join the United Nations; a key step in the overall process of legitimizing Kosovo on the world stage. Meanwhile, many other counties also announced that they would not recognize Kosovo under the current circumstances. As well as emerging regional leaders, such as India and Brazil, the list of the stated 'non-recognizers' included several European Union members, notably Cyprus, Greece, Romania, Slovakia, and Spain.[13]

In between the two opposing poles of opinion lay the majority of UN members. These were to become the 'battleground states'.[14] In some cases, resistance to recognizing Kosovo was relatively strong, but far from insurmountable. While not wishing to antagonize any side, many countries harboured deep concerns about the implications of legitimizing a unilateral act of secession. They might relent, but would have to be persuaded. In contrast, a number of other states appeared to be rather more willing to recognize, but did not want to be seen to rush into a decision for whatever reason. Without a good reason to resist, it seemed likely that many of these 'undeclared' states would eventually relent under the growing pressure being brought to bear on them by the United States, Britain, and France—the three countries leading international efforts to secure recognition.[15] At the heart of their tactics for winning over wavering states lay the argument that Kosovo was a unique case ('*sui generis*') in international politics. This was significant as it seemingly offered reassurance that the decision to recognize Kosovo would not have any spill-over effects elsewhere.[16] This in turn made the situation all the more

[10] In addition to the United States, Britain, France, Germany, and Italy, the Western members of the Contact Group overseeing Kosovo's status process, it was recognized by 14 other EU members as well as by, inter alia, Japan, Australia, South Korea, Turkey, Switzerland, Canada, and Norway.
[11] 'Statement by Russia's Ministry of Foreign Affairs on Kosovo', 216-17-02-2008, The Ministry of Foreign Affairs of the Russian Federation, 17 February 2008.
[12] 'Foreign Ministry Spokesperson Liu Jianchao's Remarks on Kosovo's Unilateral Declaration of Independence', Ministry of Foreign Affairs of the People's Republic of China, 18 February 2008.
[13] See, for example, 'Romania will not recognize Kosovo independence', *Reuters*, 19 February 2008; '"Cyprus doesn't recognize Kosovo independence"', *B92*, 26 March 2008. A few other EU members, such as Malta and Portugal, did not recognize Kosovo in the immediate weeks that followed the declaration of independence, but had done so by the end of 2008.
[14] For more on the view of various states, see James Ker-Lindsay, 'Sovereignty and the Subversion of UN Authority', in Aidan Hehir (ed), *Kosovo, Intervention and Statebuilding: The International Community and the Transition to Independence* (Abingdon: Routledge, 2010).
[15] Both the United Kingdom and the United States launched a major diplomatic initiative following the declaration of independence to persuade countries to recognize Kosovo. For example, the Foreign and Commonwealth Office even had an official dedicated to coordinating recognition efforts (comments by an FCO official to the author, 2011).
[16] The 'unique case argument' became the centrepiece of efforts to encourage states to recognize Kosovo. See, inter alia, 'Kosovo case unique, says Miliband', *BBC News*, 19 February 2008;

difficult for Serbia as it provided a seemingly plausible cover for states if they did wish to join the ranks of the recognizers; even though many countries appeared to understand that the assertion that Kosovo was *sui generis* was essentially a political, and not a legal, claim.[17]

Given this combination of strong diplomatic pressure and the 'unique case' argument, Serbia had little choice but to formulate a strategy that would challenge this argument head on before the ICJ. The difficulty facing the Serbian Government was that this was fraught with danger. While a decision by the Court in its favour could have a major positive effect, and might even result in some countries reversing their initial decision to recognize Kosovo,[18] there was always the possibility that the ICJ could come down in favour of Kosovo. This would almost certainly open the flood gates to further recognition. Ultimately, though, Belgrade had little choice but to pursue the ICJ option. By failing to act at all, it would not only allow the pressure on countries to recognize Kosovo to go unchecked, it could also send out the message that Serbia had either decided that it did not have a strong case, or that it was effectively signalling that it had given up on Kosovo. Balanced against this risk, however, Belgrade also realized that, regardless of the eventual outcome of the case, a referral to the Court would almost certainly deprive Kosovo of a lot of the recognition momentum it had established in the initial weeks after the declaration of independence. For as long as the question of Kosovo's independence was before the Court, it would be perfectly reasonable for Serbia to ask states to defer their decision on recognition, despite the pressure that they were facing—a tactic that would in fact prove to be broadly successful.[19] Regardless of the eventual outcome, the decision to refer the matter to the International Court of Justice therefore came to be seen as a cornerstone of Belgrade's wider diplomatic strategy to prevent recognition.

Simultaneously, the decision to pursue a case before the ICJ also played an important role in domestic Serbian politics. The declaration of independence had led to major demonstrations in Serbia and there was still considerable public unhappiness at the way in which Serbia had been treated by the United States and the main EU members. By referring the matter to the Court, the government would buy valuable time at home to allow popular feeling to subside while still being able to claim that it had taken a decisive step to protect the country's national interests. To this extent, the element of delay would prove to be a crucial factor underlying the decision from both a domestic and foreign policy angle.

---

'The Case for Kosovo', US State Department (Last accessed 10 November 2014: <http://www.state. gov/p/eur/ci/kv/c24701.htm>). For an analysis of this argument, see James Ker-Lindsay, 'Preventing the Emergence of Self-Determination as a Norm of Secession: An Assessment of the Kosovo "Unique Case" Argument', *Europe-Asia Studies*, Volume 65, Number 5, 2013.

[17] Even a number of officials from recognizing states have admitted that there is very little justification to the 'unique case' argument. It was essentially put together when it became clear that there was no alternative to granting Kosovo independence, but that such a move could have wider spill-over effects.

[18] For example, Costa Rica, just prior to the UN General Assembly vote, reportedly told Serbia that it would rescind its recognition if the Court decided the declaration of independence was contrary to international law. 'Kosovo recognitions "will be retracted"', *Balkan Insight*, 2 October 2008.

[19] '"ICJ case delays recognition process"', *B92*, 23 April 2010.

## 3. The Decision to Question Recognition or Secession

Having decided on the importance of pursuing a case before the ICJ, Serbia now had to decide on the specific approach it wished to take. It faced several choices. One option was, however, always off the table. There was never any possibility of bringing a case against Kosovo directly. In part, this was because Kosovo was not a state party to the Statute of the Court. However, it was also understood that, 'such action would represent a tacit acknowledgment of Kosovo's statehood'.[20] This left two other main options. On the one hand, Belgrade could challenge the legality of the decision by one or more states to recognize Kosovo in contentious proceedings. On the other, they could seek an advisory opinion on the legality of the declaration of independence itself.

Assuming the Court eventually came down in Serbia's favour, the first option was widely viewed as being much the better route. As far as Belgrade was concerned, the decision of states to recognize Kosovo amounted to a clear breach of international obligations to respect the territorial integrity of the Republic of Serbia. Moreover, it was the best choice in terms of achieving the specific goal of forcing states that had recognized Kosovo to reverse their decision as well as preventing further recognition. But it also presented several major drawbacks. In the first instance, it was hardly practical to go against every state that had recognized Kosovo.[21] Of course, Serbia could instead pursue a case against a small number of states. Here again, the options were limited. While the most obvious targets were the United States or the key EU members, a decision to focus on them would almost certainly have grave implications. While Belgrade may have been extremely unhappy at the way in which Washington had supported Kosovo's secession, Serbian officials were nevertheless keen to ensure that the diplomatic fallout with Washington and the EU was minimized. The United States was seen as a crucial strategic and economic partner for Serbia. Any attempt to bring a case against the US would have seriously harmed bilateral relations. As for the EU members, there was a real possibility that the states in question would retaliate by blocking Serbia's EU integration process. This would run counter to the explicitly stated policy of the Serbian Government to pursue the twin goals of 'Kosovo and EU membership'. Certainly within the Democratic Party (DS) elements of the government, there was never any question of relinquishing EU accession for Kosovo (nor vice versa).[22]

Another option would have been to bring a case against a small non-EU country in the hope that if Serbia won it would then force the other countries to change their positions. But this too was impractical. For a start, such an approach would

---

[20] Vidan Hadzi-Vidanovic, 'Conflict Settlement by the International Court of Justice', paper presented at the international symposium 'Problems and Procedures of National and International Conflict Settlement: South Eastern Europe as Conflict Area and Other Examples', Inter-University Centre Berlin/Split, Free University of Berlin, 9–10 July 2010. Available at SSRN: <http://ssrn.com/abstract=1988922> or <http://dx.doi.org/10.2139/ssrn.1988922>.

[21] 'Serbia to go to ICJ over Kosovo', *B92*, 26 March 2008.

[22] 'Tadić: Serbia wants both Kosovo and EU', *B92*, 10 January 2008.

still have posed a challenge to the decisions taken by the US and the EU recognizers inasmuch as a successful outcome for Serbia would have had an impact on their recognition decisions. It would also have damaged Serbia's credibility more widely. There was a real chance that Belgrade would be seen as being too cowardly to face the big powers, and so had decided to bully a smaller state. This would be especially damaging for Serbia given that much of its counter-recognition activity was now aimed at trying to win support from various African, Asian, and Latin American states. It could not afford to alienate this group.

Therefore, while the option of challenging the decision of one or more countries to recognize Kosovo was favoured by many in Serbia, most notably the caretaker prime minister, Vojislav Koštunica,[23] it was deemed to be too politically costly by both the president and the foreign minister, who were ultimately the key decision makers on this issue.[24] As a result, Serbia decided against any direct challenge to the decision of states to recognize Kosovo. This in turn meant that Serbia now had only one other route. If Belgrade was not going to pursue a contentious case against a state directly, it had no alternative but to seek an advisory opinion on some aspect of the legality of Kosovo's secession.

## 4. International Opposition to the Case

On 26 March 2008, the Serbian Government announced that it would pursue an advisory opinion on the legality of Kosovo's declaration of independence.[25] As the ICJ could only issue an advisory opinion if asked to do so by the Security Council or the General Assembly,[26] or by an organ authorized to do so by the General Assembly,[27] attention now turned to securing a General Assembly resolution referring the matter to the Court.[28]

Despite the fact that Belgrade had chosen to pursue a less confrontational route, the announcement by the Serbian Government that it intended to secure a General Assembly resolution bringing the matter before the International Court of Justice nevertheless brought about a strongly negative reaction from a number of countries. The United States immediately made it clear that it felt that the move was not only unhelpful, but would have little practical effect. Washington insisted that even if the case were to be brought to the Court, and the judges issued an opinion against Kosovo, it would have no effect on its decision to recognize Kosovo. As far as the US Government was concerned, and in line with its long held policy, recognition remained a sovereign political decision. Within the European Union, the position was a little less certain. For a start, there was a much greater reluctance to

---

[23] 'Koštunica favors lawsuits over Kosovo', *Beta*, 27 October 2008.
[24] Comments by a Serbian official to the author, August 2013.
[25] 'Serbia to go to ICJ over Kosovo', *B92*, 26 March 2008.
[26] Chapter XIV, Article 96, paragraph 1, Charter of the United Nations.
[27] Chapter XIV, Article 96, paragraph 2, Charter of the United Nations.
[28] A Security Council resolution referring the matter to the Court would not have been a feasible option as it would have been vetoed by the United States, and possibly by France and Britain as well.

dismiss any outcome of the Court. When pressed on the point, British officials, for example, refused to be drawn on whether they would be as willing as the United States to disregard an advisory opinion of the ICJ. To this extent, several of the key EU members that had recognized Kosovo, most notably Britain and France, decided that a more worthwhile approach to the matter would be to try to persuade Serbia to change its mind. To that end, several senior officials made it clear that Belgrade's decision to proceed with the application for an advisory opinion could have a very harmful effect on its quest for EU accession. Indeed, it was even suggested that it could bring the process to a halt entirely.[29]

The problem for the European Union was that its attempts to dissuade Serbia from pursuing the case had the potential to put it in a very difficult position on the international stage. For a start, and most obviously, by trying to stop Serbia from going to the ICJ, it would rather suggest that members actually harboured real doubts over the legality of their decision to recognize Kosovo. If they were so sure about the validity of their decision, as many states were publicly insisting, then surely they would have little to fear if it went before the ICJ. Of course, it was not as simple as this. A decision could turn against either side, no matter how watertight they felt their arguments were. Nevertheless, by being seen to be opposing an advisory opinion, there was a real danger that this would inevitably be read as a sign of the intrinsic weakness of their case, which might well have deterred some of those countries from sitting on the fence from recognizing Kosovo. Second, when looked at from a wider perspective, at a time when EU members were attempting to emphasize the importance of international law in global politics, and were seeking to strengthen the institutions of international justice, it would have sent out the message that they are unwilling to subject their own actions to legal oversight. They would run the risk of being accused of double standards. This accusation of double standards would have been especially strong in the case of Serbia. Having taken an uncompromising stand on Belgrade's full cooperation with the International Criminal Tribunal for the Former Yugoslavia (ICTY) as a precondition for membership of the Union, it would not look good for EU members to demand that their own actions be exempt from legal scrutiny on the grounds of political expediency. Finally, it would have had possibly unwelcome implications for the EU's ability to handle peace and security in South East Europe. After insisting that the states of the Western Balkans must not resort to armed force in managing their disputes, and having explicitly warned Serbia not to do so in the case of Kosovo, it would have been illogical, if not fundamentally wrong, to try to close off the most peaceful and legitimate methods of conflict resolution.

Therefore, while the United States remained adamantly opposed to any effort to bring the matter before the ICJ, for the reasons stated above, the European Union soon realized that it would be counter-productive to issue any further threats against Serbia, or otherwise try to pressure Belgrade to desist from seeking an advisory opinion.

---

[29] 'A June tide', *The Economist*, 19 June 2008; 'Kouchner calls on Serbia to drop ICJ plans', *B92*, 23 July 2008; '"ICJ move direct challenge to EU"', *B92*, 3 August 2008.

## 5. The UN General Assembly Resolution

Once Serbia had opted to pursue the advisory opinion route, it needed to decide the exact question to be put to the Court. Once again, there were several options available. These essentially broke down into two categories. Belgrade could either question the legality of the declaration of independence or it could ask whether the declaration of Kosovo had brought into effect a new state. The latter question was perhaps the more risky inasmuch as it would force the Court to take a very clear stand on the actual status of Kosovo as a political entity. If the Court found in Kosovo's favour, then the way would be open for widespread recognition to follow. The former question, on the legality of the declaration of independence, therefore seemed less risky. But even then, there were further decisions to be made about the exact question to be asked. On the one hand, a very specific question could be formulated that closely matched the one put to the Canadian Supreme Court over Quebec.[30] Again, this would offer a much greater chance of a clear outcome. The problem is that this outcome could go against Serbia, in which case Belgrade's room for manoeuvre would be severely curtailed. In contrast, a far more ambiguous question would offer plenty of room for the judges to offer a less precise answer, thereby make it less likely that Serbia would find itself trapped by a wholly unfavourable decision. In the end, the Serbian Government decided against a highly specific question. On 15 August 2008, the Serbian Government unveiled the text of the proposed resolution. The exact question to be addressed to the Court was as follows: 'Is the unilateral declaration of independence by the Provisional Institutions of Self-Government of Kosovo in accordance with international law?'

In the weeks that followed, a vigorous diplomatic campaign took place as the various parties tried to lobby countries to vote in their favour. In an attempt to build support for its position, Serbian officials held over 50 bilateral meetings with foreign officials.[31] In doing so, it sought to emphasize the dangers of the Kosovo precedent and allowing it to go unchallenged. For example, following a meeting with the UN Secretary-General, Tadić stated, 'to vote against means to accept that nothing could be done when secessionists in whichever part of the world proclaim the uniqueness of their cause, and claim exception to the universal scope of international law'.[32] Meanwhile, the United States actively encouraged countries to vote against the draft resolution. However, the European Union decided not to follow the US position. Having so openly

---

[30] 'Does international law give the National Assembly, legislature or government of Quebec the right to effect the secession of Quebec from Canada unilaterally? In this regard, is there a right to self-determination under international law that would give the National Assembly, legislature or government of Quebec the right to effect the secession of Quebec from Canada unilaterally?', Supreme Court of Canada, 20 July 1998, Reference re Secession of Quebec, [1998] 2 S.C.R. 217.

[31] 'Serbia receives UN backing on Kosovo in trial vote', *Euractiv*, 28 September 2008.

[32] 'Kosovo issue could undermine international system, Serbian leader tells UN', *UN News Centre*, 23 September 2008.

supported the ICJ, and international law, as a mechanism for resolving conflict, the EU could not be seen to be voting against an effort to bring a matter that they were closely involved with before the Court. Nor could EU members be seen to be trying to persuade others to vote against the resolution. For this reason, it was agreed that those EU members that did not plan to vote in favour of the resolution, notably the members that had not recognized Kosovo, should instead abstain.

In the weeks that followed, many other states also chose to take the same position as the European Union. As a result, by the day of the vote, 8 October 2008, it was widely understood that there were likely to be few votes cast against the resolution. Along with the EU members, most of the other recognizing states, which by this point amounted to 47 countries, approximately a quarter of the UN, had also opted either to abstain or not to participate at all. Meanwhile, Serbia had managed to muster considerable support for its case. In addition to Russia and China and the EU states that had chosen not to recognize Kosovo, it also managed to gather support from a number of other countries, including at least one recognizing state—Norway.[33] Nevertheless, the vote was preceded by a strong debate. For example, the US Deputy Permanent Representative to the UN insisted that Kosovo's independence was in accordance with international law and that the resolution was 'unnecessary and unhelpful'.[34] Meanwhile, the British Permanent Representative to the UN, Sir John Sawers, accused Serbia of pursuing the case, 'primarily for political rather than legal reasons.'[35]

In the end, 77 countries voted in favour of the resolution.[36] As well as Russia, China, and the remaining five non-recognizing EU members,[37] the resolution was supported by Brazil, India, Indonesia, Nigeria, and South Africa. By contrast, just six countries voted against the resolution: the United States; Albania; and four Pacific island states. 74 states, including all the members of the European Union that had by this point recognized Kosovo, abstained. The remaining 34 members—including Turkey and Bosnia-Herzegovina—decided not to participate in the vote at all.[38]

---

[33] As Hakon Blankenborg, the Norwegian Ambassador in Belgrade, later explained, 'Norway has voted for Kosovo's independence, but realizing how complicated the issue is we voted in the UN General Assembly in favor of taking the case before the International Court of Justice in The Hague': 'Norway awaits court decision', *B92*, 21 December 2008.

[34] 'Backing Request by Serbia, General Assembly Decides to Seek International Court of Justice Ruling on Legality of Kosovo's Independence', Department of Public Information, News and Media Division, New York, 8 October 2008.

[35] 'UN General Assembly backs Serbia's initiative on Kosovo', *Southeast European Times*, 9 October 2008.

[36] General Assembly resolution A/RES/63/3 (A/63/L.2), 8 October 2008.

[37] The most recent EU members to recognize Kosovo had been Malta, in August, and Portugal, which recognized Kosovo the day before the UN General Assembly vote.

[38] Turkey strongly supported Kosovo's independence, and had been one of the first countries to recognize it, but, by this point, Ankara was working closely with Serbia on addressing political problems in Bosnia. As a result, Turkey had agreed not to lobby for Kosovo's independence any further. As for Bosnia, the decision not to vote at all was driven by deep differences between the tripartite presidency over the issue.

In Serbia, there was jubilation at the decision. The result was hailed by Serbian Prime Minister Mirko Cvetković as 'a big success'.[39] The next day, the Secretary General, Ban Ki-Moon, officially conveyed the request of the General Assembly to the International Court of Justice confirming that under Article 65, Paragraph 2, of the Statute of the Court the UN Secretariat was preparing a dossier for the Court containing all relevant documents and that this would be transmitted 'as soon as possible'.[40]

## 6. Conclusion

In examining Serbia's decision to refer the matter to the ICJ, it is evident that this had always been viewed as a potential element of a wider counter-secession strategy. This was openly stated even before Kosovo declared independence. Nevertheless, relatively quickly it also became an act of necessity. Quite apart from the fact that Belgrade had to show that it was doing everything in its power to maintain a claim to Kosovo, it was obvious that it did not have the political and diplomatic strength to counter a concerted campaign by a number of major international states, most notably the United States and key members of the European Union, to press for Kosovo's recognition on the international stage. Faced with a strong campaign to persuade countries that Kosovo was a unique case in international politics, Serbia had little choice but use international law to challenge this argument. Meanwhile, the decision to pursue a case before the ICJ was also crucial as a delaying tactic. It was important that Serbia slow down the pace of recognitions after the initial flurry that occurred in the immediate weeks following the declaration of independence. By taking the matter before the Court, regardless of the eventual outcome, Serbia gave countries a legitimate reason to resist external pressure to recognize Kosovo. Simultaneously, at the domestic level, the decision to take the matter before the ICJ was not only tangible proof that the government was fighting the Kosovo cause as best it could, it also provided a very welcome way of letting the significant tensions that had emerged from within society over Kosovo's declaration of independence, and Western support for the move, subside. Bearing this in mind, and regardless of the eventual outcome of the case, the strategy of pursuing a case before the ICJ should be broadly regarded as having been successful in at least two senses. The pace of recognitions did slow, as acknowledged by Kosovo itself, and public anger did diminish.

Having opted to pursue the ICJ route, Belgrade proved to be exceedingly cautious in how it pursued the matter from there. It avoided steps that could be seen to be overtly confrontational towards either the United States or the key sponsors of Kosovo's independence within the European Union. In line with

---

[39] 'UN General Assembly backs Serbia's initiative on Kosovo', *Southeast European Times*, 9 October 2008.

[40] Request for an Advisory Opinion transmitted to the Court pursuant to General Assembly resolution A/RES/63/3 (A/63/L.2) of 8 October 2008.

Belgrade's openly stated policy of 'both Kosovo and the European Union', the Serbian Government ensured that in taking a course of action that was unpopular amongst the main EU members, it did not unduly antagonize them. This explains why it avoided the route that many thought offered the greatest potential for victory: questioning the decision of states to recognize Kosovo. Instead, it chose to call into question the legality of Kosovo's declaration of independence in advisory proceedings. While this is understandable, what is less easy to explain is the reasoning behind the decision to ask a question that focused on the legality of the declaration of independence, rather than focus on another legal aspect of the situation, such as Kosovo's claim to statehood. In part, it could perhaps be explained as part of a policy of potential loss minimization. If a very precise question had been asked that gave the Court little room to manoeuvre, it is possible that it would have come down against Belgrade. Serbia would have faced an all or nothing outcome. But even if it won, it would be a pyrrhic victory. It would still be left in a situation whereby its close allies in the EU would have been painted into a corner. Told that Kosovo's secession was illegal, they would have faced the uncomfortable and potential destabilizing prospect of having to reopen status talks. In such a situation, EU members may have taken an even more uncompromising position regarding Serbia: effectively demanding that either Belgrade accept Kosovo's independence or accept the end of its EU accession prospects. To this end, and somewhat paradoxically, a victory before the ICJ would almost certainly have forced Serbia into a situation where it would have to accept Kosovo's independence. In contrast, a question that allowed for a more ambiguous result could, and indeed eventually did, provide for a result that would allow everyone to claim victory, or at least avoid being seen as having lost.[41]

This leads to a final question: why did Serbia not cave in to the pressure from lead members of the European Union to drop the case altogether? In part, this is perhaps tied to the relative speed with which the calls for it to do so subsided. One can only guess whether Belgrade would have eventually relented had the European Union members maintained their threats to block Serbia's EU course if it pursued the case. As a counterfactual it is an interesting question, and one that is hard to answer. On the one hand, the way in which Serbia eventually relented on a further resolution calling for more status talks at the end of the ICJ opinion, in 2010, would suggest that it may have done so. However, the fact that this took place at a very early stage, when Serbia was fighting particularly hard to prevent recognition, and public emotions were still riding high, suggests that it might not have been willing, or politically able, to reverse its course; even if key members demanded it. In the event, Serbia was saved from having to make this decision by the fact that the European Union had no choice but to relent and allow the vote for fear of

---

[41] The outcome of the case will be explored later in this volume. However, for other works that examine elements, particularly the political aspects, of the case, see James Ker-Lindsay, 'Not such a "sui generis" case after all: assessing the ICJ opinion on Kosovo', *Nationalities Papers*, Volume 39, Number 1, 2011; Etain Tannam, 'The EU's Response to the ICJ's Judgement on Kosovo', *Europe-Asia Studies*, Volume 65, Number 5, 2013.

undermining its credibility as a key voice on the international stage for the international rule of law and respect for international institutions. Having set in motion a process that the leading members of the European Union evidently opposed, Serbia was eventually saved by the fact that the decision to pursue a case before the ICJ was in fact in accordance with certain key principles that the EU has sought to encourage. Even though this may have been more by accident than design, Belgrade put the EU in the uncomfortable position of being open to accusations of double standards. In doing so, it was able to win a major victory by securing a General Assembly resolution referring Kosovo's declaration of independence to the International Court of Justice.

# 3

# Arguing the *Kosovo* Case

*Marko Milanović**

## 1. Introduction

This chapter looks at how the *Kosovo* case was argued by the parties appearing before the International Court of Justice (ICJ) in the various stages of its advisory proceedings. My point in doing so is not to establish whether particular arguments were right or wrong, or to re-argue the case in any way. Rather, I am interested in the discursive shift that transpired once the issue of Kosovo's independence (at least partly) moved from the political arena to the judicial one. In other words, I want to look at how those justifying or opposing Kosovo's independence had to adjust their arguments, or develop new ones, once the case came before the Court.

In doing so, I am not claiming that there is a sharp divide between the legal and the political—quite the contrary. For example, while states made their decisions to support, oppose, or be neutral towards Kosovo's independence on the basis of a political assessment of their own interests, that assessment was to varying degrees informed and perhaps even bounded by the legal advice that the officials concerned received. Accordingly, the conceptual language of international law as an argumentative practice[1] at the very least formed the background for the political justification of any given state's attitude towards Kosovo's claimed independence. Similarly, in discussing Kosovo's independence, officials frequently had to respond to arguments about its putative illegality, and they did so before, during, and after the ICJ advisory proceedings.

But, having said that, the highly formalized setting of the ICJ did require significant adjustments to arguments made either in support of or in opposition to independence, as lawyers took over from the politicians and tried to make their points in a language that the Court could not only understand, but could also adopt as its own when writing its opinion. Some previously deployed lines of argument thus

* While I have had the privilege of being an advisor to the Serbian legal team in the advisory proceedings, this chapter is written strictly in my personal capacity and is based on publicly available information only. I am grateful to James Crawford, Vladimir Djerić, Sean Murphy, and Michael Wood for reading the piece in draft. The substantive content of the chapter was finalized in December 2013.
[1] M. Koskenniemi, *From Apology to Utopia* (CUP, 2005).

had to be dropped, others transformed, and yet others invented purely for the sake of the advisory proceedings. In other words, arguments that were persuasive in one context did not necessarily work in another. For instance, the frequent assertion of the supporters of Kosovo's independence that Kosovo was a special or *sui generis* case had to be reframed before the ICJ in order to be truly persuasive. Similarly, whereas the interplay between two broad legal and political principles—the territorial integrity of states and the self-determination of peoples—was considered by many as being crucial for assessing Kosovo's claim to independence before the advisory proceedings were initiated, these principles became increasingly marginalized as the proceedings progressed.

My goal in this chapter, therefore, is to observe the evolution of the argumentative strategies of the parties appearing before the Court and to establish the driving factors for this evolution. In doing so, I mostly focus on the written and oral pleadings before the Court, their structure, and the nature of the arguments made. The advisory opinion itself will generally be of interest to me only to the extent that it reflects the pleadings and the opposing litigation strategies. What concerns me here, in other words, is not what the Court decided, but how and why it got there.

## 2. The Pleadings in Brief

The pleadings in the Kosovo advisory proceedings consisted of two written rounds and one oral round. In the first written round, 36 states, including Serbia, submitted written statements, while the 'authors of the unilateral declaration of independence by the Provisional Institutions of Self-Government of Kosovo [PISG]' were authorized by the Court to submit a written contribution.[2] This difference in terminology was meant both to track the language of the General Assembly's resolution posing the question to the Court and to avoid prejudging the issue of Kosovo's statehood, while the identity of the 'authors' became a point of contention over the course of the proceedings.[3] For the sake of the English language, I will from now on use 'Kosovo' and 'authors' interchangeably, Kosovo's contested status notwithstanding. In the second written round, 14 states filed written comments on the statements submitted in the first round, while Kosovo filed a further written contribution. All of these 14 states had submitted written statements in the first round.[4] In the oral round, the Court heard statements from Serbia, the authors/Kosovo, and 27 other states. Of the 27, 7 had not participated in the written rounds of the proceedings.[5]

---

[2] All case materials are available at <http://www.icj-cij.org/docket/index.php?p1=3&p2=4&code=kos&case=141&k=21&p3=0>.

[3] See *infra*, Section 7.

[4] A note on citation: the written statements and comments by states will be cited with the name of the state followed by WS or WC as the case may be, e.g. Serbia WS and Serbia WC. Kosovo's two written contributions will be cited as Kosovo WC1 and Kosovo WC2. Verbatim records of oral proceedings will be cited according to the Court's own mode of citation, e.g. CR 2009/24. The opinion itself will be cited as *Kosovo AO*.

[5] Namely, Saudi Arabia, Belarus, Bulgaria, Burundi, Croatia, Jordan, and Vietnam.

In sum, 43 states plus Kosovo made submissions before the Court, which is by any measure a decent chunk of the international community, especially when bearing in mind that these included some very influential states, among them all five permanent members of the UN Security Council. Their various statements are a valuable source of *opinio juris* on a number of issues of general international law, some of which I will turn to below. They also form a complex web of argument that ultimately served to frame the Court's opinion—even though there is always a gap between arguments made by the parties and the Court's own appraisal of the case, which was indeed significant with regard to some of the issues, as we will see. These arguments cannot be truly appreciated statically, but only as a flow through time. In the first written round of pleadings, the parties set out their own starting positions and anticipated possible counter-arguments,[6] while the second written round and the oral round were directly responsive. Positions and arguments thus inevitably evolved over the course of the proceedings.

A distinctive (although not unique) feature of the Kosovo proceedings was that while they were nominally advisory in character, they also dealt with an underlying (bilateral) dispute, between Serbia and Kosovo, who inevitably had more interest in the outcome of the proceedings than other parties. That was reflected, *inter alia*, in the length of the written pleadings[7] and in the Court allowing Serbia and Kosovo a maximum of three hours each during the oral rounds, while allocating 45 minutes to each of the other participants.[8] This also meant that the 42 states participating in the proceedings in addition to Kosovo and Serbia split into two big camps: the supporters and opponents of Kosovo's independence. One state that participated in the proceedings—Egypt—remained somewhat bizarrely neutral.

Each of the two big camps had more and less important or involved players, in addition to Kosovo and Serbia—both of which obviously cared about having as many supporters as possible and made extensive lobbying efforts in that regard. Both particularly valued support from the great powers, the EU member states, and the countries in the immediate region. Some states had more interest in actively taking part in the proceedings, as well as more resources and sheer lawyerly firepower.

Similarly, there was a significant level of coordination within each camp, both at the more general inter-governmental level and at the more particular level of the relationship between the members of the different legal teams—with this coordination varying in intensity depending on the parties in question and the specific point of time in the proceedings.[9] A division of labour was most pronounced in the pro-Kosovo camp, where, for instance, France and Albania took the lead in making jurisdictional or other procedural arguments, while Kosovo itself focused

---

[6] By 'anticipate' I mean responding pre-emptively to an argument that is likely to be made by the opposing parties. That an argument was not anticipated in that sense does not necessarily mean that the counsel concerned were not *aware* that it could be made; they could just as easily have made a strategic choice not to respond to it pre-emptively.

[7] For instance, Bolivia's written statement was only one page in length, Latvia's and Brazil's were two, whereas Serbia's and Kosovo's statements ranged in the hundreds of pages, with annexes.

[8] See CR 2009/24, p. 30.

[9] For more, see Qudsi Rasheed's and Michael Wood's contribution to this volume at Chapter 4.

**Table 3.1** Countries' legal involvement in the case: pro-Serbia

|  | Pro-Serbia camp | 15 |
| --- | --- | --- |
| Three rounds of pleadings | Argentina, Bolivia, Cyprus, Spain | 4 |
| Two rounds of pleadings | Azerbaijan, Brazil, China, Romania, Russia, Venezuela | 6 |
| One round of pleadings | Belarus, Iran, Libya, Slovakia, Vietnam | 5 |

**Table 3.2** Countries' legal involvement in the case: pro-Kosovo

|  | Pro-Kosovo camp | 26 |
| --- | --- | --- |
| Three rounds of pleadings | Albania, France, Germany, Netherlands, Norway, United States, United Kingdom | 7 |
| Two rounds of pleadings | Austria, Denmark, Finland, Slovenia, Switzerland | 5 |
| One round of pleadings | Bulgaria, Burundi, Croatia, Czech Republic, Estonia, Ireland, Japan, Jordan, Latvia, Luxembourg, Maldives, Poland, Saudi Arabia, Sierra Leone | 14 |

on the substantive issues, e.g. the interpretation of resolution 1244 (to what extent this division of labour was deliberate is of course hard to say from the outside). However, because the level of coordination and involvement varied, because of the difference in lawyerly firepower, and because the interests of states belonging to either camp did not align fully, there were some significant differences in how states within each camp chose to argue their case, as I will explain below.

Tables 3.1 and 3.2 sets out the two camps, divided up by how many rounds of pleadings each of Serbia's and Kosovo's allies took part in, as a somewhat simplistic measure of these state's involvement in the case. Generally speaking, the most involved states not only had the most perceived self-interest to actively take part in the proceedings politically, but had also retained the services of the largest legal teams or those with most experience in arguing before the ICJ or other international courts.

The pro-Kosovo camp was in absolute numbers significantly larger than the pro-Serbia one, but that advantage was the greatest with regard to the least involved states. If we were to identify the cores of the two camps, in the case of Kosovo it accurately reflects those states that took part in all three rounds of pleadings, while in the case of Serbia we would have to add Russia and China to these, and possibly remove Bolivia. The level of coordination within these core groups was undoubtedly the greatest, as the analysis of the pleadings themselves will show.

## 3. Outline of Arguments

The substantive content of the pleadings can be divided into five broad groups of arguments:

(1) political and historical arguments about Kosovo's independence that did not employ the formal language of international law, i.e. did not invoke

a legal rule that applies to the specific facts of the Kosovo situation in a given way;

(2) arguments about the Court's jurisdiction to issue the advisory opinion and the propriety of it doing so;

(3) arguments about the scope of the question posed to the Court by the General Assembly;

(4) arguments about the compatibility of the declaration of independence (DoI) with general international law; and

(5) arguments about the compatibility of the DoI with Security Council resolution 1244 and the legal regime created under that resolution.

This general structure of argument was predictable from the outset, but the variations and nuances were many. With regard to category (1), some parties made extensive arguments and others very little, and there were significant differences with regard to their relevance and transition to legal arguments. Serbia and Kosovo each spent an enormous amount of their written pleadings in trying to weave their alternative political and historical narratives of the whole Kosovo situation, culminating in the declaration of independence. The great powers among their allies also went to great lengths in giving their own versions of history, including especially that of their own involvement, while states in the region (e.g. Croatia and Slovenia) provided their official narratives of the breakup of the former Yugoslavia and Kosovo's place within that process, and of Yugoslavia's constitutional framework and its attitude towards secession and self-determination. It is highly questionable whether such extensive examinations of who did what to whom in the recent or not so recent past had any direct bearing on the case, at least if they could not fit within a legal argument made later on (e.g. self-determination).[10] Though these conflicting narratives are fascinating—I especially wonder what historians would make of history as presented for the purpose of judicial proceedings[11]—I will for reasons of space not examine them any further.

Arguments about jurisdiction and propriety in category (2) were more or less straightforward and, during the course of the pleadings, were generally not thought very likely to be of much interest to the Court—yet in fact, as we will see, the case almost turned on the propriety of the exercise of jurisdiction. The case of course *did* turn on (3), the interpretation of the question posed to the Court by the General Assembly: 'Is the unilateral declaration of independence by the Provisional Institutions of Self-Government of Kosovo in accordance with international law?' The framing of virtually every other argument in the case flowed in one way or another from the interpretation to be given to the question, and

---

[10] This is not to say that the Court was not *aware* of the recent past, especially since it has had first-hand experience with some of the fallout from the breakup of the former Yugoslavia. I think it is fair to say that Serbia in no way came across as a particularly appealing litigant. But I submit that there was little any of the parties could say that would have changed the judges' own perception of events.

[11] There is some experience of such historiography in the context of criminal proceedings before the International Criminal Tribunal for the Former Yugoslavia.

virtually every single word in the question required an examination. When the question refers to the declaration of independence, is the reference to the declaration as a piece of paper, a purely verbal act, or rather to the act of secession more generally? 'By the Provisional Institutions of Self-Government of Kosovo (PISG)'—we will come to the whole issue of who the authors of the DoI were later on. 'In accordance with'—what does that mean exactly? The Court ultimately chose to interpret this as 'not prohibited by', the consequence being that, in order to win, Serbia had to show that the authors, who were in Serbia's own view a non-state actor, were somehow directly bound by a prohibitive norm of international law. And finally, 'international law'—is, say, the UNMIK Constitutional Framework 'international law'?[12]

In hindsight, the full complexity of the 'question question' today seems obvious, though it did not appear to be so to many parties until the advisory proceedings were well underway. And while it is certainly true that every question will require interpretation, *this* particular question was, if I can put it diplomatically, somewhat improvidently drafted.[13] For example, had the question been 'Did the PISG have the *right* to secede from Serbia?', the whole posture of the case would have been much more favourable for Serbia, as it would not have been enough for Kosovo to argue that there was an absence of a prohibition, nor would the question have been limited to the DoI as a piece of paper.

The formulation of the question undoubtedly shaped arguments in categories (4) and (5). With regard to general international law, the issue of Kosovo's independence was suddenly no longer seen in terms of a conflict between two grand principles of international law: the self-determination of peoples and the territorial integrity of states. Rather, if the question was whether the authors, a non-state actor, were bound by a norm of general international law that *prohibited* their declaration of independence, the issue became whether the principle of territorial integrity operated only *between* states, or also *within* them, thus creating a wide-ranging prohibition of secession. This key shift in perspective was again not equally appreciated by all parties in the proceedings, as we will see. With regard to resolution 1244, in addition to more or less obvious arguments about how the resolution is to be properly interpreted, a number of other lines of inquiry opened up that were really not considered seriously before the advisory proceedings started: whether Security Council resolutions can bind non-state actors, and if so, when do they do so; what was the nature of the legal regime established by UNMIK in Kosovo, i.e. whether it belonged to international law;

---

[12] One could even ask whether the opening 'is' in the question was in fact a 'was'.

[13] For the avoidance of doubt, the question itself was *not* drafted by any of the lawyers later representing Serbia in the advisory proceedings. The main purpose behind the draft was apparently to exclude issues such as recognition from the scope of the question, and thus increase the likelihood of the question being accepted by the General Assembly, but this was certainly not the only such formulation available. In other words, the features of the question that made it so detrimental to Serbia's position once the case was underway were not necessarily the same features that rendered the question appealing to the General Assembly.

whether any possible violation of the resolution 1244 regime was mitigated or even cured by the failure of the Council and the Secretary-General's Special Representative in Kosovo to condemn it, i.e. their acquiescence in the DoI; and what was the identity of the 'authors', i.e. were they the PISG or something else entirely?

I will now look at all these arguments in detail, looking in particular at how they evolved over time.

## 4. Jurisdiction, Propriety, and the 'Question Question'

Respondents in contentious cases routinely make preliminary objections challenging the ICJ's jurisdiction. This is also frequently the case in advisory proceedings, where there are usually some parties who would prefer that there be no opinion at all. Here the whole advisory proceedings were an initiative of Serbia, which Kosovo and its supporters would by and large rather have avoided. There are two basic types of such objections in advisory cases. First, that the Court lacks jurisdiction to render an opinion, normally because the body requesting the opinion was not properly authorized under the UN Charter to do so or exceeded the scope of the authorization it was given. Second, that even if the Court has jurisdiction, it should exercise its discretion to decline providing an opinion, normally on the basis of some defect in terms of judicial propriety.[14]

These matters of jurisdiction and propriety are generally very tedious, both academically and in pleading the case. They had to be made, anticipated, or responded almost *de rigueur*, yet at the time the arguments that the Court lacked jurisdiction to render the opinion or that it should exercise its discretion not to give it seemed bound to fail. While there have been cases in which the Court found that it lacked jurisdiction to give an advisory opinion,[15] constructing an argument that the General Assembly lacked the authority to pose a question to the Court seemed difficult at best.[16] As for propriety, the Court has *never* refused to answer a question on the basis of its discretion, and this is mainly because of how its judges quite consistently conceptualized the nature of this discretion in the wider context of the Court's advisory function. When, in invoking Article 65 of its Statute, it says that it *may* give an advisory opinion, the Court does not interpret this discretion in the same way in which, say, the US Supreme Court has discretion whether or not

---

[14] See generally J. Frowein and K. Oellers-Frahm, 'Article 65', in A. Zimmermann et al (eds), *The Statute of the International Court of Justice: A Commentary* (OUP, 2nd ed, 2012) 1605, at marginal numbers (MN), 12–43.

[15] Perhaps most notably regarding the WHO in *Legality of the Use by a State of Nuclear Weapons in Armed Conflict*, ICJ Reports 1996, p. 66.

[16] Bearing in mind that Article 96(1) of the Charter provides that '[t]he General Assembly or the Security Council may request the International Court of Justice to give an advisory opinion on *any* legal question' (emphasis added). See also *Legal Consequences of the Construction of a Wall in the Occupied Palestinian Territory, Advisory Opinion, I.C.J. Reports 2004*, p. 136, paras. 15–17, 24–28.

to grant *certiorari* in a case, i.e. as a total liberty whether or not to do so. Rather, the Court sees its discretion as essentially a safeguard against abuse of process, and would require 'compelling reasons' for refusing to respond to a properly made request for an advisory opinion.[17]

In fact, though, the *Kosovo* opinion almost turned on the discretion issue; the Court was *very* close to refusing to answer the question posed to it on grounds of propriety. The decision to give the opinion was made by 9 votes to 5. That seems like a four-person majority, but it is actually only *two* judges—had two judges changed their minds, the split would have been 7 to 7, with the President having the casting vote, from the Court's collective perspective generally a situation to be avoided. I am now only speculating, but considering the closeness of the vote and the extent to which the discretion issue is argued in the advisory opinion and the judges' separate opinions, at some point during the deliberations, there may even have been something close to a majority to refuse to give the opinion. And it was one particular discretion argument that the judges in the minority found persuasive: that the opinion was requested by the General Assembly on matters hitherto dealt with almost entirely by the Security Council, with the key question in the case being the interpretation of a Security Council resolution, and that it should, accordingly, have been properly for the Council to ask for the opinion or not.[18]

In essence, this was a constitutional argument about the separation of powers within the UN and the comity that its principal organs should extend to one another, so that one organ should not substantively impinge on the affairs of another even if it could formally do so.[19] But again, during the pleadings this did not seem to be a point that was so persuasive, so compelling, so qualitatively different from a number of other discretion arguments made, that it would have led the Court to refuse, for the very first time, to give an advisory opinion on grounds of propriety. Note, however, that the judges who (conditionally) voted for Serbia on the merits, i.e. who dissented from the opinion's substantive holdings, would in fact have decided not to give an opinion in the first place.[20] In other words, the question ultimately before the Court was not whether Serbia should *win*, but how

---

[17]  See, e.g., *Kosovo* AO, paras. 29–30.

[18]  See especially *Kosovo* AO, Separate Opinion of Judge Keith. For further discussion of jurisdiction and propriety arguments in the case, see Vladimir Djerić's contribution to this book (Chapter 6).

[19]  Note that in this respect, this argument is different from a cruder, more simplistic objection that Article 12 of the Charter precludes the exercise of jurisdiction by the Court. Article 12(1) provides that '[w]hile the Security Council is exercising in respect of any dispute or situation the functions assigned to it in the present Charter, the General Assembly shall not make any recommendation with regard to that dispute or situation unless the Security Council so requests'. In response to similar challenges in earlier cases, the Court has held that a request by the General Assembly to the Court for an advisory opinion is not a 'recommendation' in the sense of Article 12(1), although it would examine whether the Assembly acted *ultra vires* the Charter—see, e.g., *Wall*, para. 25 ff.

[20]  See *Kosovo* AO, para. 123(2); Declaration of Vice-President Tomka, paras. 2–9; Dissenting Opinion of Judge Koroma, para. 1 (stating somewhat strangely that he voted in favour of acceding to the request for an advisory opinion, even though that is contradicted by the operative paragraph of the *Kosovo* AO itself); Separate Opinion of Judge Keith (wholly devoted to the discretion issue and agreeing with the majority on the merits); Dissenting Opinion of Judge Bennouna, paras. 1–26; Dissenting Opinion of Judge Skotnikov, paras. 1–12.

it should *lose*. In the final analysis, *no* judge was willing to give Serbia the kind of opinion it wanted.

Why was this so? The answer to that question, as always, is in the internal politics of coalition-building and the formation of majorities within a collegial court, which evolve through the several stages of the deliberations, in which some voices are stronger than others. In that regard, the less appealing the possible substantive outcome was for a particular judge, the more the discretion option beckoned. The discretion option would have allowed the Court to make a grand gesture about the importance of comity between the principal organs of the United Nations, avoid saying anything about Kosovo, and do so in a seemingly neutral (and very proper and formal) kind of way.

In other words, not all jurisdiction and discretion arguments were equally compelling, and the task of counsel was to anticipate which would be. Some were clearly pre-empted by the Court's own jurisprudence and were easily dismissed: with regard to the political character of the question; the motives of Serbia in asking the General Assembly to request an advisory opinion; or that it would serve no useful purpose; and so on.[21]

Yet that last argument was made by some states in a particularly brutal way: that no matter what the Court decided, Kosovo's independence was a reality, and that reality would not change.[22] Note the unadulterated, pure apology. It may well be *true* that the Court's opinion will have no bearing on reality, but there would be nothing more defeatist for a court to say than that it will not make a particular judgment because it will not be obeyed, and this consideration is lessened only somewhat by the formally non-binding character of the advisory proceedings. The argument itself cannot succeed even if, or especially if, it is true. No court would ever openly admit its own powerlessness, nor could law, being normative, internally accept its inability to force the powerful to adhere to it. Which is not to say that the judges did not listen, were blind to the reality on the ground, or had not been faced with such existential problems before, most notably in the *Nuclear Weapons* advisory opinion where the world's nuclear powers would certainly not have disarmed on the Court's say-so.[23] And just as in the *Nuclear Weapons* case the apology/utopia dynamic determined the outcome of the case, so the Court in *Kosovo* had to find a way of not being oblivious to the reality on the ground without becoming an apologist for that reality.

The ingeniousness of the argument about the comity between the Assembly and the Council was precisely that it tapped into this dynamic, while being relatively novel and not precluded by earlier case law, enabling the Court to tick all the boxes and say something without appearing too cowardly. But not all of the participants saw that there was room to make such an argument. Of the 37 parties (including

---

[21] *Kosovo* AO, paras. 27, 33–35.

[22] See, e.g. (as an almost random sampling), Czech Republic WS, p. 5; France WC, para. 12; United Kingdom, CR 2009/32, p. 38, para. 7: 'A cardinal concern of every court must be to address whether the decision that is asked of it is capable of meaningful implementation. Courts strive not to order the unsustainable.'

[23] *Legality of the Threat or Use of Nuclear Weapons*, ICJ Reports 1996, p. 226.

Serbia and Kosovo) who participated in the first round of written pleadings, only 3 referred to the (almost winning) comity argument, and among these only France argued it at any length, without revisiting it in the subsequent rounds.[24] Kosovo, one imagines for strategic reasons, chose not to argue the jurisdiction and discretion points, merely noting in one paragraph that the Court should consider whether the exercise of its discretion would be appropriate in the circumstances of the case.[25] Serbia anticipated this argument only partially,[26] and it attracted little to no response from other states. Indeed, not a single participant in the oral rounds made any kind of detailed submissions on the comity argument, and *this* was the argument that almost carried the day.

Yet for all its ingeniousness, in the end the majority did not accept it, even though the Court discussed it at great length, indeed at far greater length than any of the other jurisdiction and propriety arguments.[27] This is yet another indication that the comity argument only gained traction after the Court had started its deliberations, with the judges engaged in their own attempts at persuasion and majority building. And once a majority was built, it found another way of ticking all the boxes—another formalist, very lawyerly kind of way—restrictively interpreting the question put before the Court, by using a door that was left wide open by the very formulation of the question.

Perhaps the most striking, indeed almost surreal, feature of the pleadings before the Court, as well as the opinion itself and the dissents, was how everybody concerned claimed that the question was clear, narrow, and precisely defined,[28] when the question was manifestly neither clear, nor necessarily narrow, nor precisely defined. As I explained above, practically every single word in the question required interpretation, and in fact allowed for several possible interpretations. For its part, from the very start of the case, Kosovo argued quite strongly that

---

[24] France WS, paras. 1.28–1.52 (although France based its argument primarily on Article 12 of the Charter, even while framing it in terms of discretion). In the second round, France merely referred back to the argument in a footnote—France WC, para. 7, fn. 10. Albania first made it with respect to jurisdiction and Article 12, and not propriety—Albania WS, paras. 48–53, then switched tack in one brief paragraph and asked the Court to exercise its discretion—Albania WS, para. 55, without following up on this argument at all in the oral round—see CR 2009/26, pp. 10–12. Ireland made a discretion argument, albeit very briefly—Ireland WS, para. 12.

[25] Kosovo WC1, p. 131, para. 7.21. See also Kosovo WC2, pp. 5–8. Some of the states supporting Kosovo explicitly argued that they saw no real issues with regard to the Court's jurisdiction and propriety—see, e.g., Switzerland WS, paras. 13–24; and Burundi, CR 2009/28, pp. 28–29. The comity argument was also *not* taken up by Kosovo in the second round, in which it relied on *other* discretion arguments—Kosovo WC2, paras. 1.12–1.17, or generally by its supporters making discretion arguments—see, e.g., United States WC, pp. 10–12.

[26] Serbia WS, pp. 33–35 (arguing that the General Assembly had an interest in the Kosovo situation and that Article 12 of the Charter did not preclude it from making a request for an advisory opinion). See also Serbia WC, pp. 33–34 (dealing with discretion on this basis in a single sentence, para. 55).

[27] *Kosovo* AO, paras. 36–48.

[28] See, e.g., *Kosovo* AO, para. 51: 'In the present case, the question posed by the General Assembly is clearly formulated. The question is narrow and specific; it asks for the Court's opinion on whether or not the declaration of independence is in accordance with international law. It does not ask about the legal consequences of that declaration. In particular, it does not ask whether or not Kosovo has achieved statehood.'

the scope of the question was limited, that it focused solely on the declaration of independence as a purely verbal act, that for the declaration not to be in accordance with international law it had to be directly prohibited by it (and that such a norm was lacking), and that the *consequences* of the declaration (e.g. whether Kosovo had managed to attain statehood) were outside the scope of the question.[29] Kosovo was supported in this narrow interpretation of the question by its allies.[30] Serbia, on the other hand, was initially content to pretend that there was no 'question question', saying only that it excluded from its scope the legality of the recognition of Kosovo by third states.[31] However, the more pressing the issue of the question became over the course of the subsequent rounds of pleadings, the more Serbia was faced with a strategic choice—should it ask the Court to reformulate the question (as the Court has consistently held it has the power to do[32]), or should it keep arguing that the question was fine as it was so long as it was not interpreted too narrowly?

The upside of the former option would have been honesty, clarity, and the possibility that the Court would have taken up the opportunity if it was offered; the downside was that it would have been tantamount to conceding that the question as posed was correctly to be interpreted as Kosovo had suggested. For good or bad, Serbia chose the latter.[33] Serbia thus argued that the reference to the DoI in the question was not to a verbal act of a non-state entity on a given day, but to 'an attempt to create a new State',[34] including the consequences of this act in terms of the legal and factual criteria for statehood, and that these were indeed the 'true legal questions' before the Court.[35] (Note how the 'true legal questions' language subtly echoes the Court's jurisprudence confirming its power to reformulate questions put before it.[36])

It is impossible to know today whether counter-factually the result would have been any different had Serbia asked the Court to reformulate the question. It is likely that it would have not, but the Court would at least have had a harder time

---

[29] Kosovo WC1, pp. 126–129, 132–139. See also Kosovo WC2, pp. 8–9.

[30] See, e.g., Germany WS, p. 8; United Kingdom WS, paras. 1.8ff; and United States WS, pp. 45–49.

[31] Serbia WS, p. 27.

[32] See, e.g., *Legal Consequences of the Construction of a Wall in the Occupied Palestinian Territory, Advisory Opinion, I.C.J. Reports 2004*, p. 136, at 153–154, para. 38 (internal references omitted):

> The Court would point out that lack of clarity in the drafting of a question does not deprive the Court of jurisdiction. Rather, such uncertainty will require clarification in interpretation, and such necessary clarifications of interpretation have frequently been given by the Court. In the past, both the Permanent Court and the present Court have observed in some cases that the wording of a request for an advisory opinion did not accurately state the question on which the Court's opinion was being sought ..., or did not correspond to the 'true legal question' under consideration .... Consequently, the Court has often been required to broaden, interpret and even reformulate the questions put.

[33] Note that, within the pro-Serbia camp, Cyprus had hinted already in the first round of pleadings that the Court may need to clarify the question—Cyprus WS, para. 60, fn. 60, while Romania did so in the oral round—CR 2009/32, p. 19.

[34] Serbia WC, p. 27.        [35] Ibid, p. 28, para. 45.        [36] *Supra* note 33.

in doing what it did.[37] The consequences of a narrow approach to the question were clear. The instant the Court chose to frame the question as narrowly as it did, so that Serbia would have to show that there was an international legal norm directly prohibiting a non-state actor from adopting a declaratory act on a given day, the general international law part of the case fell by the wayside and the resolution 1244 part of the case correspondingly became both more central and more complicated. Let me address general international law first, marginalized as it was.

## 5. Arguments under General International Law

The question allowed the Court to dispense with general international law arguments in a mere five paragraphs of its opinion,[38] finding that general international law does not prohibit declarations of independence, bearing in mind that 'the scope of the principle of territorial integrity is confined to the sphere of relations between States',[39] and that it did not need to decide whether Kosovo had the *right* to external self-determination or remedial secession from Serbia, since the question required it to establish only whether the declaration was prohibited by international law, not whether Kosovo had a positive entitlement to declare independence. This is what all the arguments about territorial integrity and self-determination ultimately boiled down to, and, for all they were worth, the Court's five paragraphs could have been even shorter.

What is remarkable here is not what the Court said, but how the political discourse about Kosovo's independence needed to transform into a legal one before the Court. Recall that the main political argument in favour of Kosovo's independence was that it somehow presented a unique, *sui generis* situation, which does not set a precedent for Abkhazia, or South Ossetia, or what have you. But in a judicial setting, this political argument is unpalatable: *every* situation is special in its own way. One cannot have legal rules if one then has to disapply them in supposedly unique situations without any clear criteria as to how and why an exception is warranted and can be made. This simple rule of law consideration did not prevent

---

[37]  See, in particular, *Kosovo* AO, paras. 50–51, esp. para. 56:

> The answer to that question turns on whether or not the applicable international law pro-hibited the declaration of independence. If the Court concludes that it did, then it must answer the question put by saying that the declaration of independence was not in accord-ance with international law. It follows that the task which the Court is called upon to perform is to determine whether or not the declaration of independence was adopted in violation of international law. The Court is not required by the question it has been asked to take a position on whether international law conferred a positive entitlement on Kosovo unilaterally to declare its independence or, *a fortiori*, on whether international law generally confers an entitlement on entities situated within a State unilaterally to break away from it. Indeed, it is entirely possible for a particular act—such as a unilateral declaration of independence—not to be in violation of international law without necessarily constituting the exercise of a right conferred by it. The Court has been asked for an opinion on the first point, not the second.

[38]  *Kosovo* AO, paras. 79–84.        [39]  Ibid., para. 80.

Kosovo's supporters from making the *sui generis* argument before the Court, but it did render the argument arbitrary and fatally unpersuasive. In order for it to become persuasive, it required translation from talking points about the special character of a particular situation into a general legal proposition. And that proposition was simply this: that non-state actors are not prohibited by international law from declaring independence, because the principle of territorial integrity extends only between states, but not within them.[40] In other words, third states could have violated the territorial integrity of Serbia by prematurely extending recognition to Kosovo, if that entity did not fulfil the legal criteria for statehood. That entity itself, on the other hand, could not have violated Serbia's territorial integrity by whatever it said or did.[41] To the extent that the Court ultimately says that general international law does not require each individual or group of individuals within a state's jurisdiction to be loyal to the state, this is perfectly sensible.

But if this is true and none of us are prohibited from seceding and/or declaring independence from states in which we live, what then is the use of having a *right* to secede, say under the rubric of external self-determination or remedial secession? To answer this question, it might be helpful to conceptualize secession within international law in a three-part model. There are cases where international law explicitly *prohibits* secession, when it is being effected through the violation of some fundamental norm of international law, such as the prohibition on the use of force or the prohibition of racial discrimination. This was the case, for example, with the Turkish Republic of Northern Cyprus or the Bantustans in South Africa.[42] Such fundamental illegality is an impediment to the achievement of statehood which otherwise satisfies the relevant factual criteria, and thus *bounds* effectiveness.[43] Then there is a middle ground, a zone of tolerance, where international law is *neutral* towards secession, neither prohibiting it nor creating a right to it.[44]

---

[40] Cf. United Kingdom WC, paras 11–14.

[41] Cf. United Kingdom, CR 2009/33, p. 47, para. 5 (Crawford):

> Mr. President, Members of the Court, I am a devoted but disgruntled South Australian. 'I hereby declare the independence of South Australia.' What has happened? Precisely nothing. Have I committed an internationally wrongful act in your presence? Of course not. Have I committed an ineffective act? Very likely. I have no representative capacity and no one will rally to my call. But does international law only condemn declarations of independence when made by representative bodies and not, for example, by military movements? Does international law only condemn declarations of independence when they are likely to be effective? It simply does not make any sense to say that unilateral declarations of independence are per se unlawful—yet no State in this case has suggested that general international law contains any more limited prohibition of such declarations; and none has been articulated in any of the sources of the law.

[42] See generally, J. Crawford, *The Creation of States in International Law* (2nd ed, OUP, 2006), 106–107, 128 ff.

[43] Note that there is a further step from saying that statehood is precluded to concluding that the non-state actors in question are directly bound by a prohibitive norm. In other words, an entity in the zone of prohibition may be legally impeded in gaining statehood, and third states may be prohibited from recognizing it as a state, but that does not necessarily entail that the non-state entity itself is prohibited from seceding or from declaring independence.

[44] See Crawford, *supra*, note 42, at 390: 'The position is that secession is neither legal nor illegal in international law, but a legally neutral act the consequences of which are regulated internationally.'

Finally, in the third part, a zone of entitlement, international law does create a *right* to secession under external self-determination or perhaps remedial secession. The argument of Serbia and most of its allies was essentially that no zone of tolerance existed between prohibition and entitlement. The argument of Kosovo and its supporters was that international law at the very least tolerated the DoI. Serbia *could* also have argued that even if the territorial integrity principle did not generally prohibit non-state actors from declaring independence, it did so here because Kosovo's independence was, as a matter of fact, enabled by an unlawful use of force contrary to the Charter by NATO in 1999. Serbia of course deliberately chose not to do so, and for three basic reasons: it did not want to antagonize the NATO powers, as this argument would inevitably do; the resolution 1244 regime came after the initial use of force and authorized the presence of international forces in Kosovo; and it was highly unlikely that the Court would want to rule on it in the context of the advisory proceedings.

How do the second and the third components of the three-part model of secession differ? Under the neutrality paradigm, an entity would need a great deal of effectiveness in order to successfully attain statehood; it would certainly need to build independent, viable, long-term institutions if it was creating a state from scratch. But this entity would need less effectiveness if it was in the third part of the model, i.e. if it had the *right* to secede. East Timor needed less effectiveness than say Abkhazia in order to become a state. Legality thus *advances effectiveness or compensates for* the lack thereof.[45] This is, in short, the difference between having the right to secede and simply not being prohibited from doing so. It lies not in the legality, *vel non*, in international law of an act such as the declaration of independence, but in its consequences, here in the creation, *vel non*, of a state, i.e. in making it easier or harder to do.

Coming back to Kosovo, it was clear from the outset that it would be quite difficult for the pro-Kosovo camp to build a persuasive argument that Kosovo had a right to external self-determination by way of remedial secession. The big question is whether a rule creating an entitlement to such secession outside the colonial context even exists. While, personally, I would like this rule to exist, it does not seem to have behind it the necessary corpus of state practice and *opinio juris* that one would normally require. No state has, for example, achieved independence pursuant to this rule, and arguments in its favour are normally based on a rather debatable reading of the safeguard clause in the Friendly Relations Declaration. And even if such a rule existed, it is highly questionable whether its requirements would have been satisfied. Was the population of Kosovo, or the Kosovo Albanians as its sub-set, a 'people' entitled to self-determination, or merely a minority within Serbia? Even if they were (bearing in mind all of the uncertainties regarding the definition of peoples in international law), and even if the level of oppression that

---

[45] Ibid., at 128: 'The secession of a self-determination unit, where self-determination is forcibly prevented by the metropolitan State, will be reinforced by the principle of self-determination, so that the degree of effectiveness required as a precondition to recognition may be substantially less than in the case of secession within a metropolitan unit.' See also ibid., at 383 ff.

they suffered under the Milošević regime in Serbia did entitle them to independence, did this entitlement lapse because of the passage of time and the regime change in Serbia? Was independence really the *ultima ratio*? And was this entitlement in any way tainted by the subsequent oppressive treatment of the Serbian minority within Kosovo? So on, and so forth.

In the advisory proceedings, both Kosovo and its core allies seemed well aware of the difficulties in persuading the Court to take the self-determination route. They were equally aware that the formulation of the question allowed for it to be avoided. They thus deliberately chose to relegate self-determination and remedial secession to a purely secondary role, or even not argue it at all. For instance, *only two pages* out of almost two hundred in the first written contribution of Kosovo concerned self-determination, and even there the main claim was that this was a point that the Court did not need to reach.[46]

Most importantly, they were aware of the possible fallout of a self-determination argument, precisely because this is an argument based on legal and moral principle, and not political expediency. Had Kosovo's allies among the great powers supported Kosovo's independence on the basis of self-determination, they would have to do so consistently with regard to every oppressed group on the planet, and that is simply not something that they want or are prepared to do, for all the lip service paid to self-determination—see, e.g., Tibet. No one wants to do the right thing *this* time, and then to *have to* do the right thing again *next* time—that was the whole point of the 'Kosovo is *sui generis*', 'Kosovo does not set a precedent', mantra repeated over and over both in the advisory proceeding and outside them. It was thus far easier, and far more expedient, to argue in the advisory proceedings that Kosovo's independence was in accordance with general international law because no norm of general international law prohibited it, even though this is not how the *political* justification for Kosovo's independence was normally framed.[47] If, however, the proposition that general international law does not prohibit secession, absent the infringement of some other fundamental rule, is correct (as I personally think it is) then the inevitable consequence of that proposition is that there may well be other Kosovos in the future. What is (relatively) unique about Kosovo, in other words, is not the *legal position* regarding its attempt at secession, but that as a matter of fact its attempt is or will be *successful*, mainly because the support of its allies allowed it not only to set up institutions of government, but also to assert its claim to independence internationally and have that claim increasingly accepted while preventing its parent state from asserting its sovereignty on the ground. The continued assertion of the 'Kosovo is *sui generis*' argument thus becomes a signal to other potential secessionists that even though they in the end *may* prove to be successful, they are not very likely to.[48]

---

[46] *Kosovo* WC1, pp. 157-158.

[47] See, e.g., the statement on the recognition of Kosovo by the then US Secretary of State, Condoleezza Rice, 18 February 2008, available at <http://2001-2009.state.gov/secretary/rm/2008/02/100973.htm>.

[48] The big question here is how high the factual threshold of effectiveness needs to be for an entity to attain statehood when it is *not* doing so in the furtherance of a right to self-determination, but

In support of my thesis about the litigation strategies of the parties, I will now provide an overview of the evolution of the general international law arguments through the course of the three rounds of pleadings, and will do so by presenting the parties' positions in Tables 3.3 and 3.4, below. Each table sets out the parties belonging to the pro-Kosovo and pro-Serbia camps, respectively, sorted firstly by the number of rounds of pleadings they participated in and, secondly, alphabetically. The tables summarize each party's arguments on self-determination and territorial integrity. I thus want to establish which of Kosovo's supporters invoked self-determination and which of Serbia's allies relied on territorial integrity; or whether they made simplistic arguments of the 'self-determination trumps territorial integrity' variety (or vice versa); or whether they realized that the key issue was whether the principle of territorial integrity bound non-state actors within a state, and the difference between the right to secede and the lack of a prohibition on secession.

In the first round of written pleadings in the pro-Kosovo camp, Kosovo, Albania, Germany, the Netherlands, Finland, Slovenia, Switzerland, Estonia, Ireland, Latvia, and Poland more or less clearly invoked remedial secession/external self-determination. While there were quite a few differences in how precisely this point was argued and what conditions were put forward by each party, these states (excluding Kosovo for the moment) have at least expressed their position in such terms that it can be qualified as *opinio juris* with regard to the existence of this right as such.[49] However, as we have seen, Kosovo argued this point quite rudimentarily, while most of Kosovo's strongest supporters did *not* take a position on remedial secession or argue that Kosovo had such a right—this was the case in the first round most notably with France, Norway, the United States, and the United Kingdom, but also Austria, Denmark, the Czech Republic, Japan, Luxembourg, the Maldives, and Sierra Leone. None of these states however explicitly argued that there was no right to remedial secession/external self-determination *in extremis*. At the same time, in the pro-Serbia camp, most states opposed a right to remedial secession: Serbia; Argentina; Cyprus; Spain; China; Iran; and Slovakia. Others took no clear position: Bolivia; Azerbaijan; Romania; Venezuela; and Libya.

Perhaps the most remarkable item from the first round is that one state in the pro-Serbia camp *did* explicitly endorse the right to remedial secession—Russia—while claiming that Kosovo did not satisfy its requirements on the facts.

---

within the zone of tolerance. For Crawford, that threshold is very high indeed: 'where the government of the predecessor State maintains its status as such, its assent to secession is necessary, at least unless and until the seceding entity has firmly established control beyond hope of recall'. Crawford, *supra* note 42, at 391. On the question of Kosovo's statehood, specifically, see Crawford's contribution to this volume.

[49]  State arguments of course have to be appreciated in the specific context of a litigation; they may qualify as (verbal) state practice, as *opinio juris*, or as something less. In this particular context, however, states have made quite clear statements that they believe a particular right exists, or not, as a matter of customary law, and under what conditions. These are therefore in my view at least expressions of *opinio juris*.

**Table 3.3** The pro-Kosovo camp's arguments about self-determination and territorial integrity

| Pro-Kosovo camp | 1st round | 2nd round | 3rd round |
|---|---|---|---|
| Kosovo | while very briefly invoking self-determination, relies primarily on the absence of a norm prohibiting declaration of independence (WC1, paras. 8.03–8.41); territorial integrity not addressed to non-state entities (para. 8.19) | reiterates that territorial integrity is not addressed to non-state actors, responding to Serbia's claims that it is (WC2, paras. 4.05–4.13; now expands on the self-determination argument, while reiterating that the Court need not reach it (paras. 4.31–4.53) | affirms and develops its previous arguments (CR 2009/25, pp. 38–46) |
| Albania | invokes external self-determination in cases of denial of internal self-determination; does not address territorial integrity within states | now seems to argue that territorial integrity applies only between states, but with some inconsistency (WC, paras. 46–48, 51); reaffirms position on self-determination | affirms its previous arguments |
| France | does not invoke self-determination; territorial integrity only extends between states; secession not prohibited (WS, paras. 2.5–2.8) | reiterates earlier arguments | reiterates earlier arguments |
| Germany | invokes remedial secession/self-determination (WS, pp. 34–37); does not explicitly argue that territorial integrity extends only between states, but claims that secession is not generally prohibited (pp. 29–30) | affirms but does not develop earlier arguments | now explicitly argues that territorial integrity does not extend to non-state actors (CR 2009/26, pp. 27–28), affirms reliance on self-determination |
| Netherlands | invokes remedial secession/self-determination in 'unique cases or cases *sui generis*' (WS, paras. 3.6, 3.20); does not address the scope of territorial integrity, but notes absence of prohibition (para.3.22) | reiterates earlier arguments | reiterates earlier arguments |
| Norway | briefly notes the absence of a prohibition of secession, as well as the theory of remedial secession/self-determination on which it does not take a position, saying that these issues are outside the scope of the question (WS, paras. 4–8) | now seems to endorse a (restrictive) theory of remedial secession (WC, paras. 4–5) | now explicitly argues that territorial integrity does not extend to non-state actors (CR 2009/31, p. 50); reiterates its previous arguments |

(*continued*)

Table 3.3 Continued

| Pro-Kosovo camp | 1st round | 2nd round | 3rd round |
|---|---|---|---|
| United States | does not invoke self-determination; secession not prohibited, international law normally regulates only relations between states (WS, pp. 50–52) | now clearly argues that territorial integrity operates only between states (WC, pp. 15–20); again expressly takes no view on self-determination (pp. 21–23) | affirms previous positions, again without taking a position on self-determination |
| United Kingdom | does not rely on self-determination, but on the absence of a prohibition, merely noting the remedial self-determination argument without stating a position on it (WS, paras. 5.30–5.32); territorial integrity applies only between states (paras. 5.8–5.11, 5.29) | again explicitly takes no position on self-determination (WC, para. 10); affirms absence of a prohibition argument (paras. 13, 33) and that territorial integrity extends only between states (paras. 39–45) | reiterates previous arguments |
| Austria | does not rely on self-determination, but on the absence of a prohibition; territorial integrity applies only between states (WS, paras. 37–40) | N/A | affirms its earlier arguments |
| Denmark | relies on the absence of a prohibition, briefly mentioning but not elaborating on self-determination (WS, pp. 3–4, 12–13) | N/A | affirms its earlier arguments |
| Finland | invokes remedial secession/self-determination (WS, pp. 34–37); does not argue that territorial integrity extends only between states | N/A | affirms reliance on self-determination; now also explicitly argues that territorial integrity does not apply within a state (CR 2009/30, pp. 59–60) |
| Slovenia | self-determination trumps territorial integrity; does not address the scope of territorial integrity | does not develop the two issues further | N/A |
| Switzerland | territorial integrity does not apply within a state (WS, para. 55); even if it does, it is only in exceptional circumstances and, in last resort, trumped by the right to self-determination, where there has been denial of this right internally (WS, paras. 66–68) | reiterates its previous arguments | N/A |

| | | |
|---|---|---|
| Bulgaria | N/A | relies on absence of a prohibition, and argues that territorial integrity extends only between states (CR 2009/28, pp. 24–25); does not take a position on self-determination |
| Burundi | N/A | no right to external self-determination outside the colonial context (CR 2009/28, pp. 38–39); takes no position on the scope of territorial integrity |
| Croatia | N/A | relies on the absence of a prohibition (CR 2009/29, p. 52); takes no position on remedial secession/self-determination |
| Czech Republic | does not rely on self-determination, but on the absence of a prohibition (WS, pp. 7–8) | N/A |
| Estonia | 'oppressed minorities' have the right to secede in cases of a severe and long-lasting denial of self-determination (WS, p. 6); does not address the scope of territorial integrity | N/A |
| Ireland | relies both on the absence of a prohibition (WS, para. 18) and on remedial self-determination in cases of gross abuses (para. 30) | N/A |
| Japan | states that the relationship between self-determination and territorial integrity is unclear, without taking a position, relying on the absence of a prohibition | N/A |
| Jordan | N/A | invokes remedial secession/ self-determination, and argues that territorial integrity does not apply within states (CR 2009/31, pp. 33–37) |
| Latvia | invokes self-determination; does not address the scope of territorial integrity | N/A |

(continued)

**Table 3.3** Continued

| Pro-Kosovo camp | 1st round | 2nd round | 3rd round |
|---|---|---|---|
| Luxembourg | does not rely on self-determination, but on the absence of a prohibition (WS, paras. 16–17) | N/A | N/A |
| Maldives | does not meaningfully address either issue | N/A | N/A |
| Poland | invokes remedial secession/self-determination (WS, paras. 6.3–6.7); does not argue that territorial integrity extends only between states | N/A | N/A |
| Saudi Arabia | N/A | N/A | very briefly mentions that Kosovo exercised its right to self-determination, but does not elaborate on this argument in any way (CR 2009/26, p. 34) |
| Sierra Leone | does not address either issue | N/A | N/A |

**Table 3.4** The pro-Serbia camp's arguments about self-determination and territorial integrity

| Pro-Serbia camp | 1st round | 2nd round | 3rd round |
|---|---|---|---|
| Serbia | no right of external self-determination or remedial secession as last resort (WS, paras. 558–569, 589–654); territorial integrity binds non-state actors (paras. 413, 440–476) | affirms and develops its previous arguments | affirms and develops its previous arguments (CR 2009/24, pp. 65–68, 77–83) |
| Argentina | territorial integrity does not apply just to states, but also to other 'international actors', such as the Kosovo Albanians (WS, para. 75); no right to remedial secession/self-determination (paras. 85–86, 97) | affirms that territorial integrity applies to non-state actors (WC, paras. 39–40), and the earlier position on self-determination (paras. 59–61) | affirms and develops its earlier arguments |
| Bolivia | does not address either issue | now argues that there is no right of external self-determination or remedial secession outside the colonial context (WC, paras. 7–18); again no argument about the scope of territorial integrity | affirms its position on self-determination, but again makes no argument about the scope of territorial integrity |
| Cyprus | no right of external self-determination or remedial secession as last resort (WS, paras. 140–146); does not explicitly address the applicability of territorial integrity to non-state actors | now clearly argues that territorial integrity extends within a state (WC, paras. 15–18); reiterates rejection of self-determination (para. 23) | affirms its earlier positions |
| Spain | self-determination does not trump territorial integrity (WS, paras. 24); does not explicitly address the applicability of territorial integrity to non-state actors | now clearly argues that territorial integrity also applies within states (WC, paras. 4–5); affirms that there is no right to remedial secession (para. 8) | affirms previous arguments |
| Azerbaijan | argues that there is no right to secede, but does not explicitly address remedial secession or the scope of territorial integrity | N/A | now explicitly says that there is no right to remedial secession/self-determination (CR 2009/27, p. 24, para. 40); affirms its previous positions |
| Brazil | does not meaningfully address either issue | N/A | again does not meaningfully address either issue |
| China | self-determination does not allow for secession; does not explicitly address the applicability of territorial integrity to non-state actors | N/A | affirms its previous positions, without clearly addressing the scope of territorial integrity |

(continued)

**Table 3.4** Continued

| Pro-Serbia camp | 1st round | 2nd round | 3rd round |
|---|---|---|---|
| Romania | does not explicitly address the applicability of territorial integrity to non-state actors, except by stating that the principle applies *erga omnes* (WS, para. 108); explicitly non-committal on whether remedial secession or self-determination could be allowed in principle (para. 138), because they do not apply to the case of Kosovo on the facts | N/A | now argues that secession is prohibited in the absence of a positive entitlement (CR 2009/32, p. 27); now also expressly rejects the remedial secession argument (pp. 31–36) |
| Russia | self-determination normally does not allow for remedial secession, except in 'truly extreme circumstances, such as an outright armed attack by the parent State, threatening the very existence of the people in question, (WS, para. 88, also pp. 38–40); does not explicitly address the applicability of territorial integrity to non-state actors | N/A | affirms previous positions, adding that territorial integrity is peremptory norm that binds not just states, but 'all subjects of international law' (CR 2009/30, p. 46, para. 34) |
| Venezuela | does not address either issue | N/A | opposes external self-determination outside the colonial context (CR 2009/33, pp. 12–13) |
| Belarus | N/A | N/A | appears to reject remedial secession/self-determination, but not unambiguously (CR 2009/27, p. 3); does not address the scope of territorial integrity |
| Iran | territorial integrity is *jus cogens*, and applies within states, not just between them (WS, pp. 3–4); self-determination does not allow for remedial secession (pp. 6–7) | N/A | N/A |
| Libya | does not address either issue | N/A | N/A |
| Slovakia | self-determination does not allow for remedial secession; does not explicitly address the applicability of territorial integrity to non-state actors | N/A | N/A |
| Vietnam | N/A | N/A | opposes external self-determination outside the colonial context (CR 2009/33, pp. 20–21) |

NB: The only neutral state in the first round, Egypt, did not say anything about the scope of territorial integrity, while seemingly arguing that there is no right to external self-determination outside the colonial context (Egypt WS, para. 74).

It was indeed the only member of the P-5 to do so. This is surprising not only because Russia opposed Kosovo's independence, but also because it has its own share of secessionists and went through the whole Chechnya experience. Russia, on the other hand, also has its own client separatists, and it may be this that led it to express its view that such a right existed even if Kosovo did not satisfy its requirements.

Within both camps there was little appreciation in the first round that the real issue with territorial integrity was whether it extended within states, and not only between them. However, this issue was clearly anticipated by Kosovo and Serbia, as well as by France, the United Kingdom, Austria, Switzerland, Argentina, and Iran. In the second written round, which had the fewest participants, there was a much clearer understanding of this issue. Thus, in the pro-Serbia camp, in addition to Serbia and Argentina, who had appreciated the point before, Cyprus and Spain started arguing more explicitly that territorial integrity prohibited non-state actors from declaring independence. Similarly, in the pro-Kosovo camp, the issue was argued in detail by Kosovo, Albania, the US, and the UK. While the parties generally reaffirmed their previous arguments, Bolivia now clearly expressed its opposition to remedial secession/self-determination, while Norway now endorsed it, by contrast with their earlier silence on the matter.

In the third, oral round, the core groups in each of the two camps had by and large already said all that there was to say. But there were of course some new additions to the two camps, as well as parties that had not participated in the second round, even if they did in the first. In the pro-Kosovo camp, a number of parties now explicitly started arguing that territorial integrity applied only between states—Germany, Norway, Finland, Bulgaria, and Jordan—while remedial self-determination was additionally endorsed by Jordan and Saudi Arabia, and opposed by Burundi. In the pro-Serbia camp, self-determination was now rejected by Azerbaijan, Romania, Belarus, Venezuela, and Vietnam, while Russia started arguing that territorial integrity was binding on non-state entities.

In sum, we have seen how the question of the scope of the territorial integrity principle and its application to non-state actors steadily gained traction as the proceedings progressed, with Serbia and Kosovo and some of their core allies anticipating it from the very beginning. With regard to remedial secession/self-determination, of the 43 states (excluding Kosovo) that appeared before the Court in the three rounds of pleadings, 14 asserted that this right existed in principle, 14 denied its existence, and the remaining 25 were neutral. When it comes to the five permanent members of the Security Council, Russia endorsed remedial self-determination in principle (while rejecting its applicability to Kosovo), China opposed it, while France, the UK, and the US remained neutral. If we take the views of the committed states as expressions of their *opinio juris*, we can only really say that the question of the existence of the right to remedial secession would remain inconclusive if the states appearing before the ICJ were a representative sample of the international community as a whole. The silence of the neutral states cannot be taken as an expression of *opinio juris* one way or the other, but it still speaks volumes, politically if not legally. As I explained above, when it came to general international law, the key issue with regard to Kosovo's secession was not a putative conflict between self-determination and territorial integrity, but the absence of a prohibition directly addressed to non-state actors. Only 6 out of the 43 participating states unambiguously argued that territorial integrity actually created such a prohibition, and this was not an argument that the Court was prepared to accept. Hence, the only place where such a prohibition could perhaps be found was resolution 1244, to which I will now turn.

## 6. Arguments under Resolution 1244

Philip Allott once famously defined treaties as 'disagreements reduced to writing'.[50] He might well have been writing about resolution 1244. When it comes to the final status of Kosovo, it is an exercise in deliberate ambiguity: you can read whatever you want into it.[51] And in the Kosovo proceedings, very good lawyers on all sides were doing just that. Most of the lines of argument with regard to the resolution were fairly obvious, since they were ultimately about parsing its language and there were only so many plausible ways of doing that. Thus, the pro-Serbia camp argued that the DoI was an unlawful attempt at terminating the international administration of the territory set up by resolution 1244, which is something that only the Security Council could have done, and that the references to a final or political *settlement* in the resolution ultimately required the agreement of all parties involved, including Serbia, or at the very least further action by the Council. The pro-Kosovo camp, on the other hand, argued that the wording of the resolution in no way prohibited independence, as it dealt with the provisional international administration and not final status, that the references to the Rambouillet Accords in the resolution indicated that the Council contemplated independence as a possible outcome based on the will of the people, and that there was indeed a negotiating process which was exhausted without success.

But there were at least four new lines of argument that were anything but obvious and emerged only in the context of the advisory proceedings, with some of them making full sense only in that context. First, the formulation of the question, ultimately requiring Serbia to show that there was a norm addressed to the authors of the declaration prohibiting them from making it, led to a very specific issue: whether resolutions by the UN Security Council can directly bind non-state actors and impose on them international legal obligations. This is an issue that had, until the advisory proceedings, attracted little scholarly or for

---

[50] P. Allott, 'The Concept of International Law' (1999) 10 *EJIL* 31, at 43.
[51] The resolution is far clearer when it comes to its provisions regarding the end of the 1999 conflict, which one could fairly say was its primary purpose.

that matter any other kind of attention.[52] And even if resolutions of the Council could bind non-state actors as a general matter, there was a further question of whether *this* particular resolution did so. At the start of the proceedings, very few of the parties realized that this was even an issue, and generally speaking only some of the core members within each camp developed any detailed arguments on this point.

Second, and partly in order to address this, Serbia argued that at issue was not only the DoI's compliance with resolution 1244 as such, but also with the whole legal regime established in Kosovo under that resolution, including the Constitutional Framework and other relevant UNMIK regulations. That raised a rather peculiar question of taxonomy: were the Constitutional Framework and UNMIK regulations part of the 'international law' that the DoI had to be in accordance with, or were they rather some weird species of municipal law? For Kosovo and its allies, the answer had to be in the negative: surely, one could not accept that say parking ticket violations under the relevant UNMIK regulations were violations of *international* law! For Serbia, on the other hand, this taxonomical inquiry was both sterile and false, since there was no good reason why UNMIK regulations could not at the same time be both international in character and have the force of internal law in Kosovo.[53] What mattered were not our intuitions as to what subject matter belongs to international law properly so called and what does not, but the fact that the regulations were made by UNMIK, a subsidiary body of the Security Council, acting under a Council mandate, within the UN as an international organization governed by international law.

Third, one way that Kosovo and its supporters had of defending against Serbia's arguments on the basis of resolution 1244 and the Constitutional Framework was to say that any violation of these instruments was properly within the jurisdiction of the Security Council and the Secretary-General's Special Representative (SRSG) in Kosovo as the head of UNMIK. Unlike in a number of previous instances, in which they declared acts of the Kosovo authorities to be void as infringing the resolution or the Framework,[54] here both the Council and the SRSG did absolutely nothing. This, argued the pro-Kosovo camp, was either conclusive evidence that there was no violation, a judgment to which the Court should defer, or acquiescence

---

[52]  See, e.g., the very brief analysis in J. Frowein and N. Krisch, 'Chapter VII: Introduction', in B. Simma (ed.), *The Charter of the United Nations: A Commentary* (2nd ed, OUP, 2002), at 716, MN 44, and J. Frowein and N. Krisch, 'Article 39', in Simma, ibid., at 723, MN 18.

[53]  Cf. C. Stahn, *The Law and Practice of International Territorial Administration* (CUP, 2008), at 647 ff; L. von Carlowitz, 'UNMIK Lawmaking between Effective Peace Support and Internal Self-Determination' (2003) 41 *Archiv des Völkerrechts* 336, at 341; E. de Wet, 'The Direct Administration of Territories by the United Nations and its Member States in the Post Cold War Era: Legal Bases and Implications for National Law' (2004) 8 *Max Planck UNYB* 291, at 331.

[54]  See, e.g., UN Doc. S/PRST/2002/16 (24 May 2002); UN Doc. S/PRST/2003/1 (6 February 2003). See also Report of the Secretary-General on the United Nations Interim Administration Mission in Kosovo, UN Doc. S/2004/71 (26 January 2004), at 3, para. 9; Report of the Secretary-General on the United Nations Interim Administration Mission in Kosovo, UN Doc. S/2004/613 (30 July 2004), paras. 14 and 62.

in this violation that cured any possible defect. The problem with this argument was again that it smacked of apology. Everybody knew that the Council did not react to the DoI because there was no consensus among its members, and that the SRSG's passivity was entirely due to the passivity of its political masters—indeed, in the Secretary-General's own view, the UN 'has maintained strict neutrality on the question of Kosovo's status'.[55] According this silence legal significance was qualitatively no different from arguing, say, that the Council acquiesced in the 2003 Iraq invasion by failing to condemn it. This is in turn why some parties in the pro-Kosovo camp focused more on the acquiescence of the SRSG, arguing that he had a duty to annul any acts that he thought were in violation of the resolution 1244 regime, rather than on that of the Council

Finally, we come to the key issue that managed to demolish Serbia's Constitutional Framework argument: the identity of the authors of the DoI. That issue was entirely novel. It was never raised at the time of the DoI itself, when other states recognized Kosovo, or when Serbia went to the General Assembly for it to request an opinion from the Court. When did the issue arise? When some very smart lawyers in the pro-Kosovo camp sat down to discuss litigation strategy in the ICJ advisory proceedings.[56] They saw that they had a problem—that the DoI was obviously a violation of the Constitutional Framework, if we think about this in terms of what the competences of the PISG were under that Framework. Again, previous and lesser infringements were declared to be null and void by the Council and the SRSG. They had to get away from that problem somehow. And then they looked at the text of the declaration itself, which starts its first paragraph with 'we, the democratically elected representatives of our people'. And then some really smart lawyer in that group of very smart lawyers said, 'Will you look at that, why not just say that in promulgating the DoI, they did not act as the PISG, but as the democratically elected representatives of their people who were not bound by the Constitutional Framework, but acted outside it?'

The two options are of course not mutually exclusive. By the fact that you were, say, elected a member of the Kosovo Assembly (or as President of Kosovo), you were a democratically elected representative of the people. But that is the argument these lawyers made, and they did so while (charmingly) referring to the original version of the declaration, written on parchment coupled with calligraphy and the John Hancock-like signatures of those present,[57]

---

[55] Report of the Secretary-General on the United Nations Interim Administration Mission in Kosovo, UN Doc. S/2008/458 (15 July 2008), paras. 29–30.

[56] I was obviously not present; the pro-Serbia camp of course also had its own share of very smart lawyers. I am also not excluding the possibility that the issue of the identity of the authors of the DoI was the subject of legal advice given to the Kosovo government after the adoption of the DoI, and that this advice had some bearing on the case. But it seems clear that the Kosovo authorities did not have the benefit of such advice *before* the adoption of the DoI, as it otherwise could have been very clearly stated at the time the DoI was adopted that the relevant Kosovo authorities were not acting as the PISG and were not bound by the Constitutional Framework.

[57] *Kosovo* WC1, pp. 207–209. We tend to do kitsch very well in the Balkans.

as evidence that it was not adopted by the Kosovo Assembly and President as part of the PISG.

The argument was good enough for the Court. While also accepting Serbia's arguments that the Constitutional Framework was part of international law[58] and that the Framework and resolution 1244 applied in Kosovo at the time the DoI was made,[59] the Court held that

The declaration of independence, therefore, was not intended by those who adopted it to take effect within the legal order created for the interim phase, nor was it capable of doing so. On the contrary, the Court considers that the authors of that declaration did not act, or intend to act, in the capacity of an institution created by and empowered to act within that legal order but, rather, set out to adopt a measure the significance and effects of which would lie outside that order.[60]

The Court buttressed this conclusion with a somewhat subtler—and *perhaps* less apologetic—variant of the acquiescence argument, which focuses solely on the SRSG:

The silence of the Special Representative of the Secretary-General in the face of the declaration of independence of 17 February 2008 suggests that he did not consider that the declaration was an act of the Provisional Institutions of Self-Government designed to take effect within the legal order for the supervision of which he was responsible. As the practice shows, he would have been under a duty to take action with regard to acts of the Assembly of Kosovo which he considered to be *ultra vires*.[61]

Note how the SRSG's silence is not interpreted as acquiescence in a possible violation but as evidence of the *legal order* in which the DoI was designed to operate or have effect in. The Court also found that '[t]here is no indication, in the text of Security Council resolution 1244 (1999), that the Security Council intended to impose...a specific obligation to act or a prohibition from acting, addressed to [non-state] actors',[62] thus assuming that the Council can indeed bind non-state actors when it wants to,[63] but that here it rather imposed obligations on member states and set out the duties of the international military and civilian presences in Kosovo. Bearing in mind the ambiguity of the resolution's language, the Court concluded, it could not be interpreted as prohibiting the authors from adopting the declaration.[64]

Let me reiterate that my purpose in writing this chapter is not to re-argue the case or evaluate the correctness of the Court's conclusions. I certainly do not think that the Court went beyond the bounds of reasonableness when it comes to the

---

[58] *Kosovo* AO, para. 88.    [59] Ibid., para. 91.
[60] Ibid., para. 105.    [61] Ibid., para. 108. See also paras. 120–121.
[62] Ibid., para. 115.
[63] See also M. Divac Oberg, 'The Legal Effect of United Nations Resolutions in the *Kosovo* Advisory Opinion', (2011) 105 *AJIL* 81; on binding non-state actors through instruments to which they are not parties, see generally S. Sivakumaran, 'Binding Armed Opposition Groups', (2006) 55 *ICLQ* 369, M. Milanovic, 'Is the Rome Statute Binding on Individuals? (And Why We Should Care)', (2011) 9 *JICJ* 25.
[64] Ibid., paras. 118–119.

interpretation of the resolution as such. The real question, as a matter of policy, of course, is who got to decide on Kosovo's independence. The Court's approach ultimately led to the result that a UN regime of territorial administration could be terminated—perhaps not formally but certainly in essence—through the acts of one of the parties to the conflict without explicit Security Council approval. Serbia aside, that result is, I think, troubling from an institutional UN perspective and will have consequences for future cases of international territorial administration. But again, I do not think that the language of the resolution as such precludes the result that the Court reached.

The only part of the Court's analysis that I do find troubling is this conclusion that the authors of the DoI did not act (or *intend* to act) in their capacity as the PISG and that, *therefore*, they could not have violated the Constitutional Framework. The manifest *non sequitur* aside, what makes this point so troubling is precisely that it is nothing more than, as Judge Tomka aptly put it, a post-hoc intellectual construct.[65] Even worse, it was *obviously* a post-hoc intellectual construct: the identity of the authors was simply never an issue before the proceedings started. Indeed, as I will show below, no state in the pro-Serbia camp anticipated this argument in the first round of pleadings, and only some in the pro-Kosovo camp made it (and not even all of Kosovo's core allies did so), with the argument steadily gaining traction in the pro-Kosovo camp as the proceedings went on.

Strangely enough, the Court could have reached the same result through less debatable means. It is of course a truism that any secession violates the existing constitutional order. In terms of international law, there is simply no problem with that. The only reason why the Court needed this whole device was that it had previously classified the Constitutional Framework as part of the 'international law' that the DoI had to be 'in accordance with', per the terms of the question put to the Court by the General Assembly. Had the Court decided that the Constitutional Framework was not international law, it could have avoided this whole authors business altogether.[66] That aside, even if the Constitutional Framework *was* violated—and I think it was, and quite blatantly so—that does not necessarily mean that Kosovo's statehood is precluded as a matter of international law. Not *every* violation of international law (assuming, as the Court decided, that the Framework was international law) would have had such a strict a consequence.

Tables 3.5 and 3.6 below are ordered like the ones in the previous section, and show which parties dealt with the four novel lines of argument that I identified above, and how and when they did so. These were: the binding effect of Security Council resolutions on non-state actors; the legal nature of the Constitutional framework; the acquiescence of the Council and the SRSG; and the identity of the authors.

---

[65] *Kosovo* AO, Declaration of Vice-President Tomka, para. 12.
[66] Cf. *Kosovo* AO, Separate Opinion of Judge Yusuf, paras. 18–21.

**Table 3.5** Pro-Kosovo camp's handling of novel lines of argument

| Pro-Kosovo camp | 1st round | 2nd round | 3rd round |
|---|---|---|---|
| Kosovo | authors are not the PISG, but the democratically elected representatives of the people of Kosovo, not subject to UNMIK (WC1, para 6.01 ff; 9.18); UNSC resolutions are addressed to states; incapable of directly imposing obligations upon a non-state actor (para. 9.02); SRSG's lack of condemnation of the declaration evidence that it was not a violation (paras. 9.20–9.28); does not expressly deal with the legal nature of the Constitutional Framework | reiterates the authors argument (WC2, paras. 1.22–1.24, 5.62); reiterates the acquiescence argument, saying that considerable deference should be paid to the SRSG's decision not to annul the declaration (paras. 5.58–5.59, 5.65); now explicitly argues that the Constitutional Framework was not part of international law (para. 5.66); expands on the position that non-state actors cannot be bound by UNSC resolutions, or that at the very least the UNSC must do so expressly (paras. 5.67–5.74) | affirms and develops its previous arguments on the identity of the authors (CR 2009/25, pp. 34–37), acquiescence of the UNSC/SRSG (pp. 60–62); briefly reiterates that the Constitutional Framework is not international law (pp. 62–63); does not deal with UNSC binding non-state actors |
| Albania | authors were not the PISG, but the democratically elected representatives of the people of Kosovo (WS, p. 4, fn. 1, paras. 40, 94, 103 ff); failure of the UNSC and the SRSG to condemn the declaration is a reason for the Court to exercise its discretion and not give an opinion, as well as evidence there was no violation (WS, paras. 59–64, 100); does not address the other two issues | reaffirms arguments on authors and acquiescence (WC, paras. 79, 90); does not address the other two issues | reiterates earlier arguments without developing them further |
| France | declaration officially approved by the Assembly of Kosovo (WS, paras. 10, 26, 2.64); lack of condemnation from the UNSC or the SRSG conclusive evidence that there was no violation (WS, paras. 2.70–2.82); does not address the other two issues | does not address any of the four issues, focusing on preliminary objections regarding jurisdiction and propriety | now briefly says that Kosovo 'a choisi de se declarer indépendant par la voie de ses représentants démocratiquement élus' (CR 2009/31, p. 14, para. 15); reiterates acquiescence argument (pp. 24–25); does not address the other two issues |
| Germany | authors are not the PISG, but the democratically elected representatives of the people of Kosovo (WS, pp. 6–7); lack of objections by the UNSC and the SRSG confirms that there was no violation (p. 42); does not address the other two issues | reiterates the authors argument (WC, p. 7); does not address other issues | reiterates the authors argument (CR 2009/26, p. 26) |

(*continued*)

**Table 3.5** Continued

| Pro-Kosovo camp | 1st round | 2nd round | 3rd round |
|---|---|---|---|
| Netherlands | appears to assume that the authors are the PISG, but not clearly so (WS, para. 1.1); the UN's position of strict neutrality entails that the declaration did not violate resolution 1244 (para. 2.5); does not address other issues | again lack of clarity on the authors issue (WC, paras. 1.1, 2.2); Constitutional Framework not international law (para. 2.3); does not address the other issues | does not address the four issues |
| Norway | authors are not the PISG, but the democratically elected representatives of the people of Kosovo (WS, para. 13); notes that neither the UNSC nor other UN organs condemned the declaration (para. 17); does not address other issues | reaffirms its position on the identity of the authors (WC, para. 9); expresses doubts that UNSC resolutions could bind non-state actors (para. 13) | reaffirms its position on the identity of the authors and again expresses doubts that UNSC resolutions can bind non-state actors (CR 2009/31 pp. 45–46, 48); |
| United Kingdom | authors are not the PISG, but the democratically elected representatives of the people of Kosovo (WS, paras. 1.12–1.13, 4.5); notes the absence of condemnation by the UNSC and the SRSG as indications of the declaration's compatibility with international law (paras. 4.6, 6.45, 6.70); does not address the issue of the legal nature of the UNMIK regulations clearly, but states that both Serbian law and 'the law applied in Kosovo before the declaration' irrelevant for its DoI's lawfulness under international law (para. 6.71); does not at all address the binding effect of UNSC resolutions on non-state actors; | reaffirms the authors argument (WC, paras. 24–26); assumes without arguing that the UNSC can bind non-state actors, but claims that when it wishes to do so it does so explicitly (paras. 22, 30); reiterates absence of condemnation argument (para. 27); now clearly argues that the Constitutional Framework was a 'municipal instrument', nor international law (para. 32) | reiterates previous arguments |
| United States | does not have a developed argument that the PISG are not the authors, but states that this is irrelevant (WS, p. 57, fn. 231); it is irrelevant because the UNSC and the SRSG have not objected to the declaration, a judgment to which the Court should give considerable weight (pp. 84–89); does not address the other two issues | now seems to argue that the authors were not the PISG or did not act in such capacity (WC, p. 38); expresses doubts that UNSC resolutions could be binding on non-state actors (p. 35, fn. 110); now clearly and at length argues that UNMIK regulations have the character of domestic law (pp. 39–42); reiterates the acquiescence/deference argument (pp. 43–45) | affirms all previous arguments |

| | | | |
|---|---|---|---|
| Austria | authors are not the PISG, but the democratically elected representatives of the people of Kosovo; they were not bound by resolution 1244, as they were not subjects of international law, but says nothing else about binding non-state actors (WS, para. 16); failure of the UNSC or the SRSG to object cured any defect (paras. 19–21, 41–42); does not address the binding effect of UNSC resolutions on non-state actors | N/A | affirms its earlier arguments |
| Denmark | does not address any of the four issues | N/A | does not address any of the four issues |
| Finland | declaration adopted by the Assembly of Kosovo/PISG (WS, paras. 2, 4, 17); does not address the other issues | N/A | now argues that the authors were not the PISG (CR 2009/30, p. 55); does not address the other issues |
| Slovenia | does not address any of the four issues | does not address any of the four issues | N/A |
| Switzerland | seems to studiously avoid the issue of the author's identity, stating only that the declaration was made 'by Kosovo' (WS, para. 96); does not address the other issues | now argues that the authors are not the PISG, but the democratically elected representatives of the people of Kosovo (WC, para. 3); does not address the other issues | N/A |
| Bulgaria | N/A | N/A | briefly states, without arguing, that the declaration was adopted by the elected representatives of the people (CR 2009/28, p. 22, para. 15); does not address the other issues |
| Burundi | N/A | N/A | accepts that the authors are the PISG (CR 2009/29, p. 35); does not address the other issues |
| Croatia | N/A | N/A | briefly argues that the authors were not acting as the PISG (CR 2009/29, p. 64); does not address the other issues |

*(continued)*

Table 3.5 Continued

| Pro-Kosovo camp | 1st round | 2nd round | 3rd round |
|---|---|---|---|
| Czech Republic | assumes that the authors are the PISG (WS, p. 6); absence of condemnation by the UNSC should be taken as a clear signal that there was no violation (WS, p. 11) | N/A | N/A |
| Estonia | authors not the PISG, but the Assembly of Kosovo consisting of representatives of the people (WS, pp. 3–4); lack of condemnation by the SRSG evidence of no violation (p. 14); does not address the other issues | N/A | N/A |
| Ireland | does not address any of the four issues | N/A | N/A |
| Japan | does not address any of the four issues | N/A | N/A |
| Jordan | N/A | N/A | briefly asserts that the authors were not the PISG, as well as the acquiescence argument (CR 2009/31, p. 31, para. 16); does not address the other issues |
| Latvia | assumes that authors are the PISG (WS, p. 2); does not address the other issues | N/A | N/A |
| Luxembourg | authors are not the PISG, but the democratically elected representatives of the people of Kosovo (WS, para. 13); simply notes that the SRSG did not annul the declaration (para. 25); does not address the other issues | N/A | N/A |
| Maldives | does not address any of the four issues | N/A | N/A |
| Poland | authors were not acting as the PISG, but as the democratically elected leaders of the people of Kosovo (WS, para. 3.41); does not address the other issues | N/A | N/A |
| Saudi Arabia | N/A | N/A | does not address any of the four issues |
| Sierra Leone | does not address any of the four issues | N/A | N/A |

**Table 3.6** Pro-Serbia camp's handling of novel lines of argument

| Pro-Serbia camp | 1st round | 2nd round | 3rd round |
|---|---|---|---|
| Serbia | assumes that the authors are the PISG; UNMIK regulations part of the international legal regime applicable in Kosovo binding on the PISG (WS, paras. 712, 876); does not address the other two issues | responds at length to the authors argument, insisting that they were the PISG (WC, paras. 31–42); develops the point of UNSC binding non-state actors, asserting that the authors would have been bound even if they were *not* acting as the PISG, and that the Constitutional Framework was part of the international legal regime (paras. 368–389); responds to the acquiescence argument (paras. 486–494) | deals with the authors issue at length (CR 2009/24, pp. 41–43); resolution 1244 binds the authors and all relevant actors, and does not need to do so explicitly (pp. 43–47); Constitutional Framework is international law because the issuing authority is international (pp. 48–49); no acquiescence by UNSC, the SG, or the SRSG (pp. 60–61) |
| Argentina | assumes that authors are the PISG (WS, paras. 18, 39, 62); Constitutional Framework part of the international resolution 1244 legal regime (paras. 65–68); because they were created by virtue of the resolution the PISG are bound by it (para. 116 ff); UNSC can impose obligations on non-state actors (para. 124) | argues emphatically that the authors are indeed the PISG (WC, paras. 26–27), and that events after the declaration cannot cure its illegality (paras. 62–66); does not address the other two issues | affirms and develops it earlier arguments on authors (CR 2009/26, pp. 38–40) and the irrelevance of subsequent events; does not address the other two issues |
| Bolivia | assumes that authors are PISG; does not address the other issues | N/A | again assumes, without arguing, that authors are PISG; does not address the other issues |
| Cyprus | binding effect of UNSC resolutions on non-state actors not addressed clearly, but argues that the PISG were themselves created by international law (WS paras. 70 ff, 106 ff); assumes that authors are the PISG (paras. 60, 62, 70ff); does not address the other two issues | argues that the authors are the PISG (WC, paras. 3–7); seems to argue that UNSC decisions can bind non-state actors (para. 18); states that the Constitutional Framework is an 'international instrument' (para. 11); briefly rejects the acquiescence argument (para. 25) | affirms its earlier positions, without further argument on the four issues |

(continued)

**Table 3.6** Continued

| Pro-Serbia camp | 1st round | 2nd round | 3rd round |
|---|---|---|---|
| Spain | assumes that authors are the PISG (WS, paras. 4–6, 14–18); PISG subject to resolution 1244 (para. 66 ff), which created a special legal regime, further developed by UNMIK (para. 59 ff) | continues assuming, without arguing, that the authors are the PISG; no acts subsequent to the declaration should be taken into account in assessing its legality, and the UNSC/SRSG's silence should not be interpreted as acquiescence (WC, paras. 9–12); does not address the other two issues | continues assuming, without arguing, that the authors are the PISG; PISG bound by all international norms part of the 1244 regime (CR 2009/30, p. 15, para. 30); rejects the acquiescence argument (pp. 19–21) |
| Azerbaijan | assumes that authors are the PISG (WS, paras. 1, 27); does not address the other issues | N/A | does not address any of the four issues |
| Brazil | assumes that the authors are the PISG; does not address other issues | N/A | again assumes, without arguing, that authors are PISG; does not address the other issues |
| China | does not address any of the four issues | N/A | does not address any of the four issues |
| Romania | assumes that the authors are the PISG (WS, para. 4); states that resolution 1244 binds the PISG (para. 14) and defines their competences (para. 58–61), but does not explicitly address the non-state actor issue or the other two issues | N/A | responds to the acquiescence argument (CR 2009/32, pp. 25–26); expressly argues that the identity of authors is irrelevant as all actors are bound by the same obligations (p. 30) |
| Russia | assumes that the DoI was adopted by the Assembly of Kosovo (WS, para. 10); states that the provisions of resolution 1244 are 'unambiguously addressed to the Kosovo Albanian leadership and hence are binding on them', but does not argue the point further (para. 24); resolution 1244 and Constitutional Framework part of a special legal regime (paras. 27–28) | N/A | rejects the 'authors are not the PISG' argument, and states that even if this were true, the resolution 1244 regime would bind any other group or gathering (CR 2009/30, p. 45, para. 29); does not address the other two issues |

| | | | |
|---|---|---|---|
| Venezuela | does not address any of the four issues | N/A | assumes without arguing that the authors are the PISG; does not address the other issues |
| Belarus | N/A | N/A | does not address any of the four issues |
| Iran | assumes that the authors were the PISG; does not address other issues | N/A | N/A |
| Libya | assumes that the authors were the PISG; does not address other issues | N/A | N/A |
| Slovakia | assumes that authors are the PISG, arguing that they acted contrary to the Constitutional Framework (WS, paras. 1 & 25); does not address the other issues | N/A | N/A |
| Vietnam | N/A | N/A | assumes without arguing that the authors are the PISG; does not address the other issues |

NB: The sole neutral state in the written pleadings, Egypt, did not address any of the four issues.

In the first written round, there was clearly a high degree of coordination in the pro-Kosovo camp regarding the 'identity of the authors' issue, with a number of parties arguing that the authors were not acting as the PISG but as the democratically elected representatives of the people: Kosovo; Albania; Germany; Norway; UK; Austria; Estonia (if in a somewhat garbled form); Luxembourg; and Poland. The high degree of coordination is also evident from the similarity in the language used by these parties when making the argument. What is most intriguing here is how some of Kosovo's supporters did not seem to get the memo, as it were, or did not find the argument to be particularly persuasive. Among its core allies, France did not raise the authors issue at all, stating that the declaration was adopted by the Kosovo Assembly, while the US relegated it to a footnote and treated it as mostly irrelevant. Among its other allies, the Netherlands, Finland, the Czech Republic, and Latvia at least appeared to assume that the authors were the PISG, while Denmark, Slovenia, Ireland, Japan, Maldives, and Sierra Leone did not express any views on the authors' identity (deliberately or not). In the pro-Serbia camp, with the exception of China and Venezuela, which do not clearly say anything about the authors, the parties simply assumed that the authors were the PISG. None seemed to anticipate the argument that the authors were something else as a device for avoiding the binding effect of resolution 1244 or the Constitutional Framework. In brief, of the 37 parties (including Kosovo and Egypt) appearing before the Court in the first round, only nine, all from the pro-Kosovo camp, thought that there was an open issue about the authors' identity. Nor, apparently, was the authors issue anticipated by the Court itself: in its first order inviting participants to make written statements to the Court, the name that the Court gave to the case was 'Accordance with International Law of the Unilateral Declaration of Independence by the Provisional Institutions of Self-Government of Kosovo'.[67] It was only when the opinion was delivered that the Court changed the name of the case into 'Accordance with International Law of the Unilateral Declaration of Independence *in Respect of Kosovo*'.[68]

Similarly, there was little awareness in the first round of the question whether Security Council resolutions can directly bind non-state actors, with only four parties making explicit arguments in that regard: Kosovo; Austria (only partially); Argentina; and Russia (also only partially). Most states in the pro-Serbia camp, including Serbia, Cyprus, Spain, and Romania, argued or proceeded from the assumption that the PISG derived their powers from the SRSG and resolution 1244, and were accordingly bound by that legal regime. The parties also generally did not address the legal nature of the Constitutional Framework and whether it formed a part of international law. The pro-Serbia camp generally seemed to proceed from the assumption that it did, while most of the pro-Kosovo camp focused on the authors issue. Similarly, the pro-Kosovo camp's acquiescence by the UNSC and/or the SRSG argument was generally not anticipated by the pro-Serbia camp.

---

[67] Order of 17 October 2008, ICJ Reports 2008, p. 409.
[68] Generally, on the naming of cases before the ICJ see S. Yee, 'Article 40', in Zimmermann et al, *supra* note 14, 922, MN 79–82.

The four issues gained much traction in the second written round. This was above all the case with the question of the authors' identity, which, as we have seen, the pro-Serbia camp did not anticipate in the first round. This was also true to a somewhat lesser extent with regard to the different varieties of the acquiescence issue. In the pro-Kosovo camp, the United States and Switzerland joined the rest of the team in claiming that the authors were not the PISG, while Kosovo, the Netherlands, the UK, and the US began arguing that the Constitutional Framework was domestic, rather than international law.

Perhaps the most interesting point here was whether Security Council resolutions can bind non-state actors, and whether resolution 1244 in particular did so. In the pro-Serbia camp, this issue was still being addressed in detail only by Serbia, and to a much lesser extent by Cyprus. In the pro-Kosovo camp, on the other hand, we encounter a variety of different responses: Kosovo argues that the Council cannot bind non-state actors, Norway and the US express doubts that it can do so, while the UK assumes that it can but that it has to do so clearly, *expressis verbis*, and that resolution 1244 does not do so. The issue gains much importance for Serbia, in particular. Its primary argument is that the authors are bound by the resolution because they are creatures of the Constitutional Framework, and the Framework itself derives its authority from the resolution. But what if Kosovo's argument that the authors were not the PISG were to be accepted, for all its artificiality? Serbia, of course, responds to that argument in detail, but it also needs an alternative. And its theory about how the authors were bound by the resolutions runs into an obvious counter-factual—what if the DoI were *not* in fact adopted by the Kosovo Assembly, but an ad hoc group of people that came together in some kind of constituent assembly which was clearly not part of the PISG? Would this hypothetical group of people, a non-PISG non-state actor, still be bound by the Constitutional Framework and resolution 1244?[69] In the second round, Serbia thus developed in great detail the argument that *all* relevant actors in Kosovo would have been bound by the resolution 1244 legal regime.

In the oral round, the authors argument was picked up by almost all members of the pro-Kosovo camp who had not done this so far, including France and Finland, the latter even doing so in open contradiction to its position in the first written round of pleadings. Little else was said on the binding effect of Security Council resolutions on non-state actors, and the Court's ultimate ruling on this point completely left open the conceptual basis for such an effect. As we have seen, the Court was content to observe that resolution 1244 when properly interpreted did not do so, without saying, on the other hand, that the Council has to bind non-state actors explicitly. Similarly, while accepting Serbia's argument that the Constitutional Framework was part of international law, the Court killed off that challenge by adopting the arguments about the identity of the authors and the acquiescence by the SRSG.

---

[69] Cf. United States WC, p. 38.

## 7. Conclusion

I hope that this brief *post mortem* of the course of argument in the Kosovo case proved to be interesting. I also think that it allows us to draw some lessons that are of general value. First, that the shift from the political to the judicial arena necessitated a shift in the arguments used to support or oppose Kosovo's independence. Some of these arguments simply got more sophisticated, as for instance with the interpretation of resolution 1244 in favour of one side or the other. Others emerged only in the context of the proceedings, and these in fact seemed especially influential—above all on the scope of the question, but also arguments about discretion and propriety and the identity of the authors of the DoI. The Court—including both the majority and the minority—was in the end very taken with all three, and their appeal lay precisely in how their very lawyerly, formalistic character allowed for the shaping of the issues to be answered, or to be avoided. The 'question question' in particular was determinative of the whole case.

Second, how this transformative effect of formalism was most pronounced when it came to the general international law part of the case. It was simply no longer enough for Kosovo's supporters to argue that it was *sui generis*. They of course did so, and did so repeatedly, but that argument made little to no impact on the opinion itself. Kosovo may well be unique in its own way, but this essentially political argument was really nothing more than damage control, designed to discourage other seekers of independence. For it to gain traction *judicially*, it was necessary to advance a general legal proposition: that international law normally prohibits neither secession nor declaration of independence, and that this absence of a prohibition does not require, and is not tantamount to, a positive entitlement to independence. The refusal of some of Kosovo's most important allies to endorse remedial secession or self-determination was similarly telling. On one hand, therefore, the pro-Kosovo camp succeeded in getting an advisory opinion that does not set a precedent for any other situation. It was indeed *designed* not to set such a precedent, reducible as it is to the trite statement that international law does not prohibit declarations of independence. From the Court's standpoint, the whole point of the opinion is that it is not memorable. But, on the other hand, even if few of its paragraphs are worthy of citation, the opinion's reliance on the absence of a prohibition inevitably sent a message that in *some* cases secession may be successful even when it is not in the furtherance of self-determination. And if there is anything that the whole Kosovo episode teaches us then, it is that powerful allies are a key ingredient to any successful secession.

Third, we could also see how allies are equally important in the judicial setting. Some arguments gained plausibility through repetition, and clearly both Kosovo and Serbia worked hard to persuade their allies to take up particular positions or arguments. This is perhaps most apparent from the pro-Kosovo camp's gradual adoption of the 'identity of the authors' argument, and the high degree of coordination between the core members of that camp, starting with the first round of written pleadings, in which regard the pro-Kosovo camp was certainly stronger than the pro-Serbia one. We can similarly observe how there is a significant cor-relation between the level of experience in arguing before the ICJ among the mem-bers of particular legal teams and their ability to anticipate some of the key, yet non-obvious, issues in the case. Not everybody saw every thrust and parry at the same time, nor made them as skilfully.

Finally, we can also see quite clearly how unpredictable the final course of the case was even for those with the most experience and skill. The pro-Kosovo camp, for instance, had no way of knowing whether their authors argument would ultimately work or not, just as no one in the pro-Serbia camp had anticipated it before it was made. Perhaps most instructive in that regard is how little attention was given by those arguing on either side to the discretion argument on comity between the Security Council and the General Assembly, which as we have seen in the end almost carried the day. It is remarkable how practically all those sitting on the other side of the bar completely disregarded what would prove to be a key point of contention between the judges in their deliberations. If anything, this shows that it is not just conversations between politicians and lawyers that can get lost in translation.

# 4

# The Practicalities of Representing a Client in Complex Multiparty Proceedings

## The Example of Kosovo

*Qudsi Rasheed and Michael Wood*

The present chapter deals in turn with certain practical aspects of the *Kosovo* advisory proceedings: (1) the lead-up to the request for an advisory opinion, especially at the United Nations; (2) certain practical considerations that may arise when advising a government in relation to such a case, particularly one with no experience of international litigation; (3) the key matter of securing Kosovo's participation in the proceedings on an equal footing with Serbia; and (4) special features of a multiparty international litigation, including the exchanges among the supporters of Kosovo's independence.

## 1. The Lead-Up to the Request

Before turning to the handling of the case and the process of coordination that took place among those participants supporting Kosovo, it is worth recalling how the request for an advisory opinion came about.[1] The positions of some states on the legal as well as the policy aspects of the request for an advisory opinion became apparent during the debate in the UN General Assembly in October 2008.

On 17 February 2008 the 'democratically-elected leaders' of the people of Kosovo declared independence.[2] This was the final step in the culmination of a series of events dating as far back, at least for some, as the Battle of Kosovo in 1389.[3] However, rather than just being the final act completing a process towards independence, the declaration of independence itself was the spark which gave rise to a new series of

---

[1] See also Ker-Lindsay in this volume.

[2] The operative part of the Declaration begins, 'We, the democratically-elected leaders of our people…'.

[3] The mythical significance of this battle can hardly be overstated. It is exemplified in the epic nineteenth century verses transcribed by Vuk Karadžić, concerning the Emperor Lazar who 'chose the

events, including a request by the General Assembly of the United Nations to the International Court of Justice (ICJ), the principal judicial organ of the United Nations.

In order fully to understand the declaration of independence, it is essential to recognize its place in the wider historical context, in particular the recent history of the region, flowing from the disintegration of Yugoslavia and the conflicts in the former Yugoslavia of the early 1990s. Whilst, as a province of Serbia, Kosovo itself was not, as such, a direct participant in the Balkans War, it was this context that provided the backdrop to the Rambouillet negotiations and the NATO military intervention of 1999, and Security Council resolution (SCR) 1244 (1999) of 10 June 1999.

Much has been written about these matters, in particular in relation to the NATO intervention and SCR 1244. Here is not the place to attempt to describe or analyse those developments. Suffice it to note three key aspects of SCR 1244 which are crucial to understanding the declaration of independence itself and seeing it in its appropriate context, rather than in a political or legal vacuum: the establishment of the Provisional Institutions of Self-Government of Kosovo (PISG); international supervision by UNMIK; and the resolution's silence on future status.

The declaration of independence was adopted on 17 February 2008. Who exactly adopted it, while seemingly a simple and neutral question of fact, took on its own story of controversy and became a significant legal question, which is discussed in other chapters in this book. Suffice to say at this stage that the declaration was adopted at a meeting of the Assembly of Kosovo—a provisional institution established by the regime created under the auspices of the United Nations and SCR 1244.

On 18 February 2008, the day after Kosovo's declaration of independence, the National Assembly of the Republic of Serbia declared the declaration invalid in light of the decision of the Constitutional Court of Serbia finding that the declaration was unlawful, being contrary to the UN Charter, the Constitution of Serbia, the Helsinki Final Act, SCR 1244, and the Badinter Commission's opinions.[4]

Eight UN member states recognized Kosovo as a new state immediately, on 18 February 2008, with a further 13 states recognizing Kosovo by the end of February 2008, and another 14 states recognizing it during March 2008.

Whilst a number of states expressly recognized Kosovo following the declaration of independence, some expressly rejected the declaration. China, Russia, and India, for example, issued a joint statement on 15 May 2008 stating that 'the unilateral declaration of independence by Kosovo contradicts resolution 1244. Russia, India and China encourage Belgrade and Pristina to resume talks within the framework

---

empire of the heaven above the empire of the earth'. For an Albanian poetic view, see A. Di Lellio, *The Battle of Kosovo 1389. An Albanian Epic* (L.B.Tauris, 2009).

[4] Decision of the National Assembly of the Republic of Serbia on the endorsement of the Decision of the Government of the Republic of Serbia on the annulment of the illegal act of the provisional institutions of self-government in Kosovo and Metohija regarding the unilateral declaration of independence, *Official Gazette of the Republic of Serbia*, No. 19/2008 (Annex 4 to Serbia's Written Statement).

of international law and hope they reach an agreement on all problems of that Serbian territory'.

It was evident that the declaration was polarizing the international community, with many of the views taken by states being couched in legal terminology and arguments. The first mention of the declaration being considered and potentially resolved by the International Court of Justice was an announcement made by Serbia on 26 March 2008, in which it called upon the ICJ to rule on the issue.[5]

Given the absence of a clear steer from the UN Security Council, the UN Secretary-General took what came to be referred to as a 'status-neutral' position in the immediate aftermath of the declaration. This was all the more significant given the central place of SCR 1244 and the role of UNMIK in the administration of Kosovo. On 15 July 2008, the Secretary-General stated: 'In the light of the fact that the Security Council is unable to provide guidance, I have instructed my Special Representative to move forward with the reconfiguration of UNMIK … in order to adapt UNMIK to a changed reality' and that the 'United Nations has maintained a position of strict neutrality on the question of Kosovo's status'.[6]

The first formal step towards bringing the Kosovo issue to the ICJ was Serbia's letter of 15 August 2008 to the Secretary-General,[7] requesting the inclusion of a supplementary item in the agenda of the sixty-third session of the General Assembly entitled 'Request for an advisory opinion of the International Court of Justice on whether the unilateral declaration of independence of Kosovo is in accordance with international law'. The letter was accompanied by an explanatory memorandum indicating the Serbian intentions behind the inclusion of this item in the General Assembly's agenda:

We hold that the most principled, sensible way to overcome the potentially destabilizing consequences of Kosovo's unilateral declaration of independence is to transfer the issue from the political to the juridical arena. Aside from reducing the diplomatic tensions that have arisen since the unilateral declaration of independence, such an approach would contribute to strengthening the rule of law in international relations. With this in mind, Serbia considers that the United Nations General Assembly, in view of the powers and functions conferred on it by the Charter of the United Nations, in particular by Articles 10, 13 and 96, has a crucial role to play in this regard.

The Republic of Serbia believes that an advisory opinion of the principal judicial organ of the United Nations—the International Court of Justice—would be particularly appropriate in the specific case of determining whether Kosovo's unilateral declaration of independence is in accordance with international law.

The international community considers the Court's impartial advisory opinions to be the most authoritative interpretations of the principles of the international legal order. Member States share a deep commitment to the safeguarding of these principles, yet some

---

[5] Joint Communiqué on the outcome of the Meeting of the foreign ministers of the Russian Federation, the People's Republic of China and the Republic of India (15 May 2008) (Annex 74 to Serbia's Written Statement).

[6] Report of the Secretary-General on the United Nations Interim Administration Mission in Kosovo, 15 July 2008 (S/2008/458).

[7] A/63/195.

are uncertain as to which arguments involving these principles they can rely on in this particular case.

Many Member States would benefit from the legal guidance an advisory opinion of the International Court of Justice would confer. It would enable them to make a more thorough judgement on the issue.

Finally, an advisory opinion of the International Court of Justice, rendered in a non-contestable, non-adversarial manner, would go a long way towards calming tensions created by Kosovo's unilateral declaration of independence, avoiding further negative developments in the region and beyond and facilitating efforts at reconciliation among all parties involved. By having recourse to the International Court of Justice, the General Assembly would ensure that the Kosovo issue becomes a symbol of renewed resolve concerning adherence to the rule of law by the international community.

On 17 September 2018, the General Committee of the General Assembly recommended the inclusion of the supplementary item proposed by Serbia.[8] On 19 September 2008, the recommendation was accepted by the General Assembly, with only the United States speaking on the item.[9]

On 23 September 2008, Serbia circulated a draft resolution containing the question to be asked of the ICJ:

'Is the unilateral declaration of independence by the Provisional Institutions of Self-Government of Kosovo in accordance with international law?'[10]

On 1 October 2008, the United Kingdom wrote to the President of the General Assembly, with a 'note of issues',[11] setting out the importance of the context in which the declaration of independence was made, including the events between 1999 and 2008. In addition, the letter made the first reference to the potential future participation of Kosovo in any contemplated ICJ proceedings stating:

Should the General Assembly decide to request an advisory opinion, we would expect that, as a matter of basic fairness, Kosovo will be permitted to participate in the proceedings and present arguments to the Court. In our view it would be entirely appropriate and would assist the Court if the General Assembly made this clear in the text of the resolution.

In its 'note of issues', the United Kingdom raised the discrepancy between the terms of the agenda item proposed by Serbia and the question in the draft resolution, in particular, the reference to the Provisional Institutions of Self-Government in the latter. The UK's note stated:

The United Kingdom would also welcome consideration of the formulation of the question in the draft resolution. The agenda item proposed by Serbia requests an advisory opinion on the question of whether 'the unilateral declaration of independence of Kosovo is in accordance with international law'. In contrast, the question formulated in the draft resolution is cast in terms of whether 'the unilateral declaration of independence by the Provisional Institutions of Self-Government of Kosovo [is] in accordance with international law'. It would be useful to know whether Serbia is seeking to focus on a narrower question

---

[8] Report of the General Committee, para. 61 (A/63/250).    [9] A/63/PV.2, p. 4
[10] A/63/L.2.    [11] A/63/461.

about the competence of the Provisional Institutions of Self-Government of Kosovo, and, if so, precisely how that question relates to Kosovo's status at the present time.

This early focus on the mention of the PISG is interesting, given that this was to become central to the ICJ's ultimate reasoning in its Opinion.

The United Kingdom also set out its view that the question was only concerned with the issue of the declaration itself and not any consequences of the declaration, whether recognition or status:

'An advisory opinion addressing the emergence to independence of Kosovo could not therefore by itself be determinative of Kosovo's present or future status or the effect or recognition of that independence by other States.'

The General Assembly considered Serbia's draft resolution on 8 October 2008 in a two-hour plenary session,[12] which began with the presentation of the draft resolution by the Serbian Foreign Minister. Jeremić explained that Serbia had chosen to seek an advisory opinion as a 'non-confrontational approach', and in order to 'prevent the Kosovo crisis from serving as a deeply problematic precedent in any part of the globe where secessionist ambitions are harboured'. He stated that the ICJ would be able to provide 'politically neutral, yet judicially authoritative, guidance to many countries still deliberating how to approach unilateral declarations of independence in line with international law'. He noted that the question posed in the draft resolution was 'amply clear' and refrained from taking political positions on the Kosovo issue, that the resolution was 'entirely non-controversial' and 'represents the lowest common denominator of the positions of the Member States on the question, and hence there is no need for any changes or additions'.[13]

Speaking next, the United Kingdom raised its concerns about the Serbian request, in particular that the request was being made 'primarily for political rather than legal reasons ... designed to slow down Kosovo's emergence' as a state. Sir John Sawers highlighted that '[m]any members of the United Nations emerged into independence during what, at the time, were controversial circumstances' which 'normalize over time and the clock of history is rarely turned back'. In addition, the UK noted its regret at the 'minimal debate about the issues'. The United Kingdom reasserted its view that Kosovo 'should be able to present arguments [to the ICJ] on an equal footing'.[14]

Albania, Turkey, USA, and Mexico also spoke in the debate.[15] In addition, a considerable number of states explained their position before or after the vote.[16]

A number of distinct themes may be seen in the interventions in the plenary debate, foreshadowing arguments later put to the Court. First, there was plainly a difference of views between states on whether the declaration of independence was unique in its nature, given the historical, political, and legal context or alternatively whether there was a risk of it setting a precedent. The so-called *sui generis* position, that is, that Kosovo was special, indeed unique, and therefore not a precedent, was

---

[12] UN Doc., A/63/PV.22, 8 October 2008.      [13] Ibid., pp. 1–2.
[14] Ibid., pp. 2–3 and 11.      [15] Ibid., pp. 3–6.      [16] Ibid., pp. 6–15.

on the whole taken by states that were favourably inclined towards Kosovo's independence, whereas those opposed to *Kosovo's* independence, including those who had what they saw as similar territorial disputes or secessionist movements in their own countries, tended to regard it as potentially precedent-setting.

Second, a number of states were opposed or at least unfavourably inclined towards the request for an advisory opinion as they saw the issue as a political not a legal one, and therefore inappropriate for resolution in the ICJ. Conversely, a range of states saw the issue as a distinctively legal one, which could be helpfully considered by the ICJ. A strange point made by a number of states was the alleged 'right' of any state to have the question addressed by the ICJ.

A third theme was the view taken by a number of states that their voting position on the resolution did not relate necessarily to their attitude to the recognition of Kosovo's independence. Indeed, a number of states who voted for the resolution had already recognized Kosovo.

Finally, a significant number of states were clear in their view that Kosovo should be entitled to take part in the ICJ proceedings.

When the draft resolution was put to a vote in the General Assembly, 77 states voted in favour of the resolution, 6 states voted against, and 74 states abstained. The supporters of Kosovo independence were spread among those voting 'no' and those abstaining, with some even voting in favour. The question referred to the ICJ pursuant to General Assembly resolution 63/3 was in exactly the terms proposed by Serbia in its draft resolution. There had been no negotiation over the text.

## 2. Practical Arrangements for Handling the Case

Five practical matters concerning the arrangements for handling any inter-state case may be illustrated by the Kosovo case.[17] First, very early decisions about handling are often important. There is no need to rush to form a full legal team, but legal advice, given right from the outset, can be crucial. That was certainly so with the *Kosovo* advisory proceedings, where a decision had to be taken on participation within a couple of days of the General Assembly's request. That is not easy for a small and newly independent state, with a recent history of conflict, a coalition government, and no experience of international litigation.

Second, care is needed in the selection of a legal team. As soon as the request was made, the Government of Kosovo moved to put its legal team in place. Kosovo could not afford to pay a great deal, so the team was lean: three foreign lawyers and an assistant. In addition one, later two, excellent international lawyers working for the Kosovo Government were closely involved. Many others offered their services, usually *pro bono*. This was quite moving, at least in the case of the many young Kosovo lawyers who were very anxious to be involved. But it was essential to keep

---

[17] See also M. Wood, 'The Role of Public International Lawyers in Government', in D. Feldman (ed), *Law in Politics, Politics in Law* (Hart, 2013), 109 at 112–13.

the team small and coherent, and all such offers of assistance were declined. The relatively small number of lawyers involved was a good thing. And at no time did the team feel the need for additional assistance. It might have been otherwise had the case involved a heavy factual element.[18]

Third, a key decision—perhaps the key decision—was to write to the Court requesting to participate, and to do so very quickly, before the Court took the decisions reflected in its first procedural Order. Kosovo's Foreign Minister transmitted such a letter to the Court on 15 October 2008, just seven days after the General Assembly had voted to request the opinion (see Section 3 below). The Court's procedural Order inviting Kosovo ('the authors of the unilateral declaration of independence') to take part was made just two days later, on 17 October 2008.[19]

Fourth, it is very important to have clear lines of instruction from a client. Kosovo had a coalition government. The President of the Republic, President Sedjiu, was from Rugova's party, while Prime Minister Thaçi was from the party that had emerged from the Kosovo Liberation Army (*UÇK*). There was talk, briefly, of setting up some sort of a commission to oversee the handling of the case. But it was made clear that the legal team had to be able to take instructions from one person, who most naturally would be the designated representative of Kosovo before the Court (Foreign Minister Hyseni). That was swiftly agreed. A key coordinating role within the Kosovo administration was played by a senior adviser to the President of the Republic, Ms Vjosa Osmani, herself an international lawyer. In the event, everyone worked well together on the case, and there was no difficulty in securing clear instructions.

There was a quite exceptional degree of interest and commitment on the part of the highest state officials (perhaps not that surprising given the existential nature of the proceedings for the new state). At all key moments, the approach (in general and in detail) was considered and agreed by all key political figures, including in addition to the Foreign Minister, the President of the Republic, the Prime Minister, the Deputy Prime Minister and the President of the Assembly. This involved reading aloud, through an interpreter, large parts of the written pleadings to the assembled senior officials.

And fifth, relations with the media are important, not so much for the court proceedings themselves, but for the client. They need to be carefully handled. This is particularly so given the confidentiality of the written pleadings until otherwise decided by the Court at the opening of the oral hearing. In addition, it is important not to appear to be seeking to influence the Court indirectly through the media, and to avoid 'trial by media'. Contacts with the media are usually best not handled directly by the lawyers, and the Kosovo authorities came to accept their

---

[18] There is a tendency in international litigation for governments, perhaps out of a misguided abundance of caution, to take on teams that are too large. If the matter is not done entirely in house, it is often better to start with a couple of outside lawyers and only add names if it becomes apparent that it is necessary to do so.

[19] *Accordance with International Law of the Unilateral Declaration of Independence by the Provisional Institutions of Self-Government of Kosovo, Order of 17 October 2008,* ICJ Reports *2008,* p. 409.

lawyers' reticence in that regard. As it turned out, the Kosovo media were highly responsible, readily accepting that not much could be said publicly over the period of almost two years between the General Assembly's request of 8 October 2008 and the International Court's Opinion of 22 July 2010.

## 3. Kosovo's Participation in the Proceedings

Returning to the key question of Kosovo's participation in the proceedings, the Kosovo Foreign Minister's letter of 15 October 2008 stated that '[t]he question submitted to the Court is one in which Kosovo self-evidently has a profound and direct interest'. It recalled that 'the importance of Kosovo being able to present its views to the Court...was stressed by a considerable number of representatives who spoke in the General Assembly debate on 8 October 2008'. A key passage then read:

It is respectfully submitted that, if the Court is to consider the request submitted by the General Assembly, and at the same time remain true to its judicial character, it is important that Kosovo be invited to participate on an equal footing with others, including Serbia, in the interests of the proper administration of justice. As the Court said in *Eastern Carelia*, '[t]he Court, being a Court of Justice, cannot, even in giving advisory opinions, depart from the essential rules guiding their activity as a Court' (*P.C.I.J. Ser. B, No. 5*, p. 29).

The letter went on to refer to the Court's 'considerable discretion in the organization of advisory proceedings', and mentioned in this connection the *Wall* Advisory Opinion, as well as to the fundamental principles of equality of the parties and *audi alteram partem*, including in advisory opinion proceedings.[20] Finally, the letter stressed that Kosovo would 'be able to furnish the Court with relevant information essential to any consideration of the request'. The letter concluded by requesting

the Court to invite the Republic of Kosovo, as a party that is directly interested and able to furnish relevant information, to participate in the proceedings, on a footing of equality with others, including the Republic of Serbia, both in the written stage and at any oral hearing.[21]

In its Order of 17 October 2008,[22] made without dissent, the Court effectively acceded to this request, in carefully worded language:

4. *Decides* further that, taking account of the fact that the unilateral declaration of independence by the Provisional Institutions of Self-Government of Kosovo of 17 February

---

[20] For a later strong reaffirmation of these principles in an advisory opinion, albeit in a very different context, see *Judgment No. 2867 of the Administrative Tribunal of the International Labour Organization upon a Complaint Filed against the International Fund for Agricultural Development*, Advisory Opinion, *ICJ Reports 2012*, p. 10, at pp. 24–31, paras. 33–48; and Judge Greenwood's Declaration, at pp. 94–7.

[21] The full text of the letter is reproduced in Ministry of Foreign Affairs of the Republic of Kosovo (2010), *Kosovo in the International Court of Justice/Kosova në Gjykatën Ndërkombëtare të Drejtësisë*, pp. 17–20. This volume includes other correspondence between the Representative of the Republic of Kosovo before the International Court of Justice, H.E. Mr. Skender Hyseni, and the Registrar of the Court.

[22] *Accordance with International Law of the Unilateral Declaration of Independence by the Provisional Institutions of Self-Government of Kosovo, Order of 17 October 2008, I.C.J. Reports 2008*, p. 409.

2008 is the subject of the question submitted to the Court for an advisory opinion, the authors of the above declaration are considered likely to be able to furnish information on the question; and decides therefore to invite them to make written contributions to the Court within the above time-limits'.

It will be seen that Kosovo was referred to as 'the authors of the unilateral declaration of independence', not 'Republic of Kosovo', thus leaving open its precise status. The written pleadings of Kosovo were referred to as 'written contributions', not 'written statements' or 'written comments', and the oral pleading was also referred to as a 'contribution'.[23] These were differences of nomenclature, not substance. It is noteworthy that Serbia and 'the authors of the unilateral declaration of independence' spoke at the beginning of the oral hearing, and each did so for a full half-day (whereas other participants were allocated 45 minutes).

Thus the Court did indeed allow the representatives of Kosovo 'to participate in the proceedings, on a footing of equality with others, including the Republic of Serbia', as requested by Kosovo in its letter of 15 October 2008. The basis on which it did so was not made explicit: Paulus probably gets as close as one can when he suggests (in respect of both Kosovo and Palestine) that 'the participations were based on a limited extension of Art. 66, para. 2 justified by procedural fairness in the fulfilment of the Court's advisory function'.[24] The Court's emphasis in paragraph 4 of its Order on the furnishing of information is entirely in line with the main object of any participation in advisory proceedings.

## 4. Exchanges Among Like-Minded States

The idea of interest groups or groups of like-minded states is well-known in the context of multilateral negotiations, such as at the Third United Nations Conference on the Law of the Sea. The same may occur in connection with 'multiparty' inter-state litigation, but is less known.

By 'multiparty' litigation we mean proceedings before an international court or tribunal involving more than two states.[25] This is routinely the case with advisory proceedings. It is less common, though by no means unusual, in contentious cases, where there may be more than one applicant or respondent, and where cases may

---

[23] According to Andreas Paulus, '[t]he relevance of this terminology remains unclear, but distinguishes the authors from the official "statements" by states provided for by Art. 66, para. 2', in A. Zimmermann et al (eds), *The Statute of the International Court of Justice. A Commentary* (2nd ed, OUP, 2012), p. 1646 (Art. 66, MN 13).

[24] Ibid., p. 1648 (Art. 66, MN 15).

[25] The term 'multiparty' litigation, used for convenience, it is not entirely accurate. Properly speaking, there are no 'parties' in advisory proceedings, though often the dynamics may seem otherwise. For example, '[w]here an advisory opinion is requested upon a legal question actually pending between two or more States', judges ad hoc may be appointed (Rules of Court, Art. 102.3; *Western Sahara* Advisory Opinion; Zimmermann et al, *The Statute of the International Court of Justice. A Commentary*

be joined. Even without formal joinder, two or more cases may raise the same or similar issues, and may therefore be dealt with in parallel, for example at a joint hearing. And where a state intervenes or seeks to intervene (though an intervening state is usually not a party to the case) a number of states will be directly concerned in a single case.

States participating in multiparty litigation may well have at least some shared legal and policy interests. This may lead to varying degrees of cooperation, or at least an exchange of views, more or less detailed, at various stages of the proceedings. But there is a wider problem. States may well have a profound interest in the outcome of a case in which they are not in any way involved, an interest either in the particular dispute which is the subject of the proceedings, or more generally and perhaps more often—given the potential precedential significance of decisions of international courts and tribunals—an interest in some of the legal points at issue.[26] An example of the former is the arbitration between Mauritius and the United Kingdom concerning the British Indian Ocean Territory/Chagos Archipelago, in the outcome of which the USA no doubt has a keen interest.[27] Examples of the latter include many of the decisions of the European Court of Human Rights, which affect all parties to the European Convention.[28]

Current or recent examples of multiparty litigation include, in addition to the *Kosovo* case, the *Nuclear Weapons*[29] and *Wall*[30] advisory proceedings, the two requests for advisory proceedings that have been addressed to the International Tribunal for the Law of the Sea,[31] the two *Lockerbie* cases,[32] the three (potentially nine) *Nuclear Disarmament* cases brought by the Republic of the Marshall Islands,[33]

(2nd ed, OUP, 2012), Cot, 'Article 68', MN 23–30). That did not happen in the *Kosovo* case, though one may assume that Kosovo and possibly Serbia considered the matter.

[26] See D. Bethlehem, 'The Secret Life of International Law', (2012) 1 *Cambridge Journal of International and Comparative Law* 23, at 31–3.

[27] <http://www.pca-cpa.org/showpage.asp?pag_id=1429>.

[28] One response, limited to the field of public international law, to the precedential effect of ECtHR decisions is that the Council of Europe Committee of Legal Advisers on Public International Law (CAHDI) has on its regular agenda an item entitled *Cases before the European Court of Human Rights involving issues of public international law.*

[29] *Legality of the Threat or Use of Nuclear Weapons,* Advisory Opinion, ICJ Reports 1996, p. 226; *Legality of the Use by a State of Nuclear Weapons in Armed Conflict*, Advisory Opinion, ICJ Reports 1996, p. 66.

[30] *Legal Consequences of the Construction of a Wall in the Occupied Palestinian Territory*, Advisory Opinion, ICJ Reports 2004, p. 136.

[31] *Responsibilities and obligations of States with respect to activities in the Area,* Advisory Opinion, 1 February 2011, *ITLOS Reports* 2011, p. 10; *Request for an advisory opinion submitted by the Sub-Regional Fisheries Commission (SRFC).*

[32] *Questions of Interpretation and Application of the 1971 Montreal Convention arising from the Aerial Incident at Lockerbie (Libyan Arab Jamahiriya v. United Kingdom); Questions of Interpretation and Application of the 1971 Montreal Convention arising from the Aerial Incident at Lockerbie (Libyan Arab Jamahiriya v. United States of America).*

[33] *Obligations concerning Negotiations relating to Cessation of the Nuclear Arms Race and to Nuclear Disarmament (Marshall Islands v. India); Obligations concerning Negotiations relating to Cessation of the Nuclear Arms Race and to Nuclear Disarmament (Marshall Islands v. Pakistan); Obligations concerning Negotiations relating to Cessation of the Nuclear Arms Race and to Nuclear Disarmament (Marshall Islands v. United Kingdom).* Applications were also made by the Republic of the Marshall Islands against China, Democratic People's Republic of Korea, France, Israel, Russia, and the USA, but because there

and the *Legality of Use of Force* cases brought by the Federal Republic of Yugoslavia against ten NATO states in 1999.[34]

The *Kosovo* case was particularly apt for a degree of coordination.[35] The case itself was but one link in a chain of an intense international crisis over Kosovo (itself part of the wider Yugoslav crisis) that lasted from the early 1990s and which is still not completely resolved.[36] By the early 2000s, there were two broad camps in relation to Kosovo: those supporting Kosovo against the claims of Serbia, on the one hand, and Serbia and its allies, principal among whom was Russia, on the other. When efforts to bridge the gap, through bodies such as the Contact Group, failed, states divided broadly into those which supported the statehood of Kosovo (25 of which formed the International Steering Group—ISG), those which opposed it, and those which avoided taking a position. States were divided along political lines, but the strongest opponents of Kosovo's statehood were those which feared secessions at home. The European Union, for example, was and is divided, with 22 (now 23) Member States recognizing Kosovo and five (Cyprus, Greece, Romania, Slovakia, Spain) refusing to do so. So too were the permanent members of the UN Security Council.

The number of states that participated in the advisory proceedings was high: more than in *Nuclear Weapons* but less than in *Wall*. In addition to Kosovo ('the authors of the unilateral declaration of independence'), 43 states participated at one or both stages. Thirty-six states filed written statements[37] (14 of whom also filed written comments in reply), and 28 took part in the oral phase,[38] which lasted from 1 to 11 December 2009. For the first time, all five permanent members of the Security Council took part in proceedings at the International Court, and did so in both the written and the oral phases.

Regular and detailed exchanges of views between legal teams representing states which have essentially common views may be of great value. The sooner such exchanges begin the better. Someone has to take the initiative in proposing and

---

is no basis for jurisdiction have not been entered in the Court's List: see Press Release No. 2014/18 of 25 April 2014 (<http://www.icj-cij.org/presscom/files/0/18300.pdf>).

[34] *Legality of Use of Force (Serbia and Montenegro v. Belgium)*, and nine others.

[35] See also the contribution of Marko Milanović in this volume.

[36] The issue of Kosovo within the Yugoslav federation goes back well beyond the 1990s: amongst the extensive literature, see N. Malcolm, *Kosovo. A Short History* (New York University Press, 1998); T. Judah, *Kosovo. What Everyone Needs to Know* (OUP, 2008). For the period between 1989 and 2008, see M. Weller, *Contested Statehood: Kosovo's Struggle for Independence* (OUP, 2009).

[37] In order of receipt: *Czech Republic*; France; Cyprus; China; *Switzerland*; Romania; Albania; Austria; *Egypt*; Germany; *Slovakia*; Russia; Finland; *Poland; Luxembourg; Libya*; UK; USA; Serbia; Spain; *Iran; Estonia*; Norway; Netherlands; *Slovenia; Latvia; Japan*; Brazil; *Ireland*; Denmark; Argentina; Azerbaijan; *Maldives; Sierra Leone*; Bolivia; Venezuela; as well as Kosovo. The following submitted written comments: France; Norway; Cyprus; Serbia; Argentina; Germany; Netherlands; Albania; *Slovenia; Switzerland*; Bolivia; UK; USA; Spain; as well as Kosovo. (These in italics did not participate at the oral phase.)

[38] In order of speaking, the participants were: Serbia; Kosovo; (thereafter in French alphabetical order) Albania; Germany; *Saudi Arabia*; Argentina; Austria; Azerbaijan; *Belarus*; Bolivia; Brazil; *Bulgaria; Burundi*; China; Cyprus; *Croatia*; Denmark; Spain; USA; Russia; Finland; France; *Jordan*; Norway; Netherlands; Romania; UK; Venezuela; *Viet Nam*. (Those in italics had not participated at the written phase.)

hosting such exchanges. And it may only gradually become apparent which states are going to participate. It was not clear how many of those in the Kosovo camp would in fact participate in the court proceedings. A large number of states had shown their support, including by recognizing Kosovo's statehood, in the General Assembly debate of 8 October 2008, in the Security Council, or as members of the International Steering Group. There were unexpected participants in the proceedings on Kosovo's side, and even more unexpected absences (such as Turkey, Canada, and Sweden). Of particular note were Slovenia's absence from the oral hearing, and Croatia's presence at the oral stage. No doubt domestic political considerations and other pressures played their part in some of the absences, as did particular issues with possible secession even among one or two of Kosovo's supporters. One important activity was to persuade states to take part, which was done with some success on Kosovo's part, either bilaterally or though forums such as the IGS. On the other hand, at no time did Kosovo seek to put pressure on states not to participate.

While the earliest possible exchange of views amongst like-minded states would seem desirable, in practice it is likely to evolve and become more intense as the case proceeds. Interest in, and attitudes towards, the litigation may well only become apparent gradually. At the earliest stages, such as at the pre-litigation phase, there may be little awareness of the significance of the case, and it may take some time to decide whether or not to participate. During the preparation of the written pleadings cooperation may be easier and seen as particularly useful, and this is even more so at the intensive oral phase, when the legal teams will be gathered in The Hague for a week or more. That is certainly how things looked during the *Kosovo* proceedings.

Lawyers from a group of about ten states which supported Kosovo, and which indicated to each other early on that they expected to participate in the case, met regularly and from quite an early stage, with one or other taking the initiative to arrange and host meetings to exchange views on all aspects of the case, including on tactics, and the main legal arguments to be deployed. As others indicated an interest, rather than enlarging the group which could have made it unwieldy, it fell to one or other participant in the main group, often lawyers representing Kosovo, to discuss matters bilaterally with them.

Marko Milanović's chapter has examined in some detail the substantive issues on which each 'camp' appears to have coordinated, showing in particular how the views expressed became clearer and closer with each stage of the proceedings. There is no need to repeat what he has said. One might only add that presenting the Court with a range of views and arguments is often no bad thing.

On the Kosovo side, a major tactical question was how far to treat the question as a narrow one, without getting into such controversial matters as remedial secession (which it was thought the Court would wish to avoid if it could). Another was whether, and if so how far, to argue that the Court was without jurisdiction or should exercise its discretion not to answer the request. Lack of jurisdiction seemed an obvious non-starter, but this did not deter Albania and France from so arguing, both in writing and orally. That may have been good tactics, on the basis that it may well be good to give the Court some ground on which to find for the other side in the hope that it will find for your side on the points that really matter.

On the issue of discretion, five judges voted against the decision to reply to the request, giving cogent reasons.[39] It might, therefore, be regarded as having been a tactical mistake on the part of some states (and the authors of the declaration) not to have majored on this. On the other hand, there is nothing to indicate that had they done so this would have changed the eventual vote on this matter. It would have required two further judges to have joined the five.[40]

In the end, even within the core group, tactics varied, no doubt for reasons good and bad, including domestic reasons.[41] But even when tactics varied it was important to avoid, so far as possible, direct contradiction of substantive positions being taken, for example on the identity of the authors of the declaration of independence. In this states on Kosovo's side were largely successful. That required careful liaison and a detailed exchange of views. Above all, such exchanges of views can enrich the contributions of the participating states, all of whom learn from each other.

## 5. Conclusion

It can be said with some certainty that for all involved, no matter which side they were on and no matter whom they represented, the *Kosovo* proceedings held important lessons on how to conduct multiparty international litigation. The legal issues were, potentially, of great significance (even if in the end the Court managed to sidestep most of them), the political stakes were high (or seemed so at the time), and the result was hard to predict. The proceedings themselves were *sui generis*, even if the circumstances of Kosovo's status were not properly so described. Nevertheless, the experience of cooperation in court proceedings could be put to good use, as some of us recently found in the very different context of the latest request for an advisory opinion from the International Tribunal for the Law of the Sea.[42]

---

[39] See, in particular, the Separate Opinion of Judge Keith, *ICJ Reports 2010*, pp. 482–90.

[40] On the assumption that the President's casting vote would then have decided the matter against answering the request.

[41] Some states, such as Switzerland, had justified domestically their recognition of Kosovo on the basis of remedial secession, and so may have felt a political necessity to argue that matter in The Hague.

[42] *Request for an advisory opinion submitted by the Sub-Regional Fisheries Commission (SRFC).*

# 5

# The Settling of a Self-Determination Conflict?

## Kosovo's Status Process and the 2010 Advisory Opinion of the ICJ

*Bernhard Knoll-Tudor*

## 1. Introduction

To international lawyers struggling to reconcile a people's rights to external self-determination with respect for the territorial integrity of the 'old' sovereign, Kosovo has proven a fascinating case study in polity formation. The past decade saw the intertwining of a number of threads of activity: direct negotiations facilitated by multilateral diplomacy; great power arrangements; the import of broad value schemes into a domestic constitutional order; as well as aspects of legal arbitration that were accompanied by attempts at regional integration through the significant involvement of the European Union.

This chapter reflects on the multilateral process through which organs of the international community attempted to exercise collective authority to regulate, condition and finally advise on a case of new state creation. With efforts having failed to achieve a settlement agreeable to both parties, dynamics turned inwards towards effectuating a claim to external self-determination, through Kosovo's declaration of independence. This, in turn, gave rise to an international legal dispute which was, to a very limited degree, resolved by the ICJ in 2010.

Reading history backwards from the final denouement—the ICJ's advisory opinion—yields interesting insights. At the outset it is worth recalling that the question of Kosovo's future status in international law was—according to UN Security Council resolution 1244—never intended to be submitted to a judicial body. Resolution 1244 created an interim regime not only to create Kosovo's governance capacity but to channel a process to establish its final status, through a 'political settlement'.[1] Presumably, recognitions would have followed such a 'settlement' had it endorsed Kosovo's path towards independence. This, as we all know, is

---

[1] UNSCR 1299, UN Dec. S/RES/1244 (1999), 10 June 1999, §11(c).

not what happened. A political process needed to transform into a legal discourse, in order to transmogrify back to a policy process.

Whatever the underlying political-normative choices were to place Kosovo on the trajectory to statehood, there are ample opportunities for international lawyers to analyse a very ambiguous case in the history of state creation. While the period of status negotiations cannot be neatly packaged into political manoeuvres and international legal initiatives, one can make an argument that the Advisory Opinion[2] represented an inflection point from where the diplomatic track, powered this time by the European Union, continued. Yet a discussion of the International Court's opinion can—especially when the subject matters the Court was asked to pronounce itself on are intrinsically tied to the realm of politics—only be fully appreciated if the political considerations that preceded and accompanied it are brought out in the open. Reflecting on the sometimes contradictory efforts of a global diplomatic machinery to confirm Kosovo's path towards independence and securing the approval of its 'parent state' to this effect also highlights the experimental nature of what overall has been, and continues to be, an exercise in state building.

## 2. Statehood or Stasis? UNOSEK and the Contact Group

Up until its declaration of independence in 2008,[3] Kosovo had, for almost a decade, been a territory in limbo.[4] The international community had, some would argue, operated in naive denial of the continued relevance of self-reliant statehood. The internal contradictions of its policy were exposed in the course of the 'standards before status' approach, fashioned by the United Nations Interim Administration Mission in Kosovo (UNMIK).[5] In effect, the 'standards before status' policy had reinforced a climate of heightened insecurity in which the conflict remained frozen rather than resolved. Ever since the publication of the (first) *Eide Report* in 2004,[6] resolving the international legal status of Kosovo had become a priority on the international agenda. This process culminated in the report of the UN Secretary-General's Special Envoy, Martti Ahtisaari, in 2007. The international community, so it seemed, had understood that it needed to close the sovereignty gap that had opened up when it assumed transitional governance functions in 1999 for an unspecified period of time.

---

[2] *Accordance with International Law of the Unilateral Declaration of Independence in Respect of Kosovo*, Advisory Opinion of 22 July 2010, ICJ Reports 2010 (hereafter ICJ *Kosovo* AO).

[3] Declaration of independence of Kosovo, 17 February 2008.

[4] For a discussion of Kosovo's international legal status under Security Council resolution 1244 of 10 June 1999, see, generally, Bernhard Knoll, *The Legal Status of Territories Subject to Administration by International Organisations* (CUP, 2008), Chapter V.

[5] Cf. Bernhard Knoll, 'From Benchmarking to Final Status? Kosovo and the Problem of an International Administration's Open-Ended Mandate', 4 *EJIL* (2005), 637–60.

[6] Special Envoy of the UN Secretary-General, 'The Situation in Kosovo', Report to the UN Secretary-General undertaken pursuant to the UN Secretary General's Reports of 30 April 2004, S/2004/348, and 6 August 2004, S/2004/932, 20 November 2004.

At the outset of diplomatic efforts to start the Kosovo status process, there stood a larger design, according to which mediation efforts conducted by a third party would ideally result in an endorsement, by the Security Council, of a settlement between the parties in a resolution based on Chapter VII of the UN Charter. Parties to the process to determine the future permanent political boundaries of the territory of Kosovo had to include Serbia, the holder of a reversionary title to the exercise of sovereign powers, as well as Kosovo's local institutions, supported in some form or other by UNMIK. Such an accord, concluded under the auspices of the Contact Group (Germany, Italy, United States, United Kingdom, France, and the Russian Federation) and a UN mediation body, could have effectively ended the status of the 'international trust' and resolved the sovereignty puzzle.

Martti Ahtisaari, who was appointed Special Envoy on 14 November 2005, after the Security Council had 'welcomed'[7] this proposal, had maximum leeway to 'start a political process to determine Kosovo's future status', as it was up to him to determine the pace and duration of the process on the basis of consultations with the Secretary-General, taking into account the cooperation of the parties and the situation on the ground.[8] Only the most basic framework was established to guide the efforts of what was termed the Office of the Special Envoy of the Secretary-General of the United Nations for the Future Status Process for Kosovo (UNOSEK). Indeed, the Contact Group's ten guiding principles—annexed to the letter confirming Ahtisaari's appointment as Special Envoy[9]—outlined merely that a settlement was to promote stability, non-partition, multiethnicity, democracy, and human rights. They represented the first in a series of messages that the Contact Group planned to send to the parties with the intention of steering the process and focusing it on key priorities. Importantly, the Contact Group emphasized that the settlement had to 'conform with European standards and contribute to [realizing] the European perspective of Kosovo'.[10] At that time, the Contact Group had already defined its own role in the status negotiations and had agreed that it would actively support the UN-led process by identifying substantive status issues[11] and providing technical expertise.

---

[7] Cf. Letter of Ambassador Andrey Denisov, President of the Security Council, to Secretary-General Kofi Annan, S/2005/709, 10 November 2005. The modalities leading to the appointment of the Special Envoy were chosen with care, since Russia had earlier insisted on a formal Security Council resolution requiring unanimity.

[8] Cf. 'Terms of Reference for the Special Envoy of the Secretary General for the Future Status Process for Kosovo', Annex to a letter from the Secretary-General to the President of the Security Council, Ambassador Mihnea Ioan Motoc, S/2005/689, 31 October 2005, §3.

[9] The Guiding Principles of the Contact Group for a Settlement of the Status of Kosovo were finalized at the meeting of Contact Group political directors in Washington, DC, on 2 November 2005 (in attendance: Special Envoy Ahtisaari and his deputy, Albert Rohan), submitted to the Security Council on 7 November 2005, and politically endorsed in the UN framework by the letter of UN Security Council President Ambassador Denisov to the Secretary-General, *supra* note 7.

[10] Ibid., Principle 2.

[11] Thirteen core issues ranging from cultural heritage, decentralization, and the economy to minority and property rights and returns were first grouped together by the US and suggested to the Contact Group at its 2 November meeting in Washington, DC.

The *modus operandi* of the Contact Group that cranked into action after several years of inactivity following NATO's intervention in the spring of 1999[12] was, for each meeting, to focus on a set of issues to be introduced in a discussion paper. Meetings were held approximately once a month between the division heads, political directors or ministers from foreign ministries, and regularly involved representatives of NATO, the European Commission and the EU presidency (the 'extended' Contact Group), as well as UNOSEK and UNMIK.[13] The Contact Group's primary occupation consisted in planning the future international presence and merging its civil and military tracks. Already at the outset of the status negotiations, it had become clear that the status process had to be accompanied by a 'dual transition' in Prishtina: although it was considered to be imperative that UNMIK should maintain its responsibilities until a new civilian presence was mandated and found its role, the transfer of authority had to be outlined and the EU had to take on responsibility for operational planning.[14] Second, the Contact Group assumed a key role in the discussions about the phasing-out of UNMIK, particularly concerning the transfer of rule-of-law-related competencies to Kosovar institutions and the reform of the security sector.

Following Special Envoy Ahtisaari's first visit to the region at the end of November 2005, the parties were encouraged to set up negotiation teams, provide an outline of their positions and agree on common platforms.[15] As the Kosovar negotiation team struggled to devise a strategy while domestic politics threatened the team's unity, Serbia's proposals were, from the start, characterized by two mostly reinforcing currents. Within the Serbian body politic, energies were focused on using the status process as a means of galvanizing the electorate in support of the government and the 'moderate nationalism' exhibited by Prime Minister Koštunica in order to counter the threat from the far-right Serbian Radical Party (SRS) and the *revanchiste* Socialist Party of Serbia (SPS).

The weeks preceding the commencement of direct negotiations were the time to build a case. While the Kosovo Albanians mourned the death of their president and icon, Ibrahim Rugova, the Serbian Government mobilized its public relations machinery in Brussels and Washington. But January 2006 was also the time when the international community resolved to take things forward. First, it decided to follow Special Envoy Ahtisaari's suggestion to deliver clear 'private messages' on the status process in its bilateral contacts with the parties, urging them to start

---

[12]  For an original insight into the Contact Group's attempts at resolving the Kosovo crisis between 1997 and 1999, see Chapter VII.2.1 of Jochen Prantl, *The UN Security Council and Informal Groups of States: Complementing or Competing for Governance?* (OUP, 2006).

[13]  This flexible organizational arrangement was put in place at the end of 2005 and lasted until the Contact-Group-initiated EU-USA-Russia Troika took over the process in August 2007 following failed attempts to pass a Security Council resolution on the basis of Ahtisaari's Comprehensive Proposal (see below).

[14]  In this regard, see Annex 1.1 (Elements of Cooperation between UNMIK and ICO in the Transition Period), International Civilian Office/European Union Special Representative (ICO/EUSR) Preparatory Team, 'Second Report to the Political and Security Committee', 20 February 2007.

[15]  Both the Kosovo PISG platform and that of the Serbian negotiation team are reprinted in *Kosovo Perspectives Weekly Bulletin* (VIP News Service), 17 February 2006, 8–11 and 14–15, respectively.

preparing the public opinion of the people they represented. This was held to be particularly important for Serbia, to which the first of Ahtisaari's private messages was addressed: 'The unconstitutional abolition of Kosovo's autonomy in 1989 and the ensuing tragic events resulting in the international administration of Kosovo have led to a situation in which a return of Kosovo to Belgrade's rule is not a viable option'.[16]

Second, and just a few weeks before the beginning of direct technical talks, the Contact Group, this time in ministerial formation, delivered a statement at the London Afghanistan conference whose significance can hardly be overstated. It stressed that 'the character of the Kosovo problem, shaped by the disintegration of Yugoslavia and consequent conflicts, ethnic cleansing and the events of 1999, and the extended period of international administration under UNSCR 1244, must be fully taken into account in settling Kosovo's status'. Even more importantly, ministers reminded Belgrade that 'the settlement needs, inter alia, to be acceptable to the people of Kosovo. The disastrous policies of the past lie at the heart of the current problems'.[17] In Prishtina, this statement was received enthusiastically, as it clearly tilted the balance to the Kosovar side. But it also heightened the role of the Contact Group in laying the foundations for UNOSEK's engagement in the months to come.

On the practical side, the Contact Group set itself the task of finalizing a conceptual blueprint of the new international presence by June 2006 that included its mandate and competences, structure, funding, and transition strategy. The discussions revealed a tentative consensus that the future presence should have a light footprint and might, in implementing the eventual settlement, make use of corrective powers.[18] Its substitution powers would be restricted to a necessary minimum to allow for a high degree of local ownership. Governance functions were to be formally separated from capacity-building, while the International Civilian Office (ICO) was to assume a strong coordination mandate to ensure coherence and efficiency in the latter field. At a meeting with Contact Group ambassadors at the time, Deputy Envoy Albert Rohan summed up the preferences of UNOSEK and the EU Council Secretariat as follows: 'as light as possible, as heavy as necessary'. Agreement was also reached regarding the need to base the new international

---

[16] UNOSEK's suggested private messages from Contact Group representatives on the Kosovo status process were discussed at the Contact Group meeting in Vienna on 16 January 2006. The messages did not stay private for long. See the public statements that a former political director of the British Foreign Office, John Sawers, made during his visit to Kosovo and Belgrade on 6 and 7 February 2006: 'British diplomat sparks Serb protest over Kosovo', *Agence France-Presse*, 7 February 2006; and 'Unbequeme Wahrheiten für Serbien', *Neue Zürcher Zeitung,* 9 February 2006, 3.

[17] Statement by the Contact Group on the Future of Kosovo, Foreign and Commonwealth Office, press release, London, 31 January 2006, §§6, 7.

[18] See the two joint papers by Secretary-General/High Representative Javier Solana and Commissioner Olli Rehn, 'The Future EU Role and Contribution in Kosovo', 7 June 2005, Chapter 4; and 'Joint Paper on Kosovo', 6 December 2005, Chapter 3. In 2006, the discussions within the extended Contact Group on the question of a follow-up presence (both civil and military) were conducted on the basis of a number of options papers presented by France, the UK, the US, UNOSEK, NATO, the European Commission, and the EU Council Secretariat. The papers have been made available to this author.

presence on a fresh Security Council resolution and to institute a steering group comprising key stakeholders to support and guide the presence.

## 3. Miscalculations and Flawed Premises

Progress in the deliberations of the Contact Group was, however, not replicated in the 'bottom-up approach' that UNOSEK pursued with the parties. A number of structural factors contributed to the extraordinarily slow progress on issues such as minority rights and decentralization. First, the proximity talks and technical negotiations could not be clearly separated from the larger status question. UNOSEK's insistence that the four negotiation tracks[19] revolve around issues that required a solution regardless of the direction in which Kosovo's international legal status tilted was a means of focusing the parties' attention on technicalities. Nonetheless, it was clear that a number of the solutions that were found could be realistically implemented only within a sovereign state—a conclusion that enraged Serbia's government.[20]

The international community's battle plan also relied on a set of flawed premises concerning its dealings with Belgrade, and on the success of messages to Prishtina. As Special Envoy Ahtisaari put it at the outset of the negotiations, Belgrade had to accept that Kosovo would not return to its control; and Kosovars would have to understand that they had to 'earn' their objective by moving forward on standards:

While today's democratic leadership of Serbia cannot be held accountable for the policies of the Milosevic regime, [it] must come to terms with Milosevic's legacy…Milosevic's dark past can neither hold them prisoner nor should it prevent them from demonstrating political courage and the vision necessary to come forward with *realistic proposals* for the future of both Kosovo and Serbia…In Kosovo it is the responsibility of the Kosovo Albanians to ensure that conditions and foundations are created for a sustainable and multi-ethnic, democratic society…The results achieved in…implementation of standards will be a *decisive factor in determining the pace of the political process* designed to settle Kosovo's future status.[21]

As to the first premise, Belgrade simply did not play along, maintaining throughout the negotiations and in private that a change in regional borders would not only work against their interests, but would also bring Serbian radicals to power

---

[19] These were: (1) decentralization; (2) cultural heritage and holy sites; (3) standards, minority rights, and returns; (4) economy and property issues.

[20] Cf. the joint letter by President Boris Tadić and the then Prime Minister, Vojislav Koštunica, to Mr Ahtisaari, 06-00-01549/2006-01, 18 May 2006: 'We entered into the negotiations believing that discussion of concrete issues before addressing the central question of future status might help build confidence and thus pave the way to a mutually acceptable solution. So far, our proposals on decentralization have been met with scant respect for the genuine fears of the Serb community. In fact, the Pristina delegation in Vienna has shown little interest in discussing matters in the status-neutral way you have urged, and this has blocked the talks and made it difficult to explore the possibilities of compromise'.

[21] Statement of the Special Envoy, EU Foreign Ministers' Gymnich Meeting, 11 March 2006, §§4–6 (emphasis added).

and present risks to neighbouring countries. The belief that Serbia would be cooperative and come forward with 'realistic proposals' (diplomatic speak for agreeing to Kosovo's sovereign statehood), encouraged by the promise of a strategic partnership—bilateral initiatives, Partnership for Peace-related activities and the genuine possibility of EU integration—was rooted more in the realm of wishful thinking than in a realistic appraisal of the state of Serbian politics. In particular, Serbia refused to be part of a barter that required it to exchange Kosovo for fast-track integration into Euro-Atlantic structures. Assuming that it would, which Brussels and Washington largely did, was a serious misjudgement, which exaggerated the 'soft power' of the prospect of accession.[22] Serbia's leadership neither took advantage of the opportunity to place the blame for the loss of Kosovo on Slobodan Milošević and Tomislav Nikolić of the SRS, the government's main challenger at the time, nor did it educate the Serbian public on 'realistic' scenarios. In short, the incentive structure provided by the Quint (France, Germany, Italy, the United Kingdom, and the United States)—forward-looking and designed to assist a 'country in denial' to move forward along the trajectory of European integration—was simply less tangible than, and outweighed by, Russia's promise of diplomatic support for Serbia's sovereignty.[23]

The messages sent to Prishtina in the course of the negotiations were, on the other hand, not devised in good faith and, consequently, gave rise to expectations that could not be fulfilled as the process came to a close. The Contact Group's prioritization and 'deadlinization' of certain standards[24] was intended to make the Kosovo Albanian public trust that tangible progress in standards implementation would bring them closer to their objective. However, both UNOSEK and Contact Group envoys understood perfectly well that the resolution of Kosovo's status and the process designed to yield it was completely disassociated from whether or not Kosovo's Provisional Institutions of Self-Government (PISG) moved

---

[22] Cf. for instance, the testimony of Under Secretary of State Nicholas Burns to the US Congress: 'We have been explicit with Belgrade: constructive engagement in the Kosovo status process…and a constructive regional role…would help clear the path to EU and NATO membership'. (in 'Kosovo: Current and Future Status', Hearing before the Committee on International Relations, House of Representatives, 18 May 2006, Washington, DC, 15). This message, namely that Serbia would be judged on how much it adopted a 'realistic approach' and a 'constructive attitude', had been amplified by EU officials ever since the status negotiations had opened. In response, Serbia's Foreign Minister, Vuk Jeremić, maintained that 'there have been messages to Serbia from some quarters to choose between Europe and Kosovo…This is an unacceptable choice and an indecent offer, to say the least, in 21st century Europe'. Cited in *VIP Daily News Report,* 30 August 2007.

[23] See, much later, the statement of the Russian Federation submitted to the ICJ on the question posed by the UN General Assembly in Resolution 63/3 (Request for Advisory Opinion—written proceedings), 16 April 2009, 15: 'Could anyone acting in good faith blame Serbia for not having agreed to the [Ahtisaari] proposal that was manifestly against the very basis of its sovereignty…?'

[24] In coordination with UNMIK, the Contact Group identified a list of priority action items ranging from the passing of 'internationally accepted laws' on languages and cultural heritage, via the completion of a public-transportation strategy for minorities and the reconstruction of commercial property damaged during the 2004 riots, to the allocation of funds for returns. The list was handed over to Kosovo's former Prime Minister, Agim Çeku, on 9 June 2006. Requests (including one to support the inclusion of Kosovo Serbs into Kosovo institutions) were simultaneously delivered to Belgrade. Since Kosovo's Government was not in a position to report on progress on priority standards

standards implementation into the centre of their activities. As the UNMIK Special Representative of the Secretary-General (SRSG) noted with concern, the causality also worked in the opposite direction: 'It is important to acknowledge that further progress on standards implementation, and the sustainability and consolidation of what has been achieved thus far, will require both a sustained momentum in the future status process and concrete prospects for a conclusion of the process'.[25]

The re-employment, by Western diplomats, of the notion of 'earned status'—which had already caused confusion in the period during which UNMIK was devising government benchmarks[26]—may have convinced their capitals that pressure on the Kosovo negotiation team would be maintained. Yet there was no automatic assurance that a positive assessment of governance indicators would lead to a favourable determination by the Security Council; this was a political process open to spoilers who could, at the stroke of a pen, veto any resolution endorsing an eventual settlement emerging from the process.

Those structural deficiencies in the UN-led process did not cause the Kosovo Albanians to adopt unconstructive positions; buoyed by the private messages of diplomatic envoys, their negotiation team's attitude remained constructive.[27] Yet the lack of a credible incentive structure for Prishtina—a firm link between standards implementation and a favourable Security Council resolution—led Quint diplomats and UNOSEK officials to promise more than they could deliver on a number of occasions. Their faith that a multilateral solution would eventually be found that would endorse the special envoy's proposal of an independent Kosovo restrained by a new civil and military presence was not merely a diplomatic ruse to prod the Kosovo Albanian delegation into showing more flexibility; more worryingly, it was based on a miscalculation as to the motives and strategies underlying Russia's actions. Russia had, through its Contact Group envoy, Aleksandr Botsan-Kharchenko, walked a long way with the Quint. Despite his criticism of the envisaged 'artificial' negotiation deadline of the end of 2006, his continued insistence on a negotiated solution, and his cursory references to the precedent that Kosovo's independence might set, he had at no point signaled outright objection to any of the issues discussed under the Contact Group's work plan.

directly in key sessions of the Security Council, regular updates were delivered in writing. See, for example, the paper on 'Key Recent Achievements', Annex to the Letter of Prime Minister Çeku to Ambassador Ellen Margrethe Løj (Denmark), President of the UN Security Council (No.130/06), 16 June 2006.

[25] UN Secretary-General, 'Report of the UN Secretary-General on the United Nations Interim Administration Mission in Kosovo', S/2007/134, 9 March 2007, §23.

[26] The last version of the 'Kosovo Standards Implementation Plan' comprised 120 pages. For its endorsement by the UN Security Council, see United Nations, 'Security Council Reiterates that Kosovo Standards Plan Should Be Basis for Reassessing PISG', UN/PR/SC/8082, 30 April 2004.

[27] On the other hand, the disappointment with Belgrade's obstructionism was palpable in the Contact Group statement of 24 July 2006 following the first round of direct talks between President Tadić and Prime Minister Koštunica, on the one side, and President Fatmir Sejdiu and the Kosovo Unity Team, on the other. It noted that: 'Prishtina has shown flexibility in the decentralisation talks. However, Prishtina will need to be even more forthcoming on many issues before the status process can be brought to a successful conclusion … Belgrade needs to demonstrate much greater flexibility in the talks than it has done so far. Belgrade needs to begin considering reasonable and workable compromises for many issues under consideration, particularly decentralisation.'

## 4. Challenges to Serbia's Position

Serbia and Montenegro (as it was called then) was, in the course of the status process, unfortunate to be represented by a foreign minister whose exuberance and charisma were matched only by his comic inconsistency. Minister Drašković's prime foreign-policy instrument was the art of the metaphor. Why, he maintained, would the international community rush into building a roof for the common house of Kosovo (status), if its foundations (standards) had not even been laid? The Kosovo Albanian approach was a recipe for failure, he declared, like demanding a university diploma before starting to study. Second, he excelled in utilizing parallels devoid of similarity to the case under consideration. His first policy pronouncement after the initiation of the status process openly contradicted the president's suggestion to constitute Kosovo as two entities within the Serbian state, itself a simulacrum of the Dayton model.[28] Minister Drašković offered 'real sovereignty' and 'internal independence' to Kosovars based on the internationally brokered peace plan for Croatia (Zagreb-4, Z-4) of early 1995, which foresaw the incremental inclusion of the *Republika Srpska Krajina (RSK)* into Croatia's jurisdiction.[29]

His reference to the failed attempts of the mini-Contact Group to integrate an irredentist community into the Croat state that was at war with Serbia was, of course, a dreadful way of advertising his 'more than autonomy, less than independence' solution for Kosovo. His offer, designed along the same lines as the Z-4 Plan, came a decade too late and suffered from a number of flaws. Comparing the position of RSK renegades with that of a population that had been governed under the 'sacred trust' of the international community and that already enjoyed a much larger measure of self-government than the Krajina Serbs would have gained under the Z-4 arrangement displayed extraordinary frivolity, particularly in failing to propose how a Kosovo entity could exercise its substantial autonomy within, and partake of, the Serbian state and its institutions.[30]

On whichever side of the status debate one found oneself, Serbia's proposal to vest Kosovo with 'more than autonomy, less than independence' never seemed to gain support among the powers (excluding Russia) that were arbitrating Kosovo's fate. Indeed, the forcible reincorporation of two million hostile Kosovo Albanians into a seven-million-strong Serbian polity had always appeared to them as running against the latter's true interests.

Yet what should we have made of Serbia's own argument that it was entitled to the protection of its territorial integrity under international law? Could one not

---

[28] Cf. *Beta Week,* 24 November 2005, No.500, 2.

[29] Minister Drašković, quoted in *Frankfurter Rundschau,* 16 November 2005. See also his comments to the *Tanjug* news agency, 2 June 2005: 'That what Z-4 guaranteed to the Serbs in Krajina, now it would guarantee to Albanians. What it guaranteed to the Croats, it should now guarantee to the Serbs in Kosovo'.

[30] The inclusion of Kosovo Albanian politicians in Serbia's central government was 'not envisaged', said the deputy head of Serbia's negotiation team (Leon Kojen, 'Kosovos Zukunft aus serbischer Sicht', *Neue Zürcher Zeitung,* 1 June 2006). Indeed, the Serbian negotiation platform did not include an offer

have given credence to the Serbian Government's intention to invite its estranged Kosovo Albanian cousins back into its state, based on equality and non-discrimination, in recognition of their cultural identity and on the basis of full respect for their internal autonomous arrangements? Could the prerequisites for the true need to secede have faded away with the evolution of events and the passage of time, as Rosalyn Higgins once suggested?[31] After all, NATO's bombing campaign relieved the Kosovo Albanian population of the threat of persecution and, possibly with it, weakened their claim to external self-determination.[32]

Notwithstanding its references to the inviolability of its borders, Serbia was never able to make a persuasive political case as to why a population should be part of, and pay allegiance to, a state that had treated that population the way it had. Serbia's argument was wide open to challenge on grounds of its constitutional choices. Had Serbia been serious in its intention to grant 'Kosovo and Metohija' the widest possible range of autonomous rights within its state, as announced by the then Prime Minister Koštunica in the wake of the status process,[33] it could have entrenched them in its 2006 Constitution. But it did nothing of the sort. The new constitution, whose preamble defined Kosovo as an integral part of Serbia, provided for the possibility of autonomous rights being severely restricted, by means of ordinary legislation, in the fields of territorial boundaries, human and minority rights, the management of provincial assets, levels and kinds of central taxation, etc. Its contents further convinced the West that Serbia could not at this stage genuinely commit to a comprehensive autonomy regime. In an apparent tangent to the second commission that addressed the Åland Island question in 1921,[34] the Council of Europe's Venice Commission opined in 2007 that Serbia's constitution 'does not at all guarantee substantial autonomy for Kosovo, for it entirely depends on the willingness of the National Assembly of the Republic of Serbia whether self-government will be realized or not'.[35]

of participatory rights at the 'central' level. For the opinion of the Venice Commission on Serbia's 2006 Constitution and its 'guarantee' of autonomy, see *infra* note 34.

[31] Judge Rosalyn Higgins, 'Self-determination and Secession', in Julie Dahlitz (ed), *Secession and International Law* (Asser Press, The Hague, 2003), 21–38, at 37.

[32] The argument is neatly summarized by Srđan Cvijić in 'Self-determination as a Challenge to the Legitimacy of Humanitarian Interventions: The Case of Kosovo', 8(1) *German Law Journal* (2007), 57–79, at 74: 'Milošević's regime certainly misgoverned Kosovo, but one can justifiably ask why the Serbian democratic government should have to pay the price for the abuses of Milošević's authoritarian regime'.

[33] Statement by the Prime Minister of the Republic of Serbia at the Security Council meeting on 24 October 2005, at 6: 'our political efforts will be directed to defining a specific and viable form of substantial autonomy for Kosovo and Metohjia, whereby legitimate interests of Kosovo Albanians will be fully acknowledged'.

[34] 'The separation of a minority from the State of which it forms a part and its incorporation in another State can only be considered as an altogether exceptional solution, a last resort when the State lacks either the will or the power to enact and apply just and effective guarantees'. Commission of Rapporteurs, 'Report of the Commission of Rapporteurs Presented to the Council of the League', League of Nations Document B.7.21/68/106, 16 April 1921.

[35] European Commission for Democracy through Law, 'Opinion on the Constitution of Serbia', No.405/2006, 70th Session, Venice, 17–18 March 2007, §8.

## 5. Spoiling the Party

Discussions in the first half of 2006 furthered a collective understanding on the part of the Quint that Ahtisaari's end product would be subject to a political trade-off with Russia on other international issues prior to its endorsement by the Security Council. As former US Under-Secretary of State for Political Affairs Nicholas Burns noted in a meeting with Special Envoy Ahtisaari, Russia 'will be unhelpful in the Contact Group and the UN [Security Council]. Although we have a commitment that they will not block a Security Council Resolution on the status, they will make it very difficult throughout the process'.[36] Halfway into UNOSEK's efforts to produce a settlement, this was a general perception shared by Quint governments. For instance, one of their ambassadors reported from a lunch with the Russian Foreign Minister, Sergei Lavrov, that, while one should be wary about his intentions of applying aspects of Kosovo's anticipated independence to the frozen conflicts of Transnistria, Nagorno-Karabakh, and South Ossetia/Abkhazia, 'we are receiving hints that they may attempt to extract a price elsewhere. Provided we do everything we can to play their sensitivity about being treated as a member of a club, a serious power who should be fully involved in negotiating the eventual outcome, the thing should be doable [sic]'.[37]

Such were the opinions held in the wake of a series of *démarches* in all Quint capitals in which Russian diplomats made clear their serious dissatisfaction with the direction the status process was taking. They criticized the tendency to lay the blame for the lack of progress in the negotiations squarely on Belgrade; they insisted firmly on the priority of a negotiated solution; and they refused to accept a settlement imposed upon Belgrade. Further, they urged the abandonment of a deadline to the negotiations, and demanded that UNOSEK's 'favorable treatment' of the Kosovo Albanian side cease. Russia quickly backtracked from its earlier declared intention to maintain unity within the Contact Group, gradually distanced itself from Ahtisaari's ideas and began to reveal its true face: an escalating rhetoric in uncompromising support of Serbia's position,[38] which the latter used as a cover for its inflexibility. This stance hardened further in the course of the following year. The West, however, maintained its belief that Russia could be convinced to at least abstain from a vote in the Security Council, as China had on 10 June 1999 when resolution 1244 was passed. As we know with the benefit of hindsight, this is not what happened.

---

[36] Burns quoted by a UNOSEK official (in an interview with the author) who attended a meeting between Condoleezza Rice and Special Envoy Ahtisaari, Washington, DC, 11 May 2006.

[37] Personal interview with a senior Quint official, Moscow, 8 June 2006.

[38] The position of the Russian Ambassador, Vitaly Churkin, at the 13 December 2006 Security Council meeting was illustrative in this regard. He chided the former UNMIK SRSG, Joachim Rücker, for having gone beyond his mandate by advocating a quick status decision, defended Belgrade against the criticism that it was unconstructive and inflexible, and insisted that only a negotiated solution would pass the Council; cf. Transcript of the 5588th Meeting, 'Kosovo Envoy Tells Security Council Delay of Status Proposal Raised Tension', SC/8900, 13 December 2006.

The Quint had, shortly before the beginning of the 'political' status talks in July 2006, adopted a firm position on 'limited sovereignty' for Kosovo under the working assumption that no negotiated settlement would be reached between the parties. But to the surprise of the US and the EU, Russia challenged the axiom that Kosovo represented a *sui generis* case devoid of precedent in international law. Moscow's lingering opposition to the Western standpoint was not a mere face-saving exercise for a Slav cousin in need. It represented a high point in Russia's new global assertiveness at the time. In the words of one commentator, when it had already become clear that Russia had little incentive to seek a compromise with the West on this issue: 'Moscow has assumed the role of a judge: a guarantor of international law, protector of human rights and commentator who bears no direct responsibility for the current and future situation on the ground'.[39] In the guise of defending the principle of territorial integrity, it asserted two coveted yet under-rated factors in the psychology of international relations: respect for its status as a major power that could not be ignored, and revenge—in this case for the humiliation over Russia's failure to prevent the NATO bombing of Serbia in 1999.

As a consequence of the Quint's miscalculation of Moscow's intent, all five draft resolutions proposed in the Security Council during June and July 2007 had to be withdrawn following the credible threat of a Russian veto.[40] The EU had at this point not yet realized that this was one of the moments in which it had to demonstrate unity and vision if it were to be a credible external actor, particularly with regard to the stability of the Western Balkans and the region's European future. Torn between two contradictory positions taken by the US and Russia, this principal regional stakeholder adopted one of its favourite tactics when faced with international difficulties: it called for an extended period of time in which negotiations should be resumed.

The 120-day deliberations that followed were led by Contact Group-mandated negotiators (representing the EU, the US, and Russia, respectively) and aimed to 'facilitate a period of further discussions between the parties'.[41] Essentially, the 'Kosovo Troika', as it was called, repeated the shuttling between capitals that was witnessed when UNOSEK led the process, and provided for six additional occasions for face-to-face negotiations. At all of the joint sessions—probably to distance itself from the methodology employed by Special Envoy Ahtisaari—the Troika reiterated that it was not making proposals of its own, but was merely asking questions to ensure that all options were being examined by the parties. The Troika indeed had no intention of imposing a solution: 'instead, the burden was on each party to convince the other side of the merits of its position'.[42]

---

[39] Oksana Antonenko, 'Russia and the Deadlock over Kosovo', 49 (3) *Survival* (2007), 91–105, at 101.

[40] The deadlock in the Security Council is described in International Crisis Group (ICG), 'Breaking the Kosovo Stalemate: Europe's Responsibility', *Europe Report* No.185, 21 August 2007, 2–3.

[41] Statement of the Contact Group Ministers, New York, 27 September 2007. See, also UN Secretary General, 'Statement on the New Period of Engagement on Kosovo', SG/SM/11111, New York, 1 August 2007. The Troika's negotiation method is recounted in both ICG, 'Kosovo Countdown: a Blueprint for Transition', *Europe Report* No.188, 6 December 2007, 2–5; and Marc Weller, 'Negotiating the Final Status of Kosovo', *Chaillot Paper* (December 2008) No.114, 57–67.

[42] European Union/United States/Russian Federation Troika, 'Report of the European Union/United States/Russian Federation Troika on Kosovo', 4 December 2007, attached to a letter from the

Such fresh idealism could not conceal the true purpose of the trilateral effort: to buy time, from August 2007 onwards, in which a 'critical mass' of EU member states could assemble to recognize an independent Kosovo following the eventual failure of the talks.[43] Of the myriad diplomatic initiatives that have accompanied the protracted dissolution of the former Yugoslavia since 1991, the Kosovo Troika may indeed stand out as the most futile. In hindsight, the Troika's attempts at brokering an agreement at any price, however implausible, and 'to leave no stone unturned'[44] in the process at times bordered on the comic: its proposals on a temporary 'neutral status'[45] and on a 'loose confederation' between Serbia and Kosovo,[46] and the consideration it gave to adapting the one-state-two-systems 'Hong Kong model', proposed by Belgrade to secure its long-term claim to sovereignty,[47] all sent confusing messages that threatened to undermine efforts undertaken by European and UN actors.

Most worryingly, the Troika 'broached' the issue of territorial exchanges[48]—trading Serb-inhabited northern Kosovo for independence—and thus felt at liberty to operate outside the Contact Group's Guiding Principles and, in particular, its sixth principle, which, excluding any possibility of territorial adjustments, stipulated that 'there will be no changes in the current territory of Kosovo, i.e. no partition of Kosovo and no union of Kosovo with any country or part of any country'.[49]

In essence, the Troika, in its efforts to avoid a complete disaster, explored options that appeared to open up the entire negotiation process again, compromising not only the work of UNOSEK but, more broadly, that of the European Union. Take, for instance, the Troika's treatment of Kosovo's 'European perspective', which the European Commission and UNMIK had tried hard over the years to secure and turn into a concrete and tangible promise. While Kosovo's international administration had—with varying degrees of success and despite its misguided 'standards before status' policy—kept the territory on track with regard to its obligations assumed under the Stabilisation and Association Process, the Troika's chief envoy, Wolfgang Ischinger, clearly exceeded the terms of his mandate when he established an explicit linkage between the imperative of concluding a horizontal status agreement with Belgrade and Kosovo's further integration into European structures: 'In [the] absence of such an agreement the European door will not be as open as I'm sure everyone here in this region would hope it to be'.[50]

---

UN Secretary-General to Ambassador Marcello Spatafora, President of the UN Security Council, 10 December 2007, §6.

[43] The Troika-led negotiations eventually failed in November 2007. Cf. Contact Group Troika press communiqué, Baden Conference, Baden, 28 November 2007.

[44] Troika press statement, Vienna, 5 November 2007.

[45] Cf. the negative reaction to the 'neutral status' proposal in *B92,* 15 November 2007.

[46] Cf. 'Lippenbekenntnisse im Kosovo-Streit', *Neue Zürcher Zeitung,* 2 October 2007, 6.

[47] Cf. 'Go slow on Kosovo?', Economist Intelligence Unit Briefing, 3 October 2007.

[48] Letter dated 10 December 2007 from the Secretary-General to the President of the Security Council, S/2007/723, enclosing the 'Report of the European Union/United States/Russian Federation Troika on Kosovo', 4 December 2007, §10.

[49] Cf. *supra* note 9. See, also, Weller, *supra* note 41, 60; as well as 'Diskussion um eine Teilung Kosovos', *Neue Zürcher Zeitung,* 17 August 2007, 3; and 'Kosovo drifts towards partition', *Balkan Insight* (BIRN) No. 104, 20 September 2007.

[50] Wolfgang Ischinger, quoted in 'EU pressures rivals to reach Kosovo deal', *International Herald Tribune,* 13 August 2007, 3.

Overall, the opening of status negotiations in late 2005 certainly was a political prerequisite for what a former political director within the German Foreign Ministry called the creation of a sustainable political foundation for the future of the territory.[51] The two years of negotiations were characterized by the intensified use of informal groups that conducted crisis management at times autonomously from the Security Council. Due to the impasse there, the process as designed by the UN Secretary-General and the Contact Group could not deliver the results: a multilateral endorsement of a status solution as devised by UNOSEK. At key points, the process allowed politicians and diplomats to promise too much, with respect to both the speed with which it had to be brought to an end and, more importantly, the outcome. UNOSEK's emphatic distancing from both Serbian and Albanian nationalisms may have facilitated the elaboration of a decentralization concept, which the mediators pursued with scientific zeal and, as some may claim, naive optimism. However, the mandate that UNOSEK and the Kosovo Troika both had—to facilitate direct negotiations, propose summaries, identify mutual standpoints, and report their findings to the UN Secretary-General—proved insufficient to make up for the unavailability of a compulsory dispute-settlement mechanism for statehood questions.[52]

## 6. UNOSEK's Settlement Proposal

Halfway through UNOSEK's direct technical talks, in one of his regular reports to the UN Secretary-General on the progress of the negotiations on decentralization, Ahtisaari remarked candidly:

In recent expert-level discussions with the sides, Pristina representatives have adopted a largely constructive approach, and seem ready to discuss concrete options… Belgrade representatives have, instead, focused more on the process itself—with an emphasis on the format of the talks and the modalities for the way forward—and have declined to discuss practical proposals related to specific locations of possible new municipalities. They have raised the issue of the 'slow pace of the talks so far' (rather inconsistently, since they carry at least part of the responsibility for delays), and of insufficient room being allowed for negotiations as such (here, also, they share responsibilities…) Belgrade's attitude has so far been to unduly prolong the talks on the practical issues by, *inter alia:* i) not concretely focusing on specifics of the territorial delineation of new municipalities; ii) by preventing an early May meeting on religious sites; iii) by not yet having delivered an overview of their claims in the economic field; and iv) by objecting to a meeting devoted to minority protection. This approach goes hand in hand with its repeated calls to move the talks immediately to status, thereby suggesting that the 'bottom-up' approach has failed, while clearly disregarding its own role in the procrastination.[53]

[51]  Michael Schaefer, 'German Foreign Policy and the Western Balkans', in Johanna Deimel and Wim van Meurs (eds), *The Balkan Prism. A Retrospective by Policy-Makers and Analysts* (Verlag Otto Sagner, Munich, 2007), 65–80, at 70.
[52]  Colin Warbrick, 'States and Recognition in International Law', in Malcolm D. Evans (ed.), *International Law* (OUP, New York, NY, 2006), 217–75, at 241.
[53]  UNOSEK, 'Overview of Recent Developments', Code Cable, 24 April 2006, §§2, 3, and 6.

From Ahtisaari's point of view, Belgrade's refusal to be part of any constructive negotiations demonstrated a deeper unwillingness to enter into a novel arrangement that would enable the various ethnic communities to coexist. It allowed itself, and by extension the international community, to be held hostage by retrograde political forces, on the basis of short-term political calculations. Although Ahtisaari also criticized Prishtina's focus on unnecessary details and noted a tendency for the ethnic Albanian side to say what UNOSEK officials wanted to hear without following up with action, he reproached Belgrade for having become *the* key obstacle to improving the situation in Kosovo through preventing Kosovo Serb participation in the PISG—a charge that did not go down well with the Russian Federation.

Shortly before delivering his proposal to the UN Secretary-General, Ahtisaari added an even gloomier note, observing that 'there has been a lot of talk about reaching a compromise. In practice, however, compromise has meant that *you* want the other side to accept *your* position. No amount of delays and meetings will bring a change to this behaviour'.[54] Yet, despite the unproductive negotiations he facilitated in over a dozen meetings in various Viennese Baroque palaces, he believed that the parties had indicated options for *rapprochement* of their irreconcilable and mutually exclusive positions. They are contained in UNOSEK's Comprehensive Proposal, which Ahtisaari submitted through the UN Secretary-General to the Security Council in March 2007.[55] The Kosovo Assembly accepted the Comprehensive Proposal and committed to its full implementation only two weeks later, in its declaration of 5 April 2007.

## 7. A Declaration of Independence, a New Constitution

The external process of status determination had to be accompanied by attempts to build deliberative legitimacy from within. The status framework was to be backed from within by a deep commitment to international law. By including strong pre-commitment devices, UNOSEK had followed the tradition of international efforts to resolve nationalist conflict and its aftermath, but departed from its illustrious precursors—the regime for Upper Silesia, the International Governing Commission for the Saarland and the Office of the High Representative in Bosnia, as mandated by the Dayton Peace Accords—in significant ways. In the absence of a horizontal status settlement, Special Envoy Ahtisaari's settlement proposed only

---

[54] Statement of the Special Envoy; Meeting of the OSCE Permanent Council, Vienna, 20 February 2007, 5 (emphasis in original). In his final speech as special envoy to the Security Council on 3 April 2007, he added: 'No additional talks—no matter how long they last, and no matter the format in which they are conducted—will change this. This is a fact one has to accept.'

[55] Special Envoy of the Secretary-General, 'Comprehensive Proposal for the Kosovo Status Settlement', Annex to the 'Report of the Special Envoy of the Secretary-General on Kosovo's Future Status', S/2007/168/Add.1, 26 March 2007 (hereafter 'Comprehensive Proposal'). On the same day, Secretary-General Ban Ki-Moon conveyed the proposal, with his full support, to the President of the UN Security Council, Ambassador Dumisani Kumalo. For a discussion of the Proposal, see Jean d'Aspremont, 'Regulating Statehood: The Kosovo Status Settlement', 20 (3) *LJIL* (2007), 649–68.

key elements of a new constitutional structure around which local institutions were to frame a locally owned text. This was felt to be especially relevant for measures to enhance minority protection and representation.[56] While the constitutional process was not limited to the issues, such as decentralization and minority protection, that were discussed in Vienna and elsewhere, the settlement imposed clear limits on the constitutional imagination of Kosovars and their ideas about political organization.

At the level of applicable law, the draft settlement stipulated that all UNMIK-promulgated legislation, including administrative directions and executive decisions, were part of the new legal order and should remain in force 'until their validity expires, or until they are revoked or replaced by legislation regulating the same subject matter in accordance with the provisions of this Settlement'.[57] James Pettifer rightly observed in one of the first analyses of Ahtisaari's proposal that this was the key paragraph in the entire document; were the proposal to be implemented, the panoply of post-crisis-period administrative regulations would remain in place for an indeterminate period.[58] And they did. In the same spirit, UNOSEK suggested limiting local competencies in the area of external relations in an apparent departure from the post-colonial rule of *tabula rasa*. In concrete terms, UNOSEK's settlement proposed that 'Kosovo shall continue to be bound...by all international agreements and other arrangements in the area of international co-operation that were concluded by UNMIK for and [on] behalf of Kosovo'.[59] The proposal's explicit reference to a speedy accession to the Council of Europe and its instruments[60] was designed to predetermine the new sovereign state's choices, emulating recent practice in Eastern Europe that clearly confirmed the trend of automatic succession to human rights treaties.

Like its predecessor, the 2001 Constitutional Framework imposed by UNMIK,[61] the new Kosovo Constitution of 15 June 2008 is a hybrid regime, combining indigenous elements and those guaranteed by the Comprehensive Proposal. The two components were merged with the intention of reducing the obvious tensions between ethnic decentralization and the unified jurisdiction of the nascent state; between representation in the legislature based on ethnicity and universal suffrage; between the rights of 'communities' and individual rights; between the imperative of creating conditions for a stable political landscape and the need to build and sustain democratic opposition; and between empowerment of local actors and limitations on the same as prescribed by the settlement—in particular between the expanded jurisdiction of the local executive branch and its international oversight in key areas. Accordingly, the establishment of a Constitutional Commission, mandated to draft the document in consultation

---

[56] See the Comprehensive Proposal's Annex 1 which stipulated that a new constitution shall incorporate a large number of minority rights and standards that 'shall be directly applicable in Kosovo' (Art.2(3)).

[57] Ibid., Art.15(2)(1) (main text).

[58] Cf. James Pettifer, 'The Ahtisaari Report—Totem & Taboo', Conflict Studies Research Centre, *Defence Academy of the United Kingdom Paper* No.07/08, February 2007, 3.

[59] Comprehensive Proposal, *supra* note 55, Art.15(2)(2).     [60] Cf. ibid., Art.2(1).

[61] UNMIK, 'On a Constitutional Framework for Self-Government', UNMIK/REG/2001/9, 15 May 2001.

with the international community,[62] was intended to build broad local ownership around a number of issues: minority representation in the legislature[63] and within the executive branch;[64] the extent of, and limits to, decentralization;[65] the type of electoral system and the composition of the new Central Election Commission;[66] and the concept and content of 'community rights'.[67]

Kosovo's declaration of independence in February 2008 and the subsequent adoption of a constitution in June that year effectively opened an area of contestation within Kosovo's politico-legal sphere. Grounding the legitimacy of the entire new polity on a set of international values that were endorsed by the document naturally posed problems with regard to the relationship between external and local actors, between foreign and domestic solutions and between outside and inside arrangements. Institutional actors, domestic and international, were uncomfortably positioned in their quest for overall authority. Who, actually, was in charge here? According to the Ahtisaari proposal, as endorsed by the constitution, corrective powers were firmly situated with the International Civilian Office (ICO). On the other hand, and in accordance with the authority vested in him by Resolution 1244, the SRSG retained the power to change, repeal, or suspend laws that are incompatible with the mandate, aims, or purposes of UNMIK.[68]

The euphoria following the adoption of the constitution thus vanished rapidly. The domestic institutional architecture it put in place stood in a bizarre relation to the international institutions that were meant to supervise it. First, the effective relegation of civil administration tasks from UNMIK to Kosovo's state institutions by the new constitution considerably compromised the legitimacy of the former, leading Kosovo's leaders to frequently question its authority. It continued to be headed by an SRSG 'unable to enforce this authority' due to UNMIK's status-neutral mandate.[69] On the opposite end of the international structure, the ICO assisted Kosovo's Government in its journey to sovereignty in accordance with the Ahtisaari settlement, as endorsed by Kosovo's constitution.[70] Third, the

---

[62] Cf. Comprehensive Proposal, *supra* note 55, Art.10(4). The Constitutional Commission, subdivided into ten working groups, was established in June 2007 by the President of Kosovo.

[63] Ibid., Annex I, Art.3(2), as well as Annex II, Art.4.　　[64] Ibid., Annex I, Art.5.

[65] Ibid., Annex III.　　　[66] Ibid., Annex I, Art.7.　　[67] Ibid., Annex II, Art.3.

[68] UN Secretary-General, 'Report of the Secretary-General on the United Nations Interim Administration Mission in Kosovo', S/1999/779, 12 July 1999, §39.

[69] UN Secretary-General, 'Report of the UN Secretary-General on the United Nations Interim Administration Mission in Kosovo', S/2008/692, 24 November 2008, §21. This assessment was also confirmed by the UNMIK SRSG who had earlier, at the Security Council, emphasized that: 'Since the entry into force of the Kosovo Constitution, exercising my legal powers under resolution 1244 (1999) has become increasingly difficult in practice...The Assembly of Kosovo continues to pass legislation, which is now promulgated by the President of Kosovo without reference to my powers under [1244] or the constitutional framework...While I am still formally vested with executive authority under [1244], I have no tools to enforce such authority' (UN Security Council, 'Verbatim Record of the 5944th Meeting of the United Nations Security Council, S/PV.5944, 25 August 2008, 2–5). The admission that Kosovo's institutions consolidated their control and authority—reiterated by SRSG Lamberto Zannier in his Security Council appearance on 26 November 2008 (S/PV.6025, 3)—may be interpreted as a testimony to the effectiveness of government and control over territory, key criteria for the assumption of rights and duties by states (Art.1, 1933 Montevideo Convention).

[70] Chapter XIII, Art.143.

deployment of EULEX under the overall authority of the United Nations clearly contributed to its separation from the ICO and gave rise to a controversy over whether its mandate was at all reconcilable with resolution 1244.[71] The configuration of EULEX—coexisting with, rather than substituting for, UNMIK—repeated the dilemma well known since the early days of UNMIK's deployment in summer 1999, where a mission designed to monitor and mentor Kosovo's state institutions was paradoxically prevented from endorsing the legitimacy of that very state.[72]

In hindsight, the June 2008 constitution may have attempted to fulfil too many functions at once: a promise of a reasonable balance of power between the international community and those that lived for almost a decade under its tutelage; an international guarantee extended to minority communities; and a social contract among the citizens of a new polity with respect to their security, welfare, and representation, regardless of their ethnicity.

## 8. The ICJ's Advisory Opinion

Irrespective of whether Kosovo will be politically containable in a secure box marked *'sui generis'*, or serve as a precedent for the resolution of 'frozen conflicts', or as an inspiration for a wider group of disgruntled minorities, the status process has left a number of reference points for the future resolution of territorial conflict. The statements of the Contact Group clearly hinted at the Federal Republic of Yugoslavia's minimal state responsibility for policies affecting its citizens. In this light, the notion of supreme state authority appears somewhat circumscribed by performance criteria. A target state may—may—forfeit its jurisdiction over territory when it does not meet the latter. Such minimal responsibility—if recognized and acted upon by outsiders—could place an obligation upon a state to ensure the physical security of the political community, thus limiting its monopoly on the legitimate use of force domestically.

On the international legal plane, the Advisory Opinion by the ICJ was eagerly expected not only by the many states that participated in its proceedings but generally by anyone interested in the law of self-determination in a post-colonial setting. A sense of relief and vindication were certainly palpable not only in Prishtina but in the capitals of those states that had supported Kosovo's path toward independence.[73] To its critics, the opinion—that international law does not contain a prohibition on declarations on independence—suggested that law itself had taken a back seat in that it remained silent in the face of state creation and its consequences, including recognitions. Law, as one pair of authors put it, has been

---

[71] Robert Muharremi, 'The European Union Rule of Law Mission in Kosovo (EULEX) from the Perspective of Kosovo Constitutional Law', 70 *Zeitschrift für ausländisches öffentliches Recht und Völkerrecht* (2010), 357–79; Erika de Wet, 'The Governance of Kosovo: Security Council Resolution 1244 and the Establishment and Functioning of EULEX', 103 *AJIL* (2009), 83–96.

[72] Cf. 'Kosovo und die Quadratur des Zirkels', *Neue Zürcher Zeitung*, 17 February 2009.

[73] See ICO Lessons Learned Report, *State Building and Exit: The International Civilian Office and Kosovo's Supervised Independence 2008-2012*, Prishtina, 2012, 50.

sidelined by national recognition practice which is 'diplomatic parlance for political expediency.'[74]

While other contributions to this volume will provide a much more substantial analysis of the Court's views, a few comments are in order. The status process itself—the Contact Group's pronunciations as well as Ahtisaari's proposal—had certainly kindled expectations that the Court would tackle what were held to be the key questions underlying Kosovo's sovereignty puzzle: the contested issue of secession in international law, and related to it, the 'emerging norm' of a collective responsibility to protect and a putatively corresponding right to self-determination following instances of grievous human rights violations. Some even suggested that the Court would 'resurrect' Kosovo's entitlement to self-determination that was presumed to have laid dormant for a decade, muted under the heavy blanket of multilateral activism. Once UNOSEK's settlement proposal was floated, and a meaningful dialogue on status issues exhausted, they maintained, one could have presumed that Kosovo's claim would be invigorated and the Court would, at a minimum, engage in balancing it against the tenet of territorial integrity contained in Article 2(4) of the UN Charter.[75]

To the disappointment of those (including this author) who hoped for substantial guidance on these matters, the Court merely investigated whether the political pronunciation of the Kosovo Assembly was in line with general international law and with the international legal regime that the Security Council had imposed on the territory in 1999. The facts of the case—human rights violations on a massive scale, the length of time Kosovo was administered by UNMIK, the years of internationally sponsored negotiations—were not held relevant to feed into the Court's legal analysis.

In fact, the Court maintained absolute silence on the question of rights and entitlements. Instead, it cautiously built argumentative blocks to encase the pink elephant in the room: '[I]t is entirely possible for a particular act—such as a [unilateral declaration of independence] not to be in violation of international law without necessarily constituting the exercise of a right conferred to it'.[76] Overall, the ICJ left the presumption against the admissibility of secession—and in favour of maintaining the territorial status quo—largely intact and the discourse on 'remedial secessions' somewhat awkwardly hanging in the air.

Equally baffling was the positivist turn the Court took when concluding that '[t]he scope of the principle of territorial integrity is confined to the sphere of relations between states'.[77] What appears, at first sight, to be a dry re-statement of the classic intra-state paradigm reveals itself in the further course of the Opinion as a method of drilling a hole into the holiest of grails: a state, the Court said, cannot invoke an entitlement to territorial integrity vis-à-vis non-state territorial entities

---

[74] Cedric Ryngaert and Sven Sobrie, 'Recognition of States: International Law or Realpolitik? The Practice of Recognition in the Wake of Kosovo, South Ossetia, and Abkhazia', 24 *LJIL* (2011) 467–90, at 480.
[75] See Oliver Corten, 'Territorial Integrity Narrowly Interpreted: Reasserting the Classical Inter-State Paradigm of International Law', 24 (1) *LJIL* (2011) 87–108, at 93.
[76] ICJ *Kosovo* AO, *supra* note 2, §156.     [77] Ibid., §80.

as it cannot oppose a right to a group which has no obligation to respect it.[78] That is indeed a surprising turn and it leaves the spectator breathless as to the applicability, to a non-state entity, of the 1970 Declaration on Principles of International Law Concerning Friendly Relations, which—referring to the right of self-determination—explicitly denies legitimacy to 'any action which would dismember or impair . . . the territorial integrity or political unity of sovereign states'.[79] Until the 2010 ICJ Opinion, there had been a lively debate on whether the addressees of this exhortation were only states themselves or also those non-state actors intent on determining their future outside of recognized territorial boundaries, including by using violent means.[80]

The Court's confinement of the principle of territorial integrity to the interstate realm may actually be the most significant and lasting contribution to legal doctrine, with entirely unclear consequences for prohibitory norms derived from this principle, such as the use of force by secessionist groups.[81] Sardonically, Ralph Wilde revealed some of the circular thinking the Court may have engaged in: 'For Kosovo to be bound to respect the right of territorial integrity of Serbia, it would have to be a state, and if it is a state then it no longer forms part of Serbia's territory, and so no basis exists for its territorial claim to impinge on the sovereign rights of Serbia.'[82]

The Court has been blamed for a narrowly constructed and formalistic opinion that avoided contentious issues such as whether the UDI had any legal consequences on the international legal plane. In the political sphere, its conclusion paved the way for a second chain of recognitions, a total of 110 to date.

## 9. Conclusion

In the long story of colonial expansion, the task of jurists had been to develop a taxonomy according to which every entity encountered in the scramble for territory could be properly categorized. The legal capacity of each entity was to be 'objectively' established by the 'degree of civilization' it had attained, before the

---

[78] Unless, of course, their organs breach a peremptory norm of *jus cogens*. See Ralph Wilde, 'Self-Determination, Secession, and Dispute Settlement after the Kosovo Advisory Opinion', 24 (1) *LJIL* 149.

[79] United Nations General Assembly, A/RES/25/2625 (XXV), 24 October 1970, Principle V. The 'savings clause' which has often been held to allow for a doctrine of remedial secession to emerge—namely, that states which arbitrarily exclude inhabitants from any share in government would not be protected by the principle of territorial integrity—will not be discussed here. The ICJ opined that the debates regarding the existence of any 'right to remedial secession' are 'beyond the scope of the question posed by the General Assembly'. Kosovo AO, *supra* note 2, at §83.

[80] See Iñigo Urrutia Libarona, 'Territorial Integrity and Self-Determination: The Approach of the International Court of Justice in the Advisory Opinion on Kosovo', 16 *Revista d'Estudis Autonòmics i Federals* (2012) 107–40, at 112–14.

[81] For a discussion, see Anne Peters, 'Does Kosovo Lie in the Lotus-Land of Freedom?', 24 (1) *LJIL* (2011) 95–108, at 106–7, as well as Corten, *supra* note 75, at 88–91.

[82] 'International Decisions', 105 *AJIL* (2011) 301–7, at 305.

metropolitan power bestowed recognition upon it.[83] The methodology of standardizing progress along an axis of 'civilization' was carried over into League of Nations practice as colonial territories were transformed into sovereign states under the protection of the Mandate system and, later, the UN's Trusteeship system.

Today's organized international community has conscientiously built upon this practice. The 'move to institutions' helped expand legal and administrative techniques so that they could operate and intervene in a way that not merely assessed but transformed the inherent capacities of entities that exist in the twilight of international personality. The eventual marginalization of the Security Council in the management of Kosovo's status does not necessarily diminish this role, or precipitate a 'crisis' of Article 24, which arrogates to the Security Council the 'primary responsibility for the maintenance of international peace and security'. Quite the contrary. The overarching leadership of the Security-Council-mandated Contact Group provided an effective interface between unilateral temptation and multilateral commitment. Before Russia's isolation in this context became apparent and the interplay between the Security Council and the Contact Group reached a dead-end in July 2007, the latter had set remarkable standards for its involvement in self-determination issues. Its pronouncement that a settlement must be acceptable to the 'people of Kosovo' was nothing less than revolutionary.

The Contact Group also narrowed down the range of possible outcomes in negotiations and decided upon successive arrangements that would limit the future state's scope of domestic competences. This further demonstrated that the concept of 'earned sovereignty', emphatically postulated by some as a panacea to problems associated with self-determination, has not significantly influenced the way in which an entity may *itself* contribute to the finalization of its status. The ward, after all, may mature into statehood only by parental decision, not by reaching certain benchmarks.

In its 2010 Opinion, the ICJ refused to become embroiled in questions of statehood or pronounce on the validity or legal effects, if any, of the recognition that Kosovo had received from an ever-growing number of states. It clearly did not see itself situated within the continuity of a UN-steered process that had for almost a decade made reference to international law, and a political process that has erroneously referred to Kosovo as a 'unique' case to which the rule of law would not apply. Yet despite or because of its silences, the ICJ's Advisory Opinion has undoubtedly enriched the notion of an international authority that assumed the role of a supreme arbitrator in attempting to resolve territorial disputes. The ICJ has done so through the back door, by insisting on the inter-state character of Article 2(4) of the UN Charter, implicitly opening argumentative spaces beyond the bland concept of 'legal neutrality' in relation to declarations of independence and unilateral non-violent secessions.

---

[83] Antony Anghie, *Imperialism, Sovereignty and the Making of International Law* (CUP, Cambridge, 2005), 77–8, with reference to Westlake and Lorimer.

The recognition of Kosovo's fuzzy statehood by a large 'coalition of the willing' in the aftermath of Kosovo's declaration of independence confirmed what had long been conventional wisdom: resolution 1244 was no longer a guarantee but had rather become an obstacle to the maintenance of international peace and the security of the region. The process of internationalization of territory through an essentially 'de-territorializing' Security Council resolution has given way to a process of 're-territorialization', through which an important part of the international community actively transformed Kosovo into a 'state *in statu nascendi*'.

This process of 're-territorialization' was aided by a subsidiary organ of the UN Secretary-General that helped a non-state territorial entity to emerge as a full-blown personality. The Ahtisaari proposal, as Peter Hilpold remarked, represented a sophisticated edifice of international and constitutional provisions which attempted to 'ensure the sustainability of a multi-ethnic state coming to life under extremely precarious conditions'.[84] One of its key proposals consisted in endowing Kosovo with the capacity to enter into contractual relations with other subjects of international law.[85] The proposal, thus, attempted to expand upon a presumed capacity that is traditionally seen as a consequence of statehood. While remaining silent on the question of 'external independence', the settlement proposal provided one of its key constitutive building blocks.[86]

Special Envoy Ahtisaari's report accompanying UNOSEK's Comprehensive Proposal of March 2007 neatly summed up the motivations underlying his recommendation—a *mélange* of (a) a recognition of past injustice; (b) the territory's protected status and the realities flowing from it; (c) the communal responsibility to thwart threats to international peace and security; and (d) the past pursuit of all conceivable avenues that could have yielded a horizontal settlement in line with a traditional understanding of Article 2(7) of the UN Charter.[87]

Not only was this the most pragmatic course of action available, it must also be seen from the vantage point of modern international law's devotion to furthering social goals and the current needs of present-day society—a principal trait that

---

[84] *Kosovo and International Law: The ICJ Advisory Opinion of 22 July 2010* (ed Peter Hilpold), (Brill: Leiden, 2012), at 19.

[85] The right to negotiate and conclude international agreements and to seek membership of international organizations featured among the proposal's General Principles (Art.5). Indeed, the proposal expected Kosovo to take all necessary measures towards ratifying the ECHR and its Protocols (Art.2(1)).

[86] Other building blocks included: the right to establish a security force under the auspices of the International Military Presence (Annex VIII, Art.5); the assumption of external debts (Annex VI); air-space control (Annex VIII, Art.7); the right to have a flag, seal, and anthem (General Principles, Art.1(7)); the right to obtain Kosovo citizenship (Annex I, Art.1(6)); and the obligation to invite an international mission (General Principles, Art.1(11)). In addition, the proposal did not provide restrictions as to the conduct of foreign affairs, which suggested that it be treated as a competence to be transferred to local authorities in due course.

[87] 'My recommendation of independence, supervised initially by the international community, takes into account Kosovo's recent history, the realities of Kosovo today and the need for political and economic stability in Kosovo. My Settlement proposal, upon which such independence will be based, builds upon the positions of the parties in the negotiating process and offers compromises on many issues to achieve a durable solution.' Report of the Special Envoy of the Secretary-General on Kosovo's Future Status, *supra* note 55, §16.

in the American tradition of international law has been termed the 'sentiment of solidarity'.[88] Indeed, it has been extraordinary to observe that an emerging community interest in achieving regional security and stability became a policy vehicle for supporting the essentially autonomous character of local government structures and their claim towards external self-determination.

Kosovo continues to be an entity that at the same time has, and does not have, an international legal personality. International law, it seems, continues to provide little—and if any, only indirect—normative guidance on the legal consequences of declarations of independence which can only be given effect through recognition. In this polyphonic narrative, in which participating voices vie for equality and independence, the case of Kosovo may well represent a *contrapunctus*: an event that stands out in its specificity, but which may in due course integrate itself into the laws of harmony and its progressions.

---

[88] Alejandro Alvarez, 'Latin America and International Law', 3 *AJIL* (1909), 269–353, at 270.

# PART II
# THE OPINION

# 6

# Questions of Jurisdiction and the Discretion to Decline a Request for an Advisory Opinion

*Vladimir Djerić\**

## 1. Introduction

Before dealing with the merits of the request for an advisory opinion, the Court had to decide that it had jurisdiction to give the opinion and, if so, whether 'there is any reason why the Court, in its discretion, should decline to exercise any such jurisdiction'.[1] While the questions of jurisdiction and discretion had certainly not been the main focus of the written and oral submissions of the participants in the advisory proceedings,[2] it is obvious from the Opinion and the appended separate and dissenting opinions of judges that the question of discretion was a major point of contention during their deliberations. After unanimously finding that it had jurisdiction to deal with the request for an advisory opinion, the Court decided to comply with it, i.e. not to decline the opinion, by a majority of nine judges in favour and five against.[3] Interestingly, the four judges who were in the minority on the substantive question, as they considered that Kosovo's declaration of independence (DoI) was not in accordance with international law, thought that the Court should decline the opinion.[4]

I will discuss the findings of the Court on jurisdiction and discretion and then examine if and how they respond to arguments raised by participants in the

---

\* While I acted as counsel for Serbia in the advisory proceedings concerning the declaration of independence in respect of Kosovo, opinions expressed in this article are mine alone and given solely in my personal capacity.

[1] *Accordance with International Law of the Unilateral Declaration of Independence in Respect of Kosovo*, ICJ Reports 2010, 403 (hereinafter: 'Opinion'), para. 17.

[2] For more on this, see the contribution of Marko Milanović to this volume.

[3] Opinion, para. 123 (2).

[4] Judge Keith considered that the Court should decline the opinion and was in the minority on that issue, but was part of the majority of ten judges who decided that the DoI was in accordance with international law, see Opinion, para. 123 (2). Judge Koroma was indicated in the operative part of the Opinion as having voted against the decision on discretion, but his separate opinion indicated that he had voted 'in favor of the decision to accede to the request for an advisory opinion'. See, ibid. and Diss. Op. of Judge Koroma, para. 1.

proceedings and, in particular, by the judges who were in the minority on the question of discretion. I will also discuss the repercussions of the Court's decision to give the opinion regardless of various objections as to the propriety of doing so.

## 2. Jurisdiction

A great majority of the participants in the proceedings, including those from the pro-Kosovo camp, supported[5] or at least did not expressly challenge[6] the Court's jurisdiction to provide the opinion. Objections to the jurisdiction were raised solely by Albania and France.[7]

Kosovo, as well as most of the states who were supporting its position, did not expressly raise the question of jurisdiction, but in carefully drafted language questioned the power of the General Assembly to request the opinion and invited the Court to consider whether it should exercise its discretion to accede to the request.[8] Thus, instead of directly challenging the competence of the Court, Kosovo challenged the competence of the General Assembly. One can only speculate that a direct jurisdictional objection by Kosovo could have been perceived as a sign of weakness, implying that Kosovo wanted to avoid the Court's pronouncement on the DoI. In order to avoid this impression, jurisdiction was not questioned, at least not expressly (except by Albania and France). On the other hand, a challenge that appealed to the Court's discretion to refuse an opinion did not raise the same perception of weakness. Being in part based on the argument that Serbia had manipulated the General Assembly to request the opinion,[9] this challenge had the appearance of being motivated by a desire to safeguard the integrity of the Court and the General Assembly, and not by a desire to avoid the Court's opinion on the DoI.

On the question of jurisdiction, the Court first reiterated that its power to give an advisory opinion was based on Article 65, paragraph 1, of the Statute.[10] Then

---

[5] Argentina, Azerbaijan, Cyprus, Egypt, Iran, Ireland, Russia, Serbia, Spain, and Switzerland.

[6] Austria, Bolivia, Brazil, China, Denmark, Estonia, Finland, Germany, Japan, Latvia, Luxembourg, Libya, the Maldives, the Netherlands, Norway, Poland, Romania, Sierra Leone, Slovakia, Slovenia, United Kingdom, and Venezuela.

[7] See Albania WS, para. 41 *et seq.* and France WS, para. 1.1 *et seq.* In the first round of oral proceedings, participating states submitted 'written statements' ('WS'), while in the second round they submitted 'written comments' ('WCM'). 'Authors of the unilateral declaration of independence' submitted 'written contributions' ('WC'). The formula 'authors of the unilateral declaration of independence' was introduced by the Court in order to enable the participation of Kosovo authorities in the proceedings while, at the same time, marking them as clearly distinct from participating states and not taking a position on Kosovo's statehood (see *Accordance with International Law of the Unilateral Declaration of Independence in Respect of Kosovo*, ICJ Reports (2008) 409, at 410, para. 4). The formula closely follows the language of resolution 63/3 by which the General Assembly requested an advisory opinion on DoI. Serbia suggested that the authors should make their submissions under the auspices of UNMIK (Serbia WS, para. 18), which was not accepted by the Court. For the sake of brevity, I will use the term 'Kosovo'.

[8] *Kosovo* WC, para. 7.21.

[9] 'The Republic of Serbia has chosen the way of advisory proceedings in order to influence the actions of Member States rather than the activities of the General Assembly', *Kosovo* WC, para. 7.19.

[10] Opinion, para. 18.

it quoted one of its previous pronouncements on the preconditions for its advisory competence stating that the advisory opinion should be requested by an organ duly authorized under the Charter, that it should be requested on a legal question, and that the question should, except in the case of the General Assembly or the Security Council, be one arising within the scope of the activities of the requesting organ.[11]

After quoting Article 96 of the Charter and referring to its paragraph 1, which authorizes the General Assembly to request an advisory opinion from the Court 'on any legal question', the Court nevertheless indicated that it 'has sometimes in the past given certain indications as to the relationship between the question which is the subject of a request for an advisory opinion and the activities of the General Assembly'.[12] This sentence was a stepping stone for the Court to list provisions of the Charter stipulating activities of the General Assembly: Article 10; Article 11, paragraph 2; and Article 12, paragraph 1. The Court however did not elaborate on how the request would fall under each of these provisions.

Here, one should mark the choice of words used by the Court. 'Sometimes in the past' implies 'not always', while the phrase 'given certain indications' is much softer than saying, for example, 'determined'. This wording indicates that the Court considered that there was no legal requirement to establish in a definitive manner the existence of relationship between the question and the General Assembly activities. At the same time, the issue of whether there should be some relationship between General Assembly activities and the question asked has nevertheless been left open, for otherwise what else would be the purpose of the Court's examination of this relationship?

Neither the Opinion nor previous advisory opinions answer this question, which bears on the interpretation of Article 96 of the Charter. This provision clearly makes a distinction between other United Nations organs and specialized agencies, which may request advisory opinions 'arising within the scope of their activities', and the General Assembly and the Security Council to which this limitation does not apply.[13] On its face, the wording indicates that there is no jurisdictional requirement for there to be a relationship between the subject matter of the opinion and the activities of the General Assembly and the Security Council. The Statute of the Court also does not contain this requirement.

Nevertheless, in *Nuclear Weapons*, some states argued that the General Assembly and the Security Council were not entitled to ask for opinions on matters totally unrelated to their work. The Court declined to say whether this was a correct interpretation of Article 96, paragraph 1, of the Charter, stating that the General

---

[11] Opinion, para. 19 (quoting advisory opinion in *Application for Review of Judgment No. 273 of the United Nations Administrative Tribunal*).

[12] Opinion, para. 21, with references to the Court's case law. This has been criticized: 'The reference to occasional past practice of the Court hardly constitutes a solid foundation for legal analysis', Jacobs, 'International Court of Justice, Accordance with International Law of the Unilateral Declaration of Independence in Respect of Kosovo, Advisory Opinion of 22 July 2010', 60 *ICLQ* (2011) 799, at 800.

[13] 'The General Assembly and the Security Council may request the International Court of Justice to give an advisory opinion on any legal question' (Art. 96, para. 1 of the Charter).

Assembly was in any case competent to ask the question.[14] It further stated that the question had relevance 'to many of the activities and concerns' of the General Assembly and noted its long standing interest in the matter.[15] The same argument about the link between the General Assembly activities and the request was made in the *Wall* case. It was there that the Court first used the non-committal formula also used in the *Kosovo* case[16] and indicated the relevant competences of the General Assembly and its interest in the matter.[17]

In all three advisory opinions, instead of clearly interpreting Article 96, paragraph 1, the Court chose to look for the link between the request and the General Assembly activities. By this it seems that the Court has not excluded, at least not definitively, an interpretation of Article 96, paragraph 1, which would require that there is at least some link between the subject matter of the question asked and the activities of the General Assembly or the Security Council. But the practical consequences of such interpretation would be extremely limited in advisory proceedings initiated by the General Assembly, since the link is likely to be found considering the wide scope of its activities under the Charter.[18]

Albania challenged the competence of the General Assembly to request an opinion on the basis that it was precluded from doing so by Article 12, paragraph 1, of the Charter.[19] This provision prevents the General Assembly from making recommendations with regard to a dispute or situation in respect of which the Security Council is exercising the functions assigned to it in the Charter. Thus, Albania's argument was not that the request was outside the scope of the General Assembly's activities, but that the General Assembly was precluded from making the request by operation of Article 12 of the Charter, because the Security Council was dealing with the matter.

In the *Wall* case, the Court had rejected a challenge that Article 12 of the Charter prevents the General Assembly from seeking an advisory opinion on the matter that was under consideration of the Security Council, and did so after an extensive analysis. Thus, the issue had by and large already been settled. In the *Kosovo* Opinion, the Court dispensed with Albania's Article 12 challenge in one paragraph. With reference to *Wall*, it reiterated that a request for an advisory opinion was not a recommendation within the meaning of Article 12. It then continued by stating that this provision did not in itself limit the authorization to request an advisory opinion, while it might limit the subsequent action of the General Assembly, after the opinion was delivered.[20]

---

[14] *Legality of the Threat or Use of Nuclear Weapons*, ICJ Reports 1996 226 (hereinafter '*Nuclear Weapons*'), at 233, para. 11. See Griffith and Staker, 'The Jurisdiction and Merits Phases Distinguished', in L. Boisson de Chayournes and P. Sands (eds), *International Law, The International Court of Justice and Nuclear Weapons* (Cambridge University Press, 1999) 59, at 67.

[15] *Nuclear Weapons*, para. 12.

[16] *Legal Consequences of the Construction of a Wall in the Occupied Palestinian Territory*, ICJ Reports (2004) 136 (hereinafter: '*Wall*'), at 145, para. 16.

[17] Ibid., para. 17.

[18] See, also, S. Rosenne, *The Law and Practice of the International Court 1920-2005* (Martinus Nijhoff Publishers, 2006) 991; Griffith and Staker, *supra* note 14, at 76.

[19] Albania WS, para. 48 *et seq.*

[20] Opinion, para. 24.

Of course, Albania was aware of *Wall* and tried to distinguish it from the present case.[21] It argued that the only question DoI could raise under international law was its compatibility with Security Council resolution 1244.[22] Assuming that the Court would scrutinize the Security Council resolution as to its compatibility with the Charter and its effect on the question of the DoI, 'this could well create a contradiction with the action of the Security Council'.[23] Essentially, it was asserted that by requesting an advisory opinion on the DoI, the General Assembly would, through the Court's opinion, influence the action of the Security Council, which was precluded by Article 12 of the Charter. This was framed as a jurisdictional challenge, but alternatively was mentioned as an element that needed to be taken into account when the Court was exercising its discretion whether to provide the opinion.[24] From the jurisdictional perspective, this was an attempt to bring Article 12 back into play as a consideration in establishing advisory jurisdiction. However, by saying that the Court, prodded by the General Assembly, may affect the Security Council's exercise of its functions, this argument in fact rewrites Article 12, whose purpose is to prevent the General Assembly, not the Court, from encroaching on the functions of the Security Council. For this reason, this argument is much stronger as a policy consideration in the context of the Court's discretion than as a requirement for jurisdiction.

The Court also addressed the issue whether the question was a 'legal question' as required by Article 96 of the Charter and Article 65 of the Statute. It remarked that the question posed was whether the DoI was in accordance with international law and concluded that '[a] question which expressly asks the Court whether or not a particular action is compatible with international law certainly appears to be a legal question'.[25] In this regard, it invoked its earlier pronouncement in the *Western Sahara* Advisory Opinion that questions 'framed in terms of law and raisi[ing] problems of international law ... are by their very nature susceptible of a reply based on law'.[26]

The Court then addressed a challenge made by France and Albania that the question posed was not in reality a legal question (of international law). In sum, they made the following argument: since international law was not concerned with the conditions in which a State was formed, including the circumstances in which it was 'proclaimed', the question before the Court was not a legal question, as it could not be answered within a genuinely legal framework (*sur un terrain véritablement juridique*), nor should the Court be tasked with determining the validity of

---

[21] France also made an extensive argument distinguishing the *Wall* case, but this was done in the context of discretion and will be discussed below, see France WS, para. 1.28 *et seq.*

[22] Albania WS, para. 50. It also somewhat contradictorily argued that DoI was an internal act, not regulated by international law, and was a matter essentially within the domestic jurisdiction in the sense of Article 2, paragraph 7, of the Charter, see ibid., para. 47. This jurisdictional challenge will be discussed below.

[23] Ibid., para. 52.

[24] See ibid., para. 53; Albania WCM, para. 37. This issue will be discussed below.

[25] Opinion, para. 25      [26] Ibid.

the DoI within any domestic legal order.[27] The Court briefly responded to this by stating that it '[could] respond to [the] question by reference to international law without the need to enquire into any system of domestic law'.[28] When discussing the possible influence of political aspects of the question to its jurisdiction, the Court also noted that it could not refuse to respond to 'the legal elements of the question which invites it to discharge an essentially judicial task, namely, in the present case, an assessment of an act by reference to international law'.[29] The Court's answer and its reiteration of the previous case law indicate that it is ready to interpret the category of 'legal question' in the broadest terms.

Finally, the Court also stated, with reference to its previous opinions, that it was not concerned with the political motives of the question or the political implications its opinion might have.[30] The Court's affirmation of its previous case law confirms the expectation that any challenges concerning the political nature of the question asked from the Court will be rejected in the future.[31]

## 3. Discretion

After finding that it had jurisdiction to answer the request of the General Assembly, the Court turned to the question of its discretion.[32] For clarity, I will summarize the views of the Court and the minority, and will do so in two parts: first, I will discuss how the Court dealt with well-known arguments concerning discretion, such as motives behind the request, its purpose etc.; second, I will deal with the 'separation of powers' argument which was new in the context of discretion.

### A. Restatement and refinement of the basic rules

The Court began by stating its long-held position that the fact that it had jurisdiction did not mean that it was obliged to exercise it. This was followed by a quote from the *Wall* opinion emphasizing the word 'may' in Article 65, paragraph 1, of the Statute and stating that this should be interpreted to mean 'that the Court has a discretionary power to decline to give an advisory opinion even if the conditions of jurisdiction are met'.[33]

---

[27] France WS, paras 1.4–1.5; see, also, Albania WS, paras 41–47. France accepted that international law was concerned with the formation of a new state as a result of the illegitimate use of armed force, but considered that this was not applicable in the case of Kosovo.

[28] Opinion, para. 26.        [29] Ibid., para. 27.        [30] Ibid., para. 27.

[31] See Frowein and Oellers-Frahm, 'Article 65', in A. Zimmermann et al (eds), *The Statute of the International Court of Justice* (2nd edition, OUP, 2012) 1605, at 1615.

[32] The Court firmly adheres to the term 'discretion' in this context, although this has been criticized on the basis that it is not a 'discretionary power' that the Court is exercising but rather application of general conditions of admissibility, see Abi-Saab, 'On Discretion', in L. Boisson de Chayournes and P. Sands (eds), *International Law, The International Court of Justice and Nuclear Weapons* (Cambridge University Press, 1999) 36, at 45. A similar point is also made in the Separate Opinion of Judge Cançado-Trindade, para. 26.

[33] Opinion, para. 29 (quoting *Wall*, para. 44, which in turn refers to *Nuclear Weapons*, para. 14).

Then Court defined the purpose of this discretionary power and did so in the following way:

> The discretion whether or not to respond to a request for an advisory opinion exists so as to protect the integrity of the Court's judicial function and its nature as the principal judicial organ of the United Nations.[34]

The Court viewed its discretion in advisory proceedings as being concerned with two requirements: first, the integrity of its judicial function and, second, its nature as the principal judicial organ of the United Nations. The first requirement was in essence, if not in exact wording, invoked in previous cases as a reason for which the Court could decline an advisory opinion.[35] The second one—the nature of the Court as the principal judicial organ of the United Nations—had previously been invoked as an important consideration *requiring* the Court to provide an advisory opinion. In the *Kosovo* Opinion, the Court also reiterated its previous pronouncements that its answer to a request for an opinion represented its participation in the activities of the United Nations and, in principle, should not be refused, except for 'compelling reasons'.[36] However, by also saying that the 'discretion whether or *not* to respond to a request exists so as to *protect* ... [the Court's] nature as the principal judicial organ of the United Nations' (emphasis added), the Court seems to have allowed that this could also be a justification for refusing to answer a request for an advisory opinion. This may be related to the fact that the institutional balance among the United Nations organs, in which the Court's role as the principal judicial organ plays an important part, was invoked during the deliberations as a reason compelling the Court to exercise its jurisdiction to refuse an opinion.

It should be noted that this pronouncement, although followed by a list of references to previous opinions, from *Eastern Carelia* to *Wall*, is neither a quote nor a paraphrase. Rather, the Court has refined and built upon its previous case law and for the first time articulated in this way the purpose of its discretion in advisory proceedings.[37] Importantly, the essence of this pronouncement was also accepted by the three additional judges who were in a minority on the issue of discretion.[38] In a subsequent advisory opinion, the Court has again referred to the two reasons

---

[34] Ibid., para. 29.

[35] The Court previously used different formulae, as can be seen from the opinions it quotes in this connection in para. 30 of the Opinion. In *Wall*, it referred to its duty to satisfy itself as to the propriety of the exercise of its judicial function, see *Wall*, para. 45. In the cases concerning decisions of UN Administrative Tribunal, the Court spoke of the requirements of its judicial character, see *Application for Review of Judgment No. 158 of the United Nations Administrative Tribunal*, ICJ Reports (1973) 166, at 175, para. 24 and *Application for Review of Judgment No. 273 of the United Nations Administrative Tribunal*, ICJ Reports (1982) 325, at 334, para. 22. Finally, in *Eastern Carelia*, the PCIJ said that '[t]he Court, being a Court of Justice, cannot, even in giving advisory opinions, depart from the essential rules guiding their activity as a Court', *Status of Eastern Carelia*, 1923 PCIJ Series B, No. 5, p. 29.

[36] Opinion, para. 30.

[37] However, the idea that the Court's discretion is guided by these two elements is not a novelty, see S. Rosenne, *supra* note 18, at 975 *et seq.*

[38] See Separate Opinion of Judge Keith, para. 4; Declaration of Judge Tomka, para. 2; Dissenting Opinion of Judge Skotnikov, para. 7.

for its discretion whether to reply to a request for an advisory opinion, but has not used the same formula as in the Opinion in the *Kosovo* case.[39]

The Court's pronouncement on the reasons for the exercise of its discretion is rather general, for which it has been criticized,[40] but it is hard to see how the Court could be more specific without unnecessarily limiting itself in the future. Also, it is submitted that the Court's case law provides sufficient guidelines at least as to what could *not* be considered a compelling reason to exercise discretion to refuse an advisory opinion.

## B.  Old arguments rejected

The Court discussed, and refused to accept, several arguments pointing out why it should exercise its discretion and refuse an opinion. Some of them were relatively easily dismissed in the Opinion, with reference to the Court's previous case law. These will be discussed first.

Many written statements pointed to motives behind the request which was in fact sought 'solely for the benefit of individual States'.[41] They pointed out that Serbia was the sole sponsor of resolution 63/3 by which the General Assembly requested an advisory opinion in the present case. This argument implied that Serbia instrumentalized the General Assembly into requesting and would, by extension, instrumentalize the Court into giving an opinion. Hence, the opinion should be refused. This was illustrated by a helpful statement from Serbia's own foreign minister Jeremić during the General Assembly debate on resolution 63/3, which was also quoted in the Opinion, when he talked about 'the right of any Member State' of the United Nations 'to pose a simple, basic question on a matter it considers vitally important to the Court' and that a vote against the resolution 'would be in effect a vote to deny the right of any country to seek … judicial recourse through the United Nations system'.[42] Nevertheless, the Court stuck to its earlier constant case law that motives of states which sponsored or voted in favour of the request were irrelevant for exercising discretion, as were the origins or the political history of the request.[43]

Similarly, the Court, in one paragraph, rejected the arguments that the General Assembly did not indicate the purpose for which it needed an opinion and that the opinion would not have any useful effect. In this regard, the Court refused to substitute itself for the General Assembly and assess the purpose for which the latter sought the opinion.[44] This was in line with its previous position in *Nuclear*

---

[39] 'In exercising that discretion, the Court has to have regard to its character, both as a principal organ of the United Nations and as a judicial body', *Judgment No. 2867 of the Administrative Tribunal of the International Labor Organization upon a Complaint Filed Against the International Fund for Agricultural Development* (1 February 2012), para. 33.

[40] See Jacobs and Radi, 'Waiting for Godot: An Analysis of the Advisory Opinion on Kosovo', 24 *LJIL* (2011) 331, at 338.

[41] See, e.g., United States WS, p. 44.

[42] A/63/PV.22 (8 Oct. 2008), at 1, quoted in Opinion, para. 32.

[43] Opinion, paras 33–34.          [44] Ibid., para. 34.

*Weapons* and *Wall* advisory opinions, which it quoted. The Court also rejected the argument that the opinion might lead to adverse political consequences. It again refused to substitute itself for the General Assembly in assessing what the consequences of the opinion could be.[45] This position was also based on the Court's previous case law. Two reasons may be invoked in support of this approach. The first is the need to maintain an institutional division between the United Nations organs. Second, if the Court were to assess the purposes and effects of its opinion, this would be a speculative exercise hardly in line with its judicial function, which is to identify, interpret, and apply the law.[46]

## C. A new argument, also rejected

Finally, arguments were made that the Court's opinion would disturb the institutional balance within the United Nations and for that reason should be refused. This was, in effect, a 'separation of powers' argument, which was new and fresh and not pre-empted by the previous advisory opinions. In the context of jurisdiction and discretion, this issue was the one that had drawn most attention during the deliberations of the Court, which is obvious from the space given to it in the Opinion and in separate and dissenting opinions.

The argument itself had not been formulated in the written and oral proceedings in the way it emerged during the deliberations. While the written statement of France contained a discussion trying to distinguish the present case from the *Wall* case with respect to the operation of Article 12 of the Charter,[47] it did not squarely raise the question of the relationship between the principal organs of the United Nations in a way that was to become a major point of contention within the Court. Rather, France's argument was that a number of considerations compelled the Court to decline the opinion, only one of which was that Article 12 of the Charter prevented the General Assembly from taking any action after the opinion (others were: the absence of interest of the requesting organ; the lack of an indication about the use for the opinion; and the lack of activity by the requesting organ with respect to Kosovo).[48] It appears that the 'separation of powers' argument truly gained significance only during the deliberations of the Court, although the debate was obviously inspired by the submissions, in particular those of France, and built upon them. In other words, the full impact of this argument was not really anticipated by the participants in the proceedings.

The Court first noted that this argument was made with reference to the fact that the Security Council had dealt with the situation in Kosovo for more than ten years, exercising its responsibility for the maintenance of international peace and security, and had discussed the DoI but had taken no action in respect to it. At the same time, after Security Council resolution 1244 (1999), the General Assembly adopted only one resolution on the situation of human rights in Kosovo, and a

---

[45] Ibid., para. 35.      [46] See, e.g., *Nuclear Weapons, supra* note 14, at p. 234, para. 13.
[47] See France WS, 1.28–1.42.      48 Ibid., para. 1.42.

number of resolutions dealing with financing of UNMIK, while the broader situation in Kosovo was not part of its agenda at the time DoI was adopted.[49] Against this background and given the respective powers of the two organs, the request should rather have been made by the Security Council. The fact that it was not, was said to constitute a compelling reason to decline the opinion.[50] The Court noted that this conclusion was said to follow from two factors: the nature of the Security Council's involvement in the situation of Kosovo and the fact that the Court would necessarily have to interpret and apply Security Council resolution 1244 (1999) in order to answer the request.[51]

The discussion within the Court had two prongs. On the one hand, it considered the impact of the request and the Court's opinion on the relationship between the General Assembly and the Security Council. On the other hand, it considered the relationship between the Court and the Security Council.

### 1. *Discretion and the relationship between the General Assembly and the Security Council*

The first line of argument in this context essentially concerned the relationship between the two political organs of the United Nations: the nature of Security Council involvement in Kosovo and, connected with it, the lack of Assembly interest in the matter.

This was elaborately discussed in the separate opinion of Judge Keith.[52] He started from the proposition that in exercising its discretion the Court considers 'both its character as a principal organ of the United Nations and its character as a judicial body',[53] which broadly corresponds to the standard accepted by the majority. But then he added that maintaining the Court's integrity as a judicial body, which had so far been emphasized by the Court, was not the only factor that should be considered as a reason to exercise the discretion: '[s]o too may other considerations, including the interest of the requesting organ and the relative interests of other United Nations organs'.[54] For him, the issue before the Court was the appropriateness 'of an organ requesting an opinion if the request is essentially concerned with the actual exercise of special powers by another organ under the Charter, in relation to the matter which is the subject of the request'.[55] After a discussion pointing to the limited involvement of the General Assembly and 'the almost exclusive role' of the Security Council with respect to Kosovo, the separate opinion concluded that, '[g]iven the centrality of that role for the substantive question asked' and the apparent lack of an Assembly interest, the Court should refuse to answer the question.[56] This conclusion was also supported by the argument that, in the absence of the interest of the requesting organ, the duty of the Court

---

[49]  Opinion, paras 38–39.      [50]  Sep. op. Keith, para. 6.      [51]  Opinion, para. 39.
[52]  Judge Keith in 1971 published a book on the advisory jurisdiction of the Court, see K.J. Keith, *The Extent of the Advisory Jurisdiction of the International Court of Justice* (Sijthoff, 1971).
[53]  Sep. op. Keith, para. 4.      [54]  Ibid.      [55]  Ibid., para. 6.      [56]  Ibid., para. 17.

to answer the request disappeared.[57] For Keith, this was the reason why the Court in practice had determined ('if the issue arises'), whether the requesting organ had or claimed to have a sufficient interest in the subject matter of the request.[58]

The Court however thought that the General Assembly did have a legitimate interest in the question, although the request concerned one aspect of a situation which the Security Council characterized as a threat to international peace and security and which continued to be on its agenda. In support of its position, the Court referred to Articles 10 and 11 of the Charter which gave the General Assembly a broad power to discuss matters within the scope of UN activities, including international peace and security, and Article 25 which provided the Security Council with 'primary' but not 'exclusive' responsibility for the maintenance of international peace and security.[59] Further, with reference to *Wall*, the Court noted that Article 12 of the Charter did not bar all action by the General Assembly in respect of threats to international peace and security which were before the Security Council and noted an increasing tendency of the two organs to deal with the same matters in parallel, the General Assembly taking a broader view of the matter, considering its humanitarian, social, and economic aspects.[60]

The Court pointed out that the analysis of the relationship between the Security Council and the General Assembly in the *Wall* opinion had been made in the context of jurisdiction, but that it was equally applicable to the issue of discretion in the present case.[61] The fact that the matter fell within the primary responsibility of the Security Council for the maintenance of international peace and security, and that this organ was dealing with it, did not preclude the General Assembly from addressing the situation or making recommendations within the limits of Article 12. Here, as in *Wall*, the Court also mentioned 'Uniting for Peace' resolution 377A(V) of the General Assembly, which provided that the General Assembly could recommend collective measures to restore international peace and security when the Security Council was unable to act due to the veto of one of its permanent members. This reference made sense because it was precisely because of the lack of unanimity of the permanent members that the Security Council did not make any pronouncement, let alone take any action, with respect to the DoI.[62]

In this context, it should be mentioned that the Court rejected France's argument, which distinguished the situation in *Wall* from the situation of Kosovo *inter alia* on the basis that in the present case the Assembly had not discussed the matter until it considered the request for an advisory opinion, while the Security Council was actively seized of it.[63] This was not considered to be a compelling reason to refuse an opinion, because the purpose of the advisory jurisdiction was to enable the future activity of UN organs. The General Assembly was thus entitled to

---

[57] Ibid., para. 16 and, also, para. 4 (referring to the Court's declaration that the exercise of its judicial function represents its participation in the activities of the Organization and, in principle, should not be refused).

[58] Sep. op. Keith, para. 15.     [59] Opinion, para. 40.     [60] Ibid., para. 41.

[61] Ibid., para. 42.     [62] See ibid., para. 37.     [63] France WS, paras 133 and 137.

discuss the DoI and take action as far as allowed by Article 12 of the Charter.[64] The Court refrained from discussing what that future action might be.

It should be noted that those arguing that the General Assembly had no interest in the subject matter of the request for an advisory opinion pointed both to the Assembly's past activity with respect to Kosovo, i.e. lack thereof, and to the actual impossibility of future activity due to Article 12 of the Charter. The Court, however, did not make any pronouncements on the possible relevance of the past (in)activity of the Assembly. While it referred to the (limited) Assembly activities with respect to Kosovo and noted that the broader situation in Kosovo was not part of its agenda at the time the DoI was adopted,[65] it avoided making any assessment of this fact. It simply moved on, and referred to Articles 10 and 11 as evidence that the General Assembly had sufficient interest in the matter. Of course, this could only be an argument with respect to the existence of such interest in the future but said nothing about the General Assembly's past interest.

Should the Court have taken into account the past activity of the Assembly as the requesting organ, with respect to the subject matter of the request? I think not. An advisory opinion may be sought with the purpose of informing the *future* activity of the requesting organ. In such a situation, it does not make sense to hold the lack of *past* interest against the requesting organ. It is only appropriate to assess whether the requesting organ can take an action in the future on the basis of an opinion. This is exactly what the Court did by looking at the relevant competences of the General Assembly. In addition, there is always a possibility that an assessment of the past interest of a requesting organ in the subject matter of an advisory opinion may lead to examination of that organ's motives or considerations in submitting the request, which is something that the Court has refused to do.[66]

With respect to future action by the General Assembly, the Court was reluctant to be drawn into any substantial assessment of what specific action the Assembly could take or whether it would be possible in light of Article 12 of the Charter. The Court was content that the relevant Charter provisions provide, at least in theory, sufficient formal bases for future action of the Assembly. In my opinion, this approach is unobjectionable. The Court could not, and did not, make any substantial assessment of the General Assembly's future interest and possible activity in the matter, because otherwise it would put itself into the place of this political organ,[67] which, in itself, would disturb the institutional balance within the United Nations and jeopardize the Court's integrity and its judicial function.

Finally, it should be recalled in this context that the Court made a similar inquiry when examining its jurisdiction, where it discussed, with reference to Article 96, paragraph 1, of the Charter, whether there was a relationship between the General

---

[64] Opinion, para. 44.    [65] Ibid., para. 38.

[66] *Admission of a State to the United Nations (Charter, Art. 4)*, ICJ Reports (1948) 57, at 61. See, also, *Interpretation of the Agreement of 25 March 1951 between the WHO and Egypt*, ICJ Reports (1980) 73, at 87, para. 33; *Nuclear Weapons,* at 234, para. 13.

[67] 'The Court cannot determine what steps the General Assembly may wish to take after receiving the Court's opinion or what effect that opinion may have in relation to those steps'. Opinion, para. 44.

Assembly activities and the subject matter of the opinion.[68] A determination of the existence of such relationship, however, appears more appropriate as a consideration in the context of the discretion to refuse an advisory opinion than in the context of jurisdiction. Not only is such an examination relevant in terms of establishing the future interest of the requesting organ, but it also does not entail interpretational difficulties which arise in the context of jurisdiction. As already discussed, these difficulties stem from the language of Article 96 of the Charter, which does not lend much support to construing the existence of such relationship as a precondition for the Court's advisory jurisdiction.

## 2. Discretion and the relationship between the Court and the Security Council

The second line of argument in the context of the 'separation of powers' discussion concerned the relationship between the Court itself and the Security Council. The general point of this argument was that the Court should not make a determination on the compatibility of the DoI with the Security Council resolution 1244 (1999) and the legal regime established thereunder because in this way it would encroach onto the sphere reserved for the Security Council. This was raised in the opinions of Judges Tomka, Skotnikov, and Bennouna, although their reasons were not identical.

In a succinct discussion, Judge Tomka pointed out that, in order to answer the question of the General Assembly, the Court would have not only to interpret but also to apply Security Council resolution 1244, since it would have to make a determination whether the DoI was in accordance with the resolution and the measures adopted thereunder.[69] This determination had not been made by the Security Council, which remained actively seized of the matter.[70] According to Tomka, '[w]ith the answer offered by the majority, the Court takes sides while it would have been judicially proper for it to refrain from doing so'.[71] By answering the General Assembly question, the Court would prejudice the determination, still to be made by the Security Council, on the conformity of the DoI with resolution 1244 and the international regime of territorial administration established thereunder.[72] In support of his argument, he also quoted the words of Manfred Lachs, then President of the Court, in the *Lockerbie* case, that the Security Council and the Court, as the two main organs with the power of binding decisions, should act in harmony when both were performing their functions with respect to a situation or dispute 'different aspects of which appear on the agenda of each, *without prejudicing the exercise of the other's powers*'.[73]

Judge Skotnikov thought that '[w]hen the Court makes a determination as to the compatibility of the DoI with resolution 1244 ... without a request from the

---

[68] See above, text accompanying notes 12–18.     [69] Decl. Tomka, para. 3.

[70] Ibid., para. 4.     [71] Ibid., para. 6.     [72] Ibid., para. 8.

[73] Ibid., para. 7, quoting *Questions of Interpretation and Application of the 1971 Montreal Convention arising from the Aerial Incident at Lockerbie (Libyan Arab Jamahiriya v. United Kingdom)*, ICJ Reports (1992) 3, at 27, (emphasis added by Judge Tomka).

Council, it substitutes itself for the Security Council'.[74] He argued that a determination of the compatibility of an act with a resolution of the Security Council should be made by the Security Council itself, since the resolutions are political decisions and the determination of compatibility is 'largely political'. Thus, according to Skotnikov, 'even if a determination made by the Court were correct in a purely legal sense (which it is not in the present case), it may still not be a right determination from the political perspective of the Security Council'.[75] He also compared the present situation with the one in the cases involving the Federal Republic of Yugoslavia (FRY), where the Court, according to him, refrained from interpreting the relevant resolutions of the General Assembly and Security Council concerning this state's status in the UN, because 'it was clearly not authorized to make a determination on the issue' until the status was clarified with the FRY becoming a UN member in 2000.[76]

However, the Court stated that the fact that it would have to interpret and apply Security Council resolution 1244 (1999) did not constitute a compelling reason not to respond to the question posed by the General Assembly. Starting from its long-standing position that it was, in the first place, the responsibility of the political organs to interpret and apply their decisions, the Court reiterated that, as the principal judicial organ of the United Nations, it had been frequently required to consider the interpretation and legal effects of such decisions.[77] To do so in the present case was therefore not incompatible with the integrity of the judicial function. This conclusion was not affected by the fact that the request did not come from the organ that adopted the decision in question. According to the Court, the situation was similar in two other advisory proceedings, the *Certain Expenses* case and the *Admission* case.[78] Finally, the Court concluded:

> Where, as here, the General Assembly has a legitimate interest in the answer to a question, the fact that that answer may turn, in part, on a decision of the Security Council is not sufficient to justify the Court in declining to give its opinion to the General Assembly.[79]

It appears that the Court confined its reasoning to the general, and rather uncontroversial, question of whether it can interpret and apply decisions of the political

---

[74] Diss. op. Skotnikov, para. 9. He also emphasized the unprecedented nature of the present advisory proceedings, where one organ of the United Nations (General Assembly) posed a question the answer to which was entirely dependent on the interpretation of a decision taken by another United Nations organ (Security Council). With reference to Article 12, he further stated that the General Assembly simply could not benefit from an opinion, because it would be precluded from making any recommendations with regard to the subject matter of the request. Ibid., paras 1–3.

[75] Ibid., para. 9

[76] Ibid., paras 10–11. This analogy is a bit strained as it concerns contentious cases before the ICJ and the issue of access to the Court, and not advisory proceedings and the issue of propriety. Further, the fact that the Court did not make a definitive determination about the status of the Federal Republic of Yugoslavia vis-à-vis the United Nations does not mean that it thought it was not authorized to do so. Indeed, it considered the relevant resolutions of the Security Council and General Assembly but thought that it was not necessary to resolve the issue in a definitive manner when deciding on preliminary measures: see *Application of the Convention on the Prevention and Punishment of the Crime of Genocide (Bosnia and Herzegovina* v. *Yugoslavia)*, ICJ Reports (1993) 3, at 12–14, paras 15–18; see, also, *Legality of Use of Force (Serbia and Montenegro* v. *Belgium)*, ICJ Reports (2004) 279, at 309, para. 74.

[77] Opinion, para. 46.       [78] Ibid., para. 47.       [79] Ibid., para. 47.

organs, *viz.* Security Council resolutions. But it did not address the essential points made by Judges Tomka and Skotnikov—that, in the circumstances of *this* case, the Court's opinion would be an unwarranted and prejudicial intrusion into the internal Security Council process of assessing the DoI (Tomka); or that, by giving the opinion, the Court would substitute itself for the Security Council, which was the only organ that could properly assess the political aspects of such a decision (Skotnikov). In other words, the issue was not whether the Court could interpret and apply a Security Council resolution, as the majority framed it, but whether it should do so when the Security Council was seized of the matter and the request came from the General Assembly.

In this context, one general point needs to be made at the outset. Advisory opinions have no binding force, although they do have the authority of the principal judicial organ of the United Nations behind them.[80] As such, they would certainly be a factor in Security Council deliberations, but, again, an advisory opinion does not bind the Council to adopt a certain decision or prevent it from doing so. Thus, by providing an opinion, the Court would not substitute itself for the Security Council, nor could the opinion, properly speaking, prejudice the Security Council deliberations, although it would undoubtedly be an important factor to be considered by its members.

Moreover, it should be noted that the Court has its own responsibilities in the maintenance of international peace and security. Unlike the General Assembly, which is constrained by Article 12 of the Charter, the Court is not expressly prevented from taking a decision or providing an opinion in a matter which is part of any dispute or situation in relation to which the Security Council is exercising its functions.[81] This was noted in the *United States Diplomatic and Consular Staff in Tehran* case, where the Court stated that the reasons behind this distinction were related to its role as the principal judicial organ of the United Nations, whose task was to resolve any legal questions that might be at issue between the parties and that 'the resolution of such legal questions by the Court may be an important, and sometimes decisive, factor in promoting the peaceful settlement of the dispute'.[82] This was affirmed in the jurisdiction and admissibility judgment in the *Nicaragua* case, where the Court rejected an objection to the admissibility of Nicaragua's application in which the United States *inter alia* claimed that the Security Council was acting with respect to virtually identical claims by Nicaragua and that the matter was essentially one for the Security Council since it concerned a complaint involving the use of force. The Court also stated 'that the fact that a matter is before the Security Council should not prevent it being dealt with by the Court

---

[80] *Interpretation of Peace Treaties*, ICJ Reports (1950) 65, at 71 ('The Court's reply is only of an advisory character: as such, it has no binding force'). See, also, Frowein and Oellers-Frahm, *supra* note 31, at 1415; Aust, 'Advisory Opinions', 1 *Journal of International Dispute Settlement* (2010) 123, at 133.

[81] This point was emphasized by Judge Sepúlveda-Amor, who thought the Court had a duty to exercise its advisory function when the question related to Chapter VII situations, see Sep. op. Sepúlveda-Amor *passim*.

[82] *United States Diplomatic and Consular Staff in Tehran*, ICJ Reports (1980) 3, at 22, para. 40.

and that both proceedings could be pursued *pari passu*'.[83] This position, taken in the context of contentious jurisdiction, seems even more pertinent in the context of requests for an advisory opinion under Article 96, paragraph 1, of the Charter, where the Court's advisory function is triggered by a political organ of the United Nations, and not by individual states. In light of these considerations, the separation of powers arguments invoked by Judges Tomka and Skotnikov lose much of their appeal, which makes it all the more puzzling why they were not answered directly by the Court.

In addition to these general considerations, one should also take into account the specific circumstances of a particular case. Of course, it is desirable that a decision is applied by the political organ that adopted it. However, it is also important that the decision is applied—full stop. In the case under consideration, the Security Council was deadlocked and had been unable to take any decision concerning the status of Kosovo: first, with regard to the Ahtisaari plan[84] and, second, with regard to the proclamation of the DoI.[85] This factor further changes the perspective with respect to the propriety of the Court's refusal to exercise its discretion and deny its opinion in the case at hand. The danger that the Court would affect, let alone prejudice, a determination by the Security Council simply did not exist in the case of the DoI, because the Council was unable to take any decision. In such situation, it was not improper for the Court to render an opinion on the legality of the DoI. Indeed, as the principal judicial organ of the United Nations, having its own responsibilities in the maintenance of international peace and security, it had an additional duty to do so. When all this is taken into account, the decision of the Court not to exercise its discretion to refuse an opinion in the *Kosovo* case seems justified, although the Court's reasoning provided no real answer to the arguments made by Judges Tomka and Skotnikov.

Finally, a related but slightly different line of argument was that, by answering the request, the Court would be dragged into a political debate between supporters and opponents of Kosovo's independence. According to Judge Bennouna, the Court should have declined an opinion in order to protect the integrity of its judicial function. For him, the issue was, above all, to protect the Court against attempts to exploit it in a political debate, rather than protecting the balance between the General Assembly and the Security Council. He lamented that the Court did not decline the request as it could have put a stop to similar 'frivolous' requests that the political

---

[83] *Paramilitary and Military Activities in and against Nicaragua (Nicaragua v. United States)*, ICJ Reports (1984) 392, at 433, para. 93. For a critique of the Court's position and a review of contemporaneous debate, see Norton, 'The *Nicaragua* Case: Political Questions Before the International Court of Justice', 27 *Va. J. Int'l L.* (1986–1987) 459.

[84] See 'Statement issued on 20 July 2007 by Belgium, France, Germany, Italy, United Kingdom and the United States of America, co-sponsors of the draft resolution on Kosovo presented to the UNSC on 17 July', available at <http://www.unosek.org/unosek/en/docref.html> (visited 31 October 2013).

[85] See Opinion, para. 37.

organs might be tempted to submit in the future.[86] He thought that the request in fact asked the Court to set itself up as a political decision-maker, in the place of the Security Council, and to take on the functions of that organ, which the latter had not been able to carry out.[87] Further, the Court could not pronounce on this question without interfering in the political process of maintaining peace and security established by the Security Council with respect to Kosovo.[88]

This argument was not directly answered by the Court, but what the Opinion stated in the context of jurisdiction can be applied here, too. When discussing its jurisdiction, the Court reiterated its long-standing position that the fact that a question had political aspects did not deprive it of its legal character and that the political motives or implications of the question were of no concern.[89]

What here comes to mind are 'political question' considerations on the basis of which courts in some national jurisdictions, notably the United States and England, may decline to deal with a case.[90] It should be noted, however, that not all national jurisdictions adopt this concept, while there are also many differences among and within the jurisdictions where it is adopted.[91] This alone, may be a reason against following this approach, because the Court could find it rather difficult to distil a legal rule from divergent national legal traditions. In any case, this has not been the subject of discussion in the proceedings so, interesting as it may be, further analysis of the 'political question' doctrine and the Court is beyond the scope of this text.

So far, the political dimension of the matter before the Court has not been considered as preventing it from discharging its judicial task with respect to either the contentious or advisory jurisdiction.[92] In the latter context, the Court perceives itself as furnishing the political organs with 'elements of legal character' relevant for their further treatment of the matter.[93] It was not infrequently that advisory cases before the Court had strong political dimensions, starting from the first one, the *Admission* case, dealing with the behaviour of Security Council members in a

---

[86] Diss. Op. of Judge Bennouna, paras 3 and 21; see, also, Sep. op. Tomka, para. 6 ('… the Court has become immersed in the disagreements prevailing in the Security Council …').

[87] Diss. Op. Bennouna, para. 7.     [88] Ibid., para. 16.

[89] Opinion, para. 27. But, see, Aust, *supra* note 80, at 145–51, arguing that exactly this should be the reason for the Court to exercise its discretion and decline an opinion.

[90] For a comparative review of the political question approaches in the United States, England and Israel, see Cohn, 'Form, Formula and Constitutional Ethos: The Political Question/Justiciability Doctrine in Three Common Law Systems' 59 *Am. J. Comp. L.* (2011) 675.

[91] In the United States, the Supreme Court provided general criteria for the 'political question' doctrine in *Baker v. Carr*, 369 US 691, at 317 (1962) but there are disagreements about their application, see, e.g., *Zivotofsky v. Clinton*, 10-699 (2012), concurring opinion of Justice Sotomayor, at 1. In England and Israel, which also adopt a similar doctrine, there is no agreement on the criteria for its application, see Cohn, *supra* note 90, at 688–712.

[92] See United Nations Diplomatic and Consular Staff in Tehran, ICJ Reports (1980) 3, at 20, para. 37, see, also, *Interpretation of the Agreement of 25 March 1951 between the WHO and Egypt*, ICJ Reports (1980) 73, at 87, para. 33.

[93] *Western Sahara*, ICJ Reports (1975) 12, at 37, para. 72.

deadlock over admission of new states members to the United Nations, which was a bitter and politically charged Cold War confrontation.[94] It is also not unusual that political organs or, rather, states which participate in their decisions attempt to use the Court's opinions in their political debate. But it is hard to see how it could be otherwise in the United Nations system, which is inherently politicized. In other words, the Court is dealing with the United Nations organs that are political organs, whose debates are political debates among states, and whose questions have political aspects, which 'in the nature of things, is the case with so many questions which arise in international life'.[95] In that sense, the political character of a legal question before the Court is, unlike in the national legal systems, a rule rather than an exception, so there is even less reason to consider it as a factor of inadmissibility than in the national context, where it is also often not considered as an obstacle to judicial involvement in a case.

## 4. Conclusion

The questions of the Court's jurisdiction and competence in advisory cases may come across as technical, perhaps even dull, and having a rather predictable answer. In the *Kosovo* case, the answer was, again, rather predictable—the Court found that it had jurisdiction and that there were no compelling reasons to prevent it from giving an opinion—but the road to this answer was bumpier than usual. While the Court found unanimously that it had jurisdiction to deal with the General Assembly request, the question whether it should exercise its discretion to decline an opinion in the circumstances of the case sparked a rather interesting debate and resulted in the Court being divided 9:5.

The Opinion has confirmed that the questions of the Court's advisory jurisdiction are by and large settled. What remains an open question is the purpose and effect of the Court's inquiry into the relationship between the General Assembly activities and the subject matter of the opinion in the context of Article 96, paragraph 1, of the Charter. As has been discussed, the Court has so far avoided addressing the issue whether Article 96, paragraph 1, requires that such a relationship must exist. Instead, it has looked for a link between the request and General Assembly activities in the case under consideration, without attempting to interpret this provision. However, this unsettled issue is of a rather limited practical effect, considering the wide scope of the General Assembly activities set out in Articles 10–11 of the Charter.

---

[94] See *Conditions of Admission of a State to Membership in the United Nations (Article 4 of the Charter), supra* note 66.

[95] *Nuclear Weapons,* p. 234, para. 13. Similarly, in the context of a contentious case, the Court stated that 'legal disputes between sovereign States by their very nature are likely to occur in political contexts, and often form only one element in a wider and longstanding political dispute between the States concerned': *United Nations Diplomatic and Consular Staff in Tehran,* ICJ Reports (1980) 3, at 20, para. 37.

With respect to its discretion, the Court reaffirmed its power to decline an opinion for compelling reasons, but, as in previous cases, decided that it should not exercise it. The Court has also refined its previous statements on the purpose of such discretion by stating that it existed to protect the integrity of the Court's judicial function and its nature as the principal judicial organ of the United Nations.

As has been seen, the debate inside the Court primarily focused on whether it should exercise its discretion in order to preserve the institutional balance within the United Nations. The arguments of the judges supporting the exercise of the discretion were twofold and concerned the institutional balance between the General Assembly and the Security Council, on the one hand, and between the Court and the Security Council, on the other.

The Court's approach towards the first issue was rather deferential with respect to the General Assembly. Building upon its previous case law, the Court refrained from drawing any consequences from the considerable lack of interest and (in)activity of the General Assembly with respect to the situation in Kosovo in the past, where the Security Council had continuously been dealing with the matter under Chapter VII of the Charter. The future activity and interest of the General Assembly were assessed only in so far as it was necessary to determine the existence of a legal basis for its future action but the Court refrained from speculating on what that action might be. This shows that the Court approached the issue of the General Assembly interest and action only by looking at its formal competences, which are sufficiently broad to cover almost any request. Apart from that, the Court refrained from considering the impact of the opinion on the relationship between the General Assembly, as the requesting organ, and the Security Council, as the organ seized of the matter under Chapter VII of the Charter. This deferential approach indicates that this path for convincing the Court to refuse an advisory opinion probably cannot be expected to be fruitful in the future.

As regards the second issue—the relationship between the Court and the Security Council—the Opinion framed it as an issue of the interpretation and application of Security Council resolution 1244 (1999) and affirmed that this task was an exercise of its judicial function, so there was no reason to use discretion and decline an opinion. The Court, however, did not address the arguments that by rendering an opinion it would prejudice the Council decision on the DoI or even substitute itself for the Council. Nevertheless, as has been discussed above, the Court's decision not to exercise its discretion was justified.

The perspective from which the Court chose to approach this question and the fact that it had actually not answered some of the pertinent arguments means that this path for invoking the Court's discretion remains open, although ultimately it may not be successful, as the preceding analysis has shown.

# 7

# The Question Question

*Daniel Müller**

## 1. Introduction

The question addressed to the Court in advisory proceedings, and its formulation, is of utmost importance. Indeed, as recalled by the Statute, the 'Court may give an advisory opinion on any legal question' (Article 65, paragraph 1). Its mission is to respond to a specific question and not just to opine on a legal problem, difference, or dispute. Therefore, the requesting body needs to submit 'a written request containing an exact statement of the question upon which an opinion is required' (Article 65, paragraph 2).

The question in advisory proceedings is indeed much more than a simple procedural pre-condition. The formulation and the understanding of the question are essential and crucial because they determine the scope of the opinion and the Court's mission in the proceedings; it also fixes the limits of the Court's task and the issues to be considered.[1] In the absence of a clearly formulated question, the Permanent Court considered that it was necessary and even

essential that it should determine what this question is and formulate an exact statement of it, in order more particularly to avoid dealing with points of law upon which it was not the intention of the Council or the Commission to obtain its opinion.[2]

In the case at hand, the Permanent Court considered that it could undertake this task and itself formulate the question given the relatively simple nature of the case. But it pointed out that 'this, however, may not always be so'.[3]

If, in principle, the Court is bound by the formulation of the question by the requesting body,[4] the Court, as a court of justice, needs also to consider 'whether, in

---

* In the proceedings before the ICJ concerning the *Accordance with International Law of the Unilateral Declaration of Independence in Respect of Kosovo*, the author acted as counsel and advocate representing the Republic of Kosovo. The views and opinions expressed herein are strictly personal and are solely those of the author.

[1] *Voting Procedure on Questions relating to Reports and Petitions concerning the Territory of South West Africa*, Advisory Opinion, ICJ Reports 1955, p. 67, at pp. 71–2.

[2] *Interpretation of the Greco-Turkish Agreement of 1 December 1926 (Final Protocol, Article IV)*, Advisory Opinion, 1928, PCIJ, Series B, No. 16, p. 14.

[3] Ibid.

[4] *Application for Review of Judgment No. 158 of the United Nations Administrative Tribunal*, Advisory Opinion, ICJ Reports 1973, p. 166, at p. 184 (para. 41).

the form in which it has been submitted, [the question] is one which the Court can properly answer'.[5] Under the well-established case law the Court disposes of some liberty in interpreting and clarifying questions which were not adequately formulated.[6] It has even assumed responsibility for reformulating a question in order to give a useful and effective reply on the legal questions really at issue.[7]

The question submitted by the General Assembly under resolution 63/3 of 8 October 2009 concerning the Kosovo issue was relatively short and simple:

Is the unilateral declaration of independence by the Provisional Institutions of Self-Government of Kosovo in accordance with international law?

The Court considered that 'the question posed by the General Assembly [was] clearly formulated'.[8] Nevertheless, it deemed it necessary to discuss some further issues which had arisen during the proceedings. The Court refused to broaden the scope of the question or to reformulate it (Section 2). Nevertheless, and despite the alleged clarity of the terms of the question, the Court deemed it necessary to correct slightly the wording of the question (Section 3) and even to re-interpret some of its aspects (Section 4).

## 2. The Court's Refusal to Broaden the Scope of the Question

Considering the question submitted by the General Assembly, the Court did not deem it necessary to broaden or to reformulate it. It affirmed at the outset that the question was 'narrow and specific',[9] asking 'whether or not the declaration of independence is in accordance with international law'.[10]

A great number of those participating in the proceedings shared this basic understanding about the scope of the question submitted to the scrutiny of the Court. During the written proceedings, most of the participating States,[11] including Serbia as the author of the question,[12] as well as the authors of the declaration

---

[5] *Application for Review of Judgment No. 273 of the United Nations Administrative Tribunal*, Advisory Opinion, ICJ Reports 1982, p. 325, at p. 348 (para. 46).

[6] *Legal Consequences of the Construction of a Wall in the Occupied Palestinian Territory*, Advisory Opinion, ICJ Reports 2004, pp. 153–4 (para. 38).

[7] *Application for Review of Judgment No. 273 of the United Nations Administrative Tribunal*, Advisory Opinion, ICJ Reports 1982, p. 325, at p. 349 (para. 47). See also *Interpretation of the Agreement of 25 March 1951 between the WHO and Egypt, Advisory Opinion*, ICJ Reports 1980, p. 73, at p. 89 (para. 35).

[8] *Accordance with International Law of the Unilateral Declaration of Independence in Respect of Kosovo*, Advisory Opinion, ICJ Reports 2010, p. 403, at p. 423 (para. 51).

[9] Ibid.    [10] Ibid.

[11] Written Statements of the Czech Republic, p. 6; of France, p. 36, para. 2.3; of Austria, p. 3, para. 2; of Egypt, pp. 3–4, para. 7; of Germany, pp. 5–6; of Poland, p. 4, para. 2.1; of Luxembourg, pp. 5–6, paras. 9–12; of the United Kingdom, p. 25, para. 1.16; of the United States of America, pp. 45–6; of Spain, p. 7, para. 6 (iii); of Estonia, p. 2; of Japan, pp. 1 and 2; and of Denmark, p. 2. See also the Written Comments of Norway, p. 3, para. 7; of Germany, p. 3; of the Netherlands, p. 2, para. 2.1; of the United Kingdom, p. 5, para. 9; and of the United States of America, p. 10.

[12] Written Statement of Serbia, pp. 26–27, paras. 19–23; Written Comments of Serbia, p. 28, para. 45.

of independence,[13] recognized that the question was narrow and precise. This was repeated during the oral proceedings.[14]

This overall agreement between the participants to the proceedings concerning the narrowness of the question rather hid the quite obvious disagreements about what the question entailed and what the Court would have to address. In particular, Serbia and those supporting its position submitted that, while the question was narrowly formulated, addressing the legality of the declaration of independence involved not only the declaration per se, but also its intended consequences and effects and their legality under international law.

This position emerged only during the written proceedings. In its first Written Statement, Serbia as the sole sponsor of General Assembly Resolution 63/3 still observed that 'the present request is confined to legal issues and concerns the legality of the [unilateral declaration of independence] under applicable rules of international law. It is no more and no less than this'.[15] Curiously, this was exactly the position of the states that argued that the question should be understood only in its very narrow meaning, i.e., that 'the question here was specifically framed to address solely the act of the declaration of independence'.[16] This very narrow understanding of the question, widely shared, triggered Serbia and its supporters to develop a slightly different argument on the scope of the question. Without openly admitting that the formulation of the question might indeed have been too narrow, Serbia submitted in its Written Comments that 'the [unilateral declaration of independence] is not merely a declaratory act; it is also an attempt to create a new State',[17] and that 'in order to fully consider the question submitted by the General Assembly, the Court should deal with the [unilateral declaration of independence] in a comprehensive manner'.[18] The comprehensive understanding of the narrow question implied, in the view of Serbia and its supporters, quite a lot:

This involves an analysis of the [unilateral declaration of independence] as an act aimed, *inter alia*, at creating a new State and purporting to terminate Serbia's sovereignty and the United Nations administration of Kosovo, as well as the future status process. This immediately raises the question of whether a State was indeed created—as claimed by the authors of the [unilateral declaration of independence] and the States that have recognized

[13] Written Contribution of the Republic of Kosovo, p. 125, para. 7.03, p. 129, para. 7.12 and p. 191, para. 10.16; Further Written Contribution of the Republic of Kosovo, pp. 8–9, paras. 1.18–1.20 and p. 130, para. 6.19.

[14] CR 2009/24, 1 December 2009, p. 41, para. 17 (Djerić (Serbia)); CR 2009/25, 1 December 2009, p. 14, para. 5 (Wood (Kosovo)) and p. 32, para. 7 (Müller (Kosovo)); CR 2009/26, 2 December 2009, p. 10, para. 7 (Frowein (Albania)) and p. 25, para. 4 (Wasum-Rainer (Germany)); CR 2009/27, 3 December 2009, p. 6, para. 3 (Tichy (Austria)); CR 2009/28, 4 December 2009, p. 23, para. 18 (Dimitroff (Bulgaria)); CR 2009/29, 7 December 2009, p. 52, para. 10 (Metelko-Zgombić (Croatia)) and p. 67 (Winkler (Denmark)); CR 2009/30, 8 December 2009, p. 23, para. 2 and p. 36, para. 35 (Koh (United States of America)), p. 40, para. 4 (Gevorgian (Russian Federation)); CR 2009/31, 9 December 2009, p. 9, paras. 4–5 (Belliard (France)), p. 27, para. 3 (Zeid (Jordan)) and p. 44, para. 10 (Fife (Norway)); CR 2009/32, 10 December 2009, p. 46, paras. 1–2 (Crawford (United Kingdom)).

[15] Written Statement of Serbia, p. 26, para. 19. See also Written Statement of Spain, p. 7, para. 6 (iii).

[16] Written Statement of the United States of America, p. 46.

[17] Written Comments of Serbia, p. 27, para. 43.    [18] Ibid., p. 28, para. 45.

the so-called 'Republic of Kosovo'—which leads to an examination that entails both factual and legal elements: whether the so-called constituent elements of statehood are present in the case of the so-called 'Republic of Kosovo', and whether this attempt at creating a new State was in accordance with applicable rules of international law.[19]

Serbia further submitted that 'the question requires the Court to address various aspects of the [unilateral declaration of independence] and the legality of these aspects under international law. These, indeed, [were] the true legal questions that [were] before the Court'.[20] In other words, the conformity of the declaration of independence should have been assessed by the Court against the effects intended and produced by that declaration.

Through this shift of position, Serbia and its supporters confessed that the question, which of course did not refer to the consequences or the legal effects of the declaration of independence and their respective legality under international law, was perhaps formulated too narrowly.[21] However, Serbia did not openly request the Court to broaden the question; this would indeed have been a very strange step by the sole author of the question and the sole sponsor of General Assembly resolution 63/3. Counsel for Serbia preferred to re-introduce the issue of the effects of the declaration as an indispensable element of the assessment of the legality of the declaration itself.

Whether the legal effects of a given act contribute to the issue of the legality of that act is, however, more than doubtful. Serbia itself could not but admit that these were indeed two different issues and confirmed that the question of the legality of the declaration conditions the issue of its legal effects and not *vice versa*: '[S]i la déclaration unilatérale d'indépendance n'est pas conforme au droit international, il s'ensuit qu'elle ne produit pas d'effets'.[22]

The Court came to the conclusion that any issues about the possible consequences of the declaration of independence were not part of the question as formulated. It is noteworthy that the Court did not discuss Serbia's argument concerning an alleged inherent link between the legality of the declaration and the legality of its consequences. It did not even deal with the argument according to which a declaration of independence did not produce any effects under international law because it was an 'ineffective act'.[23] It simply inferred that it was not necessary 'to address such issues as whether or not the declaration has led to the creation of a State or the status of the acts of recognition in order to answer the question put by the General Assembly'.[24] This conclusion was drawn from the mere fact that the General Assembly did

not ask about the legal consequences of that declaration. In particular, it [did] not ask whether or not Kosovo has achieved statehood. Nor [did] it ask about the validity or legal

---

[19] Ibid., pp. 27–28, para. 44. See also Written Comments of Argentina, p. 16, para. 28.

[20] Written Comments of Serbia, p. 28, para. 45.

[21] See also Written Statement of Cyprus, p. 18, para. 73.

[22] CR 2009/24, 1 December 2009, pp. 87–8, para. 30 (Kohen) ('If the Unilateral Declaration of Independence is not in accordance with international law it follows that it is devoid of effect').

[23] See, e.g., CR 2009/32, 10 December 2009, p. 47, para. 5 (Crawford (United Kingdom)).

[24] *Accordance with International Law of the Unilateral Declaration of Independence in Respect of Kosovo*, Advisory Opinion, ICJ Reports 2010, p. 403, at p. 424 (para. 51).

effects of the recognition of Kosovo by those States which have recognized it as an independent State.[25]

The formulation of the question was indeed in sharp contrast to other requests for advisory opinions in which the Assembly expressly sought clarification of the consequences of certain acts or facts.[26]

Of course, '[t]he General Assembly has the right to decide for itself on the usefulness of an opinion in the light of its own needs',[27] and therefore on the formulation of the question submitted. Consequently, 'in giving its opinion the Court is, in principle, bound by the terms of the questions formulated in the request'.[28] However, the Court always reserved the right to modify the scope of the question if that was required by its specific function as a court of justice. In particular, the Court explained:

[I]f it is to remain faithful to the requirements of its judicial character in the exercise of its advisory jurisdiction, it must ascertain what are the legal questions really in issue in questions formulated in a request ... [T]he Court could not adequately discharge the obligation incumbent upon it in the present case if, in replying to the request, it did not take into consideration all the pertinent legal issues involved in the matter to which the questions are addressed.[29]

The judges of the majority reaffirmed the Court's right to depart from the formulation of a question submitted to it 'where the Court determined, on the basis of its examination of the background to the request, that the request did not reflect the "legal questions really in issue"'.[30]

The Court was aware of and could not ignore the fact that the legal questions raised in regard to Kosovo were much broader than the accordance of the declaration of independence per se, and raised difficult and extremely sensitive issues like the status of Kosovo after the declaration of independence. Even if Serbia did not deem it appropriate to include these issues expressly in the formulation of the question—perhaps in order not to damage its chances of gaining the approval of its draft text by the General Assembly, or perhaps in order to avoid any negative implications of an answer by the Court concerning Kosovo's statehood which Serbia's authorities were not ready to accept—the author of the question still tried

---

[25]  Ibid., p. 423 (para. 51).

[26]  See *Legal Consequences for States of the Continued Presence of South Africa in Namibia (South West Africa) notwithstanding Security Council resolution 276 (1970),* Advisory Opinion, ICJ Reports 1971, p. 16 and *Legal Consequences of the Construction of a Wall in the Occupied Palestinian Territory,* Advisory Opinion, ICJ Reports 2004, p. 136.

[27]  *Legality of the Threat or Use of Nuclear Weapons,* Advisory Opinion, ICJ Reports 1996, p. 226, at p. 237 (para. 16).

[28]  *Application for Review of Judgment No. 158 of the United Nations Administrative Tribunal,* Advisory Opinion, ICJ Reports 1973, p. 166, at p. 184 (para. 41); *Voting Procedure on Questions relating to Reports and Petitions concerning the Territory of South West Africa,* Advisory Opinion, ICJ Reports 1955, p. 67, at pp. 71–2. See also Written Statement of Luxembourg, p. 5, paras. 9–10.

[29]  *Interpretation of the Agreement of 25 March 1951 between the WHO and Egypt,* Advisory Opinion, ICJ Reports 1980, p. 73, at pp. 88–9 (para. 35).

[30]  *Accordance with International Law of the Unilateral Declaration of Independence in Respect of Kosovo,* Advisory Opinion, ICJ Reports 2010, p. 403, at p. 423 (para. 50).

to point the Court to the 'true legal questions' in its written[31] and oral pleadings,[32] using the terms of the Court's own case law.

The Court's refusal to assess these 'true legal questions' and its decision to retain the very narrow scope of the question as formulated are probably justified by reasons of judicial policy and judicial economy. It was not the first time that the Court, exercising a sensitive and pragmatic judgment, declined to pronounce on issues which—albeit central, and maybe even the 'legal questions really in issue'— remained very delicate for many states. As early as 1950, the Court declined to respond to the real issue and the true legal question underlying the request for an opinion on the *Competence of the General Assembly for the Admission of a State to the United Nations*, and limited itself to a narrow interpretation of the question submitted to it.[33]

The Court's very limited approach to the question concerning the legality of the declaration of independence might seem unsatisfactory: quite a number of legal problems surrounding the case of Kosovo remained, and still remain, unanswered. But even within Article 96 of the Charter, the Court does not become a gathering of legal scholars which could give their opinion on every interesting or controversial issue of international law. It remains a 'court of justice'[34] and the principal judicial organ of the United Nations, which needs to take into account its role and authority. Under these considerations, the limited and narrow way the Court understood the scope of the question certainly constituted a proper way to navigate around very delicate and controversial issues like the role of international law in the creation of a new state, and Kosovo's statehood or status, in particular in relation to the United Nations and UNMIK. Any other approach would most certainly have jeopardized not only the possibility of reaching a decision by a relatively large majority, but also the chances for the opinion of the Court to be accepted by those directly concerned and, in the end, to be implemented properly. In this regard, it is noteworthy that Serbia's Minister of Foreign Affairs, when himself addressing the General Assembly, had presented the draft resolution and the question as 'represent[ing] the lowest common denominator of the positions of the Member States on this question, and hence there is no need for any changes or additions'.[35]

---

[31] Written Comments of Serbia, p. 28, para. 45. See also note 20 above.

[32] CR 2009/24, 1 December 2009, p. 41, para. 17 (Djerić).

[33] *Competence of the General Assembly for the Admission of a State to the United Nations*, Advisory Opinion, ICJ Reports 1950, p. 4, at p. 7 ('It is not the object of the Request to determine how the Security Council should apply the rules governing its voting procedure in regard to admissions or, in particular, that the Court should examine whether the negative vote of a permanent Member is effective to defeat a recommendation which has obtained seven or more votes').

[34] *Status of Eastern Carelia*, Advisory Opinion, 1923, PCIJ, Series B, No. 5, p. 29; *Constitution of the Maritime Safety Committee of the Inter-Governmental Maritime Consultative Organization*, Advisory Opinion, ICJ Reports 1960, p. 150, at p. 153.

[35] *Official Records of the General Assembly*, Sixty-third session, 22nd plenary meeting, 8 October 2008, A/63/PV.22, p. 2. See also Written Statement of the United States of America, p. 45.

## 3. The Court's 'Corrections' to the Formulation of the Question

Even if the Court did not consider it necessary or appropriate to broaden the scope of the question submitted by the General Assembly, there remained some 'aspects' which, according to the Court, required comment. In particular, the Court was not convinced that, despite the clear and specific formulation of the question, it was appropriate to answer it lock, stock, and barrel.

The principal issue concerned the reference in the question to the 'unilateral declaration of independence by *the Provisional Institutions of Self-Government of Kosovo*' (emphasis added). Indeed, the formulation of the question and the General Assembly resolution containing the request[36] suggested that the identity of the authors of the declaration of independence was beyond any doubt and, therefore, not open to discussion.

However, during the proceedings, the issue concerning the authorship of the declaration of independence emerged as being highly disputed.

Even before the adoption of resolution 63/3 by the General Assembly, the language introduced by Serbia as the sole sponsor of that resolution had attracted comment. In particular, the United Kingdom pointed to the fact that this language and the resulting qualification of the declaration of independence and its authorship was unexplained and 'its relevance and significance remain[ed] unclear'.[37] The United Kingdom drew the attention of the General Assembly to this part of the draft question and to the significant shift that this formulation would possibly entail with regard to the scope and the meaning of the question submitted to the Court:

The agenda item proposed by Serbia requests an advisory opinion on the question of whether 'the unilateral declaration of independence of Kosovo is in accordance with international law'. In contrast, the question formulated in the draft resolution is cast in terms of whether 'the unilateral declaration of independence by the Provisional Institutions of Self-Government of Kosovo [is] in accordance with international law'. It would be useful to know whether Serbia is seeking to focus on a narrower question about the competence of the Provisional Institutions of Self-Government of Kosovo, and, if so, precisely how that question relates to Kosovo's status at the present time.[38]

This statement demonstrates that the formulation of the question by Serbia was far from being 'entirely non-controversial', as Serbia's Minister for Foreign Affairs said during the consideration of the issue in the General Assembly.[39] Indeed, at no

---

[36] As the Court recalled in its opinion, the 'the third preambular paragraph of the General Assembly resolution "[r]ecall[s] that on 17 February 2008 the Provisional Institutions of Self-Government of Kosovo declared independence from Serbia"' (*Accordance with International Law of the Unilateral Declaration of Independence in Respect of Kosovo*, Advisory Opinion, ICJ Reports, p. 403, at p. 424 (para. 52)).

[37] Written Statement of the United Kingdom, p. 18, para. 1.2.

[38] Letter dated 1 October 2008 from the Permanent Representative of the United Kingdom of Great Britain and Northern Ireland to the United Nations addressed to the President of the General Assembly, UN Doc. A/63/461, Annex, para. 7.

[39] *Official Records of the General Assembly*, Sixty-third session, 22nd plenary meeting, 8 October 2008, A/63/PV.22, p. 2.

point was the formulation of the question, and even less the qualification of the declaration of independence, a matter that was discussed by the Assembly or the member states.[40] The Assembly simply endorsed what Serbia considered—wrongly as the Court established on the substance—to be the qualification of the declaration of independence and of its authorship.

Against this background and the extensive arguments put forward during the proceedings concerning the identity of the authors of the declaration of independence, the Court considered it inappropriate to simply rely on this qualification of the declaration of independence as contained in General Assembly resolution 63/3. It opined:

It would be incompatible with the proper exercise of the judicial function for the Court to treat that matter as having been determined by the General Assembly.[41]

As a matter of legal logic, in order to determine whether the declaration of independence was in accordance with international law, the identity of the authors of the declaration cannot just be presumed. This issue constitutes one element which, of course, needed to be taken into account and which was capable, in the abstract, 'of affecting the answer to the question whether that declaration was in accordance with international law'.[42] Independently of the Court's determination of who the authors actually were—which is certainly open to debate and criticism[43]—it remained an issue to be determined by the Court. Ignoring the qualification of the authorship of the declaration, as expressed in the question submitted to the Court, constituted, therefore, a necessary step in order for the Court to dispose of its 'full liberty to consider all relevant data available to it in forming an opinion on a question posed to it for an advisory opinion'.[44]

From the outset, the Court showed some prudence concerning the delicate question of the identification of the authors of the declaration of independence. As early as its Order of 17 October 2008 concerning the organization of the written proceedings, it carefully abstained from expressing any position on that issue and remained eminently neutral in its analysis and wording. Rather than inviting the 'Provisional Institutions of Self-Government of Kosovo' (or the 'Republic of Kosovo') to participate in the proceedings, the Court considered that 'the *authors* of the above declaration are considered likely to be able to furnish information on the question … and decide[d] therefore to invite them to make written contributions to the Court'.[45] During the

---

[40] See ibid., at p. 4 (Albania) and at p. 11 (United Kingdom). See also *Accordance with International Law of the Unilateral Declaration of Independence in Respect of Kosovo*, Advisory Opinion, ICJ Reports 2010, p. 403, at p. 425 (para. 53).

[41] Ibid., p. 424 (para. 52).  [42] Ibid.

[43] See also the contribution of Sean Murphy to this volume.

[44] *Certain Expenses of the United Nations (Article 17, paragraph 2, of the Charter)*, Advisory Opinion, ICJ Reports 1962, p. 151, at p. 157. See also *Accordance with International Law of the Unilateral Declaration of Independence in Respect of Kosovo*, Advisory Opinion, ICJ Reports 2010, p. 403, at p. 425 (para. 54).

[45] *Accordance with International Law of the Unilateral Declaration of Independence by the Provisional Institutions of Self-Government of Kosovo*, Order of 17 October 2008, ICJ Reports 2008, p. 409, at p. 410 (emphasis added).

oral proceedings, the President of the Court continued to refer simply to the 'authors of the Unilateral Declaration of Independence'[46] or even to the 'authors of the unilateral declaration of independence by the Provisional Institutions of Self-Government of Kosovo'.[47] Of course, this formula was most certainly adopted in order to avoid naming the Republic of Kosovo or giving it any appearance as a proper state in the proceedings and prejudging issues to be decided upon. But it is equally remarkable that, with the notable exception of Serbia,[48] no protests were logged against the participation of the authorities of the Republic of Kosovo under the umbrella of the 'authors of the declaration of independence'.

The question remains whether the Court actually modified the question submitted to it by the General Assembly?

Contrary to what Judge Koroma suggested in his dissenting opinion,[49] the Court did not *ab initio* revise the question by enquiring into the issue of the authorship of the existing declaration of independence and by substituting its own assessment for the terms of the question. As far as the interpretation and understanding of the question is concerned, the Court simply put aside the issue of who the real authors of the declaration were. This was treated as a question of the merits only, and indeed, only as far as it was deemed to be relevant under the terms and provisions of Security Council resolution 1244 (1999) and the relevant regulations enforced by UNMIK.[50] The issue was not whether the question was correctly or incorrectly formulated.[51] The question simply included language and qualifications which the Court—rightly—considered to be open to its own judicial assessment, and which therefore were to be disregarded.

This is best shown in the title of the case as modified by the Court *ex post facto*. Indeed, up to the hearings in these advisory proceedings, the name given by the Court to the case was very close to the formulation of the question in General Assembly resolution 63/3: '*Accordance with International Law of the Unilateral Declaration of Independence by the Provisional Institutions of Self-Government of Kosovo*'. Without giving any explanation, a slightly modified title was then adopted for the case which takes account of the Court's 'correction' of the question: '*Accordance with International Law of the Unilateral Declaration of Independence in Respect of Kosovo*'. This new title demonstrates that the Court

---

[46] CR 2009/25, 1 December 2009, p. 6 (President).

[47] CR 2009/24, 1 December 2009, p. 30 (President).

[48] Written Statement of Serbia, p. 26 (para. 18): '[I]nformation by the "authors" of the [unilateral declaration of independence] should be furnished to the Court under the auspices of UNMIK. The participation by the "authors" of the [unilateral declaration of independence] in the present proceedings constitutes a considerable departure from the previous practice of the Court, and raises significant issues under Article 93 of the Charter, as well as Articles 34, 35, and 66, paragraph 2, of the Statute of the Court. Serbia reserves its rights in respect to any participation of the "authors" of the [unilateral declaration of independence] in a way which would be incompatible with Security Council resolution 1244 (1999), general international law and the Statute of the Court'.

[49] Dissenting Opinion of Judge Koroma, ICJ Reports 2010, p. 467, at pp. 467–8 (para. 3).

[50] *Accordance with International Law of the Unilateral Declaration of Independence in Respect of Kosovo*, Advisory Opinion, ICJ Reports 2010, p. 403, at pp. 444–52 (paras. 101–21).

[51] See however, Declaration of Vice-President Tomka, ICJ Reports 2010, p. 454, at p. 460 (para. 21).

did not requalify or modify the qualification of the authors of the declaration by substituting it with its own findings. Simply, the issue of the authorship was not considered to be pre-determined within the formulation of the question.

But did the elimination of this part of the question as such change the meaning and scope of the question submitted by the General Assembly? In his dissenting opinion, Judge Bennouna considered that the majority 'deemed itself authorized to *modify* the wording of the request, to the point of completely altering its meaning and scope'.[52] He was of the opinion that '[t]he General Assembly did not request the Court to give its opinion on just any declaration of independence, but on the one adopted on 17 February 2008 by the Provisional Institutions of Self-Government of Kosovo'. But of course, here is exactly the problem: What if no such declaration was issued by these Provisional Institutions of Self-Government on that date? This was a point which had been made by the authors of the declaration of independence,[53] and which was endorsed by the Court's own independent assessment of the authorship issue?[54] In that case, the Court could at best have opined on the accordance with international law of a non-existent, hypothetical declaration of independence by the Provisional Institutions of Self-Government and, ultimately, on the issue of the competence of the Provisional Institutions of Self-Government established pursuant to the Constitutional Framework on Interim Self-Government adopted as UNMIK Regulation 2001/9. This is obviously a very different question than the one actually submitted by the General Assembly. Even if the Court is certainly empowered within its advisory function to opine on the interpretation of legal instruments in the abstract—and has done so in the past—'the General Assembly does not expect the Court to provide its legal opinion on a question which it has not put to it'.[55]

Not ignoring the qualification concerning the authorship of the declaration of independence contained in the question submitted by General Assembly resolution 63/3 would ultimately have had the unavoidable consequence of converting the question into a purely hypothetical and abstract one. *De facto*, the Provisional Institutions of Self-Government no longer existed at the time the Court was seized by the General Assembly. The Court would certainly have been better advised, under these circumstances, to 'exercise its discretionary power and decline to respond to a question that would no longer have any content or scope'[56]—or at least a very different hypothetical content or scope.

By ignoring the part of the question purporting to name the authors of the declaration of independence, the Court was able to address the 'true legal question'.[57]

---

[52] Dissenting Opinion of Judge Bennouna, ICJ Reports 2010, p. 500, at p. 505 (para. 27) (emphasis added).

[53] See, e.g., CR 2009/25, 1 December 2009, p. 34, para. 11 (Müller (Kosovo)).

[54] *Accordance with International Law of the Unilateral Declaration of Independence in Respect of Kosovo*, Advisory Opinion, ICJ Reports 2010, p. 403, at pp. 444–8 (paras. 102–9). See also the contribution of Sean Murphy to this volume.

[55] Dissenting Opinion of Judge Bennouna, ICJ Reports 2010, p. 500, at p. 507 (para. 32).

[56] Ibid., pp. 506–7 (para. 32).

[57] *Interpretation of the Agreement of 25 March 1951 between the WHO and Egypt*, Advisory Opinion, ICJ Reports 1980, p. 73, at p. 88 (para. 35).

It was most certainly not the intention of the General Assembly to seek an opinion on the issue whether this or that body, however named and established, had or would have been able under international law to declare the independence of Kosovo. Without any doubt, the request concerned the actual declaration issued on 17 February 2008.[58] As the authors of the declaration submitted:

The question before the Court concerns a particular Declaration of Independence that was issued on a particular day in February 2008.[59]

The Court found some support for this proposition in the fact that the title of the agenda item under which resolution 63/3 was discussed and adopted by the General Assembly—and which did not say anything about the authors of the declaration of independence—and the question actually contained in the General Assembly resolution contain one 'common element', i.e., 'whether the declaration of independence is in accordance with international law'.[60] This was the legal question submitted to the Court. Ignoring some parts of the language of the question was indeed a necessary step that the Court was empowered to undertake given that 'the question was not adequately formulated'.[61]

## 4. The Court's 'Interpretation' of the Meaning of the Question

The last issue the Court dealt with concerning the formulation and the meaning of the question submitted by the General Assembly was the understanding of the term 'in accordance with international law'.

Serbia as the author of the question submitted through the General Assembly remained eminently vague on the meaning of 'in accordance with international law'. In its Written Statement, Serbia submitted that 'the present request is confined to legal issues and concerns the legality of the [unilateral declaration of independence] under applicable rules of international law. It is no more and no less than this'.[62] Later, in its Written Comments, the author of the question changed his mind and suggested that 'the question put before the Court is not only limited to determining the legality or illegality of the [unilateral declaration of independence], but more broadly its conformity with international law'.[63] This, it continued, implied that the Court could also examine 'if the [unilateral declaration of independence] by the Provisional Institutions of Self-Government has its legal ground on the basis of a purported right to independence of a so-called "Kosovar people", or whether the existence of the constitutive elements of the State allowed

---

[58] See also Letter dated 15 August 2008 from the Permanent Representative of Serbia to the United Nations addressed to the Secretary-General, Explanatory Memorandum, UN Doc. A/63/195.

[59] CR 2009/25, 1 December 2009, p. 6, para. 2 (Hyseni (Kosovo)).

[60] *Accordance with International Law of the Unilateral Declaration of Independence in Respect of Kosovo*, Advisory Opinion, ICJ Reports 2010, p. 403, at pp. 424–5 (para. 53).

[61] Ibid., at p. 423 (para. 50).

[62] Written Statement of Serbia, p. 26 (para. 19).

[63] Written Comment of Serbia, p. 92 (para. 205).

the authors of the [unilateral declaration of independence] to proclaim their existence as an independent State'.[64]

Others, and in particular those supporting Kosovo, maintained that the question did not require the Court to inquire into the existence of a right or an international law entitlement under which the declaration of independence was authorized.[65] For instance, '[i]n Austria's view the question submitted to this Court is of limited scope: it refers only to the Declaration of Independence and its *legality* under international law ... [T]he question is not whether there exists a *permissive* rule of international law enabling declarations of independence to be made, but whether international law *prohibits* such declarations'.[66] Albania expressed the position that the 'legality of the Declaration of Independence in no way depends upon the necessity of an entitlement to independence for Kosovo based on the right of self-determination'.[67]

The Court largely avoided pronouncing on the issue, as it had done in comparable circumstances before.[68] It simply noted that, contrary to the question submitted to the Supreme Court of Canada, which inquired whether there was a *right* to secession, the General Assembly 'has asked whether the declaration of independence was "in accordance with" international law'.[69] And it continued:

The answer to that question turns on whether or not the applicable international law *prohibited* [in French: *interdisait*] the declaration of independence.[70]

In other words, the Court limited the meaning of the question and of its opinion to whether the declaration of independence in relation to Kosovo violated any rule or principle of international law or, as the Court put it, 'whether or not the declaration of independence was adopted in violation of international law'.[71] It further confirmed that it was

not required by the question it has been asked to take a position on whether international law conferred a positive entitlement on Kosovo unilaterally to declare its independence or, *a fortiori*, on whether international law generally confers an entitlement on entities situated within a State unilaterally to break away from it.[72]

Indeed, it refused to make any comments or finding on the issue of an eventual right for the people of Kosovo to declare independence because, in the opinion of the Court, 'that issue is beyond the scope of the question posed by the General Assembly'.[73]

---

[64] Ibid.
[65] Written Statements of the United Kingdom, p. 24, paras. 1.14–1.15; of Germany, p. 8; of France, p. 36, para. 2.3; of Luxembourg, p. 6, para. 15; of Norway, p. 4, para. 8; or of Ireland, p. 5, para. 18. See also Written Comments of Norway, p. 3, para. 7.
[66] CR 2009/27, 3 December 2009, p. 6, para. 3 (Tichy (Austria)) (emphasis added). See also CR 2009/32, 10 December 2009, p. 37, para. 2 (Bethlehem (United Kingdom)) and Written Comments of Albania, p. 27, para. 45.
[67] CR 2009/26, 2 December 2009, p. 18, para. 3 (Gill (Albania)). See also and CR 2009/25, 1 December 2009, p. 38, para. 18 (Müller (Kosovo)).
[68] *Legality of the Threat or Use of Nuclear Weapons*, Advisory Opinion, ICJ Reports 1996, p. 226, at p. 239 (para. 22).
[69] *Accordance with International Law of the Unilateral Declaration of Independence in Respect of Kosovo*, Advisory Opinion, ICJ Reports 2010, p. 403, at p. 425 (para. 56).
[70] Ibid (emphasis added).   [71] Ibid.   [72] Ibid.   [73] Ibid., p. 438 (para. 83).

This interpretation of the meaning of the question and of the task the Court was entrusted with by the General Assembly is certainly narrow. The term 'in accordance with' has a broader meaning[74] and did not, at the outset, preclude the Court from addressing the existence of a prohibitive rule as well as the possible existence of a permissive rule concerning the declaration of independence. Obviously, the majority of the Court did not want to deal with the extremely sensitive issues of the extent and scope of the right of self-determination or of the existence of a right to remedial secession, and this despite the fact that these points (and others) were extensively referred to and discussed during the proceedings, even by the authors of the declaration of independence—at least as a secondary argument.[75] Whether 'a more comprehensive answer, assessing both permissive and prohibitive rules of international law' would have been necessary and, indeed, beneficial for the authority of the Court's Opinion[76] is difficult to assess in the abstract. There is some merit in the view that, having demonstrated that the declaration of independence did not contravene any rules of international law, answering the question whether the declaration was warranted or authorized by any permissive rule of international law was not necessary in order to provide a useful reply to the General Assembly. But it is certainly possible to doubt whether the outright exclusion of these considerations concerning the more positive aspect of the term 'in accordance with' through a very narrow and formal interpretation of the question was the right way to circumvent—again—more difficult issues.

More damaging is the impression the Court has given on the underlying rationale of its interpretation of the question. In his Separate Opinion, Judge Simma pointed out that the Court, through this interpretation, upheld the *Lotus* principle by equating 'the absence of a prohibition with the existence of a permissive rule'.[77] In other words, the Court based its conclusion on the understanding that because the declaration of independence is not prohibited by international law, it is authorized.

This position was indeed shared by some of the participants in the proceedings. In particular, Croatia suggested:

> By taking into account the presumption of permissibility endorsed by this Court and its predecessor in the cases in which the international legality of a contested action was assessed (such as the *Lotus* case, *Judgment No. 9, 1927, P.C.I.J., Series A, No. 10*) and the *Nuclear Weapons* Advisory Opinion (*I.C.J. Reports 1996 (I)*), Croatia submits that this Declaration is not contrary to international law. In this way it may be said to be 'in accordance with international law'.[78]

Germany presented a comparable analysis on this point and concluded that '[s]ince the Declaration of Independence is not forbidden by international law, it is in accordance with international law'.[79]

---

[74]  Declaration of Judge Simma, ICJ Reports 2010, p. 478, at p. 479 (para. 4).
[75]  CR 2009/25, 1 December 2009, pp. 45–6, paras. 32–3 (Müller).
[76]  Declaration of Judge Simma, ICJ Reports 2010, p. 478, at p. 480 (para. 7); Separate Opinion of Judge Yusuf, ibid., p. 618, at pp. 618–19 (para. 2).
[77]  Declaration of Judge Simma, ibid., p. 478, at p. 479 (para. 3).
[78]  CR 2009/29, 7 December 2009, p. 52, para. 10 (Metelko-Zgombić).
[79]  CR 2009/26, 2 December 2009, p. 29, para. 22 (Wasum-Rainer). See also Written Statement of Germany, p. 8.

It is widely considered that this conception of international law as being simply a residual *corpus* of prohibitive rules limiting the otherwise existing freedom does not correspond to the present-day structure of the international legal order. It is based on an oversimplified and incomplete understanding of the ruling of the Permanent Court in the *Lotus* case.[80] But even if the Permanent Court had established a presumption of freedom—which it did not[81]—that freedom was the direct consequence of sovereignty.[82] It can therefore hardly be transposed to any other actors in the international community—and certainly not to secessionist movements.[83]

The Court did not presume or confirm the existence of such a 'principle of freedom' in its *Kosovo* opinion. A careful reading of the Court's Opinion does not support the conclusion that, not having violated international law, the declaration of independence of Kosovo was authorized by international law or, even, 'in accordance with international law'. The majority framed its response as restrictively as it understood the question:

[T]he declaration of independence of Kosovo adopted on 17 February 2008 *did not violate* international law [*n'a pas violé le droit international*].[84]

It is remarkable that the Court did not deem it necessary or appropriate to draw any other conclusions from its examination of the relevant rules of general international law and Security Council resolution 1244 (1999). In particular, it did not opine that this outcome would necessarily mean that the declaration of independence is in accordance with international law or even that it was authorized under international law. As the majority has pointed out

it is entirely possible for a particular act—such as a unilateral declaration of independence—not to be in violation of international law without necessarily constituting the exercise of a right conferred by it.[85]

In conclusion, it appears that the Court did not simply interpret the ambiguous notion of 'in accordance with international law'. It openly limited the scope of the

---

[80] See Alain Pellet, '*Lotus* que de sottises on profère en ton nom!', in *Mélanges en l'honneur de Jean-Pierre Puissochet: l'État souverain dans le monde d'aujourd'hui* (Paris, 2008), 215–30.

[81] See Ole Spiermann, *International Legal Argument in the Permanent Court of International Justice: the Rise of the International Judiciary* (Cambridge, 2005), 254 ('Literally, the *Lotus* statement did not give expression to a presumption of freedom: it rejected a presumption against freedom. The general principle, which was clearly expressed elsewhere in the judgment, was the residual principle of state freedom ("*liberté*"), not a presumption' (footnotes omitted)).

[82] *Lotus*, Judgment, 1927, PCIJ, Series A, No. 10, p. 4, at p. 18: 'International law governs relations between *independent States*. The rules of law binding upon States therefore emanate from their own free will as expressed in conventions or by usages generally accepted as expressing principles of law and established in order to regulate the relations between these co-existing independent communities or with a view to the achievement of common aims. Restrictions upon *the independence of States* cannot therefore be presumed' (emphasis added).

[83] In this sense, see James Crawford, 'Response to Experts Reports of the Amicus Curiae', in Anne F. Bayefsky (ed.), *Self-Determination in International Law. Quebec and Lessons Learned* (The Hague, 2000), 153–71, at 162.

[84] *Accordance with International Law of the Unilateral Declaration of Independence in Respect of Kosovo*, Advisory Opinion, ICJ Reports 2010, p. 403, at p. 453 (para. 123(3)) (emphasis added). See also ibid., p. 453 (para. 122).

[85] Ibid., p. 426 (para. 56).

question, bringing it down to the issue of illegality and non-illegality. This was the position of many of the participants in the advisory proceedings. And of course, it would have been very difficult for the Court to conclude that the declaration of independence was in accordance with international law: not being within the scope of international law and its rules, it could at best have been not 'not in accordance with international law'. A more open approach to the question itself could indeed have permitted the Court to explore 'the great shades of nuance that permeate international law'.[86] As Judge Simma rightly pointed out in his Separate Opinion:

[T]he Court could have explored whether international law can be deliberately neutral or silent on a certain issue, and whether it allows for the concept of toleration, something which breaks from the binary understanding of permission/prohibition and which allows for a range of non-prohibited options. That an act might be 'tolerated' would not necessarily mean that it is 'legal', but rather that it is 'not illegal' ... Furthermore, that the international legal order might be consciously silent or neutral on a specific fact or act has nothing to do with *non liquet*, which concerns a judicial institution being unable to pronounce itself on a point of law because it concludes that the law is not clear. The neutrality of international law on a certain point simply suggests that there are areas where international law has not yet come to regulate, or indeed, will never come to regulate.[87]

## 5. Concluding Remarks

There is no doubt that the Court showed some sensitivity to the many legal arguments and positions developed during the proceedings concerning the formulation and the scope of the question submitted to it. At the end, the question was not as clearly formulated as one could have thought and as the Court itself pointed out.[88]

The Court commented extensively on the formulation and the scope of the question, as well as about some assumptions, i.e., the identity of the authors of the declaration of independence. It refashioned the question by excluding some elements, i.e., the authorship point, and by restricting the scope of the request to the sole issue of the existence of a violation under international law, rather than accordance with international law.

It is difficult to accept, however, that, in exercising its powers, the Court adjusted beforehand the question 'in order to make it fit a certain mould'[89] or, to put it bluntly, that the Court accommodated its understanding of the question to the answer it was willing to give.[90] On the contrary, it was only the Court's

---

[86] Declaration of Judge Simma, ICJ Reports 2010, p. 478, at p. 481 (para. 9).

[87] Ibid.

[88] *Accordance with International Law of the Unilateral Declaration of Independence in Respect of Kosovo*, Advisory Opinion, ICJ Reports 2010, p. 403, at p. 423 (para. 51).

[89] Dissenting Opinion of Judge Benounna, ICJ Reports 2010, p. 500, at p. 507 (para. 35).

[90] See, e.g., Peter Hilpold, 'The International Court of Justice's Advisory Opinion on Kosovo: Perspectives of a Delicate Question', 14 *Austrian Review of International and European Law* 259–310 (2009), at 289.

interpretation and correction of the question, in particular the issue of the authors of the declaration of independence, which permitted the Court to reply properly to the legal question—or at least one of the legal questions—at issue.

Of course, the Court's Opinion leaves a rather unpleasant aftertaste of incompleteness. Many issues resulting from, or in relation to, the conflict in and about Kosovo were expected to be discussed by the Court. The scope of the principle of self-determination, the right to secession, or the existence of a remedial secession, the powers of the Security Council, the question of statehood and its implications for other States, including recognition, are only some of them.

But here again, it is difficult to blame the Court alone for having reduced the meaning of the question to nothing. The question was not broad in itself. Rather, as the discussions demonstrated, it was an 'anomalous and narrow' question[91] which, obviously, missed the point. From the point of view of Serbia, it was not the right question. Certainly it was a mistake not to discuss the formulation of the question in the General Assembly, at least in order to assess its advantages and inconveniences. With confidence, Serbia submitted itself to the sovereign, but always pragmatic and a little reluctant, judgment of the Court:

We are confident that the Court will know what to do, and that it will take into account the opinions of all interested Member States and international organizations.[92]

Serbia would certainly have been better advised to take into account the position of the United Kingdom, which reflects a sound approach, given the Court's case law concerning the interpretation and reformulation of a question submitted to its scrutiny:

[T]he General Assembly will need to consider carefully the precise formulation of the question submitted to the Court in order to ensure that the Court's answer will be of the greatest value.[93]

---

[91] CR 2009/30, 8 December 2009, p. 37, para. 35 (Koh (United States)).

[92] *Official Records of the General Assembly*, Sixty-third session, 22nd plenary meeting, 8 October 2008, A/63/PV.22, p. 2.

[93] Letter dated 1 October 2008 from the Permanent Representative of the United Kingdom of Great Britain and Northern Ireland to the United Nations addressed to the President of the General Assembly, UN Doc. A/63/461, Annex, para. 7.

# 8

# Reflections on the ICJ Advisory Opinion on Kosovo

## Interpreting Security Council Resolution 1244 (1999)

*Sean Murphy**

## 1. Introduction

A key aspect of the substantive legal arguments in the advisory opinion proceedings, and the focus of paragraphs 85–121 of the Court's opinion, were the meaning and effects of Security Council resolution 1244 (1999) of 10 June 1999.[1] Adopted immediately after the cessation of NATO's bombing campaign against the Federal Republic of Yugoslavia (FRY), which had forced the FRY to agree to withdraw its military and police forces from Kosovo, the resolution served several purposes. First, it brought the United Nations back into play as the central institution for authorizing measures to maintain peace and security in the Balkans. Having been sidelined during the NATO intervention, the Council and the Secretary-General resumed their roles as key decision makers charged with stabilizing the situation in Kosovo.

Second, the resolution set forth the central elements for achieving that objective, notably the deployment of both a military component (NATO's international security force in Kosovo or KFOR) to Kosovo and a civilian component (the UN Mission in Kosovo or UNMIK). The dominant concern of the Council at the time was to establish the role of the international community during the interim period, meaning the period before Kosovo's final status was resolved. In paragraph 1 of resolution 1244, the Council stated that a political solution to the 1999 Kosovo crisis would be based on the general principles expressed in Annexes 1 and 2 to the resolution, which were the principles on which NATO's military campaign was brought to a close. Those principles spoke to ending violence in Kosovo, withdrawal of FRY and Serbian military and police forces from Kosovo,

---

* The author represented Kosovo in the proceedings before the Court, but the views expressed herein are his own. The author expresses his thanks to Anthony Kuhn, G.W. J.D./M.A. '15, who provided outstanding research assistance for this chapter.
[1] SC Res. 1244 (1999).

the deployment of UNMIK and KFOR to Kosovo, the safe return of refugees, the establishment of an interim political framework for the self-government of Kosovo, and efforts toward the economic development of Kosovo. Paragraphs 2 through 4 of the resolution then indicated the various steps for the withdrawal of FRY and Serbian forces, while paragraphs 5 through 11 elaborated on the deployment of the international military and civilian presences to Kosovo. In short, most of the resolution was devoted to the immediate post-conflict phase, detailing the basic elements for the foreign military and civilian presences that would deploy to Kosovo, thereby filling the vacuum brought about by the withdrawal of FRY and Serbian governmental authority.

Third, the resolution briefly addressed the process for determining Kosovo's long-term fate, but this portion of the resolution was vague and under-developed. The only operative part of the resolution relating to final status appears in paragraph 11, which set forth the responsibilities of the international civilian presence. Though most of paragraph 11 is concerned with the interim period, subparagraphs 11(e) and (f) provide that the international civilian presence's responsibilities include:

(e) Facilitating a political process designed to determine Kosovo's future status, taking into account the Rambouillet accords (S/1999/648);

(f) In a final stage, overseeing the transfer of authority from Kosovo's provisional institutions to institutions established under a political settlement.

Hence, a key problem for both sides in the Kosovo proceedings was that most of resolution 1244 was simply not directed at the issue of Kosovo's final status, and the few provisions that were so directed provided little detail.

Even so, in the aftermath of Kosovo's declaration of independence on 18 February 2008, resolution 1244 emerged as a lightning rod for legal arguments on both sides. The resolution was adopted under Chapter VII of the UN Charter and the decisions contained therein were directly binding on all UN Member States. Yet because its language with respect to the final status of Kosovo was vague and incomplete, neither side could make an unassailable argument that resolution 1244 supported its position.

Further, while both sides sought to use the resolution to their advantage, they were fully aware that the Court would approach its interpretation from a perspective that transcended the confines of the case. Neither side could craft its position in a way that impugned the power or authority of the Security Council or of the Secretary-General, for doing so risked an adverse decision from a Court that, in all likelihood, would be disposed to protect the prerogatives of its collateral UN organs. Neither side could advance interpretations of the resolution that were seen as promoting secessionist movements in other contexts, such as Northern Cyprus or Republika Srpska. Further, both sides were aware that if the Court was forced to find that the Council had prohibited Kosovo's declaration, then that would likely necessitate the Court's further consideration of whether Kosovo had a right to 'remedial secession', an issue the Court might prefer to avoid. Indeed, addressing that issue might require the Court to opine on whether a Security Council decision under Chapter VII is invalid if it contravenes a right of self-determination, often viewed as a rule that has acquired the status of *jus cogens*. Finally, both sides had to grapple with the unusual circumstance of applying the resolution to the conduct of a non-state actor. While Security Council resolutions may clearly bind UN Member States, whether they can and do bind persons or groups of persons is far less clear.

This chapter addresses the arguments of both sides and the advisory opinion's substantive ruling on the consistency of Kosovo's declaration with Security Council resolution 1244. Section 2 addresses the five core arguments regarding the legality of the declaration in relation to resolution 1244. Section 3 then examines several ramifications of this portion of the advisory opinion for future interpretation of Security Council resolutions.

## 2. Core Legal Arguments Concerning the Consistency of the Declaration of Independence with Resolution 1244

Although there were many variations in the legal arguments that were made to the Court regarding the interpretation of resolution 1244, there were five core arguments around which those variations revolved. First, did resolution 1244 contain a prohibition, express or implied, on Kosovo's declaration, at least in the absence of Serbia's consent? Second, given that resolution 1244 provided that the final status process must take into account the March 1999 Rambouillet accords, did those accords require Serbian consent to the determination of Kosovo's final status? Third, did the final status process envisaged by resolution 1244, which commenced in 2005 under the auspices of the Special Envoy of the UN Secretary-General (former Finnish President Martti Ahtisaari), conclude prior to the issuance of the declaration, or was it not yet completed such that the declaration was an unlawful interference in that process? Fourth, even if the declaration did not directly violate resolution 1244, was it nevertheless a violation of the legal regime set up in Kosovo under the resolution (e.g., an *ultra vires* act of the Provisional Institutions of Self-Government (PISG) or a contravention of Kosovo's Constitutional Framework for Provisional Self-Government promulgated by the Secretary-General's Special Representative in Kosovo (SRSG) in May 2001)? Finally, what implication, if any, might be drawn from the fact that UN officials—who were authorized to set aside inconsistent measures by authorities in Kosovo—did not set aside the declaration? Did this support the proposition that the issuance of the declaration did not violate resolution 1244 or was it irrelevant to the declaration's legality?

### A. Did resolution 1244 directly prohibit the declaration?

Serbia and those states supporting Serbia's position asserted that resolution 1244 directly prohibited Kosovo's declaration of independence. In advancing this position, Serbia and its supporters emphasized three points.

First, the resolution's preamble reaffirmed 'the commitment of all Member States to the sovereignty and territorial integrity of the Federal Republic of Yugoslavia'.[2] That affirmation was an express recognition by the Security Council that the territorial arrangements in existence as of 1999 would remain intact, at least in the absence of some agreement by the FRY regarding Kosovo's secession. Although the FRY would change over time, renaming itself 'Serbia and Montenegro' in 2003 and consenting to the independence of Montenegro in 2006, the same general principle remained concerning the territorial integrity of Serbia in 2008. As such, the resolution expressly precluded the issuance of Kosovo's declaration of independence.[3] Other aspects of the resolution were also stressed, such as the reference to resolving the humanitarian situation in 'Kosovo, Federal Republic of Yugoslavia' in the fourth paragraph of resolution 1244's preamble,[4] the reference to Kosovo enjoying substantial autonomy 'within the Federal Republic of Yugoslavia' in the tenth operative paragraph,[5] and the provisions allowing for small numbers of Yugoslav and Serbian military and police personnel to return to Kosovo and perform tasks clearly linked with sovereignty.[6]

Second, Serbia and its supporters made extensive reference to the background of resolution 1244, noting that prior UN Security Council resolutions addressing the conflict in Kosovo—such as resolutions 1160 (1998), 1190 (1998), 1203 (1998), and 1239 (1999)—had also expressed a commitment to the sovereignty and territorial integrity of the FRY.[7] Similarly, they pointed to statements made by the Contact Group,[8] the President of the Security Council,[9] the chairman of the meeting of G-8 foreign ministers,[10] and the Military Technical Agreement at the end of NATO's bombing campaign between the KFOR and the FRY[11] as confirming the latter's sovereignty and territorial integrity.

Third, Serbia and its supporters drew a distinction between resolution 1244 and a Security Council resolution adopted the following day,[12] resolution 1246, on the international legal status of East Timor.[13] Resolution 1246 established a UN Mission in East Timor (UNAMET) 'to organize and conduct a popular consultation ... on the basis of a direct, secret and universal ballot, in order to ascertain

---

[2] SC Res. 1244, pmbl. and para. 10.

[3] See First Written Statement of the Government of the Republic of Serbia (17 April 2009), 249, paras. 675–6, *available at* <http://www.icj-cij.org/docket/files/141/15642.pdf> (Serbia First Written Statement); see also First Written Statement of the Republic of Cyprus (17 April 2009), 23, para. 92, *available at* <http://www.icj-cij.org/docket/files/141/15609.pdf> (Cyprus First Written Statement) (stating the 'sovereignty and territorial integrity of Serbia is unambiguously confirmed' in the preamble to resolution 1244 and 'provides the lens through which all other provisions should be interpreted').

[4] See, e.g., First Written Statement of the Kingdom of Spain (14 April 2009), 25, para. 37, available at <http://www.icj-cij.org/docket/files/141/15644.pdf> (Spain First Written Statement).

[5] Ibid.    [6] Ibid.

[7] Ibid., 24, para. 35; Verbatim Record of the Oral Argument of the Government of Serbia (1 December 2009) CR 2009/24, 68, paras. 15–16, available at <http://www.icj-cij.org/docket/files/141/15710.pdf> (Serbia Oral Argument).

[8] Serbia First Written Statement (n 3), 244, para. 658 (noting that the Contact Group—comprising France, Germany, Italy, Russia, the United Kingdom, and the United States—issued a statement supporting an enhanced status for Kosovo within the Federal Republic of Yugoslavia).

[9] Ibid., 244–5, para. 659.    [10] Ibid., 247, para. 667.    [11] Ibid., para. 668.

[12] See Serbia Oral Argument (n 7), 51, para. 9.    [13] SC Res. 1246 (1999).

whether the East Timorese people accept the proposed constitutional framework providing for a special autonomy for East Timor within the unitary Republic of Indonesia or reject the proposed special autonomy for East Timor, leading to East Timor's separation from Indonesia'.[14] According to Serbia, the fact that 'no such provision had been inserted in resolution 1244' showed a lack of support in the Security Council for allowing the unilateral separation of Kosovo.[15] Moreover, Serbia argued that the lack of any such provision, when coupled with the formal reaffirmation of its territorial integrity in 1244, necessarily 'precluded the possibility of Kosovo unilaterally seceding'.[16]

By contrast, Kosovo and those states supporting its position argued that no such prohibition existed in resolution 1244. They noted that there was no reference of any kind in resolution 1244 to a declaration or statement by Kosovo leaders, let alone a reference that prohibited such a declaration. With respect to the preambular language on 'territorial integrity,' Kosovo and its supporters argued that such language referred to territorial integrity 'as set out in Annex 2' of the resolution. In Annex 2, the issue of 'territorial integrity' related solely to the 'interim political framework', not to the point of achieving a final status. As such, the preambular language was relevant to the establishment of the Constitutional Framework for 'Provisional Self-Government' in Kosovo by the SRSG in 2001,[17] which did respect the concept of Kosovo being a part of the FRY during the interim period. Yet, according to Kosovo and its supporters, neither this Constitutional Framework, nor the references to 'territorial integrity' in resolution 1244, purported to address the issue of Kosovo's *final* status. Other arguments were also deployed regarding the preambular language, such as its reference to the 'Federal Republic of Yugoslavia' and not 'Serbia,' and that the principle of territorial integrity related to inter-state relations, not to conduct within a state of a non-state entity.[18]

Kosovo and its supporters also drew contrasts between resolution 1244 and other Security Council resolutions, focusing on resolutions where the Council adopted language that appeared to preclude or at least disfavour the emergence of a new state. Thus, a contrast was made with Security Council resolution 787, which was adopted in 1992.[19] In paragraph 3 of that resolution, the Council considered the possibility of a declaration of independence by the leaders of Republika Srpska within Bosnia-Herzegovina. Apparently concerned that such a declaration might be issued, the Security Council expressly affirmed that it would not accept 'any entities unilaterally declared'. According to Kosovo and its supporters, the lack of any such language in resolution 1244 made clear that the Council did not preclude the possible issuance of a declaration of independence by the representatives of the

---

[14] Ibid., para. 1.      [15] Serbia Oral Argument (n 7), 51, para. 10.      [16] Ibid., para. 11.

[17] Constitutional Framework for Provisional Self-Government in Kosovo, UNMIK Regulation No. 2001/9, 15 May 2001, in Dossier Submitted on Behalf of the Secretary-General pursuant to Article 65, paragraph 2, of the Statute of the International Court of Justice (Dossier), at No. 156.

[18] First Written Contribution of the Republic of Kosovo (17 April 2009), paras. 9.29–9.36, available at <http://www.icj-cij.org/docket/files/141/15678.pdf> (KWC).

[19] SC Res. 787, para. 3 (1992); see *infra* Section 3(D).

people of Kosovo. Further, the Council's approach in resolution 787 (stating that it would not *accept* the declaration rather than forbidding the declaration) was consistent with the contention of Kosovo and its supporters that generally the Security Council does not seek to regulate entities other than states.[20]

To similar effect, contrast was made with resolution 1251 (1999), which was adopted in the same month as resolution 1244. In resolution 1251, the Council considered the situation of northern Cyprus and stated, in paragraph 11, that:

a Cyprus settlement must be based on a State of Cyprus with a single sovereignty and international personality and a single citizenship, with its independence and territorial integrity safeguarded, and comprising two politically equal communities as described in the relevant Security Council resolutions, in a bi-communal and bi-zonal federation, and that such a settlement must exclude union in whole or in part with any other country or any form of partition or secession.[21]

In resolution 1244, by contrast, there was no language indicating that a political settlement for Kosovo had to be based on Serbia or the FRY with a 'single sovereignty and international personality', or that the political settlement must 'exclude secession'.

A third contrast was made with respect to the situation that unfolded in Georgia in 1999. In resolution 1225 of January 1999 and in resolution 1255 of July 1999, the Council expressly called for a 'settlement on the political status of Abkhazia *within the State of* Georgia'.[22] In other words, the Council expressly stated that the settlement must be one that involved Abkhazia remaining within the sovereign state of Georgia. Yet no similar language existed in resolution 1244.

The problem faced by Kosovo and its supporters was that resolution 1244 did not expressly envisage a determination of Kosovo's final status based solely upon a referendum or other measure taken by the people of Kosovo. Yet the problem faced by Serbia and its supporters was that resolution 1244 did not expressly preclude any such outcome. While many states in 1999 probably expected that Kosovo would ultimately remain within Serbia as a (perhaps highly) autonomous province, a different final status of independence was also possible. Hence, Kosovo and its supporters made ample use of statements by relevant actors that resolution 1244 did not, by itself, determine Kosovo's final status.[23] Indeed, many of the key participants in the process, including the Secretary-General,[24] the SRSG,[25] Members of the Security

---

[20] Second Written Contribution of the Republic of Kosovo (17 July 2009), paras. 5.67–5.74, available at <http://www.icj-cij.org/docket/files/141/15708.pdf> (KWC (Second)).

[21] SC Res. 1251, para. 11 (1999).

[22] SC Res. 1225, para. 3 (1999); SC Res. 1255, para. 5 (1999) (emphasis added).

[23] For example, the Legal Counsel of the United Nations at the time, Hans Corell, later opined (in his private capacity) that resolution 1244 per se 'does not guarantee that Serbia would have maintained Kosovo within its border' and 'that the resolution does not foresee that Kosovo should remain within the borders of Serbia'. Corell, 'Remarks', *Proc. Am. Soc. Int'l L.* (2008) 134.

[24] See, e.g., UN Doc. S/2009/300, para. 6.   [25] See, e.g., UN Doc. S/PV.6144, at 4.

Council,[26] and even Serbia itself, referred to resolution 1244 as establishing a 'status-neutral' framework.[27]

Ultimately, the Court accepted the position advanced by Kosovo and its supporters that the resolution did not forbid a declaration of independence. First, the Court agreed that the resolution's preamble did not, in terms, forbid such a declaration. While resolution 1244 'was essentially designed to create an interim régime' for governing Kosovo with a view to settling Kosovo's final status through a political process, it 'did not contain any provision dealing with the final status of Kosovo or with the conditions for its achievement'.[28] Second, citing resolution 1251 on the situation in Cyprus as an example, the Court held that the contemporaneous practice of the Security Council had shown that when it decided to set restrictive conditions on the permanent status of a territory, it specified those conditions in the relevant resolution.[29] Unlike resolution 1251, the Court reasoned that the terms of resolution 1244 'did not reserve for [the Security Council] the final determination of the situation in Kosovo and remained silent on the conditions for the final status of Kosovo'.[30] Third, the Court concluded that resolution 1244 was primarily concerned with creating obligations for UN Member States and UN organs, with two exceptions not relevant to the declaration of independence.[31] Thus, resolution 1244 did not intend to impose 'a specific obligation to act or a prohibition from acting'[32] that would apply to the authors of Kosovo's declaration of independence.[33]

Given that resolution 1244 did not expressly forbid a declaration of independence, Serbia and its supporters also advanced a variation of this argument. Since resolution 1244 contemplated a final status process, conclusion of that process necessarily entailed consent by Serbia (the state in whose territory Kosovo existed) or at least acceptance by the Security Council. Specifically, the terms 'political process' in subparagraph 11(e) and 'political settlement' in subparagraph 11(f) of the resolution had to envisage Serbian consent to Kosovo's final status because the establishment of a political process 'implies that all parties ... have to find a mutually agreeable solution through negotiation'.[34] The fact that resolution 1244 only provided for power to transfer from Kosovo's provisional institutions to institutions established under a 'political settlement' necessarily meant there must be an 'agreement, not a unilateral measure taken by one of the parties'.[35] Moreover,

---

[26] See, e.g., ibid., at 10 (Vietnam); ibid., at 15 (China); ibid., at 19 (Uganda); UN Doc. S/PV.6202, at 20 (China).

[27] See, e.g., UN Doc. S/PV.6202, at 7 (statement of Serbian Foreign Minister Jeremić).

[28] *Accordance with International Law of the Unilateral Declaration of Independence in Respect of Kosovo*, Advisory Opinion, ICJ Reports 2010, 403, 449, para. 114 (*Kosovo* Advisory Opinion); but see Dissenting Op. Judge Koroma, ICJ Reports 2010, 467, 470, para. 11 (finding that 'the declaration of independence violates the provision of that resolution calling for a political solution based on respect for the territorial integrity of the Federal Republic of Yugoslavia and the autonomy of Kosovo'); ibid., 471, para. 13.

[29] *Kosovo* Advisory Opinion (n 28), 449, para. 114.        [30] Ibid.

[31] Ibid., 449–50, para. 115.        [32] Ibid., 450, para. 115.        [33] Ibid., 451, para. 118.

[34] Serbia First Written Statement (n 3), 269, para. 753.

[35] Ibid., para. 754; see also Second Written Statement of the Government of the Republic of Serbia (14 July 2009), 177, para. 437, available at <http://www.icj-cij.org/docket/files/141/15686.pdf> (Serbia Second Written Statement) (noting the term 'settlement' used in resolution 1244 is the same used in the UN Charter, where it precludes unilateral methods).

Serbia and its supporters argued that respect for state sovereignty and territorial integrity is a rule of *jus cogens*, which cannot be undermined by a Security Council resolution without the consent of the state.[36]

In the alternative, they maintained that the interim status of Kosovo under UN administration within Serbia remained in force until the Security Council decided differently.[37] Otherwise, Serbia asked the Court, why would the Security Council have contemplated negotiations in the first place if one side could unilaterally terminate them at will, and why did resolution 1244 provide for the interim regime to stay in place until the Security Council terminated it?[38] This argument maintained that it is not the declaration of independence per se that violated resolution 1244 but, instead, the issuance of such a declaration without Serbia's consent or prior to a Security Council decision to end the final status settlement process.

In response, Kosovo and its supporters maintained that resolution 1244 nowhere provided for approval by Serbia of Kosovo's final status. Had the Security Council decided that such consent must exist prior to resolution of Kosovo's status, they argued that the Council could have said so, but did not. Among other things, they noted that Council resolutions pre-dating resolution 1244 had gone so far as to call for negotiations between Belgrade and Pristina,[39] but that in resolution 1244 even that language was dropped. When the time came—as contemplated by resolution 1244—the United Nations facilitated the final status talks that were launched in 2005 and concluded in 2007, without any resistance or interference from Kosovo authorities.

The Court did not view resolution 1244 as requiring Serbia's consent to Kosovo's independence. Rather, it decided that 'resolution 1244 (1999) clearly establishes an interim régime; it cannot be understood as putting in place a permanent institutional framework in the territory of Kosovo. This resolution mandated UNMIK merely to facilitate the desired negotiated solution for Kosovo's future status, without prejudging the outcome of the negotiating process'.[40] Although it may have been expected that the final status of Kosovo would be developed with the framework established by resolution 1244, the Court appears to have agreed within Kosovo that the resolution only required that UNMIK facilitate a political process and oversee a final transition, while leaving open the contours and outcome of the final settlement process.

## B. Did resolution 1244 indirectly prohibit the declaration through its reference to the Rambouillet accords?

As noted above, paragraph 11(e) of resolution 1244 referred to 'a political process designed to determine Kosovo's future status, taking into account the Rambouillet accords'. The Rambouillet accords were a key backdrop to NATO's intervention

---

[36] Serbia Second Written Statement (n 35), 122, paras. 288–9.
[37] Serbia First Written Statement (n 3), 282–8, paras. 800–23.
[38] Serbia Oral Argument (n 7), 54, para. 26.   [39] KWC (n 18), para. 5.32.
[40] *Kosovo* Advisory Opinion (n 28), 444, para. 99; but see Dissenting Op. Judge Koroma, ICJ Reports 2010, 467, 473, para. 16 (finding that 'reference to a future "settlement" of the conflict, in my view, excludes the making of the unilateral declaration of independence. By definition, "settlement" in this context contemplates a resolution brought about by negotiation').

in Kosovo. In 1998, as the crisis began unfolding in Kosovo, the 'Contact Group' (consisting of France, Germany, Italy, Russia, the United Kingdom, and the United States) tasked US Ambassador Christopher Hill with achieving an agreement that would stabilize the unfolding Kosovo crisis. Hill's efforts led to a draft agreement commonly referred to as the Rambouillet accords, after the château where the negotiations were conducted. Like resolution 1244, the Rambouillet accords envisaged an interim period of substantial Kosovo autonomy followed by a final settlement; indeed, the formal title of the accords was 'Interim Agreement for Peace and Self-Government in Kosovo'. Though never signed by Serbia, and therefore never brought into force, the accords were known to the members of the Security Council in 1999 when they adopted resolution 1244 and hence the reference in paragraph 11(e). Both sides appearing before the Court sought to use those accords to their advantage.

Serbia and its supporters approached the Rambouillet accords by noting that they recalled 'the commitment of the international community to the sovereignty and territorial integrity of the Federal Republic of Yugoslavia',[41] thus supporting the idea that Kosovo would remain a unit within the FRY (or later Serbia). Additionally, they noted that the Rambouillet accords incorporated the Helsinki Final Act as a legal parameter for determining the final status of Kosovo, which *inter alia* provided that 'the frontiers of all States in Europe shall be inviolable',[42] again signalling a desire not to impinge upon the territorial integrity of the FRY. Thus, when resolution 1244 provided for the Rambouillet accords to be taken into account in the political process to determine Kosovo's status, it meant that the Security Council envisaged Kosovo remaining within the sovereignty of the FRY.[43]

For their part, Kosovo and its supporters parsed closely the relevant texts of the four drafts considered during the so-called 'Hill Process' that presaged the Rambouillet accords, in an effort to show that the idea of a Belgrade-Pristina mutual agreement on final status was rejected and replaced with the idea of a final status settlement based on various factors, the first of which was the 'will of the people' of Kosovo.[44] Like resolution 1244 itself, they noted that all four drafts were principally focused on establishing an interim solution, one designed to create the immediate conditions for a return to a peaceful and normal life for the inhabitants of Kosovo. Near the end of the Hill drafts, however, a single clause briefly addressed the process for Kosovo's final status. The first Hill proposal included an express requirement that the final status determination would

---

[41] Serbia First Written Statement (n 3), 277, para. 782 (quoting the Interim Agreement for Peace and Self-Government in Kosovo, pmbl. and para. 4 (Rambouillet accords)); Cyprus First Written Statement (n 3), 23, para. 93.

[42] Ibid. Serbia First Written Statement (n 3), 277, para. 783.

[43] Ibid., para. 784; see also Serbia Oral Argument (n 7), 71–2, para. 25 (arguing the lack of a prohibition on Kosovo declaring independence in the Rambouillet accords was not significant because the territorial integrity of the Federal Republic of Yugoslavia had been repeatedly reaffirmed and it 'would in reality have been redundant to prohibit expressly any attempt at unilateral independence').

[44] KWC (Second) (n 20), paras. 5.05–5.18.

require the 'mutual agreement' of both Belgrade and Pristina.[45] The second[46] and third[47] Hill proposals repeated this final provision almost verbatim. The fourth and final Hill proposal of 27 January 1999, however, was different. Though placed in brackets, it read:

'In three years, there shall be a comprehensive assessment of this Agreement under international auspices with the aim of improving its implementation and determining whether to implement proposals by either side for additional steps, by a procedure to be determined taking into account the Parties' roles in and compliance with this Agreement.'[48]

Kosovo and its supporters noted that in this last version of the Hill proposals, reference to the 'mutual agreement' was dropped, replaced by an approach to Kosovo's final status that would involve a 'comprehensive assessment' under 'international auspices' by a 'procedure' that would 'take into account' the two sides' roles and compliance with the agreement.

Two days later, the Contact Group called upon the parties to meet at Rambouillet for further negotiations. Kosovo and its supporters noted that, like the final Hill proposal, the initial draft of the Rambouillet Interim Agreement did not assert that Kosovo's final status should be determined by 'mutual agreement' between Kosovo and Serbia, or otherwise required Serbia's consent; rather, it drew upon the relevant clause from the final Hill proposal.[49] For the final version of the Rambouillet accords, the clause was further amended to read:

Three years after the entry into force of this Agreement, an international meeting shall be convened to determine a mechanism for a final settlement for Kosovo, *on the basis of the will of the people*, opinions of relevant authorities, each Party's efforts regarding the implementation of this Agreement, and the Helsinki Final Act, and to undertake a comprehensive assessment of the implementation of this Agreement and to consider proposals by any Party for additional measures.[50]

For Kosovo and its supporters, the progression of the text from the first Hill proposal of October 1998 to the final version of the Rambouillet accords of March

---

[45] In the first Hill proposal of 1 October 1998, the relevant clause stated: 'In three years, the sides will undertake a comprehensive assessment of the Agreement, with the aim of improving its implementation and considering proposals by either side for additional steps, *which will require mutual agreement for adoption*'. KWC (Second) (n 20), para. 5.07 (emphasis added).

[46] In the second Hill proposal of 1 November 1998, the relevant clause stated: 'In three years, the sides will undertake a comprehensive assessment of the Agreement, with the aim of improving the implementation and considering proposals by either side for additional steps, which will require mutual agreement for adoption.' KWC (Second) (n 20), para. 5.07.

[47] In the third Hill proposal of 2 December 1998, the relevant clause stated: 'In three years, the Parties will undertake a comprehensive assessment of the Agreement, with the aim of improving its implementation and considering proposals by either side for additional steps, which will require mutual agreement for adoption.' KWC (Second) (n 20), para. 5.07.

[48] Ibid., para. 5.08 (emphasis added).

[49] The first draft of the Rambouillet Interim Agreement, dated 6 February 1999, stated: 'In three years, there shall be a comprehensive assessment of the Agreement under international auspices with the aim of improving its implementation and determining whether to implement proposals by either side for additional steps.' KWC (Second) (n 20), para. 5.12.

[50] Interim Agreement for Peace and Self-Government in Kosovo, 23 Feb. 1999, Chapter 8, Article I(3), in Dossier (n 17) at No. 30 (emphasis added).

1999 demonstrated that the concept of a Belgrade-Pristina mutual agreement on final status had been dropped, and replaced with the idea of a final status settlement based on various factors, the first of which was the 'will of the people' of Kosovo.[51] That interpretation, they contended, was confirmed by Serbia's failed effort to revise the clause noted above so as to read as follows:

After three years, the signatories shall comprehensively review this Agreement with a view to improving its implementation and shall consider the proposals of any signatory for additional measures, *whose adoption shall require the consent of all signatories.*[52]

Since that proposal was rejected at Rambouillet, in part prompting Serbia to reject the Rambouillet accords, Kosovo and its supporters maintained that the accords contemplated a final status process in which the 'will of the people' was assigned a pivotal role, and in which there was no requirement of Serbian consent.

Part of the difficulty for Serbia and its supporters in trying to use the Rambouillet accords to their advantage before the Court was Serbia's rejection of those accords. Indeed, Serbia had stated to the Security Council shortly after the Rambouillet meeting that the 'solution' proposed constituted an 'ultimatum' in which Belgrade was being asked to voluntarily give up Kosovo.[53] Further, in explaining to the Council its rejection of the Rambouillet accords, Belgrade asserted that it 'cannot agree to the secession of Kosovo and Metohija, either immediately or after the interim period of three years'.[54] Kosovo and its supporters pointed to such statements as admissions by Serbia that the Rambouillet accords could not be interpreted as requiring Serbian consent to independence.

The Court seemingly accepted the position advanced by Kosovo and its supporters that the reference to the Rambouillet accords in resolution 1244 did not signal a requirement that Serbia consent to the resolution of Kosovo's final status. After noting that the references to the Rambouillet accords could support the view that resolution 1244 contemplated the possibility of a declaration of independence,[55] the Court avoided discussing the issue in detail by simply deciding that the Security Council did not intend by such a reference to create legal obligations prohibiting the authors of the declaration from proclaiming independence.[56]

---

[51] Judge Skotnikov, after reviewing this language of the Rambouillet accords, found that by 'no stretch of the imagination can a "unilateral statement" be read into this clear policy statement endorsed by the Security Council in its resolution 1244'. Dissenting Op. Judge Skotnikov, ICJ Reports 2010, 515, 520, para. 14.

[52] KWC (n 18), para. 5.13; FRY Revised Draft Agreement, 15 March 1999, Chapter 8, Article 1 (4), reprinted in M. Weller, *The Crisis in Kosovo 1989—1999* (1999), at 489–90 (emphasis added).

[53] UN Doc. S/PV.3989, at 11.

[54] UN Doc. S/PV.3988, at 14.

[55] *Kosovo* Advisory Opinion (n 28), 448, para. 112; but see Dissenting Op. Judge Koroma, ICJ Reports 2010, 467, 471, para. 13 (finding that the Rambouillet accords 'also affirm the sovereignty and territorial integrity of the Federal Republic of Yugoslavia').

[56] *Kosovo* Advisory Opinion (n 28), 450–1.

## C. Was the declaration inconsistent with the political process for final status envisaged by resolution 1244?

If resolution 1244 did not itself directly or indirectly prohibit the issuance of the declaration, might it be said that the resolution nevertheless envisaged the unfolding of a political process for the resolution of Kosovo's final status, a process that was never fulfilled and was even aborted by Kosovo's declaration? If so, then it might be said that the declaration was not 'in accordance' with resolution 1244.

The basic process that occurred was as follows. The Secretary-General's Special Envoy in Kosovo, Ambassador Kai Eide, in October 2005 reported that the interim situation in Kosovo was no longer sustainable and that the final status process should commence, an assessment shared by the Secretary-General.[57] After reviewing Eide's report, the Security Council agreed with that assessment and stated that it supported 'the Secretary-General's intention to start a political process to determine Kosovo's Future Status, as foreseen in Security Council resolution 1244 (1999)' and that it welcomed 'the Secretary-General's readiness to appoint a Special Envoy to lead the Future Status process'.[58]

The Secretary-General proposed the appointment of Ahtisaari as his Special Envoy for supervising the process,[59] an appointment welcomed by the President of the Security Council.[60] In addition, the Security Council provided the Secretary-General, for his 'reference', certain 'guiding principles' for the final status talks that had been developed by the Contact Group. Those principles called for the 'launch' of a 'process to determine the future status of Kosovo in accordance with Security Council resolution 1244' and made clear that this was a process that the Special Envoy would 'lead'. [61] The principles asserted that any 'solution that is unilateral or results from the use of force would be unacceptable', and that the 'final decision on the status of Kosovo "should" be endorsed by the Security Council', but also stated that '[o]nce the process has started, it cannot be blocked and must be brought to a conclusion'.[62] Ahtisaari's terms of reference provided that it was he who would determine the 'duration' of the process.[63]

After receiving his instructions, Ahtisaari set to work and, over the course of fifteen months, conducted extensive negotiations with all the relevant parties,

---

[57] Letter dated 7 October 2005 from the Secretary-General addressed to the President of the Security Council, UN Doc. S/2005/635 (2005), in Dossier (n 17) at No. 193.

[58] Statement by the President of the Security Council, UN Doc. S/PRST/2005/51 (24 Oct. 2005), in Dossier (n 17) at No. 195.

[59] Letter dated 31 October from the Secretary-General addressed to the President of the Security Council, UN Doc. S/2005/708 (10 Nov. 2005), in Dossier (n 17) at No. 196.

[60] Letter dated 10 November 2005 from the President of the Security Council addressed to the Secretary-General, UN Doc. S/2005/709 (10 Nov. 2005), in Dossier (n 17) at No. 197.

[61] Guiding Principles of the Contact Group for a Settlement of the Status of Kosovo, Annex to Letter dated 10 November 2005 from the President of the Security Council addressed to the Secretary-General, UN Doc. S/2005/709 (10 Nov. 2005), in Dossier (n 17) at No. 197.

[62] Ibid.

[63] Letter of Appointment dated 14 November 2005 from the Secretary-General to Martti Ahtisaari with attached Terms of Reference, in Dossier (n 17) at No. 198.

including authorities in Belgrade and Pristina. Most of these meetings took place in Vienna, and while Kosovo and Serbia were clearly central to them, the meetings also involved a wide array of experts from the European Union, NATO, the Council of Europe, the OSCE, international financial institutions, and others. Progress was made on certain issues that needed to be dealt with relating to final status, such as on protection of religious heritage, community rights, decentralization, and economic issues. But on the issue of autonomy versus independence, the two sides' positions remained thoroughly entrenched and diametrically opposed. The government in Belgrade insisted that Kosovo remain a part of Serbia, while the Kosovo authorities, reflecting the long-standing desire of the people of Kosovo, would accept nothing less than independence.

President Ahtisaari determined in March 2007 that nothing more could be accomplished through negotiations. The potential for 'any mutually agreeable outcome' was 'exhausted'. No 'additional talks, whatever the format could overcome the "impasse"'.[64] Rather, Ahtisaari concluded that 'the only viable option' for Kosovo was independence.[65] Consequently, he advanced a 'Comprehensive Proposal for the Kosovo Status Settlement' and recommended independence—a proposal and recommendation supported by the Secretary-General.[66] Efforts to secure Serbian cooperation with that proposal (through a Security Council mission to the region and through the efforts of the Troika) failed. In September 2007, the Secretary-General indicated that there was a 'real risk of progress beginning to unravel and of instability in Kosovo and the region'.[67] In February 2008, Kosovo's leaders declared independence.

Serbia and its supporters argued forcefully that this process was clearly not the one envisaged in resolution 1244. For them, the Contact Group had issued principles for the final status negotiations that did not pre-determine independence for Kosovo; indeed, they stressed key language in those principles to the effect that '[a]ny solution that is unilateral or results from the use of force would be unacceptable' and that the 'Security Council will remain actively seized of the matter. The final decision on the status of Kosovo should be endorsed by the Security Council'.[68] Moreover, they maintained that, from the very beginning of the process, Ahtisaari took the view that independence was the only viable option and thus approached the negotiations in a biased and unfair manner.[69] Hence, the actions of Ahtisaari and certain members of the Contact Group created a setting where Kosovo 'did not have any incentive to consider any compromise solution to

---

[64] Letter dated 26 March 2007 from the Secretary-General addressed to the President of the Security Council, attachment, UN Doc. S/2007/168 (26 Mar. 2007), in Dossier (n 17) at No. 203.

[65] Ibid.

[66] Letter dated 26 March 2007 from the Secretary-General addressed to the President of the Security Council, Addendum, Comprehensive Proposal for the Kosovo Status Settlement, UN Doc. S/2007/168/Add.1 (26 Mar. 2007), in Dossier (n 17) at No. 204.

[67] Report of the Secretary-General on the United Nations Interim Administration Mission in Kosovo, UN Doc. S/2007/582, para. 29 (28 Sept. 2007), in Dossier (n 17) at No. 82.

[68] Serbia Second Written Statement (n 35), 54–5, paras. 103–5.

[69] Ibid., 55–7, paras. 106–9.

the future status but stuck to its position that independence was the only option'.[70] In fact, Serbia and its supporters asserted that the process had not been exhausted: Serbia expressed its continued willingness to negotiate with Kosovo on a wide range of options for the latter's autonomy and self-governance.[71] Finally, despite Ahtisaari's assertions, the Security Council—which had assumed the central role with respect to Kosovo's fate—had not yet determined that negotiations were exhausted,[72] and the refusal of many states to recognize Kosovo as a sovereign state demonstrated that such a determination was necessary. If a stalemate could be said to exist at the Security Council, that alone could not justify unilateral action by one side to resolve Kosovo's status. Thus, the declaration of independence and its unilateral termination of the political process were not in accordance with resolution 1244.

By contrast, Kosovo and its supporters maintained that the political process outlined above was fully in accordance with resolution 1244. Based on the language of the 'Guiding Principles', they argued that the Security Council fully understood in 2005, even in the face of strongly held and quite possibly irreconcilable positions in Belgrade and Pristina, that the Council was launching a political process that could not be blocked and that would have to reach a conclusion at the end of the process. Further, based on the terms of reference given to Ahtisaari, Kosovo and its supporters maintained there was no doubt that Ahtisaari was tasked with deciding when and whether the process had run its course.

Moreover, they emphasized that nowhere in the Secretary-General's recommendation and appointment in 2005 of the Special Envoy, nor in his terms of reference, was it stated that Kosovo's status could only be determined with the approval of Serbia or by a Belgrade-Pristina agreement, nor that final status could only be determined by a further decision of the Security Council. The Council had on many occasions, of course, included in its resolutions a decision that before a particular step could be taken, the matter must come back to the Council for approval. Yet, Kosovo and its supporters noted, no such decision was contained in resolution 1244. Further, they stressed that the conclusion by Ahtisaari about the futility of further negotiations was consistent with the Court's recognition in the *South West* Africa cases that there comes a time in negotiations when 'a deadlock' is reached—when 'both sides remain adamant' in their positions—in which case 'there is no reason to think that

---

[70] Ibid., 58, para. 112; see also Serbia Oral Argument (n 7), 57, para. 44 (stating 'negotiations must not only be based on international law, but must also be facilitated in an unbiased manner').

[71] Serbia Second Written Statement (n 35), 186, para. 467.

[72] Ibid., 189–91, paras. 477–83; Serbia Oral Argument (n 7), 58–9, paras. 48–53 ('[I]t was the Security Council that reinstated its primacy for the maintenance of international peace and security after the unilateral use of military force against the [Federal Republic of Yugoslavia] by adopting resolution 1244. It was the Security Council which, acting under Chapter VII, adopted resolution 1244 and created the current legal status of Kosovo. It was the Security Council that decided that resolution 1244 will continue to be in force until the Council decides otherwise. It was the Security Council that decided to remain actively seised of the matter. It was the Security Council that started the political process for the settlement of the future status of Kosovo. And it is also for the Security Council to decide when this process has come to an end and to then endorse the outcome of the process') (internal citations and paragraph numbering omitted).

the dispute can be settled by further negotiations between the Parties'.[73] Under such circumstances, it could not be said that the declaration contravened paragraph 11 of resolution 1244. Rather, the declaration was an obvious and necessary next step for achieving a final settlement of Kosovo's status, one that flowed directly from the conclusions by the very authorities charged by the Security Council with leading the final status process.

Kosovo's position, however, raised an important question. By issuing the declaration, did Kosovo violate resolution 1244 by terminating, in essence, the functions of UNMIK, a step presumably only the Security Council could take?[74] Kosovo and its supporters noted that the declaration did not in fact terminate or purport to terminate UNMIK's functions, and further stressed that resolution 1244 contemplated a role for UNMIK in the post-interim period, which UNMIK continued to fulfil even after issuance of the declaration. Further, Kosovo pointed out that Serbia itself had accepted that the declaration did not set aside the mandate of UNMIK and that UNMIK continued to perform certain functions after its adoption.[75]

The Court basically accepted the position advanced by Kosovo and its supporters that the issuance of the declaration of independence did not contravene the 'facilitation' of a political process as envisaged in resolution 1244.[76] In the background section of the advisory opinion, the Court found *inter alia* that after Ambassador Eide had submitted his report on Kosovo in 2005 the Security Council had reached consensus that the final status process should begin;[77] that the Secretary-General had then appointed Ahtisaari as his Special Envoy for the process;[78] that several rounds of negotiation between delegates from Serbia and Kosovo were held over

---

[73] *South West Africa (Ethiopia v. South Africa; Liberia v. South Africa), Preliminary Objections,* Judgment, ICJ Reports 1962, 319, 346; see *Mavrommatis Palestine Concessions,* PCIJ Reports 1924, Ser. A, No. 2, 6, 13 (the same); see also R. Jennings and A. Watts (eds), *Oppenheim's International Law* (9th ed 1992), vol. 1, 1182–3 (states 'are under no legal obligation to reach an agreement; nor does any obligation to negotiate necessarily involve an obligation to pursue lengthy negotiations if the circumstances show that such negotiations would be superfluous').

[74] See Dissenting Op. Judge Koroma, ICJ Reports 2010, 467, 470, para. 11 (finding that 'the unilateral declaration of independence is an attempt to bring to an end the international presence in Kosovo established by Security Council resolution 1244 (1999), a result which could only be effected by the Security Council itself'). Judge Koroma pressed the point even further, asserting that 'Kosovo cannot be declared independent while the international civil presence continues to exist and operate in the province. The resolution does not grant the international civil presence the right to alter or terminate the Federal Republic of Yugoslavia's sovereignty over its territory of Kosovo . . .'). Ibid., 472, para. 14.

[75] Serbia First Written Statement (n 3), paras. 827 and 834.

[76] But see Decl. Vice-President Tomka, ICJ Reports 2010, 454, 462, para. 28 ('The notion of a "final settlement" cannot mean anything else than the resolution of the dispute between the parties (i.e., the Belgrade authorities and the Pristina authorities), either by an agreement reached between them or by a decision of an organ having competence to do so. But the notion of a settlement is clearly incompatible with the unilateral step-taking by one of the parties aiming at the resolution of the dispute against the will of the other'); Dissenting Op. Judge Bennouna, ICJ Reports 2010, 500, 513, para. 62 (finding the resolution unlawful because it 'is unilateral, whereas Kosovo's final status must be approved by the Security Council'); Dissenting Op. Judge Koroma, ICJ Reports 2010, 467, 470, para. 11 (stating the 'resolution calls for a negotiated settlement, meaning the agreement of all the parties concerned with regard to the status of Kosovo, which the authors of the declaration of independence have circumvented').

[77] *Kosovo* Advisory Opinion (n 28), 430, para. 64.        [78] Ibid., para. 65.

the course of 2006 and 2007;[79] that Ahtisaari had determined in March 2007 that no amount of talks between the parties would result in an agreement on Kosovo's future status; and that he recommended independence for Kosovo.[80] With this history in mind, the Court held that the declaration of independence did not contravene resolution 1244 because 'the specific contours, let alone the outcome, of the final status process were left open by Security Council resolution 1244', and thus the declaration was not prohibited even though 'it was expected that the final status of Kosovo would flow from ... the framework set up by the resolution'.[81] Judge Skotnikov disagreed: '[T]he Security Council, in the view of the majority, has created a giant loophole in the régime it established under resolution 1244 by allowing for a unilateral "political settlement" of the final status issue.'[82]

## D. Was the declaration inconsistent with the legal regime in Kosovo?

If resolution 1244 did not itself prohibit the declaration of independence, then a further possibility was that the declaration was not 'in accordance with' international law because it was inconsistent with the legal regime in Kosovo, perhaps as an *ultra vires* act of the PISG or a contravention of the regulations adopted by the SRSG on behalf of UNMIK, including the 2001 Constitutional Framework.[83] This line of argument principally entailed two issues: first, was a violation of the legal regime set up in Kosovo after 1999 a violation of *international* law (as referred to in the question put forward by the General Assembly) or was it more akin to a violation of national law?, And, second, if it was the former, were the authors of the declaration actors bound by that regime?

### 1. Kosovo's legal regime as international law

Kosovo and its supporters claimed that, even if *arguendo* the declaration constituted an *ultra vires* act by the PISG or violated the 2001 Constitutional Framework, such action was not a violation of *international* law, but was a violation of the *national* law applicable in Kosovo (that is local law established for the interim administration of Kosovo). In this respect, the declaration would have been *ultra vires* only in the same way that most declarations of independence are—as a contravention of the constitutional or other national law of the state concerned, but not as a contravention of international law.[84]

By contrast, Serbia and its supporters argued that UNMIK regulations, including the Constitutional Framework, were international law. Resolution 1244 established UNMIK as the international civilian presence in Kosovo and empowered the

---

[79] Ibid., 431, paras. 67–8.    [80] Ibid., 431–2, paras. 68–9.
[81] Ibid., 445, para. 104.
[82] Dissenting Op. Judge Skotnikov, ICJ Reports 2010, 515, 520, para. 14.
[83] Constitutional Framework, in Dossier (n 17) at No. 156.
[84] KWC (Second) (n 20), paras. 5.66, 5.73, and 6.34.

SRSG to issue regulations on behalf of UNMIK. Among other things, UNMIK established the PISG and placed the SRSG in a position to oversee compliance of the PISG with the interim arrangements, including the protection of international human rights. UNMIK, therefore, was a subsidiary body of the United Nations and its regulations had an international nature to them.[85] Such regulations were clearly pursuant to UN legal authority, not pursuant to any national or local authority, and hence the nature of the legal regime was international.

Here the Court accepted the position advanced by Serbia and its supporters, finding that:

UNMIK regulations, including regulation 2001/9, which promulgated the Constitutional Framework, are adopted by the Special Representative of the Secretary-General on the basis of the authority derived from Security Council resolution 1244 (1999), notably its paragraphs 6, 10, and 11, and thus ultimately from the United Nations Charter. This Constitutional Framework derives its binding force from the binding character of resolution 1244 (1999) and thus from international law. In that sense it possesses an international legal character.[86]

The Court went on to state that resolution 1244 and the Constitutional Framework 'constituted the international law application to the situation prevailing in Kosovo on 17 February 2008'.[87]

At the same time, in the course of this part of its analysis, the Court indicated that the 'Constitutional Framework functions as part of a specific legal order ... which is applicable only in Kosovo and the purpose of which is to regulate, *during the interim phase* established by resolution 1244 (1999), matters which would ordinarily be the subject of internal, rather than international law'.[88] The Court's emphasis on the limited scope of such 'international law'—geographically limited to Kosovo and temporally limited to just the interim period—was consistent with its characterization of resolution 1244 itself as establishing 'a temporary, exceptional régime', and appears to have played an important part when considering the specific actor that declared independence, as discussed in the next sub-section. In short, the Court appears to have viewed such law as a *sui generis* international legal order.[89]

In his separate opinion, Judge Yusuf disagreed with the Court's analysis; he felt the Constitutional Framework was not a part of international law. In his view, the Court was conflating 'the source of the authority for the promulgation of the Kosovo regulations and the nature of the regulations themselves'.[90] International administrators of territory have a 'dual capacity', such that while 'they act under the authority of international institutions such as the United Nations, the regulations they adopt belong to the domestic legal order of the territory under international

---

[85]  Serbia Oral Argument (n 7), 48, para. 39.
[86]  *Kosovo* Advisory Opinion (n 28), 440, para. 88.     [87]  Ibid., 441, para. 91.
[88]  Ibid., 440, para. 89 (emphasis added).
[89]  See Jacobs and Radi, 'Waiting for Godot: An Analysis of the Advisory Opinion on Kosovo', 24 *Leiden J. Int'l L.* (2011) 331, 341.
[90]  Judge Yusuf, Sep. Op., ICJ Reports 2010, 618, 625, para. 18.

administration'.[91] Among other things, he noted that UNMIK's regulations operated in tandem with the local law in force in Kosovo as of March 1989[92] and that the regulations were simply a 'part of a territorially-based legislation which was enacted solely and exclusively for the administration of that territory'.[93] As such, for Judge Yusuf, there was no need to reach the issue of whether the authors of the declaration were part of the PISG; even if they were, there was no violation of international law.

## 2. *Applicability of Kosovo's legal regime to the authors of the declaration*

Having determined that Kosovo's legal regime was a form of international law, the Court then addressed whether that regime precluded the authors of the declaration from acting as they did. This issue turned principally on whether the authors were acting as the PISG or whether the authors were instead simply a group of democratically-elected leaders of Kosovo undertaking an act that was not an exercise of PISG authority. In addressing that issue, two elements ultimately proved important: what was the entity trying to do and how did it do it?

According to Serbia and its supporters, there was no question that the declaration had been adopted by the PISG. The PISG's Assembly met in its chamber and adopted the declaration on 17 February 2008. Subsequent practice in the form of statements by a variety of relevant actors, including governments, the SRSG, and the Secretary-General, all confirmed the view that it was the PISG Assembly that declared independence. Even the UN General Assembly, when it posed its question to the Court, saw no difficulty in regarding the relevant actor as the PISG.[94] Since resolution 1244 had detailed the scope of the powers to be exercised by the PISG and had conferred on it 'substantial autonomy' and 'self-governance', but not a power to declare independence, then the declaration violated the resolution.[95] Likewise, the Constitutional Framework adopted by the SRSG limited the extent of the external powers to be exercised by the PISG,[96] limitations the declaration flagrantly violated.[97] Finally, Serbia and its supporters also maintained that even if the authors of the declaration were not the PISG, they were still bound by the international legal regime that had been established for Kosovo.[98]

By contrast, Kosovo and its supporters maintained that the declaration was not adopted by the PISG. They noted that the PISG were a series of institutions that

---

[91] Ibid.

[92] Section 1 of UNMIK Regulation 1999/24, as amended by UNMIK Regulation 2000/59, provided that, in addition to UNMIK regulations, the law applicable in Kosovo would be the law in force prior to the abrogation of Kosovo's autonomous status by the FRY in March 1989.

[93] Judge Yusuf Sep. Op., ICJ Reports 2010, 618, 625–6, para. 19.

[94] Serbia Second Written Statement (n 35), 22–6, paras. 32–41.

[95] Serbia First Written Statement (n 3), 306, para. 874.

[96] Ibid., 307, para. 878.     [97] Ibid., 306, paras. 876–7.

[98] Ibid., 26, para. 42; see also Kohen and Del Mar, 'The Kosovo Advisory Opinion and UNSCR 1244 (1999): A Declaration of "Independence from International Law?"' 24 *Leiden J. Int'l L.* (2011) 109, 115.

did not act as a collective, even in their normal functioning. Moreover, even if the Court was to focus on a portion of the PISG (such as the Assembly), Kosovo and its supporters argued that—given the form and content of the declaration and the procedure for adopting it—the declaration differed from the legislative acts normally adopted by the PISG Assembly. Rather, this particular action was of a special and extraordinary nature that simply could not be judged as the act of a body established under the SRSG's provisional Constitutional Framework and charged with day-to-day governing responsibilities in Kosovo during the interim period.[99]

In addition to focusing on the process for adopting the declaration, Kosovo and its supporters emphasized the objective of the declaration. Even if this action of the representatives of Kosovo, meeting as a constituent body, were to be regarded as an action of the PISG Assembly, Kosovo and its supporters maintained that the legality of that action could not be judged against standards set forth in either resolution 1244 or UNMIK regulations for governance during the *interim* period. Since the final status settlement process had concluded, issuance of the declaration was not an act of an interim institution transgressing its limited authority; rather, it was an act of a constituent body declaring in the name of the people its readiness to exercise governing authority on a permanent basis, as contemplated by the political process that unfolded pursuant to resolution 1244.[100]

The Court agreed with Kosovo and its supporters on this point. Interestingly, the Court paid somewhat less attention to the form and procedure for adopting the declaration, and more to the content and purpose of the declaration. The Court agreed that there were some indications that the issuance of the declaration was an act of the PISG Assembly and President of Kosovo, but the Court asserted that the 'larger context' was that the final status negotiations relating to Kosovo had run their course, leaving a situation where resolution of that status was at hand.[101] Resolution 1244 set forth no 'specific contours' for the resolution of that status[102] nor did the Constitutional Framework which, by definition, was concerned with the interim period. By contrast, the declaration, in content and purpose, concerned Kosovo's *final* status, as the Court explained in a key passage:

The declaration of independence reflects the awareness of its authors that the final status negotiations had failed and that a critical moment for the future of Kosovo had been reached. The preamble of the declaration refers to the 'years of internationally-sponsored negotiations between Belgrade and Pristina over the question of our future political status' and expressly puts the declaration in the context of the failure of the final status negotiations, inasmuch as it states that 'no mutually acceptable status outcome was possible' (tenth and eleventh preambular paragraphs). Proceeding from there, the authors of the declaration of independence emphasize their determination to 'resolve' the status of Kosovo and to give the people of Kosovo 'clarity about their future' (thirteenth preambular paragraph). This language indicates that the authors of the declaration did not seek to act within the standard

---

[99]  KWC (n 18), paras. 6.03–6.20.
[100]  Ibid., paras. 6.21–6.33.
[101]  *Kosovo* Advisory Opinion (n 28), 445, para. 104.
[102]  Ibid.

framework of interim self-administration of Kosovo, but aimed at establishing Kosovo 'as an independent and sovereign State' (para. 1). The declaration of independence, therefore, was not intended by those who adopted it to take effect within the legal order created for the interim phase, nor was it capable of doing so. On the contrary, the Court considers that the authors of that declaration did not act, or intend to act, in the capacity of an institution created by and empowered to act within that legal order but, rather, set out to adopt a measure the significance and effects of which would lie outside that order.[103]

The Court went on to note certain aspects of the form and procedure for adopting the resolution, which also suggested that it was not the work of the PISG Assembly as such.[104] Ultimately, the Court concluded that, 'taking all factors together, the authors of the declaration of independence of 17 February 2008 did not act as one of the Provisional Institutions of Self-Government within the Constitutional Framework, but rather as persons who acted together in their capacity as representatives of the people of Kosovo outside the framework of the interim administration'.[105] Given that fact, it followed 'that the authors of the declaration of independence were not bound by the framework of powers and responsibilities established to govern the conduct' of the PISG and that the declaration 'did not violate the Constitutional Framework'.[106] Consequently, there was no need to reach the issue of whether such an act by the PISG would violate Kosovo's legal regime.

This portion of the Court's opinion elicited the greatest and sharpest substantive disagreement among the judges, and also appears to have elicited the greatest criticism from commentators. Vice-President Tomka felt that the Court's conclusion had 'no sound basis in the facts relating to the adoption of the declaration, and is nothing more than a *post hoc* intellectual construct'.[107] Judge Koroma chastised the Court for its reliance on the 'perceived intent' of the authors; relying 'on such intent leads to absurd results, as any given group—secessionists, insurgents—could circumvent international legal norms specifically targeting them by claiming to have reorganized themselves under another name'.[108] For him, such reasoning was 'a kind of judicial sleight-of-hand'.[109] Similarly, Judge Bennouna dryly observed that if the Court's 'reasoning is followed to its end, it would be enough to become an outlaw, as it were, in order to escape having to comply with the law'.[110] Judge Skotnikov agreed, lamenting that the Court did 'not explain the difference between acting outside the legal order and violating it'.[111] Judge Sepúlveda-Amor, who supported the outcome, felt that a more plausible reading of the record, despite the linguistic and procedural peculiarities of the declaration, was that the PISG Assembly *did* adopt the declaration, and therefore the Court should have proceeded to assess the legality of the declaration under Kosovo's legal regime.[112]

| | |
|---|---|
| [103] Ibid., 445–6, para. 105. | [104] Ibid., 446–7, para. 107. |
| [105] Ibid., 447–8, para. 109. | [106] Ibid., 452, para. 121. |

[107] Decl. Vice-President Tomka, ICJ Reports 2010, 454, 456, para. 12.
[108] Dissenting Op. Judge Koroma, ICJ Reports 2010, 467, 469, para. 5.
[109] Ibid., 474, para. 19.   [110] Ibid., 510, para. 46.
[111] Dissenting Op. Judge Skotnikov, ICJ Reports 2010, 515, 521, para. 15.
[112] See, e.g., Sep. Op. Judge Sepúlveda-Amor, ICJ Reports 2010, 491, 498, para. 32.

Two further aspects of this part of the Court's opinion merit mention. First, the Court did not see itself as bound by the factual assertion of the General Assembly contained in the resolution that asked for the Court's advice. The Assembly's resolution recalled that 'on 17 February 2008 the Provisional Institutions of Self-Government of Kosovo declared independence from Serbia' and then asked the Court whether the declaration 'by the Provisional Institutions of Self-Government' was in accordance with international law.[113] Judges Bennouna and Koroma regarded the General Assembly's resolution as evidence that it was the PISG that issued the declaration.[114] The Court, however, stated that it 'would be incompatible with the proper exercise of the judicial function for the Court to treat that matter as having been determined by the General Assembly',[115] and that it must 'examine the entire record and decide for itself'.[116] The Court did not indicate, however, whether such statements were limited to this particular context (a request for advice from the General Assembly regarding conduct of an institution established under Security Council authority) or were equally applicable in other contexts (such as a request for advice from the Security Council that implicated a factual determination in a Chapter VII resolution).

Second, although the Court did not say as much, its conclusion that the authors of the declaration 'acted together in their capacity as representatives of the people of Kosovo'[117] may have been necessary so as to distinguish the situation in Kosovo from other situations where a minority regime has declared a new state for the purpose of minority rule, as occurred in 1965 in Southern Rhodesia.[118] Yet, as one critic notes, while 'pointing out that the authors of the declaration had the capacity to act as representatives of the people of Kosovo, the Court ignored the crucial question, namely from where this capacity derives. It derives from the institutions of self-government'.[119]

### E. What significance should be accorded to the reactions of UN officials charged with overseeing implementation of resolution 1244?

Resolution 1244 charged the international civilian presence in Kosovo with 'overseeing the development of provisional democratic self-governing institutions in Kosovo'.[120] Further, the Constitutional Framework adopted by the SRSG stated that he would take 'appropriate measures whenever [PISG] actions are inconsistent with UNSCR 1244 (1999) or this Constitutional Framework'.[121] Prior to the

---

[113] GA Res. 63/3 (2008).
[114] Dissenting Op. Judge Bennouna, ICJ Reports 2010, 500, 506, para. 29; Dissenting Op. Judge Koroma, ICJ Reports 2010, 467, 468, para. 3.
[115] *Kosovo* Advisory Opinion (n 28), 424, para. 52.
[116] Ibid., 425, para. 54.      [117] *Supra* note 109.      [118] See *infra* Section 3(D).
[119] Vidmar, 'The Kosovo Advisory Opinion Scrutinized', 24 *Leiden J. Int'l L.* (2011) 355, 361.
[120] SC Res. 1244, para. 11(c) (1999).
[121] Constitutional Framework, Chapter 12, in Dossier (n 17) at No. 156.

2008 declaration of independence, the SRSG had taken steps on several occasions to prevent or set aside actions or declarations by Kosovo authorities that constituted a move toward independence.[122] Yet neither the SRSG nor the Secretary-General himself set aside the 2008 declaration or declared it null and void. Thus, the two sides in the Kosovo proceedings were confronted with an important issue: what significance should be accorded to such inaction?

Serbia and its supporters argued that the inaction was simply not relevant when assessing the legality of the declaration. For them, the Secretary-General and the SRSG were acting—or rather not acting—in Kosovo under the overall authority of the Security Council, and it was common knowledge that its members disagreed on the question of whether the declaration was legal or illegal.[123] As such, the Secretary-General and the SRSG were simply acting neutrally and nothing could be surmised from that posture. Furthermore, resolution 1244 did not oblige the Security Council to act to identify a breach of that resolution. When coupled with the inability to act due to the divergent views of its members, the Security Council's inaction could not be interpreted as tacit recognition of the legality of the declaration.[124] They also asserted that, after the declaration, the SRSG had continued to amend draft laws of the PISG, which demonstrated that the SRSG did not accept Kosovo as now independent,[125] and that the Secretary-General and the SRSG were waiting for a legal opinion on Kosovo's declaration from the Undersecretary-General for Legal Affairs of the United Nations, which could explain their inaction.[126]

By contrast, Kosovo and its supporters argued that the failure by the 'supreme administrative authority'[127] in Kosovo to set aside the declaration had to weigh heavily against Serbia's claim that the declaration violated resolution 1244. They noted that the SRSG and other UN officials were fully aware of the declaration and the possibility that it violated the UN civilian presence in Kosovo. Indeed, after issuance of the declaration, Serbia formally demanded that the Secretary-General take steps to have the declaration set aside by instructing the SRSG to that effect. The Secretary-General did not do so. Nor did the Security Council, either by resolution or through a statement of its President, take any steps to instruct the Secretary-General or his representatives to set aside the declaration. As such, according to Kosovo and its supporters, such inaction supported the proposition that the issuance of the declaration did not violate resolution 1244.[128]

The Court found that the silence of the SRSG in the face of the declaration of independence was of 'some significance' because it suggested the SRSG did not consider the declaration to be an act of the PISG designed to take effect under resolution 1244's legal order.[129] Had the SRSG thought otherwise, the Court

---

[122] KWC (n 18), paras. 9.24–9.26.
[123] Serbia Second Written Statement (n 35), 192–3, para. 488.
[124] Ibid., 195, paras. 493–4.     [125] Ibid., 192, para. 487.
[126] Ibid., 194, para. 490.
[127] Serbia First Written Statement (n 3), paras. 895–6.
[128] KWC (n 18), paras. 9.20–9.28.
[129] *Kosovo* Advisory Opinion (n 28), 447, para. 108.

reasoned, practice had shown the SRSG would have found the act to be incompatible with the Constitutional Framework.[130] Judge Bennouna, however, was not convinced, finding that:

the deadlock in the United Nations bodies during the process to determine Kosovo's future status does not justify the conclusion that a unilateral declaration of independence hitherto not in accordance with international law is suddenly deserving of an imprimatur of compliance. In fact, the reason why the Special Representative of the Secretary-General took no action was not that he considered the declaration to be in accordance with international law, but simply that the political body to which he was answerable was unable to reach a decision on advancing in the process under way to determine the future status of Kosovo.[131]

Likewise, in his declaration, Vice-President Tomka highlighted what he saw as a conundrum with the Court's position: 'why acts which were considered as going beyond the competences of the Provisional Institutions in the period 2002–2005, would no longer have any such character in 2008, despite the fact that provisions of the Constitutional Framework on the competencies of these institutions have not been amended and have remained the same in February 2008 as they were in 2005'.[132]

## 3. Broader Ramifications of the Advisory Opinion for Interpretation and Application of Security Council Resolutions

Having recounted in some detail the five core arguments regarding the legality of the declaration in relation to resolution 1244, this part turns to several especially important ramifications of the Court's analysis for future interpretation and application of Security Council resolutions.

### A. Security Council resolutions as *lex specialis*

While this chapter is not focused on the Court's treatment of general international law, the Court's approach to that law in relation to resolution 1244 bears mention. Arguably, resolution 1244 constituted a form of *lex specialis* that should have largely or wholly displaced general international law. Even if resolution 1244 left open the determination of Kosovo's final status, the Security Council had 'entered the field' sufficiently—in its displacement of FRY military and police authority in Kosovo, its establishment of an internationally-administered interim regime, and its assigning to the SRSG the task of promoting the final status negotiations—such that whatever rules of general international law that normally exist had now been overtaken.

---

[130] Ibid.; but see Vidmar (n 119), at 380 (suggesting an alternative possibility: the SRSG did not think the declaration violated the existing legal regime whether or not it was issued by the PISG).
[131] Dissenting Op. Judge Bennouna, ICJ Reports 2010, 500, 512–13, para. 60.
[132] Decl. Vice-President Tomka, ICJ Reports 2010, 454, 466, para. 34.

The Court, however, did not view resolution 1244 as a *lex specialis* that displaced all other rules of international law. Rather, the Court turned first[133] to 'certain questions concerning the lawfulness of declarations of independence under general international law, against the background of which the question posed falls to be considered, and Security Council resolution 1244 (1999) is to be understood and applied'.[134] This approach suggests that, when construing a Security Council resolution, it may be important to consider the baseline of international law within which the Council is operating, as it may provide insights into the assumed premises upon which the resolution was predicated. The Council adopted resolution 1244 in 1999 against a background where 'general international law contains no applicable prohibition of declarations of independence',[135] which made it even more plausible to assert that any such prohibition, if intended, should have been expressly stated in the resolution. Such an approach is well-considered: in circumstances where the Council's resolution is ambiguous or open-textured, it seems likely that the special rules of the resolution are meant to be applying general international law rather than modifying, overruling, or setting aside that law.[136]

## B. Methodology when interpreting Security Council resolutions

The Court's advisory opinion provides some guidance on the proper methodology for interpreting Security Council resolutions.[137] First, the Court viewed Articles 31 and 32 of the Vienna Convention on the Law of Treaties (VCLT)[138] as being capable of providing 'guidance' for the interpretation of Security Council resolutions,[139] an approach consistent with the Court's prior jurisprudence and that of some other international tribunals.[140] As such, the Court appears to favour a good faith interpretation of the ordinary meaning of the terms of a Security Council resolution. To that end, the Court asserted that it was engaging in 'a careful reading' of resolution 1244[141]

---

[133] *Kosovo* Advisory Opinion (n 28), 436–9, paras. 79–84.

[134] Ibid., 436, para. 78.     [135] Ibid., 438, para. 84.

[136] See International Law Commission, *Fragmentation of International Law: Difficulties Arising from the Diversification and Expansion of International Law—Report of the Study Group of the International Law Commission,* UN Doc. A/CN.4/L.682, paras. 88–107 (13 Apr. 2006), as corrected UN Doc. A/CN.4/L.682/Corr.1 (Aug. 11, 2006) (finalized by Martti Koskenniemi).

[137] For a general analysis of this issue, see Wood, 'The Interpretation of Security Council Resolutions', 2 *Max Planck Y.B. of UN Law* (1998) 73.

[138] Vienna Convention on the Law of Treaties, 23 May 1969, 1155 UNTS 331 (VCLT).

[139] *Kosovo* Advisory Opinion (n 28), 442, para. 94; see Yee, 'Note on the International Court of Justice (Part 4): the *Kosovo* Advisory Opinion', 9 *Chinese J. Int'l L.* (2010) 763, 774 ('this paragraph is destined to be cited frequently in the future'). The Court did not indicate whether VCLT (n 138) Article 33 (regarding interpretation of treaties authenticated in two or more languages) also provided guidance.

[140] See, e.g., *Prosecutor v. Tadic (Protective Measures for Victims and Witnesses)*, 105 ILR 599, 607–8, para.18 (Int'l Crim. Trib. for former Yugoslavia 1998); UN Compensation Commission, Report and Recommendation Made by the Panel of Commissioners concerning the First Installment of 'E2' Claims, UN Doc. S/AC. 26/1998/7, para. 54 (1998).

[141] *Kosovo* Advisory Opinion (n 28), 449, para. 113.

and parsed the specific wording of several provisions of the resolution, both for what they said[142] and what they did not say.[143]

Further, the Court's reference to the Vienna Convention suggests that the terms of the resolution should be considered in context (e.g., with regard to the preamble and annexes) and in light of the resolution's object and purpose. In fact, the Court read the provisions of resolution 1244 in conjunction with its Annexes 1 and 2,[144] and identified 'three distinct features of that resolution [that] are relevant for discerning its object and purpose',[145] which the Court concluded 'was to establish a temporary, exceptional régime which, save to the extent that it expressly preserved it, superseded the Serbian legal order and which aimed at the stabilization of Kosovo, and that it was designed to do so on an interim basis'.[146] This view of the object and purpose of the resolution proved important to the Court's determination that the resolution operated 'on a different level' from the declaration: the former focused on the interim period and the latter focused on Kosovo's final status.[147]

Finally, the Court's assessment of general international law (as noted in the prior section) might reflect an interpretive approach that takes into account 'relevant rules of international law applicable'[148] to those affected by the resolution, though the Court did not characterize its analysis in those terms.

Second, the Court also indicated 'other factors to be taken into account' that are specific to the interpretation of a Security Council resolution, by stating that such interpretation 'may require the Court to analyse statements made at the time of their adoption, other resolutions of the Security Council on the same issue, as well as the subsequent practice of the relevant United Nations organs and of States affected by those given resolutions'.[149] As previously noted, the Court compared the language of resolution 1244 with the Council's contemporaneous adoption of resolution 1251 (1999) relating to Cyprus,[150] compared it with prior resolutions relating to Kosovo,[151] and took into account for interpretive purposes the actions of the Secretary-General and the SRSG to implement the resolution.[152] The Court did not, however, refer to any statements made by the members of the Council at the time resolution 1244 was adopted.

Third, the Court listed, with apparent approval, the methodology it used in prior cases for interpreting and applying Security Council resolutions.[153] In particular, the

---

[142] See, e.g., ibid., 449–50, para. 115 (finding that the resolution 'is mostly concerned with creating obligations and authorizations for United Nations Member States as well as for organs of the United Nations' not for other actors).

[143] See, e.g., ibid., 449, para. 114 (finding that 'under the terms of resolution 1244 (1999) the Security Council did not reserve for itself the final determination of the situation in Kosovo and remained silent on the conditions for the final status of Kosovo').

[144] Ibid., 442–3, para. 95.        [145] Ibid., 443–4, paras. 96–8.

[146] Ibid., 444, para. 99.

[147] Ibid., 449, para. 114; see also ibid., 451, para. 118.

[148] VCLT (n 138) art. 31.3(c).

[149] *Kosovo* Advisory Opinion (n 28), 442, para. 94.

[150] Ibid., 449, para. 114.        [151] Ibid., 450, para. 116.

[152] Ibid., 443, para. 97; ibid., 447, para. 108.

[153] Ibid., 439, para. 85 (citing *Legal Consequences for States of the Continued Presence of South Africa in Namibia (South West Africa) notwithstanding Security Council Resolution 276 (1970), Advisory*

Court confirmed its view in the *South West Africa* Advisory Opinion that the interpretation of a resolution must be undertaken 'on a case-by-case basis, considering all relevant circumstances', not just when determining whether the Council intended to create a binding legal obligation, but for other interpretive purposes as well.[154]

## C. Judicial deference when reviewing Security Council resolutions

There is little doubt that the Court is properly engaged in the exercise of its judicial function when interpreting a Security Council resolution, if necessary for deciding a case or issuing an advisory opinion. Even so, an important question arises as to whether there should be special deference or caution exercised by the Court, given the Council's status as a collateral UN organ, one that is often engaged in politically difficult and sensitive issues of peace and security. The Court is no doubt wary of misinterpreting a Council resolution or ascribing to the Council or its Members views that they did not in fact hold, especially if doing so might have serious and adverse consequences. Such deference might implicitly be seen in two aspects of the *Kosovo* Advisory Opinion.

First, given that a central aspect of the Advisory Opinion was the interpretation of a Security Council resolution, a plausible basis for the Court to decline to answer the question was the fact that the request came from the General Assembly. Indeed, Vice-President Tomka in his declaration, Judge Keith in his separate opinion, and Judges Bennouna and Skotnikov in their dissenting opinions all asserted that for this reason the Court should have declined to answer the question.[155] The only prior advisory opinion where the interpretation of a Security Council resolution was central to the disposition of the issue—the *South West Africa* Advisory Opinion—involved a request from the Council, not the Assembly.[156]

In *Kosovo*, the Court did not decline to answer the question; indeed, some judges thought that interpretation of *any* Council resolution related to peace and security was an appropriate basis for the Court to engage in its advisory function, regardless

---

*Opinion*, ICJ Reports 1992, 16; *Questions of Interpretation and Application of the 1971 Montreal Convention arising from the Aerial Incident at Lockerbie (Libya v. United Kingdom)*, Provisional Measures, ICJ Reports 1992, 15, paras. 39–41; *Questions of Interpretation and Application of the 1971 Montreal Convention arising from the Aerial Incident at Lockerbie (Libya v. United States)*, Provisional Measures, ICJ Reports 1992, 126–7, paras. 42–4)).

[154] *Kosovo* Advisory Opinion (n 28), 451, para. 117 (citing *Legal Consequences for States of the Continued Presence of South Africa in Namibia (South West Africa)* (n 153), 53, para. 114).

[155] Decl. Vice-President Tomka, ICJ Reports 2010, 454, 455, paras. 5–6 ('Through the question put to it by the *General Assembly*, the Court has become immersed in the disagreements prevailing in the *Security Council* on this issue, the Council having been still actively seised of the matter but not requesting any advice from the Court'). Sep. Op. Judge Keith, ICJ Reports 2010, 482, 483–4, para. 6 (questioning 'the appropriateness of an organ requesting an opinion if the request is essentially concerned with the actual exercise of special powers by another organ under the Charter, in relation to the matter which is the subject of the request'). Dissenting Op. Judge Bennouna, ICJ Reports 2010, 500, 502–3, paras. 13–14; Dissenting Op. Judge Skotnikov, ICJ Reports 2010, 515, 515–19, paras. 1–12.

[156] *Advisory Opinion on Legal Consequences for States of the Continued Presence of South Africa in Namibia (South West Africa)* (n 153).

of who asked the question.[157] As Richard Falk notes, the decision 'seemed partly to reflect a sense of institutional responsibility, namely, that the Court should always do its best not to rely on its discretion to decline to respond whenever a major UN organ poses an international law question to it'.[158] Nevertheless, the Court took this issue seriously, spending several paragraphs of the opinion explaining why the question could be answered notwithstanding that the request emanated from the Assembly.[159] As such, the posture of the case may have led the Court to be especially cautious in reaching a decision that ascribed views to the Council that were not readily apparent from the resolution, such as a view that any unilateral declaration was prohibited, that the Council had to approve Kosovo's independence, or that the Council expected Serbia's consent prior to independence.

Second, Kosovo and its supporters had argued that it fell to the SRSG to determine whether the declaration was an *ultra vires* act or an act that violated the Constitutional Framework. Since the SRSG took no such action, they maintained that the declaration was not such an act. As noted above,[160] the Court accepted that position, finding that the SRSG was 'under a duty to take action with regard to the acts of the Assembly of Kosovo which he considered to be *ultra vires*'.[161] Since the SRSG did not take action, the Court concluded that the actor at issue was not the Assembly or the PISG as a whole.

In reaching that conclusion, the Court may have been influenced by the fact that the Security Council had delegated authority to the Secretary-General and his Special Representative and, in so doing, provided those officials with authority to interpret the Council's resolution as the need arose in theatre. While inaction by the Council itself might readily be viewed as purely a product of a political deadlock, the Court may have seen it as necessary to regard the conduct of the Secretary-General and his representatives as different—as more apolitical in nature. In other words, perhaps the Court felt it necessary to preserve the idea that international civil servants are charged with implementing UN institutional law to the best of their abilities, without regard to the political consequences. As such, in considering whether there was a transgression in theatre of the rules adopted by the SRSG to regulate local matters (such as the provisional Constitutional Framework), considerable weight should be accorded to that representative to interpret whether a transgression has occurred and, if so, to correct it. In this instance, the Court may have viewed the SRSG's decision not to declare null or set aside the declaration as an *ultra vires* act of the PISG, or a violation of the Constitutional Framework, as an authoritative or highly persuasive interpretation of resolution 1244 to which the Court should defer, at least in the absence of strong reasons to the contrary. One might argue that the SRSG's failure to act was 'a breach of his mandate',[162] but that

---

[157] See, e.g., Sep. Op. Judge Sepúlveda-Amor, ICJ Reports 2010, 491–2, para. 2, 496, para. 22; Sep. Op. Judge Cançado Trindade, ICJ Reports 2010, 523, 527, paras. 6–7.

[158] Falk, 'The Kosovo Advisory Opinion: Conflict Resolution and Precedent' 105 *Am. J. Int'l L.* (2011) 50, 55.

[159] *Kosovo* Advisory Opinion (n 28), 418–23, paras. 36–48.          [160] *Supra* Section 2(E).

[161] *Kosovo* Advisory Opinion (n 28), 447, para. 108.

[162] Kohen and Del Mar (n 98), 122.

leads to the question of why the Secretary-General did not act to correct the SRSG, which in turn leads to a question of whether the Secretary-General violated his mandate.[163] Presumably the Court would only reluctantly go down such a path.

## D. Ability of the Security Council to bind non-state actors

Chapter VII of the UN Charter empowers the Security Council to decide upon measures to be taken to maintain or restore international peace and security.[164] Notably in this context, it 'may decide what measures not involving the use of armed force are to be employed to give effect to its decisions, and it may call upon the Members of the United Nations to apply such measures'.[165] UN member states agree to accept and carry out those decisions.[166] While such provisions clearly empower the Council to order or authorize states to take action, they do not expressly address whether the Council can order or authorize other actors, including non-member states,[167] international organizations, non-governmental organizations, or persons to take action.

Even so, the Council at times addresses its resolutions to non-state actors and the failure of those actors to abide by the resolution might be regarded as a violation of international law. In resolution 1244, the Council demanded 'that the KLA and other armed Kosovo Albanian groups end immediately all offensive actions and comply with the requirements for demilitarization as laid down by the head of the international security presence',[168] just as it demanded 'that the Federal Republic of Yugoslavia put an immediate and verifiable end to violence and repression in Kosovo'.[169] Perhaps a failure of the KLA to end offensive actions would violate resolution 1244 in the same way that a failure of the FRY to end violence and repression in Kosovo would violate resolution 1244.

Yet, given that the Council normally regulates states and not non-state actors, it is appropriate to scrutinize carefully any resolution to see whether it binds a non-state actor and, if so, in what way. Interestingly, in situations involving a declaration of independence, the Council (or the General Assembly) typically does not demand that the relevant actor refrain from issuing a declaration or withdraw a declaration that has been issued, nor decide that the declaration as such violates international law.[170] Rather, the Council condemns the issuance of a declaration

---

[163] Jacobs and Radi (n 89), 344–9.     [164] UN Charter, arts. 39, 41–2.
[165] Ibid., art. 41.     [166] Ibid., art. 25.
[167] UN Charter, art. 2.5 provides that the United Nations 'shall ensure that states which are not Members of the United Nations act in accordance with these Principles so far as may be necessary for the maintenance of international peace and security'. Nevertheless, it has been argued that Council resolutions do not have a direct binding effect on non-Member States since treaties cannot bind non-parties. See Widdows, 'Security Council Resolutions and Non-Members of the United Nations' 27 *Int'l and Comp. L.Q.* (1978) 459, 461–2.
[168] SC Res 1244, para. 15 (1999).     [169] Ibid., para. 3.
[170] The Council, of course, can react to various facts that are not themselves a violation of international law, but that do threaten peace and security. See J. Alvarez, *International Organizations as*

and decides that it should not be given legal effect by the United Nations or Member States.[171] In other words, the approach taken is not to impose an obligation on the non-state actor but, rather, to make a determination as to the legal effect of that actor's conduct.[172]

For example, in 1965, the Security Council (without invoking Chapter VII) condemned 'the unilateral declaration of independence made by a racist minority in Southern Rhodesia', decided to call upon 'all States not to recognize this illegal racist minority régime',[173] and regarded 'the declaration of independence by it as having no legal validity'.[174] No part of the relevant resolutions ordered the minority regime to undertake any specific acts. The reference to 'illegal' regime and an 'invalid' declaration might be interpreted as recognition that the action *per se* violated national law,[175] though the Court in the *Kosovo* case saw it as arising from the act's connection to egregious human rights violations.[176] After Southern Rhodesia proclaimed itself a republic, the Council invoked Chapter VII, condemned the 'illegal proclamation of republican status,' and called upon states to refrain from recognition,[177] but again issued no decision or demand was directed at the minority regime.

Similarly, in 1983, the Council considered the declaration of independence by Turkish Cypriot authorities as incompatible with certain treaty commitments and, for that reason, the attempt to create a new state was 'legally invalid'; the Council further called upon 'all States not to recognize any Cypriot State other than the Republic of Cyprus'.[178] Again, the resolution did not order the Turkish Cypriot authorities to take or refrain from taking any specific acts. More recently, the Security Council adopted a resolution relating to Bosnia and Herzegovina in which it addressed the possibility of the issuance of a declaration of independence for the establishment of a new State of Republika Srpska. Resolution 787 provided that the Security Council '[st]rongly reaffirms its call on all parties and others concerned to respect strictly the territorial integrity of Bosnia and Herzegovina, and affirms that any entities unilaterally declared or arrangements imposed in contravention thereof will not be accepted'.[179] Again, the Security Council did not directly address the

---

*Law-makers* (2005) 187 ('The Charter leaves its enforcement arm with considerable discretion to act whenever the "international peace" is threatened, regardless of whether the threatening act violates international law …').

[171] See, e.g., GA Res. 2024 (1965), SC Res. 216 (1965), and SC Res. 217 (1965) (with respect to Southern Rhodesia); GA Res. 31/6 (A) (1976) and SC Res. 402 (1976) (with respect to South Africa bantustans).

[172] On this general distinction, see Öberg, 'The Legal Effects of Resolutions of the UN Security Council and General Assembly in the Jurisprudence of the ICJ', 16 *EJIL* (2005) 879, 881–2.

[173] SC Res. 216, paras. 1–2 (1965).

[174] SC Res. 217, para. 3 (1965).

[175] Ibid., pmbl. (1965) ('*Considering* that the illegal authorities in Southern Rhodesia have proclaimed independence and that the Government of the United Kingdom of Great Britain and Northern Ireland, as the administering Power, looks upon this as an act of rebellion').

[176] *Kosovo* Advisory Opinion (n 28), 437, para. 81.

[177] SC Res. 277, pmbl., and paras. 1–2 (1970).

[178] SC Res. 541, pmbl. and paras. 2, 7 (1983).

[179] SC Res. 787, para. 3 (1992); see *supra* Section 2(A).

relevant non-state actor or address the legality of a potential declaration but, rather, simply indicated that the Council would not accept such an act.

In the *Kosovo* Advisory Opinion, the Court apparently accepted that the Council had the power to 'make demands' upon non-state actors, but concluded that, in resolution 1244, the Council in fact did not issue any demand directed at the Kosovo Albanian leadership with respect to a declaration of independence. As such, the Court could not 'accept the argument' that the resolution contained 'a prohibition, binding on the authors of the declaration of independence, against declaring independence'.[180] Moreover, the Court may have been influenced by the fact that the declaration—rather than being the work of a non-state actor advancing egregious human rights violations—sought to incorporate the human rights and other provisions proposed by Ahtisaari for the final settlement.[181] In so deciding, the Court did not reach the issue of whether such Security Council demands in fact establish binding legal obligations for non-state actors and, if so, whether the contravention of those demands violates international law.[182]

Judge Bennouna asserted that resolution 1244 was binding upon 'non-State actors in Kosovo', but indicated that it was binding 'as a result of the territory [of Kosovo] having been placed under United Nations administration'.[183] Even if the declaration was issued by a group of individuals representing the people of Kosovo (and not the PISG), he asked 'how is it possible for them to have been able to violate the legal order established by UNMIK under the Constitutional Framework, *which all inhabitants of Kosovo are supposed to respect?*'.[184] Judge Skotnikov also appears to have viewed the resolution as directly binding upon non-state actors in Kosovo. He cited a statement made by the UK Government, when resolution 1244 was adopted, to the effect that the resolution 'applies also in full to the Kosovo Albanians' and that the 'Kosovo Albanian people and its leadership must rise to the challenge of peace by accepting the obligations of the resolution'.[185]

## E. International territorial administration

International administration of territory is not a new phenomenon in the history of international law,[186] but recent interventions in places such as Kosovo, East Timor, Eastern Slavonia, and elsewhere have given new significance to the phenomenon.[187]

---

[180] *Kosovo* Advisory Opinion (n 28), 451, para. 118.

[181] See Weller, 'Modesty Can Be a Virtue: Judicial Economy in the ICJ Kosovo Opinion', 24 *Leiden J. Int'l L.* (2011) 127, 142–3.

[182] See Öberg, 'The Legal Effects of United Nations Resolutions in the *Kosovo* Advisory Opinion', 105 *Am. J. Int'l L.* (2011) 81, 86 (contending 'one cannot conclude that [the Court] has found that the Security Council can bind nonstate actors').

[183] Dissenting Op. Judge Bennouna, ICJ Reports 2010, 500, 513, para. 62.

[184] Ibid., 513, para. 63 (emphasis added).

[185] Dissenting Op. Judge Skotnikov, ICJ Reports 2010, 515, 520, para. 13.

[186] D. Smyrek, *Internationally Administered Territories—International Protectorates?* (2006), at 57–117 (surveying examples such as the Free City of Danzig, the Saar Territory, Leticia, the Free Territory of Trieste, Jerusalem, West Irian, and Namibia).

[187] See generally G. Fox, *Humanitarian Occupation* (2008).

Moreover, the assumption of direct administrative authority by the United Nations appears to be a new development; prior practice, such as under the trusteeship system, did not involve the United Nations itself as an administering authority.[188] Three aspects of the Court's opinion seem especially important for this issue.

First, in the immediate aftermath of the deployment of UNMIK (and comparable deployments elsewhere), questions were raised as to whether the Security Council had the power to establish such an international administration, given its considerable intrusiveness into national sovereignty.[189] Although the issue was not directly raised in the proceedings, the Court's opinion implicitly accepts that the United Nations, at least through a Chapter VII decision of the Security Council, is empowered to engage in such administration of territory—a dramatic and perhaps revolutionary assumption of sovereign power—notwithstanding a lack of express authority in the UN Charter. To what extent that acceptance is based on a theory of maintaining peace and security under Chapter VII, or upon a theory of trusteeship,[190] cannot be discerned from the opinion. Nevertheless, such acceptance, in conjunction with the tacit acceptance by states generally, suggests a 'new normal' for UN territorial administration. At the same time, the Court did not reach the more difficult issue of whether the Council may order the final political status of a territory in the absence of the agreement of the relevant parties.[191]

Second, the Court's approach also accepted the ability of the Security Council to delegate to the Secretary-General the power of creating the international civilian presence (UNMIK). Previously the Court had implicitly accepted the power of the Council itself to create a freestanding body such as the International Criminal Tribunal for the former Yugoslavia.[192] Here, the Council implicitly accepted—albeit for an interim period—the ability of the Secretary-General under the authority of the Council to create and establish the responsibilities of an entity that exercised core sovereign functions within the administered territory, with cascading effects that flowed to the SRSG and PISG.[193]

Third, the Court's conclusion that the legal regime associated with UNMIK's presence in Kosovo was a form of international law[194] provides some guidance on

---

[188]  See Matheson, 'United Nations Governance in Postconflict Societies', 95 *Am. J. Int'l L.* (2001) 76, 76 ('Prior to the end of the Cold War, the United Nations ... had relatively little experience in the actual governance of territories'); Yannis, 'The UN as Government in Kosovo', 10 *Global Governance* (2004) 67, 67 ('In terms of scope and substance, UNMIK's mandate was almost unprecedented by the standards of UN field operations'); Tomuschat, 'Yugoslavia's Damaged Sovereignty over the Province of Kosovo', in G. Kreijen (ed), *State Sovereignty, and International Governance* (2002) 323, 338 ('It is truly an innovation in the practice of the Security Council to prohibit a government from exercising its authority in part of the country').

[189]  See, e.g., Ruffert, 'The Administration of Kosovo and East-Timor by the International Community', 50 *Int'l and Comp. L.Q.* (2001) 613, 614–22.

[190]  See von Carlowitz, 'UNMIK Lawmaking between Effective Peace Support and Internal Self-Determination', 41 *Archiv des Völkerrechts* (2003) 336, 362–74.

[191]  For a discussion, see Matheson (n 188), 85.

[192]  Application of the Convention on the Prevention and Punishment of the Crime of Genocide (Bosnia and Herzegovina v. Serbia and Montenegro) ICJ Reports 2007, paras. 444–5.

[193]  See Öberg (note 182), 87–90.     [194]  See *supra* section 2(D)(1).

how to view such deployments, and appears consistent with the views that were expressed in the academic community prior to issuance of the opinion. Writing in 2001, Carsten Stahn characterized UNMIK regulations as 'a specific source of law, placing Kosovo ... provisionally under the legal order of the United Nations'.[195] Although such regulations also constitute 'internal acts of the administered "internationalized" territories', the ultimate result was arguably a fusion of municipal and UN law so as to create a 'law of the internationalized territory which constitutes a legal entity of its own, separate from the United Nations'.[196] Similarly, Erika de Wet asserted in 2004 that such regulations, though possessing a 'dual character,' nevertheless 'belong to the legal order of the United Nations as they are enacted by subsidiary organs of the Security Council within the meaning of Article 29 of the Charter'.[197] As such, while the law may possess a dual character, the Court's assessment that violation of that law *could* be 'not in accordance with international law' seems entirely plausible.

In the aftermath of the opinion, some commentators have asserted that the Court's approach meant that, in essence, the Court assumed the role of the 'Constitutional Court' of Kosovo.[198] However, such a position seems overdrawn. Most issues concerning laws operative in internationally-administered territory will be resolved by the institutions operating within that territory, where the characterization of the law as 'international' or not has no real significance. In rare circumstances where the Court has jurisdiction and an issue is presented that requires it to deliberate upon an aspect of such law, then the Court may well regard the law as having an international character. Even so, it remains possible that particular types of regulations—due to their origin or nature—might be seen as possessing such a dominantly local character (e.g., a rule barring trucks on certain roads) that they do not truly implicate international law. Such circumstances simply were not at issue in the *Kosovo* case, and the opinion provides no guidance in that respect.

## 4. Conclusion

The Court's findings in the Kosovo advisory opinion with respect to resolution 1244 provide a rich mosaic of issues, some of which were specific to the situation of Kosovo and others that have ramifications for the interpretation and application

---

[195] Stahn, 'The United Nations Transitional Administrations in Kosovo and East Timor; A First Analysis', 5 *Max Planck Y.B. of UN Law* (2001) 105, 146; see also C. Stahn, *The Law and Practice of International Territorial Administration* (2008).

[196] Ibid. Stahn, 'A First Analysis' (n 195), 147–8.

[197] De Wet, 'The Direct Administration of Territories by the United Nations and its Member States in the Post Cold War Era: Legal Bases and Implications for National Law', 8 *Max Planck Y.B. of UN Law* (2004) 291, 331; see also Bothe and Marauhn, 'UN Administration of Kosovo and East Timor: Concept, Legality and Limitations of Security', in C. Tomuschat (ed), *Kosovo and the International Community: A Legal Assessment* (2002), 217, 228–9; Ruffert (n 189), 622–7.

[198] See, e.g., Jacobs and Radi (n 89), 341; Jacobs, 'International Court of Justice, *Accordance with International Law of the Unilateral Declaration of Independence in Respect of Kosovo*, Advisory Opinion of 22 July 2010', 60 *Int'l and Comp. L.Q.* (2011) 799, 806.

of Security Council resolutions more generally. While doubts and disagreements with the Court's decision can be fairly expressed, the Court rather systematically addressed the principal legal arguments placed before it, and there is nothing about the opinion that operates outside the realm of plausible judicial reasoning. Though the Court was faced with the difficult situation of an ambiguous resolution and a divided Council, as well as blocs of states with diametrically opposed views, the Court assumed its responsibility of answering the question and answered it clearly, without unleashing any apparent adverse consequences for the United Nations, for the Balkans, or for the field of international law generally.

# 9

# The UN Secretary-General and the Advisory Opinion

*Mathias Forteau**

## 1. Introduction

The International Court of Justice and the UN Secretariat, which are both principal organs of the United Nations under Article 7 of the Charter, enjoy quite strong relationships at the administrative level. Even though the ICJ has its own Registrar whose tasks are mainly administrative according to Article 26 of the Rules of Court, it also needs in many respects the complementary administrative or executive assistance of the UN Secretariat.[1] This is true for both contentious and advisory proceedings. When the requesting organ under Article 96 of the Charter is a UN organ, the UN Secretariat is in particular requested to transmit to the Court 'all documents likely to throw light upon the question'.[2] In that regard, the UN Secretary-General (UNSG) can be seen as playing a key role in providing the Court with unbiased data in advisory proceedings. At first sight, this administrative function is in full accordance with the independent nature of the UN Secretariat's role as reflected in Article 100, paragraph 1, of the UN Charter.[3]

On the other hand, the UNSG has been entrusted with political or diplomatic functions on many occasions since 1945, in particular by the UN Security Council under Article 98 of the UN Charter.[4] The UNSG has notably received

---

* The present article benefited from the research assistance of Ms Elizabeth Boomer. I wish to express my thanks for her valuable aid. For the sake of transparency, I must state that I appeared before the Court in the Kosovo case on behalf of France. The views expressed in the present chapter are my own personal views. In particular, nothing in the present paper can be attributed to the French Government.

[1] See I. S. Kerno, 'L'Organisation des Nations Unies et la Cour internationale de Justice', *Collected Courses of the Hague Academy of International Law*, Vol. 78 (1951), p. 555.

[2] This is nowadays a common practice, based on Article 65(2) of the Statute of the Court. On this practice, see below, Section 2.B.

[3] 'In the performance of their duties the Secretary-General and the staff shall not seek or receive instructions from any government or from any other authority external to the Organization. They shall refrain from any action which might reflect on their position as international officials responsible only to the Organization'.

[4] On the diplomatic and political role of the UNSG, see in particular M. Virally, 'Le rôle politique du Secrétaire général des Nations Unies', *AFDI*, 1958, pp. 360–99 (in particular p. 372 where

delegated powers under Chapter VII from the UN Security Council in many situations endangering international peace and security, i.e. broad, discretionary powers.[5] These diplomatic and political responsibilities gave rise, in particular, to the proposal that the UNSG be accorded the right to request advisory opinions on his own.[6]

Due to the dual nature of the functions of the UNSG (i.e. as both 'a Secretary and a General', as it has often been said[7]), it can happen that administrative and political tasks conflict with each other in a given situation. Such a scenario could have been the case in the *Kosovo* advisory proceedings where the UNSG was required to give its administrative assistance to the Court, while at the same time acting in the Kosovo political process both as chief of UNMIK and supervisor of the negotiations on the final status of Kosovo.[8] As a result, the Court had to rule, to some extent, on the actions of the UNSG in Kosovo while being simultaneously assisted by the UNSG in the management of the advisory proceedings, including the gathering of relevant documents 'likely to throw light upon the question'. One can legitimately ask whether such a situation was in full conformity with the requirements of the Court's judicial function.

Admittedly, the advisory function of the Court is not the same as in contentious cases. According to Article 102(2) of the Rules of Court, which defines the applicable rules for advisory proceedings, '[t]he Court shall ... be guided by the provisions of the Statute and of these Rules which apply in contentious cases *to the extent to which it recognizes them to be applicable*'.[9] In 1963, the Court made clear however that 'the Court's authority to give advisory opinions must be exercised as a judicial function'.[10] The advisory proceedings have then to be conducted in a manner which does not depart from the applicable standards for the independence and impartiality of courts and tribunals.[11]

---

he refers to the idea that the UNSG could be considered in fact as another (informal) member of the UN Security Council (UNSC)); Th. M. Franck, 'The Secretary-General's Role in Conflict Resolution: Past, Present and Pure Conjecture', *EJIL*, 1995, pp. 360–387.

[5]   The scope and limits of delegation of Chapter VII powers by the UNSC to the UNSG have been analysed in particular by D. Sarooshi, especially in 'The Role of the United Nations Secretary-General in United Nations Peace-Keeping Operations', *Australian Yearbook of International Law*, 1999, pp. 282 *ff.*

[6]   See P. Tavernier, 'Le Secrétaire général de l'ONU et la sécurité collective', in Société française pour le droit international, *Les métamorphoses de la sécurité collective*, Pedone, Paris, 2005, at pp. 48–9; P. Szasz, 'The Role of the UN Secretary-General', *N.Y.U. Jl. I.& P.*, 1991, Vol. 24, at pp. 192–4; C.-A. Fleischhauer, 'The Constitutional Relationship between the Secretary-General of the United Nations and the International Court of Justice', *in Boutros Boutros-Ghali, amicorum discipulorumque liber. Paix, développement, démocratie*, Bruylant, Bruxelles, 1998, p. 456.

[7]   See for instance A.-L. Vaurs-Chaumette, 'Article 98', *in* J.-P. Cot, A. Pellet, M. Forteau (eds), *La Charte des Nations Unies, commentaire article par article*, Economica, 2005, especially p. 2036.

[8]   See below, Section 2.A.          [9]   Emphasis added.

[10]   *Northern Cameroons (Cameroon v. United Kingdom), Preliminary Objections*, Judgment, ICJ Reports 1963, p. 30.

[11]   On these standards and their application to international courts and tribunals, including the ICJ, see in particular the *Reasoned Decision on Challenge*, dated 30 November 2011, in the Arbitration, *The Republic of Mauritius v. The United Kingdom of Great Britain and Northern Ireland*, <http://www.pca-cpa.org>.

These requirements have been considered by the Court, as evidenced by its latest advisory opinion, as quite stringent ones. The opinion concerned the specific case of a dispute between an international organization and one of its agents. In its opinion, the ICJ decided to take steps 'to reduce the inequality in the [advisory] proceedings before it' (the individual having no direct access on her own to the Court) in order to take into account 'the development of the principle of equality of access to courts and tribunals since 1946'.[12] According to the Court,

'[t]he principle of equality of the parties follows from the requirements of good administration of justice' (*1956 Advisory Opinion, I.C.J Reports 1956*, p.86). That principle must now be understood as including access on an equal basis to available appellate or similar remedies unless an exception can be justified on objective and reasonable grounds.[13]

Similarly, the requirement of 'equality of the parties in judicial proceedings' led the Court in the *Kosovo* case (as in the *Wall* case) to invite the authors of the declaration of independence (as it did for Palestine) to participate in the proceedings although not a State or an international organization.[14]

One may ask in light of the above whether the dual functions of the UNSG in the *Kosovo* case were compatible with judicial standards. Given the central role of the UNSG in the Kosovo crisis and the interim administration of Kosovo, it seemed at first sight quite impossible to consider the Secretariat as a mere administrative organ assisting the Court in the advisory proceedings (Section 2). The possible conflict between administrative and political functions of the UNSG was overcome by the UNSG asserting its neutrality with regard to both the final status of Kosovo and its functions in the advisory proceedings (Section 3).

## 2. Not a Mere Secretariat

As the Court pointed out in the 2010 Advisory Opinion on Kosovo, the Secretary-General has been a core actor in the Kosovo situation, as it has been handled by the UNSC, since 1999 under Chapter VII of the Charter (see sub-section A). Since, at the same time, the UNSG's assistance plays an important role in advisory proceedings (see sub-section B), the UNSG could not be seen in the present case as simply a 'secretariat', at least if the objective standard of the appearance of independence is applied ('justice should not only be done but should manifestly and undoubtedly

---

[12] *Judgment No.2867 of the Administrative Tribunal of the International Labour Organization upon a Complaint Filed against the International Fund for Agricultural Development* (Request for Advisory Opinion), ICJ Reports 2012, p. 10 at p. 31, para. 48; p. 27, para. 39.

[13] Ibid., p. 29, para. 44.

[14] See H. Thirlway, 'The Law and Procedure of the ICJ. Supplement 2010', *BYBIL*, 2010, pp. 162–164, reproduced in H. Thirlway, *The Law and Procedure of the International Court of Justice, Fifty Years of Jurisprudence* (2013), pp. 1726–7.

be seen to be done'). Obviously, it was something more than a secretariat in the present case.

## A. The Secretary-General as a core actor in the Kosovo situation

As explained in the *Repertory of Practice of United Nations Organs,* the UNSG has been exercising 'functions … with respect to political and security matters … in connection with the situation in Kosovo'.[15] In its Advisory Opinion, the Court underlined the very important role played by the UNSG in the very specific, quite exceptional political framework imposed on Serbia by the UNSC in Kosovo since 1999.

### 1. *The UNSG and the international administration of Kosovo*

First of all, the Court recalled that the UNSG had been entrusted by the UNSC with the task of establishing the interim administration of Kosovo following the 1999 use of force by NATO members against Serbia, aimed at ending the serious violations of human rights committed by Serbian forces. The Court pointed out at paragraph 58 of its Opinion that in resolution 1244 (1999),

the Security Council, 'determined to resolve the grave humanitarian situation' which it had identified (see the fourth preambular paragraph) and to put an end to the armed conflict in Kosovo, authorized the United Nations Secretary-General to establish an international civil presence in Kosovo in order to provide 'an interim administration for Kosovo … which will provide transitional administration while establishing and overseeing the development of provisional democratic self-governing institutions.[16]

The Court went on to specify that the UNSG accordingly establish the UNMIK, which has been, since its creation and on the proposal of the UNSG, 'headed by a Special Representative of the Secretary-General, to be appointed by the Secretary-General in consultation with the Security Council'.[17] In other words, the UNSG was not only requested to help in creating the international administration of Kosovo, it was also entrusted with leading this very exceptional international administration which, according to UNMIK Regulation 1999/1, was granted '[a]ll legislative and executive authority with respect to Kosovo'—i.e. all the powers a State possesses on its territory. To that extent, the UNSG, through UNMIK and his Special Representative, acted as the functional equivalent of a state in Kosovo, beginning in 1999. As the Court pointed out, '[o]n 25 July 1999, the first Special Representative of the Secretary-General promulgated UNMIK Regulation 1999/1, which provided in its Section 1.1 that "[a]ll legislative and executive authority with respect to Kosovo, including the administration of the

---

[15] *Supplement No. 9 (1995-1999),* 'Article 98', paras. 65–71.
[16] Kosovo Advisory Opinion, ICJ Reports 2010, p. 426.
[17] *Kosovo* Advisory Opinion, ICJ Reports 2010, p. 428, para. 60.

judiciary, is vested in UNMIK and is exercised by the Special Representative of the Secretary-General"'.[18]

The Court recalled in addition in its advisory opinion that the powers and responsibilities thus laid out in Security Council resolution 1244 (1999) were set out in more detail in UNMIK Regulation 2001/9 of 15 May 2001 in a Constitutional Framework for Provisional Self-Government (hereinafter 'Constitutional Framework'), which defined the responsibilities relating to the administration of Kosovo between the Special Representative of the Secretary-General and the Provisional Institutions of Self-Government of Kosovo. And, with regard to the role entrusted to the Special Representative of the Secretary-General under Chapter 12 of the Constitutional Framework, that

[t]he exercise of the responsibilities of the Provisional Institutions of Self-Government under this Constitutional Framework shall not affect or diminish the authority of the SRSG to ensure full implementation of UNSCR 1244 (1999), including overseeing the Provisional Institutions of Self-Government, its officials and its agencies, and taking appropriate measures whenever their actions are inconsistent with UNSCR 1244 (1999) or this Constitutional Framework.[19]

Similarly, according to the ninth preambular paragraph of the Constitutional Framework,

the exercise of the responsibilities of the Provisional Institutions of Self-Government in Kosovo shall not in any way affect or diminish the ultimate authority of the SRSG for the implementation of UNSCR 1244 (1999).[20]

The Court equally pointed out that,

under the régime of the Constitutional Framework, all matters relating to the management of the external relations of Kosovo were the exclusive prerogative of the Special Representative of the Secretary-General … with the Special Representative of the Secretary-General only consulting and co-operating with the Provisional Institutions of Self-Government in these matters.[21]

It eventually led the Court to conclude that 'both Security Council resolution 1244 (1999) and the Constitutional Framework entrust the Special Representative of the Secretary-General with considerable supervisory powers with regard to the Provisional Institutions of Self-Government established under the authority of the

---

[18] *Kosovo* Advisory Opinion, ICJ Reports 2010, p. 428, para. 61.

[19] *Kosovo* Advisory Opinion, ICJ Reports 2010, p. 429, para. 62.

[20] Ibid. The Court added that 'In his periodical report to the Security Council of 7 June 2001, the Secretary-General stated that the Constitutional Framework contained "broad authority for my Special Representative to intervene and correct any actions of the provisional institutions of self-government that are inconsistent with Security Council resolution 1244 (1999), including the power to veto Assembly legislation, where necessary"' (ibid., p. 429, para. 62). See also p. 440, para. 89: 'In particular, the Assembly of Kosovo was empowered to adopt legislation which would have the force of law within that legal order, subject always to the overriding authority of the Special Representative of the Secretary-General'.

[21] *Kosovo* Advisory Opinion, ICJ Reports 2010, p. 446, para. 106.

United Nations Interim Administration Mission in Kosovo'.[22] Some states argued consequently that as in previous cases, careful consideration must be given by the Court to the decisions of the UNSG or his Special Representative.[23]

In addition, the Court considered that the UNSG has been acting in Kosovo as a proxy of the UNSC. According to the Court, UNMIK's Regulations, adopted by the Special Representative of the UNSG, have the same (exceptional) value as binding resolutions of the UNSC acting under Chapter VII of the Charter.[24] The exceptional nature of the corresponding decisions adopted in Kosovo since 1999 by the UNSC, the UNSG and his Special Representative was emphasized by the Court in the following terms:

[v]iewed together, resolution 1244 (1999) and UNMIK regulation 1999/1 therefore had the effect of superseding the legal order in force at that time in the territory of Kosovo and setting up an international territorial administration. For this reason, the establishment of civil and security presences in Kosovo deployed on the basis of resolution 1244 (1999) must be understood as an exceptional measure relating to civil, political and security aspects and aimed at addressing the crisis existing in that territory in 1999.[25]

## 2. *The UNSG and the final status of Kosovo*

The UNSG was also involved in the determination of the final status of Kosovo. In fact, he played an important role in the negotiations on the final status and its 'outcome', in particular by appointing Special Envoys who were in charge of helping Serbian and Kosovar authorities in negotiating and finding a solution with regard to the fate of Kosovo (whether as an independent State or as an autonomous territory under Serbia's sovereignty).

In particular:

- In June 2005, the Secretary-General appointed Kai Eide, Permanent Representative of Norway to the North Atlantic Treaty Organization, as his Special Envoy to carry out a comprehensive review of Kosovo. In the wake of the Comprehensive Review report that he submitted to the Secretary-General (attached to United Nations doc. S/2005/635 (7 October 2005)), there was consensus within the Security Council that the final status process should be commenced[26]

---

[22] *Kosovo* Advisory Opinion, ICJ Reports 2010, pp. 440–1, para. 90.

[23] See Written Comments of the United States of America, 17 July 2009, <http://www.icj-cij. org>, pp. 43–5; see also Written Comments of France, 6 July 2009, <http://www.icj-cij.org>, para. 8.

[24] *Kosovo* Advisory Opinion, ICJ Reports 2010, p. 440, para. 88: 'The Court observes that UNMIK regulations, including regulation 2001/9, which promulgated the Constitutional Framework, are adopted by the Special Representative of the Secretary-General on the basis of the authority derived from Security Council resolution 1244 (1999), notably its paragraphs 6, 10, and 11, and thus ultimately from the United Nations Charter. The Constitutional Framework derives its binding force from the binding character of resolution 1244 (1999) and thus from international law'.

[25] *Kosovo* Advisory Opinion, ICJ Reports 2010, p. 443, para. 97.

[26] *Kosovo* Advisory Opinion, ICJ Reports 2010, p. 430, para. 64.

- In November 2005, the Secretary-General appointed Mr Martti Ahtisaari, former President of Finland, as his Special Envoy for the future status process for Kosovo. This appointment was endorsed by the Security Council (see Letter dated 10 November 2005 from the President of the Security Council addressed to the Secretary-General, United Nations doc. S/2005/709). Mr Ahtisaari's Letter of Appointment included, as an annex to it, a document entitled 'Terms of Reference', which stated that the Special Envoy 'is expected to revert to the Secretary-General at all stages of the process'. Furthermore, '[t]he pace and duration of the future status process will be determined by the Special Envoy on the basis of consultations with the Secretary-General, taking into account the co-operation of the parties and the situation on the ground'[27]
- The UNSG made regular reports to the UNSC on these negotiations[28]
- Following Special Envoy Martti Ahtisaari's submission of a finalized 'Comprehensive Proposal for the Kosovo Status Settlement', which later formed the basis of the Declaration of Independence of Kosovo,[29] and which was not accepted by Serbia, as Serbia informed the UNSG promptly,[30] the UNSG officially stated that he 'fully support[ed] both the recommendation made by [his] Special Envoy in his report on Kosovo's future status and the Comprehensive Proposal for the Kosovo Status Settlement'.[31]

In light of the above, it is quite clear that the UNSG could not be considered as acting as a pure 'secretariat' in Kosovo. He was granted a 'pouvoir exorbitant' of a political nature in the administration of Kosovo through UNMIK and the 'ultimate authority of the SRSG for the implementation of UNSCR 1244 (1999)', and by intervening quite intensively in the negotiations on the final status of Kosovo. In these circumstances, it seems at first sight quite odd that the UNSG was requested *at the same time* to intervene as an administrative organ assisting the Court in the *Kosovo* proceedings.

---

[27] *Kosovo* Advisory Opinion, ICJ Reports 2010, p. 430, para. 65. See also pp. 430–1, para. 66, on the approval by the UNSC of this appointment and the Terms of Reference.

[28] *Kosovo* Advisory Opinion, ICJ Reports 2010, pp. 431 *ff.,* paras. 67 *ff.*

[29] See ibid., p. 434, para. 75, quoting Paragraph 1 of the Declaration of Independence: 'We, the democratically-elected leaders of our people, hereby declare Kosovo to be an independent and sovereign state. This declaration reflects the will of our people and it is in full accordance with the recommendations of UN Special Envoy Martti Ahtisaari and his Comprehensive Proposal for the Kosovo Status Settlement'.

[30] See ibid., p. 435, para. 77: 'After the declaration of independence was issued, the Republic of Serbia informed the Secretary-General that it had adopted a decision stating that that declaration represented a forceful and unilateral secession of a part of the territory of Serbia, and did not produce legal effects either in Serbia or in the international legal order'.

[31] See Letter dated 26 March 2007 from the Secretary-General addressed to the President of the Security Council, S/2007/168, as quoted in *Kosovo* Advisory Opinion, *ICJ Reports 2010,* p. 433, para. 71.

## B. The Secretary-General as an assistant of the ICJ in the *Kosovo* advisory proceedings

According to the Statute of the ICJ and the Rules of Court, as well as well-established practice, the UNSG assisted the ICJ in two respects in the Kosovo proceedings.

First, since the request for an advisory opinion emanated from the UN General Assembly, it had to be 'transmitted to the Court by the Secretary-General of the United Nations'.[32] In the first paragraph of its advisory opinion, the Court accordingly indicated that the question on which the advisory opinion of the Court was requested, as set forth in resolution 63/3 adopted by the General Assembly of the United Nations on 8 October 2008, had been communicated to the Court the following day, '[b]y a letter dated 9 October 2008 of the UNSG received in the Registry by facsimile on 10 October, the original of which was received in the Registry on 15 October2008'.[33] The transmission of the request was a purely formal act, which did not involve any discretionary power.

Second, according to Article 104 of the Rules of Court, the UNSG was requested to transmit to the Court 'the documents referred to in Article 65, paragraph 2, of the Statute[34] ... at the same time as the request or as soon as possible thereafter, in the number of copies required by the Registry'.[35] These documents were communicated to the Court on 30 January 2009, before being 'subsequently placed on the Court's website'.[36] The 'Introductory Note (including the structure of the Dossier)' of the UNSG noted at paragraph 2 that the Dossier had been 'prepared pursuant to the Order of the President of the International Court of Justice of 17 October 2008 and paragraph 2 of Article 65 of the Statute of the Court'.

The Rules of Court do not specify that the 'Dossier' has to (or even can) be sent to the states or entities participating in the proceedings (contrary to what has to be done by the Registry with regard to written statements[37]). The publication of the Dossier on the website of the Court shows however that it was not supposed to be confidential—actually the Dossier did not contain any confidential information.[38] It did not prevent states submitting a written statement from quoting or relying on it, which in fact many of them did.[39]

---

[32] Rules of Court, Article 104, first sentence.
[33] *Kosovo* Advisory Opinion, ICJ Reports 2010, p. 407.
[34] According to Article 65(2), 'Questions upon which the advisory opinion of the Court is asked shall be laid before the Court by means of a written request containing an exact statement of the question upon which an opinion is required, and accompanied by all documents likely to throw light upon the question'.
[35] Rules of Court, Article 104, second sentence.
[36] *Kosovo* Advisory Opinion, ICJ Reports 2010, p. 408, para. 5.
[37] See Article 105, paragraph 1, of the Rules of Court: 'Written statements submitted to the Court shall be communicated by the Registrar to any States and organizations which have submitted such statements'.
[38] As reflected in the list of documents contained in the Introductory Note of the Dossier. According moreover to G. Guyomar, '[e]n général, la liste des documents est transmise aux Etats avec les exposés écrits et elle est imprimée dans les volumes C.I.J., *Mémoires*. Mais les documents eux-mêmes ne sont pas transmis ni imprimés, car ils sont, en principe, dans le domaine public' (*Commentaire du Règlement de la Cour internationale de Justice*, Pedone, Paris, 1983, at p. 670).
[39] See for instance France, Written Statement, 17 April 2009, fn. 39.

The role of the UNSG in the preparation of the Dossier evidences the '*sui generis* character'[40] of his functions in advisory proceedings before the Court. In fact, it involves a 'more substantive [role] than his role in contentious cases before the Court' and 'goes beyond the execution of mere formalities'.[41] Ultimately, it can even be seen as quite an ambiguous role, since the UNSG is required to assist the Court in an objective manner while the purpose of the submission of a Dossier is—to some extent—comparable to the one assigned to the Application and written pleadings of the Applicant in contentious proceedings, so far at least as the production of the documents adduced in support of the contentions contained in the pleadings is concerned.[42]

As a former Legal Counsel of the UN pointed out, the dossiers prepared by the Secretariat are 'usually quite voluminous' and the UNSG 'has a considerable discretion in deciding where he wishes to draw the line' between relevant and non-relevant documents, given the fact especially that '[n]o regulations have been adopted in this respect'.[43]

In addition, selection of relevant facts is a decisive issue with regard to the merits in many cases. It led some commentators to consider that even though the compilation of the relevant documents does not equate to being an *amicus curiae*, it nonetheless cannot be considered as a purely objective task and should not be underestimated.[44] To some extent, the same is true with regard to statements submitted to the Court by UNSG, whose content is presented as purely factual.[45] Actually, the selection of

---

[40] C.-A. Fleischhauer, 'The Constitutional Relationship between the Secretary-General of the United Nations and the International Court of Justice', in *Boutros Boutros-Ghali, amicorum discipulorumque liber. Paix, développement, démocratie*, Bruylant, Bruxelles, 1998, p. 462.

[41] Ibid., p. 464 and p. 466.

[42] See notably Article 50 of the Rules of Court, and J. Frowein, K. Oellers-Frahm, 'Article 65', in A. Zimmermann and others (eds), *The Statute of the International Court of Justice. A Commentary*, OUP, 2012, p. 1628, according to which the submission of 'all documents likely to throw light upon the question' 'corresponds to what is required for instituting contentious procedures'. However, a main difference results from the fact that the Dossier submitted by the UNSG does not include any statement of the relevant facts and of law, nor any statement of grounds on which the claim is based nor any submission.

[43] C.-A. Fleischhauer, 'The Constitutional Relationship between the Secretary-General of the United Nations and the International Court of Justice', in *Boutros Boutros-Ghali, amicorum discipulorumque liber. Paix, développement, démocratie*, Bruylant, Bruxelles, 1998, p. 465. The former Legal Counsel added that 'the establishment of the "dossier", which is carried out in the Secretariat by the Office of Legal Affairs, is a time-consuming affair. That is so because the documents to be transmitted under Article 65, paragraph 2, are by no means limited to the text of the resolution containing the question on which the advisory opinion is requested and the documents mentioned in that resolution: the term 'all documents likely to throw light on the question' has from the beginning been quite extensively interpreted by the Secretary-General'.

[44] See P. Daillier, 'L'intervention du Secrétaire général des Nations Unies dans la procédure consultative de la Cour internationale de Justice', *AFDI*, 1973, Vol. 19, p. 393.

[45] See for instance the oral statement of M. Kerno on behalf of the UNSG, in the *Peace Treaties* advisory proceedings: 'La Cour reconnaîtra que dans cette question le Secrétaire général des Nations Unies occupe une position très spéciale. Aux termes des Traités de paix, il peut être invité à désigner le troisième membre d'une commission. L'essence même de cette procédure est d'assurer que la désignation du troisième membre soit faite sans que le moindre soupçon de partialité soit possible. Le Secrétaire général ne peut donc prendre position ni sur le fond de l'affaire ni sur les questions soumises à la Cour. En exprimant un avis quelconque, il risquerait d'influencer l'opinion des Parties concernant

the relevant documents is of crucial importance since the opinion of the Court is dependent on the facts submitted to it. On the other hand, it must be observed that in the *Kosovo* case the main issues were less fact-oriented than in previous cases, in particular the *Wall* Opinion, and that most of the relevant documents were in the public domain.

In 1975 in *Western Sahara*, the Court pointed out that it is 'decisive … [that] the Court has before it sufficient information and evidence to enable it to arrive at a judicial conclusion upon any disputed questions of fact the determination of which is necessary for it to give an opinion in conditions compatible with its judicial character'.[46] In its advisory opinion of 23 July 1923 on the *Status of Eastern Carelia,* the PCIJ significantly considered in that respect that

> there are other cogent reasons which render it very inexpedient that the Court should attempt to deal with the present question. The question whether Finland and Russia contracted on the terms of the Declaration as to the nature of the autonomy of Eastern Carelia is really one of fact. To answer it would involve the duty of ascertaining what evidence might throw light upon the contentions which have been put forward on this subject by Finland and Russia respectively, and of securing the attendance of such witnesses as might be necessary. The Court would, of course, be at a very great disadvantage in such an enquiry, owing to the fact that Russia refuses to take part in it. It appears now to be very doubtful whether there would be available to the Court materials sufficient to enable it to arrive at any judicial conclusion upon the question of fact: What did the parties agree to? The Court does not say that there is an absolute rule that the request for an advisory opinion may not involve some enquiry as to facts, but, under ordinary circumstances, it is certainly expedient that the facts upon which the opinion of the Court is desired should not be in controversy, and it should not be left to the Court itself to ascertain what they are.[47]

One may ask whether the UNSG is better equipped, or more legitimate, than the Court in this respect.

The reliance on the Dossier prepared by the UN Secretariat is particularly problematic when there is no real adversarial process due to the refusal of one of the interested parties to participate in the proceedings.[48] Such was the case, for instance, of Israel in the *Wall* advisory proceedings. In the *Kosovo* case on the other hand, both Serbia and Kosovo were invited by the Court to submit written statements and written comments and to present an oral statement, and both of them availed themselves of this opportunity. As a result, the question submitted to the Court proceeded like a contentious case and therefore, there was little risk that the selection made by the Secretariat would distort the proceedings.

---

son impartialité … Telles sont les raisons, Monsieur le Président, qui ont conduit le Secrétaire général à me demander de limiter l'exposé que je fais en son nom à une présentation des faits' (Oral Statement, 28 February 1950, *in ICJ Pleadings, Oral Arguments, Documents. Interpretation of Peace Treaties with Bulgaria, Hungary and Romania*, p. 256).

   [46] Advisory Opinion, 16 October 1975, ICJ Reports 1975, pp. 28–9, para. 46.
   [47] *Series B No. 5*, p. 28.
   [48] See on this point H. Thirlway, 'The Law and Procedure of the ICJ. Supplement 2010', *BYBIL*, 2010, pp. 153–4 and 166–8.

In any event, in the *Wall* opinion, the Court decided that, even though Israel (which appeared, on the substantive level, as a Defendant State, since the question submitted to the Court purported to determine whether Israel had complied with international law) refused to fully participate in the proceeding, it had before it 'sufficient information and evidence to enable it to give the advisory opinion requested', relying in particular on the 'voluminous dossier' submitted by the UNSG.[49] It shows both that according to the Court, the Dossier of the Secretariat is a crucial piece of the proceedings, in particular when factual issues are debated among the parties, and that the Court considers it legitimate to rely on the Dossier as an objective, impartial statement of facts.

This having been said, the Court did not rely exclusively on the Dossier of the UNSG in the *Wall* case. The Court also noted that 'numerous other participants have submitted to the Court written statements which contain information relevant to a response to the question put by the General Assembly. The Court notes in particular that Israel's Written Statement, although limited to issues of jurisdiction and judicial propriety, contained observations on other matters, including Israel's concerns in terms of security, and was accompanied by corresponding annexes; many other documents issued by the Israeli Government on those matters are in the public domain'.[50] It shows that the Court is well aware too of the necessity that its findings result from *some kind* of adversarial process when disputed facts are in issue, or in case of an underlying dispute.

In any case, as for any fact or document, it is for the Court to decide on its probative value, including with respect to the documents submitted by the UNSG.[51] In the *Kosovo* Opinion, the Court, for instance, did not take into account the translations provided by the Secretariat of the unilateral declaration of independence, on which many states relied in their written statements, on the ground that they did not correspond to the original version of the declaration.[52]

The degree of 'apparent impartiality' of the UNSG in the selection of relevant documents depends of course on the nature and degree of involvement of the UNSG with regard to the substantive issues to be dealt with by the Court in its Opinion. There are in that regard three possible situations. The first two situations

---

[49]  ICJ Reports 2004, pp. 161–2, paras. 57–8. Among the numerous documents submitted to the Court by the UNSG, there were reports of the UNSG himself—see Documents No. 48 to 52 of the Dossier, accessible on the website of the Court.

[50]  Ibid.

[51]  See, *mutatis mutandis*, ICJ, *Pulp Mills on the River Uruguay (Argentina v. Uruguay),* Judgment, 20 April 2010, ICJ Reports 2010, pp. 72–3, para. 168.

[52]  ICJ Reports 2010, p. 446, para. 107: 'Certain features of the text of the declaration and the circumstances of its adoption also point to the same conclusion. Nowhere in the original Albanian text of the declaration (which is the sole authentic text) is any reference made to the declaration being the work of the Assembly of Kosovo. The words "Assembly of Kosovo" appear at the head of the declaration only in the English and French translations contained in the dossier submitted on behalf of the Secretary-General.'

are unequivocal with regard to the status of the UNSG in the proceedings. To begin with, in some cases the UNSG is not at all concerned by the question submitted to the Court, since he did not intervene directly within the UN on the issues which have to be discussed before the Court. Such was largely the case for instance in the 1996 Opinion on *Nuclear Weapons*. In other cases, the UNSG is directly involved as a 'party' in the question submitted to the Court, whether as the chief administrative officer representing the UN or as a principal organ having a disagreement with another principal organ of the United Nations. In this set of situations, it is not possible for the UNSG to claim neutrality. Actually, he is not expected to do it since, obviously, he acts as a party in the case.[53]

The third category is more equivocal. It concerns cases in which the object of the question submitted to the Court is not about the conduct of the UN or of the UNSG as such but, nonetheless, the Court has to assess, or at least has to take into account, the said conduct to answer the question. In such a situation, the UNSG cannot act as if it were a party to the case, but it also cannot act as if it has no interest in the resolution of the case. This was the situation in the *Kosovo* advisory proceedings where the question was about the accordance with international law of the unilateral declaration of independence of Kosovo, but where the conduct of the UNSG in Kosovo was not without effect on the decision with regard to the conduct of Kosovo's authorities. This tension could explain why the UNSG adopted a clear stance of neutrality in this case (among other—certainly more important, political—reasons, in particular, the absence of agreement among the members of the UNSC on the final status of Kosovo).

## 3. Neutrality as a Solution

Since it was clearly impossible, for political and diplomatic reasons, for the UNSG to endorse the view of Kosovo against Serbia or of Serbia against Kosovo, the UNSG's policy consisted of claiming strict neutrality both with regard to the final status of Kosovo (sub-section A) and with regard to his role in the proceedings before the Court (sub-section B). To some extent, this neutrality results from a political decision. As such, it can be seen as partly artificial, given the fact in particular that the UNSG 'fully supported' Ahtisaari's Plan.[54] Be that as it may, the UNSG could hardly adopt another position without affecting his status as Secretary-General of the UN—that is, of all the United Nations.

---

[53] See for instance the *Reparation* case, the *UNAT* case, the *Headquarters Agreement* case, or the *Privileges and Immunities Convention* case, as notably analysed by Rosenne in 'The Secretary-General of the United Nations and the International Court of Justice', in S. Rosenne, *Essays in International Law and Practice*, Nijhoff, Leiden, 2007, pp. 214–18.

[54] See *supra*, Section 2.A.2.

## A. The neutral position of UNSG with regard to the final status of Kosovo

On many occasions, both before and after the declaration of independence, the UNSG, or his Special Representative, made it clear that in their views, the United Nations had to remain 'neutral'; on the final status of Kosovo, in conformity with the fact that resolution 1244 (1999) itself remained neutral on this issue. In his Report on UNMIK dated 10 June 1999, the UNSG reaffirmed for instance that '[i]n line with my reports of 24 November 2008 (S/2008/692) and 17 March 2009 (S/2009/149) and the Security Council's presidential statement of 26 November 2008 (S/PRST/2008/44), the European Union Rule of Law Mission in Kosovo (EULEX) has continued to operate under the overall authority of the United Nations and within the status-neutral framework of Security Council resolution 1244 (1999)' and that '[t]he United Nations will continue to adopt a position of strict neutrality on the question of Kosovo's status'.[55]

The same position was adopted by the UNSG after the delivery of the Opinion of the Court. In his Report on UNMIK dated 29 July 2010, the UNSG pointed out that he had forwarded the advisory opinion to the General Assembly, which had requested it, and 'which will determine how to proceed on this matter'. The UNSG only encouraged the parties 'to engage in a constructive dialogue'.[56] On 9 September 2010, the UNGA adopted resolution 64/298 entitled *Request for an advisory opinion of the International Court of Justice on whether the unilateral declaration of independence of Kosovo is in accordance with international law,* which is limited to 'acknowledg[ing] the content of the Advisory Opinion' and '[w]elcomes the readiness of the European Union to facilitate a process of dialogue between the parties'. No further action (in particular from the UNSG) was contemplated by the UNGA.[57] To date, the UNGA has not adopted any other resolution on this issue. In his 29 October 2010 Report on UNMIK and subsequent reports, the UNSG indicated that 'UNMIK status remained unaffected by the advisory opinion of the International Court of Justice (ICJ), delivered on 22 July 2010'.[58]

This being said, to be neutral is not necessarily a neutral position. In particular, the *silence* the UNSG maintained with regard to the conformity with international law of the declaration of independence has been the object of

---

[55] S/2009/300, paras. 6 and 40. See also Cyprus, Written Statement, 3 April 2009, paras. 59, fn. 49, and para. 63.

[56] S/2010/401, para. 55; see also para. 11, with regard to the role of the European Union in promoting this dialogue.

[57] Contrary to what happened, in particular, in the *Wall* advisory process: see the UNGA resolution dated 20 July 2004, A/RES/ES-10/15, *Advisory opinion of the International Court of Justice on the Legal Consequences of the Construction of a Wall in the Occupied Palestinian Territory, including in and around East Jerusalem,* which paragraph 4 'Requests the Secretary-General to establish a register of damage caused to all natural or legal persons concerned in connection with paragraphs 152 and 153 of the advisory opinion'.

[58] S/2010/562, para. 2; and the last Report of the UNSG on UNMIK, dated 30 January 2014, S/2014/68.

diverging interpretations before the Court. Some states argued that such a silence confirmed the legality of the declaration of independence since, according to the Constitutional Framework, the SRSG was supposed to object to any *ultra vires* act of the Assembly of Kosovo (as he actually did several times before 2005, that is to say before the official start of the negotiations on the final status). The lack of objection was interpreted *a contrario* by these states as proving that the declaration of independence was not incompatible with the Constitutional Framework and international law.[59] The same could have been said with regard to the reconfiguration of UNMIK decided by the UNSG following the declaration of independence.[60] On the other hand, the states opposed to Kosovo's unilateral declaration of independence argued that the silence of the UNSG and his Special Representative was only of a temporary nature, while waiting for political directives from the UNSC; that, in any case, they have no power with regard to the final status of Kosovo; and that moreover nothing could be legally deduced from a silence, which is always open to divergent interpretations.[61]

To some extent, the Court endorsed the views of the states which had argued that the silence of the UN, the UNSG and his Special Representative was a relevant fact.

First, the Court endorsed the interpretation of resolution 1244 (1999) as being without prejudice to the final status of Kosovo. According to the Court,

[t]he resolution did not contain any provision dealing with the final status of Kosovo or with the conditions for its achievement [and] under the terms of resolution 1244 (1999) the Security Council did not reserve for itself the final determination of the situation in Kosovo and remained silent on the conditions for the final status of Kosovo. Resolution 1244 (1999) thus does not preclude the issuance of the declaration of independence of 17 February 2008.[62]

---

[59] See for instance the Written Statements of Austria, 16 April 2009, para. 41; France, 7 April 2009, paras. 2.70 *ff*.; Germany, 15 April 2009, p. 42; Spain, 14 April 2009, para. 43 (iv) and (v) and paras. 67–71; United Kingdom, 17 April 2009, paras. 6.45–6.46; United States, 17 April 2009, pp. 24 and 85–6; Kosovo, 17 April 2009, paras. 9.24–9.27.

[60] See *Repertory of Practice of United Nations Organs, Supplement No. 10* (2000-2009), 'Article 98', which does not mention the Kosovo advisory proceedings but points out that: '[t]he Secretary-General clarified the diminished and reconfigured role of UNMIK in the aftermath of Kosovo's declaration of independence and the coming into force of Kosovo's constitution. Despite reconfiguration of the UNMIK offices, and operations, the Secretary-General noted that "while my Special Representative is still formally vested with executive authority under resolution 1244 (1999), he is unable to enforce this authority". In his last report during the period under review, the Secretary-General noted that, while UNMIK's mandate under resolution 1244 (1999) remained in force unless the Security Council decides otherwise, changing circumstances on the ground and greater involvement by non-UN actors had led to a gradual adjustment of the profile and size of the Mission' (paras. 38–9).

[61] See, in particular, the Written Comments of Serbia, 15 July 2009, paras. 477–83 and 486–94; Cyprus, 8 July 2009, paras. 24–5; Spain, 17 July 2009, para. 12, and the Written Comments of Argentina, 15 July 2009, para. 23. See also, during the oral proceedings, CR 2009/24 (Serbia), Public sitting held on Tuesday 1 December 2009, at 10 a.m, p. 39, para. 11 (Djerić) and p. 61, para. 66 (Zimmermann). See also in that regard the Judgment of the Court in the *East Timor* case, 30 June 1995 (*Portugal v. Australia*), ICJ Reports 1995, p. 104, para. 32.

[62] *Kosovo* Advisory Opinion, ICJ Reports 2010, p. 449, para. 113.

Second, the Court considered that the unilateral declaration of independence could not violate the Constitutional Framework since

[t]he silence of the Special Representative of the Secretary-General in the face of the declaration of independence of 17 February 2008 suggests that he did not consider that the declaration was an act of the Provisional Institutions of Self-Government designed to take effect within the legal order for the supervision of which he was responsible. As the practice shows, he would have been under a duty to take action with regard to acts of the Assembly of Kosovo which he considered to be *ultra vires*.

The Court thus arrives at the conclusion that, taking all factors together, the authors of the declaration of independence of 17 February 2008 did not act as one of the Provisional Institutions of Self-Government within the Constitutional Framework, but rather as persons who acted together in their capacity as representatives of the people of Kosovo outside the framework of the interim administration.[63]

The interpretation reached by the Court has been criticized by some judges on the ground that other declarations of the SRSG went in the opposite direction by mentioning the Assembly of Kosovo's Provisional Institutions of Self-Government as the real author of the declaration of independence[64] and that in any case it is always 'delicate ... to interpret an actor's 'silence' in international law'.[65]

Whatever the soundness of Court's conclusion, the diverging interpretations of the neutrality and silence of the UNSG and his Special Representative do confirm that when the UNSG is entrusted with political tasks, as he has been in Kosovo since 1999, it is quite impossible to consider his acts or conducts as being neutral on the legal opinion to be delivered by the Court. He is necessarily involved in the case, even if his official position consists in neutrality.

## B. The neutral stance of the UNSG in assisting the Court

In the light of the above, it was appropriate for the UNSG to be as cautious as possible when assisting the Court in the advisory process. Since the UNSG could be considered a party in the case, at least as an interested actor in the situation on which the Court had to pronounce, it had to intervene before the Court in the most impartial and neutral way.

With regard to the 'Dossier', one may regret that the UNSG did not explain the methodology it used in selecting the 245 documents in it. The Introductory Note of the Dossier indicates that it 'contains the documents and other material of the United Nations as well as international instruments likely to throw light upon

---

[63] *Kosovo* Advisory Opinion, ICJ Reports 2010, pp. 447–8, paras. 108–9; see also the Disssenting Opinion of Judge Koroma, ibid., p. 469, para. 6.

[64] See the Declaration of Judge Tomka, ICJ Reports 2010, pp. 458–9, para. 17. See also pp. 464–6, paras. 32–5. See also M. Kohen and K. Del Mar, 'The Kosovo Advisory Opinion and UNSCR 1244 (1999): "A Declaration of Independence from International Law?"', *Leiden Journal of International Law*, 2011, pp. 121–3.

[65] See the Dissenting Opinion of Judge Bennouna, ICJ Reports 2010, pp. 510–11, paras. 48–51, and pp. 512–14, paras. 59–64.

the question on which the advisory opinion of the Court is requested' but then specifies in a rather equivocal way that '[t]he approach taken to the preparation of the Dossier is "comprehensive but relevant"' and that, in particular, '[w]ith the exception of Section C of Part II, which includes all Secretary-General's reports on UNMIK, all other Sections include a selective choice of documents prefaced by an explanatory paragraph'.[66] That a selection had to be made is perfectly understandable. The problem is that the UNSG did not systematically explain in the Dossier and in particular in the explanatory paragraphs *the ground on which* the selection had been made. In particular, while Section C of Part II includes all UNSG's Reports on UNMIK, which addresses concerns of transparency, other sections include documents of the UNSG, SRSG, or UNMIK without providing information on whether or not the selection was exhaustive or on what basis it had been established.[67]

To conform to a high standard of impartiality in a judicial process as well as to provide reliable documentation, it would have been a better option to be transparent regarding the methodology used to compile the 'relevant' documents. This is even more important given the fact that the methodology used for the selection of relevant facts is decisive for the assessment of the probative value of any material submitted to the Court. In the *Genocide* case for instance, the Court granted the 1999 Report of the UNSG on the 'Fall of Srebrenica' to be of 'considerable authority' because of the 'care taken in preparing the report, its comprehensive sources and the independence of those responsible for its preparation'.[68]

But the most interesting feature of UNSG's conduct before the Court lies in his decision not to submit any written or oral statement, as he could have done. As in previous cases, the ICJ decided by its Order dated 17 October 2008 that '*the United Nations* and its Member States are considered likely to be able to furnish information on the question submitted to the Court for an advisory opinion'.[69] Thus the UNSG could have submitted to the Court a written statement. Similarly, the Court recalled in its advisory opinion that '[b]y letters dated 8 June

---

[66] See paras. 2 and 4 of the Introductory Note of the 'Dossier'.

[67] See for instance Section II.G: 'This Section includes a *selection* of international agreements, bilateral and multilateral, concluded by UNMIK on behalf of Kosovo, a Note Verbale from the UN Office of Legal Affairs explaining the treaty making power of UNMIK (limited to the extent necessary for the administration of the territory) and related official communications from the Permanent Representative of the Federal Republic of Yugoslavia, and later, the Republic of Serbia and Montenegro, to the United Nations, to the Secretary-General and the President of the Security Council. They provide a representative example of the powers exercised by UNMIK pursuant to Security Council resolution 1244 (1999) in external relations'. The issue in judicial proceedings however is not only to provide 'representative' examples of the practice, but also any relevant material on the practice, which could be different in some cases (for instance if the practice has not been entirely consistent). In the same vein, the Dossier did not include General Assembly resolutions adopted with regard to specific non-self governing territories throughout the era of decolonization. It focused on 'relevant General Assembly resolutions of a general nature addressing in different contexts, aspects of the question of self-determination and territorial integrity of States' (see paras. 218 and 232 of the Introductory Note of the Dossier).

[68] ICJ, Judgment, 26 February 2007, ICJ Reports 2007, pp. 135–7, paras. 228–30.

[69] See Order, ICJ Reports 2008, para. 1.

2009, the Registrar informed *the United Nations* and its Member States that the Court had decided to hold hearings, opening on 1 December 2009, at which they could present oral statements and comments, regardless of whether or not they had submitted written statements and, as the case may be, written comments. *The United Nations* and its Member States were invited to inform the Registry, by 15 September 2009, if they intended to take part in the oral proceedings'.[70] The UNSG did not take part in the oral proceedings either.

This stance is not unprecedented. Since 1945, there have been 26 requests for advisory opinions, of which 21 concerned the United Nations. In each case, the UNSG transmitted to the Court a compilation of documents as required under Article 65(2) of the Statute. In addition, the UNSG submitted only a written statement in four cases.[71] He presented only an oral statement in four other cases.[72] Finally, he presented both a written and an oral statement in six cases.[73] On the other hand, the UNSG did not intervene at all in the proceedings in seven cases.[74] But it has to be noted that for the first three of the cases where the UNSG did not intervene, the UNSG did not receive a formal invitation to submit written or oral statements.[75]

It has thus been said that there is no consistency in the approach of the UNSG towards advisory opinions and that '[i]t is not clear why some advisory proceedings are considered worthy of appearance but not others'.[76]

---

[70] *ICJ* Reports 2010, p. 408, para. 8.

[71] See *Competence of the General Assembly for the Admission of a State to the United Nations; Application for Review of Judgment No. 158 of the United Nations Administrative Tribunal; Application for Review of Judgment No. 333 of the United Nations Administrative Tribunal; Legal Consequences of the Construction of a Wall in the Occupied Palestinian Territory.*

[72] See *Conditions of Admission of a State to Membership in the United Nations (Article 4 of the Charter); Reparation for Injuries Suffered in the Service of the United Nations; Interpretation of Peace Treaties with Bulgaria, Hungary and Romania; International Status of South West Africa.*

[73] See *Reservations to the Convention on the Prevention and Punishment of the Crime of Genocide; Effect of Awards of Compensation Made by the United Nations Administrative Tribunal; Legal Consequences for States of the Continued Presence of South Africa in Namibia (South West Africa) notwithstanding Security Council Resolution 276 (1970); Applicability of the Obligation to Arbitrate under Section 21 of the United Nations Headquarters Agreement of 26 June 1947; Applicability of Article VI, Section 22, of the Convention on the Privileges and Immunities of the United Nations; Difference Relating to Immunity from Legal Process of a Special Rapporteur of the Commission on Human Rights.*

[74] See *Voting Procedure on Questions relating to Reports and Petitions concerning the Territory of South West Africa; Admissibility of Hearings of Petitioners by the Committee on South West Africa; Certain Expenses of the United Nations (Article 17, paragraph 2, of the Charter); Western Sahara; Application for Review of Judgment No. 273 of the United Nations Administrative Tribunal; Legality of the Threat or Use of Nuclear Weapons;* and, finally, the *Kosovo* case.

[75] See C.-A. Fleischhauer, 'The Constitutional Relationship between the Secretary-General of the United Nations and the International Court of Justice', *in Boutros Boutros-Ghali,* amicorum discipulorum que liber. *Paix, développement, démocratie,* Bruylant, Bruxelles, 1998, p. 466: 'Practice shows, that until 1972, in none of the advisory proceedings initiated by UN organs, the Secretary-General—or for that matter the United Nations—has received a formal invitation under Article 66, paragraph 2, of the Statute to make written or oral statements on the question presented to the Court'. But '[t]he fact that he was not formally asked to make statements in the earlier advisory proceedings has not prevented the Secretary-General from making such statements and the Court from receiving them' (p. 467).

[76] J. Dugard, 'Advisory Opinions and the Secretary-General with Special Reference to the 2004 Advisory Opinion on the Wall', in L. Boisson de Chazournes, M. Kohen (eds), *International Law and the Quest for its Implementation: liber amicorum Vera Gowlland-Debbas,* Brill, Leiden, 2010, p. 413.

One explanation could be that, unlike the mere compilation of documents, any statement, whether written or oral, cannot be limited to a mere 'exposé historique des faits qui soit à la fois objectif, complet, clair et précis'.[77] In fact, as the practice has shown since 1945, such a statement quite inevitably leads to the presentation of some legal or factual arguments or personal views, then some 'plaidoiries juridiques'.[78] Hence the necessity for the UNSG, whose decision to present a statement is one 'arrived at his own discretion',[79] to carefully assess the appropriateness of doing so, taking into account that he has to 'bring before the Court the "international" point of view as seen by the Secretariat'[80] except when the question arises out of a situation in which the UN, or the UNSG, is involved. Practice shows in that regard that, on many occasions, there have been 'departures from strict neutrality', with the UNSG entering into the substantive debate between the members of the United Nations.[81] This runs contrary to the specific nature of the UNSG and his duty of impartiality, which supposes 'plus des attitudes d'abstention et de réserve de la part du Secrétaire général que des initiatives hardies'.[82]

The *Kosovo* case bears some resemblance in that regard to the *Reservations* case. In both cases, there was some conflict between, on the one hand, the role of the UNSG as a representative of the UN and the UN General Assembly, and in assisting the ICJ, and, on the other hand, its own operational functions (as a depositary in the *Reservations* case, as a person entrusted with specific functions by the UNSC in the *Kosovo* case). In both cases, the UNSG was, to some extent, 'juge et partie'.[83] In the *Reservations* case, the UNSG submitted a written statement and presented an oral statement. His statement 'was a spirited defence of the practice followed by the

---

[77] I. S. Kerno, 'L'Organisation des Nations Unies et la Cour internationale de Justice', *Collected Courses of the Hague Academy of International Law*, Vol. 78 (1951), pp. 561–2. Such is not however automatically the case. In the *Wall* case, for instance, the UNSG only submitted to the Court, in addition to the 'Dossier', a written statement comprising factual data only. This being said, even a factual inquiry supposed an assessment of the relevant facts. See also *supra*, n 45.

[78] I. S. Kerno, 'L'Organisation des Nations Unies et la Cour internationale de Justice', *Collected Courses of the Hague Academy of International Law*, Vol. 78 (1951), p. 562.

[79] C.-A. Fleischhauer, 'The Constitutional Relationship between the Secretary-General of the United Nations and the International Court of Justice', in *Boutros Boutros-Ghali, amicorum discipulorumque liber. Paix, développement, démocratie*, Bruylant, Bruxelles, 1998, p. 467.

[80] Ibid., at p. 468 (quoting Rosenne).

[81] See S. Rosenne, 'The Secretary-General of the United Nations and the Advisory Procedure of the International Court of Justice', in K. Wellens (ed), *International Law: Theory and Practice. Essays in Honour of Eric Suy*, Kluwer, La Haye, 1998, pp. 709–11. According to Rosenne, '[t]hose very exceptional circumstances may be found to justify the departure from a strictly neutral position which in principle ought to characterize any legal position taken by the Secretary-General in advisory proceedings before the Court, when the requesting organ is seeking guidance as to its own future action' (ibid., at p. 711).

[82] P. Daillier, 'L'intervention du Secrétaire général des Nations Unies dans la procédure consultative de la Cour internationale de Justice', *AFDI*, 1973, Vol. 19, p. 381. See, more generally, the full study, pp. 376–410, which is very illuminating on the necessity for the UNSG to remain as neutral as possible before the Court and thus the necessity of not intervening before the Court, as far as possible.

[83] P. Daillier, 'L'intervention du Secrétaire général des Nations Unies dans la procédure consultative de la Cour internationale de Justice', *AFDI*, 1973, Vol. 19, p. 396.

Secretary-General', but it was rejected by the Court. It has been 'regarded as the most serious "defeat" of the Secretary-General in the Court'.[84]

To use the language of 'victory' or 'defeat' with regard to a principal organ of the UN, whose tasks are in principle of an administrative nature and who is supposed to assist the Court in the course of the advisory proceedings, reveals that something is problematic in the current organization of these proceedings before the Court, which does not anymore match the reality of the twenty-first century powers and functions of the UNSG. In retrospect, the decision of the UNSG not to intervene before the Court in *Kosovo* proved to be very wise and should perhaps inspire a modification of the Statute, the Rules, or at least the practice of the Court in order to better separate the administrative parts of the judicial process and the substantive issues dealt with by the Court as a judicial organ.

In its latest Advisory Opinion, the Court considered that,

[a]s the Court said, on the only other occasion in which a specialized agency sought an opinion in terms of Article XII of the Annex to the Statute of the ILOAT, '[t]he principle of equality of the parties follows from the requirements of good administration of justice' (1956 Advisory Opinion, *I.C.J Reports 1956*, p. 86). That principle must now be understood as including access on an equal basis to available appellate or similar remedies unless an exception can be justified on objective and reasonable grounds ... For the reasons given, questions may now properly be asked whether the system established in 1946 meets the present-day principle of equality of access to courts and tribunals. While the Court is not in a position to reform this system, it can attempt to ensure, so far as possible, that there is equality in the proceedings before it.[85]

The Court then took some 'steps ... to reduce the inequality in the proceedings before it', which enabled it eventually to conclude that 'the unequal position before the Court of the employing institution and its official, arising from provisions of the Court's Statute, has been substantially alleviated by' its procedural decisions and that as a result, there were no more compelling reasons to refuse to deliver the advisory opinion.[86]

The Study Group of the International Law Association on the Practice and Procedure of International Courts and Tribunals has recently adopted 'The Burgh House Principles on the Independence of the International Judiciary'. Principle 2.1 contains the following guideline: 'Where a court is established as an organ or under the auspices of an international organization, the court and judges shall exercise their judicial functions free from interference from other organs or authorities of that organization. This freedom shall apply both to the judicial process in pending cases, including the assignment of cases to particular judges, and to the operation of the court and its registry'.[87] The delicate situation of the UNSG in

---

[84] S. Rosenne, 'The Secretary-General of the United Nations and the International Court of Justice', in S. Rosenne, *Essays in International Law and Practice*, Nijhoff, Leiden, 2007, pp. 215–16.

[85] *Judgment No.2867 of the Administrative Tribunal of the International Labour Organization upon a Complaint Filed against the International Fund for Agricultural Development (Request for Advisory Opinion)*, ICJ Reports 2012, p. 10 at p. 29, para. 44.

[86] Ibid., pp. 30, para. 45 and p. 31, para. 48.

[87] Available at <http://www.ila-hq.org/en/committees/study_groups.cfm/cid/1012>.

the *Kosovo* advisory proceedings shows that the current practice of the Court is not entirely compatible with this guideline—at least if a high standard of impartiality is adopted.[88]

Nothing in the current wording of Article 65 of the Statute or Article 104 of the Rules of Court makes it mandatory to have recourse to the UNSG to establish a complete record of the relevant documents. Nothing in the Statute or the Rules of Court obliges the Court either to ask, in any situation involving the United Nations, the UNSG to submit a written statement or present an oral one. It could then be appropriate for the Court in the light of the *Kosovo* case, and even if no problem of impartiality has been raised during the proceedings in this case, to assess whether a different procedural organization could be established in order to clarify the role of the UNSG within the advisory proceedings and to harmonize it with his increasing political and diplomatic functions.

---

[88] See, as a comparison, the comment made by the Court in the *Pulp Mills* case, which is of some interest in the present case: 'The Court indeed considers that those persons who provide before the Court evidence based on their scientific or technical knowledge and on their personal experience should testify before the Court, as experts, witnesses or in some cases in both capacities, rather than Counsel, so that they may be submitted to questioning by the other Party as well as by the Court' (Judgment, 20 April 2010, ICJ Reports 2010, p. 72, para. 167; see also Judge Greenwood's separate opinion, ibid., p. 231, para. 27).

# 10

# The Sounds of Silence

## Making Sense of the Supposed Gaps in the *Kosovo* Opinion

*Marc Weller**

## 1. Introduction

It is usual for a court to be criticized for its pronouncements. It is perhaps less usual for a judicial body to be criticized for pronouncements it did not make. The criticism triggered by the ICJ's Advisory Opinion on the *Accordance with International Law of the Unilateral Declaration of Independence in Respect of Kosovo* of 2010 has mainly focused on what was left unsaid.[1]

Of course, there are those who argue that the Court should not have given an opinion at all.[2] Instead, it should have exercised its judicial discretion and refused to answer the request from the General Assembly—a request made with an unconvincing majority of 77 votes in favour, six against, and 74 abstentions. In answering the question, it has been asserted, the Court interfered in the exercise by the Security Council of its primary responsibility relating to international peace and security. Moreover, in something of an abuse of the legal process, the Court was put in the position of making a ruling (albeit one in advisory form) on an issue that had proven to be divisive among states. Indeed, governments had been unable to resolve the issue, also in view of the uncertainties of the law on self-determination and secession. Hence, it was argued, the Court would be manoeuvred into the role of law-giver when pronouncing on these issues, rather than the interpreter of the law, as the law appeared unsettled.

Among those taking issue with the substance of the Court's pronouncements, two perspectives have dominated the debate. In fact, these two perspectives were already evident in the separate and dissenting opinions offered by the ICJ Judges themselves.

* I am grateful to Jake Rylatt for his research and editorial assistance, and to Dr Tiina Pajuste for her comments on an earlier draft of this chapter.
[1] *Accordance with International Law of the Unilateral Declaration of Independence in Respect of Kosovo*, ICJ Reports 2010, 403.
[2] Ibid., Declaration of Judge Tomka, at para 2; Ibid., Separate Opinion of Judge Keith; Ibid., Dissenting Opinion of Judge Bennouna, at para 14; Ibid., Dissenting Opinion of Judge Skotnikov, at para 1.

On the one side is a vocal group of dissenters within the Court, and of scholars commenting upon the Opinion, who felt generally unsettled by the Kosovo episode and its eventual outcome.[3] They saw in Kosovo's independence, which was consolidated by the Opinion, an unlawful act vis-à-vis Serbia, the former territorial sovereign. Moreover, they feared at the time that the Opinion would irresponsibly encourage secessionist movements in other regions, placing at risk peace and stability.[4] As Judge Koroma put it in his Dissent: 'The Court's opinion will serve as a guide and instruction manual for secessionist groups the world over, and the stability of international law will be severely undermined.'[5]

On the other side stand those sympathetic to the case of the Kosovars for independence. They may well have agreed in large measure with the outcome of the case. However, they complained that the Court had missed a unique opportunity to clarify or advance the law in this instance, in particular as it relates to the issue of self-determination outside the colonial context.[6]

This chapter will consider what was left unsaid by the Court. There are three types of silence that will be considered:

- First, there are quite major determinations by the Court which are stated, but not supported by a deeper analysis of their legal basis. An example is furnished by the finding that the doctrine of territorial integrity only applies in relations among states, rather than also in relations between governments and those within the state seeking secession.

- Second, there are issues which are noted by the Court, but no decision is given. This occurred, for instance, in relation to the doctrine of remedial secession.

- Finally, there are issues that appeared to many observers, and to several judges in their separate and dissenting opinions, as necessary elements in forming the Opinion, but which were altogether ignored by the Court. This concerns, for instance, the question of whether or not secession requires the consent of the government concerned, or in the alternative, a positive legal entitlement to independence on the basis of a right to self-determination.

Of course, the principal criticism of the Opinion is that is purports to answer, quite narrowly, the question asked of the Court. The question answered by the

---

[3] E.g. Kohen and del Mar, 'Kosovo's Advisory Opinion and UNSCR 1244 (1999)', 24 *Leiden Journal of International Law* (2011) 109; Hannum, 'The Advisory Opinion on Kosovo: An Opportunity Lost, or a Poisoned Chalice Refused?', 24 *Leiden Journal of International Law* (2011) 155.

[4] E.g. Trifunovska, 'The Impact of the "Kosovo Precedent" on Self-determination Struggles', in J. Summers (ed), *Kosovo: A Precedent* (Brill, 2011) 375.

[5] *Kosovo* Advisory Opinion, *supra* note 1, Dissenting Opinion of Judge Koroma, at para 2. See also, *Kosovo* Advisory Opinion, *supra* note 1, Dissenting Opinion of Judge Bennouna, at para 40, referring to the approach of the Court as one of sophism.

[6] Ibid., Declaration of Judge Simma, at para 1; ibid., Separate Opinion of Judge Sepulveda-Amor, at para 23; ibid., Separate Opinion of Judge Yusuf, at para 2; ibid., Separate Opinion of Judge Cançado-Trindade, at para 2. An example from scholarship is furnished by Burri, 'The Kosovo Opinion and Secession: The Sounds of Silence and Missing Links', 11 *German Law Journal* (2010) 881.

Court was whether or not the unilateral declaration of independence was unlawful, instead of the broader issue of the implications or consequences of the declaration of independence:

… the task which the Court is called upon to perform is to determine whether or not the declaration of independence was adopted in violation of international law. The Court is not required by the question it has been asked to take a position on whether international law conferred a positive entitlement on Kosovo unilaterally to declare its independence or, *a fortiori*, on whether international law generally confers an entitlement on entities situated within a State unilaterally to break away from it.[7]

In addressing itself to the narrow question of whether or not the declaration of independence was unlawful, the Court moved into territory where it could offer a clear answer, and one backed by a solid majority. As issuing any declaration by a group of persons within a state is unlikely to be regulated by general international law, it is possible to conclude relatively easily that such a declaration does not offend against international law. However convenient this approach may have been in disposing of the issue, at least where general international law was concerned, it risked rendering the opinion something of an irrelevance.[8] After all, as Judge Yusuf observed in his Separate Opinion:

since a declaration of independence is not per se regulated by international law, there is no point in assessing its legality, as such, under international law.[9]

Moreover, it may not be quite so easy to divide the question of the lawfulness of the issuance of a declaration of independence from the lawfulness of declaring independence as the Court suggested. To many observers, the question of whether independence was obtained lawfully in this instance was the real question at issue in this case.[10] As Judge Skotnikov put it, '[d]eclarations of independence may become relevant in terms of general international law only when considered together with the underlying claim for statehood and independence'.[11] Of course, the question of whether independent statehood can be obtained without the consent of the relevant states and, if so, under what circumstances, and what the modalities for secession might be in such a case, would indeed require further legal analysis. As Judge Yusuf noted:

The declaration of independence of Kosovo is the expression of a claim to separate statehood and part of a process to create a new State. The question put to the Court by the General Assembly concerns the accordance with international law of the action undertaken by the representatives of the people of Kosovo with the aim of establishing such a new State without the consent of the parent State. In other words, the Court was asked to assess whether or not the process by which the people of Kosovo were seeking to establish

---

[7] *Kosovo* Advisory Opinion, *supra* note 1, at para 56.
[8] Oeter, 'Secession, Territorial Integrity and the Security Council', in Hilpold (ed), *Kosovo and International Law* (Brill, 2012) 109, at 112.
[9] *Kosovo* Advisory Opinion, *supra* note 1, Separate Opinion of Judge Yusuf, at para 5.
[10] E.g. Guliyeva, 'Kosovo's Independence', in Summers (ed), *Kosovo: A Precedent* (Brill, 2011), 296; Kohen and del Mar, *supra* note 3, at 113; particularly trenchant is Hannum, *supra* note 3, at 156.
[11] *Kosovo* Advisory Opinion, *supra* note 1, Dissenting Opinion of Judge Skotnikov, at para 17.

their own State involved a violation of international law, or whether that process could be considered consistent with international law in view of the possible existence of a positive right of the people of Kosovo in the specific circumstances which prevailed in that territory.[12]

On the other hand, one would have presumed that the question put to the Court was formulated with some care by Serbia, the initiator of the request by the General Assembly for an advisory opinion, opening the door to the avenue the Court eventually took. It seems somewhat unfair to criticize the Court for answering just that question.

Nevertheless, it is an interesting question to investigate how the Court's limited pronouncements, and the supposed gaps in the opinion, affect the broader question of self-determination and secession. In addition, it appears worthwhile to consider to what extent some of the pronouncements of the Court made with reference to the narrow context of the declaration of independence might also apply to the broader issues of self-determination and secession. In order to do so, this chapter will consider the following issues raised by the Kosovo case:

- Is there a prohibition of unilateral secession in international law?
- Is it necessary to rely on a positive right to self-determination?
- Is there a right to self-determination in the sense of secession outside the colonial context?
- What is a 'People'?
- Was there a particular prohibition of secession imposed by the Security Council?
- What is the impact of process-based legitimacy on claims to secession?
- What are the implications of the use of force by NATO that preceded the eventual declaration of independence?

Given the number of interesting issues that arise from the Opinion, it will only be possible to consider each of these items fairly briefly.

## 2.  Is there a Prohibition of Unilateral Secession in International Law?

International documents addressing aspects of self-determination are replete with references to the territorial integrity and unity of states.[13] The UN Security Council and other bodies will also routinely refer to territorial integrity and unity when addressing instances of attempted secession.[14]

In the Opinion, the Court noted that several participants in the proceedings before the Court had contended that a prohibition of unilateral declarations of

---

[12] Ibid., Separate Opinion of Judge Yusuf, at para 2.      [13] See, *infra* note 25.
[14] See, *infra* note 29.

independence is 'implicit in the principle of territorial integrity'.[15] Accordingly, it considered the question of whether there is a prohibition of unilateral declarations of independence in international law. It found that 'the scope of the principle of territorial integrity is confined to the sphere of relations between States'.[16]

While many other elements of the Court's pronouncement were focused particularly on the act of declaring independence, as had been suggested by the question put to it, this pronouncement at least is clearly of general application. As the scope of the principle of territorial integrity is, according to the Court, confined to relations between states, it would neither bar a declaration of independence, nor any other conduct at the sub-state level, such as the act of effecting a secession.

This approach has been criticized for three reasons. First, the Court has been accused of following the arguably outdated *Lotus* principle in investigating whether or not an exclusionary rule exists in relation to declaration of independence. Second, there is the substantive question of whether or not a prohibition relating to unilateral independence (or declarations) exists. Third, there is the possibility of a presumption against unilateral independence—a presumption that may however be overturned.

## A. The *Lotus* approach

In its Opinion, the Court notes that:

… the General Assembly has asked whether the declaration of independence was 'in accordance with' international law. The answer to that question turns on whether or not the applicable international law prohibited the declaration of independence.[17]

Based on this approach, the Court could easily turn its finding 'that general international law contains no applicable prohibition of declarations of independence' into the conclusion that the declaration accordingly did 'not violate international law'.[18] This, in turn, was deemed a sufficient answer to the question asked by the General Assembly, which was in fact slightly different. The Assembly had asked whether the declaration was 'in accordance with' international law.

Judge Simma in particular criticized the Court for adopting what he considered an antiquated approach based on the *Lotus* principle. To his mind, this approach foreclosed a more refined reading of contemporary international law, which might also offer additional categories, such as 'tolerated' and 'desirable', in addition to permissible and impermissible.[19] Breaking away from the 'binary' operation of international law, a more subtle approach might have revealed that certain acts might be tolerated, which would not necessarily mean that they are legal, but rather that they are 'not illegal'.[20]

---

[15] *Kosovo* Advisory Opinion, *supra* note 1, at para 80.     [16] Ibid.
[17] Ibid., at para 56.     [18] Ibid., at paras 84, 122.
[19] Ibid., Declaration of Judge Simma, at para 5.
[20] See A. Peters, 'Does Kosovo Lie in the Lotus-Land of Freedom?', 24 *Leiden Journal of International Law* (2011) 95.

Whether or not a question is regulated through a permissive norm, or an exclusionary one, or perhaps through a practice of toleration, as Judge Simma suggests, depends of course on the issue at hand. The Court may well in general be minded to follow a broader, traditional approach based on the *Lotus* presumption that that which is not prohibited is permitted. However, in the particular context of this case, it is less a question of whether a *Lotus* approach to international law in general would be appropriate. Rather, it is a question of whether or not the particular issue of a declaration of independence, or in a broader context, of secession, is governed by a prohibitive or permissive rule, or by no rule at all.

The ICJ had encountered a similar issue in the *Nuclear Weapons* Advisory Opinion, where it had been asked to determine whether the threat or use of nuclear weapons would be 'permitted' under any circumstance in international law. Rather than searching for a 'permission' for the threat or use of nuclear weapons in international law, the Court had instead determined that, in relation to the issue at hand, state practice shows that the illegality of the use of certain weapons as such does not result from an absence of authorization but, on the contrary, is formulated in terms of prohibition.[21]

In this case, submissions to the Court had relied on such a purported prohibition as had, indeed, some of its members expressing themselves in individual opinions. As Judge Koroma put it in his strongly worded Dissent:

The truth is that international law upholds the territorial integrity of a State. One of the fundamental principles of contemporary international law is that of respect for the sovereignty and territorial integrity of States. This principle entails an obligation to respect the definition, delineation and territorial integrity of an existing State ... The unilateral declaration of independence involves a claim to a territory which is part of the Federal Republic of Yugoslavia (Serbia). Attempting to dismember or amputate part of the territory of a State, in this case the Federal Republic of Yugoslavia (Serbia), by dint of the unilateral declaration of independence of 17 February 2008, is neither in conformity with international law nor with the principles of the Charter of the United Nations, nor with resolution 1244 (1999).[22]

Judge Yusuf offered a more nuanced position, which will be considered in greater detail below. However, he also took the view that international law 'primarily protects, and gives priority to, the territorial preservation of States and seeks to avoid the fragmentation or disintegration due to separatist forces'.[23] Given the strength of the belief in the application of the doctrine of territorial integrity as a bar to unilateral declarations of independence, or to unilateral independence evidenced in statements of this kind, including submissions made by states to the Court, it would be difficult to criticize the Court for testing this claim and investigating whether such a prohibition actually exists as a rule framed in the negative, rather than searching for a permissive rule.

---

[21] *Legality of the Threat or Use of Nuclear Weapons*, ICJ Reports (1996) 226, at para 52.
[22] *Kosovo* Advisory Opinion, *supra* note 1, Dissenting Opinion of Judge Koroma, at para 21.
[23] Ibid., Separate Opinion of Judge Yusuf, at para 12.

## B. Determining Whether a Prohibition Exists

The Court did investigate whether a prohibition of unilateral declarations of independence exists in international law. In this sense, the issue represents less a gap in its Opinion, but more an instance of highly condensed presentation, and perhaps insufficient reasoning in support of it. The Court offered three lines of argument:

- The relevant international standards do not address themselves to sub-state actors;
- International practice does not support the view that unilateral declarations of independence are prohibited;
- Security Council practice, in particular, implicitly confirms that declarations of independence are not prohibited.

Each of these arguments is treated in no more than a paragraph or two. Hence, it is appropriate to consider each of them at slightly greater length in turn.

### 1. Relevant international standards

In addressing the question of whether international law prohibits unilateral declarations of independence, the Court considered the principal international instruments addressing territorial integrity and territorial unity. In particular, it referred to Article 2(4) of the UN Charter, the Friendly Relations Declaration 2625 (XXV) of the General Assembly, and the Helsinki Final Act.

As was already noted above, on the basis of these instruments, the Court determined very swiftly that the scope of the principle of territorial integrity 'is confined to the sphere of relations between States'.[24] It based this finding on the wording of the relevant instruments, which referred to UN 'Members', to 'States', or to 'participating States' respectively. As those seeking secession could not (yet) be considered state-actors, their actions, including a unilateral declaration of independence, were not proscribed by the principle of territorial integrity or unity set out in these standards.

The Court's swift disposal of the issue might be subject to attack, given its brevity. This point was clearly an important field of battle in the proceedings before the Court.

While most international standards do refer specifically to states, as the Court had noted, others do in fact feature a more open wording. Several texts appear to proscribe 'any attempt' or 'any action' directed against the territorial integrity and unity of states, without mentioning the state as the specific or exclusive addressee of the respective provision.[25] A more detailed analysis of this language, and of the

---

[24] *Kosovo* Advisory Opinion, supra note 1, at para. 80.
[25] GA Res. 1514 (XV), 14 December 1960, at para 6: 'Any attempt aimed at the partial or total disruption of the national unity and the territorial integrity of a country is incompatible with the purposes and principles of the Charter of the United Nations'; GA Res. 2625 (XXV), 24 October 1970, at para 1: 'Nothing in the foregoing paragraphs shall be construed as authorizing or encouraging

context in which it is used, confirms that the provisions in question are in fact focused on any attempt or action undertaken by a state. But that argument would need to be made in each instance that was invoked by the believers in the application of the doctrine of territorial integrity to non-state actors.

## 2. *International practice*

The Court countered the presumption of the existence of a prohibition of unilateral declarations of independence, or secessions, with the empirical finding that a great many states had come into existence as a result of the exercise of the colonial right of self-determination. It added:

> There were, however, also instances of declarations of independence outside this context. The practice of States in these latter cases does not point to the emergence in international law of a new rule prohibiting the making of a declaration of independence in such cases.[26]

It is interesting that the Court assumed that there would need to be a 'new' rule, prohibiting declarations of independence. Several states might have presumed, to the contrary, that such a prohibition was part of classical international law. Moreover, there are in fact but a few instances where new states have come into being through unilateral, opposed secession. At least until fairly recently, most attempted cases of unilateral opposed secession outside of the colonial context have either ended in a defeat of the attempt at the hands of the central government (classically, Biafra and Katanga, more recently, North East Sri Lanka (Tamils)), or protracted conflict and eventual stalemate.[27] This wide-spread practice could be (mis-)taken as an indication that unilateral opposed secession is a wrong which can be forcibly addressed by the respective government.

Of course, the true answer on this point concerns the level of international privilege bestowed upon secessionist groups. Outside of the colonial context, secessionist entities benefit merely from a minimum catalogue of legal entitlements in human rights law and in humanitarian law. However, a lack of legal privilege is not the same as being internationally proscribed, as will be clarified further in Section 3 of this Chapter.

## 3. *Security Council practice*

The Court also considered instances placed before it, where the Security Council appeared to have determined unilateral declarations of independence (in fact,

---

any action which would dismember or impair, totally or in part, the territorial integrity or political unity ...'

[26] *Kosovo* Advisory Opinion, *supra* note 1, at para 79.

[27] See the illuminating study offered by Professor James Crawford in the context of the Quebec Supreme Court reference: Crawford, 'State Practice and International Law in Relation to Secession', 69 *BYIL* (1998) 85.

unilateral secessions) unlawful. However, in those instances, the illegality of the conduct in question did not stem from the unilateral act of separation in itself. Rather:

The Court notes, however, that in all of those instances the Security Council was making a determination as regards the concrete situation existing at the time that those declarations of independence were made; the illegality attached to the declarations of independence thus stemmed not from the unilateral character of these declarations as such, but from the fact that they were, or would have been, connected with the unlawful use of force or other egregious violations of norms of general international law, in particular those of a peremptory character (*jus cogens*). In the context of Kosovo, the Security Council has never taken this position.[28]

Indeed, the Court turned this argument against unilateral opposed secession on its head. As the Security Council had determined such illegality only where the unilateral separation was associated with a *jus cogens* violation, one might assume that separations not tainted by *jus cogens* violations are not prohibited:

The exceptional character of the resolutions enumerated above appears to the Court to confirm that no general prohibition against unilateral declarations of independence may be inferred from the practice of the Security Council.[29]

This finding is also, ultimately, correct. However, it may not be fully persuasive unless one also considers the large number of instances where the UN Security Council has expressed itself in favour of the territorial integrity and unity of states, even where no *jus cogens* violation was involved.[30] The answer in relation to those instances would be that the Council does indeed routinely express itself in favour of the maintenance of territorial integrity and unity. This even also extends to non-state actors—in fact invariably so, given that it will be non-state actors who threaten the existing integrity of unity of states in circumstances of potential secession. However, those pronouncements would be reflective of a policy preference within the Council, exercising its political function as the principal organ charged with the maintenance of international peace and security. They are not legal, injunctive pronouncements, as could be expected if the Council had encountered a violation of a binding legal prohibition of secession in those instances. This is proven by the fact that the Council has repeatedly endorsed the eventual independence of entities that emerged from secessionist situations or conflicts, despite having expressed its earlier preference in favour of continued territorial unity.[31]

---

[28] Kosovo Advisory Opinion, supra note 1, at para 80.

[29] *Kosovo* Advisory Opinion, *supra* note 1, at para 81.

[30] These include: SC Res. 1790 (2007) on Iraq; SC Res. 1345 (2001) on Macedonia; SC Res. 1831 (2008) on Somalia; SC Res. 2100 (2013) on Mali.

[31] This applies to the former Yugoslav Republics that obtained unilateral independence (Croatia, Bosnia and Herzegovina, Macedonia, Slovenia), and to South Sudan.

# 3. Is it Necessary to Rely on a Positive Right to Self-determination?

The somewhat rushed examination of the scope of application of the doctrine of territorial integrity and territorial unity is in fact in accordance with the dominant view in legal scholarship.[32] As Professor Crawford points out:

In particular, the reason why seceding groups are not bound by the international rule of territorial integrity is not that international law in any sense favours secession. It is simply that such groups are not subject to international law at all, in the way that states are, even if they benefit from certain minimum rules of human rights and humanitarian law.[33]

Or, as Professor Abi-Saab adds:

However, if international law does not recognize a right of secession outside the context of self-determination ... this does not mean that it prohibits secession. Secession remains basically a phenomenon not regulated by international law.[34]

Yet, it is difficult to deny that governments generally discourage threats to the unity of the state they represent; and it is governments that make international law. Hence, one might indeed have expected that the international legal system reflects that preference. Indeed, as one author puts it, the absence of such a rule would be 'astounding'.[35]

Accordingly, Judge Yusuf asserted:

... international law disfavours the fragmentation of existing States and seeks to protect their boundaries from foreign aggression and intervention. It also promotes stability within the borders of States, although, in view of its growing emphasis on human rights and the welfare of peoples within State borders, it pays close attention to acts involving atrocities, persecution, discrimination and crimes against humanity committed inside a state.

... claims to external self-determination by such ethnically or racially distinct groups pose a challenge to international law as well as to their own State, and most often to the wider community of States.

... so long as a sovereign and independent State complies with the principle of equal rights and self-determination of peoples, its territorial integrity and national unity should neither be impaired nor infringed upon. It therefore primarily protects, and gives priority to, the

---

[32] See Corten, 'Territorial Integrity Narrowly Interpreted: Reasserting the Classical Inter-State Paradigm of International Law', 24 *Leiden Journal of International Law* (2011) 89; Urrutia Libarona, 'Territorial Integrity and Self-determination: The Approach of the International Court of Justice in the Advisory Opinion on Kosovo', 16 *Revista d'Estudis Autonomics i Federals* (Oct 2012) 107.

[33] Crawford, 'The Right of Self-determination in International Law', in Alston (ed), *People's Rights* (OUP, 2001), 50; *Contra* Orakhelashvili, 'Statehood, Recognition and the United Nations System: A Unilateral Declaration of Independence in Kosovo', 12 *Max Planck Yearbook of United Nations Law* (2008) 12.

[34] Abi-Saab, 'Conclusion', in Kohen (ed), *Secession: International Law Perspectives* (CUP, 2006) 470, at 474.

[35] Hilpold, 'Secession in International Law', in Hilpold (ed), *supra* note 8, 47, at 54.

territorial preservation of States and seeks to avoid their fragmentation or disintegration due to separatist forces.[36]

This emphasis of the international system on the aim of preserving the status quo, with a view to maintaining stability, is perhaps not fully captured by the Advisory Opinion. It is not easy to see how the international system can accommodate the prioritization of territorial unity, while at the same time admitting to the possibility of unilateral declarations of independence, or self-determination broadly conceived and unilateral secession. Generally, it is understood that this tension is managed through the balancing of the preference for the status quo with a limited, or carefully circumscribed right of self-determination and secession focused only on colonial and analogous situations. In fact, in addition to the claim to territorial integrity and unity, and the counter-vailing doctrine of self-determination, there is a third element to be considered in this context. This is the question of whether secession can only take place in the exercise of a right to self-determination. To some extent, such a view might be seen to be inherent in the very existence of the doctrine of self-determination. As the Canadian Supreme Court indicated in the *Quebec* reference:

International law contains neither a right of unilateral secession nor the explicit denial of such a right, although such a denial is, to some extent, implicit in the exceptional circumstances required for secession to be permitted under the right of a people to self-determination . . . [37]

In other words, if there is an exception to the rule (self-determination), then presumably there must be a rule to which that exception relates (territorial unity). If, on the other hand, it has been demonstrated that there is no rule of territorial integrity or unity applicable in this instance, as the Court had asserted, why then would there need to be an exception providing positive grounds for transgressing the (non-existent) rule? The answer to this conundrum lies in the fact that in this instance there exists a third way, as Judge Simma had suggested.[38] In addition to 'prohibited' and 'permitted as a matter of right', there is an additional option. This is the option of the neutrality of the law on the matter at hand.

The Court itself acknowledged the fact that there are more than two sides to this particular coin, as it were. It noted that 'it is entirely possible for a particular act—such as a unilateral declaration of independence—not to be in violation of international law without necessarily constituting the exercise of a right conferred by it'.[39]

In order to better understand this phenomenon, it is helpful to distinguish between three different concepts. First, there are instances of secession that offend against the international public order. As was noted above, an entity that acquires the attributes of statehood (population, territory, effective government)

---

[36] *Kosovo* Advisory Opinion, *supra* note 1, Separate Opinion of Judge Yusuf, at paras. 7, 10 and 12.
[37] *Reference re Secession of Quebec*, [1998] *SCR* 217, at para 112.     [38] See *supra* note 19.
[39] *Kosovo* Advisory Opinion, *supra* note 1, at para 56.

nevertheless cannot develop into a state if its birth was the consequence of a serious violation of *jus cogens*—it remains positively a non-state, in the sense that other
states are required to withhold recognition, must not assist the offending entity in
maintaining in place the situation that was created unlawfully, and must seek to
cooperate in bringing the unlawful situation to an end.[40]

At the other end of the spectrum, there is legally privileged secession. These
are instances where international law awards to an entity a positive entitlement to
achieve statehood if that is the popular wish, even against the active opposition
of the metropolitan state. This category of cases will be considered in the section
which follows.

In addition to these two extremes, there exists a third category—that of unprivi-
leged secession. These are instances where an entity cannot rely on a positive claim
to self-determination in the sense of a right to unilateral secession. However, its
secession is not unlawful either, as the Canadian Supreme Court had confirmed in
the *Quebec* reference.[41]

In such circumstances, international law does not express a view on the lawfulness, or otherwise, of the attempted secession. True, the principle of territorial integrity prohibits external intervention by states on behalf of the seceding
entity.[42] Moreover, the principle of territorial unity, which is a political principle,
rather than a legal injunction, reflects the general preference of states to avoid
secession where possible. The entity will therefore need to establish itself in an
environment that is likely to be hostile to its campaign for statehood. This applies
in terms of international politics and, to a certain extent, to international law.

Traditionally, international law would leave it to the central state concerned
to address the attempted secession as it wishes. It might be compliant (UK and
Scotland) or it might resist separation (Spain and Catalonia). It might even fight
secession, deploying the array of tools of power and control against the secessionist
entity, although it should respect the bounds of human rights and humanitarian law.

It is then for other governments to judge whether they wish to recognize the
independence of the entity in question. This depends on the extent of the effectiveness and finality of its claimed status that the entity has achieved, in addition to
political factors. As the general failure to recognize Somaliland for a period of over
20 years has demonstrated, one important political factor remains the preference
of governments to avoid any action which would, in their view, encourage unilateral secession elsewhere. The international reluctance to recognize is principally
driven by the hope that the central government will, after all, accept the departure
of the secession entity. In that case, this would not be an instance of opposed unilateral secession. In the case of Kosovo, on the other hand, an internationalized
'Final Status Process' had taken place under the aegis of the United Nations, and
had been exhausted. A definite outcome that appeared irreversible had obtained,

---

[40] E.g. Article 41, International Law Commission, *Articles on Responsibility of States for International
Wrongful Acts*, (2001), Supplement No. 10 (6AOR A/56/10), chp.IV.E.1.
[41] See *supra* note 36.
[42] E.g. Nolte, 'Secession and External Intervention', in Kohen (ed), *supra* note 33, at 65.

with the declaration of independence of 2008, an outcome recognized by what is now the majority of states.

In essence, therefore, international law fulfils three functions in this context. First, it precludes independence where the objective criteria for statehood have been obtained through a *jus cogens* violation. Second, international law helps to enact statehood in legally privileged cases—cases of self-determination in the sense of secession. Finally, international law remains neutral in other instances, where the matter is traditionally decided according to the principle of effectiveness, with a more recent emphasis on additional criteria of legitimacy relating both to the basis of the claim to independence, and also to the process of obtaining independence.

Of course, it is to the advantage of the entity in question to claim the legal privilege of secession by right, rather than by virtue of the facts it has to create against the preference of the international system to preserve the status quo.

## 4. Is there a Right to Self-determination in the Sense of Secession Outside the Colonial Context?

As the Court confirmed again in the Advisory Opinion:

During the second half of the twentieth century, the international law of self-determination developed in such a way as to create a right to independence for the peoples of non-self-governing territories and peoples subject to alien subjugation, domination and exploitation.[43]

However, the Court was unwilling to engage with the question of self-determination outside of the colonial context:

Whether, outside the context of non-self governing territories and peoples subject to alien subjugation, domination and exploitation, the international law of self-determination confers upon part of the population of an existing state a right to separate from that State is, however, a subject on which radically different views were expressed by those taking part in the proceedings and expressing a position on the question. Similar differences existed regarding whether international law provides for a right to 'remedial secession' and, if so, in what circumstances…[44]

… The Court considers that it is not necessary to resolve these questions in the present case.[45]

Judge Yusuf asserted, to the contrary, that this was the very question the Court had been asked to answer:

In other words, the Court was asked to assess whether or not the process by which the people of Kosovo were seeking to establish their own State involved a violation of international law, or whether that process could be considered consistent with international law in view

---

[43] *Kosovo* Advisory Opinion, *supra* note 1, at para 79.   [44] Ibid., at para 82.
[45] Ibid., at para 83.

of the possible existence of a positive right of the people of Kosovo in the specific circumstances which prevailed in that territory.[46]

Echoing this view, Judge Simma also complained that the Court had failed
to consider whether international law may specifically permit or even foresee
an entitlement to declare independence when certain conditions are met. He
referred to the fact that the authors of the declarations of independence had
made reference to the 'will of [their] people, offering a fairly clear reference to
their purported exercise of self-determination'.[47] Judge Cançado Trindade added
his own, elaborate treatment of a 'law of peoples' and self-determination to the
Opinion.[48]

## A. Remedial secession

The treatment of self-determination outside of the colonial context by the Court
had been awaited with some considerable anticipation. Whatever the other uncertainties in this area of law, as the Court itself noted, this issue had remained particularly contested among governments and, indeed, scholars. While the Court
indicated that it would not be necessary to 'resolve' these issues, the very fact that
it pointed to the divergent views on this issue appeared at first sight to undermine
the position of those advocating a progressive view.[49] For, if views among governments diverge, it is difficult to argue that there exists sufficient coherence of
practice and *opinio juris* to support a new development in customary international
law on this issue.

The classical approach was exemplified by Judge Yusuf:

Surely, there is no general positive right under international law which entitles all ethnically or racially distinct groups within existing States to claim separate statehood,
as opposed to the specific right of external self-determination which is recognized by
international law in favour of the people of non-self-governing territories and peoples under alien subjugation, domination and exploitation. Thus, a racially or ethnically distinct group within a State, even if it qualifies as a people for the purposes of
self-determination, does not have the right to unilateral secession simply because it
wishes to create its own separate State, though this might be the wish of the entire
group. The availability of such a general right in international law would reduce to
naught the territorial sovereignty and integrity of States and would lead to interminable
conflicts and chaos in international relations.[50]

---

[46] Ibid., Separate Opinion of Judge Yusuf, at para 2.
[47] Ibid., Declaration of Judge Simma, at para 1.
[48] Ibid., Separate Opinion of Judge Cançado Trindade.
[49] The strongest opponent is del Mar, 'The Myth of Remedial Secession', in D. French (ed),
*Statehood and Self-determination* (CUP, 2013), 79. But see, e.g. Doehring, 'Self-determination', in
Simma (ed), *The Charter of the United Nations: A Commentary* (OUP, 1995) 66, and Simma et al
(eds), *The Charter of the United Nations: A Commentary* (3rd Edition, OUP, 2012), at 330; Cassese,
*Self-determination of Peoples* (CUP, 1998) 119.
[50] *Kosovo* Advisory Opinion, *supra* note 1, Separate Opinion of Judge Yusuf, at para 10.

However, Judge Yusuf balanced this rather strong statement with a progressive view effectively endorsing what has become known as 'remedial secession':

.... if a State fails to comport itself in accordance with the principle of equal rights and self-determination of peoples, an exceptional situation may arise whereby the ethnically or racially distinct group denied internal self-determination may claim a right of external self-determination or separation from the State which could effectively put into question the State's territorial unity and sovereignty.[51]

In view of its growing emphasis on human rights and the welfare of peoples within State borders, he asserted, international law would pay close attention to acts involving atrocities, persecution, discrimination and crimes against humanity committed inside a state. To this end, he added, it pierces the veil of sovereignty and confers certain internationally protected rights to peoples, groups, and individuals who may be subjected to such acts, and imposes obligations on their own State as well as other States. In his view, the right of self-determination, particularly in its post-colonial conception, is one of those rights.[52] Hence,

The right of peoples to self-determination may support a claim to separate statehood provided it meets the conditions prescribed by international law, in a specific situation, taking into account the historic context.[53]

Judge Cançado Trindade endorsed this view in strong terms:

It is immaterial whether ... self-determination is given the qualification of 'remedial' or another qualification. The fact remains that people cannot be targeted for atrocities, cannot live under systematic oppression. The principle of self-determination applies in new situations of systematic oppression, subjugation and tyranny.

... Territorial integrity, in its *intra-State* dimension, is an entitlement of States which act truly like States, and not like machines of destruction of human beings, of their lives and of their spirit. By the same token, self-determination is an entitlement of peoples or populations subjugated in distinct contexts (not only that of decolonization) systematically subjected to discrimination and humiliation, to tyranny and oppression ...[54]

In fact, the proposed doctrine of remedial secession raised by the Court, and discussed at some length in these two Separate Opinions, is not quite as new as may appear at first sight. It was invoked as a formal legal doctrine close to a century ago, in the *Report Presented to the Council of the League of Nations by the Commission of Rapporteurs* on the Åland Islands Issue. While the Report dismissed the right to self-determination in its purported wider sense, it endorsed with surprising clarity the doctrine of remedial secession as a last resort in altogether exceptional situations.[55]

The debate about remedial secession was nourished in the United Nations era by the language used in the General Assembly Friendly Relations Declaration 2625 of

---

[51] Ibid., at para 12.     [52] Ibid., at para 7.     [53] Ibid., at para 11.
[54] Ibid., Separate Opinion of Judge Cançado Trindade, at para 208.
[55] League of Nations Council Doc. B.7.21/68/106 (1921), at 28.

1970. In the section on self-determination, the Declaration indicated that nothing in the text should be taken as authorizing or encouraging any action which would dismember or impair, totally or in part, the territorial integrity or political unity of sovereign and independent States. However, a further clause suggested that this protection would apply only to states 'conducting themselves in compliance with the principle of equal rights and self-determination of peoples and thus possessed of a Government representing the whole people belonging to the territory without distinction as to race, creed or colour'. This provision was repeated in the Outcome Document of the 1993 World Conference of Human Rights, with the slight modification of the final coda ('without distinction of any kind').[56]

It was argued that this language suggested that a government that fails to represent the whole population belonging to a territory without distinction ceases to benefit from the doctrine of territorial integrity or unity. As Asbjørn Eide, then a UN Special Rapporteur, indicated, if a group can prove:

… that there is no prospect within the foreseeable future that the Government will become representative of the whole people, can it be entitled to demand and to receive support for a quest for independence. If it can be shown that the majority is pursuing a policy of genocide against the group, this must be seen as very strong support for the claim to independence.[57]

Remedial secession was also considered by the Canadian Supreme Court, in its important decision on the *Quebec* Reference. While acknowledging that the position of the doctrine had not consolidated in international law, the Court noted that:

The underlying proposition is that, when a people is blocked from the meaningful exercise of its right to self-determination internally, it is entitled, as a last resort, to exercise it by secession. The Vienna Declaration requirement that governments represent 'the whole people belonging to the territory without distinction of any kind' adds credence to the assertion that such a complete blockage may potentially give rise to a right to secession.[58]

Since then the doctrine of remedial secession has been formally endorsed by the African Commission of Human Rights, which accepted that human rights violations can reach such a point that 'the territorial integrity of [a state] can be called into question'. Similarly, evidence of the exclusion from government of the population of a region (in that instance, the region of Katanga in Zaire) might give rise to a claim for self-determination.[59]

The Commission reiterated this finding in a case concerning South Cameroons. Indeed, the case is particular noteworthy as the respondent government in that case formally accepted that remedial self-determination would apply if it had indeed

---

[56] *Vienna Declaration and Programme of Action, World Conference on Human Rights, Vienna,* UN Doc. A/CONF.157/24 (1993), at I.2.

[57] A. Eide, *Possible Ways and Means of Facilitating the Peaceful and Constructive Solution of Problems Involving Minorities,* U.N. Doc. E/CN.4/Sub.2/1993/43 (10 August 1993), at para 83.

[58] *Reference re Secession of Quebec, supra* note 36, at para 134.

[59] *Katangese Peoples' Congress v. Zaire,* African Commission on Human and Peoples' Rights, Comm. No. 75/92 (1995), at para 6.

'massively' violated the human rights of the people of Southern Cameroons, or excluded them systematically from government.[60]

The mere fact that the ICJ referred to remedial secession in the *Kosovo* Opinion is likely to contribute to, rather than detract from, the dynamic towards recognition of such an entitlement in international law. The reference of the Court to deep divisions among states on this issue must of course be taken seriously.[61] However, the invocation of this doctrine by a significant number of states in the pleadings is noteworthy, as are its endorsements by two strong separate opinions.[62] While the views of Judge Cançado Trindade are intellectually persuasive, the arguments put by Judge Yusuf may persuade even more. After all, he strongly defended the doctrine of territorial integrity and unity in general, but then balanced this defence with a measured endorsement of remedial secession. Moreover, in offering criteria for the application of the doctrine in cases of severe repression and of fundamental exclusion of groups from governance of the state, Judge Yusuf put forward clear limitations to the application of the doctrine:

> To determine whether a specific situation constitutes an exceptional case which may legitimize a claim to external self-determination, certain criteria have to be considered, such as the existence of discrimination against a people, its persecution due to its racial or ethnic characteristics, and the denial of autonomous political structures and access to government. A decision by the Security Council to intervene could also be an additional criterion for assessing the exceptional circumstances which might confer legitimacy on demands for external self-determination by a people denied the exercise of its right to internal self-determination. Nevertheless, even where such exceptional circumstances exist, it does not necessarily follow that the concerned people has an automatic right to separate statehood. All possible remedies for the realization of international self-determination must be exhausted before the issue is removed from the domestic jurisdiction of the state which had hitherto exercised sovereignty over the territory inhabited by the people making the claim. In this context, the role of the international community, and in particular of the Security Council and the General Assembly, is of paramount importance.[63]

## B. Constitutional self-determination

While the issue of remedial secession features at least in two important separate opinions, the other instance of self-determination outside of the colonial context is not really addressed at all. This is the doctrine of constitutional self-determination which emerged in consequence of the dissolution of the former Yugoslavia.[64] It suggests that international law will be mindful of entitlements to self-determination

---

[60] *Mgwanga Gunme v. Cameroon,* African Commission on Human and Peoples' Rights, Comm. No. 266/03 (2009), at para 187.

[61] E.g. A. Gattini, 'The ICJ and Non-state Entities', in Hilpold (ed), *supra* note 8, 233, at 239.

[62] In this vein, Dugard, *Secession of States and their Recognition in the Wake of Kosovo* (Leiden: Brill, 2014) who holds that 'Kosovo marked the coming of age for remedial secession as a component of the law on secession', at 119.

[63] *Kosovo* Advisory Opinion, *supra* note 1, Separate Opinion of Judge Yusuf, at para 16.

[64] See Weller, *Escaping the Self-determination Trap* (Brill, 2009), Chapter IV.

even if these are based within the sphere of domestic, constitutional law. For instance, where a constitution grants an express entitlement to secession to a federal-type entity, international law will place weight on such a feature of domestic law. Similarly, a grant of self-determination in the informal constitutional practice of a state may also be of relevance (say, in relation to Canada, the United Kingdom, or Denmark). Moreover, a self-determination entitlement for an entity may be established in quasi-constitutional law, such as self-determination settlements concluded within states, at times with international involvement.

In the case of Kosovo, this issue was of some relevance, given Kosovo's dual status as an autonomous province within Serbia, and as a fully-fledged federal entity in its own right under the 1974 Constitution of the Socialist Federal Republic of Yugoslavia (SFRY). On the one hand, the dominant view appeared to have been that Kosovo's dual status excluded the kind of constitutional self-determination enjoyed by the full SFRY republics upon the dissolution of the federation. On the other hand, Kosovo's case was strengthened by the fact that its far-reaching autonomy, and even its federal status, had been unconstitutionally and unilaterally abrogated by Serbia. This in itself might have been seen as a ground for an entitlement to self-determination. Moreover, after the period of severe repression, and the expulsion of much of its ethnic Albanian majority population by Serbia's authorities during the conflict of 1999, it would have seemed oppressive to return Kosovo to the very entity that had suppressed its original autonomy. That autonomy had been removed while there still existed the overall Federation, which should have offered legal protection to its subjects. After Yugoslavia had dissolved, Kosovo would have become submerged within the legal order of Serbia alone.

Throughout the twenty years of its campaign for independence, Kosovo had taken considerable care to argue its case principally on the basis of constitutional self-determination. It had done so, knowing full well that many governments might be hesitant when it comes to admitting 'new' claims to self-determination which appear to broaden the classical, restrictive understanding of colonial self-determination. While this argument had not been given much weight internationally when it appeared unlikely that Kosovo would achieve independence, the situation changed with the advent of the Final Status Process. Suddenly, the constitutionally-based argument in favour of independence appeared attractive to governments, as it would offer an alternative, essentially domestic, explanation for the impending independence of Kosovo. This would avoid a feared precedent in favour of an international right to secession outside the colonial context.[65]

As the Court avoided addressing any potential substantive entitlements of Kosovo to independence, it also did not address the issue of constitutional self-determination in this instance. Hence, from the perspective of more conservatively-minded governments and international lawyers, it missed an opportunity to explain the unilateral secession of Kosovo on the ground of 'unique circumstances',

---

[65] These developments are chronicled at some length in M. Weller, *Contested Statehood* (OUP, 2009).

grounded in the particularities of the SFRY constitution and the circumstances of the dissolution of that state.

## 5. The Definition of the 'People'

Traditionally, the right to self-determination in the sense of secession was restricted in its application to a 'people' or to 'peoples'. This technical term would either be used, or avoided, depending on whether or not self-determination in the sense of secession was to be implied. Classically, only populations living in non-self-governing territories (colonial regimes) or under alien occupation or racist regimes would be considered 'peoples'.

The delineation of a particular people would not occur on grounds of racial, ethnic, linguistic, or cultural characteristics. Instead, a 'people' would be defined by the boundaries of the colonial or analogous territory they happen to inhabit (*uti possidetis*).[66]

The ICJ has confirmed that this principle, previously applied in the context of the dissolution of the Spanish and Portuguese colonial empires in Latin America, is also accepted in the context of the decolonization of Africa. It has noted that the maintenance of the territorial *status quo* implied by the principle, on the one hand, and the aim of self-determination to overcome the consequences of colonialism, on the other, appeared to be in conflict. However, it has recognized that it had been seen as the

wisest course to preserve what had been achieved by peoples who have struggled for their independence, and to avoid a discretion which would deprive the continent of the gains achieved by so much sacrifice. The essential requirement of stability in order to survive, to develop and gradually to consolidate independence in all fields, have induced African States judiciously to consent to the respecting of colonial frontiers, and to take account of it in the interpretation of the principle of self-determination of peoples.[67]

In the context of the dissolution of the former Yugoslavia, of which Kosovo had been a part, the Badinter Commission, created to advise the EU-sponsored international peace conference on Yugoslavia, pronounced on these issues. It confirmed that ethnic minorities were entitled to minority rights and potentially autonomy. However, only fully-fledged federal units could aspire to independent statehood. This would be effected within the established *uti possidetis*, or previous, internal, boundaries. The Commission held that:

the principle is not a special rule which pertains solely to one specific system of international law. It is a general principle, which is logically connected with the phenomenon of

---

[66] In relation to Kosovo, the most detailed treatment is A. Peters, 'The Principle of *Uti Possidetis Juris*', in C. Walter, A. von Ungern-Sternberg, and K. Abushov, *Self-determination and Secession in International Law* (OUP, 2014) 95.

[67] *Frontier Dispute (Burkina Faso v Mali)*, ICJ Reports (1986) 564, at para 25.

the obtaining of independence, wherever it occurs. Its obvious purpose is to prevent the independence and stability of new states being endangered by fratricidal struggles ...[68]

The anointing of the doctrine of *uti possidetis* as a universal doctrine has proved to be controversial, in particular where its application in Europe is concerned.[69] The process of defining states in Europe at the turn of the nineteenth to the twentieth century was left incomplete by the Versailles settlement. The freezing of territorial relations at the end of World War II ensured that this situation persisted until the end of the Cold War in 1990. The ethno-territorial conflicts which ensued in the Caucasus region and in the Balkans were a reflection of this fact. An insistence on retaining the established Versailles boundaries through the application of *uti possidetis*, according to this view, leaves these conflicts unresolved once more. This makes future conflicts unavoidable, it is argued.

   The challenge to classical doctrine in relation to the concept of a 'people' as the carrier of the right to self-determination has been broadened by recent jurisprudence elsewhere. In the *Quebec* reference, the Canadian Supreme Court considered that the term 'people' does not correspond to the entirety of the state population as defined by a previous *uti possidetis* boundary. Instead, it refers to distinct elements within the state.[70] In the Southern Cameroons case, the African Commission engaged in a more detailed review of the use of the term, in the context of the African Charter which concerns expressly 'human and peoples' rights. It applied the term 'people' outside of the traditional context:

The Commission states that after thorough analysis of the arguments and literature, it finds that the people of Southern Cameroon can legitimately claim to be a 'people'. Besides the individual rights due to Southern Cameroon[ians], they have a distinct identity which attracts certain collective rights. The UNESCO Group of Experts report referred to hereinabove, states that for a collective of individuals to constitute a 'people' they need to manifest some, or all the identified attributes. The Commission agrees with the Respondent State that a 'people' may manifest ethno-anthropological attributes. Ethno-anthropological attributes may be added to the characteristics of a 'people'. Such attributes are necessary only when determining indigenology of a 'people', but cannot be used as the only determinant factor to accord or deny the enjoyment or protection of peoples' rights.[71]

Hence, in addition to the traditional, territorial definition of a population that is legally privileged through the label 'people', two alternative approaches have come to the surface more recently. On the one hand, there is the proposal that a people might, after all, be defined through racial, ethnic, linguistic, and cultural criteria. This would pose a fundamental challenge to the doctrine of *uti possidetis*. However, the second, complementary proposition, would be that rights derived from the

---

[68]  Opinions of the Badinter Commission, 31 *ILM* (1992) 1488, Opinion 3, at para 3.
[69]  In this context, e.g. Allen and Guntrip, 'The Kosovo Question and Uti Possidetis', in J. Summers (ed), *supra* note 4, 303.
[70]  *Reference re Secession of Quebec, supra* note 36, at paras 123–5.
[71]  *Southern Cameroons, supra* note 59, at para 178.

doctrine of self-determination are mainly exercisable within the state, rather than through secession.

It is now widely accepted that self-determination is a complex entitlement that applies in different ways in different contexts. In relation to individuals, self-determination is seen on the one hand as a right to personal autonomy and choice in relation to matters affecting the person and his or her immediate environment. On the other hand, it is a right to democratic governance and participation in it. In relation to groups, self-determination implies a right to exercise the rights of individuals through a collectivity. Minorities enjoy rights relating to their existence and identity, and rights concerning full equality, including full and effective participation in public life. In relation to indigenous peoples, self-determination grants particular rights of autonomy and self-governance, including special rights relating to land, the environment and natural resources.

The Court confirmed its understanding of self-determination in the classical sense, as being focused on a right to independent statehood in the colonial context.[72] It avoided expressing itself on the application of the right outside of the colonial context. However, it also failed to note the increasing emphasis on the exercise of the right internally. As Judge Yusuf put it:

In this post-colonial conception, the right of self-determination chiefly operates inside the boundaries of existing States in various forms and guides, particularly as a right of the entire population of the State to determine its own political, economic and social destiny and to choose a representative government; and equally, as a right of a defined part of the population, which has distinctive characteristics on the basis of race or ethnicity, to participate in the political life of the State, to be represented in its government and not to be discriminated against. These rights are to be exercised within the State in which the population or the ethnic group live, and thus constitute internal rights of self-determination. They offer a variety of entitlements to the concerned peoples within the borders of the State without threatening its sovereignty.[73]

Had the Court dealt with self-determination in a more substantive way, it would undoubtedly have paid considerable attention to this more nuanced reading of the right and of its implication.

## 6. Recognition of the People as Actors

In its Opinion, the Court:

… thus arrives at the conclusion that, taking all factors together, the authors of the declaration of independence of 17 February 2008 did not act as one of the Provisional Institutions of Self-Government with the Constitutional Framework, but rather as persons who acted

---

[72] *Kosovo* Advisory Opinion, *supra* note 1, at para 79.
[73] Ibid., Separate Opinion of Judge Yusuf, at para 9.

together in their capacity as representatives of the people of Kosovo outside the framework of the interim administration.[74]

Judge Bennouna challenged the assertion that the declaration of independence had been issued outside of the Constitutional Framework established in accordance, and under the authority of, Resolution 1244 (1999). He asked: '… even if it is assumed that the declaration of 17 February 2008 was issued by a hundred or so individuals having proclaimed themselves representatives of the people of Kosovo, how is it possible for them to have been able to violate the legal order established by UNMIK under the Constitutional Framework, which all inhabitants of Kosovo are supposed to respect?'[75]

This aspect of the case turned on the question of whether or not the authors of the unilateral declaration of independence had acted in their capacity as members of the Kosovo Assembly (or parliament), or in another capacity. The individuals were principally the members of parliament, assembled in parliament, following a call to a special session of parliament, attending a meeting chaired by the Speaker of Parliament. It might have been just possible to consider that they acted as the parliament.[76]

The Court concluded that they acted in a different capacity, and hence were outside of the limitations imposed upon the Assembly by the Constitutional Framework of Kosovo, in a number of ways. This included the fact that their declaration was not published in the *Official Gazette*, was not nullified by the UN Special Representative, etc. However, there was also a more fundamental issue. Where a population, or their representatives, declare themselves independent, they reject at that very moment the jurisdiction that previously applied to them. As the Court held:

the Court considers that the authors of that declaration did not act, or intend to act, in the capacity of an institution created by and empowered to act within that legal order, but, rather, set out to adopt a measure the significance and effects of which would lie outside of that order.[77]

This finding adds to considerations already offered by the Canadian Supreme Court in the *Quebec* reference. There, the Court takes a unilateral declaration of independence for what it really is, at least where the central government opposes this step—it is a revolutionary act:

If the principle of 'effectivity' is no more than that 'successful revolution begets its own legality' … it necessarily means that legality follows and does not precede the successful revolution. *Ex hypothesi*, the successful revolution took place outside of the constitutional framework of the predecessor state, otherwise it would not be characterized as 'a revolution'.[78]

---

[74] *Kosovo* Advisory Opinion, *supra* note 1, at para 109.
[75] Ibid., Dissenting Opinion of Judge Bennouna, at para 63.
[76] See A.X.M. Ntovas, 'The Paradox of Kosovo's Parallel Legal Orders in the Reasoning of the Court's Advisory Opinion', in D. French (ed), *supra* note 48, 139.
[77] *Kosovo* Advisory Opinion, *supra* note 1, at para 105.
[78] *Reference re Secession of Quebec, supra* note 36, at para 144.

Therefore, a self-constituting entity, a population constituting itself subjectively as a people, would create facts which would, ultimately, displace the pre-existing legal order of the former territorial sovereign and instead trigger legal consequences at the international level. The declaration of independence furnishes the subjective element of statehood—the will to be a state made manifest by the state population. This is backed up, where successful, by the peaceful display of state authority over territory and population.

In this instance, the question was somewhat different, though. A revolutionary act would ordinarily be directed against the home state, rejecting the application and primacy of its jurisdiction in relation to the territory in question. Here, though, the legal order applicable to Kosovo had been established in connection with a Chapter VII pronouncement of the Security Council.

One might ask whether a population can dissociate itself from a legal regime established under the authority of Chapter VII of the Charter. Presumably this would create legal difficulties where a people enjoys a clear, traditional right to self-determination. Hence, a resolution maintaining in place a colonial regime would most likely be considered to conflict with a rule of *jus cogens*. But what would be the situation in relation to an act of popular will resulting in a declaration of independence in other circumstances?

## 7. Was there a Particular Prohibition of Secession Imposed by the Security Council?

It has been noted already that the unilateral declaration of independence, or indeed a unilateral secession, is not precluded by international law. Nor does such a declaration in itself create a legal entitlement to statehood at the international level, unless augmented by legitimacy through the application of the doctrine of self-determination, and/or supported by effectiveness of independent administration to the exclusion of the previous sovereign. The exception would relate to a declaration of independence associated with serious violations of *jus cogens*.

In this case, the Court distinguished the case of Kosovo from other instances where the Security Council had determined that the entity in question was not, and could not, be a state, because these were connected with the unlawful use of force or other egregious violations of norms of general international law, in particular those of a peremptory character.[79]

Moreover, the Court noted that the Security Council had in the past addressed itself to non-state actors. This had included the Kosovo Albanian leadership. However, there was no reference to the Kosovo Albanian leadership or other actors in Security Council resolution 1244 (1999). Hence, 'the Court cannot accept the argument that Security Council resolution 1244 (1999) contains a prohibition,

---

[79] *Kosovo* Advisory Opinion, *supra* note 1, at para 81.

binding on the authors of the declaration of independence, against declaring independence'.[80]

Of course, the resolution did not only concern relations with Kosovo. The principal addressee and beneficiary of the reassuring reference to territorial integrity would have been Yugoslavia/Serbia. Its preamble reaffirms:

... the commitment of all member states to the sovereignty and territorial integrity of the Federal Republic of Yugoslavia and the other states of the region, as set out in the Helsinki Final Act and Annex 2 ...

Annex 2 referred to a political settlement, taking 'full account of the principles of sovereignty and territorial integrity of the Federal Republic of Yugoslavia and the other states of the region'.

It could be argued that the Council acted inconsistently with this pledge, or at least the likely understanding of it on the part of Yugoslavia/Serbia at the time of the adoption of resolution 1244 (1999). Subsequently, in launching the status process and the associated negotiations, the Council departed from this agenda. The eventual result was a settlement plan submitted by the UN Special Envoy in the context of his recommendation in favour of independence for Kosovo. As Judge Koroma put it:

International law is not created by non-State entities acting on their own. It is created with the assent of States. Rather than reaching a conclusion on the identity of the authors of the unilateral declaration of independence based on their subjective intent, the Court should have looked to the intent of States and, in particular in this case, the intent of the Security Council in resolution 1244 (1999) which upholds the territorial integrity of the Federal Republic of Yugoslavia (Serbia)[81]...

At the time resolution 1244 (1999) was adopted, the Federal Republic of Yugoslavia was, and it still is, an independent State exercising full and complete sovereignty over Kosovo. Neither the Security Council nor the Provisional Institutions of Self-Government of Kosovo, which are creations of the Council, are entitled to dismember the Federal Republic of Yugoslavia (Serbia) or impair totally or in part its territorial integrity or political unity without its consent.[82]

In its findings already noted above, the Court had determined that the focus of resolution 1244 (1999) was the interim phase leading up to the final status discussions involving Kosovo. This was the scope of application of the reference to territorial integrity, and also of references to the restoration of Kosovo's autonomy and of its meaningful self-governance. This did not rule out an eventual settlement of Kosovo's status in favour of independence. In addition, the reference to territorial integrity and the Helsinki Final Act in Annex 2 of the resolution was balanced by a corresponding reference to the Rambouillet accords. The accords had referred to an eventual settlement in accordance with the 'will of the people'. This could be taken as confirmation of the fact that full self-determination even in the sense

---

[80] Ibid., at para 118.     [81] Ibid., Dissenting Opinion of Judge Koroma, at para 8.
[82] Ibid., at para 24.

of secession had been envisaged as a possibility, or at least that resolution 1244 (1999) did not preclude such a possibility.

Moreover, the Council itself had in its subsequent practice contributed to this understanding. For several years, the UN Administration, acting under the supervision of the Council, had engaged in a policy of 'standards before status'. This was widely understood as an offer of possible independence to the Kosovo Albanians, provided they managed first to demonstrate their ability to engage in responsible governance, including the protection of the ethnic Serb community. This was then duly followed by a status process which was formally billed as neither including nor excluding any particular option. The result was not predetermined. Had it been otherwise, the one or other side would have refused to engage in the negotiations. Finally, the UN's own representative declared that independence was the only viable option—an assessment endorsed by the UN Secretary-General.[83]

## 8. The Negotiating Process as a Source of Legitimacy?

Of course, there is the question of whether or not unsuccessful negotiations about possible secession can eventually lead to independence. This issue was considered at some length by the Canadian Supreme Court in the *Quebec* reference. The Court had argued that a government has to negotiate in good faith with a territory whose population has clearly and overwhelmingly expressed itself in favour of secession. Those negotiations must be conducted in good faith, the outcome being open and not pre-determined by either side. But what would happen if there were no agreed outcome to the negotiations?

The Supreme Court took the view that

To the extent that a breach of the constitutional duty to negotiate in accordance with the principles described above undermines the legitimacy of a party's actions, it may have important ramifications at the international level. Thus, a failure of the duty to undertake negotiations and pursue them according to constitutional principles may undermine that government's claim to legitimacy which is generally a precondition for recognition by the international community. Conversely, violations of those principles by the federal or other provincial governments responding to the request for secession may undermine their legitimacy ... In this way, the adherence of the parties to the obligation to negotiate would be evaluated in an indirect manner on the international plane.[84]

In this instance, this principle operated immediately on the international plane, as the negotiations had been conducted by the UN in a fully international framework. The negotiations appeared to be deadlocked or frustrated. After the Ahtisaari proposal failed to achieve acceptance by Serbia, there were two more attempts by the UN to achieve a settlement, one through a troika of negotiators headed by

---

[83] See Weller, *Contested Statehood, supra* note 64, Chapters 12–13.
[84] *Reference re Secession of Quebec, supra* note 36, at para 103.

Mr Ischinger of Germany, and another through a direct mission of the UN Security Council. Neither was successful.

Following the logic of the argument in the *Quebec* case, the evident exhaustion of the negotiation process should have strengthened the case for unilateral action, be it merely a declaration of independence, or the effective secession that would be consequent upon it. Kosovo had engaged with the negotiation process throughout and offered substantive elements for a potential draft agreement, including the difficult issues of local governance and the protection of ethnic communities. It embraced the proposal emanating from the UN Final Status Process. Hence, the Court might profitably have considered this question of process-based legitimacy for claims to independent statehood in this instance.

Another issue connected with the road to independence relates to the use of force.

## 9. What are the Implications of the Use of Force by NATO that Preceded the Eventual Declaration of Independence?

It is an essential tenet of international law that no change in the status of territory can result from the unlawful use of force. This precept, derived from the pre-World War II Stimson doctrine, has consolidated in international law by virtue of the unquestioned *jus cogens* status of the prohibition of the use of force. For instance, the foundational *Friendly Relations Declaration* of the UN General Assembly reiterates that 'the territory of a State shall not be the object of acquisition by another State resulting from the threat or use of force. No territorial acquisition resulting from the threat or use of force shall be recognized as legal'.[85] This provision is also reflected in the 1974 UN General Assembly Definition of Aggression, which adds that 'no special advantage' resulting from aggression shall be recognized as legal.[86] The application of this principle was demonstrated, *inter alia*, by the UN Security Council in its response to the purported annexation of Kuwait by Iraq.[87]

In this instance, it is true that most governments insisted that the former Yugoslavia, or Serbia, would need to restore the autonomy of Kosovo that had been removed, at least before NATO's armed action of 1999. Few would have pressed, at that time, for Kosovo's independence. It was only after the armed action that it became evident to some governments that independence was probably inevitable. This culminated in the finding of the UN Special Envoy charged with conducting the final status negotiations that independence for Kosovo is 'the only viable option'.[88]

---

[85]  GA Res. 2625 (XXV), *supra* note 25.

[86]  GA Res. 3314 (XXIX), 14 December 1974, at para 5.

[87]  SC Res. 662 (1990): '1. Decides that annexation of Kuwait by Iraq under any form and whatever pretext has no legal validity, and is considered null and void; 2. Calls upon all states, international organizations and specialized agencies not to recognize that annexation, and to refrain from any action or dealing that might be interpreted as indirect recognition of the annexation.'

[88]  *Letter dated 26 March from the Secretary-General to the President of the Security Council*, UN Doc. S/2007/168, 26 March 2007, at para 5.

It could be argued that this significant shift was due, ultimately, to the use of force by NATO in 1999.[89] In consequence of the use of force, Serbia had been displaced from the exercise of effective control over Kosovo in virtually all aspects. It seemed clear that a resumption of the exercise of Serbia's purported rights would not be realistically possible, at least without a further major armed conflict. Hence, Serbia might argue that Kosovo's eventual declaration of independence was a result of the use of force.

Of course, in this instance, there were a number of other factors. NATO's armed action could be justified by the doctrine of forcible humanitarian action in general international law. While this doctrine had not been universally endorsed by states, the operation was not widely considered as unlawful. Among those who argued that there was not yet a fully formed right to forcible humanitarian action that could be invoked in this instance, there was nevertheless something of a consensus that, in view of the specific circumstances, and the developing law in this area, the operation could still be seen as legitimate.[90] The hesitancy in condemning the action as an outright violation of the prohibition on the use of force was made evident in the vote on a draft resolution seeking to condemn NATO's armed action as a flagrant violation of Article 2(4) of the Charter. It attracted only three votes, with 12 states voting against. This contrasts sharply with the recent vote in the UN Security Council on the purported change in status of Crimea in consequence of the use of force by the Russian Federation. There 13 states voted in favour of the draft resolution, with only the author of the armed action, the Russian Federation, voting against, and China abstaining.

Moreover, NATO's action in relation to Kosovo was limited to aims that had been previously established by the UN Security Council. And NATO did not, of course, occupy or even annex the territory in consequence of the operation. Instead, the UN took on its administration under the ambit of resolution 1244 (1999).

In addition, the declaration of independence did not in fact come about as a result of the use of force. Instead, it emerged in consequence of the UN-mandated status process. Indeed, the declaration referred to the Ahtisaari settlement and incorporated it as an original limitation on Kosovo's freshly declared sovereignty. Given that the declaration fully reflected the internationally negotiated status agreement put forward by the UN Envoy, it is something of a misnomer to consider it 'unilateral'. While the text was not agreed to by Serbia, it did represent the international view as to a necessary or balanced outcome put forward by the Special Envoy on behalf of the United Nations.

The argument relating to the use of force relates both to the narrow question focusing on the declaration of independence, and to the broader issue of the resulting secession. Indeed, as the Court itself noted, in the practice of the Council, the

---

[89] See S. Yee, 'Notes on the International Court of Justice: the Kosovo Advisory Opinion', 9 *Chinese Journal of International Law* (2010) 763, at 780.
[90] This debate is reviewed at length in Weller, *Contested Statehood, supra* note 64, Chapter 9.

actual declarations purporting to change the status of a territory in consequence of the use of force have been routinely declared invalid. Hence, the opinion might have been expected to clarify why Kosovo falls into a different category of case. Instead, the Court confined itself to noting that the Security Council had not treated Kosovo as a case involving the unlawful use of force.[91]

## 10. Conclusion

When considering all the criticism of what the Court said, or left unsaid, one might consider three questions

- First, did the Opinion contribute to a reduction of tension over Kosovo and assist in achieving a normalization of the situation?
- Second, did the Opinion of the Court contribute to a proliferation of secessionist campaigns around the globe, as had been feared by some?
- And third, did the Court, after all, contribute to a better understanding of the law on self-determination and independence, or did it in fact undermine whatever consensus might exist in relation to it?

While this was not a contentious case, the Court is nevertheless an organ of the United Nations. Bearing in mind that role, it is legitimate to ask whether its Opinion contributed to the aim of maintaining or restoring peace and security in the Balkan region.[92]

When seen from this perspective, it is clear that the approach of the Court worked. Analysts claimed that the Court had failed to give a sufficiently clear and detailed answer to help advance, or even end, the status debate one way or the other. But precisely because the Court kept the scope of its answer very limited, addressing merely the question of whether the adoption of the declaration of independence was lawful or unlawful, it was able to offer a very simple and, above all, a very clear answer.

Having avoided difficult areas of law that would have proved divisive for the Court, such as the implications of post-colonial self-determination, it declared by a sufficiently strong and credible majority of ten votes to four that 'the declaration of independence of Kosovo adopted on 17 February 2008 did not violate international law'.[93]

The unambiguous nature of this pronouncement proved more decisive than the argument that the Court's ruling was too limited to help settle the issue. True, it had failed also to address related questions at any length, including the

---

[91] *Kosovo* Advisory Opinion, *supra* note 1, at para 81: 'In the context of Kosovo, the Security Council has never taken this position.'

[92] C. Walter, 'The Kosovo Advisory Opinion', in C. Walter, A. von Ungern-Sternberg, and K. Abushov, *supra* note 65, 13, at 14.

[93] *Kosovo* Advisory Opinion, *supra* note 1, at para 123.

question of whether Kosovo had had a positive entitlement in international law to self-determination. But in fairness to the Kosovo side, it was Serbia which had framed the request to the Court in those limited terms. Had it so wished, the government in Belgrade could have asked a more complex question, and it would presumably have received a more hedged or finely balanced answer. Indeed, it seems unlikely that the Court would have been able to come to an easy agreement on some of the more contested issues in international law, including the difficult issue of post-colonial self-determination.

As it was, the Kosovo Advisory Opinion has been strangely successful in terms of the outcome. The request for the Opinion in itself provided a cooling off period for the public in Serbia. Turning to the Court was rightly seen as a responsible act. It meant that no more aggressive action would be undertaken in the heated months of the immediate aftermath of the declaration of independence by Kosovo.

The Opinion, when it finally came, effectively terminated Serbia's unrealistic hope that the declaration of independence of Kosovo could somehow be undone. The government in Belgrade withdrew a draft for a General Assembly resolution which would have called for a renewal of status negotiations between Serbia and Kosovo, turning the clock back by several years.[94] This proposal was simply no longer tenable. Instead, it was constrained to join the EU in sponsoring a resolution supporting the EU mediated process of promoting cooperation, and subsequently normalization, between both entities.[95] An initial step towards that aim was achieved in the First Agreement of Principles Governing the Normalization of Relations in Brussels on 19 April 2013.

Second, the Kosovo opinion has not led to an avalanche of unilateral declarations of independence the world over. Secessionist conflicts exist, at least in the first instance, because populations feel impelled to seek what they see as self-determination by a sense of identity and often of historical injustice. Their expectations and demands are generally not much shaped by pronouncements of international courts and other agencies on whether or not international law encourages their claims. Moreover, even if the Court could exercise such an influence, the very minimalist attitude of the Court, avoiding grander pronouncements on the right to self-determination, would have significantly diminished it.

The one exception is furnished by the attitude of the Russian Federation. Although Russia had strongly opposed the Kosovo declaration of independence, it had little hesitation in invoking it as a precedent when it came to justifying its actions concerning Abkhazia and South Ossetia in 2008. After the ruling of the Court, in 2014 it was once again the conduct of the Russian Federation that raised the question of whether or not Kosovo had somehow caused its actions, or whether the 'Western' response to the Kosovo issue justified Moscow's attitude. This concerned the supposed secession and subsequent purported absorption into

---

[94]  Draft Resolution on Agenda Item 77, 64th Session of the General Assembly. Last Accessed 26 August 2014 at <http://www.un.int/serbia/Statements/77.pdf>.
[95]  GA Res. 64/298, 13 October 2010.

the Russian Federation of the Ukrainian region of Crimea. However, that instance, again, concerned the use of force by the Russian Federation, and indeed the forcible incorporation of the territory in question. Consistently with the view of the Court on *jus cogens* violations, that case was therefore one of the use of force for territorial gain, resulting in an unlawful situation, and hence quite distinct from the case of Kosovo.

The third, and, for this chapter, most relevant question is whether the Advisory Opinion assisted in developing the law on self-determination or secession and statehood, or whether it disrupted the consolidation of views in this difficult area. In truth, the Court would have been unable to advance the law on this issue significantly with anything approaching unanimity. The positions within the Court were too diverse. There were those who opposed giving a substantive opinion at all, arguing that the Court should refuse to engage with an issue which states, or the UN Security Council, had been unable to resolve. Then there were those seeking to preserve the traditional, restrictive views of statehood and self-determination. Others were willing to consider more advanced views, including self-determination outside of the colonial context and the issue of remedial secession. However, even if there had been a majority in favour of a more progressive approach, it would have been quite difficult to refine such a possible trend into one common view. Each individual would have felt impelled to insist on their particular approach to the issue.

In a situation of that kind, silence is to be preferred to open disagreement. Yet, the Court did manage to clarify a number of key issues, including the scope of application of the doctrine of territorial integrity and territorial unity, and the effect of *jus cogens* violations on claims to statehood.[96] Moreover, it offered a framework which, if filled out as has been attempted in this chapter, offers a persuasive view of the relevance and content of the concepts of self-determination and secession in the post-colonial age. It leaves sufficient room for further development of doctrine in practice, and for the recognition of recent developments left unaddressed by the Court.

---

[96] See also, Tricot and Sander, 'Recent Developments: The Broader Consequences of the International Court of Justice's Advisory Opinion on the Unilateral Declaration of Independence in Respect of Kosovo', 49 *Columbia Journal of Transnational Law* (2011) 321.

# PART III

# REACTIONS AND IMPLICATIONS

# 11

# The Court and its Multiple Constituencies

## Three Perspectives on the *Kosovo* Advisory Opinion

*André Nollkaemper**

## 1. Introduction

From one angle, the International Court of Justice (the Court), by delivering the Advisory Opinion on *Accordance with International Law of the Unilateral Declaration of Independence in Respect of Kosovo* (*Kosovo* Advisory Opinion),[1] merely did what it was asked to do: provide an answer to the United Nations (UN) General Assembly and thus fulfil its task under the UN Charter.[2]

A wider perspective is possible. This Chapter explores the proposition that by rendering an advisory opinion, the Court seeks to, and needs to, maintain its authority vis-à-vis multiple constituencies that have a stake in its decisions, and on which the Court to some extent is dependent. These constituencies include: first, the political organs of the UN; second, the state or other actors whose dispute gave rise to the advisory opinion (in the case at hand, Serbia and Kosovo); and third, the wider international community that has an interest in the proper application and development of international law.

Seen from this angle, one's assessment of the *Kosovo* Advisory Opinion is, thus, not only determined by whether the legal answer given by the Court was the right one. It also depends on the perspective from which one considers the outcome: from that of the Court's role as an organ of the UN, with particular responsibilities vis-à-vis the other organs of the UN (I will call this an 'institutional perspective'); from that of the Court as a judicial body that is tasked to contribute to the peaceful settlement of disputes (a 'dispute settlement perspective'); or as an organ on which the international community at large relies to ensure the proper

* I thank Jorian Hamster and Laura Chafey for research assistance.
[1] *Accordance with International Law of the Unilateral Declaration of Independence in Respect of Kosovo* (Advisory opinion) ICJ GL No 141, ICJ Reports 2010 403, ICGJ 423 (ICJ 2010), 22nd July 2010, International Court of Justice [ICJ]) (hereafter: Advisory Opinion).
[2] Charter of the United Nations (adopted 26 June 1945) 892 UNTS 119, 59 Stat 1031, TS 993, 3 Bevans 1153, 145 BSP 805 (hereafter: UN Charter).

interpretation and development of international law (a 'guardian perspective'). Obviously, these perspectives do not exclude each other, and with one opinion or judgment the Court may serve multiple constituencies. Nonetheless, considering the Opinion from one or another perspective may explain and clarify what the Court did or did not do, and why. In that respect, these perspectives may provide useful analytical tools for enhancing our understanding and appreciation of the Advisory Opinion.

The proposition that the Court may consider and attach weight to the interests and expectations of its constituencies is neither a new nor a remarkable one. An obvious example is the *Barcelona Traction* case,[3] in which the Court attempted to undo the negative fall-out of the *South West Africa* judgment,[4] with its pronouncement on the *erga omnes* character of particular obligations, even though it had no real need to do so in order to decide that particular case. The former decision can only be explained by the Court's awareness of the need to address the interests and expectations of developing states.[5]

The *Kosovo* Advisory Opinion was not similarly preceded by judgments or opinions which were so critically received that they called for a comparable 'corrective' decision to placate disgruntled states. However, the proposition that the Court may cater to the interests of its constituencies (including the states on which it ultimately depends) does not depend on a prior controversial judgment. Also, more generally, it is a plausible proposition that the Court cannot neglect the interests of its multiple constituencies.

Four features of a constituency-based approach should be noted at the outset. First, it will often be necessary to distinguish between the short-term and long-term interests of constituencies. Answering a question posed by the General Assembly in a particular way may cater to the immediate interests of a particular constituency, but in the long term might affect the interests of other constituencies.

Second, it would be a simplification to speak of 'the' interests of constituencies. In the case of the Security Council (SC), for instance, one can construe different interests that were at stake in the *Kosovo* Advisory Opinion. The Council as such may have had an interest in the continued validity and implementation of the arrangement set in place by SC resolution 1244, and the continued protection of the legitimate expectation of states that agree to the Council's peace settlements. But given the shifting facts on the ground, it may also be argued that the Council had an interest in a political settlement that took into account and was based on the new political reality, even when that meant that the regime of resolution 1244 was upset. The point is that, in respect of each constituency, it may not only be necessary to distinguish between short-term and long-term interests, but

---

[3] *Barcelona Traction, Light and Power Company, Limited (Belgium v Spain)* (Order: removal from the list) ICJ GL No 41, [1961] ICJ Rep 9, ICGJ 163 (ICJ 1961), 10th April 1961, International Court of Justice [ICJ].

[4] *South West Africa, Ethiopia v South Africa* (Second phase judgment) ICJ GL No 46, [1966] ICJ Rep 6, ICGJ 158 (ICJ 1966), 18th July 1966, International Court of Justice [ICJ].

[5] Christian J. Tams and Antonios Tzanakopoulos, 'Barcelona Traction at 40: The ICJ as an Agent of Legal Development' (2010) 4 LJIL 781–800.

also to consider different, and possibly competing, substantive interests of each constituency.

Third, and related to the previous point, in respect of collective institutions like the General Assembly and the Security Council, a distinction may need to be drawn between the collective interest of the institution as such, on the one hand, and the interest of particular (groups of) member states of those institutions, on the other. Formally, it is apparent that only the former count, as affirmed by the Court in the *Kosovo* Advisory Opinion.[6] However, behind the veil of the collectivity, individual members will take different positions—as evidenced by the different position of the permanent members of the Security Council.[7] The question is whether the Court can, and should, entirely neglect such divisions. Formally, the Court will say that it can and should do so. But it is difficult to escape the impression that the division within the Council made it easier for the Court to give up the regime of resolution 1244.

Fourth, the Court's ability to take into account and to cater to multiple constituencies depends largely on the leeway left by the question presented to the Court. If the law were to be absolutely clear and allow only for one outcome, the Court may have no other option than following that course, whatever the interests of particular constituencies may be. However, situations where a question put to the Court leaves no choice are rare. Usually the Court will be able to interpret and construe a question put to it in a broader or narrower way. This was not any different for the question formulated by the General Assembly on the declaration of independence.[8] In that situation, it becomes relevant to identify the multiple constituencies of the Court, and to consider the extent to which the Court's construction of the question, and the answer to that question, can be understood as an attempt to serve some or all of these constituencies.

The central argument of this chapter is as follows. The fact that the Court declined to cater to the interests formally expressed by the General Assembly and the Security Council may be explained as an attempt to preserve the longer term authority of the Court vis-à-vis its constituencies. On the one hand, exposing the conflict between the declaration of independence and resolution 1244 would have disconnected the Court from political developments and would have marginalized the Court. On the other hand, a wider discussion of the question of whether the declaration was in accordance with international law would have required the Court to pronounce on highly controversial questions of secession and self-determination. By doing so, it would inevitably have divided its constituencies in a manner that likewise would have endangered its stature. The result of the decision to duck these two questions was that the Court in the short term only served the interests of Kosovo and its supporters; however, this is better understood as a side effect of its decision to serve its longer-term interests than as a strategic decision to serve this particular constituency over all others. However,

---

[6] Advisory Opinion (n 1) para. 33.    [7] See, *infra* Section 2.2.
[8] Sienho Yee, 'Notes on the International Court of Justice (Part 4): the Kosovo Advisory Opinion' (2010) 9(4) CJIL 763–782, at 770.

the choice of reading the question as it did came with a price: it could jeopardize future international arrangements to stabilize war-torn societies if the relevant actors were to realize that they can always unilaterally pull out of such arrangements, even if they have been blessed by the Security Council. From a constituency perspective, the fact that the Court was willing to pay that price may in part be explained by the fact that the actors that will have a stake in such future arrangements are unknown.

I will review the *Kosovo* Advisory Opinion from the angles of three constituency-based perspectives: an institutional perspective, in which the constituencies consist of the political organs of the United Nations (Section 2); a dispute settlement perspective, in which the focus is on Serbia and Kosovo—the parties whose dispute gave rise to the Advisory Opinion (Section 3); and a guardian perspective, focusing on the interest of the international community at large in a stable and well-functioning international legal order (Section 4). For each perspective, I discuss: first, why the Court would have to serve that particular constituency; second, how it did so in the Advisory Opinion; third, how the relevant constituency assessed the Court's Opinion; and fourth, whether the Court, by doing what it did, managed to maintain its long-term stature vis-à-vis that particular constituency.

## 2. An Institutional Perspective

The first and foremost stakeholder of any advisory opinion is the institution that asks the question: 'the purpose of the advisory function is to offer legal advice to the organs and institutions requesting the opinion'.[9] Under Article 96 of the UN Charter, the potential constituencies of the Court are the UN General Assembly, the UN Security Council, and other bodies authorized to request opinions on legal questions 'arising within the scope of their activities'.[10] In the case at hand, the question came from the General Assembly; thus, it was the primary constituency (Sub-section A). However, the Court could not entirely neglect the interests of the Security Council (Sub-section B).

### A. The General Assembly

The first question in our analytical framework (why would the Court have to serve that particular constituency?) is easily answered. The Court's first and foremost consideration had to be that it had to cater to the interests of the General Assembly to obtain an answer to the question that it had put before the Court.

The need to cater to the interests of the General Assembly does not follow from a relation of dependency. The organs of the UN are not placed in a hierarchical

---

[9] *Legality of the Threat or Use of Nuclear Weapons* (Advisory Opinion) ICJ GL No 95, ICJ Reports 1996 226, ICGJ 205 (ICJ 1996), 8th July 1996, International Court of Justice [ICJ], para 15.
[10] UN Charter (n 2).

position. While the Court does provide annual reports to the General Assembly,[11] and is dependent on the General Assembly for its budget,[12] it is only by a stretch of the imagination that an answer to a General Assembly question that would not satisfy the General Assembly could in any way, through the budget or otherwise, come back to haunt the Court.

Yet, as an organ of the UN, the Court has an interest in cooperating with the General Assembly in the pursuit of the objectives of the UN.[13] Indeed, all organs, including the General Assembly and the Court, have a mutual responsibility to ensure that each can perform their responsibilities under the UN Charter. While the Court's Statute does not formulate this in terms of a legal obligation (Article 65 of the Statute stipulates that the Court *may* give an advisory opinion on any legal question upon request),[14] in the Court's practice there is a presumption that the Court will answer a question, and thus serve this constituency, unless there are compelling reasons not to do so.[15] In the *Kosovo* Advisory Opinion the Court said that it was 'mindful of the fact that its answer to a request for an advisory opinion represents its participation in the activities of the Organization, and, in principle, should not be refused'.[16] As discussed elsewhere in this volume, in the facts of the case there was no compelling reason to decline the request for an opinion.[17]

Catering to the interests of the General Assembly requires the Court to address the interests of the General Assembly as a whole, not those of the member states. Behind the seemingly simple question posed by the General Assembly, there will generally be the multiple agendas of member states, and catering to one of them

---

[11] Rule 13 (b) of the Rules of Procedure of the United Nations General Assembly (United Nations [UN]) UN Doc A/520.

[12] UN Charter (n 2) art 17.

[13] *Interpretation of Peace Treaties with Bulgaria, Hungary and Romania* (Advisory Opinion) (first phase) ICJ GL No 8, ICJ Reports 1950 65, ICGJ 230 (ICJ 1950), 30th March 1950, International Court of Justice [ICJ] Sep. Op. Judge Azevedo, para 8 ('the Court, which has been raised to the status of a principal organ and thus more closely geared into the mechanism of the U.N.O., must do its utmost to co-operate with the other organs with a view to attaining the aims and principles that have been set forth').

[14] Statute of the International Court of Justice (International Court of Justice [ICJ]) (adopted 26 June 1945) 33 UNTS 993, UKTS 67 (1946) Cmd 7015, 3 Bevans 1179, 59 Stat 1055, 145 BSP 832, TS No 993, ch IV (hereafter: ICJ Statute). This allows for discretion not to answer the question; see *Western Sahara* (Advisory Opinion) ICJ GL No 61, ICJ Reports 1975 12, ICGJ 214 (ICJ 1975), 16th October 1975, International Court of Justice [ICJ], para 23.

[15] Advisory Opinion (n 1) para 30; *Legal Consequences of the Construction of a Wall in the Occupied Palestinian Territory* (Advisory Opinion) ICJ Reports 2004 (I), 156, para 44; *Judgments of the Administrative Tribunal of the ILO upon Complaints Made against UNESCO* (Advisory Opinion) ICJ Reports 1956 77, 86. See also *Certain Expenses of the United Nations (Article 17(2), of the Charter)* (Advisory Opinion) ICJ Reports 1962 155; *Legal Consequences for States of the Continued Presence of South Africa in Namibia (South West Africa) Notwithstanding Security Council Resolution 276 (1970)* (Advisory Opinion) ICJ Reports 1971 27; *Application for Review of Judgment No. 158 of the United Nations Administrative Tribunal* (Advisory Opinion) ICJ Reports 1973 183; *Western Sahara* (n 14); and *Applicability of Article VI, Section 22, of the Convention on the Privileges and Immunities of the United Nations* (Advisory Opinion) ICJ Reports 1989 191.

[16] Advisory Opinion (n 1) para 30; see also *Interpretation of Peace Treaties with Bulgaria, Hungary and Romania* (n 13) para 22.

[17] This is subject to the discussion of the position of the Security Council, see Section 2.2 below. For an extended discussion of jurisdiction and discretion issues in the *Kosovo* case, see the contribution by Vladimir Djerić in this volume.

may mean neglecting the others.[18] This was not any different in the case of the *Kosovo* Advisory Opinion. Some states may have had an interest in gaining clarity on the question of the legality of recognition of Kosovo, others on the question of self-determination, and still others on the legal status of Kosovo. However, these states could not get their points included in the resolution, and the only question that was asked was whether the declaration of independence was in accordance with international law.

The fact that the Court should only address the question posed by the General Assembly as a whole is primarily relevant for the decision by the Court whether to exercise its discretion to decline to answer the question.[19] But it also pertains to the substance of the Opinion: catering to the interests of the General Assembly does not mean catering to the position of (groups of) states that are not reflected in the General Assembly's question. This is a sensible approach, and the only one which allows a workable relationship between the General Assembly and the Court as far as advisory proceedings are concerned. The Court of necessity has to accept the unity, however artificial, of the General Assembly as a constituency. Any other approach would surely threaten the future relationship between the Court and the General Assembly, and more generally the authority of the Court.

The second question of our analytical framework is whether the Court did in fact cater to the interests of the General Assembly. The straightforward way for the Court to do so would have been to answer the question as given and understood by the General Assembly. That would have meant that the Court would consider the authors of the declaration of independence as the Provisional Institutions of Self-Government,[20] and would answer the question of whether the declaration was in accordance with international law.[21]

We can only speculate as to the reasons why the Court decided not to follow the understanding and the question as expressed by the General Assembly. It approached the question on the basis of a different understanding of the identity of the authors of the declaration of independence,[22] and significantly reformulated the question from 'in accordance with international law' to 'not in violation of international law'.[23] Whatever the motivations, this approach allowed the Court

---

[18] Generally, Shabtai Rosenne, *The International Court of Justice: An Essay in Political and Legal Theory* (A.W. Sijthoff, 1957) 66 (noting that '[i]n the ultimate result, the ability of the Court to perform any function in international life depends not so much on the institutional ties linking it with this or that organization or organ, or with this or that conception of the nature of its judicial task, as on the attitudes of the States towards the judicial role. There is, in this respect, no essential difference between a direct approach to the Court by States invoking the contentious jurisdiction, and indirect approach by States invoking the advisory competence. It is always in the States, individually or in groups, that the decision rests whether, and to what extent, the Court shall be used').

[19] *Legality of the Threat or Use of Nuclear Weapons* (n 9) 237, para 16.

[20] See, convincingly, Marcelo G. Kohen and Katherine Del Mar, 'The Kosovo Advisory Opinion and UNSCR 1244 (1999): A Declaration of "Independence from International Law?"' (2011) 24 LJIL 109, 114.

[21] See Yee (n 8); Kohen and Del Mar (n 20) 114.

[22] Yee (n 8) 770–1. Marc Weller, 'Modesty Can Be a Virtue: Judicial Economy in the ICJ *Kosovo* Opinion' (2011) 24(1) LJIL 127, 143.

[23] Advisory Opinion (n 1) para 56.

to avoid two outcomes that for different reasons may have been problematic. On the one hand, if the Court had proceeded on the understanding (similar to that of the General Assembly) that the authors of the declaration were the Provisional Institutions of Self-Government, it would have been very hard to escape the conclusion that the Declaration was in violation of SC resolution 1244 as the applicable *lex specialis*.[24] In view of the fact that the political process had by then reached an unstoppable momentum, this would have produced an outcome that would have been largely irrelevant to practice and, moreover, in direct opposition to three permanent members of the Security Council: the United States; the United Kingdom; and France.[25] On the other hand, the approach taken allowed the Court to duck the question of external self-determination—a question that was certain to divide states, and could thereby endanger the long-term support of states for the Court. Both matters will be explored more fully below.[26]

It may be hypothesized that the Court's deviation from the question could have undermined the long-term relationship with the General Assembly. Potential sponsors of a resolution would possibly think twice before asking a question that could be reformulated by the Court and thereby lead to quite a different answer than the one sought. Both facts may not necessarily have been beneficial to the long-term stature of the Court.

However, coming to the third question (how did the constituency in question assess the Opinion?), we can observe that the General Assembly did not censure and, indeed, appeared largely to be fine with the Court's deviation from the question. Despite the initiative by Serbia, the General Assembly showed no interest in reopening the status issue, let alone in reinterpreting or rejecting the outcome of the Advisory Opinion. This suggests that the General Assembly as a whole was satisfied with the outcome, and considered that the Court had properly done what the General Assembly had asked it to do.[27] This also suggests that the Court has substantial leeway and that catering to the interests of the General Assembly as a whole does not mean that it should do exactly what the General Assembly asks it to do.

## B. The Security Council

A separate question is whether, in responding to a question posed by the General Assembly, the Court should also have catered to the interests of the Security Council. As a general proposition, it is obvious that the Security Council is indeed a relevant constituency for the Court. The Court in its advisory function 'serves' the

---

[24] This is persuasively argued in the Separate Opinion by Vice-President Tomka, see the Advisory Opinion (n 1).

[25] 'Reaction in quotes: UN legal ruling on Kosovo' (*BBC*, 22 July 2010) <http://www.bbc.co.uk/news/world-europe-10733837> accessed 27 January 2014. 'France calls for all nations to recognize Kosovo' (*Panorama*, 17 February 2008) <http://www.panorama.am/en/politics/2010/07/23/france/> accessed 27 January 2014.

[26] Respectively Section 2.2 and Section 4.

[27] Weller (n 22) 145.

United Nations,[28] and this is surely not limited to the General Assembly. Indeed, the relation between the Court and the General Assembly necessarily has to take into account the position of the Security Council, given the fact that virtually any possible answer to the question could potentially be of considerable interest for the Security Council's future involvement with Kosovo.[29]

In formal terms, the Court was required to consider the position of the Security Council, since it had to determine whether the General Assembly, by asking the question, had interfered with the powers of the Security Council. After all, Article 12 of the UN Charter provides that '[w]hile the Security Council is exercising in respect of any dispute or situation the functions assigned to it in the present Charter, the General Assembly shall not make any recommendation with regard to that dispute or situation unless the Security Council so requests'. It was argued before the Court, in separate opinions, and in subsequent commentaries that this implied that the Court should declare itself without jurisdiction.[30] Some also argued that, given the respective powers of the Security Council and the General Assembly, the request for an Advisory Opinion should instead have been made by the Security Council and that the Court should have exercised its discretion to decline to answer the question.[31]

In conformity with earlier opinions,[32] the Court concluded that Article 12(1) does not in itself limit the authorization to request an advisory opinion which is conferred upon the General Assembly by Article 96, paragraph 1.[33] As detailed elsewhere in this volume,[34] the Court found that the fact that the Security Council was involved did not constitute a compelling reason for the Court to refuse to respond to the request from the General Assembly.[35] These positions seem to rest on good grounds.

---

[28] Karin Oellers-Frahm, 'Lawmaking through Advisory Opinions' (2011) GLJ 12, 1033.

[29] In resolution 1244 (1999), the Security Council, acting under Chapter VII of the United Nations Charter, authorized the United Nations Secretary-General to establish an international civil presence in Kosovo in order to provide 'an interim administration for Kosovo ... which will provide transitional administration while establishing and overseeing the development of provisional democratic self-governing institutions' (para 10). The powers and responsibilities thus laid out in Security Council resolution 1244 (1999) were set out in more detail in UNMIK Regulation 2001/9 of 15 May 2001 on a Constitutional Framework for Provisional Self-Government. See, for a description of the involvement of the Council, Advisory Opinion (n 1) para 37 *et seq*. See generally Alexandros Yannis, 'The UN as a Government in Kosovo' (2004) 10 GG 67–81; Bernhard Knoll, 'From Benchmarking to Final Status? Kosovo and the Problem of an International Administration's Open-Ended Mandate' (2005) 16 EJIL 637–60.

[30] Advisory Opinion (n 1) para 18–28.

[31] Advisory Opinion (n 1) para 39; Individual opinions of Judges: Tomka, para 5 ('I fail to see any "sufficient interest" for the Assembly in requesting the opinion'); Keith, paras 11–17 (who argues that the General Assembly's interest is too small, and thus that the Court should refuse to render an opinion); Bennouna, paras 2–21 (who posits that decisions relating to the status of Kosovo should not be taken by the General Assembly, but by the Security Council, under whose 'exclusive jurisdiction' the situation in Kosovo fell); Skotnikov, para 9 (who argues that the Court unjustifiably substitutes itself for the Security Council).

[32] *Legal Consequences of the Construction of a Wall in the Occupied Palestinian Territory* (n 15) 148, para 25.

[33] Advisory Opinion (n 1) para 24.

[34] See the contribution by Vladimir Djerić in Chapter 6 of this book.

[35] *Legal Consequences of the Construction of a Wall in the Occupied Palestinian Territory* (n 15) 148, paras 26–27; Advisory Opinion (n 1) paras 42, 43, 47–8.

But such a positive assessment is not so easy to make in respect of the question of whether in substance the Court sufficiently catered to the interests of the Security Council. The preliminary question here was what were the interests of the Security Council in the first place? Comparable to what was said above in relation to the Security Council, the Court could not solve this problem by considering the position of individual members of the Security Council. If it had done so, this would not have yielded any conclusive answers, since the positions of the permanent members were far apart. As can be inferred from the inability of the Security Council to act on the declaration of independence,[36] as well as the competing positions of the United States[37] and the Russian Federation,[38] there was no single position of the Security Council on the issue to which the Court could attach weight.

In this situation of divided positions within the Security Council, the only baseline for the Court was to examine the question put to it by the General Assembly in the light of the decisions and actual practice of the Security Council in relation to Kosovo.

Measured against this yardstick, the Court's reasoning on this point is problematic. Permitted by its understanding of the identity of the authors of the declaration of independence, the Court found that these authors were not covered by resolution 1244, and that hence there was no conflict with the resolution.[39] It is difficult, however, to argue with the view that the authors *were* covered by the resolution, that the Declaration did violate the resolution, and more generally, that it upset the political process set in place by the Security Council.[40] *De facto*, the Court gave its blessing to decisive steps in the political process from which there would be no return.

That the Court could so openly decline to protect a regime set in place by the Council can be explained only by the fact that while formally the Court could only consider the position of the Council as a whole, in fact it was faced with a deeply divided Security Council. The position of the Security Council as expressed in the relevant resolutions no longer corresponded to the position of the (permanent) members of the Security Council. The permanent members were now split, with the United States, France, and the United Kingdom on one side, and China and Russia on the other. It may be speculated that if all the permanent members were to have taken the position that the regime established by the Security Council

[36] The Council discussed the declaration but took no action in respect of it; Security Council, provisional verbatim record, 18 February 2008, 3 p.m. (S/PV.5839); Security Council, provisional verbatim record, 11 March 2008, 3 p.m. (S/PV.5850).

[37] White House spokesman Mike Hammer said 'We were pleased that the court agreed with the long-standing view of the United States that Kosovo's declaration of independence is in accordance with international law'. 'Reaction in quotes: UN legal ruling on Kosovo' (*BBC*, 22 July 2010) <http://www.bbc.co.uk/news/world-europe-10733837> accessed 27 January 2014.

[38] 'ICJ opens Pandora box—Russia' (*Voice of Russia*, 22 July 2010) <http://english.ruvr.ru/2010/07/22/13135117.html> accessed 27 January 2014.

[39] Advisory Opinion (n 1) paras 119–21.

[40] See e.g. Cedric Ryngaert, 'The ICJ's advisory opinion on Kosovo's Declaration of Independence: a missed opportunity?' (2010) 57 NILR 481; Ralph Wilde, 'Self-determination, Secession and Dispute Settlement after the Kosovo Advisory Opinion' (2011) 24 LJIL 149; Kohen and Del Mar (n 20).

should be kept in place and that the declaration was an unacceptable deviation from it, it would have been much more difficult for the Court to take the approach that it took—alternatively, there may in that case not have been recourse to the Court anyway.

This point is relevant, since the relationship between the Court and the Security Council may in the long term depend more on the support of the five permanent member states than on the question of whether the Court did justice to a particular position taken by the Security Council as a whole that no longer conforms to the political preferences and interests of the relevant actors. In this respect, comparable to the situation of the General Assembly, the divided position of states behind the veil of a uniform formal institutional position meant that the Court's decision to deviate from (or neglect) what the Security Council had said was without adverse effects on the long-term relationship between the Court and the Security Council.

Another aspect of this is that if the Court were to have determined that the declaration of independence was incompatible with the regime set up by the Security Council, this outcome most likely would have been irrelevant. If it was to avoid this, the Court had to leave a strict application of the SC resolution and follow political realities. From this angle, the Advisory Opinion cannot only be explained by its catering to its constituencies as static entities, but rather by its adoption of a proper reading of the political context in which these constituencies operate.

The fact that this chosen approach, deviating from the formal position of the Security Council, did not lead to outright rejection by at least some members of the Council would seem to be due to the fact that the narrow phrasing of the question allowed states to continue to take the position that they would respect the borders drawn at the end of the Bosnian civil war in 1995.[41] Russia could, without coming into conflict with anything that the Court had said, say that it did not change its position opposing Kosovo's recognition.[42] Given that the Court did not expressly pronounce on the legality of secession or the effect on the territorial integrity of Serbia, it can be said that the Court may have succeeded in satisfying, at least to some extent, the permanent members of the Security Council.[43]

While the Court may have manoeuvered around the risk of a potential conflict with the Security Council, it might have undermined a long-term interest of the

---

[41] This was, for instance, expressed by Spain—'Spanish Deputy PM: Spain won't recognize Kosovo' (*Novinite.com*, 23 July 2010). <http://www.novinite.com/view_news.php?id=118450> accessed 27 January 2014.

[42] 'UN court decision on Kosovo will not change Moscow's stance' (*RIA Novosti*, 22 July 2010) <http://en.ria.ru/world/20100722/159913797.html> accessed 27 January 2014.

[43] See for the positive responses by the US 'Reaction in quotes: UN legal ruling on Kosovo' (*BBC*, 22 July 2010) <http://www.bbc.co.uk/news/world-europe-10733837> accessed 27 January 2014; 'Remarks by Secretary Clinton: July 2010' (*U.S. Department of State*, 22 July 2010) <http://www.state.gov/secretary/rm/2010/07/145042.htm> accessed 27 January 2014. See for France, 'France calls for all nationas to recognize Kosovo' (*Panorama*, 23 July 2010) <http://www.panorama.am/en/politics/2010/07/23/france/> accessed 27 January 2014. For China, see 'Foreign Ministry Spokesperson Qin Gang's Response to the International Court of Justice's Advisory Opinion on the Kosovo Case' (*Ministry of Foreign Affairs of the People's Republic of China*, 23 July 2010) <http://www.mfa.gov.cn/eng/xwfw/s2510/t719113.htm> accessed 27 January 2014.

Council. It may be speculated that the limited weight the Court gave to the interim regime for Kosovo could be detrimental to the willingness of states to accept comparable arrangements set up by the Security Council in future. Serbia had accepted the peace plan and the arrangement set out in resolution 1244. Surely, if it could have envisaged that several years later its understanding of this arrangement to protect a political process, as well as its territorial integrity, would be worth very little, it would have thought twice before accepting the arrangement in the first place.[44] For the future, states that find themselves in comparable situations may be reluctant to accept such arrangements if the basis of their acceptance is worth little. As noted by Wilde, the Court in effect said that

in a situation in which an international legal regime, even one, as here, crafted by the Security Council and introduced via mandatory provisions of a resolution passed under Chapter VII UN Charter, creates an interim arrangement to provide the space for a 'settlement' of a dispute, one of the disputants is free to unilaterally terminate this arrangement, without having to account for whether or not the termination constitutes a lawful 'settlement' of the situation, if the disputant is a non-State actor and, as an essential part of the settlement, has to be acting in a different capacity from its identity during the dispute settlement period—a situation which is inevitable when a sub-State group reconstitutes itself as an independent State through secession.[45]

This outcome is surely not in the long-term interests of the Security Council and its ability to contribute to peace arrangements.

## 3. A Dispute Settlement Perspective

From a second perspective, we can consider the Advisory Opinion in terms of its contribution to a settlement of a dispute between Kosovo and Serbia. From this perspective, the constituent parties are primarily Kosovo and Serbia, and possibly also those states that strongly backed either of these parties.

Of course, the standard argument is that advisory opinions are not easily examined from the perspective of a settlement of disputes. Shaw observes that '[u]nlike contentious cases, the purpose of the Court's advisory jurisdiction *is not to settle*, at least directly or as such, inter-state disputes'.[46] However, by definition, a question in the General Assembly is driven by one or more states with a particular interest in that question. It may then be said that the Court, even if it addresses only the question put to it by the General Assembly as a whole, is in fact catering to the interests of these states—in the present situation, in particular, Serbia. Some participants in the proceedings, indeed, said that 'the opinion of the Court was being sought not in order to assist the General Assembly but rather to serve the interests of one State and that the Court should, therefore, decline to respond'.[47] In response, the Court inevitably maintained the image

---

[44] Yee (n 8).     [45] See (n 40).
[46] Malcolm Shaw, *International Law* (CUP, 2014) 804 (emphasis added).
[47] Advisory Opinion (n 1) para 32.

of the General Assembly in unity: its opinion is given not to states, but to the General Assembly: 'the motives of individual States which sponsor, or vote in favour of, a resolution requesting an advisory opinion are not relevant to the Court's exercise of its discretion whether or not to respond'.[48] The Court's role in advisory proceedings is thus primarily to respond to questions posed by competent organs, rather than individual states with a real stake in a particular outcome. Advisory jurisdiction is not a form of judicial recourse for states seeking the help of the Court to settle a dispute.[49]

However, the primarily advisory nature of advisory opinions does not exclude them, in a less direct way, from contributing to the settlement of disputes. Generally speaking, the prime role of the Court is its contribution, on the basis of international law, to the peaceful settlement of disputes.[50] It seems too rigid to disconnect advisory opinions entirely from that role. Advisory opinions are likely to have an effect on actual disputes—if only because they will bolster the position of some of the disputing states, and weaken the position of others. Indeed, many states did not hesitate to rely on the *Kosovo* Advisory Opinion in order to support their position.[51] In this situation, it would be too formalistic to take the position that this should be of no concern to the Court. In the *Wall* Advisory Opinion, the Court said that 'the Court does not consider that the subject-matter of the General Assembly's request can be regarded as *only* a bilateral matter between Israel and Palestine'.[52] The fact that the subject matter was not 'only' a matter for the two parties does not exclude the fact that an advisory opinion also addresses a bilateral dispute, and that the pronouncement of the Court may have relevance to the settlement of such a dispute. Interestingly, the Court could even contribute to a peaceful settlement of disputes between states and non-state actors, as was the case, at least in the eyes of some, with the facts of the *Wall* Advisory Opinion. The limitation of access to the Court by states, as it applies in contentious proceedings between states,[53] does not apply here.

The question then is what it means for the Court to contribute, in advisory proceedings, to the settlement of a dispute. In a narrow sense, settling a dispute may mean that the Court would simply say that A or B is right, and thereby (assuming that that ruling would in fact be given effect) effectively settle the dispute. But leaving aside the unlikelihood that whatever the Court said would have a direct and decisive impact on the resolution of the conflict, this of course is not what can be expected in an advisory proceeding. If the Court were to contribute to the settlement of a dispute like the one between Kosovo and Serbia, it would do so by

---

[48] Ibid., para 33.        [49] Ibid., para 39.        [50] Rosenne (n 18).

[51] E.g. Albanian Prime Minister Sali Berisha hailed the ruling as a 'historic decision' that would contribute to peace and stability in the Balkans. Berisha also called for more countries to recognize the independence of Kosovo; see 'Albania Welcomes UN Court's Backing of Kosovo' (*China Radio International*, 22 July 2010) <http://english.cri.cn/6966/2010/07/23/1461s584558.htm> accessed 27 January 2014.

[52] *Legal Consequences of the Construction of a Wall in the Occupied Palestinian Territory* (n 15) 148, para 49 (emphasis added).

[53] ICJ Statute (n 14), art 34(1).

clarifying the parameters within which the further political process would have to take place.

It has been suggested that the *Kosovo* Advisory Opinion was in fact 'driven by considerations inherent to dispute settlement: the Court acted as an arbiter between Kosovo and Serbia and showed concern for how the opinion would affect their relationship'.[54] The argument is that the Court sought a delicate compromise between the positions of the two entities and thereby 'positioned itself more as a means of dispute settlement than as a legal advisory body'.[55]

But it is difficult to assess whether, and to what extent, the Court, did, indeed, provide a contribution to the settlement of the dispute and, in that respect, cater to the interests of Kosovo and Serbia. The only criteria for making this assessment are the actual contents of the Opinion and its reception. On this point three comments can be made.

First, in the situation as it had unfolded, an agreed settlement was virtually ruled out. It was hard to see how any answer to the question could, at least in the short term, have made a productive contribution to a settlement. In this respect, the facts of the case were unfavourable to a proper application of the second perspective on a constituency-based analysis of the Advisory Opinion. Falk rightly observed that the Court deferred to geopolitical wishes by rather unexpectedly validating the Kosovo declaration.[56]

In this situation, the room for the Court to manoeuvre was very limited. While the answer it did give was hardly conducive to a political arrangement as envisaged by resolution 1244, it is not unlikely that a negative answer to the question put to the Court would have resulted in an even worse deterioration of the situation, as it may have legitimized Serbian policies to seek reintegration of Kosovo, perhaps even by military means.[57]

Second, quite unlike the normal situation in cases of contentious proceedings, in which it has often been observed that the Court attempts to provide something to both parties, quite clearly the Opinion was only favourable to one party, as can be inferred from the sharp distinction in responses by Kosovo[58] and that of Serbia.[59] For Serbia, the Court's statement that territorial integrity was not opposable to a

---

[54] Daphné Richemond-Barak, 'The International Court of Justice on Kosovo: Missed Opportunity or Dispute "Settlement"?' (2010) 23 Hague Yrbk Intl L 3, also available at <http://works.bepress.com/cgi/viewcontent.cgi?article=1001&context=daphne_richemondbarak>.

[55] Ibid.

[56] Richard Falk, 'The Kosovo Advisory Opinion: Conflict Resolution and Precedent' (2011) 105 AJIL 50.

[57] Anne Peters, 'Does Kosovo lie in the Lotus Land of Freedom?' (2011) 24 LJIL 95.

[58] After the ICJ Opinion, President Fatmir Sejdiu said the decision was positive and that it 'explicitly on all counts spoke in favour of the right to freedom and self-determination of the people of Kosovo'. He called on the countries that had not recognized Kosovo, as well as Serbia, to 'join the common vision of the countries in the region in their position regarding the bright future and speedy Euro-Atlantic integrations'. 'K. Albanians hail ICJ decision as big victory' (*b92*, 22 July 2010) <http://www.b92.net/eng/news/politics-article.php?yyyy=2010&mm=07&dd=22&nav_id=68621> accessed 27 January 2014.

[59] See statement of President of Serbia, Boris Tadić, 'Serbia rejects Kosovo court ruling' (*Al Jazeera*, 10 September 2010) <http://www.aljazeera.com/news/europe/2010/07/201072355537730152.html> accessed 27 January 2014.

non-state actor[60] did not strengthen the negotiating power of Serbia, and nor did it bring the dispute closer to a resolution in Serbia's favour.[61] The lack of appreciation of the Serbian rights in question has been noted and critiqued by many scholars.[62] At the same time, it could be said that the fact that the Court did not endorse a right of secession of Kosovo confirmed the position taken by Serbia and allowed it to argue that even though the declaration as such may not have been in violation of international law, international law did allow Serbia to rely on territorial integrity to oppose the secession and argue that Kosovo did not manage to attain statehood.

Third, it is necessary to distinguish between the short-term and the long-term interests of the constituencies. Precisely by keeping in place the principles on which Serbia could oppose secession, and by not saying anything on the status of Kosovo, the Court left open a political process that eventually could be considered as some form of settlement, though obviously one that is quite far removed from what Serbia initially had in mind.[63] This outcome was indeed emphasized by several other states, including China,[64] Germany,[65] and Spain.[66] Indeed, one can conclude that the Court, by not seeing any barrier to a unilateral declaration of independence, did not so much contribute to a settlement along the lines of the regime set in place by the Security Council, but, in effect, paved the way for a secession that, in time, Serbia could only accept, which is, of course, one way of settling the dispute.

## 4. A Guardian Perspective

A third constituency-based perspective on the Advisory Opinion is that the Court has to serve the interests of a much wider group of states (and perhaps 'the international community' and the invisible college of international lawyers, to which the judges normally belong/identify with) by developing international law. This obviously vastly heterogeneous constituency would expect, above all, the Court

---

[60]  Advisory Opinion (n 1) paras 79–84.
[61]  Roland Tricot and Barrie Sander, 'Recent Developments: the Broader Consequences of the International Court of Justice's Advisory Opinion on the Unilateral Declaration of Independence in Respect of Kosovo' (2011) 49 CJTL 2, 321–63.
[62]  Mindia Vashakmadze and Matthias Lippold, 'Nothing But a Road Towards Secession: the International Court of Justice's Advisory Opinion on Accordance with International Law of the Unilateral Declaration of Independence in Respect of Kosovo' (2010) 2(2) GoJIL 619–47; Yee (n 8).
[63]  Statement by H.E. Mr Boris Tadić, President of the Republic of Serbia, at the 65th Regular Session of the General Assembly (25 September 2010) (emphasis added), available at <http://www.un.int/serbia/Statements/82.pdf>.
[64]  'Foreign Ministry Spokesperson Qin Gang's Response to the International Court of Justice's Advisory Opinion on the Kosovo Case' (*Ministry of Foreign Affairs of the People's Republic of China*, 23 July 2010) <http://www.mfa.gov.cn/eng/xwfw/s2510/t719113.htm> accessed 27 January 2014.
[65]  'German FM: UN court ruling on Kosovo "unique decision"' (*Expatica*, 23 July 2010) <http://www.expatica.com/de/news/german-news/german-fm-un-court-ruling-on-kosovo-unique-decision-_85299.html> accessed 27 January 2014.
[66]  'España seguirá sin reconocer la independencia de Kosovo' (*Por Agencia EFE*, 22 July 2010) <http://www.google.com/hostednews/epa/article/ALeqM5gT8UtldpZk3jBcvfxvL64w8aYo1A> accessed 27 January 2014.

to properly apply international law, but also that for it to provide a contribution to the development of international law.[67] It has been observed that a number of decisions 'candidly aim at influencing the general legal discourse by establishing abstract and categorical statements as authoritative reference points for later legal practice'.[68] By and large it would seem that in the past such contributions have been accepted as valuable by states.

The Court can contribute to such developments by finding that a particular rule is or is not part of customary international law, or by identifying or clarifying a particular treaty obligation, particularly in cases of 'dynamic' treaty interpretation.[69] This role in law development also clearly applies—perhaps even more so—for advisory opinions. Indeed, in the several advisory opinions, including the *Reparation for Injuries* Advisory Opinion,[70] the *Genocide* Advisory Opinion,[71] the *Namibia* Advisory Opinion,[72] and the *Wall* Advisory Opinion,[73] the Court has made a substantial contribution to the development of international law.[74]

The margins for the Court are narrow, however, and will be guarded by the diverse interests and expectations of states. In the Advisory Opinion in *Legality of Nuclear Weapons*, some states had contended that in answering the question posed, the Court would be going beyond its judicial role and would be taking upon itself a law-making capacity. The Court made clear that in the circumstances of the case it was not called upon to legislate, but that its task rather was 'to engage in its normal judicial function of ascertaining the existence or otherwise of legal principles and rules applicable to the threat or use of nuclear weapons'.[75] It also said that

the contention that the giving of an answer to the question posed would require the Court to legislate is based on a supposition that the present corpus juris is devoid of relevant rules in this matter. The Court could not accede to this argument; it states the existing law and does not legislate. This is so even if, in stating and applying the law, the Court necessarily has to specify its scope and sometimes note its general trend.[76]

In the *Kosovo* Advisory Opinion, in view of the unclear status of the rules of international law in issue, any answer to the 'in accordance' question that would touch on questions of secession and self-determination would inevitably lie in the grey

---

[67] Hersch Lauterpacht, *The Development of International Law by the International Court* (Stevens & Sons, 1958); Hans Wehberg, *The Problem of an International Court of Justice* (Clarendon Press, 1918).

[68] Armin von Bogdandy and Ingo Venzke, 'In Whose Name? An Investigation of International Courts' Public Authority and Its Democratic Justification' (2010) 23 EJIL 7–41, at 15.

[69] Frahm (n 28) 1041–2.

[70] *Reparation for Injuries Suffered in the Service of the United Nations* (Advisory Opinion) ICJ GL No 4, ICJ Reports 1949 174, ICGJ 232 (ICJ 1949), 11th April 1949, International Court of Justice [ICJ].

[71] *Reservations to the Convention on the Prevention and Punishment of the Crime of Genocide* (Advisory Opinion) ICJ GL No 12, [1951] ICJ Rep 15, ICGJ 227 (ICJ 1951), 28th May 1951, International Court of Justice [ICJ].

[72] *Legal Consequences for States of the Continued Presence of South Africa in Namibia (South West Africa) notwithstanding Security Council Resolution 276 (1970)* (n 15).

[73] *Legal Consequences of the Construction of a Wall in the Occupied Palestinian Territory* (n 15).

[74] Oellers-Frahm (n 28) 1041–2.

[75] *Legality of the Threat or Use of Nuclear Weapons* (n 9) para 18.

[76] Ibid., para 18.

area where specification of the contents and scope of rights and duties would lead to legal development.

In such cases it will immediately appear that the interests of states and the 'indivisible college' as a homogeneous group quickly falls apart. For the question is, who benefits from the development of international law in this particular area? Development of the law is not good per se—it all depends on what interests the current law protects and what interests a development would serve. Every silence of international law, or an 'undeveloped' state of international law, also serves particular interests. So in each specific context it is to be determined whose particular interests are served by the development of international law in a particular direction.

This holds true both for the question of whether the declaration was in conformity with the *lex specialis* (the regime set forth by the Security Council) and for those points where the Court could have made a contribution to the development of international law, notably the right of self-determination, the right of secession, the right of territorial integrity in relation to recognizing states, and the question of whether non-state actors could unilaterally undermine a regime aimed at the settlement of a situation set up by the Security Council. Some have said that on these points the Court should have been more assertive in developing the law.[77] However, none of these points are (only) abstract questions that might benefit from the development of international law—an answer either way may perhaps be said in the long run to be in the collective interests of the state parties, but at the same time inevitably serve the particular interests of particular actors.

From this perspective, a few comments can be made about the *Kosovo* Advisory Opinion in relation to the regime of the Security Council and to the wider questions of territorial integrity, self-determination, and secession.

It has already been observed above that the Advisory Opinion's approach to the regime set up by the Security Council was problematic. Kohen and Del Mar noted that the Court failed to uphold the legally binding provisions of SC resolution 1244, and it did not find unlawful or invalid an act of a subsidiary body of the Security Council that was undertaken in excess of authority and contrary to the fundamental provisions of that resolution. Thereby, they argued, the Court has not fulfilled its role as 'the guardian of legality for the international community as a whole'.[78]

Opinion on the Court's silence on matters of territorial integrity, self-determination, and secession has been more mixed. Two positions can be identified. First, some commentators appeared to be satisfied by the Opinion because the Court just did what it was asked to do. On this reading, the Court was simply not asked to pronounce on the larger questions of secession and self-determination, and the decision not to go in that direction was understandable and sound. The Court avoided these dilemmas by interpreting the question posed by the General

---

[77] This is a position taken by many scholars in the aftermath of the *Kosovo* Opinion, see for example: Ryngaert (n 40) 481.

[78] Kohen and Del Mar (n 20).

Assembly narrowly, and saying that it was not necessary to resolve the questions of self-determination and remedial secession in the present case. The General Assembly had requested the Court's opinion only on whether or not the declaration of independence was in accordance with international law, and the Court found questions relating to the right to separate from a state beyond the scope of the question.[79] Several scholars have observed that the Court's response that Kosovo's declaration of independence did not violate general international law was correct and hardly surprising.[80]

However, for other commentators, the Court's failure to engage with questions of secession and self-determination was incorrect. Several Judges thought that the Court should not have declined the opportunity to contribute to the development of international law, and that doing so would in fact have been in the collective interests of states. Judge Yusuf wrote that the Court

had a unique opportunity to assess, in a specific and concrete situation, the legal conditions to be met for such a right of self-determination to materialize and give legitimacy to a claim of separation. It unfortunately failed to seize this opportunity, which would have allowed it to clarify the scope and normative content of the right to external self-determination, in its post-colonial conception, and thus to contribute, *inter alia,* to the prevention of unjustified claims to independence which may lead to instability and conflict in various parts of the world.[81]

Judge Sepúlveda-Amor argued that dealing with the underlying issues, and clarifying the law on the questions of the scope of the right to self-determination, the question of 'remedial secession', the extent of the powers of the Security Council in relation to the principle of territorial integrity, the continuation or derogation of an international civil and military administration established under Chapter VII of the Charter, the relationship between UNMIK and the Provisional Institutions of Self-Government and the progressive diminution of UNMIK's authority and responsibilities, and, finally, the effect of the recognition or non-recognition of a state in the present case would all, in fact, have benefitted not just the General Assembly, but also the Security Council and the Secretary-General of the United Nations.[82]

Scholars also have expressed disappointment that the Court did not deal with this set of issues.[83] Dugard comments that the Court adopted a fallacious reasoning on the legality of secession. He argues that the better view is that, in the context of the Kosovo problem, a unilateral declaration of independence was as

---

[79] Advisory Opinion (n 1) para 83.

[80] Hurst Hannum, 'The Advisory Opinion on Kosovo: An Opportunity Lost, or a Poisoned Chalice Refused?' (2011) 24 LJIL 155; Thomas Burri, 'The Kosovo Opinion and Secession: The Sounds of Silence and Missing Links' (2011) 11 German Law Journal 881.

[81] Advisory Opinion (n 1) para 17.    [82] Ibid., para 33.

[83] Vashakmadze and Lippold (n 58); Thomas Burri, 'The Kosovo Opinion and Secession: The Sounds of Silence and Missing Links' (2011) 11 GLJ 881; Robert Muharremi, 'A Note on the ICJ Advisory Opinion on Kosovo' (2011) 11 GLJ 867; Hannum (n 80); Alexander Orakhelashvili, 'The International Court's Advisory Opinion on the UDI in Respect of Kosovo: washing away the "Foam on the Tide of Time"' in *Max Planck Yearbook of United Nations Law* (vol 15, 2011) 65–104.

much an act of secession as a military campaign against Serbia to secure Kosovo's independence, and that as such it fell to be judged by the international law rules governing secession. The Court should therefore have enquired into questions of self-determination and its relation to territorial integrity.[84]

But it is one thing to say that the Court should have dealt with these questions, and quite something else to determine what exactly the Court should have said. Given that states have not been able to agree on clear answers to such questions, it was unrealistic to expect the Court to do so. In assessing the potential impact of any decision of the Court on the development of the law, the pertinent question is whether it could have made such a contribution to the development of international law given its expected impact on the behaviour of states:[85] 'given the formal and functional limits placed on the ICJ, its decisions only shape the law where they are taken up by other actors engaged in the process of legal development'.[86] If the Court were not to be followed, this would actually undermine its position.[87] This is a highly relevant consideration when assessing whether, if the Court had pronounced itself on self-determination and other contested issues, its Opinion could possibly have had an impact.

Inevitably, the answer would have been welcomed by some and rejected by others. While, to some extent, this may be true for all cases where the Court makes a contribution to the development of international law, the issues in this cases were particularly open and sensitive. Addressing them expressly would have risked that at least one camp would have considered the Court politically irrelevant because it was either too conservative or too utopist.

Be that as it may, the often-heard critique that the Court said nothing beyond answering the narrow question is not entirely correct. By limiting its reading of the question, the Court could not entirely prevent giving an answer of broader significance.

First, the Opinion can be read as an affirmation of the old rule that secession is not prohibited by international law.[88] Though the Court did not say this in so many words, it seems quite inconceivable that the Court would take a formalistic position that the declaration in itself was not prohibited by international law, whereas secession was prohibited, without even alluding to that principle.

Second, the Court affirmed that 'the scope of the principle of territorial integrity is confined to the sphere of relations between states'. This has been critiqued because it would be an unwelcome effect in resolving future separatist conflicts by

---

[84] John Dugard, 'The Secession of States and their Recognition in the Wake of Kosovo' (2011) 357 Recueil des cours 9–222, 184.

[85] Tams and Tzanakopoulos (n 5) 800. See also Lauterpacht (n 67) 189–90 ('judicial legislation … cannot attempt to lay down all the details of the application of the principle on which it is based. It lays down the broad principle and applies it to the case before it. Its elaboration must be left … to ordinary legislative processes or to future judicial decisions disposing of problems as they arise').

[86] Tams and Tzanakopoulos (n 5).

[87] Lauterpacht (n 67) 76; Christopher G. Weeramantry, 'The Function of the International Court of Justice in the Development of International Law' (1997) 10 LJIL 309.

[88] Michael Bothe, 'Kosovo—So What? The Holding of the International Court of Justice is not the Last Word on Kosovo's Independence' (2011) 11 GLJ 837.

rendering countries extremely sceptical of solutions of autonomy.[89] For instance, the Indian Government fears that the *Kosovo* Opinion will set a 'dangerous precedent'.[90] However, leaving aside the special situation existing under SC resolution 1244, this was surely the correct conclusion as a matter of positive international law.

Third, it can be inferred from the reasons that the Court gave for not addressing the argument that 'the population of Kosovo has the right to create an independent State either as a manifestation of a right to self-determination or pursuant to what they described as a right of "remedial secession" in the face of the situation in Kosovo', that the Court in fact took the position that there was no such right. The Court explained its decision not to address the topic by stating that this is 'a subject on which radically different views were expressed by those taking part in the proceedings and expressing a position on the question'.[91] Similar differences existed regarding whether international law provides for a right of 'remedial secession' and, if so, in what circumstances.[92] Yee observes that these reasons for not addressing the argument show precisely that there was no *opinio juris* for it, and thus no custom regarding such a right can be found here.[93] While this may be taking it a bit too far, as theoretically it may be possible that while *opinio juris* could not be inferred from the participants in the proceedings, yet could be from the wider practice of states. However, a substantial gap between these two bodies of evidence would be unlikely.

The Court's narrow approach to the question posed by the General Assembly and the somewhat understated way in which it formulated its understanding of the principle of territorial integrity in relation to self-determination may not have been an unwise one. It allowed states to consider the answer to be narrow and case-specific, which permitted them to continue their policies in relation to Serbia, but not be constrained in relation to other situations where the question of self-determination arose. Falk observes in this context that the Court behaved in a somewhat political manner, deferring to geopolitical wishes by rather unexpectedly validating the *Kosovo* Declaration, yet seeking to prevent wider policy effects.[94]

Indeed, many actors declared after the *Kosovo* Advisory Opinion was delivered that this neither affected policies in relation to Kosovo, nor policies in relation to other questions of self-determination. Assistant Secretary at the US State Department, Philip H. Gordon, said 'I would also underscore that the Court's opinion was closely tailored to the unique circumstances of Kosovo. This was about Kosovo. It was not about other regions or states. It doesn't set any precedent for other regions or states'.[95] UK Foreign Secretary William Hague welcomed the

---

[89] Theodore Christakis, 'The ICJ Advisory Opinion on Kosovo: Has International Law Something to Say about Secession?' (2011) 24 LJIL 73, 85.

[90] 'India not to recognize Kosovo' (*Sify News*, 9 August 2010) <http://www.sify.com/news/india-not-to-recognize-kosovo-news-national-kijuEcjbjdd.html> accessed 27 January 2014.

[91] Advisory Opinion (n 1) para 82.      [92] Advisory Opinion (n 1) para 82.

[93] See Yee (n 8) at 39.      [94] Falk (n 61).

[95] 'Bureau of European and Eurasian Affairs remarks' (*U.S. Department of State*, 23 July 2010) <http://www.state.gov/p/eur/rls/rm/2010/145104.htm> accessed 27 January 2014.

Advisory Opinion, but said 'Kosovo is a unique case and does not set a precedent'.[96] After the Court's Opinion, Nikolay Mladenov, Bulgaria's Foreign Minister, issued a statement that it did not change Bulgaria's position on Kosovo, which it recognized in 2008; however, he also stated that the Court's decision should not be considered as a precedent in international law.[97]

At the same time it allowed opponents to maintain their position. Spanish Foreign Minister Miguel Ángel Moratinos expressed his 'respect' for the Court's decision, but added that it will 'in no case change the position of Spain's non-recognition of Kosovo'.[98] Vishnu Prakash, spokesperson for India's external affairs ministry, disagreeing with the Court's Opinion, stated that '[i]t has been India's consistent position that the sovereignty and territorial integrity of all countries should be fully respected by all states'.[99] Markos Kyprianou, Cyprus' Foreign Minister, declared that Cyprus will not recognize the independence of Kosovo and that the Court's Opinion will not affect this position.[100] Kyprianou stated that '[t]he decision of the ICJ is restricted only to the specific question which refers to the procedure of the declaration itself'.[101] The Cyprus Government issued the following statement: 'Cyprus would like to reiterate its position of principle on the issue of Kosovo and reaffirm its unwavering position of respect to the sovereignty and territorial integrity of Serbia, which includes the Kosovo and Metohija province'.[102]

If anything, the narrow approach taken by the Court allowed these states, whose substantive positions were quite far apart, to maintain their position, and in that respect did not undermine or significantly influence the political process. The Advisory Opinion was thus not unsuccessful in satisfying most of the constituents of the Court and in maintaining the image that the Court can function as a guardian of the international legal order.

## 5. Assessment

The point of distinguishing between the three constituency-based perspectives is not so much to distinguish between alternative approaches that were or could have been taken by the Court as to provide lenses by which particular choices of the Court can be explained and/or assessed. In this sense, the three perspectives are not

---

[96] 'Foreign Secretary welcomes Kosovo ruling' (*Gov.uk*, 22 July 2010) <https://www.gov.uk/government/news/foreign-secretary-welcomes-kosovo-ruling> accessed 27 January 2014.

[97] 'Bulgaria for dialogue after ICJ decision' (*B92*, 25 July 2010) <http://www.b92.net/eng/news/politics-article.php?yyyy=2010&mm=07&dd=25&nav_id=68668> accessed 27 January 2014.

[98] 'España seguirá sin reconocer la independencia de Kosovo' (*Por Agencia EFE*, 22 July 2010) <http://www.google.com/hostednews/epa/article/ALeqM5gT8UtldpZk3jBcvfxvL64w8aYo1A> accessed 27 January 2014.

[99] Ibid.

[100] 'Cyprus foreign minister: Cyprus won't change stance on Kosovo' (*Novinite*, 26 July 2010) <http://www.novinite.com/view_news.php?id=118525> accessed 27 January 2014.

[101] Ibid.

[102] 'Reaction in quotes: UN legal ruling on Kosovo' (*BBC*, 22 July 2010) <http://www.bbc.co.uk/news/world-europe-10733837> accessed 27 January 2014.

mutually exclusive options; rather, they provide different lenses for examining one decision. They can provide useful perspectives which can shed light on particular parts of the process or substance of the advisory proceedings,[103] showing which constituencies benefited and which did not.

On the whole, however, the *Kosovo* Advisory Opinion is not an easy case for testing, developing, and comparing the three perspectives. Given the political stalemate on the ground, there was no real prospect that the Court could have contributed to the resolution of the dispute. Moreover, the legal issues lurking behind the question asked were so politically sensitive, and the positions and practices of states so divided, that this was hardly a case where the Court could have provided a useful contribution to the development of general international law.

In substance, the overriding conclusion is that the response provided by the Court may not have satisfactorily catered to the interests formally expressed by the main constituencies of the Court (the General Assembly and the Security Council), but the result may well have served to protect the stature of the Court in relation to its key constituencies.

Two considerations are particularly relevant in this context. On the one hand, exposing the conflict between the declaration of independence and SC resolution 1244 would have disconnected the Court from the political developments. This (arguably correct) approach may have marginalized the Court, which in the long run may not have been in the interests of the Court itself or its constituencies. On the other hand, a wider discussion of the question of whether the declaration was in accordance with international law would have required the Court to pronounce on highly controversial questions of secession and self-determination. Thereby, it would inevitably have divided its constituencies in a manner that likewise would have threatened its position, which in the long run would also not have been in the interests of its constituencies. The fact that in the short term the Court only served the interests of Kosovo and its supporters is probably better understood as a side-effect of its decision to serve its longer term interests than as a strategic decision to serve this particular constituency over all others.

Yet, in the end, one (undefined) constituency may have lost out. These are the peoples and states that may benefit from future international administrations that serve to maintain and build the peace in conflict areas. By allowing non-state actors to unilaterally pull out of such an arrangement so easily, the Court may well have discouraged relevant actors to enter into such arrangements on future occasions. However, the fact that these actors are as yet unknown, and that the Security Council was too divided to insist on the continuation and implementation of its arrangement, suggests that this will not harm the Court—and this is probably what the Court cared about the most.

---

[103] Not unlike Graham Allison, 'Conceptual Models and the Cuban Missile Crisis' (1969) 63 APSR 689–718; Graham Allison and Philip Zelikow, *Essence of Decision, Explaining the Cuban Missile Crisis* (2nd ed, Pearson, 1999).

# 12

# The Political Aftermath of the ICJ's *Kosovo* Opinion

*Tatjana Papić\**

## 1. Introduction

This article will discuss political responses to the Advisory Opinion of the International Court of Justice (ICJ) on the declaration of independence of Kosovo. First, it analyses how the opinion fitted into competing narratives on the independence of Kosovo. Second, it sheds light on the attempt of Serbia— pursued a week after the AO—to insist on the re-opening of the status negotiations with Kosovo through the United Nations General Assembly (UNGA). It will show how Serbia made a shift at the last moment to compromise with the EU states for the sake of its EU integration ambitions. This resulted in the adoption of the UNGA resolution welcoming the EU-led dialogue between Belgrade and Pristina. Third, the article explores the current state of affairs between Serbia and Kosovo, attempting to understand the challenges and incentives that led the process forward. One of the agreements reached by the parties during these negotiations—on regional representation and cooperation—will be discussed in more detail. This is not only due to the fact that it explicitly refers to the AO on Kosovo, but also because its adoption and implementation are indicative of the process of the EU-led dialogue. It also shows how the position of the parties can solidify or evolve and how potential EU membership dangled in front of the parties influenced the dynamics of their relations.

\* I would like to thank Milica Delević, Vladimir Djerić, and Marko Milanović for their useful comments. I am grateful to Lana Radovanović, Milica Kostić and Dušan Kanazir for their research support. All errors remain my own. Section 4 of this chapter is partly based on my article 'Fighting for a Seat at the Table: International Representation of Kosovo', (2013) 12 *Chinese Journal of International Law* 543.

## 2. Reactions to the *Kosovo* Advisory Opinion

At the very heart of the *Kosovo* advisory proceedings lay a dispute between Serbia and Kosovo over secession, with emotions running high. Because they were most interested in the outcome of the proceedings, it is important to see how Serbia and Kosovo reacted to the decision of the Court that the declaration of independence did not violate international law, but also to look at the reactions of other states and international organizations. This article examines these reactions, trying to establish to what extent the AO influenced the future policies of the concerned parties.

### A. Reactions of Serbia and Kosovo

On the eve of the advisory opinion, both Serbia and Kosovo were adamant that the ruling of the ICJ would not alter their positions on the issue of Kosovo's independence.[1] At the same time, both were confident, at least publicly, that the Court would rule to their advantage.[2] When it emerged that the opinion held that the declaration of independence of Kosovo did not violate international law, its reception was very different in Belgrade and Pristina.

Kosovo authorities jubilantly welcomed the decision of the Court, cracking open bottles of champagne,[3] while cheers erupted from cafes and bars when the ruling was announced on television.[4] The prime minister of Kosovo, Hashim Thaçi, claimed a 'historic victory'.[5] The president of Kosovo, Fatmir Sejdiu, asserted that the Court spoke 'explicitly on all counts in favor of the right to freedom and self-determination of the people of Kosovo'.[6] Kosovo officials called upon states which had not recognized Kosovo as an independent state to do so and not to fear the possible precedential effect of such action, since 'Kosovo is a special case'.[7]

There was one specific message directed towards Serbia: that it should come to terms with Kosovo's independence for the better European future of the

---

[1] Hyseni, 'Kosovo and Serbia react to ICJ ruling', *BBC* News, 22 July 2010, <http://www.bbc.co.uk/news/world-europe-10733676> (27 September 2013).

[2] Collaku, Barlovac, 'Both Kosovo, Serbia confident on Eve of ICJ Opinion', *Balkan Insight*, 21 July 2010, <http://www.balkaninsight.com/en/article/both-kosovo-serbia-confident-on-eve-of-icj-opinion> (28 September 2013).

[3] 'K[osovo] Albanians hail ICJ decision as big victory', *B92 News,* 22 July 2010, <http://www.b92.net/eng/news/politics-article.php?yyyy=2010&mm=07&dd=22&nav_id=68621> (18 September 2013).

[4] 'ICJ ruling on Kosovo; Independence Day', *The Economist*, 22 July 2010, <http://www.economist.com/blogs/easternapproaches/2010/07/icj_ruling_kosovo> (17 September 2013).

[5] See S. Dowling, 'The world from Berlin: "Belgrade must rethink Its destructive Kosovo policy"', *Spiegel Online*, 23 July 2010, <http://www.spiegel.de/international/europe/the-world-from-berlin-belgrade-must-rethink-its-destructive-kosovo-policy-a-708126.html> (10 September 2013).

[6] See the statement of the president, Fatmir Sejdiu, in 'K[osovo] Albanians hail ICJ decision as big victory', *supra* note 3.

[7] Ibid. See also the official statement by the foreign minister of Kosovo, Skënder Hyseni, 22 July 2010, <http://www.mfa-ks.net/?page=2,4,551&offset=1> (20 September 2013).

region[8] and be ready to 'discuss issues of common interest and importance',[9] on an equal footing, i.e. on a state-to-state basis.[10]

The mood in Belgrade was naturally very different. A defeat warranted a more elaborate response. The president of Serbia, Boris Tadić, said the decision of the ICJ was 'difficult for Serbia'.[11] And although the AO was a defeat, both the President and other officials tried to present it more as disappointment with the Court's narrow reading of the question posed by the UNGA. They were focusing not so much on what the Court said but on what it did not say, as can be seen from the statement of President Tadić:

It is clear that the court was not ruling on the right to secession, but that it decided to debate only the technical content of the declaration of independence. The court avoided to rule on [this] essential issue and decided to let the top UN organ debate that, and all the political implications.[12]

The Serbian foreign minister, Vuk Jeremić, echoed this statement while giving a bit more detail:

The Court neither endorsed the view that this unilateral declaration of independence was a unique case, nor Pristina's claim that Kosovo is a state. Moreover, the court failed to approve the province's avowed right of secession from Serbia, or any purported right to self-determination for Kosovo's Albanians.[13]

It was reiterated that Serbia would never recognize Kosovo, since it believed that 'unilateral and ethnically motivated secession is not in line with UN principles'.[14]

Moreover, Serbia's next moves were announced immediately: at the following regular session of the UNGA it would push for the adoption of a resolution in order to try to 'confirm the correctness of its policy' by way of 'calling for negotiations in solving this historical problem and conflict between Serbs and Albanians'.[15] This sounded as if Serbia would urge the re-opening of negotiations on the status of Kosovo, which was soon proved to be true.

Furthermore, Serbia's officials also raised a general concern for the well-being of the international order and other states in the aftermath of the AO. Playing the 'opening Pandora's box' card, they were trying to secure as much support as possible for their future move. So, they warned against misinterpretations of the Court's views as a 'legalization' of Kosovo's attempt at secession (as preached by Kosovo officials)

---

[8] President Sejdiu in 'K[osovo] Albanians hail ICJ Decision as big victory', *supra* note 3.

[9] Foreign minister Hyseni in 'K[osovo] Albanians hail ICJ decision as big victory', *supra* note 3.

[10] Foreign minister Hyseni, *supra* note 7.

[11] 'President reacts to ICJ decision', *B92 News,* 22 July 2010, <http://www.b92.net/eng/news/politics.php?yyyy=2010&mm=07&dd=22&nav_id=68619> (9 September 2013).

[12] Ibid.

[13] Vuk Jeremić, 'Kosovo's disastrous precedent', Op-Ed, *Wall Street Journal*, 28 July 2010, <http://online.wsj.com/article/SB10001424052748703977004575392901873224526.html> (21 September 2013).

[14] Ibid.; and 'President reacts to ICJ decision', *supra* note 11.

[15] In original: 'Ovakvo mišljenje Suda otvara mogućnost Srbiji da ispravnost svoje politike potvrdi na jesen u Generalnoj skupštini UN usvajanjem rezolucije koja ce pozvati da se ovaj istorijski problem i konflikt reši srpsko-albanskim pregovorima'. See 'Tadić: Nastavak miroljubive borbe' ['Tadić: continuing a peaceful policy'], *B92 News,* 22 July 2010, <http://www.b92.net/info/vesti/index.php?yyyy=2010&mm=07&dd=22&nav_category=640&nav_id=447237> (9 September 2013).

that could have major implications for secessionist movements worldwide.[16] In their mind, Kosovo was not a unique case (as claimed by many)[17] but could establish 'a universally applicable precedent that provide[d] a ready-made model for unilateral secession'[18] if interested parties failed to reach a compromise solution.

Serbian and Kosovo officials differed fundamentally when interpreting the ICJ opinion, as they did on Kosovo's independence as such. However, both sides tried to make the most of the AO for the purposes of their entrenched domestic and international political positions. Consequently, the AO was placed into their well-established narratives: Kosovo used it as hard proof that it was an independent state and Serbia used it to justify its continuing struggle against Kosovo's independence. In this way, both Serbia and Kosovo kept the promise they gave in the wake of the ICJ ruling: they were not changing their position towards Kosovo independence, regardless of the AO.

It should also be noted that there was yet another element in Serbia's and Kosovo's responses to the AO. Officials from both sides made sure they included messages on the importance of preserving the peace.[19] In such a troubled region, this was not just meaningless rhetoric.

## B. Reactions of other states

There were no surprises either with the reactions of the other states to the AO. Those who were in favour of Kosovo's independence naturally welcomed the decision and those who were against expressed reservations. Within these two camps, the substance and intensity of responses differed from state to state. Intensity depended on the extent of previous involvement in the issue of Kosovo independence, while the substance mainly echoed arguments already voiced when Kosovo declared independence.

In addition, states from the region of the Western Balkans emphasized the regional perspective in their reactions to the AO, stressing that this decision could contribute to regional peace, stability, and progress (e.g. Albania,[20] Croatia,[21] Slovenia,[22] and Montenegro[23]).

---

[16] See 'Tadić: Teška odluka' ['Tadić: Difficult decision'], *Blic*, 23 July 2010, <http://www.blic.rs/Vesti/Politika/199626/Tadic-Teska-odluka> (24 September 2012); Jeremić, Op-Ed, *Wall Street Journal, supra* note 13 and 'Tadić: Nastavak miroljubive borbe', *supra* note 15.

[17] See Chapter 3 (Marko Milanović), and *infra* notes 40–46.

[18] Jeremić, Op-Ed, *Wall Street Journal, supra* note 13.

[19] See Marzouk, Collaku, Barlovac, 'Pristina, Belgrade react to ICJ shock decision', *Balkan Insight*, 22 July 2010, <http://www.balkaninsight.com/en/article/pristina-belgrade-react-to-icj-shock-decision> and 'President Reacts to ICJ Decision', *supra* note 10 and 'Serbia looks to UN GA after ICJ ruling', B92 News, 22 July 2010, <http://www.b92.net/eng/news/politics.php?yyyy=2010&mm=07&dd=22&nav_id=68617> (23 September 2013).

[20] 'UN court says Kosovo independence legal', *Radio Free Europe*, 23 July 2010, <http://www.rferl.org/content/UN_Court_Says_Kosovo_Independence_Did_Not_Violate_International_Law/2107090.html> (28 September 2010).

[21] 'Josipović: Beograd i Priština u EU', *B92 News*, 23 July 2010, <http://www.b92.net/info/vesti/index.php?yyyy=2010&mm=07&dd=23&nav_id=447479> (26 September 2013).

[22] 'Slovenia hopes ICJ Opinion will improve Serbia-Kosovo relations', *Slovenia Press Agency*, 22 July 2010, <http://www.sta.si/en/vest.php?s=a&id=1537018? (26 September 2013).

[23] 'Reactions to ICJ Kosovo ruling: to recognise or not to recognise', *The Economist*, 29 July 2010, <http://www.economist.com/blogs/easternapproaches/2010/07/reactions_icj_kosovo_ruling> (30 September 2013).

There were three common issues around which states expressed their responses to the AO: (1) What did the AO say/not say? (2) Was Kosovo a precedent? (3) What should Serbia and Kosovo do after the AO?

Some supporters of Kosovo independence, such as the US,[24] France,[25] Germany,[26] and the Czech Republic,[27] pointed out that the Court confirmed their view of Kosovo's declaration of independence as not being contrary to international law. France,[28] the UK,[29] and the US[30] urged states which did not recognize Kosovo to do so. On the other hand, some states which had opposed Kosovo independence (these included China,[31] Cyprus,[32] India,[33] Russia,[34] Romania,[35] Slovakia,[36] Spain,[37] and Ukraine[38]), explicitly said that they would not change their stance on the issue, despite the decision of the ICJ. Some of them explained that this was due to fact that the ICJ only considered the content of Kosovo's declaration of independence but not its consequences,[39] which was in line with Serbia's arguments.

---

[24] Statement of the US Secretary of State, Hilary Clinton, 'Release of International Court of Justice Advisory Opinion on Kosovo's Declaration of Independence', 22 July 2010, <http://www.state.gov/secretary/rm/2010/07/145042.htm> (26 September 2013).

[25] Statement of the French minister of foreign and European affairs, Bernard Kouchner, 'Kosovo: ICJ Advisory Opinion', 22 July 2010, <http://www.consulfrance-newyork.org/Kosovo-ICJ-advisory-opinion> (26 September 2013).

[26] 'EU remains divided on Kosovo despite Court opinion', *EU Observer*, 27 July 2013, <http://euobserver.com/news/30541> (26 September 2013).

[27] Statement of the Czech Ministry of Foreign Affairs on the publication of the ICJ Advisory Opinion, 22 July 2010, <http://www.mzv.cz/jnp/en/issues_and_press/statements/x2010_07_22_statement_of_mfa_on_the_publication_of_the_icj_advisory_opinion.html> (26 September 2013).

[28] Statement of the French minister of foreign and European affairs, *supra* note 25.

[29] Announcement of the Foreign and Commonwealth Office, 'Foreign Secretary welcomes Kosovo ruling', 22 July 2010, <https://www.gov.uk/government/news/foreign-secretary-welcomes-kosovo-ruling> (26 September 2013).

[30] Statement of the US Secretary of State, *supra* note 24.

[31] Chinese Foreign Ministry spokesperson, Qin Gang's response to the International Court of Justice's Advisory Opinion on the *Kosovo* Case, 23 July 2010, <http://www.fmprc.gov.cn/eng//xwfw/s2510/t719113.htm> (26 September 2013). These negotiations should be led within the UN framework.

[32] 'Reaction in quotes: UN legal ruling on Kosovo', *BBC News*, 22 July 2010, <http://www.bbc.co.uk/news/world-europe-10733837> (27 September 2013).

[33] 'India not to recognize Kosovo', *Thaindian News*, 9 August 2010, <http://www.thaindian.com/newsportal/uncategorized/india-not-to-recognize-kosovo_100409649.html> (28 September 2013).

[34] Barlovac, Arslanagic, 'World reacts to ICJ Advisory ruling on Kosovo', *Balkan Insight*, 23 July 2010, <http://www.balkaninsight.com/en/article/world-reacts-to-icj-advisory-ruling-on-kosovo> (26 September 2013).

[35] Ibid.

[36] 'Washington wants EU unity over Kosovo', *B92 News*, 22 July 2010, <http://www.b92.net/eng/news/politics.php?yyyy=2010&mm=07&dd=22&nav_id=68618> (27 September 2013).

[37] 'Spain in fresh Kosovo statement', *B92 News*, 24 July 2010, <http://www.b92.net/eng/news/politics.php?yyyy=2010&mm=07&dd=24&nav_id=68664> (26 September 2013).

[38] 'Украина не признает независимости Косово' ['Ukraine does not recognize independence of Kosovo'], Коммерсантъ Украина [Kommesrant], 28 July 2010, <http://www.kommersant.ua/doc/1477476> (27 September 2013).

[39] As did Romania, see 'Cyprus, Romania on Kosovo after ICJ ruling', *B92 News*, 23 July 2010, <http://www.b92.net/eng/news/politics.php?yyyy=2010&mm=07&dd=23&nav_id=68643> (28 September 2013).

The pro-Kosovo camp again reiterated that Kosovo was a unique case, which was not to set a precedent for the future (Bulgaria,[40] France,[41] Germany,[42] UK,[43] US,[44] Canada,[45] and Italy[46]).

The same message also came from Azerbaijan,[47] a state in the opposite camp due to the fact that the AO could resonate with its internal secessionist challenges (with Nagorno-Karabakh). Other states with such challenges were prompted to stress how their situation did not resemble Kosovo's (Indonesia,[48] Moldova,[49] Spain,[50] and Cyprus[51]). This was also one of the messages that came from Bosnia and Herzegovina (BaH).[52] However, being a deeply divided state BaH did not speak with one voice. The president of the Serb entity (Republika Srpska), sent the opposite message from the one coming from Sarajevo: the ICJ's decision on Kosovo's declaration of independence had opened 'the possibility for [Republika Srpska] to secede from Bosnia-Herzegovina'.[53] At the same time he stressed that he would continue to prevent BaH from recognizing Kosovo as an independent state.[54] This schizophrenic position was in part the result of a close relationship between Republika Srpska and Serbia.

One common stance was widespread in both camps: that Serbia and Kosovo needed to negotiate. However, when it came to what they should negotiate about, the positions again diverged diametrically. While the states opposing Kosovo's independence called for negotiations on the status of Kosovo within the UNSC resolution 1244[55]

---

[40] See 'Bulgaria for dialogue after ICJ decision', *B92 News*, 25 July 2010, <http://www.b92.net/eng/news/politics-article.php?yyyy=2010&mm=07&dd=25&nav_id=68668> (26 September 2013).

[41] Statement of the French minister of foreign and European affairs, *supra* note 25.

[42] 'EU remains divided on Kosovo', *supra* note 26.

[43] Announcement of the Foreign and Commonwealth Office, *supra* note 29.

[44] Statement of the US Secretary of State, *supra* note 24.

[45] 'Quebec sovereignty threat remains very real', *KosovoCompromise*, 3 September 2010, <http://www.kosovocompromise.com/cms/item/topic/en.html?view=story&id=3013&sectionId=2> (26 September 2013).

[46] 'Italy: Kosovo talks must continue', *B92 News,* 25 July 2010, <http://www.b92.net/eng/news/politics-article.php?yyyy=2010&mm=07&dd=25&nav_id=68669 >(26 September 2013).

[47] 'Baku says UN legal ruling on Kosovo sets no precedent', *1.News.az*, 23 July 2010, <http://news.az/articles/19703> (27 September 2013).

[48] 'ICJ ruling could inspire RI separatists', *The Jakarta Post*, 27 July 2010, <http://www.thejakartapost.com/news/2010/07/27/icj-ruling-could-inspire-ri-separatists039.html> (28 September 2013).

[49] 'И.о. главы Молдавии: Косовский прецедент неприменим к Приднестровью', ['Acting head of Moldavia: Kosovo precedent does not apply to Transnistria'], *Regnum*, 23 July 2010, <http://www.regnum.ru/news/russia/1307836.html> (27 September 2013).

[50] 'Spain in fresh Kosovo Statement', *supra* note 37.

[51] 'Cyprus, Romania on Kosovo after ICJ ruling', *supra* note 39.

[52] See the statement of the president of the tripartite Presidency of Bosnia and Herzogovina, Haris Silajdžić, in Sadiković, 'Oprečna tumačenja mišljenja o Kosovu' ['Conflicting interpretation of Kosovo [Advisory] Opinion'], 23 July 2010, <http://www.slobodnaevropa.org/content/oprecna_tumacenja_misljenja_suda_msp/2108144.html> (30 September 2013).

[53] 'RS: ICJ decision and secession', *B92 News*, 25 July 2010, <http://www.b92.net/eng/news/region-article.php?yyyy=2010&mm=07&dd=25&nav_id=68674> (30 September 2013).

[54] See 'Tadić: Teška odluka', *supra* note 16.

[55] SC Res. 1244, 10 June 1999, UN doc. S/RES/1244.

framework (China,[56] Cyprus,[57] Russia,[58] Romania,[59] Spain[60]), those who supported it were adamant that this was off the table (France,[61] Germany,[62] Italy,[63] Slovenia,[64] UK,[65] and US[66]), since they viewed Kosovo independence as an irreversible matter.[67]

Thus, as was the case with Serbia and Kosovo, the AO hardly made any difference with regard to states' attitudes towards Kosovo's independence, at least when it comes to those states that had previously declared a position.

## C. Reactions of international organizations

Not many reactions came from international organizations. Only the organizations constituting the four pillars of the international presence in Kosovo—the UN, EU, NATO, and the Organization for Security and Co-operation in Europe (OSCE)—felt a need to issue a statement after the AO. All of them were careful not to take sides and were mindful of the respective roles they played in Kosovo.

The Secretary-General of the UN urged Serbia and Kosovo to engage in a constructive dialogue and 'to avoid any steps that could be seen as provocative and derail the dialogue'.[68] He also announced that he would be forwarding the Advisory Opinion to the General Assembly for it to decide on how to proceed with the matter.[69]

OSCE and NATO were succinct: they took note of the decision, stating they would continue to carry out their respective mandates in Kosovo—the former in promoting and monitoring human rights and strengthening democratic institutions,[70] and the latter in preserving security in Kosovo.[71]

The EU response was the only one with a concrete proposal for future action. Namely, after welcoming the Court's decision, the EU high representative for foreign and security policy, Baroness Catherine Ashton, stated that the EU was

---

[56] China generally referred to the UN framework. See Chinese Foreign Ministry spokesperson Qin Gang's Response, *supra* note 31.

[57] 'Spain, Romania, Cyprus and Slovakia reiterated they will not recognise Kosovo', *KosovoCompromise*, 26 July 2013, <http://www.kosovocompromise.com/cms/item/topic/en.html?view=story&id=2905&sectionId=1> (27 September 2013).

[58] 'World Reacts to ICJ Advisory Ruling on Kosovo', *supra* note 34.

[59] Ibid.

[60] 'Spain in fresh Kosovo statement', *supra* note 37.

[61] Statement of the French minister of foreign and European affairs, *supra* note 25.

[62] 'EU remains divided on Kosovo', *supra* note 26.

[63] 'Italy: Kosovo talks must continue', *supra* note 46.

[64] 'Slovenia hopes ICJ Opinion will improve Serbia-Kosovo relations', *supra* note 22.

[65] Announcement of the Foreign and Commonwealth Office, *supra* note 29.

[66] Statement of the US Secretary of State, *supra* note 24.

[67] Ibid. See also statement of the French minister of foreign and European affairs, *supra* note 25; announcement of the Foreign and Commonwealth Office, *supra* note 29; 'EU remains divided on Kosovo', *supra* note 26.

[68] Statement attributable to the spokesperson for the Secretary-General on the ICJ advisory opinion on Kosovo's independence, 22 July 2010, <http://www.un.org/sg/statements/?nid=4691> (28 September 2013).

[69] Ibid.

[70] See 'OSCE Mission in Kosovo to continue work for benefit of all communities, says OSCE Secretary General', *Press Release*, 26 July 2010, <http://www.osce.org/sg/72112> (28 September 2013)

[71] See 'Tadić: Teška odluka', *supra* note 16.

ready to facilitate a process of dialogue between Pristina and Belgrade. This dialogue would be to promote cooperation, achieve progress on the path to Europe and improve the lives of the people. The process of dialogue in itself would be a factor for peace, security and stability in the region.[72]

Hence, despite its internal split on the issue of Kosovo recognition,[73] the EU was united on the position that Belgrade and Pristina needed to negotiate. Most of the EU states which recognized Kosovo thought talks should only include technical issues, while some of the Member States which contested Kosovo's statehood were for the renewal of status talks.[74] For this reason, the EU proposal was drafted broadly and neutrally and did not specify what the substance of the dialogue it strived to facilitate would be. As will be seen, this would prove essential in building consensus in the phases that would follow.

## 3. UNGA Resolution on the *Kosovo* AO

The AO proceedings were of Serbia's own making. It was Serbia who pushed for the request to be submitted to the ICJ, and Serbia who drafted the question. Although the idea behind the AO was to buy Serbia more time to calm the crisis over Kosovo's independence, the quest for an advisory opinion raised expectations of Serbia's 'victory' as if a fully-fledged contentious case were on-going between Serbia and Kosovo. Hence, the main issue after the AO was what Serbia's next move would be.

Ever since Kosovo declared independence,[75] one of the main goals of Serbia's foreign policy[76] was to secure the re-opening of negotiations on the status of Kosovo.[77] The AO was supposed to help achieve that goal[78] and Serbian officials were confident that the ICJ would uphold the territorial integrity of Serbia, which

---

[72] Declaration by high representative, Catherine Ashton on behalf of the European Union on the International Court of Justice advisory opinion on Kosovo, EU10-153EN, 22 July 2010, <http://www.eu-un.europa.eu/articles/en/article_9973_en.htm> (28 September 2013).

[73] Cyprus, Romania and somewhat Spain, see *supra* notes 57, 58 and 37.

[74] Ibid.

[75] Kosovo Declaration of Independence, <http://www.assembly-kosova.org/?cid=2,128,1635> (8 October 2013).

[76] According to the Serbian foreign minister, Vuk Jeremić, this goal engaged all diplomatic efforts of the country. See 'International Court of Justice rules on Kosovo independence', *Radio Free Europe*, 22 July 2010, <http://www.rferl.org/content/High_UN_Court_To_Rule_On_Kosovo_Independence/2106373.html> (1 October 2013).

[77] There were already negotiations on the Kosovo status settlement between Belgrade and Pristina, led by the UN Secretary-General's Special Envoy Martti Ahtisaari, which Serbia rejected. The so-called Ahtisaari Plan envisaged internationally supervised independence for Kosovo. (See *Comprehensive Proposal for the Kosovo Status Settlement*, see UN Doc. S/2007/168/Add.1 (26 March 2007), <http://www.unosek.org/docref/Comprehensive_proposal-english.pdf> (visited 8 October 2013).) However, this plan failed, after it was not endorsed by the UNSC, primarily due to Russia's opposition to it. See MacDonald, 'Russia rejects plan for Kosovo', *Financial Times*, 13 July 2007, <http://www.ft.com/intl/cms/s/0/f3f09aae-30a0-11dc-9a81-0000779fd2ac.html#axzz1xqyDvwn9> (16 January 2013).

[78] Statement of the Serbian prime minister, Cvetković in 'Both Kosovo, Serbia confident on eve of ICJ Opinion', *supra* note 2.

would imply that Kosovo Albanians did not have the right to secede.[79] They hoped that a legal battle in the form of ICJ advisory proceedings could be won and that this would ensure the political support needed for the re-opening of status negotiations. When they learnt that the AO proceedings did not bring the result they expected, Serbian officials nevertheless decided to push for status negotiations by submitting a draft resolution to the UNGA that would call for them.

However, this could not be done without huge cost to Serbia's other major foreign policy goal: joining the EU. The idea of reopening negotiations on Kosovo's status meant a confrontation with three major EU member states, which recognized Kosovo and were vigorously opposed to new status negotiations (UK, France, and Germany).[80] At the same time, only by a unanimous decision of all EU Member States, could Serbia hope to proceed with its integration into the EU.

The following part of this article will discuss Serbia's move to lobby for the UNGA resolution and shows how and why the initial text was changed. Moreover, it will put this move and its ultimate outcome (a UNGA resolution adopted by consensus) into the broader picture of future relations between Serbia and Kosovo.

## A. Homecoming—Kosovo's return to the UNGA

When the AO was made public, Serbian president Tadić explained to the domestic audience that, *inter alia*, the ICJ let the UNGA decide on the right to secession and its political implications.[81] Therefore, he announced, Serbia would push for a resolution in the UNGA, which would call for negotiations on the status of Kosovo. That resolution was of multifold purpose: to prove Serbia was right[82] and to prevent a different interpretation of the ICJ opinion[83] and the creation of dangerous precedents in the future.[84]

This idea was supported by the Serbian Government and the Serbian Parliament.[85] On the motion of the Government, the Parliament adopted the 'Decision on Continuation of Activities of the Republic of Serbia in Defense of its Sovereignty and Territorial Integrity'.[86] It called upon the Government to continue to defend

---

[79] See the Statement of Serbian president, Boris Tadić, in 'International Court of Justice rules on Kosovo independence', *supra* note 76.

[80] See Statement of the French minister of foreign and European affairs, *supra* note 25; announcement of the Foreign and Commonwealth Office, *supra* note 29; 'EU remains divided on Kosovo', *supra* note 26.

[81] See his statement cited above, accompanying *supra* note 12

[82] See the statement of the president of Serbia, *supra* note 15.

[83] Full quote: 'There would be no opportunities for different interpretations of the opinion [once UNGA resolution adopted].' [In original: 'Nakon [usvajanja rezolucije u GS] neće više biti prostora za različite interpretacije sudskog mišljenja'.] See 'Tadić: Teška odluka', *supra* note 15.

[84] 'Serbia's chances before UNGA "almost impossible"', *B92 News*, 9 August 2010, <http://www.b92.net/eng/news/politics.php?yyyy=2010&mm=08&dd=09&nav_id=68971> (24 September 2013).

[85] 'Serbia's parliament calls for new talks on Kosovo', *Radio Free Europe*, 27 July 2010, <http://www.rferl.org/content/Serbias_Parliament_Calls_For_New_Talks_On_Kosovo/2110590.html> (30 September 2013).

[86] Odluka o nastavku aktivnosti Republike Srbije u odbrani suvereniteta i teritorijalnog integriteta Republike Srbije, *Službeni glasnik Republike Srbije* ['Decision on the continuation

the sovereignty and territorial integrity of the country (point 1), and expressed its support for 'submitting a resolution to the UN General Assembly, which adoption will open a venue for reaching a compromise solution for Kosovo-Metohija through negotiations (point 3 and 4)'.[87]

The Serbian Foreign Ministry was already working on a draft of the resolution. The foreign minister Jeremić claimed there were 'consultations … underway with Russia, China and the European Union'[88] in preparing a draft (which later proved not to be the case),[89] but that the resolution would be written by Serbia alone.[90]

While the Serbian president maintained that Serbia was not giving up its EU ambitions,[91] it was hard to reconcile this position with the fact that a draft resolution that would call for status negotiations would mean an open confrontation with the states that recognized Kosovo, which were at the same time crucial decision-makers in the process of Serbia's EU integration (UK, Germany, and France).[92] Accordingly, Serbia's two principal foreign policy goals—joining the EU and keeping Kosovo—became mutually exclusive, regardless of what its president was claiming.[93]

## B. A fast and furious draft

Within a week from the day the ICJ delivered its AO on Kosovo independence, Serbia submitted its draft resolution to the UNGA. This speed took the US and EU by surprise.[94]

The draft resolution's preamble stressed that 'one-sided secession' could not be accepted, and the operative part acknowledged the AO and called on 'the sides to find a mutually acceptable solution for *all disputed issues through peaceful dialogue*, with the aim of achieving peace, security and cooperation in the region'.[95]

Obviously, this draft was highly divisive since it called for new negotiations on the status of Kosovo, which was unacceptable to the states that recognized Kosovo. As one would expect, these states criticized Serbia for sending such a draft

---

of Serbia's activities in the defence of its sovereignty and territorial integrity', *Official Gazette of the Republic of Serbia*], No. 51/2010. Available in English at <http://www.b92.net/eng/insight/pressroom.php?yyyy=2010&mm=07&nav_id=68750> (1 October 2013).

[87] Ibid.

[88] 'Parliament backs govt. Kosovo policy', *B92 News*, 27 July 2010, <http://www.b92.net/eng/news/politics-article.php?yyyy=2010&mm=07&dd=27&nav_id=68710> (30 September 2010).

[89] See the text accompanying *infra* note 110.

[90] 'Parliament backs govt. Kosovo policy', *supra* note 88.

[91] 'Tadić o daljoj politici prema Kosovu', ['Tadić on future moves towards Kosovo'], *B92rtv*, 26 July 2010, <http://www.youtube.com/watch?v=1u7xXMBKR5Y> (4 October 2013).

[92] Cyprus, Greece, Romania, Slovakia, and Spain refused to recognize Kosovo due to their domestic concerns.

[93] 'Tadić o daljoj politici prema Kosovu', *supra* note 91.

[94] 'Serbia criticized over GA draft', *B92 News*, 29 July 2010, <http://www.b92.net/eng/news/politics.php?yyyy=2010&mm=07&dd=29&nav_id=68776> (4 October 2013).

[95] Emphasis added. 'Serbia submits Kosovo draft to UN GA', *B92 News,* 29 July 2010, <http://www.b92.net/eng/news/politics.php?yyyy=2010&mm=07&dd=28&nav_id=68748> (16 September 2013). UN Doc. A/64/L.65.

to New York,[96] especially because it did not consult the EU before doing so,[97] although Serbian foreign minister claimed the opposite.[98] Kosovo officials predictably called for the rejection of Serbia's draft resolution.[99]

Then EU states started working on their draft resolution, which would be supported by all EU member states, including those which did not recognize Kosovo.[100] Belgrade again became a hot destination for Western high officials. British Foreign Secretary, William Hague, and German foreign minister, Guido Westerwelle, travelled there to urge Serbia's officials to drop the policy of confrontation if they wanted to bring their country closer to the EU.[101] They both asked for Serbia's draft resolution to be withdrawn.[102] The same message came from the US.[103] Serbia thus came under huge political pressure, one that was largely of its own making.

## C. Sobering up

Reactions from Belgrade were mixed. On one side were those saying that Serbia could not change its stance, such as Foreign Minister Jeremić[104] and deputy prime minister for EU integration, Božidar Djelić.[105] On the other hand, the President's cabinet was apparently more flexible and issued a statement after his meeting with British Foreign Secretary Hague that Serbia was ready for a compromise, without recognizing Kosovo.[106] Some days earlier, another deputy prime minister, Ivica Dačić,[107] said Serbia was open to changes in the draft resolution. Moreover, his statement shed more light on the circumstances in which the draft resolution was submitted in the first place. Dačić said that the Serbian Foreign Minister had informed the Government[108] that the EU was consulted on the text of the resolution, but

---

[96] 'Serbia criticized over UN GA draft', *supra* note 94.

[97] Ibid.

[98] See 'Parliament backs govt. Kosovo policy', *supra* note 88.

[99] In a letter to the member states of the UN and international organizations (Council of Europe, EU, OSCE, Organization of the Islamic Conference, The Arab League, the Organization of American States, etc.), see 'Sejdiu, Thaçi call on UN to reject Serbia's resolution', *B92 News*, 16 August 2010, <http://www.b92.net/eng/news/politics.php?yyyy=2010&mm=08&dd=16&nav_id=69109> (4 October2013).

[100] 'Serbia criticized over UN GA draft', *supra* note 94.

[101] 'British FM favors withdrawal of resolution', *B92 News,* 31 August 2010, <http://www.b92.net/eng/news/politics.php?yyyy=2010&mm=08&dd=31&nav_id=69406> (4 October 2013). 'Germany urges Serbia to accept Kosovo', *SETimes.com*, 27 August 2010, <http://www.setimes.com/cocoon/setimes/xhtml/en_GB/features/setimes/features/2010/08/27/feature-01> (4 October 2013).

[102] Ibid.

[103] 'Americans request recall of Jeremic', *Blic*, 26 July 2010, <http://english.blic.rs/News/6703/Americans-request-recall-of-Jeremic> (11 October 2013).

[104] See 'British FM favors withdrawal of resolution', *supra* note 101.

[105] 'Serbia "won't withdraw Kosovo draft"', *B92 News*, 21 August 2010, <http://www.b92.net/eng/news/politics.php?yyyy=2010&mm=08&dd=23&nav_id=69233> (5 October 2013).

[106] 'British FM favors withdrawal of resolution', *supra* note 101.

[107] '"Serbia open to changes to UN GA draft"', *B92 News*, 21 August 2010, <http://www.b92.net/eng/news/politics.php?yyyy=2010&mm=08&dd=21&nav_id=69209> (4 October 2013).

[108] This was also noted in Serbian media, see *supra* note 88.

that 'clearly there was no agreement on the text of resolution'.[109] The statement of the British Foreign Secretary, William Hague, corroborates this.[110] Therefore, it seemed that the Serbian foreign minister, Jeremić, was the *spiritus movens* in entering into an open confrontation with the major EU states and the US, by submitting a draft resolution while knowing they would strenuously oppose it.

Vuk Jeremić was perceived by Western officials and diplomats as a person unwilling to compromise on the issues of Kosovo independence.[111] He vigorously opposed Kosovo's independence and was pushing to take it to the ICJ, as corroborated by the number of hours he reportedly spent up in the air.[112] His peculiar combination of energy and divisiveness earned Serbia's foreign policy the depiction of a foreign policy on steroids.[113]

During the course of the advisory proceedings, he raised the political stakes incessantly, as if a fully-fledged contentious case was on-going between Serbia and Kosovo, and as if an outcome favourable for Serbia was never in doubt. He was, beyond question, a leading star of the advisory proceedings drama. Hence the ironic headline in the form of a personal 'thank you' note[114]—written in Serbian—that appeared on the cover of a Pristina daily newspaper when the AO was announced.[115] It was a hard blow not only for Serbia but for him personally when the ICJ did not rule as he expected. Nevertheless, in the aftermath of the AO, his rhetoric did not change. His stated desire for Serbia's draft resolution was the UN concluding that the 'secessionists were not right'.[116] It seems that he allowed no room for a compromise with EU states on the draft resolution.

However, it was clear that Belgrade could not hope to go forward with integration in the EU if it followed the path set out by its foreign minister. On 2 September, a week before the UNGA session, it was reported that Belgrade wanted to establish common ground with the 22 EU member states which had recognized Kosovo.[117] First, the views of the member states within the EU were harmonized.[118] This served as 'guidelines' for reaching harmonized positions between the EU and Serbia in discussing the issue of Kosovo in the UNGA, which were presented to President Tadić in Brussels on 7 September 2010.[119]

---

[109] '"Serbia open to changes to UN GA draft"', *supra* note 107.

[110] See 'British FM favors withdrawal of resolution', *supra* note 101.

[111] 'Americans request recall of Jeremic', *supra* note 103.

[112] He claimed that he spent 700 hours in the air in 2008. See 'Serbia's busy foreign policy: Better troublesome than dull', *The Economist*, 22 October 2009, <http://www.economist.com/node/14710896> (30 September 2013).

[113] Ibid.

[114] In the original: 'Hvala Vuče'. See Pristina daily *Express* shown in *Reuters Video* at <http://article.wn.com/view/2010/07/25/ICJ_ruling_to_sober_Serbia_Kosovo_premier_says/#/video> (20 September 2013).

[115] Ibid.          [116] 'Parliament backs govt. Kosovo policy', *supra* 90.

[117] 'Spain working on changes to Kosovo resolution', *B92 News*, 2 September 2010, <http://www.b92.net/eng/news/politics.php?yyyy=2010&mm=09&dd=02&nav_id=69434> (7 October 2013).

[118] See 'EU harmonizes position on Serbian resolution', *B92 News*, 7 September 2010, <http://www.b92.net/eng/news/politics.php?yyyy=2010&mm=09&dd=07&nav_id=69544> (7 October 2013).

[119] Ibid. See also brief statement from the EU issued on 7 September 2010, A 175/10, <http://www.consilium.europa.eu/uedocs/cms_data/docs/pressdata/EN/foraff/116326.pdf> (7 October 2013).

The message was that the wording of the draft resolution needed to be amended in order to exclude views that were leading to a clear confrontation with those EU states which recognized Kosovo's independence and were against re-opening status talks.[120]

Two days later, on the very day when the UNGA was expected to discuss Serbia's draft resolution, Belgrade finally found common ground with the EU. It immediately withdrew the draft resolution (from 28 July),[121] and submitted a new one co-written and co-sponsored with the EU.

### D. The final text—Resolution 64/289 on ICJ's Advisory Opinion on Kosovo

Resolution 64/298[122] was adopted by consensus.[123] In its operative part, the General Assembly acknowledged the AO and welcomed

the readiness of the European Union to facilitate a process of dialogue between the parties; the process of dialogue in itself would be a factor for peace, security and stability in the region, and that dialogue would be to promote cooperation, achieve progress on the path to the European Union and improve the lives of the people.[124]

Phrases such as 'unilateral secession' and 'negotiation on all open issues' were gone.[125] What was left was wording that each party could interpret in line with its position on the issue of Kosovo independence, and this secured the common ground necessary for the adoption of the resolution.

The role of the EU, welcomed by the UNGA resolution, fits with the framework set by the United Nations Security Council (UNSC) presidential statement of November 2008, which welcomed the efforts of the EU 'to advance the European perspective of the whole of the Western Balkans, thereby making a decisive contribution to regional stability and prosperity'.[126]

When introducing the draft resolution, Serbian foreign minister, Jeremić, said that the document strived to put the AO 'in an appropriate international context that [would] contribute to all-around stability',[127] and that the draft was a status-neutral document.[128] The latter was particularly important for Serbia to

---

[120] 'EU harmonizes position on Serbian resolution', *supra* note 118.

[121] See *supra* note 95.

[122] UN Doc. A/RES/64/298, 13 October 2010, <http://www.un.org/en/ga/search/view_doc.asp?symbol=A/RES/64/298> (17 September 2013).

[123] Ibid. and 'Serbia, EU reach resolution compromise', *B92 News*, 9 September 2010, <http://www.b92.net/eng/news/politics.php?yyyy=2010&mm=09&dd=09&nav_id=69564> (7 October 2013).

[124] GA Res. 64/298, *supra* note 122.

[125] 'EU harmonizes position on Serbian resolution', *supra* note 118.

[126] UN Doc. S/PRST/2008/44, 26 November 2008. At the time, this presidential statement served to provide a nexus between UNSC resolution 1244 framework and the EU Council's Action Plan of February 2008, aimed to establish a civilian mission in Kosovo (European Union Rule of Law Mission in Kosovo, EULEX). European Union Council, Council Joint Action 2008/124/CFSP of 4 February 2008, OJ 2008 L 42/92, <http://www.eulex-kosovo.eu/en/info/docs/JointActionEULEX_EN.pdf> (13 October 2013).

[127] See UN Doc. A/64/PV.120, 9 September 2010, at 1.          [128] Ibid.

emphasize, since it allowed its position of not recognizing Kosovo's independence to remain intact. After reiterating that Serbia was not and would not recognize Kosovo's declaration of independence, he stated that the resolution would 'help to create an atmosphere conducive to the establishment of a comprehensive compact of peace between Serbia and Albanians through good-faith dialogue'.[129]

This was a change everyone commended.

Besides Serbia, 14 states addressed the UNGA.[130] All of them praised Serbia for its constructive approach and none, except Albania,[131] even mentioned the first draft resolution of 28 July. Everyone also welcomed the compromise and stressed that only negotiations could secure a durable peace in the Balkans.[132] However, when it came to the issue of the substance of the negotiations, participants in the debate were again divided along the lines of their position towards Kosovo's independence.

Most of the states which addressed the UNGA were of the opinion that a durable peace should be achieved through status talks (Azerbaijan, Venezuela, Argentina, Russia, Brazil, China, India, Indonesia, and Iran).[133] Two states were adamant these negotiations should only be on practical issues (US and Albania).[134] This balance was due to the fact that most of the states which participated in the debate did not recognize Kosovo.[135] This was also why the majority of the states participating in the debate emphasized the importance of the principle of territorial integrity (Azerbaijan, Venezuela, Brazil, China, India, Indonesia, and Iran)[136] or reiterated that they considered UNSC resolution 1244 to be a legal foundation for achieving a durable solution for Kosovo (Argentina, Russia, China, and Brazil).[137]

In order to retain common ground with the EU, the address of the Serbian foreign minister largely avoided these arguments. Only at the very end of his speech could one hear an echo of his past rhetoric on Kosovo:

The Assembly should not have no doubt that, come what may, Serbia's resolve shall not waver. We will not tire, because we must not fail. Although our challenges remain formidable, so do our strengths as we look to the future with conviction in the justice of our cause.[138]

---

[129] Ibid., at 2.

[130] These were Azerbaijan, Venezuela, Argentina, US, Turkey, Brazil, Russian Federation, China, India, Peru, Albania, Fiji, Indonesia, and Iran: the first three before, and the rest after, the resolution was adopted. Ibid., at 1–7.

[131] Ibid., at 5.     [132] Ibid.

[133] Ibid. Azerbaijan, Venezuela (at 2), Argentina (at 3), Russia and Brazil (at 4), China and India (at 5), Indonesia and Iran (at 7).

[134] Ibid. US (at 4) and Albania (at 5).

[135] At the time of the UNGA session, these were Azerbaijan, Venezuela, Argentina, Brazil, Russian Federation, China, India, Fiji, Indonesia, and Iran. All but Fuji have continued to maintain their position (up to the date of the completion of this chapter). See 'Ministry of Foreign Affairs, countries that have recognized the Republic of Kosova', <http://www.mfa-ks.net/?page=2,33> (12 October 2013). States which addressed the UNGA and did recognize Kosovo at the time were the US, Turkey, Albania, and Peru. Ibid.

[136] UN Doc. A/64/PV.120, *supra* note 127, Azerbaijan, Venezuela (at 2), Brazil (at 4), China and India (at 5), Indonesia and Iran (at 7).

[137] Ibid. Argentina (at 3), Russia and Brazil (at 4). More specifically, China was not referring specifically to the UNSC resolution 1244, but to the 'framework of the relevant resolutions of the Security Council' (at 5).

[138] Ibid., at 2.

One could not know for sure if Jeremić was borrowing the rather melodramatic 'we will not tire' turn of phrase from Sir Winston Churchill[139] or from George W. Bush.[140]

Nevertheless, rhetoric echoing such horrors as World War II or 9/11 was paradigmatic of Serbia's approach to the issue of Kosovo until the point of the adoption on the UNGA resolution. The rhetoric was likely more of a leftover from the speech prepared for the initial draft resolution Serbia had submitted. But such rhetoric had to be deflated if Serbia wanted to stay on the EU membership path. Moreover, if the EU-led negotiations between Belgrade and Pristina were to lead anywhere Serbia had to make some changes in its Kosovo policy. Let us now see if this in fact happened.

## 4. Relations between Belgrade and Pristina—EU Sponsored Dialogue

This part of the article will provide an overview of the developing relations between Belgrade and Pristina after the adoption of the UNGA resolution on the AO, focusing on the on-going EU-facilitated dialogue between the parties. Although, at the time of the adoption of the UNGA resolution, the substance of the future dialogue was subject to different interpretations,[141] it was undisputed that it should take place under the auspices of the EU in the light of the EU aspirations of both Serbia and Kosovo.[142] This indeed had proved to be the most powerful incentive for the parties to reach agreements that would otherwise be unattainable.

### A. Where we stand—an overview of the EU sponsored dialogue

The dialogue between Pristina and Belgrade started in March 2011,[143] and is still on-going.[144] Initially, it was led by the political director of the Ministry of Foreign Affairs of Serbia[145] and the deputy prime minister of Kosovo,[146] with

---

[139] 'Give Us the Tools Speech' given over BBC Radio on 9 February 1941 after pleading for President Roosevelt's support in the war against Nazi Germany, available at <http://www.winston-churchill.org/learn/speeches/speeches-of-winston-churchill/97-give-us-the-tools> (11 October 2013).

[140] The address to a Joint Session of Congress and the American People on 20 September 2001 after the 9/11 terrorist attack, Office of the Press Secretary, available at <http://avalon.law.yale.edu/sept11/president_025.asp> (11 October 2013).

[141] See *supra* Section 3.D.

[142] See UN Doc. A/64/PV.120, *supra* note 127.

[143] The first three meetings were held in Brussels on 8, 9, and 28 March and on 15 April 2011. See Report of the Secretary-General on the United Nations Interim Administration Mission in Kosovo, UN Doc. S/2011/281, 3 May 2011, at 3, para. 12. (Henceforth reports of the Secretary-General of the United Nations will be referred to only by their UN document number.) Some preparatory meetings were held earlier to make up for the delay in the start of negotiations due to extraordinary elections that were called in Kosovo after the collapse of the government. See UN Doc. S/2011/43, 28 January 2011, at 4, para. 15.

[144] At the time of the completion of this paper (31 October 2013).

[145] Borislav Stefanović, see UN Doc. S/2011/281, 3 May 2011, at 3, para. 12.

[146] Edita Tahiri. Ibid.

the facilitation of an advisor to the EU foreign policy chief, Baroness Ashton.[147] However, from October 2012 onwards, Ashton was personally in charge of the facilitation, which was conducted at the highest level—between the prime ministers of Serbia (Ivica Dačić)[148] and of Kosovo (Hashim Thaçi).[149] As will be shown below, this was, per se, a huge step forward in relations between Belgrade and Pristina, since Belgrade had previously refused to meet Pristina representatives at the level of head of state or prime ministers in any circumstances.[150]

On the eve of the negotiations, a high-ranking EU official stated that they would cover three main topics: regional co-operation; freedom of movement; and the rule of law.[151] Ultimately, under these three topics, the negotiations dealt with more concrete issues of: cadastral registries; civil registry; regional trade and freedom of movement of goods; freedom of movement of persons; telecommunications; electricity; customs stamps;[152] recognition of diplomas; and the management of crossing points between Kosovo and Serbia.[153]

As can be seen, these were not the status talks that Belgrade had previously insisted should be re-opened.[154] Pristina constantly emphasized that the talks in Brussels were merely technical,[155] while Belgrade pointed out that there was a political dimension to the technical topics that were being negotiated.[156] This was, in turn, persistently denied by Pristina, probably because giving a 'political

---

[147] Robert Cooper, whose official title was Counsellor of the European External Action Service. Ibid.

[148] It comes as a paradox that the first Serbian high official to meet a Kosovo high official was Dačić, since he used to be a close collaborator of Slobodan Milošević, whose policy against Kosovo Albanians prompted NATO intervention against the Socialist Federal Republic of Yugoslavia in 1999. Moreover, Dačić criticized the former Serbian president Tadić for shaking the hand of Kosovo's Prime Minister, Thaçi, just three months earlier at the Croatian Summit. See Barlovac, 'Thaci-Tadic handshake stirs controversy', *Balkan Insight*, 9 July 2012, <http://www.balkaninsight.com/en/article/thaci-tadic-handshake-stirs-controversy> (13 October 2013).

[149] See 'EU-facilitated dialogue: Catherine Ashton meets with Prime Ministers Dačić and Thaçi to discuss', <http://eeas.europa.eu/top_stories/2012/191012_ca_dacic_thaci_en.htm> (29 October 2013). See also Barlovac, 'Dacic and Thaci meet in Brussels, make history', *Balkan Insight*, 19 October 2012, <http://www.balkaninsight.com/en/article/dacic-and-thaci-make-history-attending-meeting> (12 October 2013).

[150] See *infra* Section 4.B.

[151] See '"Three main topics" in Belgrade-Priština talks', *B92 News,* 7 March 2011 <http://www.b92.net/eng/news/politics-article.php?yyyy=2011&mm=03&dd=07&nav_id=73106> (6 March 2013).

[152] UN Docs. S/2011/281, 3 May 2011, at 3 and 4, paras. 12–15; S/2011/514, 12 August 2011, at 3, paras. 11–14; S/2011/675, 31 October 2011, at 3 and 4, paras. 13–17; S/2012/72, 31 January 2012, at 3–4, paras. 17–23; S/2012/275, 27 April 2012, at 3 and 4, paras. 13–18; S/2012/603, 3 August 2012, at 3–4, paras. 13 and 14; S/2012/818, 8 November 2012, at 4–5, paras. 18 and 19; S/2013/72, 4 February 2013, at 1–2, paras. 3–8; S/2013/444, 26 July 2013, at 1–3, paras. 3–15 and S/2013/631, 28 October 2013, at 2, para. 7.

[153] UN Doc. S/2012/275, note 152, paras. 56 and 57.

[154] See *supra* Sections 3.A and 3.B.

[155] Collaku, 'Kosovo hails "Victory" with UN GA resolution', *Balkan Insight*, 13 September 2010,<http://www.balkaninsight.com/en/article/kosovo-hails-victory-with-un-ga-resolution> and 'Pristina "will not discuss division of Kosovo"', *Balkan Insight*, 26 April 2011, <http://www.balkaninsight.com/en/article/pristina-will-not-discuss-division-of-kosovo?amp> (26 October 2013).

[156] 'Belgrade: status is up for discussion', *B92 News*, 12 March 2011, <http://www.b92.net/eng/news/politics-article.php?yyyy=2011&mm=03&dd=12&nav_id=73199> (26 October 2013).

dimension' to the talks could be perceived as the introduction of status issues through the back door and a way to undermine its independence.

The negotiations have been a bumpy ride: more than a few times they seemed to reach a dead end, only for a solution to be found.[157] In these moments, the incentive of potential EU membership dangling in front of both parties proved to be a game changer: this is why they managed to find common ground and overcome deadlocks.

Ultimately, the EU-facilitated dialogue led to important and practical agreements between Belgrade and Pristina on: (1) regional cooperation; (2) civil registries; (3) freedom of movement (vehicle registration and insurance, driving licences); (4) certification of diplomas; (5) cadastre records; (6) free movement of goods (custom stamps); (7) normalization of relations between Belgrade and Pristina (integration of four northern majority-Serb municipalities); and (8) telecommunications and energy.[158] Their content is beyond the scope of this article, as is their implementation, which continues to be a challenge.[159]

Reaching these agreements was lengthy, tough, and exhausting for all parties, including EU facilitators. Bearing in mind the deep divergence between Belgrade and Pristina on almost every issue and the political risks their governments took in internal politics, nothing less could have been expected. Both governments were criticized by the opposition for agreeing to any dialogue in the first place[160] or for giving too many concessions whenever there were reports that agreement had been reached.[161] Neither government could escape domestic political challenges and pressure. These contributed to the entrenchment of the existing political narratives, despite the dialogue and despite the agreements. Each agreement always had two interpretations: Pristina would claim that Belgrade recognized Kosovo's independence by reaching an agreement on a particular topic (e.g. regional co-operation, or the four northern municipalities), while Belgrade would claim that the agreements had nothing to do with Kosovo's statehood, which it would never, ever recognize.[162] Note the paradox here in regard to the parties' initial positions on

---

[157] For example, in July 2011, a scheduled negotiation session on custom stamps was cancelled due to this. Moreover, there were violent incidents related to this issue on two crossing points (Jarinjë/Jarinje and Bërnjak/Brnjak). See more in UN Doc. S/2011/675, *supra* note 152, at 1–4, paras. 3–15.

[158] See UN Docs. S/2012/818 and S/2013/631, *supra* note 152, at 4–5, para. 19 and at 2, para. 7 respectively.

[159] Ibid.

[160] Especially heavy pressure on the Kosovo Government continues to be imposed by the radical movement, Vetëvendosje ('Self-Determination'), which opposes any talks with Belgrade and frequently protests against them. See UN Docs. S/2011/514 and S/2013/444, *supra* note 152, at 4, para. 16 and at 2, para. 9, respectively. As for Serbia, see, 'DSS traži prekid pregovora s Prištinom i nove preogovore u UN' ['Democratic Party of Serbia requests discontinuation of the negotiations with Pristina and initiation of new ones in the UN'], *Blic*, 7 November 2011, <http://www.blic.rs/Vesti/Politika/288070/DSS-trazi-prekid-dijaloga-sa-Pristinom-i-nove-pregovore-u-UN> (12 November 2013).

[161] See Brunwasser, 'Kosovo and Serbia reach key deal', *The New York Times*, 24 February 2012, <http://www.nytimes.com/2012/02/25/world/europe/25iht-kosovo25.html> (31 October 2013) and 'PM: we have chance to defend interests differently', *B92 News*, 26 April 2013, <http://www.b92.net/eng/news/politics.php?yyyy=2013&mm=04&dd=26&nav_id=85903> (13 November 2013).

[162] Cf. 'Kosovo and Serbia reach key deal', *supra* note 161 and 'Negotiator: Serbia has not recognized Kosovo', *B92 News*, 25 February 2012, <http://www.b92.net/eng/news/politics.php?yyyy=

the nature of the dialogue. Pristina insisted that negotiations were not political but technical, yet was claiming the agreements reached very political outcomes (implicit recognition of Kosovo). On the other hand, Belgrade was arguing that the negotiations were political, and not just technical in character, but was adamant that the agreements reached were ultimately only technical.

In the first half of 2012, while some agreements were negotiated, their implementation was disappointing due to a lack political will. This was indicative, especially on the part of Serbia, that there had been no true shift in attitude towards the issue of Kosovo, despite the on-going dialogue and the agreements reached.

After the elections in May 2012, a new government was formed in Serbia, which showed a political will to push the dialogue further. In the attempt to secure international legitimacy, this government, mainly made up of former nationalists, redefined the way Serbia approached the issues raised and the agreements reached within the EU-led dialogue. This can be clearly seen in the example of the regional co-operation agreement and its implementation, which will be discussed in the next part.

## B. Past, present and future of the dialogue: the regional co-operation agreement

After Kosovo declared its independence from Serbia, regional co-operation suffered a major setback.[163] Modalities of the representation of Kosovo became controversial,[164] due to conflicting attitudes of Serbia and Kosovo on the issue.

From the establishment of the international presence by UNSC resolution 1244, Kosovo's international participation was conducted through the United Nations Mission in Kosovo (UNMIK).[165] However, after the declaration of independence, Kosovo authorities argued that it was their prerogative to represent Kosovo, not UNMIK's.[166] After the AO, they actively resisted UNMIK's facilitation role, viewing it as a limitation on the sovereignty of Kosovo.[167] Consequently, they refused to participate in a number of meetings alongside UNMIK, which required its facilitation.[168] On the other side, Serbia insisted that Kosovo could only be represented by UNMIK and refused to participate in the meetings to which representatives of Kosovo were also invited.[169]

---

2012&mm=02&dd=25&nav_id=78966> (31 October 2013). See also '"We have not, and will not recognize Kosovo"', *B92 News*, 19 April 2013, <http://www.b92.net/eng/news/politics. php?yyyy=2013&mm=04&dd=19&nav_id=85798> (31 October 2013).

[163] UN Doc. S/2010/401, 29 July 2010, at 9, para. 47.

[164] UN Doc. S/2010/562, 29 October 2010, at 11, para. 54.

[165] See, for more, Papić, 'Fighting for a Seat at the Table: International Representation of Kosovo', 12 *Chinese Journal of International Law* 543 (2013), at 548–53.

[166] Ibid, at 553–7.

[167] UN Doc. S/2010/562, *supra* note 164.

[168] See, for meetings hosted by the Regional Cooperation Council (RCC), UN Docs. S/2011/43, 28 January 2011, at 10, para. 47 and S/2011/281, 3 May 2011, at 11, para. 56.

[169] For the Warsaw Summit, see Dempsey, 'Serbia insists on summit boycott', *New York Times*, 26 May 2011, <http://www.nytimes.com/2011/05/27/world/europe/27iht-east27.html?_r=1> (14

Naturally, Serbia's policy regarding joint participation in meetings with Kosovo representatives was at its most rigid immediately after Kosovo declared independence. At first, it even included leaving meetings where Kosovo representatives were present as a part of a UNMIK delegation and were given the floor by UNMIK.[170] In 2009 Serbia's policy started to soften, and was embodied in a position of not attending meetings at which Kosovo representatives were present but not part of the UNMIK delegation in accordance with resolution 1244.[171] However, even this policy was not applied consistently.[172] Moreover, it seemed that the level of government officials was crucial for Serbia in deciding whether to attend a certain meeting or not. As mentioned earlier, Serbia's representatives never attended meetings at the level of heads of state or government alongside Kosovo representatives,[173] while they sometimes attended those of foreign ministers.[174]

Serbia's policy was motivated by its refusal to recognize Kosovo as an independent state and the misconception that it could implicitly recognize Kosovo solely through joint participation at international meetings.[175] This ill-founded fear was premised on the idea that recognition can be given accidentally without an intention to recognize.[176] That dubious position was also shared on some occasions

February 2013). For Croatia Summit, see: 'Croatia Summit 2010 opens in Dubrovnik', *SE Times*, 9 July 2010, <http://www.setimes.com/cocoon/setimes/xhtml/en_GB/features/setimes/news-briefs/2010/07/09/nb-02> (14 February 2013). For meeting at Brdo near Kranj, see 'Slovenian FM: Serbia too sensitive', *B92 News,* 23 March 2010, <http://www.b92.net/eng/news/politics-article.php?yyyy=2010&mm=03&dd=23&nav_id=65996> (18 February 2013).

[170] See 'Tadić demonstrativno napustio samit' ['Tadić left the summit'], *Politika*, 22 May 2008, <http://www.politika.rs/rubrike/Svet/Tadic-demonstrativno-napustio-samit.lt.html>, (18 February 2013).

[171] See *infra* note 175.

[172] Namely, Serbia would sometimes ask for an additional condition to be met in order to attend a certain meeting (i.e. application of *Gymnich formula*, where denomination of the participants of a meeting is by their personal names, rather than by the names of the states they represent). Nevertheless, even when this criterion was met, at some occasions Serbia chose not to attend certain meetings after all (this was the case with a meeting at Brdo near Kranj, see *supra* note 169).

[173] This was the case at Warsaw Summit, Croatia Summit, meeting at Brdo near Kranj, see *supra* note 169.

[174] Sarajevo conference organized by EU in June 2010, see 'EU-Western Balkans conference in Sarajevo', *B92 News,* 2 June 2010, <http://www.b92.net/eng/news/politics-article.php?yyyy=2010&mm=06&dd=02&nav_id=67528> (13 March 2013).

[175] See the statement of the then president of Serbia, Tadić, on 14 March 2010 on the question of the participation of Serbia at the Brdo near Kranj meeting, available on the website of the Ministry of Foreign Affairs of the Republic of Serbia (<http://www.mfa.gov.rs/Srpski/Bilteni/Srpski/b150310_s.html>; summary in English: <http://www.mfa.gov.rs/Bilteni/Engleski/b150310_e.html> (18 February 2013)). This position does not have support in international law. See Lauterpacht, *Recognition in International Law* (Cambridge University Press, 1948), at 308; Ruda, 'Recognition of States and Governments' in Bedjaoui (ed), *International Law: Achievements and Prospects*, Part I (Martinus Nijhoff, 1991), at 452; Jannings-Watts, *Oppenheim's International Law* (9th ed, Longman, 1992), at 170–4; Malanczuk, *Akehurst's Modern Introduction to International Law* (7th rev. ed, Routledge, 1997), at 88; Crawford, *Brownlie's Principles of Public International Law* (8th ed, Oxford University Press, 2012), at 149; Shaw, *International Law* (5th ed., Cambridge University Press, 2003), at 387; Dixon, *Textbook on International Law* (6th ed, Oxford University Press, 2007), at 126; Aust, *Handbook of International Law* (2nd ed., Cambridge University Press, 2010), at 28.

[176] Ibid.

by Slovakia[177] and Romania,[178] states which also did not recognize Kosovo as an independent state.

Since there was no agreed template for Kosovo's representation which would reconcile conflicting positions, *ad hoc* modalities for the identification of participants at regional fora were arranged.[179] However, this also led to disputes and the absence from events of some of the invited parties.[180]

These circumstances created a major obstacle to functional and inclusive regional co-operation, which was important for the stability of the troubled region and also served as a component of the EU integration processes for the countries of the Western Balkans. Indeed, this was the reason why regional co-operation was designated as one of the three major topics to be discussed in the framework of the EU facilitated dialogue between Pristina and Belgrade.[181]

The attitude towards joint participation at international meetings with Kosovo representatives created a major challenge for Serbia's EU integration process,[182] which required inclusive and functional regional co-operation. The European Commission in its Opinion on Serbia's application for membership of the EU of 12 October 2011 stated that it was a priority for Serbia to achieve progress in this respect.[183] It was clear that Serbia needed to collaborate in finding a solution for Kosovo's regional representation. Only in this way could it hope to become a candidate country for EU membership. Against this background, with the prospect of candidacy being a major incentive for a shift in Serbia's position, a solution that would allow both Belgrade and Pristina to develop functional regional co-operation was sought and in that context it looked more attainable.

---

[177] This was the case at the Warsaw Summit in 2011: see the statement of the spokesperson for the president of Slovakia, Marek Trubac, in Pop, 'Serbia boycotts Obama meeting over Kosovo', *EU Observer*, 25 May 2001, <http://euobserver.com/887/32390> (15 March 2013).

[178] See Bryant, Cienski, and Buckley, 'Warsaw summit faces boycott', *Financial Times*, 25 May 2011, <http://www.ft.com/intl/cms/s/0/434af2ca-8705-11e0-92df-00144feabdc0.html#axzz2O5doauOA> (13 March 2013).

[179] UN Doc. S/2010/169, 6 April 2010, at 9, para. 37. As a rule, the organizers requested the presence of an UNMIK representative; generally, he was the first one to be given the floor, and then Kosovo's authorities were invited to intervene. Ibid., para. 38

[180] Ibid.          [181] See '"Three main topics" in Belgrade-Pristina talks', *supra* note 151.

[182] See European Commission, Communication from the Commission to the European Parliament and the Council, Commission Opinion on Serbia's application for membership of the European Union, Brussels, 12 October 2011, COM(2011) 668 final, {SEC(2011) 1208 final}, at 8, <http://ec.europa.eu/enlargement/pdf/key_documents/2011/package/sr_rapport_2011_en.pdf>, (18 March 2013). See also European Commission, *Commission Staff Working Paper, Analytical Report,* Accompanying the document, Communication from the Commission to the European Parliament and the Council Commission Opinion on Serbia's application for membership of the European Union, Brussels, 12 October 2011, SEC(2011) 1208, {COM(2011) 668}, at 33–5, <http://ec.europa.eu/enlargement/pdf/key_documents/2011/package/sr_analytical_rapport_2011_en.pdf>, (18 March 2013).

[183] See EC, *Serbia 2010 Progress Report*, Brussels, 9 November 2010, doc. SEC(2010) 1330, {COM(2010) 660}, at 19–20 (<http://ec.europa.eu/enlargement/pdf/key_documents/2010/package/sr_rapport_2010_en.pdf>, 18 March 2013).

## 1. *The footnote saga: Arrangements Regarding Regional Representation and Cooperation of 24 February 2012*

After long and excruciating talks, the Arrangements Regarding Regional Representation and Cooperation (ARRC)[184] were adopted on 24 February 2012.[185] This enabled the European Council to grant Serbia candidate status for membership in the EU[186] and approve a launch of Kosovo's feasibility study for a Stabilisation and Association Agreement.[187]

The EU mediation managed to bring together diametrically opposite positions—Serbia insisted that Kosovo could participate in regional co-operation only within the framework of resolution 1244[188] and Kosovo was adamant that this was not an option, since it was an independent state, a position that was, in its view, supported by the ICJ Advisory Opinion.[189] The ARRC stipulates that the only denomination to be used within the framework of regional co-operation is

'Kosovo*'

with a linked footnote that reads

'This designation is without prejudice to positions on status, and is in line with UNSC 1244 (1999) and the ICJ Opinion on the Kosovo declaration of independence'.[190]

This is an interim solution (point 11 of the ARRC) for denomination and representation of Kosovo in the *regional* context (points 4 and 10), covering regional meetings and institutional forms of regional co-operation, and existing and future agreements (point 5). The ARRC provides that Kosovo can speak on its own account (point 4). As for the agreements already signed by UNMIK on behalf of Kosovo, the ARRC states that it cannot be interpreted as prejudicial to UNMIK's legal rights and that it is for the UNMIK to decide whether to attend the meetings within their framework (point 6).

The ARRC provides that these arrangements 'should be reflected in the practical organization of regional meetings'.[191] However, the ARRC did not contain a

---

[184] ARRC, <http://www.b92.net/eng/insight/pressroom.php?yyyy=2012&mm=02&nav_id=78973> (18 September 2013).

[185] See EU, 'EU facilitated dialogue: Agreement on Regional Cooperation and IBM technical protocol', Press Statement, 24 February 2012, 5455/12, PRESSE 9, <http://www.consilium.europa.eu/uedocs/cms_data/docs/pressdata/EN/foraff/128138.pdf> (20 March 2013).

[186] Decision of 1 March 2012, EUCO 4/3/12 REV 3, 8 May 2012, <http://www.consilium.europa.eu/uedocs/cms_data/docs/pressdata/en/ec/128520.pdf> (4 March 2013).

[187] Council conclusions on Enlargement and the Stabilisation and Association Process, 3150th General Affairs Council meeting, 28 February 2012, <http://www.consilium.europa.eu/uedocs/cms_data/docs/pressdata/EN/genaff/128255.pdf> (13 November 2013). For the substance of the Study, see Communication from the Commission to the European Parliament and the Council on a Feasibility Study for a Stabilisation and Association Agreement between the European Union and Kosovo*, 10 October 2012, COM(2012) 602 final, <http://ec.europa.eu/enlargement/pdf/key_documents/2012/package/ks_feasibility_2012_en.pdf> (20 November 2013).

[188] 'Kosovo must be represented under 1244', *B92 News*, 28 January 2012, <http://www.b92.net/eng/news/politics-article.php?yyyy=2012&mm=01&dd=25&nav_id=78453> (20 March 2013).

[189] Ibid.

[190] ARRC, *supra* note 184, points 2 and 3.

[191] Ibid., point 8.

specific provision on the ways in which this footnote is to be used, which for a period of time was a major issue between the parties and prevented the ARRC's implementation.

## 2. *Different interpretations of the ARRC—What's in a name?*

Within a month of ARRC's adoption, different interpretations of its application surfaced. According to Belgrade, the Kosovo nameplate at a meeting should always include the text of the footnote,[192] while Pristina claimed that the footnote should only be included in the agreements and official documents of the relevant regional meeting or organization.[193]

Indeed, the Government of the Republic of Serbia on 20 March 2012 adopted an instruction for its representatives[194] that restricted full application of the ARRC to the informal meetings of the Balkan region organized by the EU (point 2(g) of the Instruction). As to the other meetings, it specified that the nameplate needed to be 'Kosovo*' followed by the text agreed in ARRC, which had to be 'sufficiently visible and legible, and written in English' (point 1). There should be no display of the symbols of the 'Republic of Kosovo' (point 2). If representatives of Serbia failed to secure these conditions with the host of a meeting, they were to leave (point 2(b)). This instruction not only offered an interpretation of the ARRC that was at odds with its provisions but also raised doubts as to Serbia's good faith in the application of the agreement. Moreover, it shows that attitude of Serbia towards Kosovo essentially did not change, despite the process of EU-led dialogue.

The mutually exclusive positions of Serbia and Kosovo led each of them to boycott some meetings.[195] Hence, UNMIK's decision to reduce its presence and not attend

---

[192] See 'Zaključak o Instrukciji za postupanje predstavnika Republike Srbije na određenim skupovima posvećenim regionalnoj saradnji na kojima učestvuju predstavnici Privremenih institucija samouprave u Prištini' ['Instruction for action of the representatives of the Republic of Serbia in specific meetings dedicated to regional co-operation in which representatives of the Provisional Institutions of Self-Government in Pristina'] (hereinafter: Government of Serbia Instruction of March 2012), No. 06-1954/2012-004 of 20 March 2012 (on file with author).

[193] Furthermore, Pristina insisted that the Albanian version of Kosovo's name, i.e. 'Kosova', should be used on the nameplates, which Belgrade did not agree to. (See 'Misunderstandings mire Kosovo representation agreement', *SE Times*, 16 March 2012, <http://www.setimes.com/cocoon/setimes/xhtml/en_GB/features/setimes/features/2012/03/16/feature-02> (16 March 2013); also UN Doc. S/2012/275, *supra* note 152, at 4, para. 14.) Initially, Kosovo hoped the footnote will melt 'like a snowflake, when it gets warmer'. See the statement of Edita Tahiri, the chief of Pristina team in the EU-facilitated negotiations with Belgrade in 'Edita Tahiri: Fusnota je pahuljica' ['Footnote is a snowflake'], *B92 News*, 24 February 2012, <http://www.b92.net/info/vesti/index.php?yyyy=2012&mm=02&dd=24&nav_category=640&nav_id=585368> (22 March 2013).

[194] Government of Serbia Instruction of March 2012, *supra* note 192.

[195] See Latković, 'Delegacija Srbije zbog nedostatka fusnote napustila Sarajevo, a prištinska zbog fusnote otišla iz Beograda' ['Serbia delegation left Sarajevo because there was no footnote, while Pristina delegation left Belgrade because there was'], *Blic*, 15 March 2012, <http://www.blic.rs/Vesti/Politika/312244/Delegacija-Srbije-zbog-nedostatka-fusnote-napustila-Sarajevo-a-pristinska-zbog-fusnote-otisla-iz-Beograda> (25 March 2013); Aliu, Andric, 'Kosovars storm out of regional forum in Serbia', *Balkan Insight*, 15 March 2012, <http://www.balkaninsight.com/en/article/kosovo-delegation-left-regional-forum-in-belgrade> (25 March 2013).

certain regional meetings[196] soon after the ARRC was negotiated seemed premature. As noted by the UN Secretary-General, it was clear that there were 'inherent
shortcomings in the mechanisms to ensure implementation of [ARRC]'.[197]

After the first dispute over the nameplate (March 2012), the EU sent a message that it was up to the organizers of the meeting 'to decide where to put a
footnote'.[198] Eventually, a few months later (June 2012), the EU facilitator in the
Belgrade-Pristina negotiations, Robert Cooper, took the side of Pristina, claiming
that the Belgrade authorities were misinterpreting the ARRC.[199]

However, it seems that Belgrade was not the only one to blame for the deadlock.
It was evident that the EU facilitator did not secure a clear agreement on the location of the footnote, which was crucial considering an almost complete lack of trust
between the parties and the contentiousness of the issue. Indeed, Cooper admitted
that the issue of placing the text of the footnote on the nameplates was raised by the
Belgrade team during the negotiations and that Pristina neither agreed nor completely disagreed with it, so 'it is hard to say that there was an agreement on that
issue'.[200] This indicated that the EU facilitator was aware, or must have been aware,
that the place where the text of the footnote would stand was a matter of great
concern for both parties, but apparently chose to leave it unresolved. That made
the difficulties in the ARRC's implementation at least partly the EU's own fault.

## 3. *Epilogue: the footnote and beyond*

Finally, in September 2012, the newly elected Government of Serbia changed its
interpretation of the ARRC. It adopted a new instruction,[201] which provided that

---

[196] See UN Doc. S/2012/275, *supra* note 152, para. 56. 'UNMIK to attend regional meetings "if necessary"', *B92 News*, 29 February 2012, <http://www.b92.net/eng/news/politics-article.
php?yyyy=2012&mm=02&dd=29&nav_id=79036> (4 March 2013).

[197] UN Doc. S/2012/275, *supra* note 152, at 4, para. 14.

[198] See the statement of Maja Kocijančič, spokesperson for the EU foreign policy chief, Baroness
Catherine Ashton, in Barlovac, 'EU urged to save crumbling Kosovo-Serbia deal', *Balkan Insight*,
22 March 2012, <http://www.balkaninsight.com/en/article/kosovo-serbia-interpret-brussels-d
eal-differently> (6 February 2013).

[199] 'Belgrade misinterpreting footnote deal, EU facilitator says', *B92 News*, 14 June 2012,
<http://www.b92.net/eng/news/politics-article.php?yyyy=2012&mm=06&dd=14&nav_
id=80751> (6 February 2013).

[200] Cooper continued: 'The question was raised and the answer was a silence. When we opened
this issue in the bilateral contacts in Pristina, looking for their opinion on it, we were told that it is
extremely hard for them to accept an asterisk and that it was unacceptable to them for a nameplate
to contain the text of the footnote'. Translation from the Serbian version of the interview, Đorđević,
'Kuper: Nema fusnote na pločici' ['Cooper: No footnote on nameplate'], *Večernje novosti*, 21 June
2012, <http://www.novosti.rs/vesti/naslovna/aktuelno.289.html:385261-Kuper-Nema-fusnote-na-
plocici> (6 February 2013). Published as: 'Teško je reći da je oko toga bilo sporazuma. Pitanje je bilo
potegnuto, a odgovor je bilo - ćutanje. Kada smo bilateralno u Prištini otvorili ovo pitanje, tražeći
njihov stav, rekli su nam da je za njih ekstremno teško da prihvate zvezdicu i da im je neprihvatljivo
da na pločici stoji fusnota'.

[201] See 'Instrukcija za postupanje predstavnika Republike Srbije na skupovima posvećenim
regionalnoj saradnji na kojima učestvuju predstavnici Privremenih institucija samouprave u Prištini'
['Instruction for action of the representatives of the Republic of Serbia on meetings dedicated to
regional co-operation in which representatives of the Provisional Institutions of Self-Government in

the footnote need only stand in the official documents of a meeting and not on the Kosovo nameplate (points 1 and 2).[202] Moreover, this instruction gives discretion to the Government, when there are strongly justified reasons, to allow representatives of Serbia to attend a meeting even when the conditions set in the Instruction are not met (point 7(a)).

The position of the new Serbian Government allowed both Belgrade and Pristina to jointly participate in regional meetings, breaking the tension in regional co-operation. Soon thereafter, a new phase of the EU-sponsored dialogue was launched. It was again about technical issues, but this time it was at the highest level: on 19 October 2012, the prime ministers of Serbia and Kosovo (Dačić and Thaçi, respectively), met in Brussels under the auspices of the EU foreign policy chief, Baroness Ashton.[203] Moreover, the presidents, Tomislav Nikolić of Serbia and Atifete Jahjaga of Kosovo, met on 7 February 2013.[204]

Belgrade and Pristina agreed to appoint liaison officers to monitor implementation of the agreements reached within EU-led negotiations. The liaison officers, who work at the EU premises in Belgrade and Pristina, were exchanged in mid-June 2013.[205]

The new approach of the Serbian Government signifies that Belgrade, for the sake of its EU membership aspirations, has finally managed to overcome its opposition to Kosovo's participation in regional meetings. This was not only politically motivated but it was also based on a legal misconception that Serbia could accidentally recognize Kosovo merely by encountering its officials, especially those of the highest rank.[206]

Paradoxically, this step forward was made by a, at least nominally, more nationalist government than the previous one. This new government appeared more flexible in its general approach towards the EU-led dialogue with Kosovo. It could afford to give more concessions and secure better implementation of existing agreements than its predecessor partly due to the fact that the domestic political pressure lost its edge, as the strongest party in the government was the former main nationalist opposition party which had criticized the negotiation process in the past (Serbian Progressive Party—SPP). Moreover, the past political affiliation

---

Pristina] (hereinafter: Government of Serbia Instruction of Sept. 2012), No. 06-5592/2012-004 of 2 September 2012 (on file with author).

[202] However, the September 2012 Instruction still contains provisions which are at odds with the ARRC. See more in Papić, *supra* note 165, n. 153.

[203] See 'EU-facilitated dialogue: Catherine Ashton meets with prime ministers Dačić and Thaçi to discuss', <http://eeas.europa.eu/top_stories/2012/191012_ca_dacic_thaci_en.htm>, (19 February 2013). See also Barlovac, 'Dacic and Thaci meet in Brussels, make history', *Balkan Insight*, 19 October 2012, <http://www.balkaninsight.com/en/article/dacic-and-thaci-make-history-attending-meeting> (20 February 2013).

[204] See Barlovac, 'Kosovo, Serbia Presidents hail outcome of talks', *Balkan Insight*, 7 February 2013, <http://www.balkaninsight.com/en/article/kosovo-and-serbia-presidents-pledge-to-normalise-relations> (11 February 2013).

[205] A Pristina officer sits at the EU Delegation in Belgrade and Belgrade officer at the EU Office in Kosovo. See, 'Priština appoints new liaison officer in Belgrade', *B92 News*, 21 June 2013, <http://www.b92.net/eng/news/politics.php?yyyy=2013&mm=06&dd=21&nav_id=86708> (30 July 2013).

[206] Cf. text accompanying *supra* note 173.

of SPP's leaders (president and deputy prime minister of Serbia at the time) to the Serbian Radical Party, an extreme nationalist anti-EU party whose main leader is an indicted war criminal,[207] placed them in desperate need of international legitimacy. This was also a reason why they were ready to concede more than the previous government, which had no such legitimacy challenges.

A further important step was taken on 19 April 2013 in Brussels, where Prime Ministers Dačić and Thaçi initialled the First Agreement of Principles Governing the Normalisation of Relations (also referred as the Brussels Agreement).[208] Many hailed this 15-point agreement as historic.[209] From the political perspective, it indeed signifies normalization and a thawing of relations between Belgrade and Pristina. However, despite its name, the Agreement mainly deals with the integration into the Kosovo legal system of four northern Kosovo municipalities with overwhelming Serb majority,[210] which did not recognize the Kosovo authorities. It contains only one point that can be linked to its official name—point 14— which provides 'that neither side will block, or encourage others to block, the other side's progress in the respective EU paths'.[211] This phrase represented a compromise with respect to the earlier draft that referred to 'accession to international organisations',[212] which Belgrade thought could lead it to its formal recognition of Kosovo.[213]

Immediately thereafter, the Brussels Agreement secured the opening of negotiations on EU accession to Serbia[214] and on the Stabilisation and Association Agreement with the EU to Kosovo.[215]

---

[207] Vojislav Šešelj is on trial before the ICTY.

[208] The text of the agreement is available at <http://www.b92.net/eng/news/politics.php?yyyy= 2013&mm=04&dd=19&nav_id=85799> (31 July 2013).

[209] See, e.g., the statement of the president of the European Commission, José Manuel Barroso, <http://europa.eu/rapid/press-release_MEMO-13-353_en.htm> (31 July 2013).

[210] See points 1–11 of the Brussels Agreement, *supra* note 206. These points provide for the establishment of a Community/Association of Serb municipalities with representation in central government (points 1–6); integration of judicial and police authorities within Kosovo's legal framework while there would be a regional police commander and an appellate court for these four Serb-majority municipalities (points 7–10); municipal elections to be held in them in 2013 with the facilitation of OSCE (point 11). Points 12 and 15 deal with the implemenation of the Agreement, while point 13 provides for discussion of energy and telecoms to be intensified and completed by 15 June 2013. However, at the completion of this paper this was not the case.

[211] Point 14, ibid.

[212] See '"Agreement initialed, Serbia's demands accepted"', *B92 News*, 19 April 2013, <http:// www.b92.net/eng/news/politics.php?yyyy=2013&mm=04&dd=19&nav_id=85797> (31 July 2013).

[213] See 'Dačić: Tači minirao pregovore' ['Dačić: Thaçi sabotaged negotiations'], *B92 News*, 18 April 2013, <http://www.b92.net/info/vesti/index.php?yyyy=2013&mm=04&dd=18&nav_category=640 &nav_id=706110> (31 October 2013).

[214] However, the exact date will be set in spring 2014 upon the assessment of the implementation progress and improvement in the relations between Pristina and Belgrade. See Delegation of the EU to the Republic of Serbia, *Press Release*, 'The date for the beginning of the negotiations will be granted next spring', <http://www.europa.rs/en/mediji/najnovije-vesti/1751/The+date+for+the +beginning+of+the+negotiations+will+be+granted+next+spring.html#sthash.N33pv5qi.dpuf> (20 November 2013).

[215] See European Commission, *Press Release*, 'Serbia and Kosovo*: historic agreement paves the way for decisive progress in their EU perspectives', 22 April 2013, <http://europa.eu/rapid/press-release_IP-13-347_en.htm> (31 October 2013).

While Belgrade claimed that it did not recognize Kosovo by concluding this agreement, Pristina again claimed it did.[216] As for the international community, it did not view the conclusion of the Brussels Agreement as recognition.[217] The reason is that an intention to recognize,[218] which is an indispensable element of the recognition of statehood in international law, is missing in this case. However, Serbia did recognize the legitimacy of the institutions of Kosovo, which at least psychologically brings it a step closer to recognizing Kosovo's statehood.

## 5. Conclusion

The AO itself could not and did not alter the competing narratives surrounding the issue of the independence of Kosovo. It simply fitted into them. Nevertheless, the AO proceedings did help calm the huge tensions surrounding the issue of Kosovo's declaration of independence by keeping it, at least for a while, within the ICJ. Moreover, the delivery of the AO offered possibilities for opening a new dialogue between Serbia and Kosovo.

A watershed point was UNGA resolution 64/289, adopted as a follow-up to the AO, which signified the beginning of a slow change in Serbia's policy towards Kosovo. Paradoxically, this came as a consequence of Serbia's attempt at something quite different from what was to be the ultimate outcome in the UNGA.

Initially, Serbia made an attempt to use the UNGA as a means of pressuring for the re-opening of negotiations on Kosovo's status. This was in direct opposition to the views of major EU member states which recognized Kosovo (UK, Germany, and France) and viewed Kosovo's independence as irreversible. At the same time, these states held the key to Serbia's EU aspirations. Submitting the draft resolution without prior consultation with them could have meant that Serbia had finally made a choice between its two principal foreign policy goals—keeping Kosovo and getting into the EU—and that it had chosen Kosovo over the EU: a mostly fictional hold over Kosovo over the very real benefits of EU accession. But a more likely explanation is a more pedestrian one: Serbian officials recklessly thought they could get away with this and that the submission of the draft resolution opposed by most EU member states would not influence Serbia's EU integration. When it was realized, under intense political pressure, that this was not to be, Serbia was forced to make a U-turn if it wanted to remain on the EU membership

---

[216]  See the statement of Serbian deputy prime minister, Aleksandar Vučić, and Kosovo prime minister, Hashin Thaçi, '"We have not, and will not recognize Kosovo"', *B92 News*, 19 April 2013, <http://www.b92.net/eng/news/politics.php?yyyy=2013&mm=04&dd=19&nav_id=85798> (31 July 2013).

[217]  See the statement of the US Ambassador to Belgrade, Michael Kirby, 'Kirbi: Srbija nije priznala Kosovo, a nismo to ni tražili' ['Serbia did not recognize Kosovo nor we ask for it'], *Večernje novosti*, 25 April 2013, <http://www.novosti.rs/vesti/naslovna/politika/aktuelno.289.html:431198-Kirbi-Srbija-nije-priznala-Kosovo-a-nismo-to-ni-trazili> (31 July 2013). See also 'Breakthrough at last', *The Economist*, 20 April 2013, <http://www.economist.com/blogs/easternapproaches/2013/04/serbia-and-kosovo-0> (31 July 2013).

[218]  See *supra* note 175.

track. Thus, it withdrew its draft resolution and submitted a new one, this time co-sponsored by the EU states.

The new text, which welcomed the readiness of the EU to facilitate a process of dialogue between the parties, and thereby politically opened the way for negotiations, was adopted by consensus. It was drafted so to allow all interested parties, in particular Serbia and Kosovo, to interpret it in the light of their existing narratives about the Kosovo issue. The adoption of the UNGA resolution was a political climax in the immediate aftermath of the AO proceedings. This was also a defeat of Serbia's policy of active opposition to Kosovo's independence. Moreover, this event marked Serbia's *de facto* renunciation of this policy which was the price to be paid for its EU aspirations.

The EU-facilitated negotiations that followed led to important and practical agreements between Belgrade and Pristina. Reaching these agreements was a lengthy and tough process. The incentive of EU membership proved crucial when the dialogue seemed to reach a dead end. It should be noted, however, that despite the achievements of the EU-led dialogue, the political narratives adopted by Serbia and Kosovo did not change. The parties have continued to interpret the agreements so that they fit into their overarching positions. What did change, however, was that they were willing to take practical steps on issues that needed to be resolved as a condition for their further EU integrations. Thus, there has been a huge difference between what Serbian and Kosovo officials are saying and what they are doing in practice.

Nevertheless, it would be a mistake to think that this change in the attitude of the parties was immediately brought about by the EU-facilitated dialogue. On the contrary, the negotiations frequently stumbled and agreements reached were slowly implemented or not implemented at all. As was shown on the case of the regional co-operation agreement and the Brussels agreement that followed it, the change of government in Serbia gave a new impetus to the negotiations and the implementation of the agreements between the parties. Despite this, one should be careful in describing this change as a complete departure from Serbia's previous policies towards Kosovo. Only time will show if this will, in the long run, bring the paradigm shift necessary for the long-term progress in the relations between the parties.

From today's perspective, it can be claimed that the AO, and the UNGA resolution that followed it, ultimately produced a positive effect on the relations between Serbia and Kosovo. It presented a new opportunity and gave stimulus to politicians and diplomats to initiate an EU-sponsored dialogue between the parties that has had important practical results—although for Serbian and Kosovo politicians this did not come naturally but as a consequence of international pressure. More generally, it can be said that the advisory proceedings as an instrument of the UN system have fulfilled their function and made a contribution to dealing with what seemed insurmountable challenges arising from the situation in Kosovo, which still constitutes a threat to international peace and security.

On the other hand, the on-going dialogue between Serbia and Kosovo shows that, as a mediator, the EU can deliver solutions once it has something to offer in return. However, both Serbia and Kosovo should be aware that the issues of their relations currently discussed under the regional co-operation item as a condition of their EU membership will resurface in every chapter of the progress assessment and negotiations phase they enter into with the EU. One can only hope that they will be rational enough to realize it sooner rather than later and act accordingly for the sake of the troubled region of the Western Balkans.

# 13

## Kosovo—The Questions Not Asked

### Self-Determination, Secession, and Recognition

*Alain Pellet**

### 1. Pointless Question, Semi-Answer

A silly question calls for a silly answer. This could—and from my point of view should—have been so in the case of the Advisory Opinion concerning the independence of Kosovo. In fact, the Court generously gave a very considered answer to a question which did not deserve that much attention and, while it formally stuck to a strict interpretation of the question asked, it suggested partial answers to the real underlying issues.

The question asked to the ICJ by resolution 63/3 of the General Assembly of the UN in accordance with Article 96 of the Charter and pursuant to Article 65 of the Statute of the Court reads as follows:

Is the unilateral declaration of independence by the Provisional Institutions of Self-Government of Kosovo in accordance with international law?

As explained in other contributions to this volume, the initiative to request an advisory opinion came from Serbia which clearly conceived the Opinion to be given by the Court as a support for its fight against the secession of Kosovo. Introducing the text before the General Assembly, the Serbian Minister of Foreign Affairs, Mr Vuk Jeremić, declared that sending the question to the Court 'would prevent the Kosovo crisis from serving as a deeply problematic precedent in any part of the globe where secessionist ambitions are harboured'.[1] From this statement—and others[2]—it is apparent that what was expected was a clear-cut condemnation of Kosovo's secession.

* The author acted as Counsel for France in this case. The views expressed in this paper are his own and do not commit the French Government. Many thanks to Benjamin Samson for his assistance in preparing the present paper.

[1] UN doc. A/63/PV.22 (2008), at 1.

[2] See, e.g., the declarations of the Serbian Minister of Foreign Affairs and the Serbian President in April 2009 (<http://www.b92.net/eng/news/politics.php?yyyy=2009&mm=04&dd=22&nav_id=58669> and <http://www.expatica.com/news/local_news/Serbia-expects-ICJ-to-rule-against-Kosovo-split--_51873.

Thinking they were being skillful, the Serbian Government avoided straight-forwardly asking a question on the real issue. Instead of putting before the Court the issue of the lawfulness of Kosovo's secession, they focused on the *declaration* of independence, probably with the idea that a narrow question would limit the risk of a discussion on the right to secession under international law, the result of which was no doubt risky, as will be shown later in this paper. However, they probably realized their mistake during the proceedings since Serbia abundantly pleaded (as, it is true, did several other 'participants')[3] on issues relating, e.g., to the right to self-determination or territorial sovereignty.[4] The risk of playing a game is that you may be taken at your own word. This is exactly what happened in this case. The Court strictly kept to the question asked—and rightly so; contrary to the views of some commentators[5] and of two individual Judges,[6] it is not for the Court to act as a scholar and to clarify questions because they are obscure or interesting: in its contentious role, its function is to decide disputes between states which are submitted to it; when it gives an advisory opinion, it must answer the legal question(s) asked by an authorized body—no more and no less. 'The jurisdiction of the Court in this matter was shaped by the request, and so was the—narrow—focus of its enquiry … [h]aving failed to frame the question differently may have been a miscalculation on the part of Serbia, but this failing is hardly attributable to the Court'.[7]

---

html>) and the statement of the Russian Minister of Foreign Affairs after talks with the Serbian Minister of Foreign Affairs on 5 October 2009 (<http://sofiaecho.com/2009/10/07/795947_russia-pledges-backing-for-serbia-at-icj-hearing-on-kosovo>). See also, e.g., the statements of the Representatives of Romania (UN Doc. A/63/PV. 22 (2008), at 6) or Comoros (ibid., at 9–10).

[3] Albania, CR 2009/26, at 13–16, paras. 19–32 (Mr Frowein) and at 18–23, paras. 2–16 (Mr Gill); Argentina, CR 2009/26, at 42–6, paras. 18–26 (Ms Ruiz Cerutti); Austria, CR 2009/27, at 8–12, paras. 10–23 (Mr Tichy); Azerbaijan, CR 2009/27, at 18–25, paras. 10–45 (Mr Mehdiyev); Belarus, CR 2009/27, at 27–32 (Ms Gritsenko); Bolivia, CR 2009/29, at 8–13, paras. 6–25 (Mr Calzadilla Sarmiento); Finland, CR 2009/30, at 57–64, paras. 13–26 (Mr Koskenniemi); Russia, CR 2009/30, at 41–4, paras. 8–25 and at 46–8, paras 32–43 (Mr Gevorgian); Jordan, CR 2009/31, at 33–7, paras. 22–40 (Prince Zeid Raad Zeid Al Hussein); Romania, CR 2009/32, at 20–1, paras. 10–12 (Mr Aurescu) and at 26–9, paras. 2–10 and at 30–6, paras. 13–30 (Mr Dinescu), Venezuela, CR 2009/33, at 10–16, paras. 18–40 (Mr Fleming) and Vietnam, CR 2009/33, at 17–21, paras. 5–16 (Mr Nguyen Thi Hoang Anh).

[4] CR 2009/24, at 63–74, paras. 1–32 (Mr Shaw) and at 76–85, paras. 2–22 (Mr Kohen). See also Written Statement of Serbia, at 147–242 and Written Comments of Serbia, at 101–50.

[5] See, e.g., Burri, 'The Kosovo Opinion and Secession: The Sounds of Silence and Missing Links', 11 *German Law Journal* (2011) 882, at 885–7; Crépet-Daigremont, 'Conformité au droit international de la declaration unilatérale d'indépendance relative au Kosovo', 56 *AFDI* (2010) 229, at 238 and 240–2; or Kohen and Del Mar, 'The Kosovo Advisory Opinion and UNSCR 1244 (1999): A Declaration of Independence from International Law?', 24 *LJIL* (2011) 109, at 111–12.

[6] See *Accordance with International Law of the Unilateral Declaration of Independence in Respect of Kosovo*, Separate Opinions of Judge Simma, ICJ Reports 2010, at 478–81, paras. 1–9 and *Judge Yusuf*, ICJ Reports 2010, at 619–20, paras. 4–6. Although I respectfully disagree with them on their excessively wide interpretation of the question, I fully agree with Judge Simma in his criticism of the Court's sticking to the untenable and outdated '*Lotus* principle' assimilating 'the lack of a prohibition to permissibility' (ibid.).

[7] Weller, 'Modesty Can Be a Virtue: Judicial Economy in the ICJ *Kosovo* Opinion?', 24 *LJIL* (2011), at 131–2; see also: Hilpold, 'The International Court of Justice's Advisory Opinion on Kosovo: Perspectives of a Delicate Question', 14 *Austrian Review of International and European Law* (2009) 259, at 298–300 and 302–3.

It can certainly be a source of frustration that the Court conspicuously stuck to the narrow question asked by the General Assembly—and all the more so that, as Judge Yusuf very aptly noted, 'since a declaration of independence is not per se regulated by international law, there is no point assessing its legality, as such, under international law'.[8] This is probably the right and sufficient answer to the question—and it is very neatly and convincingly given at paragraph 84 of the Opinion.[9] However, while the question is indisputably pointless, the answer given by the Court is less so and gives too much credit to the question asked since the Court went beyond what was necessary in discussing at some length some peripheral issues, including those related to the author of the declaration and, arguably, resolution 1244 (1999) of the Security Council.

While conceding that it could depart 'from the language of the question put to it where the question was not adequately formulated ... or where ... the request did not reflect the 'legal questions really in issue', or 'where the question asked was unclear or vague', the Court found that

[i]n the present case, the question posed by the General Assembly is clearly formulated. The question is narrow and specific; it asks for the Court's opinion on whether or not the declaration of independence is in accordance with international law. It does not ask about the legal consequences of that declaration. In particular, it does not ask whether or not Kosovo has achieved statehood. Nor does it ask about the validity or legal effects of the recognition of Kosovo by those States which have recognized it as an independent State ... Accordingly, the Court does not consider that it is necessary to address such issues as whether or not the declaration has led to the creation of a State or the status of the acts of recognition in order to answer the question put by the General Assembly.[10]

And in a subsequent passage of its Opinion, the Court also specified that, since '[t]he General Assembly has requested the Court's opinion only on whether or not the declaration of independence is in accordance with international law', 'the extent of the right of self-determination and the existence of any right of "remedial secession" ... concern the right to separate from a State' and are 'beyond the scope of the question posed by the General Assembly'.[11]

Moreover, the Court rightly observed 'that the question in the present case is markedly different from that posed to the Supreme Court of Canada' on the occasion of the *Reference by the Governor in Council concerning Certain Questions relating to the Secession of Quebec from Canada*:[12]

---

[8] *Accordance with International Law of the Unilateral Declaration of Independence in Respect of Kosovo*, Separate Opinion of Judge Yusuf, ICJ Reports 2010, at 620, para. 5.

[9] At p. 438: 'general international law contains no applicable prohibition of declarations of independence'.

[10] *Accordance with International Law of the Unilateral Declaration of Independence in Respect of Kosovo*, ICJ Reports 2010, 403, at 423–4, paras. 50–1.

[11] Ibid., at 438, para. 83.

[12] 2 SCR(1998)217; 161 DLR(1998) 385; 115 ILR536. The relevant question in that case was: 'Does international law give the National Assembly, legislature or government of Quebec the right to effect the secession of Quebec from Canada unilaterally? In this regard, is there a right to self-determination under international law that would give the National Assembly, legislature or government of Quebec the right to effect the secession of Quebec from Canada unilaterally?' The present writer

The question put to the Supreme Court of Canada inquired whether there was a right to 'effect secession', and whether there was a rule of international law which conferred a positive entitlement on any of the organs named. By contrast ... [t]he Court is not required by the question it has been asked to take a position on whether international law conferred a positive entitlement on Kosovo unilaterally to declare its independence or, *a fortiori*, on whether international law generally confers an entitlement on entities situated within a State unilaterally to break away from it. Indeed, it is entirely possible for a particular act—such as a unilateral declaration of independence—not to be in violation of international law without necessarily constituting the exercise of a right conferred by it. The Court has been asked for an opinion on the first point, not the second.[13]

It is therefore apparent that the right of the Kosovar people to self-determination, the right to secession under international law, and recognition by third states are the three main underlying questions which have remained unanswered by the Court—for the excellent reasons that they were not asked. The present paper very briefly deals with each of them in turn.

## 2. The Right to Self-Determination of Non-Colonial Peoples

There is no doubt that '[a]ll peoples have the right to self-determination'.[14] But this is a right of variable content. As the Court rightly notes in the *Kosovo* Opinion, '[d]uring the second half of the twentieth century, the international law of self-determination developed in such a way as to create a right to independence for the peoples of non-self-governing territories and peoples subject to alien subjugation, domination and exploitation'.[15] But the right to self-determination has not exhausted its effects with the substantial completion of the decolonization process, nor can it be alleged that it has a purely domestic connotation limiting it with a right to a democratic system[16] and/or to the right of minorities to exist within the state.[17] It is obviously not because a people is entitled to benefit from internal self-determination that it is deprived of the right to enjoy external self-determination.

---

was consulted by the *amicus curiae* appointed by the Supreme Court in this case on certain questions of international law. The present paper is largely based on his expert opinions in this case, which have been published in English in A. F. Bayefsky (ed), *Self-Determination in International Law—Quebec and Lessons Learned* (The Hague, Kluwer Law Internl, 2000), at 85–124, 185–212 and 225–30.

[13] *Accordance with International Law of the Unilateral Declaration of Independence in Respect of Kosovo*, ICJ Reports 2010, 403, at 425–6, paras. 55–6.

[14] 1966 International Covenants on Human Rights, Art. 1; see also Charter of the United Nations, Arts. 1(2) and 55.

[15] *Accordance with International Law of the Unilateral Declaration of Independence in Respect of Kosovo*, ICJ Reports 2010, 403, at 436, para. 79.

[16] See, e.g., A. Cassese, *Self-Determination of Peoples: A Legal Reappraisal* (CUP, 1995), at 101 or Rosas, 'Internal Self-Determination', in C. Tomuschat (ed), *Modern Law of Self-Determination* (Martinus Nijhoff, 1992) 225, at 232.

[17] See, e.g., Arbitration Commission for the Former Yugoslavia (text reproduced in Pellet, 'The Opinions of the Badinter Arbitration Committee—A Second Breath for the Self-Determination of Peoples', 3 *EJIL* (1992), at 184).

On the contrary, if a people is deprived of its fundamental 'internal right' to self-determination—which can most probably be described as 'a peremptory norm of general international law' (*jus cogens*)[18]—then the creation of an independent state may be the only means of ensuring that this right is achieved; it is then more in the nature of a *consequence of the violation* ('remedy') of the principle of the right of peoples to self-determination than a component of that right.

Moreover, it is this type of reasoning that is the source of the recognition of the right of colonial peoples to independence: colonialism is considered by the United Nations, at least since the famous resolution 1514(XV) of 14 December 1960, to be a 'denial of fundamental human rights, [which] is contrary to the Charter of the United Nations and is an impediment to the promotion of world peace and cooperation', and the right to freely determine political status (including the right of colonial peoples to accede to sovereignty) is regarded as an antidote to the violence done to those peoples. *Mutatis mutandis*, the reasoning may be transposed to non-colonial peoples whose existence and identity are denied by the state into which they are integrated. This is moreover what has led to the recognition of the right to sovereignty of peoples subject to alien occupation.

It can then certainly be accepted that there is a right of 'remedial secession' under contemporary international law,[19] even though, to my knowledge, there exists no clear and undisputable precedent.

In its Opinion in the case concerning *Certain Questions relating to the Secession of Quebec from Canada*, the Supreme Court of Canada concluded that 'neither the population of the province of Quebec, even if characterized in terms of "people" or "peoples", nor its representative institutions ... possess a right, under international law, to secede unilaterally from Canada', but the only reason for this position was that the exceptional circumstances in which a people is entitled to a right to external self-determination were 'manifestly inapplicable to Quebec under existing conditions'. However, the Court in Ottawa seemed to accept that when a people is 'denied the ability to exert internally [its] right to self-determination', 'as for example under foreign military occupation; or where a definable group is denied meaningful access to government to pursue their political, economic, social and cultural development', then, such a people is granted a right to external self-determination similar to that of colonial peoples, which includes the right to independence.[20]

---

[18] See, e.g., P. Daillier, M. Forteau, and A. Pellet, *Droit international public* (L.G.D.J., 8th ed, 2009), at 223 and 227 or M. Shaw, *International Law* (CUP, 7th ed, 2014), at 185–6. See also *East Timor (Portugal v. Australia)*, ICJ Reports 1995, 90, at 102, para. 29 and *Legal Consequences of the Construction of a Wall in the Occupied Palestinian Territory*, ICJ Reports 2004, 136, at 172, para. 88.

[19] See Statement of Albania, CR 2009/26, at 22–3, para. 15 (Mr Gill); Statement of Russia, CR 2009/30, at 43–4, paras. 19–22 (Mr Gevorgian) and Statement of Romania, CR 2009/32, p. 21, para. 12 (Mr Aurescu) and p. 30, para. 13 and p. 33, paras. 22–3 (Mr Dinescu); See also, e.g., Corten, 'Déclarations unilatérales d'indépendance et reconnaissances prématurées: du Kosovo à l'Ossétie du Sud et à l'Abkhazie', 112 *RGDIP* (2008) 721; Sterio, 'On the Right to External Self-Determination: "Selfistans", Secession, and the Great Powers' Rule', 19 *Minn J Int'l L* (2010) 137.

[20] SCC, Judgment, 20 August 1998, Case n° 25506, 2 SCR (1998) 217, para. 138.

Now, if one applies this reasoning to the case of Kosovo, the following elements must be kept in mind:

- On 23 March 1989, Serbia forced the Kosovo Assembly to approve the removal of Kosovo's autonomy;[21]
- On 5 July 1990, Serbia suspended the Kosovo Assembly;[22]
- In late 1990, the Kosovo Constitutional Court was abolished by Serbia;[23]
- From the early 1990s onwards, Kosovo Albanians were subject to systematic state-sanctioned discrimination, dismissed from position in both the private and public sector and replaced by Serbs, and tortured and mistreated;[24] and
- Up until the late 1990s the situation worsened and the Albanian Kosovars were victims of 'the excessive and indiscriminate use of force by Serbian security forces and the Yugoslav Army which has resulted in numerous civilian casualties'.[25]

A full discussion of these facts would exceed the limits of this paper. However, their mere enumeration, from neutral authorities, rather eloquently shows that the Kosovar people[26] was 'denied the ability to exert internally [its] right to self-determination' and that Serbia did not behave in respect to Kosovo's population as a democratic state protecting on an equal basis all its citizens. Therefore it seems that the conditions for a right to self-determination, including a right to secede, were met.

## 3. The Right to Secession *v.* Territorial Integrity

Supposing, however, that the Kosovar could not invoke a right to a 'remedial secession', it should be admitted nevertheless that international law does not prohibit secession nor does it encourage it: it takes note of it when it results in an effective statehood.

---

[21] ICTY, Trial Chamber, Judgment, 26 February 2009, *Prosecutor v. Milan Milutinović* et al., IT-05-87-T, paras. 217–221.

[22] Ibid., paras. 223–230, referring to Law on Termination of the Activity of the Assembly of the SAP of Kosovo, 5 July 1990.

[23] Ibid., referring to Decision on Relieving of Duty the Judge[s] of the Kosovo Constitutional Court, Municipal Court Judges and Judges and Officers of the Municipal Organs for Misdemeanours, and Election of Judges to the District Court and Municipal Courts in Kosovo, 28 December 1990.

[24] Ibid., para. 224, referring among others to the report on the situation of human rights in the territory of the former Yugoslavia prepared by Tadeusz Mazowiecki, Special Rapporteur of the Commission on Human Rights, 17 November 1992, paras. 99–113. See also GA Res. 47/147, 18 December 1992; 48/153, 20 December 1993; 49/204, 23 December 1994; 50/190, 22 December 1995; 51/111, 12 December 1996; 52/139, 12 December 1997; 53/164, 9 December 1998; and 54/183, 17 December 1999. See also the Report of the OSCE Kosovo Verification Mission, 'Kosovo/Kosova, As Seen/As Told', June 1999 (available at <http://www.osce.org/odihr/17772?download=true>).

[25] SC Res. 1199, 23 September 1998.

[26] I cannot discuss at any length here the question of the legal nature and characters of the people in question.

Indeed, it clearly stems from the previous Section that there is no general right to secession in international law or, as the Supreme Court of Canada put it in the case concerning *Certain Questions relating to the Secession of Quebec*, '[i]t is clear that international law does not specifically grant component parts of sovereign states the legal right to secede unilaterally from their "parent" state'.[27] However, this does not mean that secession is prohibited under international law nor, in particular, that it necessarily collides with the principle of the territorial integrity of states as existing in positive international law.

Several participants in the proceedings challenged the 'right' of Kosovo to secede as contradicting the principle of territorial integrity embodied in Article 2, paragraph 4 of the Charter. Thus, according to Argentina, 'la déclaration est en contradiction flagrante avec le respect de l'intégrité territoriale de la Serbie'.[28] And this also was one of the main Serbian arguments: 'Most importantly, the UDI has been an attempt to create an independent State, to violate Serbia's territorial integrity and to terminate or modify the international legal régime for the administration of Kosovo.'[29]

In this respect the conclusions of the five jurists which had been consulted in 1992 on the territorial integrity of Quebec in the event of the accession of Quebec to sovereignty are still entirely well-founded:

- *In the first place,* the principle of the right of peoples to self-determination does not create a right to independence of peoples that are not in a colonial or 'remedial' situation.

- *In the second place, however,* no principle of international law prohibits a people from seceding, and when such is the case, the law of nations simply takes note of the existence of the new State.[30]

Indeed, there is no doubt that secession, unlike decolonization,[31] does in fact undermine the territorial integrity of the state. Secession is, however, a fact, and it must be determined whether that fact is, or may be, in compliance with the rules of international law as they actually stand. Two powerful arguments militate in favour of an affirmative answer to this question.

In the first place, as rightly stated in the Kosovo Opinion recalling General Assembly resolution 2625(XXV) of 1970 and the 1975 Final Act of the Helsinki Conference on Security and Cooperation in Europe, 'the principle of territorial integrity is confined to the sphere of relations between States';[32] it does not concern

---

[27] SCC, Judgment, 20 August 1998, *supra* note 20, para. 111.

[28] CR 2009/26, at 38, para. 8 (Ms Ruiz Cerutti).

[29] CR 2009/24, at 41, para. 17 (Mr Djerić); see also: CR 2009/24, at 75, para. 36 (Mr Shaw).

[30] See: Franck, Higgins, Pellet, Shaw, and Tomuschat, 'The Territorial Integrity of Quebec in the Event of the Attainment of Sovereignty', Reports prepared for Québec's Ministry of International Relations, 1992, para. 4.01 (available at <http://english.republiquelibre.org/Territorial_integrity_of_Quebec_in_the_event_of_the_attainment_of_sovereignty>).

[31] As very convincingly noted by the General Assembly 'The territory of a colony or other Non-Self-Governing Territory has, under the Charter, a status separate and distinct from the territory of the State administering it' (GA Res. 2625(XXV), 24 October 1970).

[32] *Accordance with International Law of the Unilateral Declaration of Independence in Respect of Kosovo*, ICJ Reports 2010, 403, at 437, para. 80.

the relations between a single state and its own population. This is also evidenced, for example, by the wording of paragraph 4 of Article 2 of the United Nations Charter, which is the major provision establishing and regulating this principle. It follows that the principle of territorial integrity, as contemplated by the United Nations Charter, excludes any *foreign* intervention whose aim or effect is the dismemberment of a state, in particular through armed support given to a secessionist movement (as is shown, for example, by the reactions of the international community to the creation of 'Bantustans' by South Africa, to the establishment of the 'Turkish Republic of Northern Cyprus' or to Russia's hasty annexation of Crimea).

In its Opinion concerning *Certain Questions relating to the Secession of Quebec from Canada*, the Supreme Court of Canada stressed that '[t]he various international documents that support the existence of a people's right to self-determination also contain parallel statements supportive of the conclusion that the exercise of such a right must be sufficiently limited to prevent threats to an existing state's territorial integrity or the stability of relations between sovereign states' at least when sovereign and independent states conduct 'themselves in compliance with the principle of equal rights and self-determination of peoples and thus [possess] a Government representing the whole people belonging to the territory without distinction'.[33] As noted above, it is highly debatable that this was the case with Serbia before Kosovo declared its independence.

In any case, there is no basis for alleging that secession as such is condemned by international law and, as also noted in the *Kosovo* Opinion, while, in some instances, the Security Council has condemned particular declarations of independence,[34] in all of those instances 'the illegality attached to the declarations of independence ... stemmed not from the unilateral character of these declarations as such, but from the fact that they were, or would have been, connected with the unlawful use of force or other egregious violations of norms of general international law, in particular those of a peremptory character *(jus cogens)*. In the context of Kosovo, the Security Council has never taken this position'[35] neither concerning the declaration of independence, nor the secession itself.

Second, while the principle of territorial integrity is unquestionably a principle of positive law, it is not peremptory: no one would doubt that a state may, in the exercise of its sovereign jurisdiction, cede part of its territory. Therefore, there certainly is a right for the predecessor state to accept secession. And there can be no doubt that there is no legal objection to the predecessor state's agreeing to the secession of part of its territory nor that such an agreement is a powerful—usually decisive—element for a successful secession whether the concerned part of the

[33] See SCC, Judgment, 20 August 1998, *supra* note 20, paras. 127–30.
[34] The Court mentions SC Res. 216, 12 November 1965 and 217, 20 November 1965, concerning Southern Rhodesia (although it is a case of decolonization); SC Res. 541, 18 November 1983, concerning northern Cyprus; and SC Res. 787, 16 November 1992, concerning the Republika Srpska (ICJ Reports 2010, 403, at 237, para. 81).
[35] ICJ Reports 2010, 403, at 437, para. 81.

predecessor's territory joins another pre-existing state[36] or becomes itself a new sovereign state.[37]

Such an agreement amply facilitates the effectiveness of the new state; but this is not to say that the agreement of the predecessor state is an indispensable condition for the lawfulness of a secession. Even outside the framework of decolonization, many examples of successful secessions can be cited which occurred as a result of a victorious armed struggle against the state from which they have seceded. Bangladesh is an example of such a secession—but, admittedly, a rather dubious one since, notoriously, it was successful with (and probably owing to) India's strong military involvement; but there are others. Eritrea and the states resulting from the dissolution of former Yugoslavia being the most recent and topical examples. In other words, 'successful' secessions are not the secessions accepted by the predecessor state, but *de facto* secessions.

These findings are in keeping with the very definition according to which a state is a 'primary fact', 'a fact that precedes the law and that the law recognizes when it has materialized, attributing to it certain effects, including a certain legal status'.[38] As rightly explained in Opinion n° 1 of the Arbitration Commission for the Former Yugoslavia (Badinter Commission), 'the existence or disappearance of the state is a question of fact'.[39]

The international community certainly does not encourage secession, but when secession succeeds there is no example in which third states, and the United Nations, have not drawn the inferences therefrom, regardless of the attitude of the predecessor state. The new state in no way depends on the consent of the state from which it is derived for the legal justification of its existence; that justification lies in the mere fact that it exists and that it effectively and peacefully exercises state functions, that is, in accordance with the principle of effectiveness.

In the case of Kosovo, with the passage of time, it seems more and more difficult to deny that it has obtained full statehood. Indeed, when independence was declared, it could have been sustained that its independence was artificially maintained with massive assistance from the UN (through the United Nations Interim Administration Mission in Kosovo (UNMIK)), NATO (through the NATO Kosovo Force (KFOR)) and the EU through the European Union Rule of Law Mission in Kosovo (EULEX) (the mandate of which has been extended until 14

---

[36] As was the case, for example, in: Cocos (Keeling) Islands (Australia); Greenland (Denmark); Northern Cameroons (Nigeria); Northern Mariana Islands (United States); Southern Cameroons (Cameroon). (See J.R. Crawford, 'State Practice and International Law in Relation to Unilateral Secession', 19 February 1997, para. 21, reproduced in Bayefsky (ed), *supra* note 12, at 40.)

[37] See, e.g., Mali, Syria, Singapore, the Baltic States and more generally the new states resulting from the dissolutions of the former USSR or Czechoslovakia, even though in many of these cases the consensual character of these secessions can be put in doubt.

[38] Abi-Saab, 'The Effectivity Required of an Entity that Declares its Independence in Order for it to be Considered a State in International Law', 18 December 1997, in Bayefsky (ed), *supra* note 12, at 70; see also: 'Cours général de droit international public', 207 *Recueil des Cours* (1987) 9, at 68.

[39] Arbitration Commission for the Former Yugoslavia, Opinion n° 2, 29 November 1991 (text reproduced in Pellet, 'Badinter Arbitration Committee', *supra* note 17, at 182–3).

June 2016).[40] Moreover, on 10 September 2012, the 'supervised independence' of Kosovo came to an end and the Constitution of Kosovo—which was taken from 'provisions concerning international supervision of Kosovo'—became the unique legal framework.[41] Therefore, it seems hardly debatable today that Kosovo's sovereignty is a fact, and this seems progressively accepted by Serbia itself.[42]

## 4. Recognition by Other States

Kosovo has also gained recognition: 63 states had recognized Kosovo as a state at the date of the hearings on the Advisory Opinion; there were 110 by mid-August 2014. Speaking strictly from a legal point of view, this has no particular consequence.

In the first place, neither recognition nor admission to the United Nations creates a state. Either of these factors may, obviously, consolidate the existence of a state whose foundations are weak, and as the Badinter Commission noted, recognition, 'along with membership of international organizations, bears witness to these states' conviction that the political entity so recognized is a reality and confers on it certain rights and obligations under international law'.[43] Nonetheless, according to the predominant doctrine, 'recognition by other states has purely declarative effects'.[44]

Consequently and secondly, even though premature recognition cannot be excluded (and is not necessarily illegal),[45] it is normal and legitimate for them to be expressed *after* the effective inauguration of the independence of which they are not a condition, but an indication. Now, recognition is dependent upon diplomatic vicissitudes, of which the ups and downs of the recognition of the Sahrawi Arab Democratic Republic (SADR) by third states is a telling example.[46] Palestine, Israel, Chinese Taipei are other examples of back and forth recognitions (sometimes by the same state). However, in the case of Kosovo, the number of states recognizing it as a state is increasing, slowly but surely, and, to my knowledge, no recognition has been withdrawn.

Moreover, Serbia itself, while still refusing to formally recognize Kosovo, increasingly accepts relations with it. Thus, on 19 April 2013, Kosovo and Serbia initialled the 'First agreement on principles governing the normalization of relations', which 'provides for the establishment of such an association/community with a

---

[40] See, <http://www.b92.net/eng/news/politics.php?yyyy=2014&mm=06&dd=13&nav_id=90656>.

[41] See the Report of the Secretary-General on the United Nations Interim Administration Mission in Kosovo, 8 November 2012, S/2012/818, paras 6–7.

[42] See *infra* notes 46 and 47.

[43] Opinion n° 8, 4 July 1992 (text reproduced in Türk, 'Recognition of States: a Comment', 4 *EJIL* (1993) 66, at 88.

[44] Ibid. See also: the Declaration of Montevideo on the Rights and Duties of States of 26 December 1933, Art. 3: 'The political existence of the state is independent of recognition by the other states'.

[45] Verhoeven, 'La reconnaissance internationale: déclin ou renouveau', 39 *AFDI* (1993) 7. *Contra*: M. Bothe, 'Kosovo—So What? The Holding of the International Court of Justice is not the Last Word on Kosovo's Independence', 11 *German Law Journal* (2010) 837, at 838–9.

[46] The SADR had been recognized by 85 states; the number has now decreased to hardly 45.

statute and range of competences'.[47] Since then, officials of both Parties have met regularly in order to implement this agreement.[48]

The same remarks apply to admission to the United Nations. In the case of Bangladesh, the period of three years and two months that elapsed between accession to independence and that admission definitely seems very short, given the obvious and massive intervention of a third party state on the side of the Awami League. The example of the State of Palestine, which was recognized as such by the General Assembly on 29 November 2012[49] but not admitted as a Member of the United Nations while it has been admitted to several UN organizations, also shows that recognition by the 'organized international community' can be progressive.

In the case of Kosovo, no such formal step has been taken at the UN level but Kosovo has been a full member of the IMF and of the World Bank Group since 29 June 2009.[50] And, in spite of the reservations maintained by some Member States of the EU, Kosovo is listed as a potential candidate on the European Commission's webpage.[51] On 28 October 2013, the European Union and Kosovo started negotiating a Stabilisation and Association Agreement[52] which was initialled on 25 July 2014.[53] Indeed, Kosovo's admission to the UN and/or the EU, or any kind of association with these organizations as a state, would be important 'markers' of the statehood of the Kosovar entity—as, and even more decisively, would be a formal or even an unambiguous *de facto* recognition by Serbia. However, even absent such recognitions, Kosovo can be held to possess statehood as long as it meets in fact the conditions for statehood as described by the famous *dictum* of the Badinter Commission: 'the state is commonly defined as a community which consists of a territory and a population subject to an organized political authority; ... such a state is characterized by sovereignty'.[54]

---

[47] See the Report of the Secretary-General on the United Nations Interim Administration Mission in Kosovo, 30 April 2013, S/2013/254, para. 4.

[48] See the recent Reports of the Secretary-General on the United Nations Interim Administration Mission in Kosovo, 26 July 2013, S/2013/444, paras. 3–15; 28 October 2013, S/2013/631, paras. 3–11; 30 January 2014, S/2014/68, paras. 3 and 12; 29 April 2014, S/2014/405, paras. 3–4 and 1 August 2014, S/2014/558, para. 3.

[49] GA Res. 67/19.

[50] See respectively <https://www.imf.org/external/np/sec/pr/2009/pr09240.htm> and <http://web.worldbank.org/WBSITE/EXTERNAL/COUNTRIES/ECAEXT/0,,contentMDK:22230081~menuPK:258604~pagePK:2865106~piPK:2865128~theSitePK:258599,00.html>.

[51] <http://ec.europa.eu/enlargement/countries/detailed-country-information/kosovo/index_en.htm>.

[52] European Commission, MEMO/13/938, 28 October 2013 (<http://europa.eu/rapid/press-release_MEMO-13-938_en.htm>).

[53] <http://www.mei-ks.net/?page=2,5,1011>.

[54] Opinion n° 1, 29 November 1991 (text reproduced in Pellet, 'Badinter Arbitration Committee', *supra* note 16, at 182); see also Opinion n° 8, 4 July 1992 (text reproduced in Türk, *supra* note 44, at 87–88) and the 1933 Declaration of Montevideo on the Rights and Duties of States, prec., Art. 17: 'The state as a person of international law should possess the following qualifications: a) a permanent population; b) a defined territory; c) government; and d) capacity to enter into relations with the other states'.

For these reasons, had the good—or, say, the interesting—questions been put to the Court, they should probably have answered by finding that:

(1) the Kosovar people's right to self-determination included the right to secede from the Republic of Serbia as a consequence of Serbia's denial of its democratic equal rights and disproportionate repression (remedial secession);

(2) in any case, the principle of territorial integrity, which applies between states, does not exclude the possibility of a secession from a pre-existing state;

(3) although it might have been more debatable at the time of the Opinion than today, Kosovo seems to fulfil all the conditions of statehood; and

(4) the rising number of recognitions by third states, although not a condition nor sufficient evidence of statehood, tends to reinforce the conclusion above in spite of the absence of formal recognition by Serbia and the fact that Kosovo is not a member of the United Nations.

# 14

# Kosovo and the Criteria for Statehood in International Law

*James Crawford**

## 1. The Questions Avoided

The International Court's advisory opinion on *Accordance with International Law of the Unilateral Declaration of Independence with Respect to Kosovo* is as relevant for what it says as for what it does not. The Court gave a narrow answer to a question which, most would agree, had been poorly formulated. This was not the first time that the Court had been presented with a question that was either badly drafted or otherwise problematic. But what distinguishes the Court's position in *Kosovo* from that adopted in previous opinions was its insistence that the question was 'narrow and specific'.[1] On this basis the Court refrained from reformulating the question so as to give a fuller account of the legal issues arising from Kosovo's attempt to obtain independence by the declaration of 17 February 2008.[2]

There were three such issues, as the Court noted: first, 'whether or not Kosovo has achieved statehood';[3] second, 'the validity or legal effects of the recognition of

* Thanks to Fernando Bordin, Lauterpacht Centre for International Law, University of Cambridge, for his considerable assistance with this piece.

[1] *Accordance with International Law of the Unilateral Declaration of Independence in Respect of Kosovo* (Advisory Opinion) ICJ Report 2010, 403, 423, para 51 [hereafter *Kosovo*].
[2] Cases in which the Court rephrased the question submitted to it include *Interpretation of the Agreement of 25 March 1951 between the WHO and Egypt* (Advisory Opinion) ICJ Report 1980, 73, 89, para 36 and *Application for Review of Judgment No. 273 of the United Nations Administrative Tribunal* (Advisory Opinion) ICJ Report 1982, 325, 348–50, paras 46–9. In *Legality of the Threat and Use of Nuclear Weapons*, the Court did not expressly reformulate the question of whether the threat and use of nuclear weapons was 'permitted' under international law, but it noted that 'the illegality of the use of certain weapons as such does not result from an absence of authorization but, on the contrary, is formulated in terms of prohibition' and proceeded to reply to the question accordingly: ICJ Report 1996, 226, 247, para 52. Likewise, it has been suggested that the Court also reformulated the question in the *Kosovo* opinion, insofar as it replied to a question on 'the accordance' of the declaration of independence with international law by concluding that this declaration was not 'prohibited by' international law: G. Kammerhofer, 'Begging the Question: The *Kosovo* Advisory Opinion and the Reformulation of Advisory Requests' (2011) 58 *Netherlands International Law Review* 409, 418–19.
[3] *Kosovo*, 423, para 51.

Kosovo by those States which have recognized it as an independent State';[4] and third, whether 'the international law of self-determination confers upon part of the population of an existing State a right to separate from that State'.[5]

This contribution discusses the first of these questions. While the Court did not decide whether or not Kosovo was a state, the answer that it gave to the narrower question of the legality of the declaration of independence suggests that there is nothing preventing Kosovo from becoming a state so long as it fulfils the criteria for statehood in international law. Looking at the facts on the ground some years later, it appears that Kosovo does fulfil these criteria. While a final political solution to its status with respect to Serbia's claims of territorial integrity is still pending (and therefore questions remain), Kosovo can be seen as a territorial community under government possessing a sufficient degree of formal and factual independence from Serbia and from the international organizations involved in the interim administration of its territory to be considered a state.

## 2. Application of the Criteria for Statehood to Kosovo

### A. Formal and factual independence in the case of secession

The best-known (and perhaps least helpful) formulation of the basic criteria for statehood is that laid down in Article I of the1933 Montevideo Convention on the Rights and Duties of States, namely: '(a) a permanent population; (b) a defined territory; (c) government; and (d) capacity to enter into relations with other States'.[6] Few would dispute that Kosovo has a plausible claim to fulfil these criteria. It certainly has a defined territory—corresponding to the boundaries of the autonomous region of Kosovo under successive Yugoslav and Serbian constitutions—and a permanent population of around 1.7 million. It has a structured government in place under the 2008 Constitution of the Republic of Kosovo,[7] which exercises public authority over the defined territory and the permanent population, despite some instability in the northern region (mainly populated by ethnic Serbs). It has a demonstrated capacity to enter into relations with other states as evidenced, for example, by its admission to membership of the International Monetary Fund and the World Bank.[8]

The Montevideo criteria are, however, somewhat misleading and—as regards the capacity to enter into relations with *other* States—circular. As I have argued elsewhere,[9] the central criterion for statehood, which sheds light on the criteria of government

---

[4] Ibid.    [5] Ibid 438, para 82.
[6] Convention on the Rights and Duties of States, Montevideo, 26 December 1933, 165 LNTS 19.
[7] Available at <http://www.kuvendikosoves.org/?cid=2,100,48> accessed 24 March 2014.
[8] IMF, Press Release No 09/240, June 29, 2009: <http://www.imf.org/external/np/sec/pr/2009/pr09240.htm> and <http://www.worldbank.org/en/country/kosovo> accessed 24 March 2014.
[9] J. Crawford, *The Creation of States in International Law* (2nd edn, OUP 2006) 62–89 [hereinafter *Creation of States*].

and capacity to enter into international relations, is a given territorial community's *independence*. As Max Huber described it in *Island of Palmas*, independence is the right to exercise in a portion of the globe 'the functions of a State', and of doing so 'to the exclusion of any other State'.[10] An analysis of the legal status of Kosovo presupposes an assessment of the extent of its independence under the current arrangements.

Independence has both formal and factual elements or aspects. Formal independence exists where the powers of government of a territory are vested in the separate authorities of the putative state without there being any competing claims to authority by other states. Factual independence is a matter of political fact, and can be defined as the minimum degree of real governmental power at the disposal of the authorities of the putative state that is necessary for it to qualify as independent from other states. For a territorial entity to qualify as a state, it has to be formally and factually independent to a sufficient degree.

The relationship between formal and factual independence poses complex questions which are context-dependent. There are, however, trends in state practice that provide some guidance for the evaluation of particular situations. On the one hand, formally independent entities will be considered as states even if their government is more or less incapable of effectively exercising authority over the territory and the population. This is why states created through a formal transfer of sovereignty from the predecessor are deemed to emerge even before they are able to establish fully functioning institutions,[11] and why internal unrest temporarily hampering the activities of the government of an existing state does not in principle affect the latter's international status.

An entity whose formal independence is contested—as a result, for example, of a competing claim of sovereignty from the parent state—but which manages to exercise the functions of a state to the exclusion of other states will have a claim to statehood. This is a result of the position of the long-standing international law on secession—secession is neither legal nor illegal, but a legally neutral act the consequences of which are regulated internationally.[12] The Court seemingly endorsed this point in its advisory opinion, when it examined the question of the legality of unilateral declarations of independence under general international law. In particular, it rejected the most influential general argument for considering secession unlawful or otherwise limited by international law—the principle of territorial integrity. Several participants in the proceedings suggested that territorial integrity constituted a bar on attempts at secession without the consent of the parent state.[13] The Court disagreed, concluding that the scope of the principle 'is confined to the

---

[10] *Island of Palmas Case* (1928) 2 RIAA 829, 838. In his separate opinion in the *Austro-German Customs Union Case*, Judge Anzilotti has similarly defined independence as a state's attribute of not having over it any other 'authority than that of international law'; PCIJ ser A/B no 41, 57–8.

[11] This is why, for example, the Republic of Congo was considered to be a state in 1960 despite the fact that it clearly did not have an effective government; *Creation of States*, 56–7.

[12] *Creation of States*, 390. Also, H. Lauterpacht, *Recognition in International Law* (CUP, 1947) 8.

[13] E.g. Written Statement of the Republic of Cyprus, 3 April 2009, paras 88–9: <http://www.icj-cij.org/docket/files/141/15609.pdf> accessed 24 March 2014, and Written Statement of the Republic of Serbia, 17 April 2009, para 423: <http://www.icj-cij.org/docket/files/141/15642.pdf>

sphere of relations between States'.[14] In other words, it decided that territorial integrity does not protect a state from *internal* attempts at separation.[15]

Thus doubts relating to Kosovo's formal independence in light of Serbia's sovereignty claim do not prevent the former from acquiring statehood. But there is an important *caveat*: a new state attempting to secede will have to demonstrate substantial and durable independence from the state of which it formed part before it will be regarded as definitively created.[16] Unlike cases in which consent by the parent state is forthcoming or when formal independence can be claimed as a matter of right (e.g. by operation of the principle of self-determination), opposed separation outside the colonial context requires a higher degree of factual independence.

## B. Kosovo's independence in relation to Serbia

The question then arises whether Kosovo is sufficiently independent of Serbia that it can also be described as durably independent. It seems this question must be answered in the affirmative. Though claiming to have sovereign rights over Kosovo's territory, Serbia has not exercised any meaningful public authority there since the United Nations interim administration was established in 1999. On the few occasions on which it did, this was with the consent of the Kosovar authorities. For example, on 6 May 2012 parliamentary and presidential elections for Serbia were held in Kosovo's territory following extensive consultations between Pristina and Belgrade, the former having agreed to allow the Kosovar population to vote in the Serbian elections under OSCE supervision.[17] Further, the Serbian Government refrained from conducting local elections with respect to Kosovo.[18]

Kosovo's independence from Serbia has been further consolidated by recent developments. Most significantly, on 19 April 2013 Kosovo and Serbia concluded a First Agreement of Principles Governing the Normalization of Relations as a part of a political process currently being conducted under the auspices of the European Union.[19] The agreement comprises 15 principles and envisages an implementation plan which the parties have already adopted.[20] While the agreement does not address the

---

accessed 24 March 2014. This point was emphasized by Judge Koroma, to whom the principle 'entails an obligation to respect the definition, delineation and territorial integrity of an existing State' that was violated by the unilateral declaration of independence; *Kosovo*, 475, para 21 (Koroma diss).

[14] *Kosovo*, 437, para 80.

[15] This is how the dictum has been construed in the literature: see e.g. M. Weller, 'Modesty Can be a Virtue: Judicial Economy in the ICJ *Kosovo* Opinion' (2011) 24 *Leiden Journal of International Law* 127, 135–7. For a critical view, suggesting that the Court failed to consider practice pointing to the opposite conclusion, J. Dugard, 'The Secession of States and their Recognition in the Wake of Kosovo' (2013) 357 *Recueil des Cours* 9, 187–8.

[16] *Creation of States*, 63.

[17] Report of the Secretary-General on the United Nations Interim Administration Mission in Kosovo, 3 August 2012, S/2012/603, at 2, para 5.

[18] Ibid, para 6.

[19] The text of the agreement is annexed to Law No. 04/L-199, enacted by the Assembly of Kosovo and available at <http://www.kuvendikosoves.org/?cid=2,191,1057> last accessed 24 March 2014.

[20] Available at: <http://euobserver.com/media/src/0807580ad8281aefa2a89e38c49689f9.pdf> last accessed 24 March 2014.

question of Kosovo's political status and in no way implies Serbia's recognition of Kosovo's statehood, it indicates that Serbia acknowledges Kosovo's factual independence. In particular, the agreement dismantles Serbia's attempts to exercise public power in northern Kosovo via organs established by the majority of ethnic Serbs inhabiting the region. It provides that '[a]ll police in northern Kosovo shall be integrated in the Kosovo Police framework' and that the judicial authorities of northern Kosovo 'will be integrated and operate within the Kosovo legal framework'.[21] The parties have moreover agreed not to 'block, or encourage others to block, the other side's progress in their respective EU paths',[22] an undertaking by which Serbia appears to concede, for the first time, that the government in Pristina enjoys external capacity.

The trade-off for Serbia's agreement to the incorporation of northern institutions into the central government was Kosovo's consent to the establishment of an Association/Community of Serb majority municipalities in Kosovo with considerable autonomy from Pristina.[23] While this limits Pristina's say on how the affairs of the majority of ethnic Serbs in northern Kosovo will be handled in future, it represents a victory insofar as concerns the consolidation of Kosovo's formal and factual independence. It can thus be said that, given the events of the past four years, Kosovo has been exercising the functions of a state over its territory and population to the exclusion of Serbia. It has been doing so on a viable and—it would appear—irreversible basis.

## C. Kosovo's independence in relation to the United Nations

### 1. Formal and factual independence of territories under UN administration

A further complication is that Kosovo is subject to transitional administration by the United Nations under a Security Council resolution adopted under Chapter VII of the Charter. Can a territory in such circumstances *ever* be deemed independent so as to fulfil the criteria for statehood?

UNSC resolution 1244, adopted on 10 June 1999 in the aftermath of NATO's bombing campaign, authorized the Secretary-General 'to establish an international civil presence in Kosovo in order to provide an interim administration for Kosovo under which the people of Kosovo can enjoy substantial autonomy within the Federal Republic of Yugoslavia'.[24] The objective of this interim administration was to 'provide transitional administration while establishing and overseeing the development of provisional democratic self-governing institutions to ensure conditions for a peaceful and normal life for all inhabitants of Kosovo'.[25] Resolution 1244 remains in force: it can only be revoked by a further decision of the Security Council.[26]

---

[21] Cf. First Agreement of Principles Governing the Normalization of Relations, clauses 7 and 10.

[22] First Agreement of Principles Governing the Normalization of Relations, clause 14.

[23] First Agreement of Principles Governing the Normalization of Relations, clauses 1–4. Pursuant to Clause 4, '[t]he Association/Community will have full overview of the areas of economic development, education, health, urban and rural planning'.

[24] UNSC Res 1244 (1999), operative clause 10.

[25] UNSC Res 1244 (1999), operative clause 10.

[26] Ibid, para 19: 'the international civil and security presences are established for an initial period of 12 months, to continue thereafter unless the Security Council decides otherwise'.

It might be argued that because and for so long as the UN is empowered to exercise public authority over the territory of Kosovo, Kosovo is debarred from achieving statehood. The Court's advisory opinion nonetheless suggests otherwise. In assessing whether the unilateral declaration of independence was in accordance with resolution 1244 and the Constitutional Framework established thereunder, the Court made two findings. First, it decided that the declaration had not been adopted by the Assembly of Kosovo established as part of Kosovo's Provisional Institutions of Self-Government. Rather, according to the Court, 'the authors of that declaration did not act, or intend to act, in the capacity of an institution created by and empowered to act within that legal order but, rather, set out to adopt a measure the significant and effects would lie outside that order'.[27] This meant that the declaration was not invalid on the grounds that the Assembly of Kosovo lacked the competence to adopt it under the Constitutional Framework.

Second, the Court found that the authors of the declaration did not breach any obligation established under resolution 1244 and the Constitutional Framework. It had been suggested by some states participating in the advisory proceedings that, by reaffirming 'the commitment of all Member States to the sovereignty and territorial integrity of the Federal Republic of Yugoslavia', resolution 1244 contained, or at least implied, a prohibition on unilateral declarations of independence.[28] The Court disagreed, noting that 'the Security Council did not reserve for itself the final determination of the situation in Kosovo and remained silent on the conditions for the final status of Kosovo'.[29] It concluded that resolution 1244 and the declaration of independence operated 'on a different level' insofar as the latter was 'an attempt to determine finally the status of Kosovo'.[30]

While the Court purported to frame its opinion in the narrowest of terms, these findings implicitly dispose of the question whether Kosovo may be considered formally independent as a territory under transitional administration. The Court did not find that the local authorities' attempt to solve the issue of final status by purporting to establish an independent state was incompatible with the UN regime. Much criticism has been voiced, not least by the dissenting judges,[31] about the Court's artificial characterization of the Assembly of Kosovo as an institution lying outside the Constitutional Framework. But this characterization appears to be sensible when, as the Court did, one concludes that resolution 1244 is without prejudice to steps that the local institutions of Kosovo may decide to take towards establishing a new state.[32] Once this premise is accepted, there would

---

[27] *Kosovo*, 446, para 105.

[28] E.g. Written Statement of Spain, 14 April 2009, 24–6: <http://www.icj-cij.org/docket/files/141/15644.pdf> accessed 24 March 2014.

[29] *Kosovo*, 449, para 114.

[30] Ibid. The Court found, in addition, that in any event the addressees of the resolution were the 'Member States as well as … organs of the United Nations such as the Secretary-General and his Special Representative', from which it followed that the Security Council had not intended to impose 'a specific obligation to act or a prohibition from acting' addressed to other entities; ibid 450, para 115.

[31] See, in particular, the Declaration of Vice-President Tomka in *Kosovo*, 458–60, paras 16–21.

[32] The Court's finding that resolution 1244 did not prohibit the declaration of independence was not uncontroversial. For a critical approach, see M. Kohen and K. Del Mar, 'The Kosovo Opinion and

seem to be little reason to ignore the reality of Kosovo's constitutional moment by ascribing the declaration to an assembly operating within the strict confines of the Constitutional Framework. This would only provide an incentive for the representatives of Kosovo to gather again in a different location to issue a new proclamation ostensibly unconnected with the Provisional Institutions of Self-Government.

In short, the 2010 opinion suggests that the present institutions of Kosovo may exercise public authority independently from the Special Representative of the Secretary-General.[33] The question is then whether the extent of this public authority corresponds to 'the functions of a State' so that Kosovo can be said to be factually independent in relation to the UN. Over the years the United Nations Interim Administration Mission in Kosovo (UNMIK) has been transferring competences to the Kosovar authorities, a process which intensified with the declaration of independence in February 2008.[34] This process culminated on 12 December 2010, when the first elections of representatives of the Assembly of Kosovo *outside* the framework of resolution 1244 were held.[35]

The progressive autonomy of the Kosovar institutions has also extended to foreign affairs. Up to mid-2012, the reports of the Secretary-General to the Security Council on the interim administration mission contained a section on 'external representation', reporting on UNMIK's efforts to facilitate Kosovo's engagement in international and regional initiatives. From 2010 to 2012, the Secretary-General reported on Pristina's objections to UNMIK playing this role.[36] On 10 September 2012, the authorities in Kosovo, together with the International Steering Group of States that had been established to oversee Kosovo's independence in the aftermath of the 2008 declaration, proclaimed 'the end of the "supervised" independence' of Kosovo and affirmed the Constitution of Kosovo as the '"sole" legal framework'.[37] This was followed by the adoption of constitutional amendments revoking those provisions that concerned the international supervision of Kosovo by the Steering Group.[38] These were all developments that the United Nations took account of but made no attempt to undermine, still less reverse. Subsequent reports of the Secretary-General to the Security Council have omitted the 'external representation' section, implying that Pristina is in full control of Kosovo's external affairs.

---

UNSCR 1244 (1999): A Declaration of "Independence from International Law"?' (2011) 24 *Leiden Journal of International Law* 109, 123–4.

[33] Cf. also C. Tomuschat, 'Recognition of New States – The Case of Premature Recognition' in P. Hilpold (ed), *Kosovo and International Law* (Martinus Nijhoff, 2012) 38 (concluding that 'independence and UN supervision are not irreconcilable').

[34] See e.g. the paper 'UNMIK after Kosovo Independence: Exit Strategy or 'Exist' Strategy?', prepared by the Kosovo Institute of Peace in August 2013, available at <http://www.kipinstitute.org/images/publications/UNMIK%20after%20Kosovo%20Independence.pdf>, accessed 28 April 2014.

[35] Report of the Secretary-General on the United Nations Interim Administration Mission in Kosovo, 28 January 2011, S/2011/43, at 1, para 4.

[36] E.g. Report of the Secretary-General on the United Nations Interim Administration Mission in Kosovo, 3 May 2011, S/2011/281, at 11, para 55.

[37] Secretary-General on the United Nations Interim Administration Mission in Kosovo, 8 November 2012, S/2012/818, 2, para 6.

[38] Ibid 2, para 7.

That said, the international presence in Kosovo remains considerable. For one, the Kosovo Force (KFOR) formed under the auspices of the North Atlantic Treaty Organization in accordance with resolution 1244 continues to discharge its peace-building mandate, with a contingent of some 4,882 troops.[39] The European Union Rule of Law Mission (EULEX), established in the aftermath of the declaration of independence, remains active in providing assistance to the Kosovar institutions in the rule-of-law field. Alongside its advisory and capacity-building competences, EULEX comprises an Executive Division with the mandate to investigate, pros-ecute, and adjudicate cases relating *inter alia* to war crimes, terrorism, and organ-ized crime.[40] Finally, while UNMIK's participation in the administration of the territory of Kosovo has been drastically diminished, the mission retains its man-date under resolution 1244 to exercise public power as appropriate.

Yet none of these institutions have prevented or sought to prevent the institu-tions of Kosovo from exercising legislative, executive, and judicial authority—that is, from exercising for the most part the functions of a state—with respect to the territory and population of Kosovo. Rather, while international organizations have maintained a neutral position in relation to the issue of status, they have engaged in capacity-building and the progressive devolution of public authority to elected representatives of the Kosovar people. Moreover, they were conceived as tempor-ary rather than entities with a permanent mandate. In the case of EULEX, when its mandate was renewed in 2012 and extended until 14 June 2014, the posi-tion of the institutions of Kosovo was that this occurred with Kosovo's consent. The Kosovar leadership made a point of sending an invitation letter to the High Representative of the European Union for Foreign Affairs and Security Policy, and both the invitation letter and the EU's response were ratified by the Assembly of Kosovo as a treaty.[41]

## 2. Kosovo as a special case of 'internationalized territory'

While the presence of international organizations in Kosovo casts some doubt on the extent of its independence, it bears emphasizing that the criteria for statehood are flexible enough to allow a variety of entities with differing circumstances to be classified as states. It cannot be assumed that, because an entity has special or unusual characteristics, it cannot qualify as a state.[42]

A historical analogue is the Free City of Danzig. The Free City was established in 1919 to ensure Poland's access to the sea while safeguarding the interests of the mostly German-speaking inhabitants. By Article 100 of the Treaty of Versailles,

---

[39] <http://www.aco.nato.int/kfor/about-us/troop-numbers-contributions.aspx> accessed 24 March 2014.

[40] European Union, Council Joint Action E 2008/124/CFSP, 4 February 2008 on the European Union Rule of Law Mission in Kosovo, L 42/92 OJEU, art 3(d).

[41] Secretary-General on the United Nations Interim Administration Mission in Kosovo, 8 November 2012, S/2012/818, 2, para 9.

[42] For a discussion of the application of the criteria for statehood to special cases, see *Creation of States*, 196–252.

Germany renounced its rights over the territory in favour of the Principal Allied and Associated Powers, who in turn undertook by Article 102 'to establish the town of Danzig, together with the rest of the territory ... as a Free City ... under the protection of the League of Nations'.[43] The Constitution of the Free City, drawn up by its representatives in agreement with a High Commissioner appointed by the League, was also placed under League guarantee. Differences as to the Treaty provisions were to be decided in the first instance by the High Commissioner but ultimately by the League. The Treaty of Versailles also envisaged the conclusion of a treaty between Danzig and Poland providing for Poland to undertake Danzig's foreign relations, which was done in November 1920.

The question then arose whether Danzig constituted a state. Despite controversy in the literature,[44] the facts warrant an affirmative answer. Although Poland had important rights in respect of Danzig's territory, the local administration did not cease to be independent in respect of all other matters. Moreover, while Poland had charge of Danzig's foreign relations, this was through a combination of an agency arrangement with a right of veto. This point was made by the Permanent Court of International Justice, which stated that 'the rights of Poland as regards the foreign relations of the Free City [were] not absolute' as the former was not entitled 'to impose a policy on the Free City nor to take any step in connection with the foreign relations of the Free City against its will'.[45] The role that the League played as a 'protector' in relation to Danzig may have placed some restrictions on its independence, but it did not alter the position. As the Permanent Court noted, 'the interpretation of the Danzig Constitution [was] primarily an internal question of the Free City', though one that might 'involve the guarantee of the League of Nations, as interpreted by the Council and by the Court'.[46] Danzig's overall independence and control over its internal affairs, confirmed by the *jurisprudence constante* of the Permanent Court, signalled its statehood despite the special characteristics of its status given its connections with Poland and the League.

Writing in 2006, before the unilateral declaration of independence was issued, I noted that Kosovo's legal position remained that of an autonomous area under international administration—rather than that of a state—since, until then, the territorial integrity of Serbia had been preserved.[47] I distinguished Kosovo from other internationalized territories such as Danzig on the grounds that the arrangements for UN administration were transient and left the question of the final

---

[43] *Creation of States*, 238.

[44] Cf. e.g. M. Ydit, *Internationalized Territories from the 'Free City of Cracow' to the Free City of Berlin* (A.W. Sythof 1961) 224 (denying Danzig's statehood); D. Orlow, 'Of Nations Small: The Small State in International Law' (1995) 9 *Temple International & Comparative Law Journal* 115, 122 (describing Danzig as 'functionally sovereign').

[45] *Free City of Danzig and the ILO*, PCIJ ser B no 18 (1930), 13.

[46] *Consistency of Certain Danzig Legislative Decrees with the Constitution of the Free City*, PCIJ ser A/B no 65 (1935), 13. The position of Judge Anzilotti in this respect was more categorical: 'The question submitted to the Court is one purely of Danzig constitutional law: international law does not enter into it at all' (Anzilotti diss, 24).

[47] *Creation of States*, 408.

status of the territory pending.[48] The position in 2014 is very different from that in 2006. The 2008 declaration of independence, the devolution of public power to Kosovar institutions effectively operating under an autonomous legal framework and the confirmation by the International Court that this process does not contravene resolution 1244 all lead to the conclusion that Kosovo is now a state, notwithstanding its special characteristics as a territory under UN administration. If anything, Kosovo's claim to statehood is stronger than Danzig's ever was. While the ongoing negotiations regarding its final status may lead to a different solution, Kosovo's independence appears to be not only viable but also permanent.

## D. The relevance of international recognition

At the time of writing some 108 states have recognized Kosovo.[49] While recognition is not a condition for statehood in international law, it provides evidence of legal status and may be of great importance in particular cases.[50] This is even more so in the case of secession or separation outside the colonial context. Since 1945, the international community has been extremely reluctant to accept unilateral secession of parts of independent states if the secession is opposed by the government of that state.[51] Thus, for example, Somaliland has been in fact substantially independent from the Government of Somalia since 1991, but, having failed to attract any international recognition, it is not regarded as being a state. Likewise, the attempts of Abkhazia and South Ossetia to secede from Georgia have been recognized by only a handful states.[52] Georgia views South Ossetia as an 'occupied territory'[53] and is unlikely to consent to its independence in the foreseeable future.

In contrast, the situation of Kosovo is virtually unprecedented as regards international recognition. Despite Serbia's objections, over half of the membership of the United Nations has recognized Kosovo's statehood. Recognition was considerable soon after the declaration of independence (by the end of 2008, it amounted to 55 states): it increased considerably when it became clearer that Pristina possessed an effective government which functioned independently from Belgrade and the international organizations collaborating under resolution 1244. The recognition of Kosovo signifies not only that most states are of the view that Kosovo fulfils the criteria for statehood despite its special characteristics, but also that Kosovo relies on ample international support to exercise the functions of a state in respect of its territory and population.

---

[48] Ibid 252.
[49] As reported by KosovoThanksYou, a project that monitors the international recognition of Kosovo: <http://www.kosovothanksyou.com> accessed 28 April 2014. A list available on the website of Kosovo's Ministry of Foreign Affairs reports 96 recognitions as of 28 November 2012: <http://www.mfa-ks.net/?page=2,33> accessed on 28 April 2014.
[50] *Creation of States*, 93.
[51] For a review of practice up to 2006, see *Creation of States*, 391–418.
[52] For a commentary, see A. Nußberger, 'Abkhazia' (2013) *Max Planck Encyclopedia of Public International Law*, paras 31–2; and A. Nußberger, 'South Ossetia', ibid, paras 34–5.
[53] See 'The Law of Georgia on Occupied Territories', 23 October 2008, available at <http://www.smr.gov.ge/docs/doc216.pdf> accessed 24 March 2014.

## 3. Conclusion

Though Kosovo's full integration into the international community may be dependent on a final settlement of its dispute with Serbia, which would pave the way for its admission to the United Nations, the developments of the past four years indicate that it already qualifies for statehood.[54] The government in Pristina has become independent from Serbia, has been capable of exercising the functions of a state alongside—and in spite of—the international presence in the territory, and has attracted a degree of international recognition that is atypical in cases of secession or separation outside the colonial context, against the wishes of the parent state.

---

[54] Christian Tomuschat reached a similar conclusion in a study published in 2012: C. Tomuschat, 'Recognition of New States—The Case of Premature Recognition' in P. Hilpold (ed), *Kosovo and International Law* (Martinus Nijhoff 2012) 45.

# 15

# Has the Advisory Opinion's Finding that Kosovo's Declaration of Independence was not Contrary to International Law Set an Unfortunate Precedent?

*Anne Peters*

## 1. Introduction

The declaration of Crimean independence by the Supreme Rada of Crimea of 11 March 2014 explicitly relied on the ICJ's *Kosovo* Advisory Opinion by stating:

We, the members of the parliament of the Autonomous Republic of Crimea and the Sevastopol City Council … taking into consideration the confirmation of the status of Kosovo by the United Nations International Court of Justice on July 22, 2010, which says that a unilateral declaration of independence by a part of the country does not violate any international norms, make this decision.[1]

After the Crimean referendum of 16 March 2014, in which the population pronounced itself in favour of joining Russia, the Russian President, Vladimir Putin, addressed the public in a long speech in which he explained and justified the Russian action in political, historical, and legal terms. He relied particularly on the 'Kosovo precedent':

Moreover, the Crimean authorities referred to the well-known Kosovo precedent—a precedent our western colleagues created with their own hands in a very similar situation, when they agreed that the unilateral separation of Kosovo from Serbia, exactly what Crimea is doing now, was legitimate and did not require any permission from the country's central authorities … [T]he UN International Court agreed with this approach … They wrote this, disseminated it all over the world, had everyone agree and now they are outraged. Over what? The actions of Crimean people completely fit in with these instructions, as it

---

[1] Transl. by rt.com, 11 March 2014 (Rt.com, 'Crimea parliament declares independence from Ukraine ahead of referendum', <http://rt.com/news/crimea-parliament-independence-ukraine-086/0>.

were. For some reason, things that Kosovo Albanians (and we have full respect for them) were permitted to do, Russians, Ukrainians and Crimean Tatars in Crimea are not allowed. Again, one wonders why. We keep hearing from the United States and Western Europe that Kosovo is some special case. What makes it so special in the eyes of our colleagues? It turns out that it is the fact that the conflict in Kosovo resulted in so many human casualties. Is this a legal argument? The ruling of the International Court says nothing about this. This is not even double standards; this is amazing, primitive, blunt cynicism. One should not try so crudely to make everything suit their interests, calling the same thing white today and black tomorrow . . .[2]

By contrast, Kosovo's Prime Minister, Hashim Thaçi, told the News Agency Reuters: 'Under no circumstances can the Kosovo case be compared with the case of Crimea, Kosovo is a unique case'.[3] Also, the German Federal Chancellor, Angela Merkel, in a parliamentary debate on the Crimean crisis of March 2014, rejected any comparison between Kosovo and Crimea as 'shameful'.[4]

In the years after Kosovo's independence, politicians and the press of various territorial entities aspiring for independent statehood have pointed to the Kosovo 'precedent', for example: Transdniestria;[5] Nagorno-Karabakh;[6] the Republika Srpska;[7] and Palestine.[8] Overall, both in the context of the Kosovo's protracted path to formal independence, after its declaration of independence (DoI), in the course of the proceedings before the ICJ, and more recently, some political actors have time and time again highlighted the *sui generis* nature of the Kosovo issue, and denied that it would have (or should have) any precedential value, while others on the contrary relied on the 'precedent'. This chapter analyses the merits of these

---

[2] V. Putin, Address by President of the Russian Federation, 18 March 2014, transcript at http://eng.kremlin.ru/news/6889. During an informal talk with journalists amid the Crimean crisis, the Russian President moreover seemed to raise the possibility that he might recognize Kosovo if the West accepted Crimea's annexation by Russia (Borger, 'Putin offers Ukraine olive branches delivered by Russian tanks', *The Guardian*, 4 March 2014) <http://www.theguardian.com/world/2014/mar/04/putin-ukraine-olive-branches-russian-tanks>.

[3] Bytyci, 'Don't use our case to justify Crimea, Kosovo PM tells Russia' (*Reuters*, 27 March 2014) <http://www.reuters.com/article/2014/03/27/us-ukraine-crisis-kosovo-idUSBREA2Q14V20140327>.

[4] Deutscher Bundestag, 18. Wahlperiode, 20. Sitzung, Berlin, 13 March 2014, Plenarprotokoll 18/20, at 1519 D.

[5] 'Kosovo's "inevitable" independence will set important precedent for Transdniestria; Others', *The Tiraspol Times*, 30 January 2008 (The site and the article apparently no longer exist).

[6] Antidze and Mkrtchyan, 'Kosovo "will boost Karabakh recognition drive"' (*Reuters*, 16 February 2008) <http://www.reuters.com/article/2008/02/17/us-kosovo-serbia-armenia-idUSL166671420080217>.

[7] Trifunovska, 'The Impact of the "Kosovo Precedent" on Self-Determination Struggles', in J. Summers (ed), *Kosovo: A Precedent? The Declaration of Independence, the Advisory Opinion and Implications for Statehood, Self-determination and Minority Rights* (Martinus Nijhoff Publishers 2011) 375, at 393.

[8] 'Abbas aide says declaring independence a possibility', (*Reuters*, 16 February 2008) <http://www.reuters.com/article/2008/02/20/us-palestinians-israel-talks-idUSL2022795620080220>; 'Abbas cool to unilateral Palestinian independence' (*Reuters*, 16 February 2008) <http://www.reuters.com/article/2008/02/20/us-palestinians-israel-idUSL2048771220080220>. 'In his interview to Reuters, Abed Rabbo, a top aide to Palestinian President Mahmoud Abbas, said that Palestinians should declare an independent state unilaterally if peace talks with Israel continue to falter, drawing an analogy to Kosovo. "Kosovo is not better than us. We deserve independence even before Kosovo, and we ask for the backing of the United States and the European Union for our independence."'

claims. It concludes that the Advisory Opinion, while not being a precedent in a technical sense, has the unfortunate effect, due to its failure to spell out any clear limits of secession, of not preventing subsequent (erroneous) reliance on its narrow findings. With regard to the possible 'precedential' value of the DoI and its implicit endorsement by states and the Court, the chapter concludes that the denial of 'precedent' had the legal effect of stalling the formation of a general *opinio iuris* on secession, but that the legal technique of distinguishing is a sufficient and normatively preferable strategy for containing other instances of imminent secession.

## 2. Conceptual Issues: 'Uniqueness', 'Sui Generis', 'Precedent', and Distinguishing

Was Kosovo a *sui generis* case? *'Sui generis'* means 'a kind of its own', and thus essentially the same as being a unique case. That question at first sight seems to be a factual one: an observer discerns whether a situation has similar features to other ones or not. However, such a comparison relies inevitably on value judgments and choices. Each case in life is unique and differs on the facts. The observer must choose which situations to compare, and, most of all, choose some features as 'relevant', and leave others aside. Only having made these choices, can a judgment be made that two cases (for example Kosovo and Crimea) are similar (or even equal) *in the relevant respects*—or different. In the context of a legal assessment, the choice of the factors to be taken into account (the *tertium comparationis*) must be guided by legal considerations. For example, a relevant element is the presence (or absence) of a threat of military force in the process of a secession, because current international law is characterized by a prohibition on the use of force. In the context of the Kosovo situation, elements of comparison and distinction used by the relevant actors were particularly the dissolution of Yugoslavia, the massive violations of human rights of Kosovar Albanians, the NATO intervention, and the UN administration (see in detail below Section 4).

In law, the intellectual exercise of comparing situations and cases is called 'distinguishing'. According to Black's law dictionary, 'distinguishing' is '[t]o note a significant factual, procedural, or legal difference in (an earlier case) ... [t]o minimize the case's precedential effect or to show that it is inapplicable'. A case is 'distinguishable', when it is 'different from, and thereby not controlling, or applicable in, a given case or situation'.[9]

A pertinent question is: *who* distinguishes? And here the question is particularly: the court(s) or the states? In a decentralized order with no compulsory jurisdiction, there is no single authority to perform that business of distinguishing. Cyprus in its written statement in the Kosovo proceedings pointed to this fact:

As a political matter, it is always *open to a State to distinguish* one situation from another, *however alike they may seem to other States*, or to identify one situation with another, however

---

[9] *Black's Law Dictionary* (8th edn, West 2004), at 506.

different they may seem. The States recognizing Kosovo undoubtedly intended that no other group could claim to be like the Albanian population of Kosovo and thus have a right to be a State (and to have that status acknowledged by other States). However, *they are not able to bind others to their views*.[10]

Still, the World Court is in a privileged position vis-à-vis states (even if it cannot always be seized), and its pronouncements will have a higher authority than the distinctions made by individual states.

Precedents as such are not a source of international law. In a technical sense, judicial precedents exist only in the common law. Here, a precedent is (as defined by the Oxford English Dictionary) 'a previous case or legal decision that may be or ... must be followed in subsequent similar cases'.[11] In international law, the common law notion of judicial precedent, capable of generating rules with binding effect within the legal system, is not applicable, as Cyprus pointed out in the Kosovo proceedings.[12] Nevertheless, international lawyers normally seek to construct and understand the edifice of international law as a legal *order*, and therefore seek to identify a set of coherent and consistent rules across similar cases.[13] It is in that (looser) sense that international cases and judicial pronouncements on those may function as 'precedents'.[14] In that loose sense, precedents can give indications for the emergence of a new rule of customary law. Such a new rule requires a general practice over a certain period of time, accompanied by the opinion that this practice reflects law (see in detail below Section 2). Finally, 'precedent' is also a term in international relations scholarship. In that discipline, 'precedent' refers 'to a past event that could be politically persuasive or may be used in diplomatic language'.[15]

In the Kosovo debate, the buzzword 'precedent' was not only used in its (loose) legal sense, but in some instances also, or exclusively, in its political sense. It was more or less a shorthand for the question whether the situation *does* and *should* function as a *model* for future cases or not. In this context, three different points of reference of that precedent language need to be distinguished. First, at the time of the NATO intervention of 1999, the topos emerged that the *overall situation* of Kosovo was a 'unique case'. For example, the report on Kosovo, published by an international commission initiated by Sweden and endorsed by the UN Secretary-General, under the presidency of Richard Goldstone and Carl Tham, made contradictory

---

[10] *Accordance with International Law of the Unilateral Declaration of Independence in Respect of Kosovo*, Advisory Opinion of 22 July 2010, ICJ Reports 2010, 403, Written Statement of Cyprus (submitted 17 April 2009), at 19, para. 78 (emphasis added).

[11] Oxford English Dictionary (3rd edn, OUP 2010), p. 1397.

[12] *Accordance with International Law of the Unilateral Declaration of Independence in Respect of Kosovo*, Advisory Opinion of 22 July 2010, ICJ Reports 2010, 403, Written Statement of Cyprus (submitted on 17 April 2009), at 19, para. 78 (*supra* note 10). Cyprus feared potential repercussions for its so far unrecognized breakaway territory of Northern Cyprus, occupied by Turkish forces.

[13] C. J. Borgen, 'Is Kosovo a Precedent? Secession, Self-Determination and Conflict Resolution', Summary of Presentation given at an EES Noon Discussion', 13 June 2008, no pagination <http://www.wilsoncenter.org/publication/350-kosovo-precedent-secession-self-determination-and-conflict-resolution>, or <http://www.wilsoncenter.org/sites/default/files/Sept-Oct2008PDF.pdf>.

[14] See, e.g., A. Zammit Borda, 'The Direct and Indirect Approaches to Precedent in International Criminal Courts and Tribunals', *Melbourne Journal of International Law* 14 (2014), 1–32.

[15] Borgen (*supra* note 13), no pagination.

statements about the precedential value of that 'humanitarian intervention' (which it famously qualified as being 'illegal but legitimate'). On the one hand, the report noted that '[t]he Kosovo "exception" now exists, for better and worse, as a contested precedent'. On the other hand, the report concluded: 'If, therefore, we stand back from the Kosovo intervention, it becomes clear that it did not so much create a precedent for intervention elsewhere as raise vital questions about the legitimacy and practicability of the use of force to defend human rights and humanitarian values in the 21st century'.[16] And in 2003, the ICJ highlighted the '*sui generis* position' of Yugoslavia between 1992 and 2000 vis-à-vis the United Nations and international law instruments.[17] (This was in the context of state dissolution and possible succession, and did not have anything to do with Kosovo. The possible precedential value of the break-up of the state and/or the NATO intervention will not be dealt with in this chapter.)

Second, Kosovo's *unilateral declaration of independence* (DoI) of 17 February 2008 was, first of all by its authors, and then by many commentators, qualified as a 'non-precedent', as will be examined in detail below.[18] And third, the question arose whether the ICJ Advisory Opinion of 2010 constituted a precedent or not.[19] In the following, I will deal with the possibly 'precedential' value of the Advisory Opinion first (although it came later in time), because this question is less complex (Section 3). Afterwards, I will discuss the precedential value of the 2008 DoI, as 'sanctioned' by the Opinion (Section 4).

## 3. The Advisory Opinion as a Precedent?

### A. Legal effects of advisory opinions

Advisory opinions issued by the ICJ are not legally binding judicial pronouncements. It is the 'essential characteristic' of advisory opinions that they, 'as the term implies ... constitute *advice*, i.e. they do not legally bind either the requesting

---

[16] The Independent International Commission on Kosovo, *The Kosovo Report: Conflict, International Response, Lessons Learned* (OUP 2000) at 175 and 297.

[17] ICJ, *Application for Revision of the Judgment of 11 July 1996 in the Case concerning the Application of the Convention on the Prevention and Punishment of the Crime of Genocide (Bosnia and Herzegovina v. Yugoslavia)*, Preliminary Objections (Yugoslavia v. Bosnia and Herzegovina), Judgment of 3 February 2003, ICJ Reports 2003, 7, para. 71.

[18] See the references below in notes 44–73.

[19] Referring to the Advisory Opinion as a non-precedent, the German Foreign Minister (Guido Westerwelle), during a visit to Cyprus, shortly after the issuance of the opinion, stated on 26 July 2010: 'It's a unique decision in a unique situation with a unique historical background ... This was very specific expertise it has nothing to do with any other cases in the world ... It has a special historical background and this opinion of judges has something to do with this special historical background and with this specific situation ... It is not a decision for other countries or other regions in the world'. <http://www.mfa.gov.cy/mfa/mfa2006.nsf/0/88B9C658146E783DC225776C002B0777?OpenDo cument&print>; <http://www.expatica.com/de/news/german-news/german-fm-un-court-ruling-on-kosovo-unique-decision-_85299.html>. In contrast, the Russian President referred to the Advisory Opinion as a precedent in his 18 March 2014 address concerning Crimea (*supra* note 2).

party or any other body or State to take any specific action pursuant to the opinion'.[20] For this reason alone, an advisory opinion cannot constitute a precedent in the common law sense discussed above.

Advisory opinions are, however, 'judicial decisions', and thus a subsidiary source of international law in terms of Article 38(1)(d) ICJ Statute.[21] Also, advisory opinions may contribute to the identification or even formation of customary law to the extent that they manifest or confirm practice and *opinio juris* of international legal persons, notably states. Finally, the opinions enjoy a certain institutional authority, i.e. their substance is acknowledged by other participants in the system as being worthy of respect. Overall, it can be said that advisory opinions have a 'real legal significance'[22] and 'will normally have important legal effects'.[23] Statements made therein may have 'far-reaching legal consequences'.[24]

Generally speaking, decisions of the ICJ have the function of, on the one hand, resolving a concrete legal dispute (adversarial judgment) or answering a legal question (advisory opinion), and on the other hand, developing the law further (at least to a limited extent[25]). These two functions may stand in tension. Indeed, a number of advisory opinions have been crucial to the development of international law, for example the *Reparations for Injuries* Opinion (1949), the opinion concerning *Reservations to the Convention on the Prevention and Punishment of the Crime of Genocide* (1951), and the *Namibia* Opinion (1970). The ICJ itself regularly cites its own advisory opinions and relies on them in the same manner as on its previous adversial judgments. Finally, the Court itself has ascribed some *political* importance to its own opinions. For example, it stated that the *Nuclear Weapons* Advisory Opinion 'would have relevance for the continuing debate on the matter in the General Assembly and would present an additional element in the negotiations on the matter'.[26]

Overall, it would thus not be owing to the formal status and *de facto* authority of advisory opinions in general, but rather to its substance (or lack of substance),

---

[20] Thirlway, 'Advisory Opinions', *Max Planck Encyclopedia Online Edition* <http://opil.ouplaw.com/view/10.1093/law:epil/9780199231690/law-9780199231690-e4?rskey=T6AfXq&result=1&prd=EPIL>.

[21] Art. 38(1)(d) says that the Court shall apply 'judicial decisions … as subsidiary means for the determination of rules of law'.

[22] T. D. Gill et al (eds), *Rosenne's The World Court: What It is and How It Works* (6th edn, Martinus Nijhoff 2003), at 88.

[23] Frowein and Oellers-Frahm, 'Article 65', in A. Zimmermann et al (eds), *The Statute of the Intenational Court of Justice: A Commentary* (2nd edn 2012), para. 45.

[24] Ibid., para. 50.

[25] Cf. ICJ, *Legality of the Threat or Use of Nuclear Weapons* (Advisory Opinion), ICJ Reports 1996 226, para. 18: 'It is clear that the Court cannot legislate and, in the circumstances of the present case, it is not called upon to do so. Rather its task is to engage in its normal judicial function of ascertaining the existence or otherwise of legal principles and rules applicable to the threat or use of nuclear weapons. The contention that the giving of an answer to the question posed would require the Court to legislate is based on a supposition that the present *corpus juris* is devoid of relevant rules in this matter. The Court could not accede to this argument; *it states the existing law and does not legislate*. This is so even if, in stating and applying the law, the Court necessarily has to specify its scope and *sometimes note its general trend*' (emphasis added).

[26] Ibid., para. 17.

that the Kosovo Opinion might contribute a little or a lot to the development of international law, and be in that untechnical sense a 'precedent'—or not.

## B. Legal effects of the *Kosovo* opinion in particular

In the *Kosovo* case itself, the ICJ described an opinion's effects as follows: 'The advisory jurisdiction is not a form of judicial recourse for States but the means by which [organs of the UN] may obtain the Court's opinion in order to assist them in their activities'.[27] But '[t]he Court cannot determine … what effect that may have in relation to those steps' of the General Assembly.[28] This self-description relates to the political rather than to legal effects of the opinion.

One possible political effect could theoretically have been to bolster Kosovar statehood (although this was not explicitly a topic of the Opinion). The Advisory Opinion might have had a discernible effect for the recognition of Kosovo, i.e. for the international community's acknowledgment of Kosovar statehood—simply because the judicial statement on the legality of the DoI might factor in the states' legal and political considerations when deciding whether to recognize the entity or not. Before the Advisory Opinion, Kosovo had already been recognized by 69 states. One year after the Opinion, in August 2011, only 12 additional recognitions had come about (in total 81). Three years after the Opinion (in August 2013), 106 states had recognized Kosovo. So apparently, the Opinion did not really accelerate the speed of recognitions, and did not impact much on the recognition calculus of individual states.

So what about the 'precedential' value of the Opinion in the untechnical sense explained above? During the proceedings, in the camp of states opposing Kosovar independence, four states contradicted the '*sui generis*/uniqueness argument' and warned against setting an undesirable precedent through the Opinion itself (Serbia,[29] Cyprus,[30] Argentina,[31] and Bolivia[32]). Clearly, they thought such a 'precedent' to be pernicious because it accepted the fracturing of a state. In that sense, Serbia commented: 'The *destabilising factor* of this argument is immediately evident, and no argument claiming that the Kosovo case is not a precedent can cure this'.[33] From the bench, dissenting Judges Skotnikov and Koroma went in

---

[27] ICJ, *Accordance with International Law of the Unilateral Declaration of Independence in Respect of Kosovo*, Advisory Opinion of 22 July 2010, ICJ Reports 2010, 403, para. 33.

[28] Ibid., para. 44.

[29] *Accordance with International Law of the Unilateral Declaration of Independence in Respect of Kosovo*, Advisory Opinion of 22 July 2010, ICJ Reports 2010, 403, Written Comment of Serbia (submitted until 17 July 2009), at 66–8, 71, paras. 128–30, 133, 139.

[30] Cyprus, Verbatim Record (VR) (CR 2009/29 December, 7, 2009, 10 a.m.), at 47 para. 57, at 48, para. 64–5.

[31] Argentina, VR (CR 2009/26 December, 2, 2009, 10 a.m.), at 47–8, paras. 30–1.

[32] *Accordance with International Law of the Unilateral Declaration of Independence in Respect of Kosovo*, Advisory Opinion of 22 July 2010, ICJ Reports 2010, 403, Written Statement of Bolivia (submitted until 17 April 2009), at 1.

[33] *Accordance with International Law of the Unilateral Declaration of Independence in Respect of Kosovo*, Advisory Opinion of 22 July 2010, ICJ Reports 2010, 403, Written Comment of Serbia (submitted until 17 July 2009) (note 29), at 71, para. 139 (emphasis added).

the same direction. They deplored the fact that the Advisory Opinion would be relied upon later by other groups, and would in that sense constitute a bad precedent: 'The Court's Opinion will serve as a guide and instruction manual for secessionist groups the world over, and the stability of international law will be severely undermined'.[34] It would have 'an inflammatory effect'.[35]

Must we now admit, four years after the issuance of the Opinion, that these gloomy predictions have come true? We have seen that, in these few years, so far, only one state (Russia) has specifically justified a territorial alteration (Crimea) by reference to the *Kosovo* Opinion.[36] No 'parade of sovereignty' has occurred after the Opinion. Rather, the conflicts surrounding breakaway territories worldwide have remained rather stalemated. However, it is too early to predict future reliance on the Opinion.

What are possible reasons for the (so far) relatively modest effects of the *Kosovo* Opinion? First, there is one feature which relates to the dual functionality of advisory opinions of dispute resolution (in a broad sense) and developing the law. The *Kosovo* Opinion very much shied away from the latter function, and concentrated on the former. Seen in that light, it is appropriate to read the Opinion as a contribution to the solution of the Kosovo controversy rather than as an attempt at developing the law of self-determination and secession.[37] This perspective could well explain the lack of its 'precedential value' in the sense of law-making.

Second (and related to the first point), the Opinion was extremely parsimonious in legal substance. The Opinion is silent on secession, on statehood, on recognition, and on *uti possidetis*. It also largely circumvented the issue of territorial integrity by stating that the principle is not applicable to actors from inside a state. The Court did not need to address these issues because it was not explicitly asked to do so. But it would have been possible, and arguably not an overstepping of the Court's jurisdiction, to flesh out the question a bit more and give a broader (and deeper) answer.[38] Judge Bruno Simma made that point when declaring that this Advisory Opinion had little 'relevance' and little 'advisory quality'.[39] But apparently the judges could not reach a broader and deeper consensus.

---

[34] ICJ, *Accordance with International Law of the Unilateral Declaration of Independence in Respect of Kosovo*, Advisory Opinion of 22 July 2010, ICJ Reports 2010, 403 (*supra* note 27), Dissenting Opinion of Judge Koroma, para. 4.

[35] ICJ, *Accordance with International Law of the Unilateral Declaration of Independence in Respect of Kosovo*, Advisory Opinion of 22 July 2010, ICJ Reports 2010, 403 (*supra* note 27), Dissenting Opinion of Judge Skotnikov, para. 17.

[36] See *supra* note 2.

[37] Walter, 'The Kosovo Advisory Opinion: What It Says and What It Does Not Say' in C. Walter, A. von Ungern-Sternberg and K. Abushov (eds), *Self-Determination and Secession in International Law* (2014), at 25.

[38] Maybe not on all points: for example, it would have been difficult for the Court to say (with the narrow question before it) whether Kosovo was a state or not.

[39] '[T]he Court could have delivered a more intellectually satisfying opinion, and *one with greater relevance* as regards the international legal order as it has evolved into its present form, had it not interpreted the scope of the question so restrictively ... To not even enquire into whether a declaration of independence might be "tolerated" or even expressly permitted under international law does not

Had the Court's Opinion had more substance, it could have drawn a line between inadmissible and admissible secessions. Such a finding could have cut both ways: possibly (even if unintentionally), it might encourage those entities which fulfil the criteria, and discourage those entities which do not. It is a matter of psychology (and hinges on the observer's perspective on the legitimacy and perils of secession) which consequence (unintended or not) the observer (or the judges themselves) deem more likely and more pernicious: boosting secessions by drawing a line, or boosting secessions by refraining from drawing a line.

As it turns out now, the latter scenario came true. So ironically, the Kosovo Opinion seems to have constituted a 'precedent' *in a reverse sense*: it is exactly the sparseness of the Opinion (and in particular the failure of the Court to pronounce itself on the underlying issue of secession instead of concentrating on the act of declaring independence) which allowed Crimea and Russia in 2014 to rely on the ICJ Opinion in order to justify the Crimean claim for self-determination and secession.[40] Had the Court more clearly than it did condemned the involvement in processes of secession from the side of third states, or had it spelled out procedural and substantive conditions for secession, this (erroneous) usage of the Opinion, *inter alia* by the Russian President, Vladimir Putin, in his speech of 18 March 2014 explaining the incorporation of Crimea into Russia,[41] would not have been possible.

The prediction of concurring Judge Yusuf, who had called for a judicial pronouncement on the (narrow) legitimacy of secession, came true:

The fact that the Court decided to restrict its opinion to whether the declaration of independence, as such, is prohibited by international law, without assessing the underlying claim to external self-determination, *may be misinterpreted as legitimizing such declarations under international law*, by all kinds of separatist groups or entities that have either made or are planning to make declarations of independence ... The Court had a unique opportunity to assess, in a specific and concrete situation, the legal conditions to be met for such a right of self-determination to materialize and give legitimacy to a claim of separation. It has unfortunately failed to seize this opportunity, which would have allowed it to clarify the scope and normative content of the right to external self-determination, in its post-colonial conception, and thus to contribute, *inter alia*, to the *prevention* of unjustified claims to independence which may lead to instability and conflict in various parts of the world.[42]

So, in effect, while the Court read the question narrowly in order to avoid any precedential effect, it was the legalistic narrowness itself that allowed it to be relied

---

do justice to the General Assembly's request and, in my eyes, significantly reduces the *advisory* quality of this Opinion.' (ICJ, *Accordance with International Law of the Unilateral Declaration of Independence in Respect of Kosovo*, Advisory Opinion of 22 July 2010, ICJ Reports 2010, 403 (*supra* note 27), Declaration of Judge Simma, paras. 7 and 10 (emphasis partly in the original)).

[40]   Walter (*supra* note 37): 'It cannot be overlooked that the instrumental use by Russia of the declaration of independence and the referendum on the Crimea was somehow facilitated by the silence of the Court on possible limits to external involvement.'

[41]   See *supra* note 2.

[42]   ICJ, *Accordance with International Law of the Unilateral Declaration of Independence in Respect of Kosovo*, Advisory Opinion of 22 July 2010, ICJ Reports 2010, 403 (*supra* note 27), Separate Opinion of Judge Yusuf, paras. 6 and 17 (emphasis added).

on by Russia as a precedent.[43] In that sense, the Advisory Opinion did have the reverse effect of a 'bad precedent' through its silence.

## 4. The DoI as a Precedent?

### A.  Deniers of a precedent (before and after the DoI)

The Preamble to Kosovo's DoI of 17 February 2008 underlined that 'Kosovo is a special case arising from Yugoslavia's non-consensual break-up and is not a precedent for any other situation'. One day after the DoI, the EU Council Conclusions on Kosovo played the same tune.[44]

*Before the declaration of independence*, but with a view to that possible course of events, the first official documents to insist on the uniqueness of the problem had been the Final Report of the Special Envoy on Kosovo's future status of 26 March 2007, and the accompanying Secretary-General's letter to the President of the Security Council of the same date. The Special Envoy, Ahtisaari, wrote: 'Kosovo is a *unique* case that demands a *unique* solution. It does not create a *precedent* for other unresolved conflicts'.[45] The UN Secretary-General echoed this:

Kosovo is a unique case that demands a unique solution. It does not create a precedent for other unresolved conflicts. In unanimously adopting resolution 1244 (1999), the Security Council responded to Milosevic's actions in Kosovo by denying Serbia a role in its governance, placing Kosovo under temporary United Nations administration and envisaging a political process designed to determine Kosovo's future. The combination of these factors makes Kosovo's circumstances extraordinary.[46]

Some months later, in June 2007, ten former foreign ministers published an opinion piece in the *New York Times*. Under the headline, 'Kosovo must be independent', they wrote that 'the only viable option is for Kosovo to become independent under strict supervision ... Kosovo is a *unique situation* that has required a creative solution. It should *not* create a *precedent* for other unresolved conflicts'.[47]

*After the DoI*, recognitions of the new state began to trickle in. Among the 110 states which have up to now recognized Kosovo, a small number have, in official statements relating to recognition, explicitly highlighted the uniqueness of the situation. These were, in particular, states which quickly (still in the

---

[43]  Observation by Marko Milanović.

[44]  EU Council Conclusions on Kosovo, 2851st External Relations Council Meeting, Brussels, 18 February 2008, Press Release 6496/08 (Presse 41), at 7.

[45]  M. Ahtisaari, Special Envoy of the United Nations Secretary-General, 'Report of the Special Envoy of the Secretary-General on Kosovo's future status', United Nations Security Council, S/2007/168, 26 March 2007, para. 15, 'Conclusions' (emphasis added).

[46]  Letter dated 26 March 2007 from the Secretary-General addressed to the President of the Security Council, S/2007/168, para. 15.

[47]  Former foreign ministers, 'Kosovo must be independent', *New York Times*, 15 June 2007 (emphasis added) <http://www.nytimes.com/2007/06/15/opinion/15iht-edkosov.1.6153178.html>. The authors were, *inter alia,* Madeleine Albright (USA), Joschka Fischer (Germany), Helveg Petersen (Denmark), Hubert Vendrine (France).

spring of 2008) announced recognition. In chronological order of recognition these were (*inter alia*) France,[48] the UK,[49] the USA,[50] Latvia,[51] Peru,[52] Poland,[53] Switzerland,[54] Sweden,[55] Iceland,[56] Canada,[57] Hungary,[58] and Lithuania.[59] Most recognizing states preferred not to say anything on the uniqueness/precedence issue.

*In the ICJ Kosovo proceedings*, in total 20 states explicitly stated or wrote that they considered the Kosovo situation as 'unique', or *'sui generis'*.[60] Among those, 11 explained in addition that Kosovo's declaration of independence was not to constitute a 'precedent'.[61] Also, the authors of the DoI wrote: 'That the opinion of the Court might ... as some States seem to wish, create a precedent on alleged "fundamental rules and principles of international law which apply throughout the international legal order", is irrelevant ... Such characteristics are quite special in nature, such that the emergence of Kosovo as an independent State is

---

[48] French Representative to the Security Council Mr. Ripert, in the 5839th Meeting of the Security Council, 18 February 2008, UN Doc. S/PV.5839, at 19–20.

[49] British Representative to the Security Council Sir John Sawers in the 5839th Meeting of the Security Council, 18 February 2008, UN Doc. S/PV.5839, at 12–14.

[50] Statement of Secretary of State Condoleeza Rice of 18 February 2008, but not in the recognition letter from US President Bush to the President of Kosovo of the same date.

[51] Announcement by Minister of Foreign Affairs of Republic of Latvia on recognition of Kosovo's independence of 20 February 2008: 'Latvia emphasises that the case of Kosovo is unique, and it cannot be considered as a precedent for solving other frozen conflicts in the world <http://beqiraj.de/docs/independence/Lettland.pdf>.

[52] Ministerio de Relaciones Exteriores de Peru, Perú decide reconocer independencia de Kósovo, Comunicado Oficial 002-08 (22 February 2008): 'El Perú ... considera que se ha producido una situación única' <http://beqiraj.de/docs/independence/Peru.pdf>.

[53] Statement of 26 February 2008.

[54] Statement by the President of the Swiss Confederation on Recognition of Kosovo and the establishment of diplomatic relations, 27 February 2008: '... in view of the circumstances of this particular case, Switzerland's recognition of the independence of Kosovo does not constitute a precedent' <https://www.news.admin.ch/dokumentation/00002/00015/index.html?lang=en&msg-id=17497>.

[55] Ministry of Foreign Affairs of Sweden, 'Sweden recognises the Republic of Kosovo', 4 March 2008: 'In view of the conflicts in the 1990s that led to the collapse of Yugoslavia and the subsequent extended period of international administration of Kosovo, the EU also underlined that Kosovo is a sui generis case that cannot be deemed to have any effect as a precedent'.

[56] The Government of Iceland, 4 March 2008: 'Due to the unique circumstances of Kosovo, recognition of its independence cannot be viewed as a precedent.'

[57] Statement of the Canadian Minister of Foreign Affairs and International Trade of 18 March 2008.

[58] Hungarian Government, 19 March 2008: 'At the same time, the Government reaffirmed that resolving the status of Kosovo constitutes a sui generis case that does not set any precedent for other unresolved conflicts.'

[59] Resolution on the Recognition of the Republic of Kosovo, 6 May 2008.

[60] Bulgaria (Verbatim Record (VR (CR 2009/28, 4 December 2009, 10 a.m.), at 22 para. 16); Burundi (VR (CR 2009/28, 4 December 2009, 10 a.m.), at 27); Croatia (VR (CR 2009/29, 7 December 2009, 10 a.m.), at 50–1); Estonia (Written Statement, at 11–12); Ireland (Written Statement, at 10–11, paras. 33–4); Japan (Written Statement, at 5–6 and 8); Latvia (Written Statement, at 2); Luxembourg (Written Statement, at 2–3, paras. 5–8.); Maldives (Written Statement, at 1); and the states mentioned in the next note 61. (All written statements submitted before 17 April 2009.)

[61] *Albania* (Written Statement, at 38, para. 72); *Azerbaijan* (Written Statement, at 4, para. 17); *Denmark* (Written Statement, at 5–6 and 8; VR (CR 2009/29, 7 December 2009, 10 a.m.), at 66); *France* (Written Statement, at 2, para. 10, at 25, para. 2.1., at 29–30, paras. 2.17–2.19, at 35, para. 2.39, at 48, para. 2.82; VR (CR 2009/31, 9 December 2009, 10 a.m.), at 12 para. 11); *Germany* (Written Statement of Germany, at 26–7); *The Netherlands* (Written Statement, at 13, para. 3.20;

not a precedent for the emergence of other States where similar factors do not exist'.[62]

One of the statements came from the UK: 'We are very clear that the situation in Kosovo does not constitute a precedent for developments elsewhere. Kosovo's independence does not open the door for the fracturing of States more generally ... [W]e would encourage the Court to consider saying in terms in its advisory opinion that the circumstances pertaining in Kosovo are highly particular and cannot be relied upon as a precedent in any other situation'.[63] 'We do not assert a sui generis legal régime. The United Kingdom's contention is that, for reasons of the confluence of very particular factual circumstances, the situation of Kosovo does not create a precedent elsewhere'.[64]

The majority opinion of the Court did not dwell on the uniqueness argument and did not mention the term 'precedent' at all. Concurring Judge Cançado Trindade seemed to espouse the argument that the situation in Kosovo was unique, but did not draw his own conclusions from this diagnosis.[65] Dissenting Judge Skotnikov accepted that 'the present case ... is unprecedented', and concluded that the Court 'should have used its discretion to refrain from exercising its advisory jurisdiction in the rather peculiar circumstances of the present case', and should have dismissed the General Assembly's request in the first place, without entering into the merits.[66] Judge Sepúlveda-Amor mentioned that the Security Council 'has gone as far as to institute an *unprecedented* international régime of civil administration under Chapter VII of the United Nations Charter'.[67]

Many of these (and other) statements—both before and after independence, and during the ICJ proceedings—explain and justify the uniqueness of the Kosovo situation by pointing to the following four factors (with some nuances):[68]

---

VR (CR 2009/32, 10 December 2009, 10 a.m.), at 15–16, para. 29); *Norway* (VR (CR 2009/31, 9 December 2009, 10 a.m.), at 52–3, para. 33); *Poland* (Written Statement, at 5, para. 3.2; at 18, para. 3.40, at 22, para. 5.1., at 23, para. 5.2.2., at 30, para. 7.4, at 24, para. 5.2.5); *Slovenia* (Written Statement at 2; Written Comment, at 5, para. 6); the *UK* (Written Statement at 9–10, paras. 0.17–0.20, at 11–13, paras. 0.22 and 0.27, at 73, para. 4.7., at 74–6, para. 4.11; Written Comment of *UK* at 6, paras. 11–12); *USA* (VR (CR 2009/30, 8 December 2009, 10 a.m.), at 38 para. 39). (All written statements submitted before 17 April 2009; all written comments submitted until 17 July 2009.)

   [62] Written Contribution of the Authors of the Unilateral Declaration of Independence regarding the Written Statements (submitted until 17 July 2009), at 7, para. 1.15, at 126, para. 6.06 (emphasis added).

   [63] UK VR (CR 2009/32, 10 December 2009, 10 a.m.), at 40, para. 10.

   [64] Ibid., para. 11.

   [65] ICJ, *Accordance with International Law of the Unilateral Declaration of Independence in Respect of Kosovo*, Advisory Opinion of 22 July 2010, ICJ Reports 2010, 403 (*supra* note 27), Separate Opinion of Judge Cançado Trindade, paras. 45, 49, 63, 146, 227, 229.

   [66] ICJ, *Accordance with International Law of the Unilateral Declaration of Independence in Respect of Kosovo*, Advisory Opinion of 22 July 2010, ICJ Reports 2010, 403 (*supra* note 27), Dissenting Opinion of Judge Skotnikov, paras. 6 and 1.

   [67] ICJ, *Accordance with International Law of the Unilateral Declaration of Independence in Respect of Kosovo*, Advisory Opinion of 22 July 2010, ICJ Reports 2010, 403 (*supra* note 27), Separate Opinion of Judge Sepúlveda-Amor, at 495–6, para. 21 (emphasis added).

   [68] See the references to the 20 states' written and oral statements in the Kosovo proceedings before the ICJ above in notes 60–61. France, Germany, Ireland, Luxembourg, and the UK, in particular, succinctly laid out those four factors of 'uniqueness' in their written statements.

(1) The break-up of Yugoslavia (hence the specific and rare historical situation of the dismemberment of a state);[69] (2) the massive human rights violations committed against ethnic Kosovar Albanians since 1989; (3) the humanitarian intervention by NATO; and (4) the internationalization of the situation through Security Council resolution 1244,[70] which established an exceptionally comprehensive and extended UN administration of Kosovo. For example, the Assistant Secretary of State of the US State Department mentioned (one year before the DoI) all four factors:

Kosovo is a *unique* situation, because NATO was forced to intervene to stop and then reverse ethnic cleansing. The Security Council authorized effective Kosovo to be ruled effectively by the United Nations, not by Serbia. UN Council Resolution 1244 also stated that Kosovo's final status would be the subject of negotiation. Those conditions do not pertain to any of the conflicts that are usually brought up in this context. It's not applicable to Abkhazia, or South Ossetia, or Transdniestria. Nor is it applicable to Chechnya or to any separatist conflicts in Europe.[71]

Germany wrote along the same lines in its statement in the ICJ proceedings:

Several aspects combine to make Kosovo a truly unique *sui generis* case …—the anteced-ents of the conflict of the 1990s, possibly as far back as 1912, but in particular those of the late 1990s, as documented in relevant UN and other documents;—the nature and scope of what happened in 1998–1999 (as documented): massacres and pillaging, mass ethnic cleansing, necessity of international community intervention to prevent, or rather put an end to this;—the involvement of the international community and in particular its most universal institution, the UN: before and after 1999;—the earnest and intense, but ulti-mately unsuccessful search for a negotiated solution in this framework (in other words: no other avenue left open, unilateral action is *ultima ratio*).[72]

Overall, the deniers of the precedential value of the DoI, pronouncing both before and after the independence had actually come about, were all from the

---

[69] See, for example, the statement of the Permanent Representative of Belgium in the Security Council, UN Doc. S/PV.5839, at 9 (18 February 2008, emphasis added): 'Kosovo's independence is situated within a historical context that no one can ignore: the *disintegration of Yugoslavia*, which led to the creation of new independent States. The independence of Kosovo is part of this framework and can thus in no way be considered to set a precedent.'

[70] See, for example, the EU Council Conclusions on Kosovo, 2851st External Relations Council Meeting, Brussels, 18 February 2008, Press Release 6496/08 (Presse 41), at 7: 'The Council reiterates the EU's adherence to the principles of the UN Charter and the Helsinki Final Act, inter alia the principles of sovereignty and territorial integrity and all UN Security Council resolutions. It under-lines its conviction that in view of the conflict of the 1990s and the *extended period of international administration under SCR 1244*, Kosovo constitutes a *sui generis* case which does not call into question these principles and resolutions' (emphasis added). Cf. also Borgen (*supra* note 13), no pagination: 'resolution 1244 internationalized the problem and moved Kosovo from being solely under Serbian authority into a grey zone of international administration … [This] is different from assessing a claim by a separatist group that, on its own, is seeking to overturn the authority of the pre-existing state'.

[71] Council on Foreign Relations, 'Serbs Urged to Accept Kosovo Plan to Gain "European Future"', Interview with Assistant Secretary of State (US State Department) Daniel Fried, 6 February 2007 (emphasis added) <http://www.cfr.org/kosovo/serbs-urged-accept-kosovo-plan-gain-european-future/p12563>.

[72] *Accordance with International Law of the Unilateral Declaration of Independence in Respect of Kosovo*, Advisory Opinion of 22 July 2010, ICJ Reports 2010, 403, Written Statement of Germany (submitted until 17 April 2009) (*supra* note 61), at 26–7.

pro-independence camp. However, none of the four arguments they gave for the *sui generis* nature of the issue is really convincing. They are either grounded in dubious facts, or they rest on unsubstantiated legal analysis, or tend to neglect essentially similar cases that led to diametrically different outcomes.[73] At best, only the four factors in combination can be said to constitute a special case.

## B. Proponents of a precedential value of the DoI

The other side in the controversy about the status of Kosovo, those actors who opposed Kosovar independence, notably Serbia and Russia, explicitly affirmed—first, during the (ultimately futile) status negotiations and, in particular, after Kosovo's DoI—that the situation did have the quality of a 'precedent'. But, unlike the potentially secessionist territorial entities mentioned above (Transdniestria, Crimea, Palestine, and so on), the political agenda of these participants was not to promote secession in other regions of the world, but—conversely—to stress the dangerous consequences of Kosovar independence, in order to prevent that independence (unsuccessfully, as it turned out).

Thus, Serbia commented on the Kosovar DoI in the Security Council: 'this arbitrary decision represents a precedent which will cause irreparable damage to the international order [and] … runs afoul of the first principle of the Charter of the United Nations … *there are dozens of other Kosovos in the world*, and all of them are lying in wait for Kosovo's act of secession to become a reality and to be established as an acceptable norm'.[74] According to the Russian President Dimitry Medvedev, it would be impossible 'to tell the Abkhazians and Ossetians (and dozens of other groups around the world) that what was good for the Kosovo Albanians was not good for them. In international relations, you cannot have one rule for some and another rule for others'.[75] The President of the Russian Parliament (Duma), Boris Gryslov, opined that the Kosovar DoI ran against the Helsinki Accords on the inviolability of borders, and that this was 'the first precedent' (i.e. a 'precedent' in illegality).[76]

To sum up, both camps in the Kosovar status controversy (pre- and post-independence) relied on the 'precedent' argument, with exactly contrary political objectives: to favour or to oppose Kosovar independence. Interestingly, both sides agreed that they did not desire any other secessions to happen in the world. The only difference was that one side wanted Kosovar independence (and no other case of independence), while the other side wanted no entity's independence at all.

---

[73] Jovanović, 'Is Kosovo and Metohija Indeed a Unique Case?', in J. Summers (ed), *Kosovo: A Precedent? Implications for Statehood, Self-determination and Minority Rights* (2011) 345, at 348 et seq.

[74] *The Declaration of Independence, the Advisory Opinion* and the Statement of the President of Serbia in the Security Council, 18 February 2008 (UN Doc. S/PV/5839, at 5, emphasis added).

[75] Medvedev, 'Why I had to recognize Georgia's breakaway regions', *Financial Times*, 27 August 2008 <http://www.ft.com/cms/s/0/9c7ad792-7395-11dd-8a66-0000779fd18c.html#axzz2tykPdlA4>.

[76] Novosti, 1 April 2008, <http://de.ria.ru/world/20080401/102673108.html>.

## 5.  Possible Effects of 'No Precedent' Talk on the Evolution of International Customary Law

It has been asserted that the 'no precedent' talk is, as a matter of legal theory, irrelevant. States cannot in the present rule out a case serving in the future as a model.[77] Any exercise in comparison and possible legal distinguishing will be done in the future, in retrospect: 'What will be referred to as precedence tomorrow or as evidence of a newly emerging legal rule is not determined by the states that acted yesterday and especially not by the meaning that those states attribute to their actions'.[78] In the ICJ proceedings, Serbia made this point, too: 'The *mere assertion* by its authors that a fact they produced is not a "precedent" does not prevent it to be one.'[79]

This position needs to be moderated somewhat: the 'no precedent' talk does have repercussions for the international customary law on secession. Given the fact that an advisory opinion has no binding authority and no law-making effect in itself (see above Section 3.A.), its possible legal effect for the customary law reigning in the field can only be assessed in combination with the act (the DoI) on which the Opinion pronounced. It is—if at all—only that act (and the reactions of states to it) which potentially modified the law, and the Opinion, by stating that the DoI did not violate international law, could merely 'sanction' this. The reactions of states to the DoI constitute acts of state practice. Arguably, the DoI itself (being an act issued by a non-state actor), also constituted internationally relevant practice. In theory, the relationship between such a piece of practice and the extant international customary law may take either of four forms which will be discussed in what follows.

### A.  Scenarios without change of the law as it stands

First, theoretically, the practice might have correctly applied a pre-existing rule of international law. (The pre-existing rule being that international law does not prohibit individuals or groups of individuals from declaring independence from whatever state.) In that case, the practice would have had to be qualified as lawful and the state of the law would have remained unchanged. The ICJ did not exactly espouse this view: it did not qualify the DoI as lawful, but reformulated the question and said that it did not violate international law.

Second, theoretically, the inverse relationship would have been present if the pre-existing rule had been a prohibition of secession. If this (hypothetical) rule still

---

[77]  Jovanović, (*supra* note 73), at 373–4.

[78]  Christian Marxsen, 'The Crimea Crisis—An International Law Perspective', *Zeitschrift für ausländisches öffentliches Recht und Völkerrecht* 74 (2014), 367–91, 388 (footnotes omitted).

[79]  *Accordance with International Law of the Unilateral Declaration of Independence in Respect of Kosovo*, Advisory Opinion of 22 July 2010, ICJ Reports 2010, 403, Written Comment of Serbia (submitted until 17 July 2009) (*supra* note 29), at 79, para. 167 (emphasis added).

stood, it was breached by the DoI. The ICJ did not espouse this view either. But other actors were of this opinion. For example, Russia embraced this legal position in the Security Council[80] and in the advisory proceedings themselves.

The third possible interpretation of the effects of the DoI on international customary law is that no international legal rule applied to this situation, that the situation was, in other words, outside the international legal realm—hence in the political sphere or coming under the rules of domestic law only. The *'sui generis'* talk can be seen as an attempt to catapult the situation out of the legal realm.[81] The finding of the ICJ was along this line (but only with regard to the DoI, not with regard to secession): no international legal prohibition on declarations of independence existed,[82] therefore the DoI was not in violation of international law.[83] The consequence of the Opinion is that it does not stand in the way of future declarations of independence, if these are not 'connected with the unlawful use of force or other egregious violations of norms of general international law'.[84]

## B. Creation of a new international customary rule?

In contrast to the above-mentioned three possible relationships of the practice surrounding the DoI and an assumed static rule of customary international law, there is also the possibility that this practice has changed or is about to modify the law. A new rule might have been created through the DoI and notably through the reactions to it, confirmed by the Advisory Opinion. When a breach of the law is considered as, or functions as, a 'precedent', then through this precedent, the law will be developed into new (possibly undesirable) law. This is what is meant by the adage '*ex iniuria ius oritur*' (law cannot be born out of illegality). This is what Argentina and Bolivia had in mind when, in the ICJ *Kosovo* proceedings, they warned against 'un précédent fâcheux',[85] 'a bad precedent': 'if there is an acceptance of a unilateral declaration of Kosovo's independence without having a clear foundation of international law to analyze and judge in every case, *we would be establishing a bad precedent*'.[86]

Importantly, and as stated above (Section 2), such a development of the law would need a general practice, carried by *opinio juris*. Along that line, Timothy Waters opined that 'the Opinion could be read as *accepting the argument that Kosovo merits independence because of these specific circumstances*. This, in turn, could be read as indicating the shape of successful claims to secession in the future, and

---

[80] See *infra* note 93.

[81] See, in that sense, the statements of Serbia and Cyprus; see below notes 94–96.

[82] ICJ, *Accordance with International Law of the Unilateral Declaration of Independence in Respect of Kosovo*, Advisory Opinion of 22 July 2010, ICJ Reports 2010, 403 (*supra* note 27), para. 114.

[83] Ibid., paras. 84, 119–21: There was neither violation of general international law, nor of SC res. 1244, nor of the constitutional framework.

[84] Ibid., para. 81.

[85] *Accordance with International Law of the Unilateral Declaration of Independence in Respect of Kosovo*, ICJ Reports 2010, 403, VR (CR 2009/26 December, 2, 2009, 10 a.m.), at 47, para. 30.

[86] *Accordance with International Law of the Unilateral Declaration of Independence in Respect of Kosovo*, Advisory Opinion of 22 July 2010, ICJ Reports 2010, 403, Written Statement of Bolivia (submitted 17 April 2009), at 1.

creating an exceptionally high threshold for them—thus *not* a truly *sui generis* case, but *a new rule*, though in either case one that favours one substantive view of Kosovo's situation'.[87] From that perspective, the 'sanctioning' of the DoI by the Advisory Opinion did 'create' a new rule, but an extremely narrow one.

However, this reading of the events and of the Advisory Opinion faces a number of problems. First, legal theory finds it notoriously difficult to distinguish a breach of a customary norm (occurring through 'wrong' practice) from the formation of a new customary law rule (through new practice, accompanied by *opinio juris*). If we look at the practice (in our case, the DoI and the states' reactions to it) alone, we cannot tell whether the behaviour is aberrant, or whether it is 'new' and right. In order to find out whether there was a breach of the old customary law or whether—conversely—the formation of a new customary rule is going on, we need to examine the second element of customary law, the *opinio iuris* of the legal persons involved (states for simplicity's sake). However, at the point in time when the law changes, the opinion of the legal subjects that their behaviour (in our case the Kosovar representatives and the acquiescing states) is lawful can only be in error. The legal actor cannot be (rightfully) convinced that it is acting in conformity with the law, or that its behaviour is required by law, because such a legal rule does not (yet) exist. Therefore, an *opinio juris* in its strict sense (in the sense of a conviction that a permissive legal rule allows or even mandates the course of action taken) cannot exist as a matter of logic.[88] In that situation, *opinio juris* may exist (only) as to the immediate future. The *opinio* may then take 'the form of a settled conviction as to what the law should be, and would be for the proclaiming state... One can without contradiction announce the intention to live by a certain rule, if one does live by it from that time.'[89] This view means abandoning the purely static view on the law. Observers should accept and welcome the fact that, in order to be functional, law needs to be a living instrument. Once this dynamic perspective is espoused, we must acknowledge that there will be a phase of uncertainty, a grey zone during a certain period of time. The emergence of the new rule will only be identifiable in hindsight. The exact turning point of legal change cannot be pinned down with precision.

The second important point is that—even if we assume that the Kosovo episode can be qualified as the starting point of a new customary rule on secession—the exact content of the potential new rule remains slightly unclear. Is the new rule that international law does not condemn, but tolerates, some secessions *ex post*? Or does international law give a 'right' to remedial secession? But which secessions exactly and under what conditions?

[87] Waters, 'Misplaced Boldness: The Avoidance of Substance in the International Court of Justice's Kosovo Opinion', 23 *Duke Journal of Comparative & International Law* (2013) 267, at 323 (emphasis added, footnote omitted).

[88] Kelsen, 'Théorie du droit international coutumier', 1 *Revue internationale de la théorie du droit* (1939) 253, at 263.

[89] J. Crawford and T. Viles, 'International Law on a Given Day', in K. Ginther et al (eds), *Völkerrecht zwischen normativem Anspruch und politischer Realität. Festschrift für Karl Zemanek zum 65. Geburtstag* (Duncker & Humblot 1994) 45–68, at 67.

Another problem is that it might still be too early to assess a shift of the law. A (potential) shift can be identified only *ex post facto* (when new cases arise). The UN General Assembly's condemnation of the secession of Crimea in 2014,[90] does not necessarily prove that such a shift of the law has not taken place. The reason is that Crimea is again a different case: The secession was not peaceful but was rendered possible through the unlawful threat and use of force by a neighbouring state. Crimea and Kosovo can thus be quite clearly distinguished. Only if a 'similar' case to Kosovo's arose (one which displayed the four distinguishing features that were cited by so many actors as defining the unique case[91]), it would also be covered by the potential new rule (which emerged through practice, but was sanctioned by the Advisory Opinion).

A crucial objection is that, even if the requirements for the creation of new rules of customary law have been watered down in the past decades, a single case leading to a major dispute within the international community does not satisfy even lenient standards, because it does not constitute a 'general' practice and does not manifest the conviction of a number of states that this practice reflects an international legal rule. In the case of the Kosovo DoI, the ensuing ICJ proceedings were arguably a good forum for the manifestation of a (possibly changing) *opinio juris*. Importantly now, the 'no precedent' talk of so many actors prevented the formation of an *opinio juris*, even if it could not declare what happened to be a 'non-practice'. I think that this language not only prevented the formation of those actors' *own* legal conviction, but additionally made it more difficult to ascribe a legal opinion to other actors. Even those actors who did not explicitly say that they would not consider Kosovo as a precedent (but remained silent) were aware of the caveat pronounced by the others. They can thus be legitimately presumed to have relied on the fact that there would not be any change in the law, even if they themselves did not make that clear. Their silence on the matter cannot be presumed to have a law-developing character.

Finally, even if the DoI, the ensuing recognitions of Kosovo as an independent state by many other states, and the acceptance of the DoI in the Advisory Opinion were interpreted as triggering the creation of a new rule, then those states that qualified Kosovo's secession as unlawful must be considered as *persistent objectors*.[92] The Russian position in the Security Council was that the Kosovar declaration of independence was a 'blatant breach of the norms and principles of international law'.[93] Importantly, Russia is therefore precluded from relying on such a (potential) new rule herself. The law does not permit arguing that other states have violated international law and then taking the rule created by the alleged violation as a new rule and applying it (selectively) to other cases.

[90] UN GA Res. 68/L39, 27 March 2014 'Territorial Integrity of Ukraine', adopted with 100:11 votes, and 58 abstentions.

[91] See *supra* text with notes 68–72.

[92] Independent International Fact-Finding Mission on the Conflict in Georgia, report ('Tagliavini-Report') of September 2009, Chap. 3, at 140–1 <http://rt.com/files/politics/georgia-started-ossetian-war/iiffmcg-volume-ii.pdf>.

[93] Statement of the Russian Permanent Representative in the Security Council, UN Doc. S/PV/5839, at 6 (18 February 2008).

Considering all these factors, it is not persuasive to interpret the *Kosovo* case, as endorsed by the ICJ, as the emergence (or starting point of the creation) of a customary law on the matter of secession. Amongst other factors, it was also the 'no precedent' talk which had certain a stalling effect in this regard.

## 6. Normative Drawbacks of the 'No Precedent' Language

So while the 'no precedent' talk has been and continues to be legally relevant, it is at the same time normatively undesirable, because it undermines the very fabric of international law. There are three aspects to this.

### A. Abdication of the law

First, there is the danger of an abdication of the law. Law consists in norms, i.e. in prescriptions which are general and abstract and thus by definition cover future cases as well. Statements that one specific event should not be regarded as relevant amounts to stating that this particular event is *outside the realm of the law*, and—by contrast—only in the realm of politics.

Serbia and Cyprus made this point clear in the ICJ proceedings. Serbia wrote: 'If the Court were to base its opinion on a characterization of Kosovo as a situation *sui generis*, it would cease to be a court of law and would take on the role of the other principal organs of the United Nations—that of deciding how a particular situation *should be handled politically*'.[94]

If Kosovo is really a *sui generis* case, then it may be suggested that its genus would simply be defined as 'Kosovo'. This seems to be the approach taken by those advancing that this case cannot constitute a precedent. There would be just one case of 'Kosovo' and no other 'Kosovos' able to achieve independence in the future. It would be a genus containing only this one case. If this is indeed the case, then the genus of Kosovo is not a legal category *but rather an arbitrary political denomination established for purely political reasons*. To put it simply, Kosovo is considered a genus by some Powers because they have chosen not to apply international law to the case of Kosovo, and thus not to establish it as a precedent.[95]

Cyprus stated: 'The generality of the rules regulating the basic substance of international law is of as great importance as is their binding quality ... "Special cases" do not merely *dilute the quality of legality of a system: they replace it with a political element*, in which the power and commitment of individual actors becomes more significant than the legal rights that they enjoy.'[96]

---

[94] Serbia, VR (CR 2009/29, 7 December 2009, 10 a.m.), at 49, paras. 69–70 (emphasis added).
[95] Written Comment of Serbia (submitted until 17 July 2009) (*supra* note 29), at 68, para. 130 (emphasis added).
[96] Written Statement of Cyprus (submitted until 17 April 2009) (*supra* note 10), at 18–19, para. 77 (emphasis added).

The narrowness of the ICJ Opinion was criticized by scholars on exactly the same grounds: 'The Kosovo case is *thrown back again to the global political arena*, where it is supposed to be settled by political, rather than legal merits, not least due to the Court's lack of courage to tackle some substantive (legal) issues'.[97]

Of course, the acknowledgment that a given situation is outside the realm of international law need not necessarily be analytically wrong or normatively undesirable. Lawyers should not strive for over-legalization. There may be international law-free zones, and properly and beneficially so. On the other hand, it seems strange that, of all issues, a problem concerning states and boundaries, namely secession, should not have come under the purview of international law. The refusal of the 'no precedent' speakers, and of the Court, to admit that there are already international rules regulating secessions (more than the prohibition on realizing it by means of military force), amounts to a *déni de justice*.

## B. Undermining the generality of law

The attempt to catapult one single event out of the realm of the law risks undermining the very essence of law, its generality. Generality, in turn, is important, because it guarantees equal treatment, a fundamental precept of fairness.

Bruno Coppieters spelled this out as follows: 'Those who deny the relevance of the Kosovo model for other secessionist conflicts, on the basis of its unique features, *may very well end up denying that universal principles should be applied at all*, either in Kosovo or in any other similar conflict'.[98] Serbia and Cyprus raised this point, too, in the ICJ proceedings: 'Si tout cas est un "*unicum*" … dans le sens où il est différent des autres, chacun doit être apprécié à la lumière des règles de droit international général et spécial qui lui sont applicables. *Or, le droit est fait de règles abstraites qui s'appliquent à tous les membres de la société de manière égale*'.[99] Cyprus pointed out that 'the quality of the generality of the rules of international law … are at the heart of the question which the Court has been asked to address'.[100]

Finland seemed to insinuate that no abstract and general rule can be formulated on the creation of states:

[T]here are some facts that can be assessed by mechanical application of rules and other cases where many rules seem prima facie applicable and require careful attention to the facts of the situation. Or in other words, there is a difference between distributing parking tickets and legal assessment of a declaration of independence. In the former case, there is no need to examine the particularities … Independence is not like that. Here there is no routine—a recent history of the declarations of independence lists only 'more than one hundred cases', each one distinguished historically, politically and factually from the others. And here the differences are not irrelevant but at the heart of the statehood of each entity. *A State is a*

---

[97] Jovanović, (*supra* note 73), at 374 (emphasis added).

[98] Coppieters, 'The Kosovo Model: Four Lessons for the Caucasus,' *European Parliament*, 22 February 2006 (emphasis added). <http://www.europarl.europa.eu/meetdocs/2004_2009/documents/dv/afet_220206_coppieters_present_r/afet_220206_coppieters_present_rev.pdf>.

[99] Serbia, VR (CR 2009/24, 1 December 2009, 10 a.m.), at 88, para. 33 (emphasis added).

[100] *Accordance with International Law of the Unilateral Declaration of Independence in Respect of Kosovo*, ICJ Reports 2010, Written Statement of Cyprus (submitted until 17 April 2009) (note 10), at 20, para. 81.

*State because it is special*, not because it has come about by some procedural routine or some mechanical criterion. This is what those who attack the sui generis view appear to deny. As if deciding on statehood were like distributing parking tickets.[101]

This Finnish statement illustrates that there is a fine line between committing an injustice by refusing to apply a general rule (thus refusing to grant identical treatment), and safeguarding justice by being attentive to the specificity and particular features of a case. Put differently, the fair application of the general rules may well demand a differentiated treatment of situations. However, these differentiations must rely on objectively verifiable features and serve legitimate aims. The mere desire to create a legal exception would not be sufficient.

## C. Risk of double standards

Linked to the problem of generality is the following aspect: the insistence on Kosovo being a unique case is normatively undesirable because it bears the danger of creating and applying double standards. Applying double standards is pernicious for the rule of law and fairness. Again, the core element of the rule of law, namely the principle that like cases must be treated alike, is at stake. However, this principle does not require the schematically identical treatment of all situations. Rather, it hinges on the identification of relevant similarities and differences. If cases are relevantly different, then they may (and indeed must) be treated differently. So the issue boils down to identifying similarities and differences, which requires a value judgment.[102] If, for example Crimea, can and even must be properly distinguished from Kosovo, then this does not amount to applying double standards (see also Section 7).

Moreover, the principle of equal treatment cannot apply in the realm of unlawful behaviour, because this would condemn the supervising actors to perpetuating unlawfulness. Also, the principle of *tu quoque* does not apply to serious violations relating to norms on the protection of the human person (cf. the expression of this principle in Article 60(5) VCLT—and these are (*inter alia*) the ones at stake here. This means that, even if the international community's and the ICJ's (implicit) acceptance of the Kosovo secession were considered to having violated international law, this fact cannot furnish an equal treatment-type argument to do that again. There is no principle of 'precedence in illegality'.

## 7. Conclusions

In a technical sense, and independently of the unpersuasiveness of the 'no precedent' talk, there is indeed no Kosovo precedent. But the world now knows 'a Kosovo argument in international diplomacy',[103] or at least a *Kosovo rhetoric*,

---

[101]  VR (CR 2009/30, 8 December 2009, 10 a.m.), at 54–5, para. 8 (emphasis added).

[102]  See above Section 2.

[103]  Borgen (*supra* note 13), n.p.; Trifunovska (*supra* note 7), at 376; T. Fleiner, 'The Unilateral Secession of Kosovo as a Precedent in International Law', in U. Fastenrath, R. Geiger, D.-E. Kahn,

which could so far not be entirely refuted or counteracted by the 'no precedent' language.

The political intention of the states highlighting the uniqueness of Kosovo was to send a message to Catalans, Scots, Basques, Corsicans, and Quebecois that they would not be allowed to rely on the *Kosovo* case to justify their secession. But this was, as argued above, not normatively appropriate or at least has normative drawbacks (Section 6).

Moreover, the 'no precedent' talk is not even necessary in legal terms, for the following reason. If those groups are not abused and excluded from political participation (which does not seem to be the case), then they will anyway not be able to rely on the principle of remedial secession which was arguably, if only indirectly, promoted by the acknowledgment of Kosovar independence. If, however, these other groups can be reasonably qualified as a people in the sense of international law, if they are seriously abused and marginalized, if negotiations to establish internal self-determination have been seriously tried but have failed, and if the group, in a fair and free democratic procedure decides to secede, this would, exceptionally, be tolerated under international law—independently of what various actors had said about Kosovo being a precedent or not.

Likewise, the recent secession of Crimea (and its immediate fusion with Russia) can be quite easily distinguished from the Kosovar case. The unlawful threat and use of force by the neighbouring state Russia, which promoted and accompanied the breakaway of Crimea, led to a violation of the territorial integrity of Ukraine—even under the narrow terms of the Kosovo opinion.[104] A violation of that principle of territorial integrity was also inherent in the breach of several treaties which guarantee the Ukrainian territorial integrity.[105] Concomitantly, both the UN General Assembly resolution[106] and the draft Security Council resolution[107] on Crimea affirmed a commitment to the territorial integrity of Ukraine, without, however, explicitly stating that the principle had been violated. In conclusion, that territorial alteration was legally distinguishable from the establishment of an independent Kosovo: Kosovo was no 'precedent' for it.

The problem in the real world is, however, that the Kosovo argument or rhetoric (however poor it is) may still be used by a powerful state. Such a state, let us say Russia, 'is not in need of the ultimately striking legal argument—one which allows [e.g.] Russian authorities to make a case, to present arguments for the legality by

A. Paulus, S. von Schorlemer, and C. Vedder (eds), *From Bilateralism to Community Interest: Essays in Honour of Judge Bruno Simma* (OUP 2011), 877–94 (esp. at 883).

[104] ICJ, *Accordance with International Law of the Unilateral Declaration of Independence in respect of Kosovo*, Advisory Opinion of 22 July 2010, ICJ Reports 2010, 403 (*supra* note 27), paras. 80–1.

[105] Art. 1 and 2 of the Budapest memorandum of 5 December 1994; Art. 2 and 3 of the Treaty on Friendship, Cooperation, and Partnership between Ukraine and the Russian Federation of 31 May 1997.

[106] UN GA Res. A/68/L39 of 27 March 2014 'Territorial Integrity of Ukraine', para. 1: 'Affirms its commitment to the ... territorial integrity of Ukraine within its internationally recognized borders'.

[107] Security Council draft resolution (UN Doc. 189/ 2014 of 15 March 2014), para. 1: 'Reaffirms its commitment to the sovereignty, independence, unity and territorial integrity of Ukraine within its internationally recognized borders'.

further expanding the right to self-determination is already good enough for Putin to save his face while acting as a regional hegemonial power'.[108]

But—and this is the question for international lawyers—how bad may an argument get to still serve that face-saving function in international relations? Importantly, if international legal experts do not point out where the limits of an acceptable legal argument lie (assuming that there *is* a limit[109]) then a law-breaker may gain approval even by the help of an extremely bad, not tenable, pseudo-justification, at least vis-à-vis parts of his own population. So the lawyerly task is to examine (in hindsight, when new cases arise) legal factors which might constitute genuine, legally relevant and legitimate distinctions from previous cases. The futile attempt to rule out a precedential quality in either the Kosovo situation or the *Kosovo* Opinion is not necessary to achieve this, and should be omitted in order to avoid undermining the (relative) normative power of international law.

---

[108] Marxsen (*supra* note 78), 389 (footnotes ommitted).
[109] Unlike what Koskenniemi's indeterminacy argument assumes. See Koskenniemi, *From Apology to Utopia* (2nd edn, CUP 2005), at 590–1.

# PART IV
# THE ROAD AHEAD

# 16

# Some Implications of the Advisory Opinion for Resolution of the Serbia-Kosovo Conflict

*Richard Caplan\* and Stefan Wolff*

## 1. Introduction

Whatever its broader implications, the Advisory Opinion of the International Court of Justice (ICJ) regarding Kosovo's declaration of independence clearly has some bearing on prospects for resolution of the long-running conflict between Kosovo and Serbia.[1] Indeed, the Advisory Opinion could even be viewed as a political game changer, potentially if not actually, insofar as it has spurred other developments and created opportunities for state and non-state actions that have been positively consequential for resolution of the conflict. However, not all of the effects of the Advisory Opinion have necessarily been conducive to resolution of the conflict; some effects may in fact have inhibited or even militated against conflict resolution. In important respects, moreover, it may still be too early to say what the precise ramifications of the Advisory Opinion have been or are likely to be, and it is also difficult to isolate its effects from those of other associated developments.

This chapter examines the prospects for mitigation, and ultimately resolution, of the Serbia-Kosovo conflict arising from the Advisory Opinion. It explores the basis for conflict resolution inherent in an ICJ advisory opinion in general terms. It then focuses on four major developments that on balance have arguably promoted mitigation of the Serbia-Kosovo conflict to which the Advisory Opinion may have contributed, in particular: 1) the facilitation of further recognition of Kosovo statehood and its effects; 2) expanded international engagement in Serbia and Kosovo, especially on the part of the European Union; 3) shifts in domestic opinion, politics

\* Richard Caplan would like to acknowledge the support of the British Academy via the Academy's Mid-Career Fellowship scheme for his research and writing of this article.

[1] Falk, 'The *Kosovo* Advisory Opinion: Conflict Resolution and Precedent', 105 *AJIL* (2011) 1, at 50–60.

and policy in Serbia and Kosovo leading towards the normalization of relations between the two entities; and 4) the growing participation of Kosovo in the society of states.

## 2. Advisory Opinions and Conflict Resolution

When reflecting on the possible conflict-mitigating effects of the *Kosovo* Advisory Opinion, and ICJ advisory opinions in general, it is important to bear in mind the nature and intended effects of advisory opinions. While the conceivable utility of the Court as an instrument for the peaceful settlement of disputes between states is clear, the role of advisory opinions in this regard is perhaps less evident. The Court can be asked to offer its opinion on 'any legal question' put to it by the UN General Assembly, or Security Council, or other UN organs and specialized agencies authorized to do so by the General Assembly.[2] However, the advisory jurisdiction of the Court is not meant to be a form of judicial recourse for states.[3] Rather, as discussed by Nollkaemper in his contribution to this book, advisory opinions are meant to assist the General Assembly, the Security Council, and other UN bodies in the conduct of their own activities, which may include conflict management in its various manifestations.

The request for an advisory opinion may relate to a legal question actually pending between two or more states or it may be an 'abstract question' unrelated to a legal question in dispute between states.[4] With regard to the *Kosovo* Opinion, the legal question certainly pertained to a real dispute, whether between two states or between a state and a non-state entity within it, depending on one's view of Kosovo's status at the time. However, the legal question was arguably also of broad interest, as the Government of Serbia argued in its written submission to the Court, because it concerned 'respect for the Charter, in particular its purposes and principles, respect for decisions of United Nations organs, as well as compliance with norms of general international law', among other shared concerns.[5]

Notwithstanding the relevance that an advisory opinion may have to a given dispute, the Court is not governed formally by consequentialist reasoning in the formulation of its judgments. An opinion may have adverse political consequences, the Court acknowledged in its *Kosovo* Opinion, and these consequences may be apparent to the Court, but this is not a reason for the Court to refrain from offering an opinion.[6] Nor, in principle, should the political aspects of a question prevent the

---

[2] Charter of the United Nations, Art. 96; Statute of the International Court of Justice, Art. 65.

[3] *Accordance with International Law of the Unilateral Declaration of Independence in Respect of Kosovo*, Advisory Opinion (Int'l Ct. Justice, 22 July 2010), ICJ Reports 2010 403 [hereinafter the *Kosovo* Opinion], para. 33. Documents of the International Court of Justice referred to in this essay are available on the Court's website, <http://www.icj-cij.org>.

[4] Rules of the Court (1978), Art. 102.

[5] Written statement of the Government of Serbia, 15 April 2009, para. 53.

[6] *Kosovo* Opinion, para. 35. In his dissenting opinion, however, Judge Bennouna warned against attempts, in this and other cases, to exploit the Court for political purposes. See Dissenting Opinion of Judge Bennouna, para. 3.

Court from being able to execute its 'essentially judicial task' in the formulation of an opinion.[7] Whether, and to what extent, principle and practice may diverge in this regard is, however, an empirical question that lies beyond the scope of this essay.

The contribution that an advisory opinion may make to conflict mitigation depends, in part, on the stature and authority of these opinions in general. In Richard Falk's view, 'advisory opinions should be read and treated as providing the most authoritative international law assessments available, and deserve respect by affected parties and by the political organs of the United Nations, as well as scholars'.[8] Such a view, however, may be more aspirational than real. States directly implicated in an advisory opinion have frequently chosen to ignore the national policy implications of the Court's legal assessment when they have perceived their interests to be adversely affected by it.[9] States are not the only relevant parties, however: advisory opinions may also influence civil society and non-state actors who, in turn, may bring pressure to bear on governments to effect changes in their policies.

There may not always be policy implications from an advisory opinion, or the implications may not always be particularly evident. In the case of the *Kosovo* Opinion, the Court gave a very narrow interpretation of the question put to it. Specifically, the ICJ noted in its opinion that the General Assembly 'does not ask whether or not Kosovo has achieved statehood. Nor does it ask about the validity or legal effects of the recognition of Kosovo by those States which have recognized it as an independent State'. In other words, 'the Court [did] not consider... it... necessary to address such issues as whether or not the declaration has led to the creation of a State or the status of the acts of recognition'.[10]

Arguably even narrower in its answer, the Court's principal finding was that the declaration of independence that Kosovo adopted on 17 February 2008 did not breach international law or violate UN Security Council resolution 1244. Leaving aside the possible effects of that finding on state behaviour, which we discuss below, there are no obvious implications for national policy that flow from this opinion. The Court's main finding did not give a licence to states to recognize Kosovo statehood; nor did it have any implications for Serbian policy. Had the Court concluded that Kosovo's declaration of independence violated international law, however, that finding might also have entailed obligations on states not to recognize the 'illegal' situation resulting from the declaration.[11] It would almost certainly have emboldened Serbia, with the support of other UN member states, to pursue additional measures within and outside the Organization to challenge the 'illegal' declaration.

---

[7] *Legality of the Threat or Use of Nuclear Weapons in Armed Conflict*, Advisory Opinion (Int'l Ct. Justice, 8 July 1996), para. 16, ICJ Reports 1996, p. 226.

[8] Falk, *supra* note 1, at 52.

[9] As did the Soviet Union with respect to *Certain Expenses of the United Nations* (1962), and Israel with respect to *Legal Consequences of the Construction of a Wall in the Occupied Palestinian Territory* (2004).

[10] *Kosovo* Opinion, para. 51.

[11] As with *Legal Consequences of the Construction of a Wall in the Occupied Palestinian Territory* (see *supra* note 9).

## 3. Further Recognition of Kosovo and its Effects

While the Court's main finding did not give a licence to states to recognize Kosovo statehood, it arguably created a further opportunity for such action. Before the Court issued its opinion, on 22 July 2010, 69 states had recognized Kosovo. In the subsequent three years to 25 September 2013, a further 37 states extended recognition. In the absence of all relevant empirical data, we cannot know what part the Advisory Opinion may have played in the decisions of states to recognize Kosovo. A number of states—among them Oman, Niger, Côte d'Ivoire and Kuwait—invoked the Advisory Opinion as the basis for their decision to establish diplomatic relations.[12] It is reasonable to assume that in other cases, too, the opportunity created by the Advisory Opinion facilitated recognition.[13]

Recognition is, in many ways, an indicator of the success or failure of any secessionist project. However, it is not just any recognition that counts, nor is it simply a numbers game. From a political perspective, what matters ultimately is the quantity and quality of recognitions received. More than 100 states have now recognized Kosovo, among them the United States and 23 out of 28 EU member states. Given the regional and global political dynamics of, and in, the Western Balkan region, this is sufficient to secure Kosovo's survival as an independent state and, as we discuss below, its partial but increasing participation in the international community. At the same time, non-recognition, so far, by two of the five veto-wielding members of the UN Security Council, means that Kosovo has some way to go before becoming a full and equal member of the international community. In contrast, the break-away regions of South Ossetia and Abkhazia have only been recognized by one of the permanent five members of the Security Council—Russia—and a minute number of other comparatively small states.[14] While the quality of recognition by Russia, a major power, will secure the survival of both entities, their ability to participate broadly in international affairs is significantly more limited. Their survival at best takes the form of wholly dependent client states with an uncertain longer-term future.

In the case of Kosovo, recognition, including after the ICJ Opinion, has helped to consolidate independent statehood. This, in turn, has contributed to mitigation of the Serbia-Kosovo conflict and to stability in the Western Balkan region more generally. The parallel with the former Yugoslav republic of Macedonia

---

[12] Facsimiles of *notes verbales* available at <http://en.wikipedia.org/wiki/International_recognition_of_Kosovo>, accessed 14 February 2014.

[13] While the Advisory Opinion did not produce a flood of recognitions (only three states recognized Kosovo in 2010 after the Court issued its opinion), many states waited to announce their decisions on the occasion of official meetings with Kosovo diplomats.

[14] Apart from Russia, South Ossetia and Abkhazia are recognized by Nicaragua, Venezuela, Nauru, and Tuvalu. Vanuatu initially recognized Abkahzia in May 2011 but following a change in government, withdrew its recognition. In July 2013, Georgia and Vanuatu established diplomatic and consular relations, with the accompanying protocol stating that 'the Republic of Vanuatu recognizes the territorial integrity of Georgia within its internationally recognized borders, including its regions—the Autonomous Republic of Abkhazia and the Tskhinvali Region/South Ossetia'. 'Georgia, Vanuatu Establish Diplomatic Ties', *Civil Georgia* (Tbilisi: 2013).

is instructive here.[15] Macedonia, embroiled in a conflict over national identity with Greece that prevented European Community (EC) member states from extending recognition after it declared independence in September 1991, existed in a state of diplomatic limbo for nearly two years from 1991 to 1993. The lack of clarity about Macedonia's status pending recognition invited a form of 'land speculation' that arguably would have been more difficult to pursue had Macedonia been promptly and firmly constituted as a new state. Thus, in January 1992, Athens and Belgrade conducted talks about the prospect of establishing a 'joint Serbian-Greek border', while in March 1992 Branko Kostić, the vice-president of rump Yugoslavia, spoke more bluntly about the possibility of partitioning Macedonia. There were also concerns that Serbia might use the plight of the small Serbian community in Macedonia, numbering roughly 44,000 or 2 per cent of the population, as a pretext for military actions against the republic. Of course recognition had not been enough to prevent predatory advances against Bosnia-Herzegovina by Croatia and Serbia but precisely because adjustments to territory were being openly, and not so openly, discussed in the region, Macedonia's position was made even more vulnerable by its indeterminate status. As Kiro Gligorov, Macedonia's president, cautioned in June 1992: 'The EC's tendency to take a wait-and-see attitude regarding recognition… encourages all those who are interested in exploiting this unclear situation in that region or even turning to open aggression'.[16] Bulgaria, in particular, seemed to appreciate this logic and argued that recognition would discourage the use of force against Macedonia.[17]

Even more than had been the case in Macedonia, the ethnic Serb community in Kosovo—with the support of Belgrade—has exploited the ambiguity regarding Kosovo's status since the declaration of independence to challenge the extension of Pristina's authority to the northern, Serb-majority territories. When in July 2011, for instance, the Kosovo authorities sought to secure the customs posts along the border with Serbia, local Serbs blockaded the roads leading to the posts and forced the officials to retreat.[18] This confrontation—one of several—was symptomatic of the continuing disagreement over sovereignty. While the Advisory Opinion, and any recognition flowing from it, may have inflamed tensions between Belgrade and Pristina and between ethnic Serbs and Albanians within Kosovo, at least initially, over time, as we discuss below, those tensions have abated, in part as a consequence of the reality of the emergence of a sovereign, independent state of Kosovo that

[15] This paragraph is drawn from R. Caplan, *Europe and the Recognition of New States in Yugoslavia* (Cambridge University Press, 2005), Ch. 4. For a recent consideration of Macedonia in the context of Kosovo's declaration of independence and the ICJ Advisory Opinion, see Stroschein, 'Discourse in Bosnia and Macedonia on the Independence of Kosovo: When and What is a Precedent?' 65 *Europe-Asia Studies* (2013) 5, at 874–88.

[16] Cited in Ramet, 'The Macedonian Enigma', in S. P. Ramet and L. S. Adamovich (eds), *Beyond Yugoslavia: Politics, Economics, and Culture in a Shattered Community* (Westview Press, 1995), at 225.

[17] Moore, 'Diplomatic Recognition of Croatia and Slovenia', *RFE/RL Research Report*, 24 January 1992, at 14. Bulgaria was the first state to recognize Macedonia.

[18] International Crisis Group, 'Kosovo and Serbia: A Little Goodwill Could Go a Long Way', *Europe Report no. 215*, 2 February 2012, at 1.

the growing number of recognitions has made apparent.[19] While some discontent among ethnic Serbs in the Mitrovica region remains about their presumed fate of living in Kosovo, political platforms expressing such discontent have become marginalized. This became particularly evident in the context of the 2013 local elections. Although voting had to be abandoned in northern Mitrovica on 13 November 2013, due to targeted attempts by extremist factions to disrupt the elections, repeat elections on 17 November resulted in an overwhelming victory for the Serbian Civic Initiative (Gradjanska Inicijativa Srpska-GIS), a political party backed by Belgrade, which, while not (yet) accepting Kosovo's independence does not favour boycotting political engagement with Pristina either.[20]

## 4. Expanded International Engagement

The *Kosovo* Opinion has arguably been one of a number of developments that have led to expanded international engagement in Serbia and Kosovo. Since the publication of the Opinion, there has been a concerted effort by states and multilateral organizations—most notably the European Union (EU)—to shift the focus of the antagonists away from the conflict that divides them and towards the common goal of integration in the EU. On the day of the publication of the Advisory Opinion, Catherine Ashton, the EU's High Representative for Foreign Affairs and Security Policy, acknowledged that '[t]he advisory opinion opens a new phase' and declared: 'The focus should now be on the future. The future of Serbia lies in the European Union. The future of Kosovo also lies in the European Union. This is in line with the European perspective of the region and the relevant [European] Council conclusions.'[21]

Notwithstanding the fact that five of the EU's 28 member states to date have not recognized Kosovo,[22] the EU has led on efforts since the publication of the Advisory Opinion to promote cooperation between Kosovo and Serbia and the integration of both into the EU. In September 2010, the EU worked with Serbia to draft a UN General Assembly resolution, which Serbia tabled and all EU member states co-sponsored, that welcomed 'the readiness of the European Union to facilitate a process of dialogue between the parties... to promote cooperation [and] achieve progress on the path to the European Union... '.[23]

---

[19] Emblematic of this view is the statement by Serbian Prime Minister Ivica Dačić before the Serbian Parliament on 12 January 2013: 'While we debate resolutions and declarations, the process of entrenching Kosovo's independence has been going on for many years, since 1999... Serbian sovereignty is all but gone from Kosovo'. Cited in International Crisis Group, 'Serbia and Kosovo: The Path to Normalization', *Europe Report no. 223*, Brussels, 19 February 2013, at 9 (fn. 52).

[20] L. Malazogu et al, 'Integration or Isolation? Northern Kosovo in 2014 Electoral Limbo', Central European Policy Institute, Policy Brief, 13 February 2014.

[21] 'Declaration by the High Representative Catherine Ashton on behalf of the European Union on the ICJ advisory opinion', Brussels, 22 July 2010.

[22] The five 'non-recognizers' are Cyprus, Greece, Romania, Slovakia, and Spain.

[23] UN Doc. A/RES/64/298 (13 October 2010). It is worth noting that the draft resolution that Serbia first proposed condemned Kosovo's unilateral actions. See 'Serbia submits Kosovo draft to UN

The EU-facilitated dialogue envisaged in the UN resolution began on 8 March 2011, aiming 'to remove obstacles that have a negative impact on people's daily lives, to improve cooperation, and to achieve progress on the path to Europe'.[24] The Belgrade-Pristina dialogue would result in the signing of the First Agreement of Principles Governing the Normalisation of Relations, otherwise known as the Brussels Agreement, on 19 April 2013 the first major bilateral agreement between Serbia and Kosovo.[25] The details and implications of the agreement are discussed below but what it is important to appreciate at this stage is that it caps (to date) a process of rapprochement initiated and facilitated by the EU after the publication of the Advisory Opinion.

Improvements in relations between Belgrade and Pristina—as part of a broader EU-mandated political and economic reform agenda for Serbia and Kosovo—would become a key condition for the two parties to advance towards integration with the EU. Thus the European Council, on 5 December 2011, noted that the opening of accession negotiations with Serbia would be considered by the Council once the Commission had established that Serbia had achieved the necessary degree of compliance with the membership criteria, 'notably the key priority of taking steps towards a visible and sustainable improvement of relations with Kosovo'.[26] Similarly, in its 11 December 2012 Conclusions on Enlargement Strategy, the European Council stated: 'A visible and sustainable improvement in relations between Serbia and Kosovo is needed so that both can continue on their respective European paths, while avoiding that either can block the other in these efforts'.[27] On 22 April 2013—three days after the 'Brussels Agreement' was signed—the EU announced that in view of the progress achieved, the Commission was recommending to Member States that negotiations be opened with Serbia on EU accession, and with Kosovo on a Stabilization and Association Agreement (SAA).[28] On 2 May 2014, the European Commission concluded the formal negotiations for an SAA between the EU and Kosovo.

What exactly Brussels has meant by either 'a visible and sustainable improvement in relations' or the 'normalisation of relations' has never been entirely clear. This lack of clarity perhaps reflects the lack of consensus among the EU member states with respect to recognition of Kosovo. As long as member states have not been in agreement on recognition, Brussels has been unable to make it an

---

GA', *B92 News*, 28 July 2010. Serbia amended the draft under pressure from European leaders. See also J. Ker-Lindsay, *The Foreign Policy of Counter-Secession: Preventing the Recognition of Contested States* (Oxford University Press, 2012), at 136.

[24] European Union, 'EU facilitated dialogue: A positive start', press statement 7566/11, Brussels, 9 March 2011.

[25] First Agreement of Principles Governing the Normalisation of Relations, 19 April 2013, text available at <http://www.europeanvoice.com/page/3609.aspx?&blogitemid=1723>.

[26] Council of the European Union, 'Council Conclusions on Enlargement and Stabilisation and Association Process', 5 December 2011, para. 54.

[27] Council of the European Union, 'Council Conclusions on Enlargement and Stabilisation and Association Process', 11 December 2012, para. 45.

[28] European Commission, 'Serbia and Kosovo: historic agreement paves the way for decisive progress in their European perspectives', press release IP/13/347, 22 April 2013.

explicit objective or a condition for accession. Indeed, all of the EU's initiatives for this reason have had to have the appearance of being 'status neutral'. Yet at the same time, what is clear is that the EU does not want states to accede to the Union if they are implicated in any major outstanding bilateral issues, including border disputes. Another northern Cyprus scenario is completely anathema in EU enlargement and neighbourhood policy circles. In contrast to the Cypriot case, however, an amicable solution in the case of Kosovo seems more likely. On the one hand, accession is not imminent—not for Serbia and certainly not for Kosovo. Learning from the Cyprus debacle, it is unlikely that the EU would allow just one of the two to join, thus creating a powerful veto player over the accession of the other. Also, unlike Cyprus, 23 of the 28 current EU members recognize Kosovo and none recognizes the so-called Turkish Republic of Northern Cyprus. As a consequence, simultaneous admission of Kosovo and Serbia is the more likely long-term scenario.[29]

Though likely, such a scenario would not be unproblematic. As yet, there remain five EU member states that do not recognize Kosovo's statehood. As Papić has noted above, however, there is a pattern of compromise within the EU and between the EU, Serbia, and Kosovo. In the immediate aftermath of the *Kosovo* Opinion, all 28 member states of the Union agreed on the need for further dialogue and eventually the EU facilitated bilateral negotiations that paved the way towards normalization, which in turn created the opportunities for both Kosovo and Serbia to make further progress in their relations with the EU: Serbia started accession negotiations with the EU in January 2014, while Kosovo began negotiations on a Stabilization and Association Agreement (SAA) with the EU in October 2013—a necessary step along the way to membership negotiations.

Although clearly positive in one sense, this also underlines the rather differential state of 'proximity' to membership. Serbia is far more advanced in its capacity to meet the requirements of EU membership than Kosovo. While it may take Serbia several years yet to satisfy the technical requirements, Kosovo has significantly more work to do ahead of the Commission even recommending the opening of accession negotiations. This, then, poses an immediate problem of another kind: with Kosovo lagging behind, Serbian accession is likely to be delayed, not because of its own degree of readiness, but because of factors largely beyond its own control. As a consequence, rather than acting as a conflict-mitigating process, accession could potentially aggravate tensions between the sides anew, increasing Serbian resentment of its southern neighbour and thus limiting any prospects of genuine reconciliation between them.

---

[29]  On the issue of EU enlargement policy vis-à-vis Serbia and Kosovo, see, for example, Kostovicova, 'When Enlargement Meets Common Foreign and Security Policy: Serbia's Europeanization, Visa Liberalization and the Kosovo Policy', 66 *Europe-Asia Studies* (2014) 1, at 67–87; Tannam, 'The EU's Response to the International Court of Justice's Judgment on Kosovo's Declaration of Independence', 65 *Europe-Asia Studies* (2013) 5, at 946–64, and Vachudova, 'EU Leverage and National Interests in the Balkans: The Puzzles of Enlargement Ten Years On', 52 *JCMS: Journal of Common Market Studies* (2014) 1, at 122–38.

With this in mind, it would be worthwhile reconsidering the simultaneous accession scenario. One option would be to avoid a scenario in which a future Serbian government could exercise a veto over a subsequent accession by Kosovo, either by including a relevant clause in the accession treaty for Serbia or by a Council Decision on membership for both entities at the time of Serbia's accession with the proviso of Kosovo successfully completing its own negotiations.

Another option would be to treat simultaneous accession to the EU by Serbia and Kosovo as part of a broader and more comprehensive regional approach by the EU. In other words, the membership perspective of all Western Balkan countries could be realized simultaneously, in a way similar to the 2004 accession of ten Central and Eastern European countries. In such a scenario, Serbia and Kosovo would become members of the Union simultaneously with Bosnia and Herzegovina, Macedonia, and Albania. This would, in all likelihood, further delay Serbian accession beyond the point at which the country would be individually ready for membership but it would create a more complex pattern of negotiations in which singling out just one country responsible for the delay would be difficult. That said, such an approach has the potential of reinforcing a Serbian sense of victimhood that in the past has fuelled nationalistic myths in the country, namely that Serbia, since the days of King Lazar and the battle on Kosovo polje, has always suffered at the hands of its neighbours and has been short-changed by the great powers of the day.[30]

Given, in particular, the already existing complications of the EU's relations with Macedonia (and especially with existing member states Greece and Bulgaria in relation to the name issue and related aspects of Macedonian identity), and to a lesser extent Albania, an alternative to this comprehensive accession approach would be to focus on Kosovo, Serbia, and Bosnia and Herzegovina only. This approach could simultaneously offer additional incentives to Serbia to adopt a more flexible approach towards Kosovo in return for seeing its compatriots in Republika Srpska also join the EU as part of Bosnia and Herzegovina.

Regardless of which, if any, of these approaches will eventually be adopted, Serbia and Kosovo will need to find a mutually acceptable solution to resolving their relationship prior to possible future EU accession, simultaneous or otherwise. One model of relations that would fit such an approach, and that has been suggested as a possible way to square the diplomatic circle, is that of West Germany (the Federal Republic of Germany, FRG) and East Germany (the German Democratic Republic, GDR) from 1972/3 to 1990.[31] Although neither state recognized the other—and the FRG claimed to represent all of Germany—the two states, in the so-called *Grundlagenvertrag* (Basic Treaty), agreed to respect one another's sovereignty, independence, and territorial integrity. Together with the Four Powers Agreement on

---

[30] See, for example, Morus, 'The SANU Memorandum: Intellectual Authority and the Constitution of an Exclusive Serbian "People"', 4 *Communication and Critical/Cultural Studies* (2007) 2, at 142–65; Hastings, 'Special Peoples', 5 *Nations and Nationalism* (1999) 3, at 381–96; Bieber, 'Nationalist Mobilization and Stories of Serb Suffering: The Kosovo Myth from 600th Anniversary to the Present', 6 *Rethinking History* (2002) 1, at 95–110.

[31] International Crisis Group, *supra* note 19, at 5.

the status of Berlin, this bilateral arrangement between the two German states paved the way for their concurrent admission to the United Nations in September 1973. At that time, West Germany also officially renounced the Hallstein Doctrine of being the sole legitimate representative of the German nation (*Alleinvertretungsanspruch*), which enabled East Germany to join other international organizations as a member state. Such a model made it possible for both states to develop cooperative relations while maintaining their otherwise mutually incompatible notions of one another's legal status.

The 'German model', however, would only resolve the bilateral dispute over recognized statehood between Serbia and Kosovo; it does not resolve issues related to the status of Serbs in Kosovo and the presumptive role of Belgrade as their protector. While this is an issue to which we return again in the next section, it is also worth noting that, although intuitively appealing, the German model is not the only one that exists. Taiwan, recognized by only some 20 current UN member states, nonetheless enjoys a significant degree of both independence and participation in international affairs, predicated, however, on China's tacit agreement and a policy of non-retaliation against countries that trade with Taiwan, recognize its passports as valid travel documents, or accept students into their own higher education institutions.[32]

The situation is similar to northern Cyprus, whose residents benefit from relatively flexible travel arrangements and the ability to hold Turkish and (for the most part) Cypriot passports. The so-called Green Line Regulation that came into effect following the accession of Cyprus to the EU recognizes that the EU *acquis communautaire* is not currently enforced or enforceable north of the Green Line and offers a number of exemptions allowing some goods to be traded without imposing tariffs and northern Cypriots to work in the south.[33] There is a UN presence on both sides of the Green Line and in the buffer zone, and the EU has established a Programme Support Office in the northern part of Nicosia, which runs a variety of aid programmes in support of the residents of northern Cyprus.

Similarly, the Transnistrian region of Moldova remains outside the full control of the Government of Moldova, yet arrangements have been found for residents to enjoy relatively unimpeded freedom of movement, for companies to benefit from the Autonomous Trade Preferences that the EU has extended to Moldova,[34] and for international and regional organizations, such as the EU, OSCE and UNDP to have a presence in the region and run various development and humanitarian programmes and initiatives there.

---

[32] For a discussion of the two German states in the context of Kosovo's UN accession, see Efevwerhan, 'Kosovo's Chances of UN Membership: A Prognosis', 4 *GJIL* (2012) 1, at 93–130. On Taiwan, see, for example, Zaid, 'Taiwan: It Looks Like It, It Acts Like It, But Is It a State? The Ability to Achieve a Dream through Membership in International Organizations', 32 *New Eng. L. Rev.* (1998) 3, at 805–18.

[33] See Council Regulation (EC) No 866/2004 of 29 April 2004 on a regime under Article 2 of Protocol No 10 of the Act of Accession as amended by Council Resolution (EC) No 293/2005 of 17 February 2005.

[34] See Council Regulation (EC) No 55/2008 of 21 January 2008 introducing autonomous trade preferences for the Republic of Moldova and amending Regulation (EC) No 980/2005 and Commission Decision 2005/924/EC.

Dividing lines in other conflicts, however, are less porous. Contacts across the Administrative Boundary Lines in South Ossetia and Abkhazia are far more limited because of fears and resistance on all sides. Virtually no contact, other than the exchange of sniper fire, exists between Azerbaijan and Nagorno-Karabakh. In all three cases, there is no proper presence of regional or international organizations, and travel by their officials is regularly curtailed.

Compared to all of these cases, Kosovo has already achieved an internationally far more recognized status—both in the sense of actually being recognized by more than 100 UN member states and in terms of inward (and outward—see below) international engagement. This has been facilitated, albeit not solely, by the ICJ Advisory Opinion. By not framing its opinion in a way that would make engagement with Kosovo seem an infringement of international legal standards (i.e., by explicitly not pronouncing itself on this issue), the ICJ has enabled a degree of pragmatism on the part of Kosovo and Serbian leaders, as well as their regional and international partners. Short of any major change in attitude, this pragmatism has become self-sustaining and self-reinforcing and has also allowed for a gradual shift in the domestic politics of independence in Serbia and Kosovo to which we turn in the next section.

## 5. Shifts in Domestic Opinion, Politics and Policy

The Advisory Opinion, along with other subsequent developments, has arguably also contributed to shifts in domestic opinion, politics and policy in Serbia and Kosovo, and elsewhere. In the case of Serbia and Kosovo, it has led gradually towards improved relations between the two entities. However, the shifts have been uneven—especially among the Serbs—and the improvement in relations similarly has been only partial.

In some important respects the Advisory Opinion changed nothing in Serbian policy and public opinion. Serbia was and, following the ICJ opinion, has remained adamant in its refusal to recognize Kosovo's 'unilaterally proclaimed independence'. (This particular formulation has been interpreted to mean that Serbia might be willing to accept a *negotiated* independence that accommodated its interests and concerns.)[35] The Serbian Government's position enjoys broad public support in Serbia and among Kosovo Serbs. However, in an apparent effort to strengthen its prospects for accession to the EU, the Serbian Government in mid-January 2013 proposed, and the Serbian Parliament endorsed, a platform for talks with Pristina which, in a radical departure from the past, affirmed Kosovo's territorial integrity (within Serbia) and Kosovo's jurisdiction over the entire territory, thus arguably removing one option—partition of Kosovo—from consideration.[36]

Kosovo's northern Serbs—less numerous but more concentrated than the Kosovo Serb population south of the Ibar River—have tended to be more hardline

---

[35] International Crisis Group, *supra* note 19, at 10.
[36] For a discussion of the platform, see ibid., at 8–9.

than Belgrade. They organized a referendum on 14–15 February 2012 in the four predominantly Serb municipalities in which the overwhelming majority responded negatively to the question 'Do you accept the institutions of the so-called Republic of Kosovo?'[37] In an ironic twist of fate, northern Serbs have even mooted the possibility of a declaration of independence from Kosovo, claiming to find support for such an option in the ICJ advisory opinion.[38] A majority of northern Serbs also chose to boycott Kosovo-wide local elections held on 3 November 2013, although it is noteworthy that for the first time since Kosovo's 2008 declaration of independence the northern Serb-majority municipalities—with encouragement from Belgrade—agreed to participate in the elections at all.[39]

An even bigger shift occurred with the signing of the First Agreement of Principles Governing the Normalization of Relations by Prime Minister Ivica Dačić of Serbia and Prime Minister Hashim Thaçi of Kosovo in Brussels on 19 April 2013. The agreement is concerned largely with matters relating to the governance of northern Kosovo, and applies a number of principles of territorial and/or community self-governance that have been long-established in conflict management theory and policy. It allows for the establishment of an 'association/community' comprising the four northern Serb-majority municipalities, which Pristina had long resisted out of concern that such an association would constitute the embryo of a future breakaway entity. It also allows for the integration of the local police and judiciary—heretofore under Belgrade's control—within Pristina's jurisdiction. The northern Kosovo Serbs initially rejected the agreement but it remains to be seen whether their opposition will prevent implementation now that Belgrade has basically agreed to cede authority to Pristina. To date Belgrade and Pristina have achieved agreements on a number of practical matters ranging from the recognition of diplomas, car insurance and civil registries to police integration and the functioning of the justice system.

## 6. Growing Participation of Kosovo in the Society of States

Kosovo has sought, since its declaration of independence, to participate as widely as possible in the society of states, while Serbia has tried to limit its ability to do so. Naturally, these diametrically opposed strategies have aggravated tensions between the two entities at times. From Kosovo's perspective, participation in the international community as a recognized sovereign, independent state constitutes an affirmation of its status. Serbia's view is not different on this point, yet, rather than seeing Kosovo's participation on this basis as a positive development, it perceives it as further undermining Serbia's sovereignty and territorial integrity.

---

[37] 'Referendum in north: 99.74% say "No" to Priština', *B92 News*, 16 February 2012.

[38] International Crisis Group, *supra* note 19, at 11.

[39] 'Elections municipales sous tension dans la partie serbe de Mitrovica, au Kosovo', *Le Monde*, 3–4 November 2013.

The ICJ Advisory Opinion has arguably facilitated Kosovo's growing participation in the society of states, and to that extent it could be said to be laying
the foundations for mitigation and resolution of the conflict between Serbia and
Kosovo in the longer term provided that Belgrade gradually changes its stance.
As we discussed in the preceding sections, there are international precedents for
such a change in policy that relies on pragmatic cooperation between the two
sides. The continuing normalization of relations between Belgrade and Pristina
through the EU-facilitated dialogue is an indication that such an approach may
gain further traction.

Participation in the society of states takes many forms, most prominently membership in multilateral organizations. Thus far Kosovo has become a member of
the International Monetary Fund and the World Bank—both in 2009, prior to the
*Kosovo* Opinion—and the European Bank for Reconstruction and Development
(EBRD). Membership in these organizations, however, is open to entities that
are not necessarily sovereign, independent states. Kosovo is also a member of
a number of smaller regional organizations, including the Council of Europe
Development Bank (CEB), the Venice Commission and the US-Adriatic Charter.
As a consequence of an agreement brokered by the EU in 2012 between Belgrade
and Pristina—known as the 'asterisk agreement'—the Pristina Government has
been able to represent itself in regional fora as 'Kosovo*', where the asterisk is
linked to a footnote that reads: 'This designation is without prejudice to positions
on status, and is in line with UNSC 1244 and the ICJ Opinion on the Kosovo
declaration of independence'.[40] The prospect of Kosovo joining the most important international and regional organizations—notably the United Nations, the
Council of Europe (CoE), the North Atlantic Treaty Organization (NATO), and
the Organization for Security and Cooperation in Europe (OSCE)—remains
unpromising as long as Serbia persists in its objections.

While a Serbian softening on Kosovo membership in any of these international organizations is unlikely anytime soon or outside a more comprehensive
settlement, this does not exclude near-term options for Kosovo's broader outward
engagement with the international community in the form of other multilateral
organizations and individual member states. For example, it is possible for states
to participate in almost all specialized UN organizations without being a full
member of the UN itself. Here, again, the German model is instructive: West
Germany joined most specialized organizations in the 1950s and 1960s and pursued a policy of so-called active non-membership.

Taiwan has also obtained a range of memberships in international and regional
organizations, including the World Trade Organization and the International
Olympic Committee, the Asia-Pacific Economic Cooperation, the Asian
Development Bank and, not to be belittled in this day and age, the Governmental
Advisory Committee of the Internet Cooperation for Assigned Names and

---

[40] Arrangements Regarding Regional Representation and Cooperation, 24 February 2012. To date
the regional fora in which Kosovo participates are the Regional Cooperation Council (RCC) and the
Energy Community of South East Europe (ECSEE).

Numbers. Because of Chinese resistance it has failed, however, to join any significant UN specialized organizations, including, despite numerous attempts so far, the World Health Organization.

Regardless of its lack of full UN membership, Kosovo nonetheless has the capacity to enter into treaties with other states or organizations. In the same way that the EU (and all its member states) concluded an agreement with Taiwan on visa-free travel, Kosovo is similarly likely to enter into such and other arrangements with the EU. This is clearly evident already in negotiations between Kosovo and the EU on a Stabilization and Association Agreement (SAA) that began at the end of October. While Serbia is more advanced in its contractual relations with the EU (the SAA was negotiated between 2005 and 2008, signed in 2008, then ratified by Serbia and all EU member states, and eventually entered into force on 1 September 2013), this is unlikely to constitute a major roadblock for Kosovo. As it is highly improbable that the EU would accept anything but a concurrent accession of both states at some future point, both states have an interest in Kosovo catching up quickly.

Closer and more contractually-based relations between Kosovo and the EU are not in themselves a pathway to broader international recognition for Kosovo. However, much like the ICJ Opinion, they are part of a broader set of factors that help consolidate Kosovo statehood. As long as Kosovo uses these consolidation gains responsibly, and reciprocates Serbian acquiescence with more flexibility at the domestic and bilateral level in relation to its treatment of Serbs in Kosovo, the more likely is it that Kosovo's participation in the society of states will grow further. In other words, not only are Kosovo's inward and outward international engagements closely linked, but they also cannot be analysed in isolation from the important domestic dimensions of the politics of Kosovo independence in both states.

## 7. Conclusion

It would be a gross overstatement to claim that the effects of the *Kosovo* Opinion have by themselves altered the political landscape to such an extent that Kosovo is on the fast track to universal recognition of its independent statehood and full membership in the United Nations and other regional and international organizations. At the same time, part of what has been accomplished—more engagement by international actors in Kosovo, shifts in Serbian and Kosovar bilateral relations, and growing participation by Kosovo in the society of states—is clearly attributable, in part, to the ICJ Advisory Opinion.

As we have argued in this chapter, the *Kosovo* Opinion lowered the risks for regional and international organizations and their individual member states in becoming more engaged with Kosovo and allowing Kosovo greater levels of participation in international affairs. The increasing inward and outward modes of engagement have so far mutually reinforced each other, and this is likely to continue as long as neither Kosovo nor Serbia attaches status questions to such engagement. This constitutes a highly pragmatic approach by all involved.

Although perhaps not explicitly modelled on similar cases, such as the relationships between the two German states during the Cold War or to a lesser extent those between China and Taiwan, the *Kosovo* Opinion has made it possible for the two disputants, other states, and regional and international organizations to acknowledge an existing status quo and work towards making it more stable and sustainable. This is in sharp but welcome contrast to other cases, such as Cyprus and the multiple conflicts in the post-Soviet space—notably Transnistria in Moldova, Abkhazia and South Ossetia in Georgia, and Nagorno-Karabakh in Azerbaijan—precisely because in these cases status and international engagement are more overtly and controversially linked.

Crucially, though, the pragmatism that we have noted is closely connected to shifts in domestic policy and public opinion. The bilateral and regional and international 'normalization' that has characterized the situation concerning Kosovo over the past several years, due in significant measure to EU mediation between the sides, has gradually facilitated and conditioned these shifts. Thus, the April 2013 agreement between Belgrade and Pristina is a complex deal that linked improved constitutional possibilities for Serbs in Kosovo to the beginning of negotiations by Kosovo on a Stabilization and Association Agreement with the EU, and the entry into force of the Stabilization and Association Agreement for Serbia, and the EU's decision to formally open accession negotiations.

At the time of writing, six years after Kosovo's declaration of independence in February 2008, we face, in this part of the Western Balkans, a considerably improved and much more stable situation than at almost any time since the beginning of the former Yugoslavia's disintegration more than 20 years ago. The *Kosovo* Opinion has arguably been an important catalyst by creating conducive conditions for the positive developments since July 2010, which can perhaps be best described as sustained, and hopefully sustainable, pragmatism by Kosovar and Serbian leaders and their European and international partners.

# 17

# Old Problems, Fresh Frameworks:

## Kosovo, Serbia and the EU—the Virtue of a 'Free Territory'

*James Gow* *

## 1. Introduction

The International Court of Justice (ICJ) Advisory Opinion, delivered in July 2010, did little to change the situation regarding Kosovo. It rather left things exactly where they were, having layered a new grey zone upon past ones. This was a long-running statehood and sovereignty problem in need of new thinking that would dissolve some aspects of the problem and provide the conceptual and political innovation necessary for a fresh framework. The challenge for all concerned remained how to get out of the cycle of moving from one grey area to another, to another, to yet another. Kosovo spent a decade under UN formal administration. There was an effort to change that to being under EU administration. That failed and went into a messy period, which ended with a contested declaration of independence that, itself, just substituted one grey area for another. If clarification was genuinely sought when the UN General Assembly (UNGA) tasked the ICJ, following a Serbian question, to offer an advisory opinion, the outcome certainly did nothing to clarify matters.

The trend remained unchanged because the ICJ was no better placed than any other actor to address the core political question: how to reconcile Serbia's rejection of Kosovo's unilateral (but coordinated) declaration of independence with that declaration itself. How was it possible to solve this Catch-22 question and, so, to square the Kosovo circle? To do so meant finding a way forward that would allow agreement, in effect, to disagree. Such an agreement would have to allow Kosovo and the International Steering Group of states that took responsibility for super-vising Kosovo's independence and declared it fully sovereign, three weeks after its declaration of independence, as well as the 23 EU Member States recognizing

* The present contribution benefits from the assistance, advice, or research of Milena Michalski, Ernst Dijxhoorn, Julia Himmrich, Bekim Blakaj, Zoran Pajić and James Ker-Lindsay. It is based, in part, on research conducted for a project funded by the Arts and Humanities Research Council's Beyond Text Programme, 'Pictures of Peace and Justice', AHRC Award AH/H015566/1. It was completed under a Leverhulme Trust Major Research Fellowship on 'The Mladic Trial and the Legacy of the Yugoslavia Tribunal'.

Kosovo as independent (originally 22, but increased after Croatia's accession in July 2013), to maintain their perspective, on the one hand. On the other, it would have to allow Serbia, Russia, the remaining five EU members, and others to stick to their opposite perspective.

A more creative alternative was required, which would permit everyone to reach an agreement that, while also allowing different parties to agree to disagree on key points, at the same time, would clear the international blockage on Kosovo. While this would not completely remove the grey to grey movement, let alone do so immediately, it would provide the framework in which that could, eventually, happen—and possibly sooner, rather than later, and, certainly, faster than any alternative would. The purpose of the present contribution is to offer such a framework, setting out a version of what the Kosovo situation needed to move towards resolution. The substantive essence of that idea, as argued in the present study, would be to create an EU 'Free Territory'—the EU Kosovo Free Territory. The remainder of this article develops what this should have been. The first section sets the ICJ Advisory Opinion in the context of Kosovo's moving from one grey area to another, necessary to an understanding of what follows, although the ICJ ruling is a trigger for this book as a whole. Second, it briefly reviews options discussed or advocated in terms of resolving the Kosovo conundrum, as well as international engagement and peacebuilding. Finally, the article introduces the notion of the Kosovo Free Territory, situating it in wider contexts for statehood arrangements, including those within the EU, and explaining how adoption of the EU Kosovo Free Territory concept would benefit all concerned—Kosovo, the EU, and beyond.

## 2. The ICJ

In an attempt to escape the impasse, the ICJ was invoked. In October 2008, the UN General Assembly asked the International Court of Justice for an advisory opinion regarding Kosovo's declaration of independence in February that year. The request followed Serbia's bringing the matter to the General Assembly, seeking a legal view that would support its political lobbying there to persuade members of the Assembly not to recognize Kosovo as having independent international personality. At that stage, 48 countries had recognized Kosovo—and, by the time of the ICJ Advisory Opinion in July 2010, the total had become 69. Kosovo sought the recognition of 100 members of the UN, as a 'strategic goal',[1] which, it seemed to think, would confer legitimacy—and it certainly resulted in Kosovo's being given its own 'country' status by global businesses, such as Facebook.[2] It was probably thought that this figure, representing a clear majority of the UN General Assembly's membership,

---

[1] *Balkan Insight*, 25 December 2012, available at <http://www.balkaninsight.com/en/article/kosovo-one-step-closer-to-100-recognitions> (accessed 30 April 2014).

[2] *The New York Times*, 12 December 2013, available at <http://www.nytimes.com/2013/12/13/world/europe/kosovo-seeking recognition-follows-the-crowd-to-facebook-social-media.html> (accessed 30 April 2014).

would also offer sufficient legitimacy to support an application for membership—but membership would also require the support of Russia and China in the Security Council, which would not be forthcoming, as the situation stood. Some judged that it might be possible for Kosovo to overcome these vetoes, if the General Assembly could adopt a 'Uniting for Peace' type resolution. Using legal opinion, the Assembly could 'determine' whether or not the veto right had been 'abused' and, if the answer were affirmative, it could 'proceed with the admission without any recommendation by the Council'.[3] Although a veto would mean that this would still not result in actual membership, it would create a context in which moral legitimacy had been established.[4] Serbia therefore posited the following question, which the General Assembly referred to the Court: 'Is the unilateral declaration of independence by the Provisional Institutions of Self-Government of Kosovo in accordance with international law?' The question Serbia posed was very peculiar in legal terms and open to several different interpretations, with the Court choosing to read it quite narrowly even though Serbian submissions to the Court argued that it should be interpreted broadly.[5]

The opinion (supported by a 10–4 majority) was very specific and focused—including the way it made clear the areas it did not cover.[6] The chief finding of the Court, following the path of narrowly interpreting the question, was that there was nothing in general international law, or the specific bodies of law relating to Kosovo, that would prohibit Kosovo's declaration of independence. In this sense, the declaration itself was not in breach of international law, as there was no relevant law to breach. This was essentially a 'permissive' interpretation of the law—that which is not prohibited is allowed. However, one of the members of the Court, Judge Simma, argued in his declaration that because something was not explicitly prohibited does not mean that it was in accordance with the law. Taking a broader reading of the situation and the law, he suggested that the Court should have explored whether the declaration as a state-founding activity was in line with other aspects of international law, in particular, respect for sovereignty, and whether only a positive right to declare independence, possibly expressed in 'deeper analysis of whether the principle of self-determination or any other rule (perhaps expressly mentioning remedial secession) permit or even warrant independence (via secession) of certain peoples/territories', and would properly be 'in accordance' with international law.[7]

---

[3] Judge Alvarez at the ICJ in 1950, quoted by David I. Efewerhan, who develops other parts of this argument; Efewerhan, 'Kosovo's Chances of UN Membership: A Prognosis', *Goettingen Journal of International Law*, 4 (2012) 1, p. 107.

[4] The '100' figure was eventually reached in 2013 without triggering any activity of this kind, let alone a formal application by Pristina.

[5] Marko Milanović, 'Kosovo Advisory Opinion Preview', *EJIL-Talk*. Available at <http://www.ejil-talk.org/kosovo-advisory-opinion-preview/> (accessed 17 December 2010). See also the contributions by Marko Milanović and Daniel Mueller to this volume.

[6] International Court of Justice, *Accordance with International Law of the Unilateral Declaration of Independence in Respect of Kosovo, Advisory Opinion*, ICJ Reports 2010, 403, 22 July 2010.

[7] International Court of Justice, *supra* note 6, 'Declaration of Judge Simma', p. 480, available at <http://www.icj-cij.org/docket/files/141/15993.pdf> (accessed 30 April 2014).

The Court went out of its way to make it clear that it was giving a narrow answer to a narrow question and, despite Judge Simma's view on the law and the 'quality' of the opinion being offered,[8] that it was steering an essentially political course focused on the question itself—even if its answer inevitably transformed the question slightly by interpreting 'in accordance' as meaning 'not prohibited'. In making the limits of its opinion clear, the Court explicitly noted significant questions not addressed. Thus, the question, narrowly interpreted and answered, left open major issues regarding Kosovo's legal situation, which would be relevant for states considering recognizing Kosovo and for discussions of the Advisory Opinion in the UN General Assembly in September 2010.

Even though the initial reaction to the Advisory Opinion was that Serbia had lost out and the reaction in Serbia itself was generally negative,[9] in fact what happened was that it very strongly reinforced the status quo. One additional state recognized Kosovo's independence, while the UNGA discussed the case. By the end of 2010, despite the ICJ Opinion and the subsequent General Assembly discussion, that number had only crept up to 72. Over the next three years, this would creep up by a further 18. So despite the sense that the Advisory Opinion went against Serbia, the actual result was essentially just to throw everything back into the political realm, particularly that of the UN General Assembly. The chief outcome was agreement between Serbia and the EU to pursue dialogue between Pristina and Belgrade on mutual relations (see below).[10] The consequence was to have a set of political and security questions come up yet again: *plus ça change, plus c'est la même chose*. From being stuck in one bit of mud and escaping into another bit of mud, and from that one into quicksand, at each stage, there was no real sense of moving forward—even if some tiny increments of change slowly accrued. It is in this context that considering options for Kosovo became all the more imperative.

## 3. The Options for Kosovo

Discussion surrounding the EU's role in Kosovo's declaration of independence and beyond has fallen into two categories. One of these focuses on the circumstances of Kosovo's independence and the legal-political issues surrounding EULEX in relation to the UN mission formally in place and in charge in Kosovo.[11] The other focuses on the practical aspects of EULEX's role and the prospects for its mission in complicated and compromised circumstances. These included the prevailing political culture in Kosovo,[12] and friction with the UN mission on the ground,

---

[8] Ibid. p. 481.    [9] See Tatjana Papić's discussion of this reaction in Chapter 12.
[10] 'Historical agreement with EU', *B92 News*, 9 September 2010, available at <http://www.b92.net/eng/news/politics.php?yyyy=2010&mm=09&dd=09&nav_id=69566> (accessed 6 June 2014).
[11] Warbrick, 'Kosovo: the Declaration of Independence', 57, *ICLQ* (2008); Wet, 'The Governance of Kosovo: Security Council resolution 1244 and the Establishment and Functioning of Eulex', 103 *AQIL* (2009) 1; Visoka and Bolton, 'The Complex Nature and Implications of International Engagement after Kosovo's Independence', 13 *Civil Wars* (2011) 2.
[12] Pond, 'The EU's Test in Kosovo', 31 *The Washington Quarterly* (2008) 1.

as Kosovo moved from transitional administration to transitional statehood, but remained in an indeterminate, messy situation in which some countries recognized Kosovo's independence, yet the majority did not.[13] The only exception to this pattern was an attempt to tackle this latest version of the Kosovo question by Spyros Economides, James Ker-Lindsay and Dimitris Papadimitriou.[14] This was a nice effort to engage with the thorny question of what to do about Kosovo, even if, in the end, there was found to be no satisfactory option. The following paragraphs will review the four options they considered and the ways in which they were found wanting.

Option one was, in effect, more of the same. This would mean continuing with things as they were. The authors labelled this 'maintained independence'. What it meant, in effect, was that this form of muddling through was familiar and the parties were all accustomed to it. But, as the authors pointed out, quite rightly, this model was probably not sustainable forever. Of course, many situations were sustainable, in the medium and long term. But they depended on commitment and political will (often conditioned by fear of what another actor might do). Once actors have a stake in a situation, it is very difficult to walk away from it. Therefore, for all those questions of 'it might not last' there is always a contrary perspective that judges how it is always very difficult to leave a commitment. One way or another, critics and publics would question the course of action. The longer a condition endured, the more likely that people would seriously question spending large amounts of money and expending other resources on a 'going nowhere' stalemate. 'More of the same' was, in effect, a holding operation. After a while, people would begin to question holding operations. Had Kosovo been a contest within the Cold War, or an equivalent situation, there would have been a firm commitment to hold on to it, at all costs. But, if the question concerned, as it did in reality, a little province in South Eastern Europe, costing an enormous amount of money and generating a great big headache, then questions were inevitable. This option, which Economides et al. correctly assessed, maintained the grey zone surrounding Kosovo and did nothing to break out of it. The one really positive thing about it was that this option could buy time. With time, solutions can sometimes emerge.

The second idea covered in the four options was enforcement of the Ahtisaari plan. It is hard not to have a sense that this option was a sort of feeble 'straw man' to be knocked down. The idea at the core of it—going back to the Ahtisaari plan and enforcing it—was impossible in practice. Using Ahtisaari as a basis for development was feasible but implementing Ahtisaari was simply impossible. It needed UN Security Council endorsement and an enforcement resolution under Chapter VII of the UN Charter to make it work in the way that it should. These would not be forthcoming—if they were, then other problems would also disappear. Ahtisaari enforcement was not, therefore, a genuine possibility at all. This would be all the more the case if the big question of 'who implements' were added. Would it be

---

[13] Gow, 'Kosovo—the Final Frontier? From Transitional Administration to Transitional Statehood', 3 *Journal of Intervention and Statebuilding* (2009) 2.
[14] Economides et al., 'Kosovo: Four Futures', 5 *Survival* (2010) 5, at 112.

Pristina, Brussels, or back to the UN? Who would implement and under whose authority would major issues be settled?

The third option was partition, or boundary changes. This was something that had been very widely discussed and aired by commentators. Even people in senior and prominent positions could be heard, privately at least, murmuring that this might be the outcome in the end as the complete concurrence among influential serving and recently retired defence officials made very clear in focus group research: 'the solution is 11%, all it needs is 11%.'[15] Although there was not, however, any clear sense of what this meant—it was clear that Serbia needed to be 'given' something tangible—a portion of Kosovo (presumably north of the Ibar) that could ease the loss of Kosovo. It was agreed that this would probably take a long time and that 'for now it is necessary to be pragmatic and find a way around things: we are always pragmatic—if they don't have a name tag, we won't have a name tag, we want to find ways to talk and be pragmatic, to find ways round, to let things develop'.[16] However, the astute analytical judgement here was to recognize that the simple idea just to divide communities by drawing a line was rarely, if ever, anything like simple in practice, as confronted by the continuing rolling question of what happens to various sub-groups, once a territorial partition occurs. There were three main factors that militated very strongly against partition in Kosovo.[17] The first of these was that the Ahtisaari proposals and the constitution that went with them very strongly and explicitly underlined the territorial integrity of Kosovo, and that nothing should be allowed to partition it, a position backed by Kosovo and US officials. The second major hindrance to thinking on partition was that any move towards further partition would have precedential effect. This is why international society is based on the principle of mutual recognition between sovereigns, and the principle of not breaching that principle and the territorial integrity it implies, because the moment anyone starts to breach it,[18] they set a precedent for more generalized breach. In practice, while Kosovo's declaration of independence had already put this issue on the agenda, any new steps would mean designating completely new borders, based on ethnic political community, which would provoke difficulties around the world and, more acutely, in the immediate region of the Western Balkans, where the precedential effect would be felt directly on Bosnia and Herzegovina, and also on Macedonia, immediately risking regional stability. Finally, an agreement on partition seems highly unlikely, on the surface, because it would run counter to Serbia's policy of maintaining the high ground of legality and principle, on which it was backed by Russia and China, in particular. Of course, it must be recognized that Serbia could find a situation in which partition appeared to be an acceptable outcome and in which it could accept the loss of Kosovo, including the historic and symbolic cultural sites and founding places

---

[15] 'Pictures of Peace and Justice: Documentation, Evident and Impact of Visual Material in Relation to International War Crimes Prosecutions', Beyond Text Programme, Arts and Humanities Research Council, Award AH/H015566/1 PPJ FG011, Belgrade, April 2011, (hereafter PPJ FG011).

[16] PPJ FG011.

[17] These factors receive more developed discussion in Gow, *supra* note 13, at 250–1.

[18] Hedley Bull, *The Anarchical Society: A Study of Order in World Politics* (Macmillan, 1997).

of the Serbian Church, by gaining something to assuage its dignity. Some Serbian leaders might well privately harbour this notion. Whatever its attractions and challenges for Serbian actors, as already noted, any partition would also have to overcome Kosovo and US rejection of any move to breach what they regarded as Kosovo's territorial integrity (a matter of considerable irony in Serbian eyes, given Washington's role in fostering Kosovo's declaration of independence)—although Belgrade's perspective on Crimea and eastern Ukraine (as with Moscow's) did not cohere with its view on Kosovo. Thus, although events drove the issue of partitioning Kosovo onto the agenda, very strong factors served to block moves in that direction, even it were judged to be desirable. Neither the US, nor any other actor, could stand in the way of agreement between the two parties at the core of the question. Hence any Belgrade-Pristina agreement on partition would necessarily have to be endorsed internationally. However, that prospect was not at all likely, in the short term, given the strong factors militating against it—to begin with the fact that Pristina, Washington, and Brussels were all absolutely against the idea of partition (even if that stance seems philosophically inconsistent with their coordinated approach to forcing Kosovo's separation from Serbia, in 2008).

The final suggestion that Economides et al. came up with was autonomy for the Serbian areas north of the River Ibar. This was also a form of separation, albeit one that could make sense in terms of letting a political community govern itself, without necessarily leading to independent international personality for that territory. However, allowing a form of self-government would be equivalent, in principle, to that being proposed by the later democratic government in Serbia (in contrast to the false version of self-government proposed by the regime of Slobodan Milošević, during the years of Belgrade repression and war crimes). Yet, Kosovo—and its international backers—deemed that to be too little, despite its extensive scope, and rejected it as unacceptable. There was no immediate cause for thinking that something unacceptable to Kosovo's Albanians should be regarded as perfectly reasonable for a territorially condensed part of its Serbian minority. For the idea of enhanced autonomy really to work, an independent Kosovo had to be assumed, in principle, which the Serbian majority territories north of the River Ibar would not only recognize, but be ready actively to engage with. Although, in practice this is what happened to a very limited degree, following the Belgrade-Pristina Dialogue (see below), that was probably not a reasonable assumption—as the continuing tensions in 2014 confirmed.[19] Whilst the Serbian-majority communities in northern Mitrovica and its surrounding area might well begin to engage with Pristina—indeed they did so, under Serbian and UNMIK influence to a limited extent—doing this on the basis of recognizing the international independence of

[19] 'Serbs protest against election law', *B92*, available at <http://www.b92.net/eng/news/poli­tics.php?yyyy=2014&mm=03&dd=28&nav_id=89811> (accessed 19 October 2010); 'Thaci's statement "irresponsible and untrue"', *B92*, available at <http://www.b92.net/eng/news/politics.php?yyyy=2014&mm=03&dd=28&nav_id=89810> (accessed 19 October 2010); 'Brisel: Zavrseni razgovori BG-PR', *B92*, 31 March 2014, available at <http://www.b92.net/info/vesti/index.php?yyyy=2014&mm=03&dd=31&nav_category=640&nav_id= 830856> (accessed 31 March 2014).

Kosovo would require the kind of agreement that was not available and unlikely to be available in any foreseeable future, unless something wholly unforeseen emerged to transform the situation. In addition, it was hard to avoid the inference that, if this arrangement were to work at all, then why not go all the way, in terms of self-governance? That would mean a return to the question of partition (and the pitfalls that make that option unlikely were addressed above). Enhanced autonomy would probably just be a version of partition 'lite' and, as such, would leave full partition a lingering question.

Economides et al.'s review of four options found that some regime of enhanced autonomy for Serbs in northern Kosovo was perhaps the most likely outcome, but even this 'would be an extremely difficult settlement to reach'. A later assessment by two of the same authors, arrived at a (quite reasonable) back-to-the-future conclusion:[20] Kosovo's future EU accession would have to wait, and be dependent on first achieving 'standards'. This was, in effect, a new version of the 'standards before status' policy that had characterized international involvement in Kosovo under UN Special Representative of the Secretary-General, Michael Steiner until 2004, when unrest and a new approach by the new UN Special Representative of the Secretary-General, Kai Eide, led to a process of 'status before standards', in effect.[21]

In 2010, new impetus sharply forced the pace on Kosovo's status and Kosovo's position: US Secretary of State, Hilary Clinton, made a major visit to the Western Balkans, in October;[22] Serbia was given the prospect of acceding to the EU sometime between 2014 and 2016;[23] and on 25 October, the European Council referred Serbia's candidacy to the European Commission on condition, in particular, that there should be cooperation with the International Criminal Tribunal for the former Yugoslavia and that Belgrade developed positive relations with Pristina.[24] Those developing positive relations were transformed into a formal dialogue between Belgrade and Pristina, in an effort incrementally to move forward diplomatically, while setting aside the big issues, such as recognition.

That dialogue progressed through seven rounds of discussion in 2011 and,[25] after a significant pause, an historic first meeting, in October 2012, between Ivica

---

[20] Ker-Lindsay and Ecomomides, 'Standards before Accession: Kosovo's EU Perspective', 14 *Journal of Balkan and Near Eastern Studies* (2012)1.

[21] See Gow, *supra* note 13.

[22] 'Clinton ends Balkan tour in Kosovo', 14 October 2010, *B92*, available at <http://www.b92.net/eng/news/in_focus.php?id=91&start=0&nav_id=70271> (accessed 19 October 2010); 'Key days for Serbia's European path', *B92*, 16 October 2010, available at <http://www.b92.net/eng/news/in_focus.php?id=91&start=0&nav_id=70320> (accessed 19 October 2010); 'Tadic on recent violence, EU integration', *B92 News*, 17 October 2010, available at <http://www.b92.net/eng/news/politics-article.php?yyyy=2010&mm=10&dd=17&nav_id=70332> (accessed 19 October 2010).

[23] 'PM: Serbia in EU between 2014 and 2016', *B92 News*, 19 October 2010, available at <http://www.b92.net/eng/news/politics-article.php?yyyy=2010&mm=10&dd=19&nav_id=70375> (accessed 19 October 2010).

[24] The notion of bringing Serbia and others into the Union by around 2014 was not new—but it would be an ideal moment, marking the end of a century of trouble, and having great symbolic value. Gow, 'Europe and the Muslim World: European Union Enlargement and the Western Balkans', 7 *Journal of Southeast European and Black Sea Studies* (2007) 3.

[25] For further detail on the dialogue, see Chapter 12 by Tatjana Papić and *supra* note 9.

Dačić, the Serbian Prime Minister (who was elected in spring 2012), and Kosovo's Prime Minister, Hashim Thaçi.[26] This was followed by two subsequent meetings, and produced some small steps of cooperation, such as agreement on the recognition of university diplomas, cadastre, and non-marked border arrangements.[27] The Belgrade-Pristina dialogue continued, under the auspices of the EU High Representative for External Affairs, Cathy Ashton, and, after three further tough rounds of negotiation, concluded in an Agreement of Principles, between Dačić and Thaçi in April 2013 that helped normalize relations between their polities.[28] The Agreement of Principles was sufficient to satisfy the European Council, which had been insisting on positive talks, while considering whether to move beyond its offer of candidate status to Serbia, and make a commitment to start accession talks. That decision came on 28 June—on the historically fateful St. Vitus' Day, or Vidovdan[29]—when the Council endorsed a recommendation to open accession talks. That endorsement became a formal date for talks to open, six months later, when the European Council summit, in December, announced that talks would start in January. The first Inter-Governmental Conference was held on 21 January 2014.[30] While talks did open, their progress required Serbia to continue the normalization process, in addition to negotiation of the *acquis communautaire*. EU expectations were explicit: all agreements reached in the dialogue had to be implemented;[31] principles of regional co-operation had to be respected; outstanding issues had to be resolved 'through dialogue and in the spirit of compromise... on the basis of practical and sustainable solutions', requiring cooperation on the technical and legal questions necessary to resolve those issues through dialogue; and, finally, there must be cooperation with EULEX.[32] Thus, the dialogue would need to continue, as it did (with problems, inevitably),[33] in practice, despite the hiatus of elections in Serbia, during Spring 2014. The nationalist Serbian Progressive Party of President Tomislav Nikolić and Deputy Prime Minister Aleksandar Vučić

---

[26] 'Serbia-Kosovo EU-facilitated dialogue: statement by EU HR Ashton after third meeting', Brussels, EU12-417EN, 4 December 2012.

[27] European Council, 'Council conclusions on enlargement and stabilisation and association process', 3132nd General Affairs Council meeting, Brussels, 5 December 2011.

[28] <http://eeas.europa.eu/top_stories/2013/190413__eu-facilitated_dialogue_en.htm>.

[29] Vidovdan, 28 June, was by a blend of chance and deliberate action, a recurring day of momentous and historic events, including the Battle of Kosovo Polje, in 1389, the passing of the Constitution of the Kingdom of Serbs, Croats and Slovenes, in 1921, Belgrade's expulsion from the Soviet family of communist countries in 1948, and the transfer of former President Slobodan Milošević to the International Criminal Tribunal for the former Yugoslavia, in 2003.

[30] Council of the European Union, 'First Accession Conference with Serbia', Press Release, 5486/14, Brussels, 21 January 2014.

[31] In her assessment of the Agreement in her contribution to the present book, Tatjana Papić wisely notes that 14 of the 15 points in the Agreement concerned the integration of four Serb-majority municipalities within Kosovo, rather than broader issues—although she also correctly notes that it was important in 'thawing' Belgrade-Pristina relations. See Ch. 12, pp. xxx, *supra* note 9.

[32] Conference on Accession to the European Union—Serbia, 'General Position', Accession Document AD 1/14, CONF-RS-1, Brussels, 9 January 2014, pp. 10–11.

[33] 'Brisel: Zavrseni razgovori BG-PR', *B92* 31 March 2014, available at <http://www.b92.net/info/vesti/index.php?yyyy=2014&mm=03&dd=31&nav_category=640&nav_id=830856> (accessed 31 March 2014).

(increasingly, the most important figure in Serbian politics) reaped the benefits of EU progress, with the Progressives seen to have delivered EU progress while apparently standing up for Serbia (even though, in reality, it had been Socialist Prime Minister Dačić who had forced the EU agenda, making it clear that there was no alternative, and leading the Serbian side of the dialogue).

The EU's position, by insisting on the resolution of outstanding issues, in essence, meant that negotiations on accession could progress and that dialogue could continue. But, it also meant that eventual accession could be predicated on, *inter alia*, recognition of Kosovo's independent international personality, as asserted by Pristina. However, it would not necessarily have to be so, depending on prevailing interpretations of the situation, which could be expected to be divided, in any case, along the same lines that already divided the EU over Kosovo's status. All of this meant that, for all the progress made, including the significant improvement in the atmosphere of relations between the various parties, the same question would remain that had been there from the outset: how to achieve an arrangement that would allow the parties to agree to disagree, or, perhaps, to agree with diverging interpretations, or recognize without recognizing. To some extent, this had governed the situation since 2008, when the European Commission had judged that an Instrument of Pre-Accession Assistance with Kosovo, in effect since 2007, meant that a Stabilization and Association Agreement with Pristina could be discussed without prejudice to the position of the five EU states that rejected Kosovo's independence. Thus, even as accession talks progressed, there was, therefore, still a need for imagination and the kind of new thinking that could facilitate both progress and a simultaneous easing of the blockage as had been necessary from the start. Incremental movement had occurred, of course. But, essentially, everybody had stayed where they were, from one phase to another, from one year to another, from one month to another. All the actors stuck in the Kosovo maze needed to find a way out and a way forward that would make EU accession possible for Serbia and the EU, without any further delays than the negotiations themselves would bring, and that would give Kosovo a guaranteed EU perspective. (In stating this, the assumptions are that Pristina's authorities, lacking diplomatic magnanimity, believed that they could use international pressure to force Belgrade into a somewhat humiliating concession on recognition, sooner rather than later. At the same time, Belgrade could not bring itself to recognize, or see itself bullied into recognizing, Kosovo's independence in the timeframe of the accession negotiations.[34]) How could all the parties involved, including the international actors, get out of the impasse, which was present in Pristina's part-coordinated declaration of independence and from which there was no reasonable prospect of escape until Belgrade was ready to accede to the EU. A framework for transforming the impasse was necessary, which would both allow the parties to agree to disagree, while continuing to foster normality in all other respects. This is why the concept of an EU 'Free

---

[34] Personal contact with Kosovo officials has made clear the sense that the government felt no need to compromise—a key word for Serbia in the EU approach to accession—as Belgrade would eventually be obliged by their obstinacy and EU—and wider—pressure to accept the inevitabile and formally recognize Pristina as having independent international personality.

Territory', or something similar (the name is illustrative) might have the potential to facilitate resolution of the situation.

## 4. An EU 'Free Territory'

Serbia and the EU, and so all other actors involved in the Kosovo question, faced the prospect that negotiations on accession would proceed to completion, but, potentially, accession itself would continue to be stalled by the issue of recognition. Thus, all the efforts would have come back round to the point of departure. The same question remained to be answered, having not been adequately answered through all the stages of grey zone to grey zone evolution over Kosovo. How to solve a problem like Kosovo? Beyond the ICJ, which failed to solve it (and indeed refused even to make an attempt), this was a question for Kosovo itself, Serbia, the United States, the UN, and other international organizations, and the EU, for which it was both an internal and an external question. Indeed, if Kosovo could be solved as a problem for the EU, it was likely to be solved as a problem, in and of itself, for all the others involved. This is because any solution that would unblock division over Kosovo inside the Union, would pave the way for solutions on all other fronts. Internally, the Union was divided, with 23 member states recognizing Kosovo as having independent international personality, while the remaining five steadfastly opposed to recognition (Spain, Greece, Cyprus, Slovakia and Romania). As already seen, since 2007, this division made any further decisions by the EU regarding Kosovo very difficult, if not impossible. If just one—Spain—of the five states opposed to recognizing Kosovo as having independent international personality were to change its position, a swathe of Hispanic and Lusophone countries around the world would follow suit, giving Kosovo more of the support it would need to force an application to join the United Nations—even though that exercise could never be more than symbolic so long as a permanent member of the UN Security Council was ready to veto its membership. Moreover, the conditions that would make it possible for Madrid to change its position (particularly an agreement that would also end Kosovo's status under UN Security Council resolution 1244 (1999) and the formal role of UNMIK (the UN Mission in Kosovo)) would almost certainly meet the objections of the four other EU states opposed to Pristina's claimed status. The same would apply to a range of other countries, including Russia, as any agreement that led to the end of UN Security Council resolution 1244 would also have gained Moscow's acquiescence already. Any such agreement would, of course, also have to have the assent of both Kosovo and Serbia.

   One option, raised during negotiations in 2007 by Ischinger and reiterated by an MEP in 2009,[35] was to look at the idea of a 'Basic Treaty', rather as, during the

---

[35]  Weller, 'Kosovo's Final Status', 84 *International Affairs* (2008) 6, at 1227; Joost Lagendijk, MEP, *South East Europe TV*, 'Resolution on Kosovo', interview with Joost Lagendijk, 4 February 2009. Video available online: <http://seetv.blastmedia.eu/event/resolution-on-kosovo/interview-with-mep-j oost-lagendijk> (accessed 30 November 2014).

Cold War, the German Democratic Republic (the DDR) and the Federal Republic of Germany (the BRD) came to agree that neither would be a member of the UN. That particular detail was irrelevant in this case, because Serbia was already a member of the UN. But without pursuing all the details, it was possible to imagine an agreement that might permit Serbia and Kosovo to have a working relationship, setting aside, without prejudice, other questions about statehood, alliance belonging, and political development of other kinds, which would offer some scope for progress. It was a good idea. It would create new formal arrangements. It would embrace the existing stalemate. But it would also do something to help adjust the predicament and take the situation forward. However, it would still have to deal with the issue of resolution 1244 and the way in which that affected status. It would probably still need to get agreement in various quarters in order to make it possible. This would not just be about the basic direct agreement between Belgrade and Pristina. Other things would need to be agreed. This was, therefore, an interesting idea that could be a context for other things to happen. It would not be a solution, in itself, and would need to have complementary contextual developments.

Another idea appeared in a little noticed paper published by a Brussels think-tank and written by Michael Emerson.[36] His proposal was to bring Kosovo into the EU, but without EU membership. This was a curious notion—membership without membership. It would involve negotiations of a certain kind to come to an arrangement with Kosovo. Kosovo would not necessarily be independent, in the sense of being recognized as having independent international personality or becoming a member of the UN (though this would not be excluded). But, *de facto,* it would be embraced by the EU. It would become part of the EU and would have elements of EU governance and administration in operation, derived from the Ahtisaari proposals, for a period of transition. Emerson pointed to Liechtenstein in this context, which is a part of the European Economic Area, as well as being *de facto* part of Switzerland, without being formally part of either the EU or Switzerland. Liechtenstein's situation and status in the world led to other variants of the questions of self-determination, statehood and sovereignty that affect other cases around the world.[37] Liechtenstein offered something here. But, it was limited as an example because Liechtenstein already had formal sovereignty and independent international personality. Its interest lay in the way its formal sovereignty operated in terms of the exercise of rights, such that it was *de facto* part of Switzerland and *de jure* part of the EU customs zone without technically being part of either political community. But, Liechtenstein offered an inspiring lesson (questions about financial malpractice notwithstanding) in this day and age of how

---

[36] Emerson, 'Kosovo merits "special status as part of the EU"', *CEPS Policy Brief* No. 143 (2007) Brussels, Centre for European Policy Studies, October. The paper was, indeed, so little noticed, that I had not noticed it until preparing the present analysis.

[37] Liechtenstein is a great driving force and example in the area of self-determination and much of my thinking has been facilitated by my involvement with the Liechtenstein Institute on Self-Determination (LISD) at Princeton University, which Crown Prince Hans Adam endowed to allow work on issues of this kind, under the direction of Wolfgang Danspeckgruber. The idea contained in this article had its inspiration in 2007 during one of LISD's project meetings.

to think about the different ways in which states could operate and manage the exercise of sovereign rights in a world of international markets and transnational communities, especially smaller or even 'micro' states.[38] Emerson's ideas were, in a sense, incomplete—at least to the extent that he did not know quite what to call the arrangement he suggested—but, further flexible diplomatic options identified in the present contribution were also overlooked. In particular, his analysis focused on Kosovo and the EU, but did not consider Serbia and others who would be affected by, and probably would need to agree to, any such arrangement. But, he was striving to do something that went in the right direction by seeking an inventive arrangement involving Kosovo and the EU that could facilitate progress.

That right direction can be continued into the final straight by consideration of the concept of an EU 'Free Territory'. Conceptualizing in that way permits the possibility of allowing all concerned—Kosovo, Serbia, the EU, the UN, the US—to move forward while agreeing to disagree on the key point of recognition, the crucial requirement of any successful design. While the 'more of the same' model discussed by Economides et al. was actually one form of 'agreeing to disagree', it only worked by letting all parties stay, more or less, where they were and not doing anything else. In contrast, the requirement that to be addressed was how to agree to disagree on recognition for however long the disagreement might go on—and sometimes that could be centuries—yet still get on with life and, vitally, make progress. The notion of an EU 'Free Territory' could do just this.

The first reference point, as background, for this concept is the free territory of Trieste (which extended into the Istrian Peninsula) at the end of the Second World War. As with other reference points, this is not to be taken literally, because the detailed situations are different. But, there are ideas that can provide us with inspiration and can help us think creatively around the question of how to get Kosovo and Serbia out of limbo. The 'Free Territory' of Trieste was a temporary agreement to disagree, in effect, as Trieste, itself, was divided between Italy and its Western Allies, on one side, and Communist Yugoslavia, on the other. The Federal Peoples Republic of Yugoslavia, as it then was, and Italy disputed the territory divided into Zones A and B. This continued until the circumstances of the changing Cold War led to an abrupt end in 1954. (In 1953, following the appointment of Nikita Khrushchev as leader of the Soviet Union and the armistice in Korea, earlier in the year, the British and Americans decided to withdraw their troops in the Western Zone A (Zone B was in communist Yugoslav hands), to hand over Trieste to Italy, in line with their interpretation of the Tripartite Declaration at the United Nations in 1948, which Yugoslavia regarded as an act of aggression, breaking what was effectively a combined agreement to disagree and accept territorial control, on either side.)[39] But, it is still a notion of value for the contemporary quest to alter the Kosovo framework.

---

[38] H.S.H. Hans-Adam II, The Reigning Prince of Liechtenstein, *The State in the Third Millennium* (Triesen: van Eck Verlag, 2009).

[39] Duncan Wilson, *Tito's Yugoslavia* (Cambridge University Press, 1979); Beatrice Heuser, *Western Containment Policies in the Cold War: The Yugoslav Case, 1948-1953* (Routledge, 1989)..

The EU itself has a particularly rich record of innovation and invention in accommodating different needs at different times. With an array of special status territories, or special membership territories, the EU has been fantastic—whatever strengths and failings it might have otherwise—at being imaginative and inventing and devising *ad hoc* solutions to all kinds of problems. It is almost infinitely inventive in its capacity to find new forms to fit new situations. The different arrangements it has for different territories are testimony to this. Some of these territories belong to Member States, some do not belong to Member States but are associated with them, and some territories are simply associated with the EU. Examples could include the Channel Islands, associated with the UK, or the murky issue of Cyprus' membership of the EU—but with EU legislation not applying to the northern part of the island. The Faroe Islands, which belong to Denmark, are not part of the EU, nor covered by it, but have a technical special relationship with it. The EU already had so many different options that it was not a major challenge to explore different avenues.

Finally, beyond the EU context, the notion of a 'Free Territory' derives from an understanding of the 'Free Association' between the Federated States of Micronesia and the US.[40] The compact affects territories that were formerly Trust Territories of the Pacific Islands, first of all under the UN, then under the US military, and lastly under the US Department of the Interior, with a dedicated Office of Insular Affairs opened in 1995.[41] In many respects, these territories are *de facto* part of the US. They are treated in many ways as though they are part of the federal territory. But they are certainly not treated this way in all respects. There is self-government and free choice, even though Micronesia is treated as part of the US for defence purposes, which is very nice for those islands, on one level, absolving them of any responsibility for their own defence.. Of course, this arrangement is not so attractive for anyone who does not like US military bases. But even that reservation can be offset as the US basically sustains the islands financially.[42] The initial 15-year agreement came to an end in 2006 and was renewed by both Micronesia and the Marshall Islands. They are formally sovereign, independent, and, despite their practical dependency, in 'free association' with the US. The word 'free' is crucial. Despite the pragmatics involved, it is a voluntary act, in which all parties joined.

---

[40] The 'Free Association' compact first came to my attention during 2007 in the context of the Princeton Liechtenstein Institute, prior to Kosovo's declaration of independence. I began to develop thinking on this notion regarding Kosovo, which I shared with some people then, albeit, too late in the day to make a difference to those events. As time passed, I came to realize how the notion could help guide thinking on Kosovo post declaration of independence. See Government of the Federated States of Micronesia, *Compact Of Free Association* (included in U.S. Pub. Law 99–239, Compact of Free Assoc. Act of 1985, 48 USC 1681 note. 59 Stat. 1031 and amended 17 Dec. 2003 by House Jt. Res. 63; U.S. Pub. Law 108-188). Available at <http://www.fsmlaw.org/compact/> (accessed 17 December 2010).

[41] <http://www.doi.gov/oia/about/history.cfm>.

[42] United States Government Accountability Office, 2008, 'Testimony before the Insular Affairs Subcommittee, House Resources Committee, U.S. House of Representatives: Compact of Free Association Micronesia Faces Challenges to Achieving Compact Goals'. Statement of David Gootnick, Director, International Affairs and Trade, Tuesday, June 10, 2008. GAO-08-859T. Washington DC: GAO.

It is an arrangement that everybody wants to work and something to which nobody could reasonably object.

The detail of any 'free' association involving Kosovo, Serbia, the EU, and others, would, of course, have to be worked out. That detail would be important and would need to be specific. But it could be identified and negotiated without any prejudice to questions of sovereignty, or the particular positions of the parties. They could enter into an agreement to establish an EU 'Free Territory', or 'Free Association', in part, following the model of the Basic Treaty (noted above), and partly following the model of Micronesia. And this agreement could be informed by any other example or model that we might discover to have relevance to this process.

It would make sense for the agreement to be informed by the Ahtisaari proposals, in some way. After all, that was the basis on which all agreed, including Russia, until a parallel Western agenda emerged. It would make sense for agreement on an EU 'Free Territory' to include elements of Ahtisaari, or Ahtisaari-plus (recognizing that the situation has moved on considerably since 2007). Many in Pristina would cautiously resist this, however much it made painless sense without prejudice to status, as they might perceive it as 'going back' to a phase now past. The same could be said for Pristina's international backers. A 'Free Territory' or 'Free Association' agreement would confirm that Kosovo could not—and would not—'go back'.[43] Of course, it could be argued that the visual evidence of mass murder and war crimes in 1999, starting at Račak in January and continuing through the spring, had already made it impossible to 'go back'. These crimes against humanity put it out of the question for Serbia ever to embrace Kosovo again, in the eyes of most Western policy makers and observers, as well as the eyes of the Kosovo Albanians.[44] So, a 'free territory' would only be confirming the inevitable, in this sense. Given that it was previously agreed, and that EULEX existed because of it, for example, it would be perfectly reasonable to suppose that everybody should be able to agree on adopting those elements necessary to Kosovo's continuing development as part of a 'Free Association' agreement. An Ahtisaari-plus approach, fully taking into account subsequent developments and building on them, while only using those elements of Ahtisaari still judged to be relevant to continuing Kosovo's development would make sense (and no one could deny that significant development work was still needed both by internal initiative and effort and outside assistance). Nonetheless, the same path could be followed without any reference whatsoever to Ahtisaari. The key was to use the framework to foster Kosovo's development and both its own and Serbia's relationship with the EU, in a manner that would allow EU membership to come more quickly for both polities, and, in effect and practice, to be guaranteed by the agreement. Most of all, it would allow progress to be made

---

[43] I made the mistake of saying 'back to Ahtisaari' at the meeting where I first publicly aired the EU 'Free Territory' idea at a meeting in Washington DC. A representative from the Kosovo mission to the US, otherwise interested in the idea and sympathetic, said, 'No, no, we're not going back to the past'. This was not my intention, of course, as I made clear—the purpose was to make progress, rather than to make an impossible return to the *status quo ante*. 'Getting Kosovo Out of Limbo?', presentation at the Woodrow Wilson International Center for Scholars. Washington DC, 12 April 2010.

[44] Author's interview with human rights activist, Belgrade, April 2011.

more rapidly towards full normalization, as it would be made smoothly and wholly consensually, on the basis of the agreement. This would forego any further need for Brussels—or, indeed, Washington—to bully and batter Belgrade into cooperating and normalizing relations with Pristina. It would, to a large extent, represent the normalization of relations, in an EU context. While not going so far as to give formal recognition to Kosovo's full independent international personality, a 'Free Territory' agreement would offer formal and legal confirmation of Kosovo's separation and also of its, at least, partial, independent international character. Belgrade would benefit from having its EU path free from obstacles by being able to join a legal agreement to confirm Kosovo's separation. Kosovo would benefit from having Serbia's legal confirmation of separate status as a polity and from gaining inclusive EU status at an expedited rate and a formal guarantee of eventual membership.

Any agreement would also need to embrace, far more quickly and far more positively than was previously the case, a sense of how Pristina could take responsibility for its own affairs. This is because one of the lessons of the Kosovo experience (and other instances of external administration and assistance) is that outsiders are really not very good at running places, on the whole, unless they happen to be extremely good and directed politicians, with a sense of command and leadership responsibility—like Paddy Ashdown in Bosnia, or George C. Marshall, in Germany. Unfortunately, leaders of that calibre do not come along too often and, even then, they still have to fight the circumstances that they meet. While external assistance and support is necessary to a transition, and supervision might well be essential, evidence suggests that, by a four-year point, a clear shift to self-government and responsibility within a territory should have commenced, although the overall process of support would be needed for a decade or more.[45] There would really need to be a quick sense of moving to self-governance—meaning ownership. While there has been a lot of talk about ownership, in Kosovo, as in parallel situations of transitional administration, there has been little real sense of what that means, in practice, and how to go about achieving it. An agreement based on 'free association' and the establishment of an EU 'Free Territory' should be the chance to encourage the Kosovo political community and its leaders to take responsibility for themselves and their destiny.

At the same time, such an agreement would allow Pristina and its backers to argue that by using a word such as 'free', the agreement confirmed their independence, while permitting Belgrade and its backers to argue that it was not formal recognition of independent international personality as such, because of the EU context and the notion of 'association'. Because the agreement would embrace all sides, a new UN Security Council resolution to endorse it would be possible, which would explicitly replace the obstacles of contested interpretation surrounding UN Security Council resolution 1244, by deciding that both the new resolution and resolution 1244 would cease to have effect on the date that Belgrade acceded to the EU. (Of course, although more problematic, the ending of resolution 1244 and the

[45] Paul Collier, *Reducing the Security Risk in Low-Income Countries: Full Research Report* (2008), ESRC End of Award Report, RES-228-25-0055, Swindon: ESRC.

absorption of some of its elements could be decided within the adoption of any new resolution.) The new resolution would be time-, or rather, event-barred for two reasons. First, it would ensure that international commitments entered into under its auspices would not have to continue longer than necessary. Second, the fact that the new resolution and any residual effects of resolution 1244 would end at the point of EU accession would mean that any state feeling itself constrained by the continuing effect of resolution 1244 in its approach to Kosovo would no longer have to consider that constraint. Only conventional state interpretations of diplomatic relations and the foreign policy decisions of states would be relevant. Thus, a Kosovo 'Free Territory' would not only help to cement Kosovo's independence and 'freedom', it would also free many states from diplomatic-legal Triffids. Greater freedom would come, for example, with Spanish agreement within the EU. It is hard to imagine that any EU Member State would block an EU agreement supported by all the others, releasing other Hispanic countries, which demonstrated their unquestioning loyalty to Spain by withholding recognition of Kosovo (even if some might have their own agendas, as well) to act freely. The 'Free Territory' or 'Free Association' arrangement would offer a win-win-win-win way out of the impasse for all concerned, facilitating far more than simply Kosovo's confirmed, formal relationship with the EU (which would otherwise wait decades) and Serbia's accession to the Union.

## 5.  Conclusion

The 'Free Territory' concept would offer a way forward, because it would be based on 'free association' and arrangements to which everybody concerned agreed. They would agree to the arrangement precisely because it would offer a way forward. The EU 'Free Territory' would necessarily have to be endorsed by the UN Security Council, under Chapter VII of the Charter, thereby replacing resolution 1244. But, unlike the impasse of 2007 and the blocking of the Ahtisaari proposal, the voluntary nature of a 'Free Association' agreement, in this case, would remove any grounds for objection. It would be against no one's will or interests. Moreover, the agreement would also need to be linked to eventual EU membership for Kosovo, which would be explicit in the agreement and in the Security Council resolution endorsing it. That Security Council resolution would 'time out' (unlike the indefinite effect of resolution 1244), that is, it would cease to have effect, at the point where Belgrade acceded to the EU. Only at that point would any of the questions set aside in the agreement to disagree need to be revisited—and even then they could be set aside once more. All parties could reassess their positions at that point, and, even, a further new Security Council resolution could be agreed, if the parties wished. However, the likely reality would be that the Security Council resolution covering the 'Free Territory' would be an invisible stabilizer, which, at the point of its termination, would no longer be needed, as the framework would have enabled, even within two or three years, a situation in which Pristina, Belgrade, and the EU would have no need for such a prop.

It is clear that Kosovo, Serbia, and the EU, as well as other international actors, need a new perspective. The model of an EU 'Free Territory' based on 'free association' involving all of the parties and confirmed by a UN Security Council resolution under Chapter VII of the UN Charter, as sketched above, offers a chance to move forward. It could bring benefits to all concerned. For the US and the UN, if nothing else, it would bring UN Security Council resolution 1244 to an end. That would allow each of them the exit they previously envisaged in 2006–7. For the EU, it would allow all 28 Member States to agree on what to do and how to move forward. Because the new 'Free Territory' arrangement would be based on agreement involving all concerned, the EU would be able to maintain unity and consensus, while once again being in a position to take important decisions regarding the future development of Kosovo. The 'Free Territory' agreement would also be important in terms of the EU's dealings with Serbia, which would gain a stable position and a clearer and stronger sense of its path to the EU, as well as being able to meet the EU's demand that it develop positive relations with Pristina. And, yet, Serbia could be allowed to maintain its formal position on the issue of sovereignty and territorial integrity, until such a point in the future as anything else might change. For Kosovo it would mean an increasingly stable position. It would mean a firm and irrevocable EU commitment to eventual membership. It would mean developing an EU link that would see responsibility transferred more and more rapidly into the hands of Kosovo's political leaders. For the Kosovo Serbs, it would also mean stability. It would bring clarity to the situation, so far as that can possibly be achieved. And, in the creative and adaptable vein of the EU's history of invention and innovation, it might even mean another EU 'Free Territory'—a separate EU 'Free Territory' within a 'Free Territory', because one of the beauties about the EU's record of adaptation and the generation of special arrangements is that it could always be applied more than once in slightly different variations in different places. With the wit and inventiveness, that have characterized the EU throughout its history, particularly in terms of evolutionary and ingenious constitutional and security arrangements and adaptations, a way forward to benefit all concerned could be found, which would facilitate the eventual resolution of the 'independence' question.

# 18

# Reflections on the Law and Politics of the *Kosovo* Case

*Harold Hongju Koh* *

What is it about Kosovo that makes international lawyers cringe? Lawyers believe in precedent. Yet curiously, in recent years, the tiny state of Kosovo has been invoked not once, but twice, for the proposition that a watershed piece of state practice does not establish any enduring legal precedent. In the late 1990s, some believed fervently that NATO should intervene to prevent humanitarian slaughter, yet when the time came to justify it under international law, they argued that 'Kosovo is *sui generis*' and should be treated as 'illegal but legitimate'. On 22 July 2010, the International Court of Justice (ICJ) ruled by a vote of 10–4 that the February 2008 declaration of independence of Kosovo was in accordance with international law. Some now similarly read the ICJ's Advisory Opinion as standing for the proposition that 'Kosovo is *sui generis*', and has no precedential effect with respect to any other country's declaration.

I write as an international lawyer and human rights practitioner who does not believe that Kosovo's legal legacy should be 'Kosovo is *sui generis*'. On both legal issues—the international lawfulness of declarations of independence and humanitarian interventions—Kosovo establishes important precedents that international lawyers must analyse with care.

I have elsewhere argued that humanitarian intervention in Kosovo was both legal and legitimate.[1] In this essay, I reflect on the law and politics of the *Kosovo*

* This chapter is written entirely in my personal capacity and relies only on my personal recollection and public documents. It does not necessarily reflect the views of the United States Government or any of its current officials. I am particularly grateful to Marko Milanović and Emily Kimball for their comments, and to my State Department friends and colleagues Anna Mansfield, Peter Olson, and especially Todd Buchwald, who as much as any among the scores of lawyers who took part in this case, helped design the legal argument that eventually confirmed Kosovo's independence.

[1] See, e.g., Harold Hongju Koh, 'Syria and the Law of Humanitarian Intervention', Part I, Just Security Blog, <http://justsecurity.org/2013/09/26/koh-syria/>; 'Syria and the Law of Humanitarian Intervention', Part II, Just Security Blog, <http://justsecurity.org/2013/10/02/koh-syria-part2>/; 'Syria and the Law of Humanitarian Intervention', Part III, Just Security Blog, <http://justsecurity.org/2013/10/10/syria-law-humanitarian-intervention-part-iii-reply/>.

ICJ Case and the *Kosovo* precedent, in light of the essays in this volume. I do not believe, as some have suggested, that the Court has set an unfortunate precedent by its Advisory Opinion finding Kosovo's declaration of independence not contrary to international law.[2] While political considerations undoubtedly helped shape the legal arguments made to the Court, that inevitable fact did not convert the Court's decision into an exercise in pure politics. As a matter of international law, the ICJ was clearly correct in narrowly holding that Kosovo's declaration of independence was not unlawful. At the same time, the careful wording of the narrow precedent established by the Advisory Opinion—not the notion that the case is *sui generis*—rebuts Russia's later outlandish claims that the Court's opinion somehow authorized such declarations as Crimea's 2014 declaration of independence.

## 1. The *Kosovo* Case

For me, this set of issues had an unusual personal resonance. The 2010 ICJ opinion was the culmination of my 11 years of engagement with Kosovo as a human rights official and international lawyer. As Assistant Secretary of State for Democracy, Human Rights and Labor in the Clinton Administration during the late 1990s, I attended the diplomatic talks in Rambouillet. In Belgrade, I met with Serbian officials later charged and convicted of war crimes, and I visited Kosovo several times. There I witnessed stunning ethnic hatred and division, experienced the misery of the Kosovar refugee camps, and immersed myself in the US and NATO response to the human rights and humanitarian crisis there. I supported the humanitarian intervention as a necessary last resort, and helped commit US funds and energy to the creation of a post-conflict legal system in Kosovo. After the bombing stopped, I swore into office the first judges of an autonomous Kosovo. I felt a strong sense of closure when I argued one decade later in The Hague in defence of the lawfulness of Kosovo's independence.

As a lawyer and scholar committed to the even-handed application of international law rules, I never felt comfortable with the claim that 'Kosovo is *sui generis*', with respect to either the humanitarian intervention argument or the declaration of independence. Thus, when I became Legal Adviser of the US Department of State in June 2009, my aim regarding the upcoming Kosovo argument was to emphasize arguments that would not merely validate the declaration, but clarify precisely what historical circumstances made this particular declaration lawful.

Before I took office, the United States Government had already submitted lengthy written pleadings in the Kosovo case. Accordingly, I participated in the writing and editing only of the final round of pleadings and oral observations that I presented to the Court. What follows is thus not a US Government position paper, but only my own personal recollections and views based on public documents,

---

[2] See, e.g., Anne Peters, Chapter 15.

which may or may not reflect the views of the many other able lawyers with whom I worked on this memorable endeavour.[3]

In evaluating the US position, what struck me first was that—as a country famously founded with the Declaration of Independence of 1776—it was in America's national interest that our country support the lawfulness of a parallel declaration of independence for one of the world's youngest democracies.[4] Second, that consideration need not lead us to endorse the legality of *all* declarations of independence, without regard to circumstance, or to steer the Court toward the thorny issue of self-determination, particularly given the unusual legitimating historical circumstances that gave rise to Kosovo's declaration. Third, because the United States had maintained close ties to Serbia since the ouster of Milošević, we were equally determined not to have our legal filing in the ICJ case seen as an anti-Serbian diatribe. Fourth, we saw no contradiction between the peacefully declared declaration of independence and either general international law or UN Security Council resolution 1244[5]—which had not contemplated the territorial integrity of Serbia, but that of a Federal Republic of Yugoslavia that no longer existed, in which Serbia was one component part. Moreover, the resolution only had effect during the interim period of international administration in Kosovo, which had now ended. Nor, finally, did we see the declaration as violating the Kosovo Constitutional Framework, which we viewed as effectively operating as domestic law.[6]

Perhaps most clear to me was that we were looking at a case of what Americans like to call: 'if it ain't broke, don't fix it'. The simple political reality was that the UN's extensive intervention in Kosovo had worked. As a political matter, the Court should hesitate to intervene because the status quo was both working, and arguably superior to any alternative future in which the Court might declare the declaration unlawful. Our pleadings therefore sought to remind the Court that it was part of a larger UN system whose institutions had invested deeply in making Kosovo's nationhood possible. Given that the independent nation of Kosovo, which so many United Nations institutions had painstakingly midwifed, had become a reality, that equilibrium should not be lightly undone by the UN's own judicial body. Practically speaking, we argued, there was no going back.[7] The

---

[3] In addition to the many outstanding lawyers who pleaded for other governments, the extraordinary US State Department team was led by Assistant Legal Adviser for European Affairs Peter Olson, Assistant Legal Adviser for United Nations Affairs Todd Buchwald and Attorney-Adviser Anna Mansfield, and also included: Fay Hartog-Levin, Ambassador of the United States of America to the Kingdom of the Netherlands; Senior Adviser Philip Spector and Special Assistant Kristen Eichensehr; US Embassy/Hague Legal Counsellors John Kim and Karen Johnson, and Attorney-Advisers John Daley, Emily Kimball, and Jeremy Weinberg

[4] This point became particularly poignant to me as I read David Armitage's fascinating book, *The Declaration of Independence: A Global History* (Harvard University Press , 2007), while I reviewed our draft pleadings over the Independence Day holiday, 4 July 2009. That reading led to the insertion of several references to Armitage's findings into our oral observations.

[5] Indeed, 9 out of 15 Security Council members that voted for resolution 1244 later recognized Kosovo as independent.

[6] Although the Court did not accept this argument, which was elaborated in our second memorial, we thought it deserved fuller consideration.

[7] Cf. Oral Observations of Harold Hongju Koh on behalf of the United States of America, <http://www.icj-cij.org/docket/files/141/15726.pdf>, para. 40. When 'Cyprus pointedly sought to analogize

Advisory Opinion had been put to the Court by a Serbian-sponsored General Assembly resolution. Thus the question presented needed to be answered, but only as broadly as necessary to answer 'yes, this particular declaration was in fact lawful'.

Keeping all of these concerns in mind, I carefully worded my December 2009 observations to state the narrow issue this way:

Those pleading before you have discussed a broad range of issues, including the validity of recognition of Kosovo, the effectiveness of the United Nations, the legality of military actions in 1999, and the potential responsibility of non-state actors for internationally wrongful acts. Yet the precise question put to this Court is much narrower: 'Is the unilateral declaration of independence by the Provisional Institutions of Self-Government of Kosovo in accordance with international law?' The answer to that question, we submit, is yes. For as a general matter, international law does not regulate declarations of independence, nor is there anything about Kosovo's particular declaration that would render it not 'in accordance with international law.'[8] Standing alone, a declaration neither constitutes nor establishes political independence; it announces a political reality or aspiration that must then be achieved by other means... We therefore urge this Court to leave Kosovo's Declaration undisturbed—either by refusing to issue an opinion or by simply answering in the affirmative the question presented: whether Kosovo's Declaration of Independence accords with international law.[9]

To ensure that the legality of the Kosovo declaration would not be studied stripped of its unique historical context, we recalled that after the traumatic humanitarian intervention, Kosovo's supporters had helped birth the new nation with painstaking concern for international law and human rights. 'We respectfully submit[ted] that a Security Council resolution drafted with such an intent did not give birth to a declaration of independence that violates international law'.[10] Mindful of appearing to license future incidents like Crimea, we did 'not deny that international law may regulate particular declarations of independence, if they are conjoined with illegal uses of force or violate other peremptory norms, such as the prohibition against apartheid. But that is hardly the case here, where those declaring independence did not violate peremptory norms'.[11]

Finally, we made the 'no going back argument' this way:

Kosovo's declaration of independence brought a necessary and stabilizing end to a turbulent chapter in the history of the Western Balkans, and made possible a transition to a common European future for the people of Kosovo and their neighbors. The real question this Court faces is whether to support re-opening of this tragic past or whether instead to let Kosovo and Serbia look forward to this more promising future... The 2008 declaration of independence,

---

the 1244 process to the heart-wrenching, but misleading, case where a parent sends a small child off to state supervision, only to lose her forever', I argued that 'upon reflection, the far better analogy would be to acknowledge the futility of the state forcing an adult child to return to an abusive home against her will, particularly where parent and child have already long lived apart, and where repeated efforts at reconciliation have reached impasse. There, as here, declaring independence would be the only viable option, and would certainly be in accordance with law'.

[8] Koh Statement, para. 3.     [9] Ibid., at para. 38.     [10] Ibid., at para. 5.
[11] Ibid., para. 20.

and the ensuing recognition of Kosovo by many nations, brought much-needed stability to the Balkans and closed the books on the protracted break-up of what once was Yugoslavia. Kosovo's declaration of independence emanated from a process supervised by the United Nations, which through resolution 1244 and the institutions it established, was deeply involved in Kosovo's past and present. And the declaration has now made possible a future in which Kosovo is not merely independent politically, but also self-sufficient economically, administratively, and civilly... [T]his Court has no reason to upend what has become a stable equilibrium. For Kosovo is now independent. Both Kosovo and Serbia are part of Europe's future. As the principal judicial organ of the United Nations, this Court should not be conscripted into a member state's effort to roll back the clock nearly a decade, undoing a careful process accomplished under resolution 1244 and overseen by so many other United Nations bodies.[12]

In July 2010, the Court accepted several of these arguments, holding that Kosovo's unilateral declaration of independence from Serbia did not violate any applicable rule of international law. In particular, the Court held that the declaration did not breach general international law, UN Security Council resolution 1244, or the Constitutional Framework that was adopted by the Secretary-General's Special Representative on behalf of the UN Interim Administration Mission in Kosovo.

In so holding, the Court announced no sweeping rule of international law. It clearly did not adopt the general rule of presumptive illegality that Serbia had urged: 'the international law principle of territorial integrity prohibits *all* nonconsensual secessions (and *a fortiori*, all declarations of independence), except where domestic law grants a right of secession or the parent state accepts the declaration before or soon after the secession'.[13] But in announcing that Kosovo's particular declaration was in accordance with international law, the Court's advisory opinion is also glaring for all the issues it did not address. As Anne Peters has observed, 'the Opinion was extremely parsimonious in legal substance [and] silent on secession, on statehood, on recognition,... on *uti possidetis* [and] largely circumvented the issue of territorial integrity ....'[14] In particular, the Court carefully avoided any broader statement regarding the concept of self-determination through unilateral secession, because it could find no statement supported by sufficient state practice and *opinio juris*, or other relevant sources of international law.

Second, the Court held that nothing in state practice suggests that promulgating declarations of independence are questions of law rather than politics or that, standing alone, the act of promulgating the declaration should be regarded as contrary to international law. Finding no generally applicable rule of international law governing declarations of independence, the Court 'found it entirely possible for a particular act—such as a unilateral declaration of independence—not to be in violation of international law without necessarily constituting the exercise of a right conferred by' international law.[15] In so saying,

---

[12]  Ibid., para. 42.

[13]  Koh Statement, para. 19 (citing Written Statement of the Government of the Republic of Serbia ('Serbia Statement'), para. 943).

[14]  Peters, Chapter 15, *supra* note 3.       [15]  Advisory Opinion, para. 56.

the Court carefully noted that in all of the cases where the Security Council had condemned particular declarations of independence, it had responded to the 'concrete situation existing at the time that those declarations of independence were made', with 'the illegality attached to the declarations of independence thus stemm[ing] not from the unilateral character of these declarations as such, but from the fact that they were, or would have been, connected with the unlawful use of force or other egregious violations of norms of general international law, in particular those of a peremptory character (*jus cogens*)'. 'In the context of Kosovo,' the Court noted, 'the Security Council has never taken this position.'[16]

Third, finding no general rules of international law applicable to declarations of independence, the Court also found no prohibition in the *lex specialis* of the case: UN Security Council resolution 1244 and the Constitutional Framework of Kosovo. Rejecting Serbia's claims, the Court found that the former did not preclude the issuance of Kosovo's declaration of independence because the declaration of independence was a unilateral attempt to determine finally the status of Kosovo, while resolution 1244's object and purpose 'was to establish a temporary, exceptional legal regime which, save to the extent that it expressly preserved it, superseded the Serbian legal order and… aimed at the stabilization of Kosovo, and… was designed to do so on an interim basis'.[17] Moreover, the Court found that the declaration of independence did not violate the Constitutional Framework for Kosovo either, because 'the declaration of independence of 17 February 2008 was not issued by the Provisional Institutions of Self-Government, nor was it an act intended to take effect, or actually taking effect, within the legal order in which those Provisional Institutions operated', which the Constitutional Framework governed.[18]

Finally, the Court clarified that even when dealing with a matter with which other UN institutions were already seized, '[t]he purpose of the advisory jurisdiction is to enable organs of the United Nations and other authorized bodies to obtain opinions from the Court which will assist them in the future exercise of their functions. The Court cannot determine what steps the General Assembly may wish to take after receiving the Court's opinion or what effect that opinion may have in relation to those steps. As has been demonstrated, the General Assembly is entitled to discuss the declaration of independence and, within the limits considered above, to make recommendations in respect of that or other aspects of the situation in Kosovo without trespassing on the powers of the Security Council'.[19] Accordingly, Secretary-General Ban Ki-moon immediately announced that he would forward the Advisory Opinion to the General Assembly, 'strongly encourag[ing] the parties to engage in a constructive dialogue… [and] urg[ing] all sides to avoid any steps that could be seen as provocative and derail the dialogue'.[20] At the time of this writing, the Republic of

---

[16]  Ibid., para. 81.      [17]  Ibid., para. 100.      [18]  Ibid., para. 121.
[19]  Ibid., para. 44.
[20]  Secretary-General Statement on Advisory Opinion on Kosovo, July 22, 2010, available at <http://www.un.org/News/briefings/docs/2010/db100722.doc.htm> .

Kosovo has been recognized as an independent state by 109 countries, including 23 out of 28 European Union Member States.

The day after the Court's ruling, Kosovo's Prime Minister, Hashim Thaçi, came to the Office of the Legal Adviser to thank our State Department team for its work on the ICJ case. His visit brought full circle my personal participation for more than a decade in this remarkable historical episode. My colleagues and I were moved and gratified that our own country, founded with an audacious declaration of independence so many years ago, could play a historic supporting role for one of the world's youngest democracies.

## 2. The *Kosovo* Precedent

At a State Department press briefing the day that the Advisory Opinion issued, I noted:

What… happened here is that Kosovo had declared independence—[and] the fact of that independence has become a political reality. But… there [wa]s a question… put from the General Assembly to… the International Court of Justice which attempted to cast legal doubt on that independence. The court's opinion today by a vote of 10 to 4 answered those legal objections and now it's returned to the situation that it was in before, which is how to move forward toward a common European future… [21]

When asked by a journalist, but 'doesn't a fact create a precedent whether you recognize it or not?', I answered,

[A]s a lawyer I [have] carefully studied precedents and I don't read court decisions to say more than they say. They didn't say all declarations of independence are in accordance with international laws, but they said that Kosovo's declaration of independence on its particular set of facts is in accordance with international law. They pointed to, among other facts peculiar to Kosovo's situation, the fact that there was a humanitarian crisis; the fact that there was a special UN Security Council resolution to address the problem; [and] the fact that processes were created to create an international civilian and security presence.[22]

In other words, we never read the Advisory Opinion as validating under international law *all* declarations of independence—past, present or future. But neither did we read it as a *sui generis* event of no precedential weight. As the Court had made clear, legality *vel non* in any particular case would turn on the 'concrete situation existing at the time that those declarations of independence were made', with 'the illegality attached to [any particular] declarations of independence… stemm[ing] not from the unilateral character of these declarations as such, but from the fact[s]' as they existed at the time of the declaration, in particular, if 'they were, or would

---

[21] Harold Hongju Koh, Legal Adviser of the Department of State, The International Court of Justice's Advisory Opinion on Kosovo's Declaration of Independence, FPC Briefing Foreign Press Center Washington, DC, July 22, 2010, <http://fpc.state.gov/145040.htm> ('Koh Press Briefing').
[22] Ibid.

have been, connected with the unlawful use of force or other egregious violations of norms of general international law'.[23]

It was with some surprise, then, that four years later—after I had left the US Government—I learned that our Kosovo memorials were being quoted on the Kremlin website, by the Russian Minister of Foreign Affairs, and by President Putin himself.[24] Citing arguments that the ICJ and the United States had made in supporting the lawfulness of Kosovo's Declaration of Independence, Russia claimed that Crimea's 2014 DoI must also be lawful, calling the US hypocritical.

Deceptively, President Putin relied on an introductory quote from my oral observations, while pointedly omitting a key distinction that I drew just moments later in my oral presentation. Initially, I said:

… international law does not regulate every human event, and… an important measure of human liberty is the freedom of a people to conduct their own affairs. In many cases, including Kosovo's, the terms of a declaration of independence can mark a new nation's fundamental respect for international law.[25]

But soon thereafter, I followed that general statement with an explicit caveat: 'We do not deny that international law may regulate particular declarations of independence, *if they are conjoined with illegal uses of force or violate other peremptory norms* …'[26] My oral observations noted that this was not the case in Kosovo, and went on to describe three key factual circumstances that further made Kosovo's declaration distinctive: '[t]hat Declaration was the product of not one, but three overlapping historical processes, which did not preordain Kosovo's Declaration, but do help to explain it [1] the disintegration of Yugoslavia; [2] the human rights crisis within Kosovo; [and 3] the United Nations response'.

By contrast, before Crimea's declaration, Ukraine was a stable territory undergoing a change in government, whose territorial stability was challenged only after Russia's purposeful interference and use of force. The people of Kosovo declared independence only after suffering through years of bloody repression and crimes against humanity by the Serbian Government. Russia could point to no parallel human rights crisis in Crimea. Perhaps most important, Kosovo did not declare independence prematurely, but only after an exhaustive process within the UN system, which exhausted all available avenues for a mutually agreed solution, before finally concluding—in Special Envoy Martti Ahtisaari's words—that 'the only viable option for Kosovo is *independence*'.[27]

No similar process transpired in Ukraine. Crimea's declaration of independence and incorporation into Russia occurred almost overnight, and was not the

---

[23] Advisory Opinion, para. 81.

[24] <http://eng.kremlin.ru/news/6889>. I was later advised that it was the Russian media that first drew parallels between the Crimea situation, on the one hand, and the ICJ's and the US's arguments in the *Kosovo* Advisory Opinion, on the other. This led Putin to ask the Russian Ministry of Foreign Affairs for quotes from the oral arguments that he could use in his speech. See generally Milanović <http://www.ejiltalk.org/crimea-kosovo-hobgoblins-and-hypocrisy/>.

[25] Koh Statement, para. 4.     [26] Koh Statement, para. 20 (emphasis added).

[27] *See* Report of the Special Envoy of the Secretary-General on Kosovo's Future Status, S/2007/168, 26 March 2007, para. 5 (emphasis added) [Dossier No. 203]; see also US Statement, pp. 22–32; Koh

last available option reached after a lengthy attempt to find a negotiated solution with Ukraine. While Kosovo was protected by a complex legal regime established under UN Security Council resolution 1244, Crimea was illegally entered and occupied by Russian forces, which led almost immediately to Crimea's annexation into Russia. Crimean independence did not follow effective exhaustion of political remedies within the United Nations or any other intergovernmental organization. On the contrary, in Crimea, the UN General Assembly adopted a resolution calling on all parties to desist from any actions that would affect the territorial integrity of Ukraine or change Crimea's status.[28]

The three factors I cited above resembled the four-factor test offered by France, Germany, Ireland, Luxembourg, and the United Kingdom when arguing in support of the lawfulness of Kosovo's DoI.[29] Acknowledging that rare confluence of factors, we suggested that if there were a case (like the United States), where unilateral secession could be justified by self-determination considerations (as in the case of the United States' Declaration in 1776), it would be a situation where the parent state is not just inattentive to, but affirmatively violating, the human rights of the people of the breakaway nation and where all available political alternatives had been exhausted.

I summarized these considerations in the only paragraph of our oral observations that addressed self-determination:

But if the Court should find it necessary to examine Kosovo's Declaration through the lens of self-determination, it should consider the unique legal and factual circumstances of this case, which include the extensive Security Council attention given to Kosovo; the large-scale atrocities against the people of Kosovo that led to Rambouillet and the [Security Council resolution] 1244 process; the United Nations concern for the will of the people of Kosovo, their undivided territory and the unique historical, legal, cultural and linguistic attributes; the lengthy history of Kosovo's autonomy; the participation of Kosovo's representatives in the internationally led political process; the commitment of

---

Statement, para. 29. ('By the time that Kosovo declared independence in February 2008, the specific political process envisioned by resolution 1244 had ended. The future status process had run its course and the negotiations' potential to produce any mutually agreed outcome on Kosovo's status had been exhausted. With the Secretary-General's support, the Special Envoy—who was charged with determining the scope and duration of the political process—had announced that "[n]o amount of additional talks, whatever the format, will overcome this impasse" and the Envoy had specifically declared that the only viable option for Kosovo was independence.')

[28] By a vote of 100 in favour to 11 against, with 58 abstentions, the General Assembly adopted a resolution titled 'Territorial Integrity of Ukraine', <http://www.un.org/News/Press/docs/2014/ga11493.doc.htm> (March 27, 2014). This resolution called on states, international organizations and specialized agencies not to recognize any change in the status of Crimea or the Black Sea port city of Sevastopol, and to refrain from actions or dealings that might be interpreted as such. Also by the text, the Assembly called on states to 'desist and refrain' from actions aimed at disrupting Ukraine's national unity and territorial integrity, including by modifying its borders through the threat or use of force. It urged all parties immediately to pursue a peaceful resolution of the situation through direct political dialogue, to exercise restraint, and to refrain from unilateral actions and inflammatory rhetoric that could raise tensions.

[29] Peters, Chapter 15, *supra* note 3 (the four factors cited by these countries were: (1) Yugoslavia's breakup; (2) the massive human rights violations in Kosovo; (3) NATO's humanitarian intervention; and (4) the internationalization of Kosovo's situation via resolution 1244).

the people of Kosovo in their Declaration to respect prior Security Council resolutions and international law; and the decision by United Nations organs to leave undisturbed Kosovo's move to independence.[30]

As my colleague, former Assistant Secretary of State for European Affairs, Dan Fried, had noted: 'Those conditions do not pertain to any of the conflicts that are usually brought up in this context. It's not applicable to Abkhazia, or South Ossetia, or Transdniestria. Nor is it applicable to Chechnya or any separatist conflicts in Europe.'[31]

To say that these factual differences matter is not to say that particular unusual cases do not create legal precedents. Lay terms like 'unique' or 'sui generis' are confusing to lawyers because all cases resemble other cases where the same or a similar set of conditions obtain. Thus, I agree with Anne Peters' conjecture that the best reading of the Kosovo Opinion is 'as indicating the shape of successful claims to secession in the future and creating an exceptional high threshold for them—thus not a truly *sui generis* case, but a new rule … From that perspective, the "sanctioning" of the DOI by the Advisory Opinion did "create" a new rule, but an extremely narrow one'.[32]

From this perspective, the Kosovo DoI cleared a very high bar that Crimea's declaration came nowhere close to meeting. Kosovo did establish a precedent, but the narrow precedent it created was one whose factual pedigree few other declarations can match.

In the end, as Marko Milanović has noted, Putin's position on Crimea's declaration of independence proved 'ultimately contradictory and self-defeating'.[33] For even when chiding the US because it supported Kosovo's independence but challenged Crimea's, Russia herself had conspicuously argued in the *Kosovo* ICJ proceedings for a high bar for lawful declarations of independence: permitting unilateral secession, but 'limited to truly extreme circumstances, such as an outright armed attack by the parent State, threatening the very existence of the people in question'.[34] It goes without saying that the Crimean case could not remotely meet Russia's own standard for international lawfulness.

When all is said and done, the greatest lesson of the *Kosovo* ICJ case may be about the limits of mechanical jurisprudence in international law. In his fascinating oral presentation for Finland, Martti Koskenniemi put it this way:

there are some facts that can be assessed by mechanical application of rules and other cases where many rules seem prima facie applicable and require careful attention to the facts of the situation. Or in other words, there is a difference between distributing parking tickets and legal assessment of a declaration of independence. In the former case, there is no need to examine the particularities… Independence is not like that…. [H]ere the [factual]

---

[30] Koh Statement, para. 39.

[31] Interview with Assistant Secretary of State Daniel Fried, 6 February 2007, <http://www.cfr.org/kosovo/serbs-urged-accept-kosovo-plan-gain-european-future/p12563>.

[32] Peters, *supra* note 3.     [33] Milanović, *supra* note 24.

[34] Written Statement of Russian Federation, pp. 39–40.

difference [between declarations] are not irrelevant but at the heart of the statehood of each entity. *A State is a State because it is special*, not because it has come about by some procedural routine or some mechanical criterion.[35]

Put another way, declarations of independence may not be parking tickets, but they are acts of politics—sometimes 'high politics', which are constitutional and constitutive in character, and sometimes mere 'low politics', expedient statements that change no political realities or that simply mask an illegal exercise of force. It is the job of legal rules to distinguish between the moments of high politics that are of constitutional dimension, and the moments of low politics that parade as high politics.

In this context, even narrow legal precedents are useful. The fair application of general rules means articulating the rules with clarity and specificity and not treating unlike cases alike. For example, mass vehicular homicides and running red lights to get mothers in labour to the hospital may both trigger traffic tickets, but no rational observer would consider these acts to be equally unlawful. The mechanical application of bright-line rules regarding legality or illegality only coincidentally yields justice, and rarely takes sufficient account of complex facts, rich national histories or delicate political equilibria that have been painstakingly achieved.

But those who would treat Kosovo as *sui generis* make a different kind of mistake: they treat the Court's Advisory Opinion not as a traffic ticket, but as a *railway ticket*, good for this train and this trip only. By limiting its analysis to saying, in effect, that it had not been given enough cause to question the lawfulness of *this particular declaration*, the Court limited the historical value of its precedent by ducking broader, recurring questions about sovereignty, self-determination, and secession that dog our international political landscape. Judge Simma's thoughtful declaration flagged this narrowness when he criticized the Court's opinion as 'an exercise in mechanical jurisprudence'.[36] He argued:

that the General Assembly's request deserves a more comprehensive answer, assessing both permissive and prohibitive rules of international law. This would have included a deeper analysis of whether the principle of self-determination or any other rule (perhaps expressly mentioning remedial secession) permit or even warrant independence (via secession) of certain peoples/territories … [T]he Court could have delivered a more intellectually satisfying Opinion, and one with greater relevance as regards the international legal order as it has evolved into its present form, had it not interpreted the scope of the question so restrictively. To treat these questions more extensively would have demonstrated the Court's awareness of the present architecture of international law.[37]

Perhaps the best response to Judge Simma is that it is in the very nature of the Court's Advisory Opinion process that it has been asked to answer narrow questions. It is thus hardly surprising when the Court does not reach out to enunciate

---

[35] Oral Statement of Professor Martti Koskenniemi on behalf of Republic of Finland, para. 8.
[36] Declaration of Judge Simma, para. 10.        [37] Ibid., para. 7.

answers that are broader than necessary, much less elaborate 'global legal architecture'. That is not to say that 'Kosovo cases make bad law' or generate unfortunate precedents. In my judgment, they make good but narrow law, with respect to both humanitarian intervention and declarations of independence. The Kosovo precedents articulate narrow legal justifications based on unusual factual circumstances that are unlikely to recur anytime soon.

So in the end, Kosovo is about declarations of independence, not parking tickets or railway tickets. Kosovo created precedents, but narrow ones. The legal legacy of Kosovo is not that it is *sui generis*, but that it creates narrow legal precedents based on exceptional sets of facts that are not easy to replicate. We can say with confidence that Kosovo does not justify Crimea, but what is much harder to glean from the Court's opinion is precisely what other kinds of declarations of independence might be deemed lawful in the future.

Should the Court take up another case involving a declaration of independence—which seems very unlikely to happen anytime soon—it seems unlikely to have the broad array of pleadings or the kind of global interest that made the Kosovo case so unusual. In that sense, as Judge Simma noted, the case represents a missed opportunity to produce a more thoughtful, realistic and less formalistic piece of jurisprudence than the Court actually produced.

On the other hand, at the end of the day, surely it is better for the Court to be narrowly right, than overbroadly wrong. Perhaps the clearest legacy of the Kosovo case is not what the Court did, but what it did not do. In its Kosovo Advisory Opinion, the International Court of Justice did not fix what was not broken. Thus, whatever may be the shortcomings of its analysis, it satisfied the first test of legitimacy for any difficult decision: namely, 'first, do no harm'.

# Bibliography

## DOCUMENTS AND PROCEEDINGS

*Accordance with International Law of the Unilateral Declaration of Independence, in Respect of Kosovo*, Advisory Opinion, ICJ Reports 2010, p. 403

Pleadings and other case materials available at <http://www.icj-cij.org/docket/index.php?p1=3&p2=4&code=kos&case=141&k=21&p3=0>

International Crisis Group, *Kosovo and Serbia after the ICJ Opinion*, 26 August 2010, available at <http://www.crisisgroup.org/en/regions/europe/balkans/kosovo/206-kosovo-and-serbia-after-the-icj-opinion.aspx>

Ministry of Foreign Affairs of the Republic of Kosovo (2010), *Kosovo in the International Court of Justice/Kosova në Gjykatën Ndërkombëtare të Drejtësisë*

## BOOKS AND ARTICLES

U. D. Acharya, 'ICJ's Kosovo Decision: Economical Reasoning of Law and Question of Legitimacy of the Court' (2012) 12(1) *Chicago-Kent Journal of International and Comparative Law 1 Gonzaga University School of Law Research Paper No. 2011–11*

D. Akande, 'ICJ Finds that Kosovo's Declaration of Independence not in Violation of International Law' (23 July 2010) *EJIL: Talk! Blog of the European Journal of International Law*. Available at: <http://www.ejiltalk.org/icj-finds-that-kosovos-declaration-of-independence-not-in-violation-of-international-law>

M. Arcari, L. Balmond (eds), *Questions de droit international autour de l'avis consultatif de la cour internationale de justice sur le Kosovo* (Giuffrè, 2011)

B. Arp, 'The ICJ Advisory Opinion on the Accordance with International Law of the Unilateral Declaration of Independence in Respect of Kosovo and the International Protection of Minorities' (2010) 11 *German Law Journal*, pp. 847–865

N. Beal, 'Defending State Sovereignty: The I.C.J. Advisory Opinion on Kosovo and International Law' (2012) 21 *Transnational Law & Contemporary Problems*, p. 549

W. Benedek, 'Implications of the Independence of Kosovo for International Law' in I. Buffard, J. Crawford, A. Pellet, S. Wittich (eds), *International Law Between Universalism and Fragmentation*. Festschrift *in Honour of Gerhard Hafner* (Brill, 2008), pp. 391–412

F. Berisha, D. Vuniqi, 'Declaration of Independence of the Republic of Kosovo and the Issue of Assessment in the International Court of Justice' (October 21, 2013) University of Pristina, *Faculty of Law Working Paper Series*

M. Bothe, 'Kosovo—So What? The Holding of the International Court of Justice is not the Last Word on Kosovo's Independence' (2011) 11 *German Law Journal*, pp. 837–839 (being a translation of an article in the *Süddeutsche Zeitung*, 24/25 July 2010)

R. A. Brand, 'Special Report: Kosovo after the ICJ Opinion' (2013) 74 *University of Pittsburgh Law Review*, p. 595

T. Burri, 'The Kosovo Opinion and Secession: The Sounds of Silence and Missing Links' (2010) 11 *German Law Journal*, pp. 882–893

J. Cerone, 'Kosovo Advisory Opinion of the International Court of Justice' (2010) *Annals of the Faculty of Law in Belgrade*, p. 209

E. Circovic, 'An Analysis of the ICJ Advisory Opinion on Kosovo's Unilateral Declaration of Independence' (2010) 11 *German Law Journal*, pp. 896–912

T. Christakis, 'The ICJ Advisory Opinion on Kosovo: Has International Law Something to Say about Secession?' (2011) 24 *Leiden Journal of International Law,* pp. 73–86.

T. Christakis, O. Corten, 'Editors' Introduction: Symposium: The ICJ Advisory Opinion on the Unilateral Declaration of Independence of Kosovo' (2011) 24 *Leiden Journal of International Law*, pp. 71–72

E. Christie, 'Accordance with International Law of the Unilateral Declaration of Independence in respect of Kosovo, ICJ Advisory Opinion of 22 July 2010, General List No. 141' (2010) 17 *Australian International Law Journal*, pp. 205–212

O. Corten, 'Territorial Integrity Narrowly Interpreted: Reasserting the Classical Inter-State Paradigm of International Law' (2011) 24 *Leiden Journal of International Law*, pp. 87–94

J. d'Aspremont and T. Lieflä̈nder, 'Consolidating the Statehood of Kosovo: Leaving the International Law Narrative Behind' (2012) *Journal of European and International Affairs, Amsterdam Law School Research Paper* No. 2012-101; Amsterdam Center for International Law No. 2012-15.

E. De Brabandere, 'The Kosovo Advisory Proceedings and the Court's Advisory Jurisdiction as a Method of Dispute Settlement' (September 1) International Court of Justice and Kosovo: Opinion or Non-Opinion? Seminar, 2010. Available at: <http://www.haguejusticeportal.net/index.php?id=12076>

C. Del Re Emanuela, 'From the Balkans to the Caucasus: Paradoxes of the Precedents in a Post-Balkan Perspective' in D. A. Mahapatra (ed), *Conflict and Peace in Eurasia* (Routledge, 2013)

C. Escobar Hernández, 'La posición del Reino de España en el procidimiento consultiva: una aproximación general' (2011) 63 *Spanish Journal of International Law*, pp. 11–27

R. Falk, 'Agora: The ICJ's Kosovo Advisory Opinion: The Kosovo Advisory Opinion: Conflict Resolution and Precedent' (2011) 105 *The American Journal of International Law*, pp. 50–60

T. Fleiner, 'The Unilateral Secession of Kosovo as a Precedent in International Law', in U. Fastenrath and others (eds), *From Bilateralism to Community Interest. Essays in Honour of Judge Bruno Simma* (OUP, 2011), pp. 877–894

J. A. Frowein, 'Kosovo and Lotus', in U. Fastenrath and others (eds), *From Bilateralism to Community Interest. Essays in Honour of Judge Bruno Simma* (OUP, 2011), pp. 923–931

H. Hannum, 'The Avisory Opinion on Kosovo: An Opportunity Lost, or a Poisoned Chalice Refused?' (2011) 24 *Leiden Journal of International Law*, pp. 155–161

P. Hilpold 'The ICJ Advisory Opinion on Kosovo: Perspectives of a Delicate Question' (2013) 14 *Austrian Review of International and European Law*, p. 44

P. Hilpold, (ed), *Das Kosovo-Gutachten des IGH vom 22. Juli 2010* (Brill, 2011)

R. Howse, R. Teitel, 'Delphic Dictum: How Has the ICJ Contributed to the Global Rule of Law by its Ruling on Kosovo?' (2010) 11 *German Law Journal*, pp. 841–845

I. Ingravallo, 'Kosovo after the ICJ Advisory Opinion: Towards a European Perspective?' (2012) 14 *International Community Law Review*, pp. 219–241

P. Iskenderov, 'Kosovo: A Unique Case or a Dangerous Precedent?' (2011) 57(2) *International Affairs (Minneapolis)*, pp. 230–237.

D. Jacobs, Y. Radi, 'Waiting for Godot: An Analysis of the Advisory Opinion on Kosovo' (2011) 24 *Leiden Journal of International Law*, pp. 331–353

H. Jamar, M. K. Vigness, 'Applying Kosovo: Looking to Russia, China, Spain and Beyond After the International Court of Justice Opinion on Unilateral Declarations of Independence' 11 *German Law Journal* (2010), pp. 913–928

M. Kohen, K. Del Mar, 'The Kosovo Advisory Opinion and UNSCR 1244 (1999): A Declaration of Independence from International Law?' (2011) 24 *Leiden Journal of International Law*, pp. 109–126

D. Meester, 'The International Court of Justice's Kosovo Case: Assessing the Current State of International Legal Opinion on Remedial Secession' (2010) 48 *Czech Yearbook of Public & Private International Law*, pp. 215–254

S E Meiler, 'The Kosovo Case: An Argument for a Remedial Declaration of Independence' (2012) 40 *Georgia Journal of International & Comparative Law*, p. 833

M. Milanović, 'Kosovo Advisory Opinion Preview' (14 July 2010) *EJIL: Talk! Blog of the European Journal of International Law*. Available at: <http://www.ejiltalk.org/kosovo-advisory-opinion-preview/>

J. E. Moliterno, 'What the ICJ's Decision Means for the Kosovars' (2010) 11 *German Law Journal*, pp. 891–893

A. Mills, 'The Kosovo Advisory Opinion: If you don't have anything constructive to say … ?' (2011) 70 *Cambridge Law Journal*, pp. 1–4

C. Moore (ed), *Contemporary Violence: Postmodern War in Kosovo and Chechnya* (MUP, 2010)

R. Muharremi, 'A Note on the ICJ Advisory Opinion on Kosovo' (2010) 11 *German Law Journal,* pp. 867–880

A. X. M. Ntovas, 'The Paradox of Kosovo's Parallel Legal Orders in the Reasoning of the Court's Advisory Opinion' in D. French (ed), *Statehood and Self-Determination: Reconciling Tradition and Modernity in International Law*, (CUP, 2013)

M. D. Öberg, 'The Legal Effects of United Nations Resolutions in the Kosovo Advisory Opinion' (2011) 105 *The American Journal of International Law* pp. 81–90

Z. Oklopic, 'Preliminary Thoughts on the Kosovo Opinion' (26 July 2010) *EJIL: Talk! Blog of the European Journal of International Law*. Available at: <http://www.ejiltalk.org/preliminary-thoughts-on-the-kosovo-opinion/>

A. Peters, 'The Kosovo-Opinion and the Art of Saying Nothing' (*Das Kosovogutachten und die Kunst des Nichtssagens* in original German article) (2010) 126(3) *Jusletter*, p.1

A. Peters, 'Does Kosovo Lie in the Lotus-Land of Freedom?' (2011) 24 *Leiden Journal of International Law*, pp. 95–108

A. Peters, 'Statehood after 1989: '*Effectivités*' between Legality and Virtuality', in J. Crawford, S. Nouwen (eds), *Select Proceedings of the European Society of International Law: Third Volume* (Hart 2012), Ch. 13

Ch. Pippan, 'The International Court of Justice's Advisory Opinion on Kosovo's Declaration of Independence: An Exercise in the Art of Silence' (2008) 3 *Europäisches Journal für Minderheitsfragen*, pp. 149–164

D. L. Phillips, *Liberating Kosovo: Coercive Diplomacy and U.S. Intervention* (MIT Press 2012)

U. Preuß, 'Kosovo—A State *Sui Generis*?' 58 *Südosteuropa*, pp. 389–412

D. Richemond-Barak, 'The International Court of Justice on Kosovo: Missed Opportunity or Dispute "Settlement"?' (2010) 23 *Hague Yearbook of International Law*. Available open access: <http://works.bepress.com/daphne_richemondbarak/2>

C. Ryngaert, 'The ICJ's Advisory Opinion on Kosovo's Declaration of Independence: A Missed Opportunity?' (2010) 57 *Netherlands International Law Review*, pp. 481–494

D. Shelton, 'Self-determination in Regional Human Rights Law: from Kosovo to Cameroon' (2011) 105 *The American Journal of International Law*, pp. 60–81

J. Summers (ed), *Kosovo: A Precedent? The Declaration of Independence, the Advisory Opinion and Implications for Statehood, Self-Determination, and Minority Rights* (Brill, 2011)

S. Talmon, M. Weller, 'Kosovo: The ICJ Opinion—What Next?', Summary of the International Law Discussion Group meeting held at Chatham House on Tuesday, 21 September 2010. Available at: <http://www.chathamhouse.org/publications/papers/view/109474>

C. Tams 'The Kosovo Opinion' (2010) *EJIL: Talk! Blog of the European Journal of International Law*. Available at: <http://www.ejiltalk.org/the-kosovo-opinion/>

E. Tannam, 'The EU's Response to the International Court of Justice's Judgment on Kosovo's Declaration of Independence' (2013) 65 *Europe-Asia Studies*, pp. 946–964

R. Tricot, B. Sander 'Recent Developments: The Broader Consequences of the International Court of Justice's Advisory Opinion on the Unilateral Declaration of Independence in respect of Kosovo' (2011) 49 *Columbia Journal of Transnational Law*, p. 321

I. Urrutia Libarana, 'Territorial Integrity and Self-Determination: The Approach of the International Court of Justice in the Advisory Opinion on Kosovo', (2012) 16 *Revista d'Estudis Autonòmics i Federals*, pp. 107–140

J. Vidmar, 'The *Kosovo* Advisory Opinion Scrutinized' (2011) 24 *Leiden Journal of International Law*, pp. 355–382

C. Walter, 'Recent Developments: The Kosovo Advisory Opinion: What It Says and What It Does Not Say' in C. Walter, A. von Ungern-Sternberg, K. Abushov (eds), *Self-Determination and Secession in International Law* (OUP 2014)

T. W. Waters, 'Misplaced Boldness: The Avoidance of Substance in the International Court of Justice's Kosovo Opinion' (2013) 23 *Duke Journal of Comparative & International Law*, pp. 267–333

M. Weller, 'Modesty Can Be a Virtue: Judicial Economy in the ICJ Kosovo Opinion' (2011) 24 *Leiden Journal of International Law*, pp. 127–147

R. Wilde, 'Kosovo 2008: Independence, Recognition and International Law', (2008) 5(2) *Soochow Law Journal*, pp. 51–81

R. Wilde, 'Accordance with International Law of the Unilateral Declaration of Independence in Respect of Kosovo', (2011) 105 *The American Journal of International Law*, pp. 301–7

R. Wilde, 'Self-Determination, Secession and Dispute Settlement after the Kosovo Advisory Opinion', (2011) 24 *Leiden Journal of International Law*, pp. 149–154, 71–72

R. Wilde, 'Kosovo (Advisory Opinion)', in R Wolfrum (ed), *The Max Planck Encyclopedia of Public International Law*, (OUP 2012)

R.Wilde, M. Milanović, A. Peters, Q. Qerimi, 'What the Kosovo Advisory Opinion Means for the Rest of the World', (Friday 25 March 2011) *Proceedings of the American Society of International Law*, pp. 259–274

S. Wolff, 'Self-Determination after Kosovo', (2013) 65 *EuropeTAsia Studies*, pp. 799–822

R. Wolfrum, 'Advisory Opinions: Are they a Suitable Alternative for the Settlement of International Disputes?', (2013) 239 *Beiträge zum ausländischen öffentlichen Recht und Völkerrecht*, pp. 33–123

S. Yee, 'Note on the International Court of Justice (Part 4): The Kosovo Advisory Opinion', (2010) 9 *Chinese Journal of International Law*, pp. 763–783

# Index